Arguing About Metaphysics

"Rea's *Arguing About Metaphysics* is an excellent anthology which combines rigorous yet accessible essays in contemporary metaphysics with philosophically sophisticated and entertaining pieces of fiction. The result is an engaging and challenging volume certain to stimulate and introduce the philosophical novice to the delights of serious exploration in five central areas of metaphysics."

Hud Hudson, Western Washington University

Arguing About Metaphysics is a wide-ranging anthology that introduces students to one of the most fundamental areas of philosophy. It covers core topics in metaphysics such as personal identity, the nature of being, time, and the concept of freedom. The volume contains scholarly articles by Quine, Lewis, van Inwagen, and Pereboom, as well as short works of science fiction that illustrate key ideas in metaphysics.

The volume is divided into five parts, helping the student get to grips with classic and core arguments and emerging debates in:

- On What There Is
- Time and Time Travel
- Change and Identity
- Freedom
- Worlds and Worldmaking

Michael C. Rea provides lucid introductions to each section, giving an overview of the debate and outlining the arguments of each section's readings. *Arguing About Metaphysics* is a comprehensive and engaging reader for students who are new to philosophy.

Michael C. Rea is Professor of Philosophy and Director of the Center for Philosophy of Religion at Notre Dame. He is the author of *World Without Design: The Ontological Consequences of Naturalism* (2002) and co-author of *Introduction to the Philosophy of Religion* (2008).

Arguing About Philosophy

This exciting and lively series introduces key subjects in philosophy with the help of a vibrant set of readings. In contrast to many standard anthologies which often reprint the same technical and remote extracts, each volume in the *Arguing About Philosophy* series is built around essential but fresher philosophical readings, designed to attract the curiosity of students coming to the subject for the first time. A key feature of the series is the inclusion of well-known yet often neglected readings from related fields, such as popular science, film and fiction. Each volume is edited by leading figures in their chosen field and each section carefully introduced and set in context, making the series an exciting starting point for those looking to get to grips with philosophy.

Arguing About Knowledge
Edited by Duncan Pritchard and Ram Neta

Arguing About Law
Edited by Aileen Kanvanagh and
John Oberdiek

Arguing About Metaethics
Edited by Andrew Fisher and Simon Kirchin

Arguing About the Mind
Edited by Brie Gertler and Lawrence Shapiro

Arguing About Art 3rd Edition
Edited by Alex Neill and Aaron Ridley

Arguing About Metaphysics
Edited by Michael C. Rea

Forthcoming titles:
Arguing About Language
Edited by Darragh Byrne and Max Kolbel

Arguing About Political Philosophy
Edited by Matt Zwolinski

Arguing About Religion
Edited by Kevin Timpe

Arguing About Metaphysics

Edited by
Michael C. Rea

Routledge
Taylor & Francis Group

NEW YORK AND LONDON

First published 2009
by Routledge
270 Madison Ave, New York, NY 10016

Simultaneously published in the UK
by Routledge
2 Park Square, Milton Park, Abingdon, Oxon OX14 4RN

Routledge is an imprint of the Taylor & Francis Group, an informa business

Typeset in Joanna by
RefineCatch Limited, Bungay, Suffolk
Printed and bound in the United States of America on acid-free paper by
Edwards Brothers, Inc.

Library of Congress Cataloging-in-Publication Data
Arguing about metaphysics / edited by Michael C. Rea.
     p. cm. – (Arguing about philosophy)
  1. Metaphysics. I. Rea, Michael C. (Michael Cannon), 1968–
BD111.A67 2008
110 – dc22
2008025146

ISBN10: 0–415–95825–3 (hbk)
ISBN10: 0–415–95826–1 (pbk)

ISBN13: 978–0–415–95825–7 (hbk)
ISBN13: 978–0–415–95826–4 (pbk)

Dedication

To Cheryl, Jeff, and Derrick Marzano

Contents

Acknowledgements   *xi*

General Introduction   1

PART 1
On What There Is   7

    Introduction to Part 1   9

  1 *Willard V. Quine* On What There Is   11

  2 *Henry Fitzgerald* Nominalist Things   22

  3 *Peter van Inwagen* A Theory of Properties   24

  4 *D. M. Armstrong* A World of States of Affairs 45

  5 *David Lewis and Stephanie Lewis* Holes   54

  6 *Richard Routley* On What There Is Not   59

  7 *David Lewis* Truth in Fiction   78

  8 *Peter Unger* I Do Not Exist   94

PART 2
Time and Time Travel   107

    Introduction to Part 2   109

  9 *H. G. Wells* The Time Traveller's Speech   113

10 *Alan Lightman* Einstein's Dreams   116

11 *A. N. Prior* Thank Goodness That's Over   122

12 *Ned Markosian* A Defense of Presentism   127

13   *Paul Horwich* The Metaphysics of *Now*   151

14   *Donald C. Williams* The Myth of Passage   167

15   *Robert Heinlein* "—All You Zombies—"   178

16   *Robert Silverberg* Absolutely Inflexible   186

17   *David Lewis* The Paradoxes of Time Travel   193

18   *Richard Hanley* No End in Sight: Causal Loops in
     Philosophy, Physics and Fiction   203

PART 3
Change and Identity   225

     Introduction to Part 3   227

19   *Parmenides and David Lewis* Problems About Change:
     Selections from the Writings of Parmenides and
     David Lewis   231

20   *Brian Smart* How to Reidentify the Ship of Theseus   236

21   *Roderick Chisholm* Identity and Temporal Parts   239

22   *Mark Heller* Temporal Parts of Four Dimensional
     Objects   264

23   *Greg Egan* Dust   272

24   *Daryl Gregory* Second Person, Present Tense   292

25   *Derek Parfit* Personal Identity   305

26   *Eric T. Olson* An Argument for Animalism   320

PART 4
Freedom   333

     Introduction to Part 4   335

27   *Stephen Robinett* The Satyr   337

28   *Ted Chiang* What's Expected of Us   347

29   *Richard Taylor* The Story of Osmo   349

30   *Peter van Inwagen* Fatalism   351

31   *William L. Rowe* Two Concepts of Freedom   372

32   *Susan Wolf* Freedom Within Reason   387

33   *Derk Pereboom* Determinism *Al Dente*   399

34   *Peter van Inwagen* The Mystery of Metaphysical
      Freedom   420

35   *Harry G. Frankfurt* Alternate Possibilities and Moral
      Responsibility   428

PART 5
Worlds and Worldmaking   435

      Introduction to Part 5   437

36   *Max Tegmark* Parallel Universes   441

37   *John Leslie* World Ensemble, or Design   451

38   *Peter Forrest* The Tree of Life: Agency and Immortality
      in a Metaphysics Inspired by Quantum Theory   469

39   *David Lewis* A Philosopher's Paradise   483

40   *Alvin Plantinga* Two Concepts of Modality:
      Modal Realism and Modal Reductionism   518

41   *Nelson Goodman* Words, Works, Worlds   545

      Index   557

Acknowledgements

The editor and publishers wish to thank the following for permission to use copyrighted material:

American Philosophical Quarterly for J.L.Mackie, 'Causes and Conditions' in *American Philosophical Quarterly*, 2 (1965) pp. 245–64.

Blackwell Publishers for David Lewis, 'Possible Worlds' in *On the Plurality of Worlds* (1986) pp. 192–209; and David Lewis, 'Counterparts or Double Lives?' in *Counterfactuals* (1973) pp. 84–91.

Duke University Press for Derek Parfit, 'Personal Identity' in *Philosophical Review*, Vol. 80, No. 1 (1971) pp. 3–27. Copyright © 1971 by Cornell University Press.

Cambridge University Press for J. M. E. McTaggart, 'Time' in *The Nature of Existence*, Vol. 1 (1921) pp. 9–23; C. D. Broad, *Examination of McTaggart's Philosophy* (1938) pp. 309–13; Mark Heller, chapter 1 in *The Ontology of Physical Objects* (1990) pp. 1–29; material from Hilary Putnam, *Reason, Truth and History* (1981) pp. 49–56; and material from G.E.M. Anscombe, *Causality and Determination* (1971) pp. 89–104.

Gelfman Schneider Literary Agents for Alan Lightman, material from *Einstein's Dreams* (UK permission), copyright © 1993 by Alan Lightman.

Harvard University Press for Michael Dummett, 'Realism' in *Truth and Other Enigmas* (1978) pp. 145–65. Copyright © 1978 by Michael Dummett.

The Journal of Philosophy for Trenton Merricks, 'Endurance and Indiscernibility' in *Journal of Philosophy*, Vol. 91, No. 4 (1994) pp. 165–84; and W. V. Quine, 'Ontological Relativity: The Dewey Lectures 1968' in *Journal of Philosophy*, Vol. 65, No. 7 (1968) pp. 185–212.

Saul Kripke for 'Identity and Necessity' in *Identity and Individuation*, ed. Milton K. Munitz, NYU Press (1971) pp. 135–64.

Stephanie R. Lewis and The Journal of Philosophy for David Lewis, 'Causation' in *Journal of Philosophy*, Vol. 70, No. 17 (1973) pp. 556–67. This paper has also been reprinted in David Lewis, *Philosophical Papers II*, Oxford University Press (1986). That volume also includes extensive postscripts to the original paper, substantially expanding (and amending) Lewis' views.

Oxford University Press for material from Bertrand Russell, *The Problems of Philosophy*, Clarendon (1912) pp. 91–100; Max Black, 'The Identity of Indiscernibles' in *Mind*, LXI (1952); and material from David Hume, *A Treatise of Human Nature*, eds. L.A. Selby-Bigge and P.H. Nidditch (1978) pp. 73–78 and 154–72.

Pearson Education Inc. for material from Richard Taylor, *Metaphysics*, 4th edition (1992) pp. 81–90.

Alvin Plantinga for 'Actualism and Possible Worlds' in *Theoria*, Vol. 42, No. 1–3 (1976) pp. 139–60.

Mary Prior for A.N. Prior, 'The Notion of the Present' in *Studium Generale*, 23 (1970).

The Review of Metaphysics for W. V. Quine, 'On What There Is' in *Review of Metaphysics*, Vol. 2 (1948) pp. 21–38. Copyright © 1948 by The Review of Metaphysics [with additional permission from Harvard University Press for amendments included in *From a Logical Point of View* by

W. V. Quine, Harvard (1961) pp. 1–19]; and D. C. Williams, 'On the Elements of Being' in *Review of Metaphysics*, Vol. 7 (1953) pp. 3–18. Copyright © 1953 by The Review of Metaphysics.

Springer Science + Business Media for Edwin B. Allaire, 'Bare Particulars' in *Philosophical Studies*, Vol. 14, No. 1–2 (1963) pp. 1–8; James Van Cleve, 'Three Versions of the Bundle Theory' in *Philosophical Studies*, Vol. 47, No. 1 (1985) pp. 95–107; and Albert Casullo, 'A Fourth Version of the Bundle Theory' in *Philosophical Studies*, Vol. 54, No. 1 (1988) pp. 125–39.

Richard Swinburne for 'Personal Identity: The Dualist Theory' in *Personal Identity*, eds. Sydney Shoemaker and Richard Swinburne (1984) pp. 192–209.

Taylor & Francis Books UK for material from A.C. Ewing, *Fundamental Questions of Philosophy* (1951) pp. 208–15. Copyright © 1951 by Routledge; material from D.H. Mellor, *Real Time II* (1998) pp. 47–56. Copyright © 1998 by Routledge; and material from J.J.C. Smart, *Philosophy and Scientific Realism* (1963) pp. 131–42. Copyright © 1963 by Routledge.

Thomson Publishing Services for H.H. Price, 'Universals and Resemblance', chapter 1 in *Thinking and Experience*, Hutchinson's University Library (1953).

University of California Press for David Lewis, 'Survival and Identity' in *Identities of Persons*, ed. Amélie Rorty (1976) pp. 317–41. Copyright © 1976 The Regents of The University of California.

Westview Press for material from Peter Van Inwagen, *Metaphysics* (1993) pp. 56–69. Copyright © 1993 by Westview Press, a member of Perseus Books Group; and material from David Armstrong, *Universals* (1989) pp. 75–112. Copyright © 1989 by Westview Press, a member of Perseus Books Group.

Every effort has been made to contact copyright holders for their permission to reprint material in this book. The publishers would be grateful to hear from any copyright holder who is not here acknowledged and will undertake to rectify any errors or omissions in future editions of this book.

GENERAL INTRODUCTION

THE FIELD OF METAPHYSICS and its characteristic puzzles occupy a central place both in the history of philosophy and on the current philosophical landscape. But what is metaphysics? Other areas of philosophy are relatively easy to characterize. In ethics, we study morality; in logic, we study the principles of sound reasoning; in epistemology we study the nature of knowledge and related concepts; and so on. But it is much harder to explain what we are doing when we study metaphysics.

Matters are further complicated by the fact that bookstores often have entire sections devoted to "metaphysics" that are filled with books that have very little to do with what academic metaphysicians are interested in and a whole lot to do with occult topics like astrology, ghosts, psychic powers, the secret lives of plants, and the like. These latter issues are what the folks in the general public recognize as falling under the label "metaphysics." So if you tell your dental hygienist, or your seat-mate on an airplane, or your prospective in-laws that you are studying metaphysics in college or (heaven forbid) aspiring to obtain a doctoral degree in the field, they are all too likely to think that you are devoting your time and attention to something strange and frivolous rather than to a serious academic subject.

Aristotle famously characterized metaphysics as the study of *being qua being*, or of *being as such*. But this characterization is almost certain to be useless to anyone who is not already well versed in philosophy generally and in the history of metaphysics in particular. Indeed, I suspect that few professional metaphysicians have any clear idea what this characterization means; and I think that even fewer would be inclined to think of themselves as studying "being as such" in pursuing their various research projects.

According to a more common characterization, metaphysics is the study of *what there is*, or of *what there **really** is*, or of *ultimate reality*. But these characterizations too are less than helpful. Why think that it is in metaphysics rather than in, say, botany or zoology or theoretical physics, that we learn about "ultimate reality" or about "what there really is"? Why are we doing metaphysics when we ask whether there are abstract objects, but not when we ask whether there are unicorns? In what sense is the former but not the latter a question about "what there really is"? Why do questions about the nature of causation have more to do with ultimate reality than do questions about the function of a human heart, or about the defining characteristics of electrons? These questions are hard to answer.

So what *can* we metaphysicians and students of metaphysics tell our friends and family about the subject to which we are devoting so much of our time?

We do best, I think, to approach the question of what metaphysics is first by looking at what questions metaphysicians typically ask and then by asking what, if anything, those questions share in common. Here is a sample of such questions:

- When you assert something is there a some *thing* that you're asserting? If so, what kind of thing is it?
- When two things share a common property, is there some one identical *thing* that they in fact share (perhaps as a common part), or is talk of "sharing" just a manner of speaking? And if there is some actual thing that is shared, then what does the sharing amount to? Is it a kind of overlap? Or is it some sort of resemblance?
- When you talk about ways things could have been (e.g., "there's more than one way this class could turn out"), to what sorts of things (if any) does the word "ways" refer?
- What is the relation between an object and its properties? Are the properties of a thing parts or constituents of it? If not, then are we supposed to imagine that properties are somehow external to the things that have them, and are related to them simply by resemblance or some other sort of relation?
- Is change really possible? If so, what does it mean to say that something has changed?
- Is the passage of time possible? And what is time, anyway?
- What does it take to get the members of a set of objects to compose something?
- A gold statue is constituted by a lump of gold. The lump of gold still exists after it is melted down and reshaped, but the statue doesn't. So what is the relationship between the lump and the statue? Are they two different things in the same place at the same time? If not, then how do "they" have different survival conditions?
- What is an event? Can the same event happen more than once? What is involved in one event's *causing* another?
- What are human minds? Are they immaterial thinking substances, or are they material objects (brains, perhaps?), or something else entirely?
- Are human beings free? Is freedom even possible?
- Is it possible to live after death?
- Do human beings or human faculties have anything like a proper function?
- Why are there contingent beings rather than nothing at all? Is there a necessary being (a God, perhaps) who created all contingent things?

There are many more such questions; but the list just given provides a flavor for the sorts of issues with which metaphysicians typically concern themselves. As I see it, what these questions have in common is roughly this: They are non-scientific questions about what exists and about the necessary connections among certain kinds of concepts, properties, and relations. The concepts, properties, and relations in question are, roughly, those pertaining to things other than reasons, values, and mathematical objects. (Note, though, that it is not uncommon to hear philosophers talk about, say, the "metaphysics of morals." Here what they have in mind are just non-scientific questions about the *existence* of certain kinds of moral properties or about the *consequences* that certain claims in the domain of ethics might have for broader metaphysical concerns.) Metaphysics, then, may be roughly characterized as the attempt to answer such non-scientific questions in a disciplined, rigorous way.

Thus, in short: *Metaphysics* is the attempt to provide rigorously developed answers to non-scientific questions about what exists and about the necessary connections among such concepts, properties, and relations as pertain to things other than reasons, values, and mathematical objects. Moreover, we may characterize *ontology* as that branch of metaphysics which focuses on *existence* claims of the sort studied by metaphysics, and on the logical consequences thereof.

The fact that metaphysics concerns itself with *non-scientific* questions about the character and makeup of the world has made many philosophers rather uneasy with the whole enterprise. The sciences enjoy a great deal of respect as fields of inquiry, and many think that the methods of science and those methods alone are the tools by which we ought to build our theories about the world. A priori theorizing about the world—the sort of theorizing that requires no lab-equipment or experimental apparatus, but just an easy chair, a working brain, and a good chunk of time free for thinking—has long been viewed with some skepticism. According to many philosophers, metaphysical theorizing is just idle tale-spinning: when we do metaphysics, we scratch our heads and reflect on what seems obvious to us, and then we spin out stories that aren't supported by "real evidence" in an effort to make sense of our world.

One of the most well-known expressions of this sort of negative attitude toward metaphysics comes from David Hume:

> If we take in our hand any volume; of divinity or school metaphysics, for instance; let us ask, Does it contain any abstract reasoning concerning quantity or number? No. Does it contain any experimental reasoning concerning matter of fact and existence? No. Commit it then to the flames: for it can contain nothing but sophistry and illusion.
>
> (*Enquiry Concerning Human Understanding*, section XII)

Hume's attitude is characteristic of those in the empiricist tradition—those who treat empirical theorizing of the sort found in the sciences as the only way of acquiring reliable information about the world. Likewise, contemporary empiricists have had little better to say about metaphysics. Rudolf Carnap, for example, complained that metaphysicians are "like musicians without musical ability," the point being that metaphysical theories are (like music) devoid of cognitive content and (unlike good music) not even endowed with aesthetic value.[1] One might think that these concerns apply as much to ethics and epistemology as to metaphysics. But in the case of the first two disciplines, the concerns are lessened somewhat by the fact that both fields, unlike metaphysics, concern themselves with *values* and *norms* which can't really be investigated scientifically. In the case of metaphysics, on the other hand, it is hard to shake the worry that metaphysicians are often trying to do much the same thing that scientists do—namely, discover facts "about the world" (as opposed to facts about abstract values or about the relations among our ideas)—but with the wrong tools.

In light of these sorts of objections, it is easy to see why many people think that academic discussion of metaphysical topics is nothing more or less than a rather sophisticated sort of bull-session. It is easy to see why people think that metaphysics is neither serious nor important.

It is important to note, however, that this indictment of metaphysics depends crucially upon whether there really is reason to believe that metaphysical theorizing is an unreliable way of reaching the truth about things. For the fact is, metaphysicians examine and critically evaluate some of the most existentially important beliefs that human beings ever hold—beliefs that lie at the very heart of our conception of our-selves and our commonsense ways of thinking about the world we live in. It matters very much to us whether we are free in a way that would allow us to be genuinely responsible for our actions, whether we might possibly survive death, whether there might be (or must be) things—perhaps even intelligent and powerful things—beyond what we find in the material world, and so on. Moreover, many of the "drier," less universally gripping questions discussed by metaphysicians arise because they concern vital pieces of the overall framework within which we must pose and answer the more obviously important questions. If, contrary to what the objectors think, the methods of metaphysics constitute genuine ways of discovering the truth about these matters, then the practice of metaphysics is in fact one of the most important and existentially relevant intellectual endeavors we could possibly engage in.

This is not the place to try to discuss in detail the aforementioned objections against metaphysics; but two fairly general reactions to them are worth highlighting. First: Metaphysicians rely on *rational intuitions*—intellectual experiences of the sheer obviousness or necessary truth of various claims—in building their theories. And it is notoriously hard to produce an *argument* against the reliability of rational intuition or against the meaningfulness of metaphysical debates without either relying on rational intuitions or else impugning the epistemic status of a variety of non-metaphysical theories that one would otherwise have thought were perfectly respect-able. It is also notoriously hard to draw clear lines of demarcation between subjects that admit of reliable a priori investigation and subjects that do not. For this reason, many contemporary metaphysicians—especially since the revival of metaphysics in the mid-twentieth century, following the collapse of logical empiricism—have felt content simply to ignore the objections arising out of the empiricist camp, at least until those objections can be made precise enough to be persuasive.

It might be tempting to think that this reaction comes to nothing more than sticking one's head in the sand. Even so, it is exactly the reaction that many empiricists themselves have toward more general skeptical complaints—complaints that chal-lenge the evidential value of sense perception, for example. When skeptics demand evidence for the reliability of our senses, empiricists generally take themselves to be justified in ignoring the demand. We are entitled simply to trust our senses, they say. But if that is right, then shouldn't we be entitled simply to trust our rational intuitions as well? Many have thought so. In this vein, consider what Thomas Reid says to those who prioritize *reason* over *sense perception*:

> The sceptic asks me, Why do you believe the existence of the external object which you perceive? This belief, sir, is none of my manufacture; it came from the mint of Nature; it bears her image and superscription; and, if it is not right,

the fault is not mine: I even took it upon trust, and without suspicion. Reason, says the sceptic, is the only judge of truth, and you ought to throw off every opinion and every belief that is not grounded on reason. Why, sir, should I believe the faculty of reason more than that of perception?—they came both out of the same shop, and were made by the same artist; and if he puts one piece of false ware into my hands, what should hinder him from putting another?

(*Inquiry*, ch. 6, section 20, pp. 168–169)

The point here is that reason (and so presumably rational intuition as well) and sense perception ought—at least initially, absent *evidence* that one or the other is untrustworthy—to be treated as on a par. Reid, of course, is defending the trustworthiness of sense perception; but exactly the same sort of speech might as well be made in defense of the trustworthiness of intuition. To be sure, those offering Reidian speeches on behalf of metaphysics, or on behalf of a priori theorizing generally, must come to grips with the fact that there is far greater and persistent disagreement in metaphysics than in science, and (apparently) far less by way of "success" and "progress" in metaphysics as well. But many of us think that even once this difference is accounted for, the alleged reasons for abandoning metaphysics are far from compelling.

A second reaction has been to take on the empiricist preference for empirically based theorizing, along with empiricist skepticism of appeals to rational intuition, and to try to do metaphysics in a way that is roughly continuous with science and that goes beyond science as little as possible. Those who identify with the tradition of *philosophical naturalism* manifest a deep skepticism about appeals to rational intuition; and so they confine themselves to a sort of metaphysics that is best characterized as aiming simply to fill in some of the explanatory gaps in our scientific theories and to draw out and systematize some of the more interesting logical consequences of those theories. Standing at the forefront of this tradition are John Dewey and W. V. Quine; but a great many others—indeed, many of those whose work is reproduced in the present collection—see themselves as, in one way or another, associated with that tradition. This reaction, of course, concedes a lot of territory to the objectors. But, if sound, it still leaves an important place in the overall project of human inquiry for the practice of metaphysics.

What you find in this textbook is a sample of papers presenting and defending some of the most important positions in some of the most central debates in contemporary metaphysics. In accord with the goals of the "Arguing About . . ." series, readings in this volume have been chosen with an eye to making the subject matter as engaging and accessible to non-specialists as might be possible in a textbook that nevertheless aims to give balanced coverage to standard topics in the field. To this end, the volume includes not only "contemporary classics" from the academic literature, but also shorter "position papers," a few science-fiction stories, and other less specialized material that might help to raise more vividly or to motivate more effectively the issues treated in each section. In making my decisions about what to include and what to omit, I received some very valuable advice (much of which I followed) from Hud

Hudson and from three anonymous referees for Routledge. I am very grateful for their help. I am also grateful to Routledge for permission to use some of the introductory material from my *Critical Concepts in Philosophy: Metaphysics* volumes (Routledge, 2008) in the introductions to the present text. Finally, I would like to thank Alex Arnold for preparing the index, and the Institute for Scholarship in the Liberal Arts in the College of Arts and Letters at the University of Notre Dame for their financial support.

Note

1 From "The Elimination of Metaphysics Through Logical Analysis of Language," English translation in S. Sarkar (ed.), *Logical Empiricism at its Peak: Schlick, Carnap, and Neurath* (London: Routledge, 1996), p. 30.

PART 1

On What There Is

INTRODUCTION TO PART 1

MY SISTER AND I share some features in common: personality traits, certain physical features (DNA structure, facial contour), and so on. We also have shared memories. Our histories overlap; we have participated in some of the same events. In some respects we think alike. Some of the things that I believe are also things that she believes. Some of the things that she is inclined to say on various occasions are also things that I would say on similar occasions. All of this is perfectly mundane: everyone shares these sorts of things with other people. But difficult philosophical questions lurk close by.

The questions arise out of the fact that nouns are labels for things, but most of the nouns in the previous paragraph don't seem to refer to anything concrete. My sister and I share features in common; so—it would seem—there must be an x such that x is a feature, and my sister and I both *have it* (whatever that means). We share memories; so—it would seem—there must be an x such that x is a memory and x is somehow present in both my mind and hers. We have participated in some of the same events; so—it would seem—there must be an x such that x is an event. We sometimes say the same things; so—it would seem—there must be an x such that x is a *sayable* thing (whatever such a thing might be) and x is said by both me and my sister. When we were children, we used to believe in and talk about non-existent things (like Santa Claus); so—it would seem—there must be an x such that x is a non-existent thing and x was believed in and talked about by both me and my sister. And on and on we might go. But should we really take these inferences seriously? Do we really want—or need—to believe in such things (abstract things, presumably) as features, shareable mental states (like memories), events, sayable items (propositions), and the like? And if we do, then what exactly are these things? These are some of the most foundational questions in metaphysics.

The "ontological question," according to Quine, is just the question, "What is there?" Biologists, chemists, physicists, zoologists, and many others are in the business of providing (what philosophers would think of as) initial, provisional answers to this question. The answers are provisional in the sense in which the remarks in the previous paragraph about the existence of features and so on are provisional. Given some of the things we say about feature-sharing, memory-sharing, and the like, it *looks as if* there must be things like features and shareable memories and so on in order for those claims to be true. It looks that way; but maybe not. After all, it's also common to say things like "the average supermodel does not have a genius IQ." But it would be absurd to ask, "Where does this average supermodel live, and how can I meet her?" There is no such person; claims apparently about "the average supermodel" are *really* about something else. Likewise, biologists, chemists, physicists, and others give us theories that appear to refer to organisms, molecules, atoms, fundamental particles, and a lot more besides. These theories provide us with (in the best cases, obviously) empirically adequate ways of thinking and talking about the world. (They are empirically adequate in the sense that thinking and acting as if they are true will help us to make the right empirical predictions, help us to get around in and control our environment, and so on.) But it is at least partly a philosophical question whether the things apparently talked about in those theories *really exist*— i.e., whether the apparently referring expressions that appear in the canonical formulations of those theories really refer to the sorts of things to which they seem to refer. For, after all, there might be philosophical reasons for thinking that there simply *can't* be molecules (say) or atoms, in which case (if philosophical arguments can be taken seriously) theories that apparently talk about atoms will have to be understood as talking about something else.

So philosophers engaged in ontology are in the business of answering the question, "What is there?" But how shall we go about answering such questions? In the previous paragraph, I said things that suggest that the way to answer ontological questions is to ask which of the entities apparently referred to in our scientific theories or in our ordinary (and genuinely respectable) ways of talking *have* to exist in order for our scientific and (respectable) commonsense claims to be true. This is a roughly Quinean suggestion about how to proceed. (It is only roughly Quinean because Quine would not give nearly the sort of weight to common sense that I just did.) If we adopt this methodology, then a natural way of going about answering ontological questions is to look for ways of paraphrasing claims about problematic entities (like features, or sayable items, perhaps) in terms of claims about non-problematic entities (like concrete objects maybe). If we find acceptable paraphrases, one might think, then we don't have to believe in the problematic items; if we do not, then we are committed to them.

This methodology for answering ontological questions is hardly universally accepted. Dispute about it and related topics falls within the scope of *metaontology*, that area of inquiry which tries to sort out the correct way of doing ontology. The readings in this part of the book concern both ontology and metaontology. The first three selections present contrasting perspectives on the existence of properties (construed as abstract objects). Quine rejects them, claiming that sentences that apparently refer to them can all be paraphrased away. Quine's position is a version of *nominalism*—a position that is vividly and amusingly characterized in Fitzgerald's "Nominalist Things." Van Inwagen, on the other hand, defends a realist position, embracing abstract properties on the grounds that Quine's claims about paraphrasability are untenable. The remaining readings focus on other problematic items: states of affairs, non-existent objects, holes, fictional characters, and composite objects. Throughout these articles also is interwoven a dispute about metaontology, with Quine, Lewis, and van Inwagen both embracing and illustrating what I described above as the "Quinean" approach, and Routley embracing an alternative approach, according to which it makes perfect sense to talk about and quantify over "objects" that one believes not to exist.

Chapter 1

Willard V. Quine

ON WHAT THERE IS[1]

A curious thing about the ontological problem is its simplicity. It can be put in three Anglo-Saxon monosyllables: "What is there?" It can be answered, moreover, in a word – "Everything" – and everyone will accept this answer as true. However, this is merely to say that there is what there is. There remains room for disagreement over cases; and so the issue has stayed alive down the centuries.

Suppose now that two philosophers. McX and I, differ over ontology. Suppose McX maintains there is something which I maintain there is not. McX can, quite consistently with his own point of view, describe our difference of opinion by saying that I refuse to recognize certain entities. I should protest of course that he is wrong in his formulation of our disagreement, for I maintain that there are no entities, of the kind which he alleges, for me to recognize; but my finding him wrong in his formulation of our disagreement is unimportant, for I am committed to considering him wrong in his ontology anyway.

When I try to formulate our difference of opinion, on the other hand. I seem to be in a predicament. I cannot admit that there are some things which McX countenances and I do not, for in admitting that there are such things I should be contradicting my own rejection of them.

It would appear, if this reasoning were sound, that in any ontological dispute the proponent of the negative side suffers the disadvantage of not being able to admit that his opponent disagrees with him.

This is the old Platonic riddle of non-being. Non-being must in some sense be, otherwise what is it that there is not? This tangled doctrine might be nicknamed *Plato's beard*: historically it has proved tough, frequently dulling the edge of Occam's razor.

It is some such line of thought that leads philosophers like McX to impute being where they might otherwise be quite content to recognize that there is nothing. Thus, take Pegasus. If Pegasus *were* not, McX argues, we should not be talking about anything when we use the word; therefore it would be nonsense to say even that Pegasus is not. Thinking to show thus that the denial of Pegasus cannot be coherently maintained, he concludes that Pegasus is.

McX cannot, indeed, quite persuade himself that any region of space-time, near or remote, contains a flying horse of flesh and blood. Pressed for further details on Pegasus, then, he says that Pegasus is an idea in men's minds. Here, however, a confusion begins to be apparent. We may for the sake of argument concede that there is an entity, and even a unique entity (though this is rather implausible), which is the mental Pegasus-idea; but this mental entity is not what people are talking about when they deny Pegasus.

McX never confuses the Parthenon with the Parthenon-idea. The Parthenon is physical; the

Parthenon-idea is mental (according any way to McX's version of ideas, and I have no better to offer). The Parthenon is visible; the Parthenon-idea is invisible. We cannot easily imagine two things more unlike, and less liable to confusion, than the Parthenon and the Parthenon-idea. But when we shift from the Parthenon to Pegasus, the confusion sets in – for no other reason than that McX would sooner be deceived by the crudest and most flagrant counterfeit than grant the non-being of Pegasus.

The notion that Pegasus must be, because it would otherwise be nonsense to say even that Pegasus is not, has been seen to lead McX into an elementary confusion. Subtler minds, taking the same precept as their starting point, come out with theories of Pegasus which are less patently misguided than McX's, and correspondingly more difficult to eradicate. One of these subtler minds is named, let us say, Wyman. Pegasus, Wyman maintains, has his being as an unactualized possible. When we say of Pegasus that there is no such thing, we are saying, more precisely, that Pegasus does not have the special attribute of actuality. Saying that Pegasus is not actual is on a par, logically, with saying that the Parthenon is not red; in either case we are saying something about an entity whose being is unquestioned.

Wyman, by the way, is one of those philosophers who have united in ruining the good old word 'exist'. Despite his espousal of unactualized possibles, he limits the word 'existence' to actuality – thus preserving an illusion of ontological agreement between himself and us who repudiate the rest of his bloated universe. We have all been prone to say, in our common-sense usage of 'exist', that Pegasus does not exist, meaning simply that there is no such entity at all. If Pegasus existed he would indeed be in space and time, but only because the word 'Pegasus' has spatio-temporal connotations, and not because 'exists' has spatio-temporal connotations. If spatio-temporal reference is lacking when we affirm the existence of the cube root

of 27, this is simply because a cube root is not a spatio-temporal kind of thing, and not because we are being ambiguous in our use of 'exist'. However, Wyman, in an ill-conceived effort to appear agreeable, genially grants us the non-existence of Pegasus and then, contrary to what *we* meant by non-existence of Pegasus, insists that Pegasus *is*. Existence is one thing, he says, and subsistence is another. The only way I know of coping with this obfuscation of issues is to *give* Wyman the word 'exist'. I'll try not to use it again; I still have 'is'. So much for lexicography; let's get back to Wyman's ontology.

Wyman's overpopulated universe is in many ways unlovely. It offends the aesthetic sense of us who have a taste for desert landscapes, but this is not the worst of it. Wyman's slum of possibles is a breeding ground for disorderly elements. Take, for instance, the possible fat man in that doorway; and, again, the possible bald man it that doorway. Are they the same possible man, or two possible men? How do we decide? How many possible men are there in that doorway? Are there more possible thin ones than fat ones? How many of them are alike? Or would their being alike make them one? Are no two possible things alike? Is this the same as saying that it is impossible for two things to be alike? Or, finally, is the concept of identity simply inapplicable to unactualized possibles? But what sense can be found in talking of entities which cannot meaningfully be said to be identical with themselves and distinct from one another? These elements are well nigh incorrigible. By a Fregean therapy of individual concepts, some effort might be made at rehabilitation; but I feel we'd do better simply to clear Wyman's slum and be done with it.

Possibility, along with the other modalities of necessity and impossibility and contingency, raises problems upon which I do not mean to imply that we should turn our backs. But we can at least limit modalities to whole statements. We may impose the adverb "possibly" upon a statement as a whole, and we may well worry about the semantical analysis of such usage; but little real advance in such analysis is to be hoped for in expanding our universe to include so-called *possible entities*. I suspect that the main motive for this expansion is simply the old notion that Pegasus, e.g., must be because it would otherwise be nonsense to say even that he is not.

Still, all the rank luxuriance of Wyman's universe of possibles would seem to come to naught when we make a slight change in the example and speak not of Pegasus but of the round square cupola on Berkeley College. If, unless Pegasus were, it would be nonsense to say that he is not, then by the same token, unless the round square cupola on Berkeley College were, it would be nonsense to say that it is not. But, unlike Pegasus, the round square cupola on Berkeley College cannot be admitted even as an unactualized *possible*. Can we drive Wyman now to admitting also a realm of unactualizable impossibles? If so, a good many embarrassing questions could be asked about them. We might hope even to trap Wyman in contradictions, by getting him to admit that certain of these entities are at once round and square. But the wily Wyman chooses the other horn of the dilemma and concedes that it is nonsense to say that the round square cupola on Berkeley College is not. He says that the phrase 'round square cupola' is meaningless.

Wyman was not the first to embrace this alternative. The doctrine of the meaninglessness of contradictions runs away back. The tradition survives, moreover, in writers such as Wittgenstein who seem to share none of Wyman's motivations. Still I wonder whether the first temptation to such a doctrine may not have been substantially the motivation which we have observed in Wyman. Certainly the doctrine has no intrinsic appeal; and it has led its devotees to such quixotic extremes as that of challenging the method of proof by *reductio ad absurdum* – a challenge in which I seem to detect a quite striking *reductio ad absurdum eius ipsius*.

Moreover, the doctrine of meaninglessness of

contradictions has the severe methodological drawback that it makes it impossible, in principle, ever to devise an effective test of what is meaningful and what is not. It would be forever impossible for us to devise systematic ways of deciding whether a string of signs made sense – even to us individually, let alone other people – or not. For, it follows from a discovery in mathematical logic, due to Church, that there can be no generally applicable test of contradictoriness.

I have spoken disparagingly of Plato's beard, and hinted that it is tangled. I have dwelt at length on the inconveniences of putting up with it. It is time to think about taking steps.

Russell, in his theory of so-called singular descriptions, showed clearly how we might meaningfully use seeming names without supposing that the entities allegedly named be. The names to which Russell's theory directly applies are complex descriptive names such as 'the author of *Waverly*', 'the present King of France', 'the round square cupola on Berkeley College'. Russell analyzes such phrases systematically as fragments of the whole sentences in which they occur. The sentence 'The author of *Waverly* was a poet', e.g., is explained as a whole as meaning 'Someone (better: something) wrote *Waverly* and was a poet, and nothing else wrote *Waverly*'. (The point of this added clause is to affirm the uniqueness which is implicit in the word 'the', in 'the author of *Waverly*'.) The sentence 'The round square cupola on Berkeley College is pink' is explained as 'Something is round and square and is a cupola on Berkeley College and is pink, and nothing else is round and square and a cupola on Berkeley College'.

The virtue of this analysis is that the seeming name, a descriptive phrase, is paraphrased in *context* as a so-called incomplete symbol. No unified expression is offered as an analysis of the descriptive phrase, but the statement as a whole which was the context of that phrase still gets its full quota of meaning – whether true or false.

The unanalyzed statement 'The author of *Waverly* was a poet' contains a part, 'the author of *Waverly*', which is wrongly supposed by McX and Wyman to demand objective reference in order to be meaningful at all. But in Russell's translation, 'Something wrote *Waverly* and was a poet and nothing else wrote *Waverly*', the burden of objective reference which had been put upon the descriptive phrase is now taken over by words of the kind that logicians call bound variables, variables of quantification: namely, words like 'something', 'nothing', 'everything'. These words, far from purporting to be names specifically of the author of *Waverly*, do not purport to be names at all; they refer to entities generally, with a kind of studied ambiguity peculiar to themselves. These quantificational words or bound variables are of course a basic part of language, and their meaningfulness, at least in context, is not to be challenged. But their meaningfulness in no way presupposes there being either the author of *Waverly* or the round square cupola on Berkeley College or any other specifically preassigned objects.

Where descriptions are concerned, there is no longer any difficulty in affirming or denying being. 'There is the author of *Waverly*' is explained by Russell as meaning 'Someone (or, more strictly, something) wrote *Waverly* and nothing else wrote *Waverly*'. 'The author of *Waverly* is not' is explained, correspondingly, as the alternation 'Either each thing failed to write *Waverly* or two or more things wrote *Waverly*.' This alternation is false, but meaningful; and it contains no expression purporting to designate the author of *Waverly*. The statement 'The round square cupola on Berkeley College is not' is analyzed in similar fashion. So the old notion that statements of non-being defeat themselves goes by the board. When a statement of being or non-being is analyzed by Russell's theory of descriptions, it ceases to contain any expression which even purports to name the alleged entity whose being is in question, so that the meaningfulness of the statement no longer can be thought to presuppose that there be such an entity.

Now what of 'Pegasus'? This being a word

rather than a descriptive phrase, Russell's argument does not immediately apply to it. However, it can easily be made to apply. We have only to rephrase 'Pegasus' as a description, in any way that seems adequately to single out our idea: say 'the winged horse that was captured by Bellerophon'. Substituting such a phrase for 'Pegasus', we can then proceed to analyze the statement 'Pegasus is', or 'Pegasus is not', precisely on the analogy of Russell's analysis of 'The author of *Waverly* is' and 'The author of *Waverly* is not'.

In order thus to subsume a one-word name or alleged name such as 'Pegasus' under Russell's theory of description, we must of course be able first to translate the word into a description. But this is no real restriction. If the notion of Pegasus had been so obscure or so basic a one that no pat translation into a descriptive phrase had offered itself along familiar lines, we could still have availed ourselves of the following artificial and trivial-seeming device: we could have appealed to the *ex hypothesi* unanalyzable, irreducible attribute of *being Pegasus*, adopting, for its expression, the verb 'is-Pegasus', or 'pegasizes'. The noun 'Pegasus' itself could then be treated as derivative, and identified after all with a description: 'the thing that is-Pegasus', 'the thing that pegasizes'.

If the importing of such a predicate as 'pegasizes' seems to commit us to recognizing that there is a corresponding attribute, pegasizing, in Plato's heaven or in the mind of men, well and good. Neither we nor Wyman nor McX have been contending, thus far, about the being or non-being of universals, but rather about that of Pegasus. If in terms of pegasizing we can interpret the noun 'Pegasus' as a description subject to Russell's theory of descriptions, then we have disposed of the old notion that Pegasus cannot be said not to be without pre-supposing that in some sense Pegasus is.

Our argument is now quite general. McX and Wyman supposed that we could not meaningfully affirm a statement of the form 'So-and-so is not', with a simple or descriptive singular noun in place of 'so-and-so', unless so-and-so be. This supposition is now seen to be quite generally groundless, since the singular noun in question can always be expanded into a singular description, trivially or otherwise, and then analyzed out à la Russell.

We cannot conclude, however, that man is henceforth free of all ontological commitments. We commit ourselves outright to an ontology containing numbers when we say there are prime numbers between 1000 and 1010; we commit ourselves to an ontology containing centaurs when we say there are centaurs; and we commit ourselves to an ontology containing Pegasus when we say Pegasus is. But we do not commit ourselves to an ontology containing Pegasus or the author of *Waverly* or the round square cupola on Berkeley College when we say that Pegasus or the author of *Waverly* or the cupola in question is *not*. We need no longer labor under the delusion that the meaningfulness of a statement containing a singular term presupposes an entity named by the term. A singular term need not name to be significant.

An inkling of this might have dawned on Wyman and McX even without benefit of Russell if they had only noticed—as so few of us do—that there is a gulf between *meaning* and *naming* even in the case of a singular term which is genuinely a name of an object. Frege's example will serve: the phrase 'Evening Star' names a certain large physical object of spherical form, which is hurtling through space some scores of millions of miles from here. The phrase 'Morning Star' names the same thing, as was probably first established by some observant Babylonian. But the two phrases cannot be regarded as having the same meaning; otherwise that Babylonian could have dispensed with his observations and contented himself with reflecting on the meanings of his words. The meanings, then, being different from one another, must be other than the named object, which is one and the same in both cases.

Confusion of meaning with naming not only made McX think he could not meaningfully repudiate Pegasus; a continuing confusion of meaning with naming no doubt helped engender his absurd notion that Pegasus is an idea, a mental entity. The structure of his confusion is as follows. He confused the alleged *named object* Pegasus with the *meaning* of the word 'Pegasus', therefore concluding that Pegasus must be in order that the word have meaning. But what sorts of things are meanings? This is a moot point; however, one might quite plausibly explain meanings as ideas in the mind, supposing we can make clear sense in turn of the idea of ideas in the mind. Therefore Pegasus, initially confused with a meaning, ends up as an idea in the mind. It is the more remarkable that Wyman, subject to the same initial motivation as McX, should have avoided this particular blunder and wound up with unactualized possibles instead.

Now let us turn to the ontological problem of universals: the question whether there are such entities as attributes, relations, classes, numbers, functions. McX, characteristically enough, thinks there are. Speaking of attributes, he says: "There are red houses, red roses, red sunsets; this much is pre-philosophical common-sense in which we must all agree. These houses, roses, and sunsets, then, have something in common; and this which they have in common is all I mean by the attribute of redness." For McX, thus, there being attributes is even more obvious and trivial than the obvious and trivial fact of there being red houses, roses, and sunsets. This, I think, is characteristic of metaphysics, or at least of that part of metaphysics called ontology: one who regards a statement on this subject as true at all must regard it as trivially true. One's ontology is basic to the conceptual scheme by which he interprets all experiences, even the most commonplace ones. Judged within some particular conceptual scheme – and how else is judgment possible? – an ontological statement goes without saying, standing in need of no separate justification at all. Ontological statements follow immediately from all manner of casual statements of commonplace fact, just as – from the point of view, anyway, of McX's conceptual scheme – 'There is an attribute' follows from 'There are red houses, red roses, red sunsets.'

Judged in another conceptual scheme, an ontological statement which is axiomatic to McX's mind may, with equal immediacy and triviality, be adjudged false. One may admit that there are red houses, roses, and sunsets, but deny, except as a popular and misleading manner of speaking, that they have anything in common. The words 'houses', 'roses', and 'sunsets' denote each of sundry individual entities which are houses and roses and sunsets, and the word 'red' or 'red object' denotes each of sundry individual entities which are red houses, red roses, and red sunsets; but there is not, in addition, any entity whatever, individual or otherwise, which is named by the word 'redness', nor, for that matter, by the word 'househood', 'rosehood', 'sunsethood'. That the houses and roses and sunsets are all of them red may be taken as ultimate and irreducible, and it may be held that McX is no better off, in point of real explanatory power, for all the occult entities which he posits under such names as 'redness'.

One means by which McX might naturally have tried to impose his ontology of universals on us was already removed before we turned to the problem of universals. McX cannot argue that predicates such as 'red' or 'is-red', which we all concur in using, must be regarded as names each of a single universal entity in order that they be meaningful at all. For, we have seen that being a name of something is a much more special feature than being meaningful. He cannot even charge us – at least not by *that* argument – with having posited an attribute of pegasizing by our adoption of the predicate 'pegasizes'.

However, McX hits upon a different stratagem. "Let us grant," he says, "this distinction between meaning and naming of which you make so much. Let us even grant that 'is red', 'pegasizes', etc., are not names of attributes Still, you admit they have meanings. But these

meanings, whether they are *named* or not, are still universals, and I venture to say that some of them might even be the very things that I call attributes, or something to much the same purpose in the end."

For McX, this is an unusually penetrating speech; and the only way I know to counter it is by refusing to admit meanings. However, I feel no reluctance toward refusing to admit meanings, for I do not thereby deny that words and statements are meaningful. McX and I may agree to the letter in our classification of linguistic forms into the meaningful and the meaningless, even though McX construes meaningfulness as the *having* (in some sense of 'having') of some abstract entity which he calls a meaning, whereas I do not. I remain free to maintain that the fact that a given linguistic utterance is meaningful (or *significant*, as I prefer to say so as not to invite hypostasis of meanings as entities) is an ultimate and irreducible matter of fact; or, I may undertake to analyze it in terms directly of what people do in the presence of the linguistic utterance in question and other utterances similar to it.

The useful ways in which people ordinarily talk or seem to talk about meanings boil down to two: the *having* of meanings, which is significance, and *sameness* of meaning, or synonymy. What is called *giving* the meaning of an utterance is simply the uttering of a synonym, couched, ordinarily, in clearer language than the original. If we are allergic to meanings as such, we can speak directly of utterances as significant or insignificant, and as synonymous or heteronymous one with another. The problem of explaining these adjectives 'significant' and 'synonymous' with some degree of clarity and rigor – preferably, as I see it, in terms of behavior – is as difficult as it is important. But the explanatory value of special and irreducible intermediary entities called meanings is surely illusory.

Up to now I have argued that we can use singular terms significantly in sentences without presupposing that there be the entities which those terms purport to name. I have argued further that we can use general terms, e.g., predicates, without conceding them to be names of abstract entities. I have argued further that we can view utterances as significant, and as synonymous or heteronymous with one another, without countenancing a realm of entities called meanings. At this point McX begins to wonder whether there is any limit at all to our ontological immunity. Does *nothing* we may say commit us to the assumption of universals or other entities which we may find unwelcome?

I have already suggested a negative answer to this question, in speaking of bound variables, or variables of quantification, in connection with Russell's theory of descriptions. We can very easily involve ourselves in ontological commitments, by saying, e.g., that *there is something* (bound variable) which red houses and sunsets have in common; or that *there is something* which is a prime number between 1000 and 1010. But this is, essentially, the *only* way we can involve ourselves in ontological commitments: by our use of bound variables. The use of alleged names is no criterion, for we can repudiate their namehood at the drop of a hat unless the assumption of a corresponding entity can be spotted in the things we affirm in terms of bound variables. Names are in fact altogether immaterial to the ontological issue, for I have shown, in connection with 'Pegasus' and 'pegasize', that names can be converted to descriptions, and Russell has shown that descriptions can be eliminated. Whatever we say with help of names can be said in a language which shuns names altogether. To be is, purely and simply, to be the value of a variable. In terms of the categories of traditional grammar, this amounts roughly to saying that to be is to be in the range of reference of a pronoun. Pronouns are the basic media of reference; nouns might better have been named pro-pronouns. The variables of quantification, 'something', 'nothing', 'everything', range over our whole ontology, whatever it may be; and we are convicted of a particular ontological

presupposition if, and only if, the alleged presuppositum has to be reckoned among the entities over which our variables range in order to render one of our affirmations true.

We may say, e.g., that some dogs are white, and not thereby commit ourselves to recognizing either doghood or whiteness as entities. 'Some dogs are white' says that some things that are dogs are white; and, in order that this statement be true, the things over which the bound variable 'something' ranges must include some white dogs, but need not include doghood or whiteness. On the other hand, when we say that some zoölogical species are cross-fertile, we are committing ourselves to recognizing as entities the several species themselves, abstract though they be. We remain so committed at least until we devise some way of so paraphrasing the statement as to show that the seeming reference to species on the part of our bound variable was an avoidable manner of speaking.

If I have been seeming to minimize the degree to which in our philosophical and unphilosophical discourse we involve ourselves in ontological commitments, let me then emphasize that classical mathematics, as the example of primes between 1000 and 1010 clearly illustrates, is up to its neck in commitments to an ontology of abstract entities. Thus it is that the great mediaeval controversy over universals has flared up anew in the modern philosophy of mathematics. The issue is clearer now than of old, because we now have a more explicit standard whereby to decide what ontology a given theory or form of discourse is committed to: a theory is committed to those and only those entities to which the bound variables of the theory must be capable of referring in order that the affirmations made in the theory be true.

Because this standard of ontological presupposition did not emerge clearly in the philosophical tradition, the modern philosophical mathematicians have not on the whole recognized that they were debating the same old problem of universals in a newly clarified form.

But the fundamental cleavages among modern points of view on foundations of mathematics do come down pretty explicitly to disagreements as to the range of entities to which the bound variables should be permitted to refer.

The three main mediaeval points of view regarding universals are designated by historians as *realism*, *conceptualism*, and *nominalism*. Essentially these same three doctrines reappear in twentieth-century surveys of the philosophy of mathematics under the new names *logicism*, *intuitionism*, and *formalism*.

Realism, as the word is used in connection with the mediaeval controversy over universals, is the Platonic doctrine that universals or abstract entities have being independently of the mind; the mind may discover them but cannot create them. *Logicism*, represented by such latter-day Platonists as Frege, Russell, Whitehead, Church, and Carnap, condones the use of bound variables to refer to abstract entities known and unknown, specifiable and unspecifiable, indiscriminately.

Conceptualism holds that there are universals but they are mind-made. *Intuitionism*, espoused in modern times in one form or another by Poincaré, Brouwer, Weyl, and others, countenances the use of bound variables to refer to abstract entities only when those entities are capable of being cooked up individually from ingredients specified in advance. As Fraenkel has put it, logicism holds that classes are discovered while intuitionism holds that they are invented – a fair statement indeed of the old opposition between realism and conceptualism. This opposition is no mere quibble; it makes an essential difference in the amount of classical mathematics to which one is willing to subscribe. Logicists, or realists, are able on their assumptions to get Cantor's ascending orders of infinity; intuitionists are compelled to stop with the lowest order of infinity, and, as an indirect consequence, to abandon even some of the classical laws of real numbers. The modern controversy between logicism and intuitionism arose, in fact, from disagreements over infinity.

Formalism, associated with the name of Hilbert, echoes intuitionism in deploring the logicist's unbridled recourse to universals. But formalism also finds intuitionism unsatisfactory. This could happen for either of two opposite reasons. The formalist might, like the logicist, object to the crippling of classical mathematics; or he might, like the *nominalists* of old, object to admitting abstract entities at all, even in the restrained sense of mind-made entities. The upshot is the same: the formalist keeps classical mathematics as a play of insignificant notations. This play of notations can still be of utility – whatever utility it has already shown itself to have as a crutch for physicists and technologists. But utility need not imply significance, in any literal linguistic sense. Nor need the marked success of mathematicians in spinning out theorems, and in finding objective bases for agreement with one another's results, imply significance. For, an adequate basis for agreement among mathematicians can be found simply in the rules which govern the manipulation of the notations – these syntactical rules being, unlike the notations themselves, quite significant and intelligible.[2]

I have argued that the sort of ontology we adopt can be consequential—notably in connection with mathematics, although this is only an example. Now how are we to adjudicate among rival ontologies? Certainly the answer is not provided by the semantical formula "To be is to be the value of a variable"; this formula serves rather, conversely, in testing the conformity of a given remark or doctrine to a prior ontological standard. We look to bound variables in connection with ontology not in order to know what there is, but in order to know what a given remark or doctrine, ours or someone else's, *says* there is; and this much is quite properly a problem involving language. But what there is is another question.

In debating over what there is, there are still reasons for operating on a semantical plane. One reason is to escape from the predicament noted at the beginning of the paper: the predicament of my not being able to admit that there are things which McX countenances and I do not. So long as I adhere to my ontology, as opposed to McX's, I cannot allow my bound variables to refer to entities which belong to McX's ontology and not to mine. I can, however, consistently describe our disagreement by characterizing the statements which McX affirms. Provided merely that my ontology countenances linguistic forms, or at least concrete inscriptions and utterances. I can talk about McX's sentences.

Another reason for withdrawing to a semantical plane is to find common ground on which to argue. Disagreement in ontology involves basic disagreement in conceptual schemes: yet McX and I, despite these basic disagreements, find that our conceptual schemes converge sufficiently in their intermediate and upper ramifications to enable us to communicate successfully on such topics as politics, weather, and, in particular, language. In so far as our basic controversy over ontology can be translated upward into a semantical controversy about words and what to do with them, the collapse of the controversy into question-begging may be delayed.

It is no wonder, then, that ontological controversy should tend into controversy over language. But we must not jump to the conclusion that what there is depends on words. Translatability of a question into semantical terms is no indication that the question is linguistic. To see Naples is to bear a name which, when prefixed to the words 'sees Naples', yields a true sentence; still there is nothing linguistic about seeing Naples.

Our acceptance of an ontology is, I think, similar in principle to our acceptance of a scientific theory, say a system of physics: we adopt, at least insofar as we are reasonable, the simplest conceptual scheme into which the disordered fragments of raw experience can be fitted and arranged. Our ontology is determined once we have fixed upon the over-all conceptual scheme which is to accommodate science in the broadest sense; and the considerations which determine

a reasonable construction of any part of that conceptual scheme, e.g. the biological or the physical part, are not different in kind from the considerations which determine a reasonable construction of the whole. To whatever extent the adoption of any system of scientific theory may be said to be a matter of language, the same – but no more – may be said of the adoption of an ontology.

But simplicity, as a guiding principle in constructing conceptual schemes, is not a clear and unambiguous idea; and it is quite capable of presenting a double or multiple standard. Imagine, e.g., that we have devised the most economical set of concepts adequate to the play-by-play reporting of immediate experience. The entities under this scheme – the values of bound variables – are, let us suppose, individual subjective events of sensation or reflection. We should still find, no doubt, that a physicalistic conceptual scheme, purporting to talk about external objects, offers great advantages in simplifying our over-all reports. By bringing together scattered sense events and treating them as perceptions of one object, we reduce the complexity of our stream of experience to a manageable conceptual simplicity. The rule of simplicity is indeed our guiding maxim in assigning sense data to objects: we associate an earlier and a later round sensum with the same so-called penny, or with two different so-called pennies, in obedience to the demands of maximum simplicity in our total world-picture.

Here we have two competing conceptual schemes, a phenomenalistic one and a physicalistic one. Which should prevail? Each has its advantages; each has its special simplicity in its own way. Each, I suggest, deserves to be developed. Each may be said, indeed, to be the more fundamental, though in different senses: the one is epistemologically, the other physically, fundamental.

The physical conceptual scheme simplifies our account of experience because of the way myriad scattered sense events come to be associated with single so-called objects; still there is no likelihood that each sentence about physical objects can actually be translated, however deviously and complexly, into the phenomenalistic language. Physical objects are postulated entities which round out and simplify our account of the flux of experience, just as the introduction of irrational numbers simplifies laws of arithmetic. From the point of view of the conceptual scheme of the elementary arithmetic of rational numbers alone, the broader arithmetic of rational and irrational numbers would have the status of a convenient myth, simpler than the literal truth (namely the arithmetic of rationals) and yet containing that literal truth as a scattered part. Similarly, from a phenomenalistic point of view, the conceptual scheme of physical objects is a convient myth, simpler than the literal truth and yet containing that literal truth as a scattered part.

Now what of classes or attributes of physical objects, in turn? A platonistic ontology of this sort is, from the point of view of a strictly physicalistic conceptual scheme, as much of a myth as that physicalistic conceptual scheme itself was for phenomenalism. This higher myth is a good and useful one, in turn, in so far as it simplifies our account of physics. Since mathematics is an integral part of this higher myth, the utility of this myth for physical science is evident enough. In speaking of it nevertheless as a myth, I echo that philosophy of mathematics to which I alluded earlier under the name of formalism. But my present suggestion is that an attitude of formalism may with equal justice be adopted toward the physical conceptual scheme, in turn, by the pure aesthete or phenomenalist.

The analogy between the myth of mathematics and the myth of physics is, in some additional and perhaps fortuitous ways, strikingly close. Consider, for example, the crisis which was precipitated in the foundations of mathematics, at the turn of the century, by the discovery of Russell's paradox and other antinomies of set

theory. These contradictions had to be obviated by unintuitive, *ad hoc* devices; our mathematical myth-making became deliberate and evident to all. But what of physics? An antinomy arose between the undular and the corpuscular accounts of light; and if this was not as out-and-out a contradiction as Russell's paradox, I suspect that the reason is merely that physics is not as out-and-out as mathematics. Again, the second great modern crisis in the foundations of mathematics – precipitated in 1931 by Gödel's proof that there are bound to be undecidable statements in arithmetic – has its companion-piece in physics in Heisenberg's indeterminacy principle.

In earlier pages I undertook to show that some common arguments in favor of certain ontologies are fallacious. Further, I advanced an explicit standard whereby to decide what the ontological commitments of a theory are. But the question what ontology actually to adopt still stands open, and the obvious counsel is tolerance and an experimental spirit. Let us by all means see how much of the physicalistic conceptual scheme can be reduced to a phenomenalistic one; still physics also naturally demands pursuing, irreducible in *toto* though it be. Let us see how, or to what degree, natural science may be rendered independent of platonistic mathematics; but let us also pursue mathematics and delve into its platonistic foundations.

From among the various conceptual schemes best suited to these various pursuits, one – the phenomenalistic – claims epistemological priority. Viewed from within the phenomenalistic conceptual scheme, the ontologies of physical objects and mathematical objects are myths. The quality of myth, however, is relative; relative, in this case, to the epistemological point of view. This point of view is one among various, corresponding to one among our various interests and purposes.

Notes

1   This is a revised version of a paper which was presented before the Graduate Philosophy Club of Yale University on May 7, 1948. The latter paper, in turn, was a revised version of one which was presented before the Graduate Philosophical Seminary of Princeton University on March 15.

2   See Goodman and Quine, "Steps toward a constructive nominalism," *Journal of Symbolic Logic*, vol. 12 (1947), pp. 97–122.

Chapter 2

Henry Fitzgerald

NOMINALIST THINGS

Scene: bedroom in an Austrian mansion, c.1937

Gretel. I don't like his manner.
Kurt. His attitude worries me.
Lisel. I am troubled by a general air of foreboding.
Maria. Yes, children: my life is also, on occasion, clouded by manners, attitudes and airs of foreboding.
Brigita. So what do you do about it?
Maria. Why, I simply think of nominalistically respectable things instead.
Von Trapp children (together). Nominalistically respectable things? What are they?
Maria. Well, let me explain . . .

Properties, counterparts, tropes and relations,
Promises, lies and confused explanations,
Numbers and rhomboids, and this very list:
These are all items which do not exist.

Space-time and classes and Beethoven's seventh,
Earthquakes and sets and July the eleventh,
Are, like the flutter of butterflies' wings,
Nominalistically dubious things . . .

In my calm and
Lucid moments,
When I'm feeling fine,
I scorn the existence of all of this stuff,
I talk about all the time.

Maria. Come on children, tell me some nominalistically respectable things.
Kurt (doubtfully). Er . . . stones? Concrete?
Lisel (even more doubtfully). Electrons?
Maria. Well—uh—yes, but there's much more to it than that . . .

Raindrops and temporal slices of kittens,
Every third stitch in a pair of red mittens,
Mereological bundles of string:
These are all perfectly reasonable things.

Barmaids and walnuts and sand that's been hosed off,
Silver and gold and the fusion composed of
Alpha Centauri and Hitler's left knee:
All of these objects are okay by me . . .

Things substantial,
Made of matter:
They are better, far,
Than some abstract nonsense but one step removed
From Rorty and Derrida.

Frideric. Exoskeletons!
Kurt. Time-slices of undetached heads!
Lisel (getting carried away): Statues of Rottweilers! Dragons!
Remaining von Trapp children (together). Dragons??
Maria. It's all right, children! One need have no quarrel with dragons, qua nominalist! The number two would be a far greater stain on the world's ontological purity than a mere dragon!

Hobbits and wizards and weapons enchanted:
Towering trees which Galadriel planted,
Rhine maidens, giants and Nibelung rings:
These are a few of my favourite things.

Underground kingdoms and magical potions,
Atomless matter and bottomless oceans:
Though they're not terribly easy to find,
Nominalistically, no one should mind.

Can you touch it?
When you hit it,
Does it make a 'ping'?
If you answered 'yes', then, by golly, it's real:
It gets to be called a THING.

Chapter 3

Peter van Inwagen

A THEORY OF PROPERTIES

1. It Would Be Better Not to Believe in Abstract Objects if We Could Get Away with It

In their book *A Subject without an Object: Strategies for the Nominalistic Interpretation of Mathematics*[1] (the main topic of the book is well conveyed by its subtitle), John Burgess and Gideon Rosen suggest that—in fact, they argue at some length for the conclusion that—the motivation for undertaking nominalistic reconstructions of mathematics has not been clearly and persuasively formulated.[2] This seems to me to be wrong. At any rate, it seems to me that it is not hard to formulate the motivation (or a sufficient motivation) for this project clearly and persuasively. Suppose one could show this: it would be better not to believe in abstract objects if one could get away with it. Or this, if it is not the same: it would be philosophically desirable to accept only philosophical positions that do not require their adherents to affirm the existence of abstract objects. I will take it that it is evident why someone who accepted this conclusion (or either of them, if they are different) would have a strong motivation for wishing that a nominalistic reconstruction or interpretation of mathematics were available.

In this section I will present an argument for the conclusion that not believing in abstract objects would be a Good Thing—for the conclusion, that is, that one should not believe in

abstract objects unless one feels rationally compelled to by some weighty consideration or argument. If we call the thesis that there are abstract objects *platonism*, my conclusion is that a philosopher should wish not to be a platonist if it's rationally possible for the informed philosopher not to be a platonist. And I'll take it for granted that, if one takes this attitude toward platonism, one should take the same attitude toward any theory from which platonism is deducible. Thus, if a theory T entails platonism, that is a good reason not to accept that theory. (This bald statement requires qualification, however. If T is a very attractive theory, the fact that T entails platonism might be a good reason for accepting platonism. Its existence and the fact that it entailed platonism might in fact be just the "weighty reason" for accepting platonism that showed that one should, after all, be a platonist. My point is really a truism: if Theory One entails Theory Two, and is known to do so, then the question whether either of the theories should be accepted or rejected cannot be considered in isolation from the question whether the other should be accepted or rejected.) If, moreover, a theory might, for all anyone knows at present, entail platonism, that is a good reason to try to find out whether it in fact entails platonism— just as, if a theory might, for all anyone knows, entail a contradiction, that is a good reason to try to find out whether it in fact entails a contradiction.

My thesis is no clearer than the term 'abstract object', and, unfortunately, I have nothing very useful to say about what this phrase means. I will note, however, that it is possible to divide the terms and predicates we use in everyday and scientific and philosophical discourse into two exhaustive and exclusive classes by a very simple method. We stipulate that one class shall contain the terms and predicates in the following list: 'table', 'the copy of *War and Peace* on the table', 'Mont Blanc', 'the Eiffel Tower', 'Catherine the Great', 'neutron star', 'intelligent Martian', 'elf', 'ghost', 'angel', 'god', and 'God'. We stipulate that the other shall contain 'number', 'the ratio of 1 to 0', 'proposition', 'sentence' (as in 'the same offensive sentence was scrawled on every blackboard in the building') 'property', 'angle' (as in 'the sum of the opposite angles of a right triangle is equal to a right angle'), 'possibility' (as in 'that possibility is still unrealized'), 'the lion' (as in 'the lion is a large African carnivore of the genus *Felis*'), '*War and Peace*' (as in '*War and Peace* has been translated into thirty-nine languages'), 'the English language', and 'the mixolydian mode'. We then ask philosophers (it had better be philosophers; it's unlikely that anyone else will cooperate) to place each term or predicate of our discourse (let's leave mass terms out of the picture, just to simplify matters) in the class where it will be most at home. (We make it clear that the classification is not to depend on whether the person doing the classifying believes that a term to be classified denotes anything or believes that a predicate to be classified has a non-empty extension. We have, in fact, included such items as 'the ratio of 1 to 0' and 'elf' among our 'paradigms', items, that is, that by everyone's reckoning have no semantical correlates, to make our intent on this point clear.) I say that this procedure will yield pretty consistent results. Perhaps not as consistent as the results would have been if the paradigms comprised the names of twenty even numbers and twenty odd numbers and the "new" words our respondents were

asked to classify were all names of natural numbers. But pretty consistent. Some of the terms in our list of paradigms may be ambiguous and might be understood by different philosophers in different ways. And some philosophers may have idiosyncratic theories about the items in the extensions of some of these terms. (Most philosophers would put '{Catherine the Great, {the Eiffel Tower}}' in with 'property' and 'the lion'; but the author of *Parts of Classes* might be inclined to think that this term was more at home with 'Catherine the Great' and 'the Eiffel Tower'.) And some terms may just yield inconsistent responses: Amie Thomasson would say that our whole scheme of classification was in at least one respect objectionable, since '*War and Peace*' isn't a clear candidate for membership in either class—for it denotes an object that is non-spatial and has instances (like many of the items in the second list), and is, nevertheless, a contingently existing artifact (like some of the items in the first). Nicholas Wolterstorff would say that our classification scheme was unobjectionable, and that '*War and Peace*' clearly belonged right where we had put it, since it denoted something that was much more like a proposition than it was like a volume on a library shelf. He would add that the idea of a contingently existing, non-spatial object that had instances was incoherent.[3] (I don't think that either of these philosophers could be said to have a theory of the ontology of the novel that was "idiosyncratic" in the way Lewis's theory of classes is idiosyncratic.)

When all the possible qualifications and doubtful cases have been noted, however, there will be, or so I maintain, really substantial agreement as to which class any given term or predicate should be placed in. (There will also be substantial agreement on this point: every term can be placed in one list or the other.) And this implies that, with respect to most terms, most philosophers will be in substantial agreement about the truth-values of the propositions that are substitution-instances of the following schema:

If X is really, as it appears on the syntactical face of it to be, a term, and if it denotes an object, it denotes an abstract object.

Where did the words 'abstract object' come from? 'Abstract object' as I see it, is just the general term that applies to the objects denoted by the terms in the second class—provided, of course, that those terms have denotations. This is no substantive thesis, not even a substantive thesis about meaning. It is simply a stipulation. By a similar stipulation, we can call the items denoted by the terms in the first class *concrete* objects. (The word 'object', as I use it, is simply the most general count-noun. It is synonymous with 'thing' and 'item' and, no doubt, with 'entity'. That is to say, everything is an object. That is to say, 'For every x, if x is an object, then x is F' is equivalent to 'For every x, x is F' and 'For some x, x is an object and x is F' is equivalent to 'For some x, x is F'.) A similar point applies to the schema 'If X is really, as it appears on the syntactical face of it to be, a predicate, and if it has a non-empty extension, its extension comprises abstract objects.' The qualification 'if X really is a term' is a concession to anyone who thinks (and no doubt this is a very reasonable thing to think in some cases) that some words or phrases that have the syntax of terms do not really "function as denoting phrases".

This is as much as I have to say about the meaning of 'abstract object'. On such understanding of 'abstract object' as what I have said supplies, a "platonist" is someone who thinks that at least some of the linguistic items in the second class really are terms (really are predicates) and really have referents (really have non-empty extensions). If my thesis is wrong—if my lists of paradigms does *not* really partition the terms and predicates we use into two classes, if this is not even an *approximation* to the truth—then my explanation fails, owing simply to the fact that there is no such thing as what I have called 'the second class of terms'.

In my view, as I have said, it is better not to be a platonist—prima facie better, better if we can get away with it. The reason is not profound. I suppose one could classify it as an 'Occam's razor' sort of reason, though I will not make any use of this term.

Think of matters this way. The platonist must think of objects, of what there is, as falling into two exclusive and exhaustive categories, the abstract and the concrete. If x falls into one of these categories and y into the other, then no two things could be more different than x and y. According to orthodox Christian theology, no two concrete things could differ more than God and an inanimate object. But (assuming for the sake of the illustration that all three things exist) the differences between God and this pen pale into insignificance when they are compared with the differences between this pen and the number 4; indeed, the number seems no more like the pen than like God. The difference between *any* abstract object and *any* concrete object would seem to be the maximum difference any two objects could display. The difference between a topological space and the color the Taj Mahal shares with the Washington Monument is no doubt very great, but each is far more like the other than either is like this pen. (Again, of course, we are assuming for the sake of the illustration that all three things exist.)

Now it seems very puzzling that objects should fall into two exclusive and radically different categories. Rather than suppose that this is so, it would be much more appealing to suppose that at least one of these categories is empty—or that the words we have used to describe one or both of the two categories are meaningless. And we cannot suppose that the category that contains the pen, the category of concrete objects, is empty, for that is the category into which *we* fall, and, as Descartes has pointed out, we know *we* exist. (I set aside Quine's amusing reduction of supposedly concrete things to pure sets; we can't discuss everything. I shall mention this reduction again, but only as an example to illustrate a point.) It seems, moreover, that we know a lot more about concrete things than we know about abstract things. We understand them better. Maybe not *well*, but better than we understand abstract things. At least we understand *some* of them better: simple paradigms of concrete things. We do not understand even the simplest, the paradigmatic, abstract objects very well at all. You say there is such a thing as the number 4? All right, tell me what properties it has. Well, it has logical properties like self-identity and having, for no property, both that property and its complement. And it has arithmetical properties like being even and being the successor of three and numbering the Stuart kings of England. But what others? It is, no doubt, non-spatial, and perhaps non-temporal. It is perhaps necessarily existent. At about this point we trail off into uncertainty. Consider, by way of contrast, this pen. It has the same logical properties as the number. It does not have arithmetical properties, but it has functional properties, like being an instrument for making marks on surfaces, and perhaps the functional properties of an artifact are analogous to the arithmetical properties of a number. It has "metaphysical" properties, properties as abstract and general as those we ascribed to the number: it occupies space, it endures through or is extended in time, its existence is contingent. When we have said these things, these things that correspond to what we were able to say about the number, however, we do not trail off into uncertainty. There is *lots* more we can say. We could write a book about the pen, albeit not a very interesting one. We could discuss its color, its mass, its spatial and mereological structure, the chemical composition of its various parts and of the ink it contains, the devices by which ink is drawn from an internal reservoir to the rolling ball that distributes the ink on paper, and so—for practical purposes, at least—*ad infinitum*. If it is not altogether clear what I mean by saying that we have a pretty good understanding of a certain *object* ('object' as opposed to 'concept'),

this is what I mean: this ability to go on saying true things about the intrinsic features of the object till we drop. And if I say we do not have a very good understanding of the number 4, I mean simply that, if we try to describe its intrinsic features, we soon trail off in puzzlement. We may trail off in puzzlement at some point in our disquisition about the pen: when we try to specify the conditions under which it endures through time or the counterfactual situations in which it would have existed, for example. (If Sartre is right, certain speculations about the pen can lead not only to puzzlement but to nausea.) But we can go on about the pen for an awfully long time before we come to such a point. If this difference in our abilities to describe the pen and the number cannot be ascribed to "a better understanding" of the pen than of the number, what can it be ascribed to? After all, it can hardly be that the number has fewer properties than the pen. If the number and the pen both exist—if the phrases 'the number 4' and 'this pen' both really denote something—then these two objects both have the following feature: each is an object x such that, for every property, x has either that property or its complement. It must therefore be that we know a lot less about the properties of the number than we do about the properties of the pen. And that seems to me to imply that, when we talk about the pen, we have a pretty good idea of the nature of the thing we are talking about, and when we talk about the number, we have at best a radically incomplete idea of the nature of the thing we are talking about.

Platonists, therefore, must say that reality, what there is, is divided into two parts: one part *we* belong to, and everything in this part is more like us than is anything in the other part. The inhabitants of the other part are radically unlike us, much more unlike us than is anything in "our" part, and we can't really say much about what the things in the other part are like. It seems to me to be evident that it would be better not to believe in the other part of reality, the other category of things, if we could manage it. But we can't manage it. In the next section I shall try to explain why we can't get along without *one* kind of abstract object: properties.

2. We Can't Get Away with It

What reasons are there for believing in the existence of properties (qualities, attributes, characteristics, features, . . .)? I think it is fair to say that there are apparently such things as properties. There is, for example, apparently such a thing as humanity. The members of the class of human beings, as the idiom has it, "have something in common". This appears to be an existential proposition. If it is (the platonist will ask rhetorically), what could this "something" be but the property "humanity"? It could certainly not be anything physical, for—Siamese twins excepted—no two human beings have any physical thing in common. And, of course, what goes for the class of human beings goes for the class of birds, the class of white things, and the class of intermediate vector bosons: the members of each of these classes have something in common with one another—or so it appears—and what the members of a class have in common is a property—or so it appears. But, as often happens in philosophy, many philosophers deny that what is apparently the case is really the case. These philosophers—"nominalists"—contend that the apparent existence of properties is mere appearance, and that, in reality, there are no properties.

How can the dispute between those who affirm and those who deny the existence of properties (platonists and nominalists) be resolved? The ontological method invented, or at least first made explicit, by Quine and Goodman (and illustrated with wonderful ingenuity in David and Stephanie Lewis's "Holes") suggests a way to approach this question.[4] Nominalists and platonists have different beliefs about what there is. Let us therefore ask this: how should one decide what to believe about what there is? According to Quine, the problem of deciding

what to believe about what there is is a very straightforward special case of the problem of deciding what to believe. (The problem of deciding what to believe is, to be sure, no trivial problem, but it is a problem everyone is going to have somehow to come to terms with.) If we want to decide whether to believe that there are properties, Quine tells us, we should examine the beliefs we already have, the theses we have already, for whatever reason, decided to believe, and see whether they "commit us" (as Quine says) to the existence of properties. But what does this mean? Let us consider an example. Suppose we find the following proposition among our beliefs:

Spiders share some of the anatomical features of insects.

A plausible case can be made for the thesis that this belief commits us to the existence of properties. We may observe, first, that it is very hard to see what an "anatomical feature" (such as "having an exoskeleton") could be if it were not a property: 'property', 'quality', 'characteristic', 'attribute', and 'feature' are all more or less synonyms. The following question is therefore of interest: does our belief that spiders share some of the anatomical features of insects therefore commit us to the existence of "anatomical features"? If we examine the meaning of the sentence 'Spiders share some of the anatomical features of insects', we find that what it says is this:

There are anatomical features that insects have and spiders also have.

Or, in the "canonical language of quantification",

It is true of at least one thing that it is such that it is an anatomical feature and insects have it and spiders also have it.

(The canonical language of quantification does not essentially involve the symbols '∀' and '∃'.

Natural-language phrases like 'it is true of everything that it is such that' and 'it is true of at least one thing that it is such that' will do as well, for the symbols are merely shorthand ways of writing such phrases. And the canonical language of quantification does not essentially involve variables—'x', 'y' and so on. For variables are nothing more than pronouns: "variables" are simply a stock of typographically distinct third-person-singular pronouns; having such a stock at one's disposal is no more than a device for facilitating cross-reference when one makes complicated statements. In the case of the present simple statement, 'it' works as well as 'x': there is *no* difference in meaning between 'It is true of at least one thing that it is such that it is an anatomical feature and insects have it and spiders also have it' and '∃x x is an anatomical feature and insects have x and spiders also have x'.)

It is a straightforward logical consequence of this proposition that there are anatomical features: if there are anatomical features that insects have and spiders also have, then there are anatomical features that insects have; if there are anatomical features that insects have, then there are anatomical features—full stop.

Does this little argument show that anyone who believes that spiders share some of the anatomical features of insects is committed to platonism, and, more specifically, to a belief in the existence of properties? How might a nominalist respond to this little argument? Suppose we present the argument to Norma, a convinced nominalist (who believes, as most people do, that spiders share some of the anatomical features of insects). Assuming that Norma is unwilling simply to have inconsistent beliefs, there would seem to be four possible ways for her to respond to it:

(1)   She might become a platonist.
(2)   She might abandon her allegiance to the thesis that spiders share some of the anatomical features of insects.
(3)   She might attempt to show that, despite

appearances, it does not follow from this thesis that there are anatomical features.
(4)   She might admit that her beliefs (her nominalism and her belief that spiders share some of the anatomical features of insects) are apparently inconsistent, affirm her nominalistic faith that this inconsistency is apparent, not real, and confess that, although she is confident that there is some fault in our alleged demonstration that her belief about spiders and insects commits her to the existence of anatomical features, she is at present unable to discover it.

Possibility (2) is not really very attractive. It is unattractive for at least two reasons. First, it seems to be a simple fact of biology that spiders share some of the anatomical features of insects. Secondly, there are many, many "simple facts" that could have been used as the premise of an essentially identical argument for the conclusion that there are properties. (For example, elements in the same column in the Periodic Table tend to have many of the same chemical properties; some of the most important characteristics of the nineteenth-century novel are rarely present in the twentieth-century novel.) Possibility (4) is always an option, but no philosopher is likely to embrace it except as a last resort. What Norma is likely to do is to try to avail herself of possibility (3). She is likely to try to show that her belief about spiders and insects does not in fact commit her to platonism. If she does, she will attempt to find a *paraphrase* of 'Spiders share some of the anatomical features of insects', a sentence that (i) she could use in place of this sentence, and (ii) does not even *seem* to have 'There are anatomical features' as one of its logical consequences. If she can do this, she will be in a position to contend that the commitment to the existence of anatomical features that is apparently "carried by" her belief about spiders and insects is only apparent. And she will be in a position to contend—no doubt further argument would be required to establish this—that the apparent existence of anatomical features is *mere* appearance (an appearance that is due to certain forms of words we use but needn't use).

Is it possible to find such a paraphrase? (And to find paraphrases of all the other apparently true statements that seem to commit those who make them to the reality of properties?) Well, yes and no. 'Yes' because it is certainly possible to find paraphrases of the spider-insect sentence that involve quantification over some other sort of abstract object than anatomical features—that is, other than properties. One might, for example, eliminate (as the jargon has it) the quantification over properties on display in the spider-insect sentence in favor of quantification over, say, concepts. No doubt any work that could be done by the property "having an exoskeleton" could be done by the concept "thing with an exoskeleton". Neither of the two statements 'At least one thing is such that it is an anatomical feature and insects have it and spiders also have it' and 'At least one thing is such that it is an anatomical concept and insects fall under it and spiders also fall under it' would seem to enjoy any real advantage over the other as a vehicle for expressing what we know about the mutual relations of the members of the phylum *Arthropoda*; or, if one of them does, it will be some relatively minor, technical advantage. It is certain that a nominalist will be no more receptive to an ontology that contains concepts (understood in a platonic or Fregean sense, and not in some psychological sense) than to an ontology that contains properties. When I say it is not possible to get along without asserting the existence of properties, therefore, what I mean is that it is not possible to get along without asserting the existence of properties—or something that a nominalist is not going to like any better than properties.

Now the distinction between a "relatively minor, technical advantage" and a really important advantage, an advantage that can be appealed to as relevant in disputes about fundamental ontology, is not as clear as it might be. Here is an example that illustrates this point. Some philosophers, most notably Quine, would agree that we cannot eliminate quantification over abstract objects, but deny that examples like the above, or any other consideration, should convince us that there are *properties*. Quine would insist that the most that any such argument can establish is that we must allow the existence of *sets*. Quine concedes that in affirming the existence of sets he is affirming the existence of abstract objects. The set of all spiders, after all, is not a spider or a sum of spiders or any other sort of concrete object. It is true that if the only use we made of the language of set-theory was exemplified by phrases like 'the set of all spiders' and 'the set of all intermediate vector bosons', we could regard our use of such phrases as being merely a device for referring collectively to all spiders, to all intermediate vector bosons, and so on. But that is not the only use we make of such language; for, if we are going to say the things we want to say, and if we affirm the existence of no abstract objects but sets, we must quantify over sets and we must refer to (and quantify over) sets that have sets as members. (If we wish to express the facts of evolutionary biology, we must say things like 'Any spider and any insect have a common ancestor', and those who believe in no abstract objects but sets cannot say that without quantifying over sets—at least, not unless they are willing to take 'ancestor of' as undefined; if their only undefined term is 'parent of', they must affirm generalizations about individually unspecified sets to express the idea 'ancestor of'. Or we may wish to make use of the idea of *linear order*—we may, for example, wish to calculate the probability of drawing a face card, an ace, and a heart *in that order*; and those of us who believe in no abstract objects but sets must refer to sets that have sets as members to explain the idea of things-arranged-in-some-linear-order.) Sets, then, are abstract objects; but, Quine says, sets are not properties. And this statement points to a far more important fact than the statement that concepts are not properties. Sets, Quine tells us, are well-behaved in a way in which concepts and properties are not. Or, availing himself of the method of "semantic ascent", he might wish rather to say this: those who contend that general terms like 'concept' and 'property' have nonempty extensions face intractable problems of individuation, problems that do not face those who, in admitting abstract objects into their ontology, content themselves with admitting sets. I mention this position of Quine's (that an ontology that contains sets and no other abstract objects is superior, all other things being equal, to an ontology that contains properties or Fregean concepts) because it is important, but I decline to discuss it because it raises some very difficult questions, questions I cannot attempt to answer within the confines of this paper.[5]

Let us return to the topic of paraphrase. Is it possible to provide sentences like 'Spiders share some of the anatomical features of insects' with *nominalistically acceptable* paraphrases? My position is that it is not. I cannot hope to present an adequate defense of this position, for an adequate defense of this position would have to take the form of an examination of all possible candidates for nominalistically acceptable paraphrases of such sentences, and I cannot hope to do that. The question of nominalistically acceptable paraphrase will be answered, if at all, only as the outcome of an extended dialectical process, a process involving many philosophers and many years and many gallons of ink. I can do no more than look at one strand of reasoning in this complicated dialectical tapestry. My statement "We can't get away with it" must be regarded as a promissory note. But here is the ten-dollar co-payment on the debt I have incurred by issuing this note.

Suppose a nominalist were to say this: "It's easy to find a nominalistically acceptable paraphrase of 'Spiders share some of the anatomical features of insects'. For example: 'Spiders are like insects in some anatomically relevant ways'

or 'Spiders and insects are in some respects anatomically similar'." A platonist is likely to respond as follows (at least, this is what I'd say):

> But these proposed paraphrases seem to be quantifications over "ways a thing can be like a thing" or "respects in which things can be similar". If we translate them into the canonical language of quantification, we have sentences something like these:
>
> > It is true of at least one thing that it is such that it is a way in which a thing can be like a thing and it is anatomical and spiders are like insects in it.
> >
> > It is true of at least one thing that it is a respect in which things can be similar and it is anatomical and spiders and insects are similar in it.
>
> These paraphrases, therefore, can hardly be called nominalistically acceptable. If there are such objects as ways in which a thing can be like a thing or respects in which things can be similar, they must certainly be *abstract* objects.

What might the nominalist say in reply? The most plausible reply open to the nominalist seems to me to be along the following lines.

> My platonist critic is certainly a very literal-minded fellow. I didn't mean the 'some' in the open sentence 'x is like y in some anatomically relevant ways' to be taken as a *quantifier*: I didn't mean this sentence to be read '$\exists z$ (z is a way in which a thing can be like a thing and z is anatomical and x is like y in z)'. That's absurd. One might as well read 'There's more than one way to skin a cat' as '$\exists x \, \exists y$ (x is a way of skinning a cat and y is a way of skinning a cat and $x \neq y$)'. I meant this open sentence to have no internal logical structure, or none beyond that implied by the statement that two variables are free in it. It's just a form of words we learn to use by comparing

various pairs of objects in the ordinary business of life.

And here is the rejoinder to this reply:

If you take that line you confront problems it would be better not to have to confront. Consider the sentence 'x is like y in some *physiologically* relevant ways'. Surely there is some logical or structural or syntactical relation between this sentence and 'x is like y in some anatomically relevant ways'? One way to explain the relation between these two sentences is to read the former as '$\exists z$ (z is a way in which a thing can be like a thing and z is physiological and x is like y in z)' and the latter as '$\exists z$ (z is a way in which a thing can be like a thing and z is anatomical and x is like y in z)'. How would *you* explain it? Or how would you explain the relation between the sentences 'x is like y in *some* anatomically relevant ways' (which you say has no logical structure) and 'x is like y in *all* anatomically relevant ways'? If neither of these sentences has a logical structure, how do you account for the obvious validity of the following argument?

Either of two female spiders of the same species is like the other in all anatomically relevant ways.

Hence, an insect that is like a given female spider in some anatomically relevant ways is like any female spider of the same species in some anatomically relevant ways.

If the premise and conclusion of this argument are read as having the logical structure that their syntax suggests, the validity of this argument is easily demonstrable in textbook quantifier logic. If one insists that they have no logical structure, one will find it difficult to account for the validity of this argument. That is one of those problems I alluded to, one of those problems it would be better not

to have to confront (one of thousands of such problems).

I suggest that we can learn a lesson from this little exchange between an imaginary nominalist and an imaginary platonist: that one should accept the following condition of adequacy on philosophical paraphrases:

Paraphrases must not be such as to leave us without an account of the logical relations between predicates that are obviously logically related. Essentially the same constraint on paraphrase can be put in these words: a paraphrase must not leave us without an account of the validity of any obviously valid argument.

Accepting this constraint has, I believe, a significant consequence. This consequence requires a rather lengthy statement:

Apparent quantification over properties pervades our discourse. In the end, one can avoid quantifying over properties only by quantifying over other sorts of abstract object—"ways in which a thing can be like a thing", for example. But most philosophers, if forced to choose between quantifying over properties and quantifying over these other objects, would probably prefer to quantify over properties. The reason for this may be illustrated by the case of "ways in which a thing can be like a thing". If there really are such objects as ways in which a thing can be like a thing, they seem to be at once intimately connected with properties and, so to speak, more *specialized* than properties. What, after all, would a particular "way in which a thing can be like a thing" be but the sharing of a certain property? (To say this is consistent with saying that not just any property is such that sharing it is a way in which a thing can be like a thing; sharing "being green" can plausibly be described as a way in which a thing can be like a thing, but it is much less plausible to describe sharing "being either green or not round"—if there is such a property—as a way in which a thing can be like a thing.) And if this is so, surely, the best course is to accept the existence of properties and to "analyze away" all apparent quantifications over "ways in which a thing can be like a thing" in terms of quantifications over properties.

It is the content of this lengthy statement that I have abbreviated as "We can't get away with it."

This argument I have given above has some obvious points of contact with the so-called Quine-Putnam indispensability argument for mathematical realism.[6] But there are important differences between the two arguments—I mean besides the obvious fact that my argument is an argument for the existence of properties and not an argument for the existence of specifically mathematical objects. It should be noted that my argument is not that we should believe that properties exist because their existence is an indispensable postulate of science. Nor have I contended that the scientific indispensability of properties is *evidence* for the existence of properties. I have not maintained that, because of the scientific indispensability of properties, any adequate account of the success of science must affirm the existence of properties. For one thing, my argument has nothing in particular to do with science. Science does indeed provide us with plenty of examples of sentences that must in some sense, on some analysis, express truths and also, on the face of it, imply the existence of properties—for example, 'Many of the important properties of water are due to hydrogen bonding.' But our everyday, pre-scientific discourse contains a vast number of such sentences, and these will serve my purposes as well as any sentences provided by the sciences. If our spider-insect sentence is insufficiently non-scientific to support this thesis, there are lots of others. ('The royal armorer has succeeded in producing a kind of steel that has some of but not all the desirable

characteristics of Damascus steel'.) My argument could have been presented in, say, the thirteenth century, and the advent of modern science has done nothing to make it more cogent.

More importantly, I have not supposed that the fact (supposing it to be a fact) that quantification over properties is an indispensable component of our discourse is any sort of *evidence* for the existence of properties. That's as may be; I neither affirm that thesis nor deny it. It is simply not a premise of my argument, which is not an epistemological argument. Nor is my argument any sort of "transcendental" argument or any sort of inference to the best explanation; I have not contended that the success of science cannot be accounted for on nominalistic premises. Again, that's as may be. If I have appealed to any general methodological principle, it is only this: if one doesn't believe that things of a certain sort exist, one shouldn't say anything that demonstrably implies that things of that sort do exist. (Or, at any rate, one may say such things only if one is in a position to contend, and plausibly, that saying these things is a mere manner of speaking—that, however convenient it may be, it could, in principle, be dispensed with.) This methodological rule does not, I think, deserve to be controversial. We would all agree, I assume, that, if *p* demonstrably implies the existence of God, then atheists who propose to remain atheists shouldn't affirm *p*—or not, at any rate, unless they can show us how they could in principle dispense with affirming p in favor of affirming only propositions without theological implications.[7]

I suppose I ought to add—the point needs to be made somewhere—that, if one *could* show how to eliminate quantification over properties in a nominalistically acceptable way, that achievement, by itself, would have no ontological implications. After all, Quine has shown how to eliminate quantification over everything but pure sets (at least, it can be argued that he's shown how to do this), and Church has shown how to eliminate quantification over women.[8] The devices of Quine and Church would be of ontological interest if "containing only pure sets" or "not containing women" were desirable features for an ontology to have. But they're not. If what I said in the first section of this paper is right, however, "containing no abstract objects" is an advantage in an ontology.

I will close this section with a point about philosophical logic—as opposed to metaphysics. My argument fails if there is such a thing as substitutional quantification; and it fails if there is such a thing as quantification into predicate positions. (Or so I'm willing to concede. If either substitutional quantification or quantification into predicate positions is to be found in the philosopher's tool kit, then defending my thesis—"We can't get away with it"—becomes, at the very least, a much more difficult project.) I say this: substitutional quantification and quantification into non-nominal positions (including predicate positions) are both meaningless. More exactly:

(1)   Substitutional quantification is meaningless unless it is a kind of shorthand for objectual quantification over linguistic objects, taken together with some semantic predicates like 'x is true' or 'something satisfies x'. But substitutional quantification, so understood, is of no use to the nominalist; for, so understood, every existential substitutional quantification implies the existence of linguistic items (words and sentences), and those are abstract objects.

(2)   Quantification into non-nominal positions is meaningless unless (a) the non-nominal quantifiers are understood substitutionally; this case reduces to the case already dismissed; or (b) it is understood as a kind of shorthand for nominal quantification over properties, taken together with a two-place predicate (corresponding to the 'ε' of set-theory) along the lines of 'x has y' or 'x exemplifies y'. (In saying this, I'm

saying something very similar to what Quine says when he says that second-order logic is set theory in sheep's clothing—for the salient feature of the language of second-order logic is quantification into predicate positions. But, since I do not share Quine's conviction that one should admit no abstract objects but sets into one's ontology, I am free to say "Second-order logic is property theory in sheep's clothing".)

I have defended (1) elsewhere.[9] My arguments for (2) would be no more than a reproduction of Quine's animadversions on quantification into non-nominal positions.[10]

3. If We Affirm the Existence of Properties, We Ought to Have a Theory of Properties

By a "theory of properties", I mean some sort of specification of, well, the *properties* of properties. If one succeeds in showing that we cannot dispense with quantification over properties, one's achievement does not tell us much about the intrinsic features of these things. When I was presenting what I took to be the prima facie case for nominalism, I said that we didn't know much about the properties of properties. I am now making the point that the sort of argument for the existence of properties I have offered does not tell us much about the nature of properties. The whole of our discourse about things, on the face of it, defines what may be called "the property role", and our argument can be looked on as an attempt to show that something must play this role. (The property role could, in principle, be specified by the Ramsey-style methods that Lewis sets out in "How to Define Theoretical Terms."[11]) But it tells us nothing about the intrinsic properties of the things that play this role that enable them to play this role. In "Holes", Bargle argues that there must be holes, and his argument is in many ways like our argument for the existence of properties; that is, he uses some ordinary discourse about cheese and crackers to define the "hole role", and he attempts to show that one can't avoid the conclusion that something plays this role. Argle, after an initial attempt to evade Bargle's argument, accepts it. He goes on, however, to show how things acceptable to the materialist can play the hole role. In doing this, he spells out the intrinsic properties of the things he calls holes (when they are holes in a piece of cheese, they are connected, singly-perforate bits of cheese that stand in the right sort of contrast to their non-cheesy surroundings), and he, in effect, shows that things with the intrinsic properties he assigns to holes are capable of playing the role that Bargle's argument shows is played by something-we-know-not-what.

We are not in a position to do, with respect to properties, anything like what Argle has done with respect to holes, for, as I have observed, we cannot say anything much about the intrinsic properties of properties. It is of course unlikely that, if we could say anything more than the little we can about the intrinsic properties of properties, we should find that the things whose properties we had specified were acceptable to the nominalist. It would seem in fact that even the little we can say about the properties of properties is sufficient to make them unacceptable to nominalists. (If this were not so, the whole nominalist-platonist debate would have to be re-thought.) However this may be, the plain fact is: we platonists *can't* describe those something-we-know-not-what which we say play the property role in anything like the depth in which Argle describes the things that (*he* says) play the hole role. Argle can describe the things he calls 'holes' as well as he can describe anything; we platonists can describe any concrete object in incomparably greater depth than we can any property.

I wish it weren't so, but it is. Or so I say. Some will dissent from my thesis that properties are mysterious. David Lewis is a salient example. If Lewis is right about properties, the property role is played by certain *sets*, and one can describe at least some of these sets as well as one can describe any set.[12] In my view, however, Lewis is not right about properties. In the next section I will explain why I think this. (A qualification: I have said that, according to Lewis, certain sets are suitable to play the property role. In Lewis's view, however, it may be that our discourse defines at least two distinct roles that could equally well be described as "property-roles". It should be said of those sets—the sets that Lewis has pressed into service—that, although they can play *one* of the property roles, they are unsuited for the other—if there are indeed two property roles.[13])

4. Lewis's Theory of Properties as Sets (with Some Remarks on Meinongian Theories of Properties as Sets)

According to Lewis, the property "being a pig" is the set of all pigs, including those pigs that are inhabitants of other possible worlds than ours. But, in saying this, I involve myself in Lewis's notorious modal ontology. Let us, for the moment, avoid the questions raised by Lewis's modal ontology and say that Lewis's theory is one member of a species of theory according to all of which the property "being a pig" is the set of all possible pigs. Members of this species differ in their accounts of what a possible pig is. (That is to say, they differ in their accounts of what a *possible* or *possible object*, is for we are interested not only in the property "being a pig" but in properties generally. According to all theories of this kind, every property is a set of *possibilia* and every set of *possibilia* is a property.) Lewis's theory will be just the member of this species according to which possible objects are what Lewis says possible objects are, and will be like the other members of the species on all points not touching on the nature of possible objects. The other members of the species are Meinongian theories, or at least all of them I can think of are.

What is a possible object? Examination of our use of the adjective "possible" shows that it has no fixed meaning. Its meaning rather depends on the word or phrase it modifies: a possible X is an X that is possibly F, where what F is depends on what X is. A possible proposition is a proposition that is possibly true. A possible state of affairs is a state of affairs that possibly obtains. A possible property is a property that is possibly instantiated. What, then, is a possible pig? A pig can't be true or false, can't obtain or not obtain, isn't instantiated or uninstantiated. A pig just is. So—a possible pig is a pig that is possibly what? It may be that we sometimes use "possible pig" to mean not something of the form 'pig that is possibly F', but rather 'thing that is possibly a pig'; if so, this is no clue to what 'possible pig', and more generally 'possible object', mean in theories according to which the property "being a pig" is the set of all possible pigs and every set of possible objects is a property. If any such theory is correct, every possible pig must be, without qualification, a pig—and not a merely counterfactual pig or a merely potential pig. And no one, in any context, would ever want to define 'possible object' as 'something that is possibly an object', for, although it is possible not to be a pig (in fact, I've seen it done), it is not possible not to be an object. 'Possible object' must therefore, at least in statements of theories of properties like those we are considering, have a logical structure like that of 'possible proposition' or 'possible property'. A definition of 'possible object' must have the form 'thing that is an object and is also possibly F'. And of course, if the definition is to be of any interest, F must represent a characteristic that does not belong to objects as a necessary and automatic consequence of their being objects. What characteristic could satisfy this condition?

A Meinongian, or, rather, a neo-Meinongian like Terence Parsons or Richard Sylvan, has a simple answer to this question.[14] Just as a possible proposition is a proposition that is possibly true, and a possible property is a property that is possibly instantiated, a possible object is an object that is possibly existent. (We must avoid confusion on the following point. Assuming that there is such a thing as the proposition that $2 + 2 = 5$, it is a possible object and is not a possible proposition. Since all propositions are objects, it might be thought to follow that it was at once a possible object and not a possible object. But to infer that conclusion would be to commit the fallacy of ambiguity. All that follows from its being a possible object and its not being a possible proposition is that it is an object that is possibly existent and an object that is not possibly true—which is not even an apparent contradiction.) And, the neo-Meinongians maintain, objects are not necessarily and automatically existent. Although any object must be, there are objects that could fail to exist. In fact, most of the objects that are do fail to exist, and many objects that do exist might have been without existing. (Paleo-Meinongians—Meinong, for example—would not agree that any object must be: they contend that many objects, so to speak, don't be.)

What is to be said about neo-Meinongianism? What Lewis says seems to me to be exactly right: the neo-Meinongians have never explained what they mean by 'exist'.[15] We anti-Meinongians and they mean the same thing by 'be'. We anti-Meinongians say that 'exists' and 'be' mean the same thing; the neo-Meinongians say that this is wrong and 'exists' means something else, something other than 'be'. (And, they say, the meanings of the two verbs are so related that—for example—the powers that exist must form a subset of the powers that be.) Unfortunately, they have never said what this "something else" is. I would add the following remark to Lewis's trenchant critique of neo-Meinongianism. The only attempt at an explanation of the meaning of 'exists' that neo-Meinongians have offered proceeds by laying out supposed examples of things that are but do not exist. But, in my view, the right response to every such example that has ever been offered is either "That does too exist" or "There is no such thing as that." And, of course, if there is no distinction in meaning between 'be' and 'exist', then neo-Meinongianism cannot be stated without contradiction. If 'be' and 'exist' mean the same thing, then the open sentence 'x exists' is equivalent to '∃y x = y'. And, if that is so, 'There are objects that do not exist' is logically equivalent to 'Something is not identical with itself'. Since neo-Meinongians obviously do not mean to embrace a contradiction, their theory depends on the premise that 'exist' means something other than 'be'. But, so far as I can see, there is nothing for 'exists' to mean but 'be'. In the absence of further explanation, I am therefore inclined to reject their theory as meaningless. It does not, I concede, follow that 'possible object', if it means 'object that possibly exists', is meaningless. If it means that, that's what it means, and that which means something is not meaningless. It does, however, follow, that 'possible object' means the same as 'object'; at least this must be true in the sense in which, say, 'object that does not violate Leibniz's Law' or 'object that is possibly self-identical' or 'object whose being would not entail a contradiction' mean the same as 'object'. And in that case the theory that a property is a set of possible objects cannot be distinguished from the theory that a property is a set of objects *tout court*.

Let us turn to Lewis's version of the properties-as-sets-of-possible-objects theory. According to Lewis, a possible object is indeed simply an object. But some possible objects are, as he says, *actual* and some are *merely* possible. Merely possible objects are not objects that do not exist; that is, they are not objects of which we can correctly say that they do not exist "in the philosophy room". Outside the philosophy room, in the ordinary business of life, we can say, and say truly, that flying pigs do not exist, despite the fact that we say truly in the philosophy room that some possible objects are flying pigs. When we say that there are no flying pigs, our use of the quantifier is like that of someone who

looks in the fridge and says sadly, "There's no beer." When I say, in the philosophy room, "There are flying pigs, but they're one and all merely possible objects", I'm saying this: "There are [an absolutely unrestricted quantifier; the philosophy room is just that place in which all contextual restrictions on quantification are abrogated] flying pigs, and they're spatio-temporally unrelated to me."

The problem with Lewis's theory, as I see it, is that there is no reason to think that there is anything spatio-temporal that is spatio-temporally unrelated to me, and, if there *is* anything in this category, I don't see what it has to do with modality.[16] Suppose there *is* a pig that is spatio-temporally unrelated to me—or, less parochially, to us. Why should one call it a "merely possible pig"—or a "non-actual pig"? Why are those good things to call it? This is not the end of the matter, however. Even if a pig spatio-temporally unrelated to us *can't* properly be called a merely possible pig, it doesn't follow immediately that Lewis's theory of properties is wrong. If what Lewis calls the principle of plenitude is true—if, as Lewis maintains, there exists (unrestricted quantifier) a pig having, intuitively speaking, every set of properties consistent with its being a pig—then there might be something to be said for identifying the set of all pigs (including those spatio-temporally unrelated to us) with the property "being a pig". (If there exist pigs having every possible combination of features, there must be pigs that are spatially or temporally unrelated to us: if every pig were spatially and temporally related to us, there wouldn't be room for all the pigs that Lewis says there are.) There might be something to be said for this identification, that is, even if the set of all pigs couldn't properly be called 'the set of all pigs, both actual and merely possible'. But even if there are pigs spatio-temporally unrelated to us, there is, so far as I can see, no good reason to accept the principle of plenitude—even as it applies to pigs, much less in its full generality.

On the face of it, the set of pigs seems to

represent far too sparse a selection of the possible combination of characteristics a pig might have for one to be able plausibly to maintain that this set could play the role "the property of being a pig". According to both the neo-Meinongians and Lewis, the set of pigs has a membership much more diverse than most of us would have expected, a membership whose diversity is restricted only by the requirements of logical consistency (for Lewis) or is not restricted at all (for the neo-Meinongians). If I am right, both Lewis and the Meinongians have failed to provide us with any reason to accept this prima facie very uncompelling thesis.

5. A Theory of Properties

There is only one real objection to Lewis's theory of properties: it isn't true. It is a model of what a good theory should be, insofar as theoretical virtue can be divorced from truth. In this section I present a theory of properties that, or so I say, does have the virtue of truth. Alas, even if it has that virtue, it has few others. Its principal vice is that it is very nearly vacuous. It can be compared to the theory that taking opium is followed by sleep because opium possesses a dormitive virtue. That theory about the connection of opium and sleep, as Lewis points out somewhere, is not *entirely* vacuous: it is inconsistent with various theses, such as the thesis that taking opium is followed by sleep because a demon casts anyone who takes opium into sleep. The theory of properties I shall present, although it is pretty close to being vacuous, is inconsistent with various theses about properties, and some of these theses have been endorsed by well-known philosophers. (A proper presentation of this theory would treat properties as a special kind of relation.[17] But I will not attempt to discuss relations within the confines of this paper.)

The theory I shall present could be looked on as a way of specifying the property role, a way independent of and a little more informative than specifying this role via the apparent quantifications over properties that are to be found in our discourse. This theory identifies the property role with the role "thing that can be said of something". This role is a special case of the role "thing that can be said". Some things that can be said are things that can be said *period*, things that can be said *full stop*. For example: that Chicago has a population of over two million is something that can be said; another thing that can be said is that no orchid has ever filed an income-tax return. But these things— 'propositions' is the usual name for them—are not things that can be said *of* anything, not even of Chicago and orchids. One can, however, say *of* Chicago that it has a population of over two million, and one can also say this very same thing of New York. And, of course, one can say it of Sydney and of South Bend. (It can be said only falsely of South Bend, of course, but lies and honest mistakes are possible.) I will assume that anything that can be said of anything can be said of anything else. Thus, if there are such things as topological spaces, one can say of any of them that it is a city with a population of over two million, or that it has never filed an income-tax return. I don't know why anyone would, but one could.

Let us call such things, propositions and things that can be said of things, *assertibles*. The assertibles that are not propositions, the things that can be said of things, we may call *unsaturated* assertibles. I will assume that the usual logical operations apply to assertibles, so that, for example, if there are such assertibles as "that it has a population of over two million" and "that it once filed an income-tax return", there is also, automatically as it were, the assertible "that it either has a population of over two million or else has never filed an income tax return". (In a moment, I shall qualify this thesis.) It follows that the phrase I used to specify the role I wish to consider—"things that can be said of things"— cannot be taken too literally. For if there are any unsaturated assertibles, and if there are arbitrary conjunctions and disjunctions and negations of such unsaturated assertibles as there are, it will be impossible for a finite being to say most of them of anything. "Things that can be said of things" must therefore be understood in the sense "things that can in principle be said of things", or perhaps "things of a type such that some of the simpler things of that type can be said of things" or "things that can be said of things by a being without limitations". All these ways of qualifying "said of" could do with some clarification, but I cannot discuss the problems they raise here. (One possible solution to the problem raised by human limitations for our role-specification would be to substitute something like 'can be true of' or 'is true or false of' for 'can be said of' in our specification of the unsaturated-assertible role. This is, in my view, a promising suggestion, but I do think that 'can be said of' has certain advantages in an initial, intuitive presentation of the theory of properties I shall present.)

It seems to me that there are such things as unsaturated assertibles: there are things that can be said of things. It seems to me that there is an *x* such that *x* can be said of *y* and can also be said of *z*, where *z* is not identical with *y*. One of the things you can say about the Taj Mahal is that it is white, and you can say that about the Lincoln Memorial, too. (I take it that 'about' in this sentence is a mere stylistic variant on 'of'.) If, during the last presidential campaign, you had heard someone say, "All the negative things you've said about Gore are perfectly true, but don't you see that they're equally applicable to Bush?" you wouldn't have regarded this sentence as in any way problematical—not logically or syntactically or lexically problematical, anyway. (And if the speaker had said 'perfectly true of him' instead of 'perfectly true' your only objection could have been that this phrasing was wordy or pedantic.) I say it seems to me that there are such things. I certainly see almost no reason to deny that there are such things, other than the reasons we have (and which I have tried to lay out) for denying that there are abstract objects of any

sort. (For assertibles, if they exist, are certainly abstract objects.) I say 'almost no reason' because there are, I concede, powerful "Russellian" objections to admitting assertibles into our ontology. If there are things that can be said, there are things that can be said of things that can be said. We can say of a proposition that it is false or unsupported by the evidence. We can say of "that it is white" that it can be said truly of more than one thing. Now *one* of the things we can say of "that it is white" would seem to be that it isn't white. That's a thing that can be said *truly* about "that it is white"—a thing that can be said of something is obviously not a visible thing, and only a visible thing can have a color—so, *a fortiori*, it's a thing that can be said about "that it is white". It would seem, therefore, that one of the things we can say about "that it is white" is that it can't be said truly of itself. And it would seem that we can say this very same thing about, for example, "that it has a population of over two million". It seems evident therefore that, if there are things that can be said of things, one of them is "that it can't be said truly of itself". What could be more evident than that this is one of the things that can be said (whether truly or falsely) about something? But, of course, for reasons well known to us all, whatever things that can be said of things there may be, it can't be that one of them is "that it can't be said truly of itself". At any rate, there can't be such a thing if—as we are supposing—anything that can be said of something can be said of anything. If, therefore, we accept the conditional 'If there are things that can be said of things, one of them must be "that it can't be said truly of itself"', we can only conclude that there are no things that can be said of things. Well, I choose to deny the conditional. It's true that it seems self-evident. But, then, so does 'If there are sets, there is a set containing just those sets that are not members of themselves.' Everyone who accepts the existence of sets or properties is going to have to think hard about how to deal with Russell's Paradox. There are many workable ways of dealing with the paradox. (Workable in that, first, they generate a universe of abstract objects sufficient to the needs of the working mathematician, and, secondly, none of them is known to lead to a contradiction—and there's no particular reason to think that any of them does.) None of these "workable" ways of dealing with the paradox is, perhaps, entirely satisfying. In the case of first-order set- or property-theories, the workable ways of dealing with the paradox are workable ways of saying that certain open sentences must correspond to sets or properties—and leaving it an open question which, if any, of the others do. The friends of things that can be said of things can easily adapt any of the standard, workable ways of dealing with the paradox to the task of saying which open sentences must correspond to things that can be said about things. These adaptations will, I think, be neither more nor less intellectually satisfying than the "originals".

I propose, therefore, that properties be identified with unsaturated assertibles, with things that can be said of things. It seems unproblematical that unsaturated assertibles can successfully play the property role. And I would ask this: what is the property whiteness but something we, in speaking of things, occasionally predicate of some of them? And what is predicating something of something but *saying* the former of the latter? Well, perhaps someone will say that it sounds wrong or queer to say that whiteness is one of the things we can say of the Taj Mahal. I don't think that arguments that proceed from that sort of premise have much force, but I won't press the point. Anyone who thinks that unsaturated assertibles—from now on, I'll say simply "assertibles"—cannot play the property role but is otherwise friendly to my arguments may draw this conclusion from them: there are, strictly speaking, no properties, but assertibles may be pressed into service to do the work that would fall to properties if it were not for the inconvenient fact that there are no properties to do it. If we suppose that there are assertibles, and if we're unwilling to say that assertibles are properties,

what advantage should we gain by supposing that there are, in addition, things that we *are* willing to call properties?

Now if properties are assertibles, a wide range of things philosophers have said using the word 'property' make no sense. For one thing, a property, if it is an assertible, cannot be a part or a constituent of any concrete object. If this pen exists, there are no doubt lots of things that are in some sense its parts or constituents: atoms, small manufactured items . . . perhaps, indeed, every sub-region of the region of space exactly occupied by the pen at t is at t exactly occupied by a part of the pen. But "that it is a writing instrument", although it can be said truly of the pen—and is thus, in my view, one of the properties of the pen—is not one of the parts of the pen. That it is not is as evident as, say, that the pen is not a cube root of any number. Nor is "that it is a writing instrument" in any sense present in any region of space. It makes no sense, therefore, to say that "that it is a writing instrument" is "wholly present" in the space occupied by the pen. In my view, there is just nothing there but the pen and its parts (parts in the "strict and mereological sense"). There are indeed lots of things true of the pen, lots of things that could be said truly about the pen, but those things do not occupy space and cannot be said to be wholly (or partly) present anywhere.

If properties are assertibles, it makes no sense to say, as some philosophers have said, that properties are somehow more basic ontologically than the objects whose properties they are. A chair cannot, for example, be a collection or aggregate of the properties ordinary folk say are the properties of a thing that is not a property, for a chair is not a collection or aggregate of all those things one could truly say of it. Nor could the apparent presence of a chair in a region of space "really" be the co-presence in that region of the members of a set of properties—if only because there is no way in which a property can be present in a region of space. (I hope no one is going to say that if I take this position I must believe in "bare particulars". A bare particular would be a thing of which nothing could be said truly, an obviously incoherent notion.)

Properties, if they are assertibles, are not (as some philosophers have said they are) objects of sensation. If colors are properties and properties are assertibles, then the color white is the thing that one says of something when one says of it that it is white. And this assertible is not something that can be seen—just as extracting a cube root is not something you can do with a forceps. We never see properties, although we see *that* certain things have certain properties. (Looking at the pen, one can see that what one says of a things when one says it's cylindrical is a thing that can be said *truly* of the pen.) Consider sky-blue—the color of the sky. Let us suppose for the sake of the illustration that nothing—no exotic bird, no flower, no 1958 Cadillac—is sky-blue. (If I say that nothing is sky-blue, it's not to the point to tell me that the sky is sky-blue or that a reflection of the sky in a pool is sky-blue, for there is no such thing as the sky and there are no such things as reflections. And don't tell me that when I look at the sky on a fine day I perceive a sky-blue quale or visual image or sense-datum, for there are no qualia or visual images or sense-data. I may be sensing sky-bluely when I look at the sky on a fine day, but that shows at most that something has the property "sensing sky-bluely"; it does not show that something has the property "being sky-blue".) Now some philosophers have contended that if, as I have asked you to suppose, nothing is sky-blue, it must be possible to *see* the property "being sky-blue". After all (they argue), this property is in some way involved in the visual experience I have when I look at the sky, and this fact can't be explained by saying that when I look at the sky I'm seeing something that has it, for (we are supposing) nothing has it. And what is there left to say but that when I look upwards on a fine day I see the uninstantiated property "being sky-blue"? I would answer as follows: since the property "being sky-blue" is just one of those

things that can be said of a bird or a flower or a 1958 Cadillac (or, for that matter, of human blood or the Riemann curvature tensor), we obviously don't *see* it. It's involved in our sensations when we look upwards on a fine day only in this Pickwickian sense: when we do that, we sense in the way in which visitors to the airless moon would sense during the lunar day if the moon were surrounded by a shell of sky-blue glass. And why *shouldn't* we on various occasions sense in the way in which we should sense if an X were present when in fact there is no X there?

Some philosophers have said that existence is not a property. Are they right or wrong? They are wrong, I say, if there is such a thing to be said about something as that it exists. And it would seem that there is. Certainly there is this to be said of a thing: that it might not have existed. And it is hard to see how there could be such an assertible as "that it might not have existed" if there were no such assertible as "that it exists".

Some philosophers have said that there are no individual essences or haecceities, no "this-nesses" such as "being *that* object" or "being identical with Alvin Plantinga". Are they right or wrong? They are wrong, I say, if one of the things you can say about something is that it is identical with Alvin Plantinga. Is there? Well, it would seem that if Plantinga hadn't existed, it would still have been true that he might have existed. (It would seem so, but it has been denied.) And it is hard to see how there could be such a thing as the saturated assertible "that Alvin Plantinga might have existed" if there were no such thing as the unsaturated assertible "that it is Alvin Plantinga".

Some philosophers have said that, although there are obviously such properties as redness and roundness, it is equally obvious that there is no such property as "being either red or not round". They have said, to use a phrase they favor, that the world, or the Platonic heaven, is "sparsely", not "abundantly", populated with properties. Are they right? If properties are assertibles, only one answer to this question seems possible: No. If one of the things you can say about something is that it is red and another thing you can say about something is that it is round, then, surely, one of the things you can say about something is that it is either red or not round. (Mars is either red or not round, and that, the very same thing, is also true of the Taj Mahal and the number four—given, of course, that all three objects exist.) It is, of course, our answer to the question 'Is the world sparsely or abundantly supplied with properties?'—"abundantly"—that eventually leads to our troubles with Russell's Paradox. But, again, the alternative doesn't seem possible.

Some philosophers have denied the existence of uninstantiated properties. Is this a plausible thesis? If properties are assertibles, it is a very implausible thesis indeed, for there are obviously things that can be said of things but can't be said truly of anything: that it's a—non-metaphorical—fountain of youth, for example. No doubt someone, Ponce de León or some confidence trickster, has said this very thing about some spring or pool. (If there are uninstantiated properties, are there *necessarily* uninstantiated properties? Yes indeed, for one of the things you can say about Griffin's *Elementary Theory of Numbers* is that it contains a correct proof of the existence of a greatest prime. You can say it about *Tess of the D'Urbervilles*, too. It would seem, moreover, that one of the things you can say of something, one of the things that is "there" to be said about a thing, is that it is both round and square.)

Some philosophers have said that properties exist only contingently. This would obviously be true if there could not be uninstantiated properties, but it would be possible to maintain that there are uninstantiated properties and that, nevertheless, some or all properties are contingently existing things. Could this be? Well, it would certainly seem not, at least if the accessibility relation is symmetrical. One of the things you can say about something is that it is white. Are there possible worlds in which there is no

such thing to be said of anything? Suppose there is such a world. In that world, unless I'm mistaken, it's not even possibly true that something is white. Imagine, if you don't mind using this intellectual crutch, that God exists in a world in which there's no such thing to be said of a thing—not "said truly of a thing": "said of a thing *simpliciter*"—as that it is white. Then God, who is aware of every possibility, is not aware of the possibility that there be something white. (If God could be aware of or consider the possibility that there be something white, he would have to be aware that one of the things that can be said of something is that it is white.) Therefore, there must be no such possibility in that world as the possibility that there be something white. Therefore, with respect to that possible world, the possible world that is in fact actual is not even possible; that is to say, in that world, the world that is in fact the actual world doesn't exist (or exists but is impossible). But then the accessibility relation is not symmetrical. And I should want to say about the proposition that the accessibility relation is symmetrical what Gödel said of the power-set axiom of set theory: it forces itself upon the mind as true. Admittedly, there are steps in this argument that can be questioned and have been questioned—or at least, the corresponding steps in certain very similar arguments have been questioned. (I give one example of an objection, not the most important objection, that could be made to this argument: the argument at best proves that 'that it is white' denotes *an* object in, or with respect to, every possible world; it doesn't follow from this that this phrase denotes the *same* object in every possible world.) But the argument seems convincing to me. At any rate, it is the argument that will have to be got round by anyone who wants to say that properties do not exist necessarily.

There are many other interesting and important theses about properties than those I have considered. But the theses I have considered are, or so it seems to me, all the interesting and important theses to which the theory of properties as assertibles is relevant. The fact that this theory is inconsistent with various interesting and important theses about properties shows that, although it may be very close to being vacuous, it does not manage to be entirely vacuous.[18]

Notes

1 John Burgess and Gideon Rosen, *A Subject without an Object*, (Oxford University Press, 1997).

2 Ibid., Part 1A, "Introduction", *passim*.

3 For Amie Thomasson's views, see her book *Fiction and Metaphysics* (Cambridge University Press, 1999); for Nicholas Wolterstorff's, see his *Worlds and Works of Art* (Oxford University Press, 1980).

4 W. V. Quine, "On What There Is", in *From a Logical Point of View* (Harvard University Press, 1961), pp. 1–19 (originally published in the *Review of Metaphysics*, 1948.); W. V. Quine, *Word and Object* (Cambridge, MA: MIT Press, 1960), ch. VII, "Ontic Decision", pp. 233–76; Nelson Goodman and W. V. Quine, "Steps toward a Constructive Nominalism", *Journal of Symbolic Logic*, 12 (1947), pp. 105–22; David and Stephanie Lewis, "Holes", in David Lewis, *Philosophical Papers, vol. I* (Oxford University Press, 1983), pp. 3–9 (originally published in the *Australasian Journal of Philosophy*, 1970).

5 I will, however, make one remark, or one connected series of remarks, about Quine's thesis. I doubt whether having an extensional principle of individuation has the fundamental ontological significance that Quine ascribes to it. To begin with, I'm not entirely sure that the idea of a certain sort of entity's having an extensional principle of individuation makes sense. I certainly don't see how to write out a Chisholm-style *definiens* for 'the so-and-sos have an extensional principle of individuation'. And I am far from confident that, if I did understand the concept "sort of thing that has an extensional principle of individuation", I should regard falling under this concept as a mark of ontological good behavior. I don't see why the concept "abstract object of a sort that has an extensional principle of individuation" should be identified with the concept "abstract object of a sort that is well-behaved". In any case, whatever may be the case as regards the individuation of properties,

they seem to be perfectly well-behaved (Russell's paradox aside; but sets enjoy no advantage over properties in respect of Russell's paradox). It might be objected—Quine no doubt would object—that properties lack not only an extensional principle of individuation (whatever that is), but lack a principle of individuation of any sort. Properties must therefore (the objection continues) to be ruled *entia non grata* by anyone who accepts the principle "No entity without identity". I reply, first, that it is certainly possible to supply principles of individuation for properties, although any such principle will be controversial. (For example: *x* is the same property as *y* just in the case that *x* and *y* are coextensive in all possible worlds; *x* is the same property as *y* just in the case that *x* and *y* are coextensive in all possible worlds *and*, necessarily, whoever considers *x* considers *y* and whoever considers *y* considers *x*.) Second, the principle "No entity without identity" is ambiguous. It might mean "One should not quantify over entities of a given sort unless one is able explicitly to supply a principle of individuation for those entities." Or it might mean "For every *x* and for every *y*, *x* is identical with *y* or it is not the case that *x* is identical with *y*." I see no reason to accept the first of these principles. The second is certainly unobjectionable (it is a theorem of quantifier logic with identity), but there is no reason to suppose that someone who quantifies over entities of a sort for which he has not endorsed an explicit principle of individuation is committed to its denial.

6 See Hilary Putnam, *Philosophy of Logic* (New York: Harper & Row, 1971). *Philosophy of Logic* is reprinted in its entirety in Stephen Laurence and Cynthia Macdonald (eds.), *Contemporary Readings in the Foundations of Metaphysics* (Oxford: Blackwell, 1998), pp. 404–34.

7 For an important objection to this style of reasoning, see Joseph Melia, "On What There's Not", *Analysis*, 55 (1995), pp. 223–9. I intend to discuss Melia's paper elsewhere; to discuss it here would take us too far afield. I wish to thank David Manley for impressing upon me the importance of Melia's paper (and for correspondence about the issues it raises).

8 In 1958, Alonzo Church delivered a lecture at Harvard, the final seven paragraphs of which have lately been making the e-mail rounds under the

title (not Church's), "Ontological Misogyny". In these paragraphs, Church wickedly compares Goodman's attitude toward abstract objects to a misogynist's attitude toward women. ("Now a misogynist is a man who finds women difficult to understand, and who in fact considers them objectionable incongruities in an otherwise matter-of-fact and hard-headed world. Suppose then that in analogy with nominalism the misogynist is led by his dislike and distrust of women to omit them from his ontology.") Church then shows the misogynist how to eliminate women from his ontology. (In case you are curious: We avail ourselves of the fact that every woman has a unique father. Let us say that men who have female offspring have two modes of presence in the world, primary and secondary. Primary presence is what is usually called presence. In cases in which we should normally say that a woman was present at a certain place, the misogynist who avails himself of Church's proposal will say that a certain man—the man who would ordinarily be described as the woman's father—exhibits secondary presence at that place. . . .) "Ontological Misogyny" came to me by the following route: Tyler Burge, Michael Zeleny (Department of Mathematics, UCLA), James Cargile.

Quine's reduction of everything to pure sets (well, of physics to pure sets, but physics is everything for Quine) can be found in his essay "Whither Physical Objects?" which is included in R. S. Cohen, P. K. Feyerabend, and M. W. Wartofsky (eds.), *Essays in Memory of Imre Lakatos* (Dordrecht: D. Reidel, 1976), pp. 497–504. I thank Michael Rea for the reference.

9 Peter van Inwagen, "Why I Don't Understand Substitutional Quantification", *Philosophical Studies*, 39 (1981), pp. 281–5. The arguments presented in this paper are similar to the more general arguments of William G. Lycan's fine paper, "Semantic Competence and Funny Functors", *Monist*, 64 (1979). "Why I Don't Understand Substitutional

Quantification" is reprinted in my *Ontology, Identity and Modality Ontology, Identity, and Modality: Essays in Metaphysics* (Cambridge University Press, 2001).

10 See the section of W. V. Quine's *Philosophy of Logic* (Englewood Cliffs, NJ: Prentice-Hall, 1970) entitled "Set Theory in Sheep's Clothing" (pp. 66–8).

11 David Lewis, "How to Define Theoretical Terms", *Philosophical Papers*, vol. 1, Oxford University Press, 1983 pp. 78–95 (originally published in the *Journal of Philosophy*, 1970).

12 See David Lewis, *On the Plurality of Worlds* (Oxford: Blackwell, 1986), sect. 1.5, "Modal Realism at Work: Properties", pp. 50–69.

13 See David Lewis, "New Work for a Theory of Universals", in *Papers on Metaphysics and Epistemology* (Cambridge University Press, 1999), pp. 8–55 (originally published in the *Australasian Journal of Philosophy*, 1983). See especially the section entitled "Universals and Properties", pp. 10–24 in *Papers on Metaphysics and Epistemology*.

14 See Terence Parsons, *Non-Existent Objects* (Yale University Press, 1980); Richard Routley [= Richard Sylvan], *Exploring Meinong's Jungle and Beyond: An Investigation of Noneism and the Theory of Items* (Canberra: Departmental Monograph No. 3, Philosophy Department, Research School of Social Sciences, Australian National University, 1980).

15 See David Lewis, "Noneism and Allism", in *Papers in Metaphysics and Epistemology* (Cambridge University Press, 1999), pp. 152–63 (originally published in *Mind*, 1990).

16 I have gone into this matter in a great deal of detail in "Two Concepts of Possible Worlds", *Midwest Studies in Philosophy*, 11 (1986) pp. 185–213 (reprinted in *Ontology, Identity and Modality*, cited above).

17 And it would treat propositions as a special kind of relation: it would treat properties as monadic relations and propositions as 0-adic relations.

18 A condensed version of this paper (with the appropriately condensed title "Properties") will appear in a *Festschrift* for Alvin Plantinga.

Chapter 4

D. M. Armstrong

A WORLD OF STATES OF AFFAIRS

1. States of Affairs Defended

This is a position paper or trailer for a larger work in progress and having the same title. My hypothesis is that the world is a world of states of affairs. I think that I am saying the same thing as those who have held that the world is a world of facts not things. So it may be in order to begin by saying why I use the phrase 'state of affairs' rather than the word 'fact'. This is all the more in order because it is common among those who patronize facts to use 'state of affairs' to mean no more than *possible* fact. My states of affairs, however, are all existents.

In my view, the word 'fact' is much too closely tied to the notions of statement and proposition. It is natural to think of facts as the 'tautological accusatives' of true statements and propositions. Given this, to each true statement or proposition there corresponds its own peculiar fact. This is quite unsatisfactory for my purposes. I have therefore taken over the phrase 'state of affairs'. It sounds less colloquial and more like a term of art, which is desirable. Those who are lost to all shame and use acronyms in their philosophical publications can abbreviate it to 'SOA'.

The general structure of a state of affairs I take to be this. A state of affairs exists if and only if a particular has a property, or a relation holds between two or more particulars. The relations are all *external* relations, that is, in no case are they dictated by the nature of their terms. In the jargon of possible worlds, it is not the case that in each world in which the terms exist, that is, in which the related particulars exist, the relation also holds.

It is generally conceded by philosophers that what particulars exist is to be determined *a posteriori* as a result of empirical investigation. It is not so generally conceded that what properties and relations exist is also to be determined empirically, but it seems equally important that this concession should also be made. Contemporary philosophy tends to use the terms 'property' and 'relation' in such a way that properties and relations are tautological accusatives of monadic and polyadic predicates respectively. And for certain purposes this is undoubtedly convenient. I take the liberty of talking in this way myself where there is need. In that looser way of talking, properties and relations are determined in discourse, not determined empirically. But I make bold to say that the properties and relations that enter into *states of affairs* are the true or real properties and relations. Or if you recoil from such pre-Moorean language, they are the fundamental properties and relations.

States of affairs have as constituents particulars, properties and relations. I hold that the properties and relations should be taken to be *universals*, thus making it possible for different particulars to instantiate the very same property or different pairs of particulars to instantiate the very same (dyadic) relation. But for those who think that universals, even these non-semantic universals of mine, are creatures of darkness, there is an interesting alternative here. One can take the properties and relations of particulars to be particulars themselves. Using the transitive and symmetrical relation of exact resemblance one can then construct equivalence-classes of these property and relation particulars. It turns out that these equivalence-classes are able to reflect many of the properties of universals (though not all) thus perhaps 'saving the phenomena' without the need to admit universals. (See my 1989, Chap.6, Secs. V & VI.) The identification of these equivalence-classes can still be an *a posteriori* affair. For most versions of this *trope* theory, states of affairs will still be required to unite ordinary particulars with properties and relations, although the 'rules of composition' will not be exactly the same. Even if one reduces ordinary particulars to 'bundles' of trope properties, the various bundlings would still appear to be states of affairs within the meaning of the act.

Returning, though, to my preferred alternative, which is to accept universals, we find that the necessity for states of affairs may be, often is, challenged. Why is anything more needed than particulars and universals, monadic and polyadic? The answer to this comes from one of the fundamental assumptions that drive this ontology. It is the need for truths to have a truthmaker (a phrase introduced by C.B. Martin) or an ontological ground (the phrase used by Gustav Bergmann). Let it be the case that the particular *a* exists, and the property-universal F exists. It is clear, in general at least, that these two entities could exist and yet it fail to be the case that *a* is F. If the latter is to be true, then some truthmaker is required. The state of affairs of *a's being* F is suggested as that truthmaker, as the ontological ground.

A spectacular case is provided by non-symmetrical relations. It is unlikely that *loves* is a relation in the true ontological sense. The rela-

tion is surely not identical in all cases where an *x* loves a *y*, which is required for a universal. But let us here overlook this point. Let *a* love *b*, and *b* love *a*. The two states of affairs are presumably independent. Either could have occurred without the other. Yet the two different states of affairs involve exactly the same constituents. How are they to be differentiated? Only by this, it would seem: they are two different states of affairs. Hence we require states of affairs in our ontology.

Alas, one person's *modus ponens* is another person's *modus tollens*. The case just considered moves David Lewis to deny that there are any states of affairs, conceived as things composed from particulars. For, he reasons, it is impossible that two different things could be made out of *exactly* the same constituents. This leads him to assert that the only way that wholes can be composed out of parts is by that austere form of composition envisaged by the mereological calculus. For in this calculus there is one whole and one alone that a given set of parts compose. So for Lewis there can be no states of affairs. The world must be a world of things. A Quinean ontology, an ontology of the subject alone, with the predicate giving us not ontology but mere 'ideology', seems inevitable (Lewis, 1983). He might allow universals, but they will just be unusual things.

Here is a reason for thinking that mereological composition cannot be 'the cement of the universe'. Mereological wholes *supervene* upon their parts. This, indeed, follows from the fact that, given certain parts, there is only one possible whole which they compose. Different metaphysicians differ in their permissiveness with respect to what things can go together to make a whole. Some censorious persons will not let the Sydney Opera House get together with the square root of minus one. ('What next?', they say.) Lewis is completely permissive in this respect and I pretty much go along with him there. For us, Lewis and Armstrong, given that the putative parts are logically compatible, then the whole supervenes. (As indeed the parts supervene on the whole.) What supervenes, however, appears to be *ontologically* nothing more than what it supervenes upon. So, I reason, if mereology really is the only form of composition that there is, then ontologically there is no real composition in the world. This I take to be an absurd conclusion.

So I believe that we should accept the truthmaker argument from predications, non-relational and relational, to states of affairs. It is interesting, and even somewhat surprising, that these entities can differ although their constituents are exactly the same, but I recommend that we simply follow the wind of the argument. Only if someone could come forward with a non-supervenient form of composition that nevertheless allowed only one possible whole to be constructed out of exactly the same parts, would I be inclined to look critically at states of affairs.

States of affairs prove their worth at many points in ontological analysis. They illuminate the topic of causation, in particular singular causation, as will be noted in a later section. Somewhat surprisingly they seem to cast light on the nature of classes (Armstrong, 1991). But here it may be of worth to look briefly at the topic of *structural universals* which Lewis, in particular, finds a vexed one (Lewis, 1986). Consider a carbon atom, a, which is bonded in the familiar cross-shaped pattern separately to four hydrogen atoms: b, c, d, e. The particular which is the mereological sum $a + b + c + d + e$ is a methane molecule. It is straightforward, *given states of affairs*, to describe the structure of this methane molecule. With C = carbon, H = hydrogen, and B = bonding, we have Ca, Hb, Hc, Hd, He, Bab, Bac, Bad, Bae. To get a description of the (putative) structural universal *being a methane molecule* we should first substitute existential quantifiers for the particulars (together, of course, with non-identity clauses for these quantifiers). This gives us an assertion that the structural universal is instantiated. Abstracting from the assertion of instantiation we have a description of the universal: an

individual that is a carbon atom, four further individuals that are hydrogen atoms, and where . . . etc., etc. The structural universal is a certain *type* of conjunction of states of affairs. It would, of course, be open to someone to think of this as a structure of universals instead of a structural universal. But although it may not be of the first importance to resolve that dispute, one reason for going the latter way and calling it a universal is to provide for the (epistemic) possibility of 'structures all the way down'.

States of affairs are thought to labour under a certain further difficulty, though. It is a difficulty most usually articulated for the particular case of an ontology of particulars and universals, but seems to be a general one. It is the difficulty of predication, the difficulty of the nexus of instantiation (as they say in Iowa), the difficulty of the non-relational tie (W.E. Johnson and P.F. Strawson), the difficulty of the formal distinction (as Scotus put it), the difficulty of participation (as Plato had it). Is not bringing the constituents of a state of affairs, the particulars, the properties and the relations, together into states of affairs, a further relation in which all the constituents stand? But then the new relation is just a further element which requires to be integrated along with the other constituents. Most contemporary opponents of universals take comfort from this argument. Often it seems to be the only argument they have to set against the multifarious difficulties facing their particular variety of Nominalism!

Well, those of us who accept states of affairs do have to accept what one might think of as an operator that takes constituents of states of affairs to states of affairs (and, in thought, to merely possible states of affairs). But I think that we are under no compulsion to take this 'formation' of states of affairs as a further constituent, something on the same level as the original constituents. One reason for this, I suggest, is that once the putative states of affairs are reached, all further 'relations' in the regress that our Nominalist friends say that we must accept *supervene* upon the states of affairs. That a state of affairs having certain constituents exists, is, I take it, a contingent matter. But all the alleged further relations in the regress flow necessarily from the structure of the state of affairs. So I suggest that this supervenience is a sign that these 'extra' relations do not have to be taken seriously ontologically.

2. States of Affairs Rule

Having said something in defence of states of affairs, let us advance to the proposition that states of affairs are all that there is. It is not denied on this view that there are things—particulars— nor is it denied that there are properties and relations. But it is denied that there is anything that exists outside states of affairs. It is denied that there is anything that is not a *constituent* of one or more state of affairs. (A point of usage. I generally reserve the word 'part' for mereological parts, speaking instead of constituents of states of affairs. Constituents are a sort of part, too. But they do not obey the axioms of the mereological calculus, so it has seemed advisable to employ another word instead of part.)

If states of affairs are all there is, then there are no 'bare particulars' meaning by this phrase particulars conceived to exist in independence of any state of affairs. (I am here hijacking a term used by Gustav Bergmann and his followers. In their usage bare particulars can be found within states of affairs. But it seems to me that the phrase calls out to be used as I use it.) Equally, there are no uninstantiated universals. Every property is a property of some particular. Every relation holds between two or more particulars. I do not know that there is any very strong pressure to postulate bare particulars. Uninstantiated properties and relations are a different matter. There are semantic arguments for their existence. The idea is that they are required to be the meanings of predicates that, while meaningful, nevertheless fail to apply truly to anything. I think that these arguments can be treated with a certain indifference. But there is a strong *prima facie* case for uninstanti-

ated laws of nature and some of these seem to demand uninstantiated universals. Again, some philosophers have proposed to give an account of possibilities and possible worlds by appealing to uninstantiated universals (Forrest, 1986, Bigelow and Pargetter, 1990, 4.5). In a complete treatment the arguments from uninstantiated laws and from possibilities would have to be carefully considered. I have tried to deal with the argument from laws elsewhere (1983, Ch.8). Not everybody thinks I have been successful, but here I will assume this important step in my argument.

I do not suppose that those who accept that there are universals will find it too difficult an idea that properties and relations are literally, if unmereologically, parts of states of affairs. But that particulars should be in the same situation— tables and thunderstorms—may seem a strange, not to say a ratbag, view. I think that the sense of paradox is eased if we draw a distinction between the 'thin' and the 'thick' particular. Let me emphasize, however, before drawing it, that the distinction does not introduce any further entities into this ontology.

The thin particular is the particular considered in abstraction from all its properties. Although not bare, it is very thin indeed. (But you can be thin without being bare.) For me, all thin particulars, although numerically different, are, as it were, indistinguishably different. Particulars may be said to have or rather to be haecceities or thisnesses, but they have no mysterious inner and particularized essence that marks off one from another and accounts for their numerical difference. The secret of numerical difference is simply numerical difference. Different particulars may be parts of other particulars, parts which include, I hold, temporal parts, or overlap other particulars. This is the mereological sense of the word 'part' and, with Lewis (1993), I take this identity of parts to be best understood as partial identity. But that is about all that can be said about the thin particular. Notice, however, that it is not hidden, as Locke had it hidden. Even in our most basic, most elementary, perceptions we are aware of particulars, though of course particulars as having certain properties and relations, that is: particulars in states of affairs.

So much for the thin particular. The thick particular is the thin particular considered along with all of its intrinsic, that is, non-relational properties. It is a much more familiar creature. But, on the scheme proposed, what can it be except a state of affairs or conjunction of states of affairs? The existence of conjunctive universals is a somewhat controversial but not too important an affair. I allow them, provided that the conjunct universals are all instantiated by the same particular, but some philosophers do not. Suppose we allow them. Then we can roll up all the non-relational properties of a particular into a single, but far from simple, conjunctive universal. We can call it that particular's *nature*. Now consider the state of affairs of that particular's having that nature: *a's having* N. This state of affairs is the thick particular.

I will just note a pleasant anticipation of the thin/thick distinction by Herbert Hochberg. He spoke of 'Socrates' and 'big Socrates' (n.d.). In true Iowan style, however, the object he was talking about was not a philosopher but a white square patch.

To gain a somewhat more concrete grip on the doctrine that the world is nothing but a world of states of affairs let us consider another doctrine which I uphold and which I call the doctrine of Naturalism. This is the proposition that the world consists of, and is exhausted by, the single, public, spatio-temporal system. (Naturalism is not to be confused with Physicalism, the doctrine that this space-time world involves nothing more than the entities and laws recognized by a—completed—physics. A Naturalist need not be a Physicalist, although I myself accept both theses.) In the order of knowledge the doctrine of Naturalism must be accorded a higher epistemic credit-rating than the states of affairs doctrine, although I uphold both. After all, the thesis that the world is a world of states of

affairs is no more than a *philosopher's* thesis! But in the order of being, if I am right, the space-time world is nothing but a huge conjunction of states of affairs. To *exhibit* this would be a huge undertaking, and, *prima facie*, there are all sorts of ways that we could work out the identification, depending upon the answer to all sorts of scientific and philosophical questions concerning the nature of space and time. For instance, the world might turn out to consist of genuinely atomic particulars which are space-time points, perhaps having field properties, and the concatenation of these points might constitute space-time. This is just one scheme, and not one that I have any particular affection for, although I have no particular dislike of it either. But it illustrates a little more concretely, if still unexcitingly, what a world of states of affairs might be like.

It may be noted that the unity of the space-time world is not constituted by the mere conjunction of the state of affairs. A conjunctive state of affairs, as we may call such a conjunction, has a merely mereological unity, which is to say no real unity at all. The real unity is given by the fact that all the particulars are directly or recursively linked to each other by real, that is external, relations. These relations appear to be exhausted by causal and spatiotemporal relations.

The states of affairs, which includes their constituents, constitute the ultimate truthmakers for all truths. This gives occasion to say something about truth. Two theories of truth, in particular, fight in the breast of any right-minded, not to say clean-living, philosopher. I, at any rate, have oscillated between the two for many years. The first is the Correspondence theory. To say that p is true is to say that this proposition corresponds to reality. The other is the Redundancy theory. To say that p is true is, fundamentally, to say no more than to say p. My suggestion now is that both theories have got hold of part of the truth about truth. The Redundancy theory is satisfactory at the more superficial level of usage, the truth-*predicate*, formal semantics, and, I think, truth-conditions. But our statements and propositions do correspond or fail to correspond to reality. Their correspondent is the truthmaker, the ontological ground, for that statement or proposition. But it is vital to realize that the correspondence is not a one-one affair. To think so is to fall into the gravitational field of the Redundancy theory and as a result to postulate a fact peculiar to each true proposition. It is this error, I believe, that has led to dissatisfaction with the supremely natural view that truth is or involves correspondence to reality. The correspondence of truth with truthmaker is actually many-many. It is a totally disorderly affair. I now think that there must be a truthmaker for every truth, even necessary truths, although the latter do not require a great deal in the way of truthmaker. It is a, perhaps the, major metaphysical enterprise to determine the general nature of the truthmakers for the various sorts of true discourse. That the basic truthmakers are states of affairs (and of course their constituents) is, I have been arguing, the beginning of ontological wisdom.

3. Higher-order States of Affairs

One of the attractions of the metaphysics of the *Tractatus* is that the facts that constitute the world are all of the same order. There are no facts about facts. This doctrine is again upheld by Brian Skyrms in his "Tractarian Nominalism" (1981). Unlike Wittgenstein, Skyrms explicitly makes the constituents of his facts particulars and universals, the latter dividing into properties and relations. He might have been privy to my thoughts. He uses the word 'Nominalism', unwisely in my view, not to deny universals but to betoken that he denies the existence of any facts of higher-order.

It seems, however, that there is no escape from such facts (states of affairs). The knock-down case, I believe, is the one pointed to by Russell, what he called 'general facts' (1918, p. 93). I will speak of facts of totality or, in my own terminology, states of affairs of totality. Consider all

the electrons, past, present and future. Particular *a* will have properties sufficient to make it an electron. So will particular *b*, and so on. Does the conjunction of these states of affairs serve as a truthmaker for the truth that these are *all* the electrons? I don't think it can. For it is *contingent* that these are all the electrons. These states of affairs could all exist and yet not exhaust the totality of electrons.

This last point might be conceded, but, it may be objected, why not accept here a truthmaker that would fail to be a truthmaker for the same truth 'in another possible world'? My answer to this is that the truthmaking relation, although many-many, is an *internal* relation, one that supervenes upon, is necessitated by, the nature of the terms. One point here is that the correspondence relation is not a spatio-temporal or a causal relation, and Hume long ago pointed out that these are the only plausible candidates for 'relations of matters of fact' i.e. external relations (see the *Treatise*, Bk.1, Pt.1, Sec. V, & Pt.3, Sec.1). But the matter can be approached more directly. That it is true that a certain collection of electrons is *all* the electrons is surely only true because there are no more of them. If there are more, then it is not true. That there are no more of them is then part of the truthmaker. But this is a higher-order state of affairs or fact.

It seems, then, that there is allness or totality in the world. Here is one logical constant that does signify. I don't think that the notion can be *analyzed*, but I think we can categorize it a bit further. Allness appears to be a relational property of sorts, in the same sort of way that being a father is a relational property (as opposed to the relation of fathering, on which being a father supervenes). Consider the class or the aggregate (mereological whole) which happens to be the class or the aggregate of the electrons. What makes it *all* the electrons? Is it not that it stands in the totalling relation—the alling relation—to a certain property, the property of *being an electron*? The class or aggregate which happens to be the class of all the protons stands in the very same relation to the property of *being a proton*. It alls being a proton, we might say. We have a relation which is a universal here, it seems, and on it supervenes the allness of certain classes and aggregate with respect to certain properties.

If we admit such 'general facts', then that will have a considerable bearing on the vexed question whether or not to admit *negative* states of affairs. For, as is well known, given all positive states of affairs, and given the further fact of totality that these *are* all the positive states of affairs, then all negative states of affairs supervene. If so, then it would seem that we do not need to postulate the negative facts alongside positive ones. It is true that there are some arguments for negative states of affairs to be considered. There appear to be negative perceptions: perceiving that there is nobody in the room. There also appear to be cases of negative causation: lack of water causing death. Ontologically speaking, however, I think it can be made plausible that these are mere surface phenomena. It may be noted that negative properties are as suspect as negative states of affairs.

The account just sketched of totality or allness leads on to a certain view of the nature of number. Consider the salient relation that holds between *being an electron* and *being an aggregate of nineteen electrons* and also between *being a proton* and *being an aggregate of nineteen protons*. Peter Forrest and I have argued that there is a good case for identifying this relation with the natural number nineteen (Forrest and Armstrong, 1987). The account appears to generalize smoothly to the rational numbers and to the reals, thus permitting a univocal account of these sorts of number. In each case, a unit-universal stands in a certain ratio or proportion to an aggregate universal. With *being one kilogram mass* as unit-property, it stands in the 3.2 ratio to *being 3.2 kilograms mass*. That unit-property also stands in the pi relation to *being pi kilograms mass*. Perhaps the account can even be generalized to cover the infinitesimals of non-standard analysis.

Allness and the numbers turn out, on this scheme, to have at least a family resemblance to each other, reminding us of the thesis of Grossmann (1983, Secs. 137–142) that numbers fall into the category of quantifiers. But there is an important difference between allness and the numbers. The 'alling' relation is external. The numerical relations, however, are internal, flowing necessarily from the nature of their terms. That being so, the truthmakers for the holding of the relations are nothing more than the related terms. The relations are of the sort that can hold between windowless monads or the denizens of different possible worlds.

As I see it then, the integration of mathematics into the world of states of affairs should draw its inspiration from the *Tractatus* rather than from the hardline empiricism of Mill, John Anderson, Quine and others. The states of affairs are contingent, mathematical truths are necessary, and the secret of necessity lies in the reduction of its ontological content.

The consideration of number has taken us away from the topic of higher-order states of affairs, because, unlike allness, the internal relations involved do not call for higher-order states of affairs. This may be the place, nevertheless, to say a word about such mathematical entities as the higher infinite cardinal numbers. The worry here is that there may be no aggregate or class of things which can stand in the right internal relation to some unit-property. But without such a relation, on this theory of number, there would appear to be no such number. To this difficulty I reply by saying that mathematical existence is something less than full-blooded existence. For an infinite number to exist is no more than for the required aggregate or class to be a *possible* one, although this must be absolute not just epistemic possibility. This view (put forward e.g. by Putnam, 1967) is a trifle deflationary. But it does help with a difficult epistemological problem. How is it that in mathematics we can arrive at the result that a certain entity exists *a priori*, a result that, after checking of proofs, we do not regard as open to falsification, barring the unusual case of doubt being raised about the original premisses? If all we have really achieved is the weaker conclusion that something is possible, then it becomes easier to accept that such knowledge is possible *a priori*.

Getting back to higher-order states of affairs, it is plausible that causation, singular causation, this causing that, is a relation between states of affairs. It is particulars that act. But they act in virtue of their properties and the effect of their action is determined by the properties of the thing that they act upon. This strongly suggests a relation between states of affairs. Putting it in a no doubt oversimplified way, that *a* is F brings it about that *b* is G.

Causation naturally leads one on to the topic of laws of nature. Indeed it may be that all the *fundamental* laws, the laws on which all other laws supervene, are causal laws. Singular causation exhibits a fair amount of regularity, and it is a natural hypothesis that each token of a causal sequence instantiates some law. It is true that there appears to be no *a priori* argument that takes one from singular causation to law, a point emphasized by Anscombe (1971). But, as suggested by Adrian Heathcote, there do appear to be good *a posteriori* grounds for identifying singular causal sequences with instantiations of laws (Heathcote and Armstrong, 1991).

In the Humean tradition laws are identified with cosmic regularities of a certain sort: 'cosmic coincidences' as that most honest of all Humeans, Jack Smart, calls them. If this traditional Empiricist position can be maintained, then there is no call here to postulate higher-order facts in explaining causes and laws. But, building on the work of many others, I have tried to show how implausible this position is in my 1983. Suppose, instead, as I think plausible, that laws should be seen as relationships holding between universals. We then have higher-order states of affairs, and ones that differ in type from facts of totality and the links between token states of affairs *apparently* present in singular causation.

If we think of a property as a *type* of state of affairs, the property F as the *something is* F type of state of affairs, then one can think of a nomic/causal connection of properties as a state of affairs where one type of state of affairs brings about a further type of state of affairs. But this formulation is not to be understood as a universally quantified truth about tokens of the types in question. It is a 'direct' connection between the state of affairs types in question, i.e. the universals in question, a connection postulated for its explanatory value. It entails the corresponding universally quantified state of affairs, without being entailed by it. It is not supervenient upon mere first-order states of affairs. As such, it is a higher-order state of affairs.

It is interesting to note here the position of those who accept laws as relations between universals, but who hold that the relation is a necessary one. Since their laws hold in any possible world in which the 'antecedent' universal in the law is instantiated, for them laws supervene upon universals. Such a position seems incompatible with the view, which I defend, that the supervenient is ontologically nothing over and above whatever it supervenes upon. For surely what nomic connections hold between given properties is a substantial matter of fact? (Lewis has pointed out to me that those who hold that laws are necessary might well concede this point but go on to argue that the substantial matter of fact is that law-bearing universals, rather than others, are instantiated. I think I can still make my point, but it would certainly take longer.) Laws, then, I say, though relations of universals, involve higher-order states of affairs that are contingent. (By 'laws' are here to be understood the nomic connections themselves, not the true statements that such a connection holds.)

In Dretske, Tooley and Armstrong the sort of laws discussed are usually those linking two properties, generally called F and G in order to make the example as specific and concrete as possible. I think this is excusable. The issues are complex enough without having to concentrate from the beginning on some more lifelike but more tangled case. It remains true, though, that your average law of nature that has some claim to be fundamental will be a functional law that connects two or more quantities. This in turn means that a scientific or *a posteriori* realism about universals will have to concentrate particularly on universals of *quantity*. There are quite pressing problems.

Consider a quantity such as *mass* (or *rest mass*). There is a whole class of *determinate* universals, such as *one kilogram in mass* or *one ounce in mass*. What is the determinable *mass*? Is it also a universal? If it is, then is it a universal whose determinates are its instances, a universal which appears in functional mass-laws? If so, then it seems that we must postulate higher-order properties— properties of properties. A difficulty here, at least for me, is that this supposed higher-order property seems to be supervenient on the first-order properties. Determinates entail determinables. Hence I would have to say that we do not get a genuinely higher-order property. Yet we cannot treat a functional law as a mere class of laws—the class of the highly specific laws that govern the individual determinates. That would be a retreat to a Humean theory of functional laws, unacceptable to anybody who is upholding a theory of 'strong' laws.

This has been a survey, inevitably hurrying over many matters that demand a very much fuller treatment. Indeed, much that might have claimed a place has been omitted altogether. But I hope it has shown something of the attraction and, you may think, the problems, that face the metaphysical programme that seeks to exhibit the world as made up of a single sort of constituent: states of affairs having in turn as their sole constituents particulars, property-universals and relation-universals.

References

Anscombe, G.E.M. (1971) 'Causality and Determination', Cambridge: Cambridge University Press. Reprinted in *Causation and Conditionals*, ed. E. Sosa, Oxford: Oxford University Press, 1975.

Armstrong, D.M. (1983) *What is a Law of Nature?* Cambridge: Cambridge University Press.

Armstrong, D.M. (1989) *A Combinatorial Theory of Possibility*, Cambridge: Cambridge University Press.

Armstrong, D.M. (1991) 'Classes are States of Affairs', *Mind*, 100, 189–200.

Bigelow, J. & Pargetter, R. (1990) *Science and Necessity*, Cambridge: Cambridge University Press.

Forrest, P. (1986) 'Ways worlds could be', *Australasian Journal of Philosophy*, 64, 15–24.

Forrest, P. & Armstrong, D.M. (1987) 'The Nature of Number', *Philosophical Papers*, 16, 165–186.

Grossmann, R. (1983) *The Categorial Structure of the World*, Bloomington: Indiana University Press.

Heathcote, A. & Armstrong, D.M. (1991) 'Causes and Laws', *Noûs*, XV, 1, 63–74.

Hochberg, H. (n.d.) 'Things and Qualities' in *Metaphysics and Explanation*, ed. W.H. Capitan and D.D. Merrill, University of Pittsburgh Press, 82–97.

Hume, D. *A Treatise of Human Nature.*

Lewis, D.K. (1983) 'New work for a theory of Universals', *Australasian Journal of Philosophy*, 61, 343–377.

Lewis, D.K. (1986) 'Against Structural Universals', *Australasian Journal of Philosophy*, 64, 25–46.

Lewis, D.K. (1993) 'Many, but Almost One', in *Ontology, Causality and Mind: Essays in Honor of D.M. Armstrong*, ed. John Bacon, Keith Campbell and Lloyd Reinhardt, Cambridge: Cambridge University Press.

Putnam, H. (1967) 'The thesis that Mathematics is Logic', in *Bertrand Russell, Philosopher of the Century*, ed. R. Shoenman, London: Allen & Unwin. Reprinted in H. Putnam, *Philosophical Papers*, Vol.1, Cambridge: Cambridge University Press.

Skyrms, B. (1981) 'Tractarian Nominalism', *Philosophical Studies*, 40, 199–206. Reprinted as Appendix in Armstrong 1989.

Chapter 5

David Lewis and Stephanie Lewis

HOLES

Argle. I believe in nothing but concrete material objects.

Bargle. There are many of your opinions I applaud; but one of your less pleasing characteristics is your fondness for the doctrines of nominalism and materialism. Every time you get started on any such topic, I know we are in for a long argument. Where shall we start this time: numbers, colors, lengths, sets, force-fields, sensations, or what?

Argle. Fictions all! I've thought hard about every one of them.

Bargle. A long evening's work. Before we start, let me find you a snack. Will you have some crackers and cheese?

Argle. Thank you. What splendid Gruyère!

Bargle. You know, there are remarkably many holes in this piece.

Argle. There are.

Bargle. Got you!

Bargle. You admit there are many holes in that piece of cheese. Therefore, there are some holes in it. Therefore, there are some holes. In other words, holes exist. But holes are not made of matter; to the contrary, they result from the absence of matter.

Argle. I did say that there are holes in the cheese; but that is not to imply that there are holes.

Bargle. However not? If you say that there are A's that are B's, you are committed logically to the conclusion that there are A's.

Argle. When I say that there are holes in something, I mean nothing more nor less than that it is perforated. The synonymous shape-predicates '... is perforated' and 'there are holes in ...'—just like any other shape-predicate, say '... is a dodecahedron'—may truly be predicated of pieces of cheese, without any implication that perforation is due to the presence of occult, immaterial entities. I am sorry my innocent predicate confuses you by sounding like an idiom of existential quantification, so that you think that inferences involving it are valid when they are not. But I have my reasons. You, given a perforated piece of cheese and believing as you do that it is perforated because it contains immaterial entities called holes, employ an idiom of existential quantification to say falsely 'There are holes in it.' Agreeable fellow that I am, I wish to have a sentence that sounds like yours and that is true exactly when you falsely suppose your existential quantification over immaterial things to be true. That way we could talk about the cheese without philosophizing, if only you'd let me. You and I would understand our sentences differently, but the difference wouldn't interfere with our conversation until you start drawing conclusions which follow from your false sentence but not from my homonymous true sentence.[1]

Bargle. Oh, very well. But behold: there are as many holes in my piece of cheese as in yours. Do you agree?

Argle. I'll take your word for it without even counting: there are as many holes in mine as in yours. But what I mean by that is that either both pieces are singly-perforated, or both are doubly-perforated, or both are triply-perforated, and so on.

Bargle. What a lot of different shape-predicates you know! How ever did you find time to learn them all? And what does 'and so on' mean?[2]

Argle. Let me just say that the two pieces are equally-perforated. Now I have used only one two-place predicate.

Bargle. Unless I singly-perforate each of these crackers, how will you say that there are as many holes in my cheese as crackers on my plate? Be so kind as not to invent another predicate on the spot. I am quite prepared to go on until you have told me about all the predicates you have up your sleeve. I have a good imagination, and plenty of time.

Argle. Oh, dear . . . (ponders)

Argle. I was wrong. There *are* holes.

Bargle. You recant?

Argle. No. Holes are material objects.

Bargle. I expected that sooner. You are thinking, doubtless, that every hole is filled with matter: silver amalgam, air, interstellar gas, luminiferous ether or whatever it may be.

Argle. No. Perhaps there are no truly empty holes; but I cannot deny that there might be.

Bargle. How can something utterly devoid of matter be made of matter?

Argle. You're looking for the matter in the wrong place. (I mean to say, that's what you would be doing if there were any such things as places, which there aren't.) The matter isn't inside the hole. It would be absurd to say it was: nobody wants to say that holes are inside themselves. The matter surrounds the hole. The lining of a hole, you agree, is a material object. For every hole there is a hole-lining; for every hole-lining there is a hole. I say the hole-lining is the hole.

Bargle. Didn't you say that the hole-lining surrounds the hole? Things don't surround themselves.

Argle. Holes do. In my language, 'surrounds' said of a hole (described as such) means 'is identical with.' 'Surrounds' said of other things means just what you think it means.

Bargle. Doesn't it bother you that your dictionary must have two entries under 'surrounds' where mine has only one?

Argle. A little, but not much. I'm used to putting up with such things.

Bargle. Such *whats*?

Argle. Such dictionary entries. They're made of dried ink, you recall.

Bargle. Oh. I suppose you'll also say that '. . . is in . . .' or '. . . is through . . .' said of a hole means '. . . is part of . . .'.

Argle. Exactly so, Bargle.

Bargle. Then do you still say that 'There are holes in the cheese' contains an unanalyzed shape-predicate synonymous with '. . . is perforated'?

Argle. No; it is an existential quantification, as you think it is. It means that there exist material objects such that they are holes and they are parts of the piece of cheese.

Bargle. But we wouldn't say, would we, that a hole is made out of cheese?

Argle. No; but the fact that we wouldn't say it doesn't mean it isn't true. We wouldn't have occasion to say, unless philosophizing, that these walls are perpendicular to the floor; but they are. Anyhow we *do* say that caves are holes in the ground and that some of them are made out of limestone.

Bargle. Take this paper-towel roller. Spin it on a lathe. The hole-lining spins. Surely you'd never say the hole spins?

Argle. Why not?

Bargle. Even though the hole might continue to be entirely filled with a dowel that didn't spin or move at all?

Argle. What difference does that make?

Bargle. None, really. But now I have you: take a toilet-paper roller, put it inside the paper-towel roller, and spin it the other way. The big hole spins clockwise. The little hole spins counter-clockwise. But the little hole is part of the big hole, so it spins clockwise along with the rest of the big hole. So if holes can spin, as you think, the little hole turns out to be spinning in both directions at once, which is absurd.

Argle. I see why you might think that the little hole is part of the big hole, but you can't expect me to agree. The little hole is inside the big hole, but that's all. Hence I have no reason to say that the little hole is spinning clockwise.

Bargle. Consider a thin-walled hole with a gallon of water inside. The volume of the hole is at least a gallon, whereas the volume of the hole-lining is much less. If the hole is the hole-lining, then whatever was true of one would have to be true of the other. They could not differ in volume.

Argle. For 'hole' read 'bottle;' for 'hole-lining' also read 'bottle.' You have the same paradox. Holes, like bottles, have volume—or, as I'd rather say, are voluminous or equi-voluminous with other things—in two different senses. There's the volume of the hole or bottle itself, and there's the volume of the largest chunk of fluid which could be put inside the hole or bottle without compression. For holes, as for bottles, contextual clues permit us to keep track of which we mean.

Bargle. What is the volume of the hole itself? How much of the cheese do you include as part of one of these holes? And how do you decide? Arbitrarily, that's how. Don't try saying you include as little of the cheese as possible, for however much you include, you could have included less.

Argle. What we call a single hole is really many hole-linings. Some include more of the cheese, some include less. Therefore I need not decide, arbitrarily or otherwise, how much cheese is part of the hole. Many different decisions are equally correct.

Bargle. How can a single hole be identical with many hole-linings that are not identical with one another?

Argle. Really there are many different holes, and each is identical with a different hole-lining. But all these different holes are the same hole.

Bargle. You contradict yourself. Don't you mean to say that they all *surround* the same hole—where by 'surround' I mean 'surround,' not 'be identical with'?

Argle. Not at all. I would contradict myself if I said that two different holes were identical. But I didn't; what I said was that they were the same hole. Two holes are the same hole when they have a common part that is itself a hole.

Bargle. You agreed before that there were as many holes in my cheese as crackers on my plate. Are there still?

Argle. Yes; there are two of each left.

Bargle. Two crackers, to be sure, but how can you say there are two holes?

Argle. Thus: there is a hole, and there is another hole that is not the same hole, and every hole in the cheese is the same hole as one or the other.

Bargle. Be so kind as to say 'co-perforated,' not 'same,' and stop pretending to talk about identity when you are not. I understand you now: co-perforation is supposed to be an equivalence relation among hole-linings, and when you say there are two holes you are trying to say that there are two non-identical co-perforation-classes of hole-linings. Really you identify holes not with hole-linings but with *classes* of hole-linings.

Argle. I would if I could, but I can't. No; holes are hole-linings; but when I speak of them as holes, I find it convenient to use 'same' meaning 'co-perforated' wherever a man of your persuasion would use 'same' meaning 'identical.' You know my reason for this trickery: my sentences about sameness of holes will be true just when you wrongly suppose your like-sounding sentences to be. The same goes for sentences about number of holes, since we both analyze these in terms of sameness.[3]

Bargle. You still haven't told me how you say there are as many holes in my cheese as crackers on my plate, without also saying how many there are.

Argle. Here goes. There exist three things X, Y, and Z. X is part of the sum of the crackers, Y is part of the cheese, and Z is part of Y. Every maximal connected part of Y is a hole, and every hole in the cheese is the same hole as some maximal connected part of Y. X overlaps each of the crackers and Z overlaps each maximal connected part of Y. Everything which is either the intersection of X and a cracker or the intersection of Z and some maximal connected part of Y is the same size as any other such thing. X is the same size as Z.[4]

Bargle. Your devices won't work because co-perforation is not an equivalence relation. *Any* two overlapping parts of my cheese have a common part that is a hole-lining, though in most cases the hole-lining is entirely filled with cheese. To be co-perforated is therefore nothing more than to overlap, and overlapping is no equivalence relation. The result is that although, as you say, you can find two hole-linings in this cheese that are not co-perforated, you can find another one that is co-perforated with both of them.

Argle. If you were right that a hole made of cheese sould be entirely filled with the same kind of cheese, you could find far more than two non-co-perforated hole-linings; and there would be no such thing as cheese without holes in it. But you are wrong. A hole is a hole not just by virtue of its own shape but also by virtue of the way it contrasts with the matter inside it and around it. The same is true of other shape-predicates; I wouldn't say that any part of the cheese is a dodecahedron, though I admit that there are parts—parts that do not contrast with their surroundings—that are *shaped like* dodecahedra.

Bargle. Consider the paper-towel roller. How many holes?

Argle. One. You know what I mean: many, but they're all the same.

Bargle. I think you must say there are at least two. The left half and the right half are not the same hole. They have no common part, so no common part that is a hole.

Argle. They're not holes, they're two parts of a hole.

Bargle. Why aren't they holes themselves? They are singly-perforated and they are made of matter unlike the matter inside them. If I cut them apart you'd have to say they were holes?

Argle. Yes.

Bargle. You admit that a hole can be a proper part of a bigger—say, thicker-skinned—hole?

Argle. Yes.

Bargle. You admit that they are shaped like holes?

Argle. Yes, but they aren't holes. I can't say why they aren't. I know which things are holes, but I can't give you a definition. But why should I? You already know what hole-linings are. I say the two halves of the roller are only parts of a hole because I—like you—would say they are only parts of a hole-lining. What isn't a hole-lining isn't a hole.

Bargle. In that case, I admit that co-perforation may be an equivalence relation at least among singly-perforated hole-linings.

Argle. All holes are singly-perforated. A doubly-perforated thing has two holes in it that are not the same hole.

Bargle. Are you sure? Take the paper-towel roller and punch a little hole in its side. Now you have a hole in a hole-lining. You'd have to say you have a hole in a hole. You have a little hole which is part of a big hole; the big hole is not singly-perforated; and the little hole and the big hole are the same hole, since the little hole is a common part of each.

Argle. I think not. You speak of *the* big hole; but what we have are two big holes, not the same, laid end to end. There is also the little hole, not the same as either big hole, which overlaps them both. Of course we sometimes call something a hole, in a derivative sense, if it is a connected sum of holes. Any decent cave consists of many holes that are not the same hole, so I must have been speaking in this derivative sense when I said that caves are holes.

Bargle. What peculiar things you are driven to say when philosophy corrupts your mind! Tell me the truth: would you have dreamt for a moment of saying there were two big holes rather than one if you were not suffering under the influence of a philosophical theory?

Argle. No; I fear I would have remained ignorant.

Bargle. I see that I can never hope to refute you, since I no sooner reduce your position to absurdity than you embrace the absurdity.

Argle. Not absurdity; disagreement with common opinion.

Bargle. Very well. But I, for one, have more trust in common opinions than I do in any philosophical reasoning whatever. In so far as you disagree with them, you must pay a great price in the plausibility of your theories.

Argle. Agreed. We have been measuring that price. I have shown that it is not so great as you thought; I am prepared to pay it. My theories can earn credence by their clarity and economy; and if they disagree a little with common opinion, then common opinion may be corrected even by a philosopher.

Bargle. The price is still too high.

Argle. We agree in principle; we're only haggling.

Bargle. We do. And the same is true of our other debates over ontic parsimony. Indeed, this argument has served us as an illustration—novel, simple, and self-contained—of the nature of our customary disputes.

Argle. And yet the illustration has interest in its own right. Your holes, had I been less successful, would have punctured my nominalistic materialism with the greatest of ease.

Bargle. Rehearsed and refreshed, let us return to—say—the question of classes.[5]

Notes

1 Cf. W. V. Quine, "On What There Is," *From a Logical Point of View*, 2nd ed. (Cambridge, Mass: Harvard University Press, 1961), p. 13.

2 Cf. Donald Davidson, "Theories of Meaning and Learnable Languages," in Y. Bar-Hillel, *Logic, Methodology and Philosophy of Science, Proceedings of the 1964 International Congress* (Amsterdam, 1965), pp. 383–94.

3 Cf. Quine's maxim of identification of indiscernibles in "Identity, Ostension, and Hypostasis," *From a Logical Point of View*, p. 71; P.T. Geach, "Identity," *Review of Metaphysics* 21 (1967): 3–12.

4 This translation adapts a device from Nelson Goodman and W. V. Quine, "Steps toward a Constructive Nominalism," *Journal of Symbolic Logic* 12 (1947): 109–10.

5 There would be little truth to the guess that Argle is one of the authors and Bargle is the other. We thank Charles Chastain, who also is neither Argle nor Bargle, for many helpful comments.

Chapter 6

Richard Routley

ON WHAT THERE IS   NOT

Quine's ultimate ontological reduction is radical. What exists? Simply the empty set, and sets constructed by taking it as an element. One thus enters a truly desert landscape, and the reduction thus assumes the proportions of an 'ontological debacle' . . . '*A lesson to be drawn from this debacle is that ontology is not what mainly matters*' ([5], p. 189; the quotations are from Quine).

Most things do not exist. For every thing that exists, for instance Three Mile Island nuclear reactor (an odd product of the null set), there are several things that do not exist, abstractions beginning with the null set and the property of being that reactor. And there are a great many abstractions other than those directly generated by the null set and things that exist. These truths we hold to be elementary, and where not self-evident they can be argued for.[1] Quine, however, in a very bold stroke, has stolen much of the terminology we ordinarily use to state, and argue, these elementary facts – and as far as most philosophers are concerned, he has got away with it.

The theft is evident from the first lines of Quine's 'On What There Is', an influential period piece[2] from times when ontology did matter more, with the discussion of which this paper is primarily concerned. The ontological problem is there said to be formulable as 'What is there?', and answered 'Everything'; an answer 'everyone will accept as true' (p. 1). The ontological problem in question is, however, the problem as to what exists or (perhaps

differently) of what has being, which is not just a very different problem from the more easily answered question as to what things there are, what count as things, but also a problem which is not truly answered 'Everything', since many things do not exist. The theft is of the English expressions 'what', 'there is', 'is', 'thing', and 'everything', which are commonly enough used *without* existential import to consider and talk about items that do not exist and have no being. Just consider 'What is . . .?' questions concerning fictional objects or the objects of false theories, e.g. 'What is a hobbit?' 'What is a phlogiston?', or such questions as 'What is an impossible thing?', 'What is a merely possible thing as distinct from one that exists?' It is not merely ironical then that Quine should subsequently (p. 3) magnanimously give away the word 'exist', claiming that he still has 'is'.[3]

Once the stolen goods are restored it is no great feat to resolve many long-standing, but gratuitous, philosophical puzzles, beginning with the platonic riddle of non-being, that 'non-being must in some sense be, otherwise what is it what there is not?' (pp. 1–2). Consider some thing, d say, that does not exist, for example d is Meinong's round square. Then *what* does not exist is in this case d; but it in no way follows from 'd is non-existent' that 'd exists'. Such nonentities as d need have no being in any sense. It is basically because whatness and thinghood have been illicitly restricted to what exists or has being, that a puzzle seems to have arisen: for certainly we contradict ourselves if we say that what has being does not have being. There is no contradiction however in saying that what is a thing or object, e.g. d, may have no being in any sense; and this dissolves what Quine nicknames *Plato's beard*, without using or blunting, Occam's razor. For Occam's razor to remain sharp requires only that entities not be multiplied beyond necessity; but no multiplication of entities has been made, no bloating of the universe (of what exists) has occurred. Indeed the theory of objects enables a very substantial *reduction* in what is said to exist, so that what is said to exist can coincide with what really does exist, namely only certain individual objects now located in space.[4] But, more to the point, Occam's razor embodies various muddles of the very sort that it is important to remove. In particular, Occam's dictum that entities [or differently, objects] should not be multiplied beyond necessity supposes that it is in our power to increase or decrease the number of entities [or objects]: but of course in *that* sense – as opposed to the destruction or creation of objects by one's activity – it is not. What we can increase or decrease is not what exists but what we *say* exists, what we (*choose* to) *talk about*, and what our theories *commit* us to in one way or another. So the dictum, and a use like Quine's of it, confuses what exists with what we (choose to) talk about or what we, or our theories, *say* exists – a confusion that runs through into recent criteria for ontological commitment, themes of ontological relativity, and programs for ontological reduction.

Because d has no being there is no cause to try, like Quine's philosopher M[c]X, to assign some kind of being to d, e.g. ideational existence as an idea in men's minds. Pegasus and the Pegasus-idea remain, as they are, distinct items: Pegasus is a horse, the Pegasus-idea is not, since ideas are not (significantly) horses; Pegasus does not exist, but the Pegasus-idea presumably does; and so on. In fact, detailed arguments that

ideas are different from the objects they present were given by Meinong. One of these, set out more formally (as in [7], p. xxv), runs as follows:

1. Ideas are, by their very nature, of something (some object).
2. Ideas, when they occur, exist. (This premise, which is rejected in [2], is dispensable.)
3. If ideas were identical with their objects, all their objects would exist whenever someone was having an idea of them.
4. But there are objects which never exist (e.g. the *perpetuum mobile* and Pegasus).
5. Therefore, ideas are not identical with their objects.

Elsewhere, ([22], p. 199) Quine himself makes a similar distinction:

> . . . to identify the Parthenon with the Parthenon-idea is simply to confuse one thing with another; and to try to assure there being such a thing as Cerberus by identifying it with the Cerberus-idea is to make a similar confusion.

Yes, to confuse one thing with another. Quine's 'essential message' in [22], §33 repeated over and over, is however that

> Some meaningful words which are proper names from a grammatical point of view, notably 'Cerberus', do not name anything (p. 202),

otherwise briefly referred to as 'the mistaken view that "Cerberus" must name something'. In fact, but not of necessity, "Cerberus" does name something, not the Cerberus-idea, but Cerberus. There is no mistake: 'Cerberus' names Cerberus, whence, particularizing, 'Cerberus' names something. Quine's message is a plea to have us restrict quantifiers to existentially-loaded ones; for it is true that 'Cerberus' does not name anything existent. There are excellent reasons, however, for ignoring such pleas, for not so limiting quantificational apparatus. Nor does the removal of existential restrictions involve any of the mistakes Quine imagines he finds in taking nonentities in the domain of quantifiers or as named: there need be no confusion of meaning with naming (though meaning can be explicated through interpretation – which is wider than naming – in worlds); there need be no confusion of meaning with things talked about (but *naming* is a sub-species of *being about*); there need be no appeal to attempts (inspired by the Ontological Assumption)[5] to make nonentities exist somehow, for example, as shadows of entities, or as names, or somewhere, for example, in the mind, or in myth or in fiction and so on.

Similarly, because there is no need to assign some kind of being to d, the false dichotomies spawned by referential positions like empiricism, that Quine relies upon in putting the mythical M^{c}X on the spot can equally be dispensed with, e.g. that whatever has being either exists spatio-temporally, or else exists as an idea in men's minds. Since d does not exist, it does not exist in this or that way. Like other alleged problems about d the problem about how or in what way d exists vanishes given that d does not exist.

The commonsense (noneist) position being advanced should not be confused with that of Quine's other non-existent philosopher, Wyman.[6] For it is not maintained that Pegasus, for instance, 'has his being as an unactualized possible' (p. 3), or as anything else, since he simply has no being. More generally, the transformation of 'c is d' (e.g. 'what I am thinking of is Pegasus' or 'Pegasus is an unactualized possible') to 'c has its being as d' (e.g. to 'what I am thinking of has its being as Pegasus' or 'Pegasus has his being as an unactualized possible') should be rejected; for it depends on the erroneous assumption that all objects have being. Nor, for similar reasons, is it maintained, with Wyman, that Pegasus *is* (p. 3). The expression

'Pegasus is' is, like 'Pegasus likes', deviant in many English idiolects (including mine): its incompleteness is suggested by questions like 'is what?' Insofar as 'is' functions intransitively, 'x is' means, as the OED (i.e. [6]) indicates, 'x exists'. In short, *we* can give Quine the intransitive use of 'is', and so (as in the title of this paper) of 'is not'. Since the noneist position certainly does not claim that Pegasus exists, or, as Wyman puts it, subsists (i.e. exists, though perhaps in a very low-level way), it does not claim, in Wyman's way, that Pegasus is.[7] It follows, using the first account Quine gives of commitment to an ontology, according to which we commit ourselves to an ontology containing d when we say d, that noneism is *not* committed to an ontology containing items that do not exist, such as possibilia and abstractions, since, for each such x, it is true that x is *not*.[8]

As regards such impossible items as the round square cupola on Berkeley College, Wyman's position differs in kind from the theory of objects and Meinong's position (for which see e.g. [7], chapter 12). In contrast with 'purple happy number', there is nothing meaningless about 'round square cupola', which is what Quine has Wyman say (p. 5).[9] Wyman, like traditional rationalists, unjustly restricts objects which do not exist to the possible. The theory of objects in removing this restriction does not thereby admit 'a realm of unactualized possibles': 'realm', like 'universe' and '(the) real', carries ontological overtones. Although some items such as round squares are impossible, they nonetheless have (distinctive) properties. Accordingly, various different non-null sets of impossibilia can be formed; but these sets do not exist, any more than their elements or other abstract sets.

Despite the differences between Wyman's position and those of a genuinely Meinongian turn, it is widely supposed that Quine's scholastic objections to Wyman's unactualized possibles do serious, perhaps irreparable, damage to *all* these positions. Thus, for example, Kenny ([8],

p. 169): 'these objections, I think, make untenable the notion of Meinongian pure objects'.
This is far from so, as we now try to explain.
Quine's main charge (p. 4) is that possible
objects are 'disorderly' and 'well-nigh incorrigible'; and the basis of the charge is to be
found in the assumption that 'the concept of
identity is simply inapplicable to unactualized
possibles'. The assumption is unwarranted,
since identity and difference judgements concerning such objects are commonly made, both
ordinarily and in more technical discourse. Nor
are such judgements lacking in criterial under-
writing. For *the very same notions of identity* – most
importantly, extensional identity – *and distinctness
that apply to entities apply likewise to nonentities*, objects
that do not exist. The criterion for identity for
nonentities is, as for entities, coincidence in
extensional properties. Thus, for instance, Her-
cules and Heracles are identical, though some
people did not and do not know this. The criterion for distinctness is that of positively differing on extensional properties. Thus, for example,
Pegasus is distinct from Thunderhead because
Pegasus has the (extensional) property of being
winged and Thunderhead does not. Hence, nonentities *can* 'meaningfully be said to be identical
with themselves and distinct from one another'
(pace p. 4). Moreover, far from 'the concept of
identity being simply inapplicable to unactualized possibles', precisely the same criterion as
that given, and ordinarily used, is presupposed
classically – on one common theory – in such
misleading results as, for example, that Pegasus
and Chiron are one and the same because they
have the same traits (namely none). But, strictly,
what is true of nonentities classically depends on
the theory of names and descriptions adopted.[10]
On Russell's theory of descriptions all nonentities are identical, indeed all statements concerning unactualized possibilia b and c are
indeterminate because it is false that b = c and
false that b ≠ c. At this point one latent inconsistency in Quine's stance becomes apparent. For it
cannot both be false – as it is on Russell's theory,

which Quine endorses (pp. 5–6) – and meaningless, in the sense of concept inapplicability –
as Quine suggests it is – that nonentities are
identical and not distinct.

The criteria for identity given, both nonclassical and classical, also serve to meet familiar
overstatements like that of Kenny ([8], p. 168):

> The most serious – indeed the insurmount-
> able – objection to Meinongian pure objects
> is that it is impossible to provide any criterion
> of identity for them.

Since criteria compete, it is perfectly possible to
provide them, and rival criteria can be critically
assessed, for instance, in terms of their consequences. But, despite the ready availability of
criteria, the objection, that nonentities have no
(clear) identity conditions, is repeated over and
over in the literature. Another recent example,
where the objection is also used as ground for
setting aside Meinong's theory,[11] may be found
in Linsky ([23], pp. 35–36, transposed):

> Meinong comes nearest to capturing . . . our
> intuitions about reference in natural language
> and his theory does not seem to lead to con-
> tradiction as it is widely supposed to do. What
> disturbs us about his ontological population
> explosion, I believe, is that these objects have
> no clear identity conditions.

> Is the present king of France identical with the
> present king of China? There seem to be no
> principles which can be used to provide an
> answer to such questions. One answer is as
> reasonable as the other and this makes the
> very notion of an *object* seem misapplied here.

Apart from the very first claim, this requires correcting claim by claim. Although Meinong's
theory, if carefully (re-)formulated, does not
lead to contradiction, the account Linsky gives
([23], p. 34) does lead to contradiction (given
only a very minimal logic):

But Meinong insists, against Frege that what phrases of this form [$\ulcorner(\iota x)(\phi x)\urcorner$] denote is always $(\iota x)(\phi x)$. . . . The insistence that $\ulcorner(\iota)(\phi x)\urcorner$ denote the right thing leads immediately to a special case of the independence of *Sosein* from *Sein*, for it entails that $\phi(\iota x)(\phi x)$ is always true for any choice of ϕ.

That for every ϕ, $\ulcorner(\iota x)(\phi x)\urcorner$ denotes $(\iota x)(\phi x)$ is distinct from the Independence Principle (as varieties of free logic will show) and does *not* entail $\phi(\iota x)(\phi x)$ (as neutral logic countermodels will show). The unqualified Characterisation Principle, $\phi(\iota x)(\phi x)$, which Linsky (mistakenly) attributes to Meinong (p. 33, as well as p. 34), is an exceedingly damaging principle, and contrary to Linsky (p. 35) does lead to propositions of the form p & ~p. For consider the object $(\iota x)(Rx \& ~Rx)$, a for short. Then, by the above principle, Ra & ~Ra.

There is no "ontological population explosion" under Meinong's theory: to suggest so is to misrepresent the theory. The identity *conditions* for objects are clear, even if, as in the case of existing objects, it is not always clear, or determinate, whether certain objects are the same or not. Since these ordinary identity principles provide an answer to questions such as Linsky's about the kings, there certainly are principles which supply answers to such questions – and similarly theories of descriptions such as Russell's provide answers, even if wrong ones, e.g. the king of France = the king of China. In fact the king of France is Leibnitz-distinct from the king of China, since someone can think of one but not the other; and a theory which gave a different result would hardly be reasonable. And on Linsky's assumptions about Meinong's theory, the two kings are presumably extensionally distinct since one is king of France and the other not (but of China): thus as they differ in extensional respects they are in fact distinct. Accordingly, there is no solid evidence adduced, on the basis of identity-conditions, that the notion of *object* is misapplied in Meinong's theory.

As with identity, so for likeness and similarity, essentially the same accounts that apply to entities apply to nonentities, two items being alike if they have sufficiently many extensional properties in common. It is on this basis that we say that a dryad and a naiad are alike, and much more alike than a unicorn and a centaur. Thus some possible things are alike, but as in the case of entities, alikeness is in general not sufficient for identity. These simple points answer *all* Quine's alleged difficulties for objects that do not exist except those concerning the number of men in the doorway. Briefly, the concepts of identity and distinctness, likeness and difference, are applicable to nonentities, and the criteria for their application are the same as in the case of entities. Hence too set-theoretical notions are applicable to nonentities as well as entities, and numerical concepts apply. As Locke and Leibnitz argued against the scholastics and Frege reiterated ([26], p. 31), various classes of possibilia can be counted and numbered. A nonactual man in the doorway belongs to the three element class consisting of Pegasus, Heracles and a nonactual man in the doorway (not, as Frege's own theory, adopted in Quine's ML, would have it, to a one element class comprising the null set). Similarly, it may make good sense to ask 'How many objects of a given type have a given property?' even where some or none of the objects exist. The main problem, not special to nonentities, lies in determining which properties the objects in question have, not with matters of sense.

Quine, however, is suggesting (e.g. p. 4, 'What sense can be made of . . .') that such questions as 'How many possible fat men are there in that doorway?' make no sense, and accordingly, that corresponding assertions of the form 'There are n possible fat men in that doorway' are meaningless. For the question is significant if the corresponding indicatives are. But prima facie the indicatives are significant (and transformations can be used and arguments constructed which reveal that the sentences are significant): they contain no category or type mistakes. So they cannot be convincingly written off as not well-formed: even if they should strike the uninitiated as odd they require logical accommodation. Accordingly such questions, and indicatives, are just as much a problem for classical logical positions as for the nonclassical position they are directed against.

Consider now a nearest open doorway and an arbitrary fat man who never has existed, e.g. Mr. Pickwick. Ask whether Mr. Pickwick is in that doorway. The answer is, as a matter of observation, No. In literal contexts the answer is the same in the case of every other merely possible fat man. Hence, the answer to the question 'How many (merely) possible fat men are in that doorway?' is: Zero. The same answer may be expected on more theoretical grounds. By a familiar, and classically accepted, thesis attributed to Brentano, a merely possible item cannot stand in entire physical relations, such as *being in* or *standing in*, to actual items. Hence, merely possible men of any variety, fat or thin, bald or not, cannot stand in actual doorways. Thus the answer to Quine's numerical (how many?) questions is: Zero. There are zero possible men in that doorway, zero possible fat ones, and exactly the same number of merely possible thin ones.

The answers given to these last questions are, again, exactly those of classical orthodoxy, even if the reasons for the answers are of a somewhat different cast. Since classical orthodoxy has, with its very limited quantificational apparatus, serious difficulties in expressing its answers, let us articulate them for it. Since no nonentities exist, of whatever kind, there are exactly as many nonexistent fat men as thin men, namely, none, so none can be standing in any actual doorways.[12] In short, classical orthodoxy can already supply answers to what are reckoned the hardest of Quine's questions – giving the lie to such charges as that identity, difference and numerical properties cannot be meaningfully attributed to nonentities, and so removing the ground

for the further charges of disorderliness and incorrigibility.

It is not easy to avoid the impression that one of the many reasons why Quine's questions have been thought to cause especially severe difficulties for theories of nonexistent objects is because 'A possible man is in that doorway' has been confused with 'A man is possibly in that doorway', because *de re* modalities have been confused with *de dicto* modalities (in *one* sense of that vexed distinction). As the latter claim, like the pure de dicto claim 'It is logically possible that a man should be in that doorway', is usually true for open unoccupied doorways (and let us suppose for the selected one such), if the conflation were correct the answer to the question 'How many possible men are in that doorway?' – now the question 'How many men are possibly in that doorway?' – would seem to be 'At least some' since Quine is possibly in that doorway, and the determination of the exact number would – on the doubtful assumption that it is determinate at all – become a knotty, though hardly "insoluble," problem. But the conflation is not correct: the sentences have different semantical analyses, the first stating a relation of *being in* in the factual situation, whereas the second states such a relation in some possible world.

Part of the interest of Quine's question comes from the number of different answers it has been given by different philosophers, different answers induced partly by different questions, not only the de re question we have so far been concerned with, namely

(1) How many merely possible (nonactual) men are in that actual doorway? but also the questions:

(2) How many men are possibly in that doorway?

(3) How many men can possibly be in (be crowded into) that doorway?, or, more precisely, what is the largest number of men that can possibly be in that doorway?

Question (2) splits into different questions according as the collective quantifier precedes or follows the modal operator, namely

(2a) Of what numbers n of men is it true that for those n men it is possible that they are in that doorway (together)?

(2b) Of what number of men is it true that it is possible that those men are in that doorway?

The answer to question (3) sets a bound on the answer to question (2). No doubt the answer to (3) is at least, Many, but a more exact answer depends on how small humans can be and on what shape and how large the doorway is (and also on the type of modality). The answer to (2b) is then: any number between zero and the bound. For let k be any such number: then the statement "it is possible that k men are in the doorway" is true. Accordingly, the best answer to (2) is: it is indeterminate,[13] though the indeterminacy is bounded.

No doubt some conflation of modalities is encouraged by ordinary discourse. Consider, for example, 'Some clouds and a possible thunderstorm are forecast for Victoria this afternoon', where the apparent de re modality has an intended de dicto expansion. A confusion of modalities may seem to damage Parsons' answer to Quine ([10], p. 572):

... when Quine asks about "the [merely] possible fat man in the doorway", he uses a definite description which, on this account [because the uniqueness clause is not satisfied], fails to refer − for there are many possible fat men in the doorway.

It is logically possible that many fat men are in the doorway, but it would be quite invalid to infer that many possible fat men are in the doorway − nor does Parsons' analysis support such a move. For properties such as those of possibility and actuality figuring in the interpretation of 'possible fat men' and 'actual doorway' are (in the intended sense) extranuclear and so are not characterising. But what has been said is not what Parsons means. There is an ambiguity in 'possible fat man', depending upon whether 'possible' goes into the description, as supposed above, or not, i.e. is regarded as consequential. On the latter construal, there are on Parsons' theory infinitely many possible fat men in that doorway (indeed the cardinality is presumably nondenumerable), one for each consistent set of nuclear (i.e. roughly, characterising) properties which includes at least the properties of being a man, being fat, and being in the doorway.[14] Infinitely many, irrespective of the size of the fat men and perhaps that some of them will be giants who fill the doorway or more. Such results are implausible but can easily be avoided, by requiring joint possibility (in the consequential sense) of occupation of the doorway.

It is bound to be objected that any theory of (nonexistent) objects will generate many, very many, possibilia standing in that doorway. Consider the n possible fat men standing in that doorway, for an arbitrarily selected number n. Then surely, by assumptions of such theories (e.g. object characterisation postulates), some n possible fat men are standing in that doorway? Emphatically, No. Such postulates have only carefully restrained roles on any theory that can claim coherence: they do not warrant ontological arguments or the establishing of new extensional relations between what exists and what is merely possible (as [2] explains in detail). Nothing, of course, stops the design of (generally, less acceptable) theories with more sweeping characterisation postulates. Some of these theories would, like Parsons' ingenious theory, give different answers to some of Quine's questions. This is unsurprising, rather as it is unsurprising that different classical-style theories identify Pegasus with different objects, or admit different universes of sets.

A similar reply can be made to the related

objection that we can tell a variety of conflicting stories which describe fat men in the doorway. A tells one story with 3 fictional fat men fitted into the doorway. B out-does A and tells a tale in which 10 fat men are squeezed into the doorway. C tells an even taller tale. . . . How many fat men are in the doorway? On A's story 3, B's 10, and on C's tale 98 say. But in reality, as before, 0. For the world of A's story is not the real world. No characterisation postulate applies: we cannot directly determine such characteristics of the real world as what stands in actual places by story telling.[15] For these reasons too Rescher's answer (in [14]) to Quine's how many questions, namely, 'As many as are described', is inadequate (Rescher's answer is a much better answer to question (2) above, which may be the question Rescher intended to answer). Each of A, B and C describe different numbers and not all can be right, since 3 men differ from 98. That is, different, and inconsistent, descriptions may be given, and different, and inconsistent, riders may be added at a later time. Moreover, descriptions are not the only way of specifying possibilia; they may, for instance, be inferred from a theory. That the story-teller line cannot be right perhaps emerges more clearly if the story tellers use actual fat men in their accounts, e.g. A's story is about Herman Kahn and two other modern Falstaffs. A story about actual figures does not make that story true, except in appropriately indicated fictional contexts. As it is with entities, so also is it with nonentities.

The fact is that differences between entities and nonentities have been much exaggerated, especially by the enemies of the nonexistent, empiricists and idealists alike.[16] For nonentities are not as chaotic, as indeterminate, or as lacking in independence as they have been represented as being; while at the same time entities are not as totally independent, as free of indeterminacy and vagueness as has been made out. The following cloud parody, which can be reworked for a great many other natural entities, should help to bring out these points:

. . . The slum of entities is a breeding ground for disorderly elements. Take, for instance, the cloud in the sky above; and, again, the adjacent cloud in the sky. Are they the same cloud or two clouds? How are we to decide? How many clouds are there in the sky? Are there more cumulus than nimbus? How many of them are alike? Or would their being alike make them one? . . . is the concept of identity simply inapplicable to clouds? But what sense can be found in talking of entities which cannot meaningfully be said to be identical with themselves and distinct from one another? These elements are well-nigh incorrigible . . . I feel we'd do better to clear the slum of entities and be done with it.

And so to parody Kenny also: these objections make untenable the notion of an entity. What should be removed, however, is not the slum of entities and nonentities, but the classical logical economy which has reduced these solid dwellings to slums.

The parody leads to certain further points. To begin with, many of the problems which are taken to be insuperable in the case of nonentities arise equally in the case of entities, especially natural objects such as clouds and storms and waves, mountains and waterfalls and forests. But the problems are not usually seen as – and should not be seen as – discrediting entities. Thus a double standard is being applied. Questions which it is realized do not present insuperable problems for entities, are taken to do so in the case of nonentities, which are required to be determinate, distinct, and so on in a way that entities are frequently not (see further [2], chapter 9). For recall the decision questions for entities that Wittgenstein and Wisdom introduced us to, and add some more, e.g. How wide is Mt. Egmont? Where do its slopes end? How long is a leech? How long is Plato's beard? Is this a new wave? How many mountain peaks are in a range? Questions as to precise boundaries, in particular, are very common with natural entities: these are *sometimes* settled by decision or convention, and sometimes not. Sometimes they are said to call only for cheerful indecision.

An upshot is that common philosophical paradigms of entities and the resulting pictures of the universe (of entities) need considerable adjustment, or better, replacement. The paradigms of entities have too often been artefacts such as furniture and office equipment which, because human artefacts, do have sharp boundaries and determinate numerical properties, in contrast to natural objects, which frequently, in advance of specific decisions, do not. The paradigms have encouraged dicta, such as Quine's 'No entities without identity', designed (unsuccessfully) to rule out such things as attributes, which, too seriously applied, exclude many natural objects as entities. It is then the dicta, not the entities, that have to go. Likewise to be rejected as misleading is the familiar philosophical picture of entities as the 'furniture of the universe' (for a recent elaboration of this picture, see Findlay [13], pp. 328–29, on 'the universe's undeniable furniture', and Bunge [24] on 'the furniture of the world').

Why has the Identity Problem been thought to be so severe for nonentities, far more problematic than for entities? There are a number of different sources of identity anxiety, and in order to see where the sources of anxiety lie and help to remove them, it is important to separate out these different sources for the alleged Problem. For different aspects of the theory of objects are appropriately brought in to deal with different sources. Thus some anxieties are mitigated by appeal to indeterminacy, some are resolved through the theory of extensionality and of identity in intensional frames, and some by making use of features which derive from (object) characterisation postulates. There are at least these cases:

1.   Anxiety arises from indeterminacy of identity. Some identity claims concerning nonentities are indeterminate, e.g. (in advance

of a theory which decides the issue) which of the various Faustus's of the literature are the same. From this point of view identity is simply on a par with other features of nonentities. It is felt, however, that this reveals an arbitrariness and perhaps chaoticness about nonentities because the property in question, namely, identity, is a logical one. It is felt that the fact that some identities concerning nonentities are indeterminate makes nonentities unsuitable objects for logical treatment. This is not so, any more than it is so in the case of entities. It is simply that a satisfactory logical treatment will have to allow appropriately for indeterminacy. Further, this particular sort of worry should be resolved once indeterminacy and the way it is treated are grasped; and in fact it should be seen as a superior feature of a theory that it can take up and explain the data on which the anxiety is based, rather than simply using it as a reason for rejecting nonentities as outside the scope of a logical theory.

2.   Several worries derive from the issue of criteria of identity for nonentities. The first worry arises because no distinction is made between contingent and necessary identity; it is assumed that identity relations between nonentities must be necessary identities (e.g. identity of concepts), giving rise to the mistaken charge that nonentities are nothing but concepts, and thereby making them unsuitable for intensional analysis and sacrificing much of the very substantial point of having nonentities for intensional analysis (on this see [2], especially chapter 8). That the assumption is mistaken should be evident from elementary contingent identities, such as 'Pegasus is what I am thinking about'. Necessary identity is rightly perceived as generating serious problems, but the options are not perceived. The

difficulties are resolved by a theory of extensional identity (as in [16]), which applies to nonentities, just as to entities. Then, 'no therapy of concepts' is required for the 'rehabilitation of objects which do not exist' (p. 4); nor is it desirable.

A worry remains. It is thought that one cannot have contingent identities between nonentities because this is identity of reference and in the case of nonentities there is no reference to be identical. This problem is removed (in the theory of identity) by distinguishing identity of reference and extensional identity, that is identity under extensional properties. Referential identity, which can only apply truly to existing items, is defined in terms of coincidence of entities in extensional respects: it is extensional identity of entities. Thus if a and b are referentially identical 'a' and 'b' have interchangeable referential occurrences.[17] Since expressions about nonentities have no referential occurrences in true statements, nonentities cannot have identity of reference. But they can still be extensionally (or contingently) identical, since they have extensional properties, and extensional identity of nonentities is coincidence of extensional properties.

3. Perplexity derives from failure to see that nonentities can have extensional properties, with the result that it is thought that any two of them must be the same. The worry is resolved in the theory of objects through characterisation postulates which assign extensional features to nonentities on the basis of their characterisations.

4. Anxiety arises from the failure of nonentities to have distinctive identity criteria, different from those for entities. For example, Lambert (in [9], p. 252) seems to think that each sort of item should have its own distinctive identity criteria. This need not be so.[18] Different sorts of items may have the same identity criteria, e.g.

possibilia and impossibilia, or properties and intensional sets, and yet be distinguished by other features, e.g. the assumption of existence leads to inconsistency in the case of impossibilia but not of possibilia, and sets differ categorially from properties in such matters as being able to have members.

Quine suspects 'that the main motive for' including nonentities in the domain of discourse is to escape the 'riddle of non-being' (p. 4); but since that riddle can be satisfactorily disposed of, so he thinks, by way of Russell's theory of descriptions without appeal to nonentities (p. 8), there is no need or ground for such expansion of the discourse domain. According to noneism, he is wrong on both counts. Firstly, the noneist solution to the riddle is, like Meinong's, an incidental, but pleasing, by-product of a theory designed primarily for, and from, the analysis of intensional discourse about what does not exist (see [2], especially chapter 1). Secondly, Russell's theory of description is inadequate for such a task; for it sometimes delivers the intuitively wrong truth-value assignments. For example, it is true that Meinong thought that the round square is square, but whatever scope it is given on Russell's theory of description it nevertheless gets wrongly assigned value false. Once one such counterexample has been glimpsed, others are easily designed. Somewhat different counterexamples are supplied by truths such as the following yields: If the winged horse Pegasus does not exist I can nevertheless think of him and be aware that he is winged.

Noneists have no taste for grossly impoverished discourse – which is what Quine's taste for desert landscapes (p. 4) comes to and has led to – yet find no convincing case for populating the domain of reality with a profusion of abstractions such as sets in their transfinite multiplicity – after the fashion of Quine. (Indeed, one has the feeling from Quine's work that in the beginning there is *no case* for admitting that such objects as sets exist, *except* that the immensely important enterprise of scientifically essential mathematics could not get along without their existence. But, somewhat rewritten, it can: see [2], chapter 11. So the residual case collapses.)

Quine's discussion of the ontological problem of universals in [1] is much less detailed in argument and less conclusive than his discussion of the problem for particulars. The noneist critique of Quine which follows will correspondingly be more doctrinaire and less detailed in arguments for the claims advanced. The noneist thesis is, in direct contrast to M^{c}X, that there are no such entities as attributes, relations, classes, numbers, functions, propositions, and the like: none of these exist, in any sense. Even so, some items are attributes, others are numbers, and so on; and these non-existent items play an important, and sometimes essential, role in discourse and can have a major explanatory role. Such a position, anathema to most empiricists, Quine tries, in effect, to rule out as not even an option. In this he is less than successful, as is now argued.

Quine's main move is to try to foist upon us a criterion of ontological commitment in terms of use of bound variables, namely, that 'to be assumed as an entity . . . is to be reckoned as the value of a variable' (p. 13), and more explicitly,

> . . . we are convicted of a particular ontological presupposition if, and only if, the alleged presupposition *has to be* reckoned among the entities over which our variables range in order to render one of our affirmations true (p. 13, emphasis added).

The argument offered for the criterion[19] is hardly compelling. While it is true that we can easily involve ourselves in ontological commitments, i.e. commitments to the *existence* of certain things, by maintaining (saying is not enough) that *there exist* such and such things, this is not the only way in which ontological commitments can arise, nor need non-existential quantification commit us ontologically. Quine contends, however, in an inference which looks remarkably like an A-conversion, that 'use of bound variables' . . . 'is, essentially, the *only* way we can involve ourselves in ontological commitments' (p. 12). On the face of it this contention is just false: someone who maintains that such and such thing exists commits himself just as much as someone who maintains that there exist such and such things. Quine's further argument (pp. 12–13) is that the eliminability of names and descriptions shows that names, and descriptions, are 'altogether immaterial to the ontological issue'.[20] The argument is invalid: the support is irrelevant. For 'exists' is a referentially transparent predicate, and the paraphrasing of 'Pegasus', for example, as 'the thing which pegasizes' does nothing to eliminate the commitment but simply rephrases it. That Pegasus exists (or does not) remains true because it is true that the x which pegasizes exists (or not). In symbols, $p = \iota x p(x) \supset . E(\iota x p(x) \supset E(p))$. It is similar with the elimination of descriptions. Because $E(x) \equiv (\exists y) (x = y)$ and $E!(x) \equiv (\exists! y) (x = y)$ we can quite evidently involve ourselves in ontological commitments by way of names and descriptions if we can so involve ourselves through the use of bound existential variables. And all the fact that languages shunning names can be designed shows is that in such languages we should lack primitive expressive means of stating ontological commitments through names. In itself this shows nothing about the statements of such commitments in languages which are not so lacking in expressive power. The conclusion is accordingly that Quine's claim as to bound variables being the only way we can involve ourselves in ontological commitment is false.

Nor does the use of quantifiers and bound variables always involve us in ontological commitments: the use of intensionally covered quantifiers may not, and the use of non-existential or existentially neutral quantifiers does not (as [3] and [4] explain). For example, use of the neutral quantifier 'something' (which expands symbolically to 'for some object x, x . . .'), as in the claim 'something does not exist', in no way commits the claimant to the existence of anything ('anything' can also be used neutrally here). The appealing equation 'to be assumed as an entity, purely and simply, is to be reckoned as the value of a variable' (p. 13) is as false as it is simple.

Quine now acknowledges the limitations of the criterion: 'admission of additional linguistic elements can upset this ontological standard' ([21], p. 161). What is true is that 'when language is thus [severely] regimented [to the framework of referentially restricted quantification and truth functions], its ontology comprises just the objects that the variables of quantification admit as values' (p. 161). What is *not* true, however, is that 'the basic structure of the language of science' is of this severely regimented form.[21] And it is palpably false that 'It is only our [rather, this] somewhat regimented and sophisticated language of science [in contrast with the common man's idiom, for example] that has evolved in such a way as really to raise ontological questions' (p. 160). More than two millenia of nonregimented philosophical discussion of ontological questions tell against this claim, and should force its reformulation. But what Quine adds only makes things worse. 'The ontological question . . . for ordinary language generally *makes sense only* relative to agreed translations into ontologically regimented notation' (p. 161, emphasis added; also p. 168), which there may well not be. The only argument Quine indicates for this astonishing proposition (p. 162) is based on adopting his already-flawed criterion of ontological commitment: the argument, along with surrounding considerations, is perhaps better construed as a reductio ad absurdum of the adoption of the translation-to-regimented-notation as sole test for ontological commitment.

Unfortunately, the original false criterion pervades much of what Quine has to say about ontology and ontological problems, and renders it unacceptable. This applies in particular to what he has to say (especially in [1]) about the ontological commitments of conceptual schemes and about the problem of universals. The result in the case of the universals problem is that the noneist position,[22] according to which we can talk quantificationally about universals though none such exist, is entirely excluded. And the separation of neutral quantification from existence, as in noneism, removes what basis such assertions as the following may have had:

> One's ontology is basic to the conceptual scheme by which he interprets all experiences, even the most commonplace ones. Judged within some particular conceptual scheme . . . an ontological statement goes without saying, standing in need of no separate justification at all (p. 10).

A noneist conceptual scheme, or theory, may include notions such as those of time and number which items are definitely not assigned existence, and others where the question of existence is unknown or left open (and even on Quine's view the latter can happen as long as quantification is eschewed). Ontology is not so basic after all.[23] For similar reasons fixing upon an over-all conceptual scheme does not (contrary to Quine's claim on pp. 16–17) determine an ontology.

Quine attempts to use the relativity of conceptual schemes, and of what he takes to be the automatically associated ontology, to dispose of positions on universals like M^cX's (p. 10). But the rival scheme Quine sketches is hardly very compelling, and the serious weakness of some of his points becomes apparent if the working example is changed from *redness* to, for instance, *brittleness* or *solubility*. Brittle things have nothing in common 'except as a popular and misleading manner of speaking'? The grounds for assessments of brittleness extends no further than actual things that are brittle? Properties such as brittleness have no 'real explanatory power'? Even more surprisingly, predicates such as 'is red' and 'is brittle', though meaningful, have no meaning! In 'refusing to admit meanings' Quine has thereby deprived himself even of the usual semantics for applied quantificational logic which interprets predicates through universals, either attribute- or set-theoretically. M^cX, presumably, was not impressed by Quine's attempt to cool down the hot spot he put himself in with his vaunted rejection of meanings, and nor are we. Meaning does not reduce, as Quine hopes we'll allow, to sameness of meaning unless, what is at issue, attribute abstraction is also allowed; but given abstraction, through which meaning can be recovered from sameness of meaning, redness can be retrieved from things being red, and so on. Quine, no doubt, hopes that we'll allow too that 'what is called giving the meaning of an utterance is simply the uttering of a synonym'; but this (pre-Wittgensteinian suggestion) is a travesty of the range of things that would count as giving the meaning of an expression.

When it comes to the universals of mathematics and physical science, as distinct from those of commonsense, Quine's attitude suddenly changes. The 'higher myth' of numbers and classes 'is a good and useful one' (p. 18). Truth has vanished: in trying on one or other conceptual schemes or associated myths, we are only selecting, it is alleged, what is simple, economical, useful, and serves our various interests or purposes. Important issues among the problems of universals have been lost sight of, such as, what is true in classical mathematics, and which, if any, of the claims made as to the existence of universals are correct, how much of classical mathematics is myth (and how precisely is this analogy cashed out) and how much can be redeemed. Don't anticipate clear answers on such issues in [1].

Quine supposes that the intermediate and upper ramifications (the cantilevered superstructure, on a later image) of his conceptual scheme will enable him to communicate successfully with M^cX, on such topics as politics, the weather, and language (p. 16). Given Quine's assumptions as to what can be significantly said and the severe limitations on his conceptual scheme, this should strike one as extremely doubtful, and certainly as nowhere substantiated. Weather forecasts, for example, are frequently decidedly intensional and exhibit remote grades of modality: the intensional assessment of such forecasts, as discussion of the weather may involve, strikes the less credulous among us as even further beyond the pale of legitimate Quinean discourse and admissible myth.

There is much else, of less immediate relevance to noneism, to disagree with in Quine's essay 'On What There Is', especially in the last pages. There is, for example, good reason to dispute the unsupported claim (p. 19) that the phenomenalistic conceptual scheme 'claims epistemological priority'. (The reasons include those Austin has advanced in [25], and those introduced in the analysis of phenomenalism in [2], chapter 8). It is certainly highly disputable that 'we adopt, at least insofar as we are reasonable, the simplest conceptual scheme into which the disordered fragments of raw experience can be fitted and arranged' (p. 16). That is a slick, and on reflection obnoxious, empirico-pragmatic reslanting of what is accounted reasonable. Raw experience is by no means all that has to be accounted for, correctly. Much depends too on whether or not "fitting" is forcing and whether or not a classical logical straightjacket is imposed.

But Quine's position has not remained stationary, and several parts of the essay (the claim to priority of a phenomenalistic scheme is a minor example) have been abandoned in, and sabotaged by, later work. Early on Quine was tempted by nominalism (and phenomenalism), which shaped priorities and sharply delimited what existed (or what was said to exist) whatever science might require; subsequently, however, as reflected in [1], the accommodation of science became the dominating factor in determining what things exist,[24] and a physicalist ontology of physical objects *and* sets formed therefrom for scientifically essential mathematics, resulted; but recently ontology has come to matter less and less, and a new ontology, carrying ontological reduction towards a set-theoretic limit, has emerged. The tendency to superannate the ontological problem as to what exists, for instance as trivial, or as a matter for scientists, or to dispose of it in a relativistic fashion, as theory relative, was long discernible in Quine's work, but it has become more prominent with the emphasis of relativistic and reductionistic themes.

According to the theme of ontological relativity, we can enquire about the ontology of a theory *only* relative to 'the background theory with its own privately adopted and ultimately inscrutable ontology' ([13], p. 51). Total relativity Quine tries to escape by appeal to an alleged qualitative difference between ontology, which is relative, and truth, which is not. 'Sentences in their truth or falsity are what run deep, ontology is by the way ... questions of inference and ontology become incidental' ([21], p. 165). But, to all appearances, truth is relative for Quine, certainly when remote from experience, a matter to be pragmatically settled, like choice of a conceptual scheme (cf. [1], p. 18, discussed above). There is, moreover, a serious tension between the relativity thesis and Quine's theme that ontology is on the same footing as science; for instance:

What reality is like is the business of scientists, in the broadest sense, painstakingly to surmise, and what there is, what is real, is a part of that question ([10], p. 22).

Several things have gone astray: (i) science is not so relative, given that truth is not, nor therefore, given the above connection, is reality and what exists, contradicting the theory relativity of ontology. In any case, the relativity theme is prima facie implausible, and arguments for it can be faulted in the same sort of way as arguments

for the theory-dependence of all (observational) truth-claims (Cf. [12], chapter 11, where the claim that 'all entities are theoretical' is rejected). This is unremarkable, for, on referential assumptions, (ii) truth and existence are far from independent.[25] In particular, by the Ontological Assumption, if it is true that c has some property, then c exists. Thus theory relativity of existence would be reflected back in theory relativity of truth. However, (iii) what exists is by no means entirely the business or preserve of scientists. For they too may operate with mistaken referential or other (e.g. reductionistic) assumptions, and so for instance conclude from ontological reduction that only pure sets exist or from the fact that there are true statements about c's, or that c's have properties, that c's exist. There is also the crucial matter of criteria for existence, which – like the quite distinct matter of criteria for ontic commitment – are as much the business of philosophers as anyone else.

Though much is sometimes made of the difference between what a theory says and what it is committed to, the separate issues of what exists and what ontic commitments to allow ourselves are characteristically (but not invariably) conflated.

There remains the question what *there is*, or perhaps better, what ontological commitments to allow ourselves in our discourse ... this question, like any question concerning the broadest features of our scientific schematism, has to be settled pragmatically ([17], p. 159).

The matter of what exists is not open to pragmatic settlement (any more than to choice), and is, though, to a declining extent, largely beyond human technological control. The different question of what theory to adhere to is, however, sometimes a matter open to *limited* choice, but it is *not*, in important cases (such as fundamental theories or conceptual schemes), settled simply pragmatically. For theory choice is constrained by factual data *before* pragmatic factors come into play.[26] It is partly because the criteria for what is said to exist are open to haggling, and are to some extent theory-dependent, that it is thought that what exists is also open to human negotiation, and is theory relative. What is theory relative is what theories assert to exist and, differently, are committed to the existence of, not what exists. (The confusion is like that, already noted, underlying applications of Occam's razor.) Of course, what exists, and what a theory maintains exists are connected, again through truth. If a theory is true and asserts that c's exist (or is committed to the existence of c's), then c's exist.[27] But truth cannot be here whittled down in the manner of pragmatism, to acceptability or the like, without correspondingly weakening the conclusion. Yet this is precisely what Quine, and many others, have tried to do.

> Quine divided the question "What things or sorts of things exist?" into two questions: (1) What, according to a given theory, exists? (In Quinean terms: What are the *ontological commitments* of a given theory); (2) Which theories have we a good reason to accept as true? (Chihara [20]; according to Gochet [5], p. 142, 'this faithfully reports the views of Quine').

The division is illegitimate. When (2) is so varied from the *requirement* of truth, what (1) and (2) yield is not what is given, but instead: What things have we good reason to accept do exist?

Pragmatism illicitly transfers a certain softness we can find in what we have good reason to accept as existing (and, similarly, as true) to a softness in what exists (and what is true). Ontological reduction proper, as opposed to theory reformulation, presupposes such softness. Much as the question of what exists has been conflated with the question of ontological commitments of discourse and theories, so reduction upon what exists (which can hardly happen purely theoretically) has been (con-)fused with a theoretical "ontological" reduction. To affect ontological reduction in this sense is 'to delete superfluous objects in a theory's ontology without affecting the truth-values of the sentences that constitute it' ([5], p. 169). What such ontological reduction effects is precisely a reduction in the primitive subject terms of a theory, which is reflected back in the domain of objects and entities required by the theory, not any diminution of what exists. For this reason there would be no ontological debacle, no debacle as regards what exists, even if Quine's ultimate ontological reduction to pure set theory could be pulled off. Ontological reduction is not existential elimination.[28] Ontology does not cease to matter.

Appendix

While the referential paradigm prevails, "fatal" objections to theories of objects and to Meinong's theory will continue to roll off the presses. Another recent example is afforded by Cargile who contends that Meinongianism, at least as applied to sentences of a logical subject-predicate form, is 'an absurd doctrine' ([19], pp. 175–76). He gives as reasons i) 'the fact that "impossible objects" such as "the round square plane figure atop Berkeley College" are logically intolerable' and ii) that there are "permanently unanswerable questions" about such objects as the king of France and the great and wise king of France, such as whether they are the same. As with Linsky and Kenny, the reasons offered, descending from Russell through Quine, do not strictly guarantee the contention, and, more important, neither withstands investigation. As to i), objects like that mentioned are not logically intolerable: they can be included in the domain of neutral quantification logic without any serious difficulty. As to ii), incompleteness of objects is not a damaging feature, but what should be expected. However, incompleteness neither sharply separates nonentities from entities, nor is as rampant as Cargile supposes. The two kings of France, for example, differ by virtue of different properties. In fact, though he vigorously rejects Meinongianism, Cargile has no decisive arguments against it. Mostly what he presents are his own referential views as opposed to viable logical alternatives (e.g. p. 185), and travesties of Meinong (e.g. p. 178, 'even Meinong would not have called "the round square is round" true') and Meinongian alternatives.

Notes

1 Many such arguments are assembled in [2], where a full account of the underlying theory, noneism, is given. Noneism is an elaboration of the theory of objects, perhaps best known from Meinong's presentation. The present paper expands chapter 3 of [2].

2 Especially as reprinted in [1], to which '[1]' will mostly refer. All page citations without further detail are to [1].

3 Nor is ontology exactly independent of lexicography, in the way Quine here suggests – a suggestion his own subsequent discourse-relativization of "ontology" undercuts.

4 It was Meinong's thesis that any existing object has a more or less definite location in space and time. It is a corollary that abstract objects do not exist (see further [2], chapter 9).

5 This assumption, which is explained below, is criticized in detail in [2], 1.3.

6 Philosophical legend has it that Wyman is modelled on Meinong, but the serious discrepancies between Wyman's position and any but a hearsay Meinong position cast some doubt on the legend. Wyman is somewhat more like the Russell of The Principles of Mathematics.

7 Meinong's position diverges from the stream of noneism here followed: for according to Meinong possibilia such as Pegasus subsist. Insofar as this implies more than that possibilia are possible – in some or other of the commonly confused senses, e.g. that they could exist or that the supposition of their existence leads to no contradiction or that their characterisation leads to no contradiction – it should be rejected as misleading.

8 Observe that the results so obtained from the first criterion *diverge* from those obtained by applying Quine's other and better known criterion for ontological commitment, according to which ontological commitment is determined through preparedness to quantify (p. 12). In these terms noneism is ontologically committed to what it maintains does *not* exist, e.g. possibilia, abstractions, and so on. A corollary is the inadequacy of the quantificational criterion that 'to be is to be the value of a bound variable' (p. 15). The inadequacy of Quine's case for the criterion is discussed below.

9 The dilemma that Wyman is supposed to encounter is colourfully represented in [22] p. 202: "Having already cluttered the universe with an implausible lot of unactualised possibles, are we to go on and add a realm of unactualised impossibles? The tendency at this point is to choose the other horn of the supposed dilemma, and rule that expressions involving impossibility are meaningless." That is almost certainly not the main historical tendency; and it is a tendency to which there are serious objections (see [4]). The supposed dilemma is no dilemma, not for the reasons Quine offers, that 'there need be no mystery about attributing nonexistence where there is nothing [existent] to attribute it to' (and we have observed the inadequacies in reductions of talk about nonentities to talk of entities), but because the first option can be restated neutrally. There are, and need be, no additions to the universe (of entities) of new realms: the population, or number of elements, of the entity-universe is unchanged. Talk of 'cluttering', 'implausible lot', etc., reflects inappropriate referential thinking.

10 For instance, in Quine's Mathematical Logic, which includes a Fregean style theory of descriptions much inferior (in all but technical ease) to Russell's theory, nonentities have the most amazing properties. For example, Pegasus is identical with the null set – so the concept of identity is certainly applicable – and has all the same properties, e.g. Pegasus exists, but has no members, Pegasus is a subset of every set whatsoever, and all the natural numbers are simple logical constructions of Pegasus. The data concerning nonentities may be a little soft – but it is not *that* soft.

11 In general, acclaimed refutations of theories of objects and Meinong's theory are no refutations at all: see [2], chapter 4, and the Appendix.

12 On a favoured alternative account, they are all identical with the null set (or entity), which does not stand in any actual doorways. The result is as before. But other accounts from out of the classical stables differ, e.g. Hilbert's theory supplies no answer, and even Russell's theory strictly applied gives no answer to those questions which include the adjective 'possible'. Let it not be taken as an objection to nonclassical approaches, then, that different theories provide different answers to the questions.

13 This is the answer to Quine's question arrived at in the original version of [2]. It now appears to be an answer to a different, if easily confused, question, namely (2b).

14 This may be freely admitted for *Parsons doorways*, Parsons doorways being the doorways of Parsons' theory and having properties supplied by that theory. That is, a Parsons doorway is like Holmes' London – only the source book for such an object is Parsons' theory, not the requisite group of Sherlock Holmes stories. There are many interesting questions one can ask, and answer, about Parsons doorways, e.g. Do any exist? The answer is No; for if one did a merely possible object could stand in entire physical relations to an entity, contravening the Brentano thesis. Could an existing object, e.g. Parsons, stand in a Parsons doorway? On Parsons' *theory* the answer is Yes, given that Parsons is fat enough (in fact a Parsons doorway will, on the theory, contain as many existing fat men as are standing in the given doorway). But, in fact (i.e. on the theory here elaborated), the answer is, again, No; for Parsons would stand in the doorway along with, and next to, various merely possible objects, again contravening Brentano. However, Parsons' Parsons, i.e. the set with exactly Parsons' nuclear properties, could be in a Parsons doorway (e.g. in the world of Parsons' theory); but now the Brentano thesis is not violated, for, in particular, the set correlated with Parsons does not exist.

15 This is part only of a larger story concerning the truth of fiction and storytelling. Of course it is true that Mr. Pickwick wore gaiters, that Sherlock Holmes lived in London, and that phlogiston is the heat substance; and it is true that James Bond stood in, or at least passed through, various doorways; and this need not conflict with the fact that no such objects exist or ever existed. The reconciliation is (as [2], chapter 7 tries to explain) in the first place, by way of contextual differences – fictional statements are contextually intensional – in the second and associated place, by way of duplicate subjects, e.g. Bond stood in the doorway depicted in the film (which is true iff, in the world of the film, he stood in the given doorway) and, in the third and most important place, through what are called *reduced relations*.

16 Of course, when it comes to attempts to *discredit* nonentities, the reverse also happens: features of entities, such as reliability of characterisation, are inappropriately transferred intact to nonentities.

17 For a referential occurrence of a subject both existential commitment and referential transparency are required. And then truth can be assessed entirely in terms of the reference. According to the Reference Theory, all *genuine* subjects occur referentially. Much of [2] is devoted to the refutation, dismantling, and replacement of the Reference Theory.

18 Of course, differences can be contrived, e.g. referential identity is (trivially) distinctive of entities.

19 Note that the criterion is formulated in terms of ontological commitments or presuppositions of people (notably philosophers), *not* as in Quine's subsequent work, in terms of theories or discourse. Even within a referential framework, which its use is heavily biased towards, (since intensional discourse ruins its operation), the criterion encounters serious difficulties. For example, the italicized modal clause cannot be deleted without the criterion (and nontrivial extensional variants upon it) yielding unintended and unsatisfactory results, yet the needed modal qualification – like the set of conditions upon translation of discourse into an approved canonical language to test for ontological commitment – exceeds acceptable referential resources (see [12] and [15]).

20 A related argument for the commitment criterion is suggested in [17], pp. 152–53. But all the argument shows is that a test cannot be given simply in terms of singular terms, not that singular terms have no role or that with singular terms removed the question of commitment contracts just to 'the ranges of values of variables of quantification', of one sort or another. This is so only for a very limited segment of discourse.

21 For reasons advanced in [2], chapters 10 and 11.

22 Such a position, which has substantial historical roots, is developed in [2].

23 Quine has now reached a similar conclusion ([22], p. 169), but on entirely different grounds. In terms of what this does to his earlier logical point of view, the term 'debacle' is not entirely inappropriate.

24 For Quine, the three principles which govern the domain of entities are, according to Gochet ([5], p. 181), a criterion of individuation ("no entity without identity"), a nominalist principle of economy rooted in a principle of relative empiricism ("Don't venture further from the sensory evidence than you need to"), and a principle that science, i.e. scientific laws, should be preserved; 'it is necessary to economize, but *without* impoverishing science'. But we don't *choose* what exists, nor freely what we honestly *say* exists; and though someone might try to impose requirements like the above on what a well-constructed theory takes to exist, the procedure would be misguided because, for example, a worthwhile theory might, like many scientific theories, include among its objects many that do not exist, and in a way scarcely governed by considerations such as economy and relative empiricism ([2], chapters 10 and 11).

25 And often (erroneously) equated, especially in the case of propositions.

26 See [18], where it is argued that pragmatic factors are rather lightweight ones. Ayer puts part of what needs to be said nicely: 'when Quine and Goodman renounced abstract entities, were they thinking only that it would be more convenient . . . was there not a suggestion that their reason for renouncing them was that they did not believe in their existence?' ([17], p. 148).

Quine insinuates that there are no decisive rational argumentative or dialectical methods for choice of conceptual scheme, so we are 'thrown back on pragmatic considerations, or other considerations as yet unproposed' ([17], p. 159), the latter being immediately dismissed. The argument obviously lacks tightness at several points. There are rational methods of theory choice which by no means reduce to pragmatic considerations.

27 A converse connection holds for complete theories.

28 Cf. the discussion of ontic commitment above.

References

[1] W. V. Quine, *From a Logical Point of View*, Second Edition, Revised, Harvard University Press, 1961.

[2] R. Routley, *Exploring Meinong's Jungle and Beyond*, Research School of Social Sciences, Australian National University, 1979.

[3] R. Routley, 'Some Things Do Not Exist', *Notre Dame Journal of Formal Logic*, 7 (1966), 251–76.

[4] L. Goddard and R. Routley, *The Logic of Significance and Context*, Scottish Academic Press, Edinburgh, 1973.

[5] P. Gochet, *The Ascent to Truth: An Exposition and Defense of Quine's Philosophy*, typescript, Liege, 1981.

[6] *Concise Oxford English Dictionary*, Fourth Edition, Clarendon Press, Oxford, 1951.

[7] A. Meinong, *On Emotional Presentation*, translated by M. L. Schubert Kalsi, Northwestern University Press, Evanston, 1972.

[8] A. Kenny, *Descartes: A Study of His Philosophy*, Random House, New York, 1968.

[9] K. Lambert, 'On "The Durability of Impossible Objects" ', *Inquiry* 19 (1976), 251–54.

[10] W. V. Quine, *Word and Object*, MIT Press, Cambridge, Mass., 1960.

[11] T. Parsons, 'A Prolegomenon to Meinongian Semantics', *Journal of Philosophy*, 71 (1974), 561–80.

[12] R. L. Cartwright, 'Ontology and the Theory of Meaning', *Philosophy of Science*, 21 (1954), 316–25.

[13] W. V. Quine, *Ontological Relativity and Other Essays*, Columbia, New York, 1969.

[14] N. Rescher, *Topics in Philosophical Logic*, Reidel, Dordrecht, 1968.

[15] I. Scheffler and N. Chomsky, 'What Is Said to Be', *Proceedings of the Aristotelian Society*, n.s. 59 (1958), 71–82.

[16] R. Routley, 'Existence and Identity in Quantified Modal Logics', *Notre Dame Journal of Formal Logic* 10 (1969), 113–49.

[17] P. T. Geach, A. J. Ayer, W. V. Quine, 'Symposium: On What There Is', *Aristotelian Society Supplementary Vol.* 25 (1951), 125–60.

[18] R. Routley, 'The Choice of Logical Foundations', *Studia Logica* 39 (1979), 76–96.

[19] J. Cargile, *Paradoxes: A Study in Form and Predication*, Cambridge University Press, 1979.

[20] C. S. Chihara, *Ontology and the Vicious Circle Principle*, Cornell University Press, Ithaca, 1973.

[21] W. V. Quine, 'Facts of the Matter', in *Essays on the Philosophy of W. V. Quine*, (ed. R. W. Shahan and C. Swoyer), University of Oklahoma Press, Norman, 1979, 155–69.

[22] W. V. Quine, *Methods of Logic*, Revised edition, Holt, Rinehart and Winston, New York, 1959.

[23] L. Linsky, *Names and Descriptions*, University of Chicago Press, 1977.

[24] M. Bunge, *Ontology I: The Furniture of the World*, Reidel, Dordrecht, 1977.

[25] J. L. Austin, *Sense and Sensibilia*, Clarendon Press, Oxford, 1962.

[26] G. Frege, *The Foundations of Arithmetic*, translated by J. L. Austin, Blackwell, Oxford, 1950.

Chapter 7

David Lewis

TRUTH IN FICTION

We can truly say that Sherlock Holmes lived in Baker Street, and that he liked to show off his mental powers. We cannot truly say that he was a devoted family man, or that he worked in close cooperation with the police.

It would be nice if we could take such descriptions of fictional characters at their face value, ascribing to them the same subject-predicate form as parallel descriptions of real-life characters. Then the sentences "Holmes wears a silk top hat" and "Nixon wears a silk top hat" would both be false because the referent of the subject term—fictional Holmes or real-life Nixon, as the case may be—lacks the property, expressed by the predicate, of wearing a silk top hat. The only difference would be that the subject terms "Holmes" and "Nixon" have referents of radically different sorts: one a fictional character, the other a real-life person of flesh and blood.

I don't question that a treatment along these Meinongian lines could be made to work. Terence Parsons has done it.[1] But it is no simple matter to overcome the difficulties that arise. For one thing, is there not some perfectly good sense in which Holmes, like Nixon, is a real-life person of flesh and blood? There are stories about the exploits of super-heroes from other planets, hobbits, fires and storms, vaporous intelligences, and other non-persons. But what a mistake it would be to class the Holmes stories with these! Unlike Clark Kent et al., Sherlock Holmes is just a person—a person of flesh and blood, a being in the very same category as Nixon.

Consider also the problem of the chorus. We can truly say that Sir Joseph Porter, K.C.B., is attended by a chorus of his sisters and his cousins and his aunts. To make this true, it seems that the domain of fictional characters must contain not only Sir Joseph himself, but also plenty of fictional sisters and counsins and aunts. But how many—five dozen, perhaps? No, for we cannot truly say that the chorus numbers five dozen exactly. We cannot truly say anything exact about its size. Then do we perhaps have a fictional chorus, but no fictional members of this chorus and hence no number of members? No, for we can truly say some things about the size. We are told that the sisters and cousins, even without the aunts, number in dozens.

The Meinongian should not suppose that the quantifiers in descriptions of fictional characters range over all the things he thinks there are, both fictional and non-fictional; but he may not find it easy to say just how the ranges of quantification are to be restricted. Consider whether we can truly say that Holmes was more intelligent than anyone else, before or since. It is certainly appropriate to compare him with some fictional characters, such as Mycroft and Watson; but not with others, such as Poirot or "Slipstick" Libby. It may be appropriate to compare him with some non-fictional characters, such as Newton and Darwin; but probably not with others, such as Conan Doyle or Frank Ramsey. "More intelligent than anyone else" meant something like "more intelligent than anyone else in the world of Sherlock Holmes." The inhabitants of this "world" are drawn partly from the fictional side of the Meinongian domain and partly from the non-fictional side, exhausting neither.

Finally, the Meinongian must tell us why truths about fictional characters are cut off, sometimes though not always, from the consequences they ought to imply. We can truly say that Holmes lived at 221B Baker Street. I have been told[2] that the only building at 221B Baker Street, then or now, was a bank. It does not follow, and certainly is not true, that Holmes lived in a bank.

The way of the Meinongian is hard, and in this paper I shall explore a simpler alternative. Let us not take our descriptions of fictional characters at face value, but instead let us regard them as abbreviations for longer sentences beginning with an operator "In such-and-such fiction. . . ." Such a phrase is an intensional operator that may be prefixed to a sentence ϕ to form a new sentence. But then the prefixed operator may be dropped by way of abbreviation, leaving us with what sounds like the original sentence ϕ but differs from it in sense.

Thus if I say that Holmes liked to show off, you will take it that I have asserted an abbreviated version of the true sentence "In the Sherlock Holmes stories, Holmes liked to show off." As for the embedded sentence "Holmes liked to show off," taken by itself with the prefixed operator neither explicitly present nor tacitly understood, we may abandon it to the common fate of subject-predicate sentences with denotationless subject terms: automatic falsity or lack of truth value, according to taste.

Many things we might say about Holmes are potentially ambiguous. They may or may not be taken as abbreviations for sentences carrying the prefix "In the Sherlock Holmes stories. . . ." Context, content, and common sense will usually resolve the ambiguity in practice. Consider these sentences:

Holmes lived in Baker Street.
Holmes lived nearer to Paddington Station than to Waterloo Station.
Holmes was just a person—a person of flesh and blood.
Holmes really existed.
Someone lived for many years at 221B Baker Street.
London's greatest detective in 1900 used cocaine.

All of them are false if taken as unprefixed, simply because Holmes did not actually exist. (Or perhaps at least some of them lack truth value.) All are true if taken as abbreviations for prefixed sentences. The first three would probably be taken in the latter way, hence they seem true. The rest would probably be taken in the former way, hence they seem false. The sentence

No detective ever solved almost all his cases.

would probably be taken as unprefixed and hence true, though it would be false if taken as prefixed. The sentence

Holmes and Watson are identical.

is sure to be taken as prefixed and hence false, but that is no refutation of systems of free logic[3] which would count it as true if taken as unprefixed.

(I hasten to concede that some truths about Holmes are not abbreviations of prefixed sentences, and also are not true just because "Holmes" is denotationless. For instance these:

Holmes is a fictional character.
Holmes was killed off by Conan Doyle, but later resurrected.
Holmes has acquired a cultish following.
Holmes symbolizes mankind's ceaseless striving for truth.
Holmes would not have needed tapes to get the goods on Nixon.

Holmes could have solved the A.B.C. murders sooner than Poirot.

I shall have nothing to say here about the proper treatment of these sentences. If the Meinongian can handle them with no special dodges, that is an advantage of his approach over mine.)

The ambiguity of prefixing explains why truths about fictional characters are sometimes cut off from their seeming consequences. Suppose we have an argument (with zero or more premises) which is valid in the modal sense that it is impossible for the premises all to be true and the conclusion false.

$$\frac{\psi_1, \ldots, \psi_n}{\therefore \phi}$$

Then it seems clear that we obtain another valid argument if we prefix an operator "In the fiction f . . ." uniformly to each premiss and to the conclusion of the original argument. Truth in a given fiction is closed under implication.

$$\frac{\text{In f}, \psi_1, \ldots, \text{In f}, \psi_n}{\therefore \text{In f}, \phi}$$

But if we prefix the operator "In the fiction f . . ." to some of the original premises and not to others, or if we take some but not all of the premises as tacitly prefixed, then in general neither the original conclusion ϕ nor the prefixed conclusion "In the fiction f, ϕ" will follow. In the inference we considered earlier there were two premises. The premiss that Holmes lived at 221B Baker Street was true only if taken as prefixed. The premiss that the only building at 221B Baker Street was a bank, on the other hand, was true only if taken as unprefixed; for in the stories there was no bank there but rather a rooming house. Taking the premises as we naturally would in the ways that make them true, nothing follows: neither the unprefixed conclusion that Holmes lived in a bank nor the prefixed

conclusion that in the stories he lived in a bank. Taking both premises as unprefixed, the unprefixed conclusion follows but the first premiss is false. Taking both premises as prefixed, the prefixed conclusion follows but the second premiss is false.[4]

Our remaining task is to see what may be said about the analysis of the operators "In such-and-such fiction. . . ." I have already noted that truth in a given fiction is closed under implication. Such closure is the earmark of an operator of relative necessity, an intensional operator that may be analyzed as a restricted universal quantifier over possible worlds. So we might proceed as follows: a prefixed sentence "In fiction f, ϕ" is true (or, as we shall also say, ϕ is true in the fiction f) iff ϕ is true at every possible world in a certain set, this set being somehow determined by the fiction f.

As a first approximation, we might consider exactly those worlds where the plot of the fiction is enacted, where a course of events takes place that matches the story. What is true in the Sherlock Holmes stories would then be what is true at all of those possible worlds where there are characters who have the attributes, stand in the relations, and do the deeds that are ascribed in the stories to Holmes, Watson, and the rest. (Whether these characters would then *be* Holmes, Watson, and the rest is a vexed question that we must soon consider.)

I think this proposal is not quite right. For one thing, there is a threat of circularity. Even the Holmes stories, not to mention fiction written in less explicit styles, are by no means in the form of straightforward chronicles. An intelligent and informed reader can indeed discover the plot, and could write it down in the form of a fully explicit chronicle if he liked. But this extraction of plot from text is no trivial or automatic task. Perhaps the reader accomplishes it only by figuring out what is true in the stories—that is, only by exercising his tacit mastery of the very concept of truth in fiction that we are now investigating. If so, then an analysis that starts by making uncritical use of the concept of the plot of a fiction might be rather uninformative, even if correct so far as it goes.

A second problem arises out of an observation by Saul Kripke.[5] Let us assume that Conan Doyle indeed wrote the stories as pure fiction. He just made them up. He had no knowledge of anyone who did the deeds he ascribed to Holmes, nor had he even picked up any garbled information originating in any such person. It may nevertheless be, purely by coincidence, that our own world is one of the worlds where the plot of the stories is enacted. Maybe there was a man whom Conan Doyle never heard of whose actual adventures chanced to fit the stories in every detail. Maybe he even was named "Sherlock Holmes." Improbable, incredible, but surely possible! Now consider the name "Sherlock Holmes," *as used in the stories*. Does the name, so used, refer to the man whom Conan Doyle never heard of? Surely not! It is irrelevant that a homonymous name is used by some people, not including Conan Doyle, to refer to this man. We must distinguish between the homonyms, just as we would distinguish the name of London (England) from the homonymous name of London (Ontario). It is false at our world that the name, "Sherlock Holmes," as used in the stories, refers to someone. Yet it is true in the stories that this name, as used in the stories, refers to someone. So we have found something that is true in the stories but false (under our improbable supposition) at one of the worlds where the plot of the stories is enacted.

In order to avoid this difficulty, it will be helpful if we do not think of a fiction in the abstract, as a string of sentences or something of that sort. Rather, a fiction is a story told by a storyteller on a particular occasion. He may tell his tales around the campfire or he may type a manuscript and send it to his publisher, but in either case there is an act of storytelling. Different acts of storytelling, different fictions. When Pierre Menard re-tells *Don Quixote*, that is not the same fiction as Cervantes' *Don Quixote*—not even if they are in the same language and match word for word.[6] (It would have been different if Menard had copied Cervantes' fiction from memory, however; that would not have been what I call an act of storytelling at all.) One act of storytelling might, however, be the telling of two different fictions: one a harmless fantasy told to the children and the censors, the other a subversive allegory simultaneously told to the *cognoscenti*.

Storytelling is pretence. The storyteller purports to be telling the truth about matters whereof he has knowledge. He purports to be talking about characters who are known to him, and whom he refers to, typically, by means of their ordinary proper names. But if his story is fiction, he is not really doing these things. Usually his pretence has not the slightest tendency to deceive anyone, nor has he the slightest intent to deceive. Nevertheless he plays a false part, goes through a form of telling known fact when he is not doing so. This is most apparent when the fiction is told in the first person. Conan Doyle pretended to be a doctor named Watson, engaged in publishing truthful memoirs of events he himself had witnessed. But the case of third-person narrative is not essentially different. The author purports to be telling the truth about matters he has somehow come to know about, though how he has found out about them is left unsaid. That is why there is a pragmatic paradox akin to contradiction in a third-person narrative that ends ". . . and so none were left to tell the tale."

The worlds we should consider, I suggest, are the worlds where the fiction is told, but as known fact rather than fiction. The act of storytelling occurs, just as it does here at our world; but there it is what here it falsely purports to be: truthtelling about matters whereof the teller has knowledge.[7] Our own world cannot be such a world; for if it is really a fiction that we are dealing with, then the act of storytelling at our world was not what it purported to be. It does not matter if, unbeknownst to the author, our world is one where his plot is enacted. The real-life

Sherlock Holmes would not have made Conan Doyle any less of a pretender, if Conan Doyle had never heard of him. (This real-life Holmes might have had his real-life Watson who told true stories about the adventures he had witnessed. But even if his memoirs matched Conan Doyle's fiction word for word they would not be the same stories, any more than Cervantes' *Don Quixote* is the same story as Menard's. So our world would still not be one where the Holmes stories—the *same* Holmes stories that Conan Doyle told as fiction—were told as known fact.) On the other hand, any world where the story is told as known fact rather than fiction must be among the worlds where the plot of the story is enacted. Else its enactment could be neither known nor truly told of.

I rely on a notion of trans-world identity for stories; this is partly a matter of word-for-word match and partly a matter of trans-world identity (or perhaps a counterpart relation) for acts of storytelling. Here at our world we have a fiction f, told in an act *a* of storytelling; at some other world we have an act *a'* of telling the truth about known matters of fact; the stories told in *a* and *a'* match word for word, and the words have the same meaning. Does that mean that the other world is one where f is told as known fact rather than fiction? Not necessarily, as the case of Menard shows. It is also required that *a* and *a'* be the same act of storytelling (or at least counterparts). How bad is this? Surely you would like to know more about the criteria of trans-world identity (or the counterpart relation) for acts of storytelling, and so indeed would I. But I think we have enough of a grip to make it worthwhile going on. I see no threat of circularity here, since I see no way of using the concept of truth in fiction to help with the analysis of trans-world identity of acts of storytelling.

Suppose a fiction employs such names as "Sherlock Holmes." At those worlds where the same story is told as known fact rather than fiction, those names really are what they here purport to be: ordinary proper names of existing characters known to the storyteller. Here at our world, the storyteller only pretends that "Sherlock Holmes" has the semantic character of an ordinary proper name. We have no reason at all to suppose that the name, as used here at our world, really does have that character. As we use it, it may be very unlike an ordinary proper name. Indeed, it may have a highly non-rigid sense, governed largely by the descriptions of Holmes and his deeds that are found in the stories. That is what I suggest: the sense of "Sherlock Holmes" as we use it is such that, for any world w where the Holmes stories are told as known fact rather than fiction, the name denotes at w whichever inhabitant of w it is who there plays the role of Holmes. Part of that role of course, is to bear the ordinary proper name "Sherlock Holmes." But that only goes to show that "Sherlock Holmes" is used at w as an ordinary proper name, not that it is so used here.[8,9]

I also suggest, less confidently, that whenever a world w is not one of the worlds just considered, the sense of "Sherlock Holmes" as we use it is such as to assign it no denotation at w. That is so even if the plot of the fiction is enacted by inhabitants of w. If we are right that Conan Doyle told the Holmes stories as fiction, then it follows that "Sherlock Holmes" is denotationless here at our world. It does not denote the real-life Sherlock Holmes whom Conan Doyle never heard of, if such there be.

We have reached a proposal I shall call ANALYSIS 0: *A sentence of the form "In fiction f, ϕ" is true iff ϕ is true at every world where f is told as known fact rather than fiction.*

Is that right? There are some who never tire of telling us not to read anything into a fiction that is not there explicitly, and Analysis 0 will serve to capture the usage of those who hold this view in its most extreme form. I do not believe, however, that such a usage is at all common. Most of us are content to read a fiction against a background of well-known fact, "reading into" the fiction content that is not there explicitly but that comes jointly from the explicit content and the factual background. Analysis 0 disregards the background. Thereby it brings too many possible worlds into consideration, so not enough comes out true in the fiction.

For example, I claim that in the Holmes stories, Holmes lives nearer to Paddington Station than to Waterloo Station. A glance at the map will show you that his address in Baker Street is much nearer to Paddington. Yet the map is not part of the stories; and so far as I know it is never stated or implied in the stories themselves that Holmes lives nearer to Paddington. There are possible worlds where the Holmes stories are told as known fact rather than fiction which differ in all sorts of ways from ours. Among these are worlds where Holmes lives in a London arranged very differently from the London of our world, a London where Holmes's address in Baker Street is much closer to Waterloo Station than to Paddington.

(I do not suppose that such a distortion of geography need prevent the otherworldly places there called "London," "Paddington Station," . . . from being the same as, or counterparts of, their actual namesakes. But if I am wrong, that still does not challenge my claim that there are worlds where the stories are told as known fact but where it is true that Holmes lives closer to Waterloo than to Paddington. For it is open to us to regard the place-names, as used in the stories, as fictional names with non-rigid senses like the non-rigid sense I have already ascribed to "Sherlock Holmes." That would mean, incidentally, that "Paddington Station," as used in the stories, does not denote the actual station of that name.)

Similarly, I claim that it is true, though not explicit, in the stories that Holmes does not have a third nostril; that he never had a case in which the murderer turned out to be a purple gnome; that he solved his cases without the aid of divine revelation; that he never visited the moons of Saturn; and that he wears underpants. There are bizarre worlds where the Holmes stories are told as known fact but where all of these things are false.

Strictly speaking, it is fallacious to reason from a mixture of truth in fact and truth in fiction to conclusions about truth in fiction. From a mixture of prefixed and unprefixed premises, nothing follows. But in practice the fallacy is often not so bad. The factual premises in mixed reasoning may be part of the background against which we read the fiction. They may carry over into the fiction, not because there is anything explicit in the fiction to make them true, but rather because there is nothing to make them false. There is nothing in the Holmes stories, for instance, that gives us any reason to bracket our background knowledge of the broad outlines of London geography. Only a few details need changing—principally details having to do with 221B Baker Street. To move the stations around, or even to regard their locations as an open question, would be uncalled for. What's true in fact about their locations is true also in the stories. Then it is no error to reason from such facts to conclusions about what else is true in the stories.

You've heard it all before. Reasoning about truth in fiction is very like counterfactual reasoning. We make a supposition contrary to fact— what if this match had been struck? In reasoning about what would have happened in that counterfactual situation, we use factual premises. The match was dry, there was oxygen about, and so forth. But we do not use factual premises altogether freely, since some of them would fall victim to the change that takes us from actuality to the envisaged counterfactual situation. We do not use the factual premiss that the match was inside the matchbox at the time in question, or that it was at room temperature a second later. We depart from actuality as far as we must to reach a possible world where the counterfactual supposition comes true (and that might be quite far if the supposition is a fantastic one). But we do not make gratuitous changes. We hold fixed the features of actuality that do not have to be changed as part of the least disruptive way of making the supposition true. We can safely reason from the part of our factual background that is thus held fixed.

By now, several authors have treated counterfactual conditionals along the lines just sketched. Differences of detail between these treatments are unimportant for our present purposes. My own version[10] runs as follows. A counterfactual of the form "If it were that ϕ, then it would be that ψ" is non-vacuously true iff some possible world where both ϕ and ψ are true differs less from our actual world, on balance, then does any world where ϕ is true but ψ is not true. It is vacuously true iff ϕ is true at no possible worlds. (I omit accessibility restrictions for simplicity.)

Getting back to truth in fiction, recall that the trouble with Analysis 0 was that it ignored background, and thereby brought into consideration bizarre worlds that differed gratuitously from our actual world. A fiction will in general require some departures from actuality, the more so if it is a fantastic fiction. But we need to keep the departures from actuality under control. It is wrong, or at least eccentric, to read the Holmes stories as if they might for all we know be taking place at a world where three-nostrilled detectives pursue purple gnomes. The remedy is, roughly speaking, to analyze statements of truth in fiction as counterfactuals. What is true in the Sherlock Holmes stories is what would be true if those stories were told as known fact rather than fiction.

Spelling this out according to my treatment of counterfactuals, we have

ANALYSIS 1: *A sentence of the form "In the fiction f, ϕ" is non-vacuously true iff some world where f is told as known fact and ϕ is true differs less from our actual world, on balance, than does any world where f is told as known fact and ϕ is not true. It is vacuously true iff there are no possible worlds where f is told as known fact.*

(I postpone consideration of the vacuous case.)

We sometimes speak of the world of a fiction.

What is true in the Holmes stories is what is true, as we say, "in the world of Sherlock Holmes." That we speak this way should suggest that it is right to consider less than all the worlds where the plot of the stories is enacted, and less even than all the worlds where the stories are told as known fact. "In the world of Sherlock Holmes," as in actuality, Baker Street is closer to Paddington Station than to Waterloo Station and there are no purple gnomes. But it will not do to follow ordinary language to the extent of supposing that we can somehow single out a single one of the worlds where the stories are told as known fact. Is the world of Sherlock Holmes a world where Holmes has an even or an odd number of hairs on his head at the moment when he first meets Watson? What is Inspector Lestrade's blood type? It is absurd to suppose that these questions about the world of Sherlock Holmes have answers. The best explanation of that is that the worlds of Sherlock Holmes are plural, and the question have different answers at different ones. If we may assume that some of the worlds where the stories are told as known fact differ least from our world, then these are the worlds of Sherlock Homes. What is true throughout them is true in the stories; what is false throughout them is false in the stories; what is true at some and false at others is neither true nor false in the stories. Any answer to the silly questions just asked would doubtless fall in the last category. It is for the same reason that the chorus of Sir Joseph Porter's sisters and cousins and aunts has no determinate size: it has different sizes at different ones of the worlds of H.M.S. Pinafore.[11]

Under Analysis 1, truth in a given fiction depends on matters of contingent fact. I am not thinking of the remote possibility that accidental properties of the fiction might somehow enter into determining which are the worlds where that fiction is told as known fact. Rather, it is a contingent matter which of those worlds differ more from ours and which less, and which (if any) differ least. That is because it is a contingent fact—indeed it is *the* contingent fact on which all others depend—which possible world is our actual world. To the extent that the character of our world carries over into the worlds of Sherlock Holmes, what is true in the stories depends on what our world is like. If the stations of London had been differently located, it might have been true in the stories (and not because the stories would then have been different) that Holmes lived nearer to Waterloo Station than to Paddington Station.

This contingency is all very well when truth in fiction depends on well-known contingent facts about our world, as it does in the examples I have so far given to motivate Analysis I. It is more disturbing if truth in fiction turns out to depend on contingent facts that are not well known. In an article setting forth little-known facts about the movement of snakes, Carl Gans has argued as follows:

> In "The Adventure of the Speckled Band" Sherlock Holmes solves a murder mystery by showing that the victim has been killed by a Russell's viper that has climbed up a bell-rope. What Holmes did not realize was that Russell's viper is not a constrictor. The snake is therefore incapable of concertina movement and could not have climbed the rope. Either the snake reached its victim some other way or the case remains open.[12]

We may well look askance at this reasoning. But if Analysis I is correct then so is Gan's argument. The story never quite says that Holmes was right that the snake climbed the rope. Hence there are worlds where the Holmes stories are told as known fact, where the snake reached the victim some other way, and where Holmes therefore bungled. Presumably some of these worlds differ less from ours than their rivals where Holmes was right and where Russell's viper is capable of concertina movement up a rope. Holmes's infallibility, of course, is not a countervailing resemblance to actuality; our world contains no infallible Holmes.

Psychoanalysis of fictional characters provides a more important example. The critic uses (what he believes to be) little-known facts of human psychology as premises, and reasons to conclusions that are far from obvious about the childhood or the adult mental state of the fictional character. Under Analysis I his procedure is justified. Unless countervailing considerations can be found, to consider worlds where the little-known fact of psychology does not hold would be to depart gratuitously from actuality.

The psychoanalysis of fictional characters has aroused vigorous objections. So would Gans's argument, if anyone cared. I shall keep neutral in these quarrels, and try to provide for the needs of both sides. Analysis 1, or something close to it, should capture the usage of Gans and the literary psychoanalysts. Let us find an alternative analysis to capture the conflicting usage of their opponents. I shall not try to say which usage is more conducive to appreciation of fiction and critical insight.

Suppose we decide, *contra* Gans and the literary psychoanalysts, that little-known or unknown facts about our world are irrelevant to truth in fiction. But let us not fall back to Analysis 0; it is not our only alternative. Let us still recognize that it is perfectly legitimate to reason to truth in fiction from a background of well-known facts.

Must they really be facts? It seems that if little-known or unknown facts are irrelevant, then so are little-known or unknown errors in the body of shared opinion that is generally taken for fact. We think we all know that there are no purple gnomes, but what if there really are a few, unknown to anyone except themselves, living in a secluded cabin near Loch Ness? Once we set aside the usage given by Analysis 1, it seems clear that whatever purple gnomes may be hidden in odd corners of our actual world, there are still none of them in the worlds of Sherlock Holmes. We have shifted to viewing truth in fiction as the joint product of explicit content and a background of generally prevalent beliefs.

Our own beliefs? I think not. That would

mean that what is true in a fiction is constantly changing. Gans might not be right yet, but he would eventually become right about Holmes's error if enough people read his article and learned that Russell's viper could not climb a rope. When the map of Victorian London was finally forgotten, it would cease to be true that Holmes lived nearer to Paddington than to Waterloo. Strange to say, the historical scholar would be in no better position to know what was true in the fictions of his period than the ignorant layman. That cannot be right. What was true in a fiction when it was first told is true in it forevermore. It is our knowledge of what is true in the fiction that may wax or wane.

The proper background, then, consists of the beliefs that generally prevailed in the community where the fiction originated: the beliefs of the author and his intended audience. And indeed the factual premises that seemed to us acceptable in reasoning about Sherlock Holmes were generally believed in the community of origin of the stories. Everyone knew roughly where the principal stations of London were, everyone disbelieved in purple gnomes, and so forth.

One last complication. Suppose Conan Doyle was a secret believer in purple gnomes; thinking that his belief in them was not shared by anyone else he kept it carefully to himself for fear of ridicule. In particular, he left no trace of this belief in his stories. Suppose also that some of his original readers likewise were secret believers in purple gnomes. Suppose, in fact, that everyone alive at the time was a secret believer in purple gnomes, each thinking that his own belief was not shared by anyone else. Then it is clear (to the extent that anything is clear about such a strange situation) that the belief in purple gnomes does not "generally prevail" in quite the right way, and there are still no purple gnomes in the worlds of Sherlock Holmes. Call a belief *overt* in a community at a time iff more or less everyone shares it, more or less everyone thinks that more or less everyone else shares it, and so on.[13] The proper background, we may conclude,

comprises the beliefs that are overt in the community of origin of the fiction.

Assume, by way of idealization, that the beliefs overt in the community are each possible and jointly compossible. Then we can assign to the community a set of possible worlds, called the *collective belief worlds* of the community, comprising exactly those worlds where the overt beliefs all come true. Only if the community is uncommonly lucky will the actual world belong to this set. Indeed, the actual world determines the collective belief worlds of the community of origin of the fiction and then drops out of the analysis. (It is of course a contingent matter what that community is and what is overtly believed there.) We are left with two sets of worlds: the worlds where the fiction is told as known fact, and the collective belief worlds of the community of origin. The first set gives the content of the fiction; the second gives the background of prevalent beliefs.

It would be a mistake simply to consider the worlds that belong to both sets. Fictions usually contravene at least some of the community's overt beliefs. I can certainly tell a story in which there are purple gnomes, though there are none at our collective belief worlds. Further, it will usually be overtly believed in the community of origin of a fiction that the story is not told as known fact—storytellers seldom deceive—so none of the worlds where the fiction is told as known fact can be a collective belief world of the community. Even if the two sets do overlap (the fiction is plausible and the author palms it off as fact) the worlds that belong to both sets are apt to be special in ways having nothing to do with what is true in the fiction. Suppose the story tells of a bungled burglary in recent times, and suppose it ends just as the police reach the scene. Any collective belief world of ours where this story is told as known fact is a world where the burglary was successfully covered up; for it is an overt belief among us that no such burglary ever hit the news. That does not make it true in the story that the burglary was covered up.

What we need is something like Analysis I, but applied from the standpoint of the collective belief worlds rather than the actual world. What is true in the Sherlock Holmes stories is what would be true, according to the overt beliefs of the community of origin, if those stories were told as known fact rather than fiction.

Spelling this out, we have

ANALYSIS 2: *A sentence of the form "In the fiction f, ϕ" is non-vacuoûsly true iff, whenever w is one of the collective belief worlds of the community of origin of f, then some world where f is told as known fact and ϕ is true differs less from the world w, on balance, than does any world where f is told as known fact and ϕ is not true. It is vacuously true iff there are no possible worlds where f is told as known fact.*

It is Analysis 2, or something close to it, that I offer to opponents of Gans and the literary psychoanalysts.

I shall briefly consider two remaining areas of difficulty and sketch strategies for dealing with them. I shall not propose improved analyses, however; partly because I am not quite sure what changes to make, and partly because Analysis 2 is quite complicated enough already.

I have said that truth in fiction is the joint product of two sources: the explicit content of the fiction, and a background consisting either of the facts about our world (Analysis 1) or of the beliefs overt in the community of origin (Analysis 2). Perhaps there is a third source which also contributes: carry-over from other truth in fiction. There are two cases: intra-fictional and inter-fictional.

In the *Threepenny Opera*, the principal characters are a treacherous crew. They constantly betray one another, for gain or to escape danger. There is also a streetsinger. He shows up, sings the ballad of Mack the Knife, and goes about his business without betraying anyone. Is he also a treacherous fellow? The explicit content does not make him so. Real people are not so very treacherous, and even in Weimar Germany it was

not overtly believed that they were, so background does not make him so either. Yet there is a moderately good reason to say that he is treacherous: in the *Threepenny Opera*, that's how people are. In the worlds of the *Threepenny Opera*, everyone put to the test proves treacherous, the streetsinger is there along with the rest, so doubtless he too would turn out to be treacherous if we saw more of him. His treacherous nature is an intra-fictional carry-over from the treacherous natures in the story of Macheath, Polly, Tiger Brown, and the rest.

Suppose I write a story about the dragon Scrulch, a beautiful princess, a bold knight, and what not. It is a perfectly typical instance of its stylized genre, except that I never say that Scrulch breathes fire. Does he nevertheless breathe fire in my story? Perhaps so, because dragons in that sort of story do breathe fire. But the explicit content does not make him breathe fire. Neither does background, since in actuality and according to our beliefs there are no animals that breathe fire. (It just might be analytic that nothing is a dragon unless it breathes fire. But suppose I never *called* Scrulch a dragon; I merely endowed him with all the standard dragonly attributes except fire-breathing.) If Scrulch does breathe fire in my story, it is by inter-fictional carry-over from what is true of dragons in other stories.

I have spoken of Conan Doyle's Holmes stories; but many other authors also have written Holmes stories. These would have little point without inter-fictional carry-over. Surely many things are true in these satellite stories not because of the explicit content of the satellite story itself, and not because they are part of the background, but rather because they carry over from Conan Doyle's original Holmes stories. Similarly, if instead of asking what is true in the entire corpus of Conan Doyle's Holmes stories we ask what is true in "The Hound of the Baskervilles," we will doubtless find many things that are true in that story only by virtue of carry-over from Conan Doyle's other Holmes stories.

I turn finally to vacuous truth in impossible fictions. Let us call a fiction *impossible* iff there is no world where it is told as known fact rather than fiction. That might happen in either of two ways. First, the plot might be impossible. Second, a possible plot might imply that there could be nobody in a position to know or tell of the events in question. If a fiction is impossible in the second way, then to tell it as known fact would be to know its truth and tell truly something that implies that its truth could not be known; which is impossible.

According to all three of my analyses, anything whatever is vacuously true in an impossible fiction. That seems entirely satisfactory if the impossibility is blatant: if we are dealing with a fantasy about the troubles of the man who squared the circle, or with the worst sort of incoherent time-travel story. We should not expect to have a non-trivial concept of truth in blatantly impossible fiction, or perhaps we should expect to have one only under the pretence—not to be taken too seriously—that there are impossible possible worlds as well as the possible possible worlds.

But what should we do with a fiction that is not blatantly impossible, but impossible only because the author has been forgetful? I have spoken of truth in the Sherlock Holmes stories. Strictly speaking, these (taken together) are an impossible fiction. Conan Doyle contradicted himself from one story to another about the location of Watson's old war wound. Still, I do not want to say that just anything is true in the Holmes stories!

I suppose that we might proceed in two steps to say what is true in a venially impossible fiction such as the Holmes stories. First, go from the original impossible fiction to the several possible revised versions that stay closest to the original. Then say that what is true in the original is what is true, according to one of our analyses of non-vacuous truth in fiction, in all of these revised versions. Then nothing definite will be true in the Holmes stories about the location of

Watson's wound. Since Conan Doyle put it in different places, the different revised versions will differ. But at least it will be true in the stories that Watson was wounded elsewhere than in the left big toe. Conan Doyle put the wound in various places, but never there. So no revised version will put the wound in the left big toe, since that would change the story more than consistency demands.

The revised versions, like the original fiction, will be associated with acts of storytelling. The revised versions, unlike the original, will not actually be told either as fiction or as known fact. But there are worlds where they are told as fiction, and worlds where they are told as known fact.

Even when the original fiction is not quite impossible, there may be cases in which it would be better to consider not truth in the original fiction but rather truth in all suitably revised versions. We have a three-volume novel set in 1878. We learn in the first volume that the hero had lunch in Glasgow on a certain day. In the third volume, it turns out that he showed up in London that same afternoon. In no other way does this novel purport to be a fantasy of rapid transit. The author was just careless. We could without vacuity apply our analyses directly to the novel as written. Since the closest worlds where it is told as known fact are worlds with remarkable means of travel, the results would astonish anyone—for instance, our forgetful author—who had not troubled to work out a careful timetable of the hero's movements. It would be more charitable to apply the analyses not to the original story but instead to the minimally revised versions that make the hero's movements feasible by the means of travel that were available in 1878. At least, that would be best if there were ways to set the times right without major changes in the plot. There might not be, and in that case perhaps truth in the original version—surprising though some of it may be—is the best we can do.

Postscripts

A. Make-Believe Telling, Make-Believe Learning

The storyteller purports—normally, if not invariably—to be telling the truth about matters whereof he has knowledge. I take the actual telling of the story, in effect, as part of the story itself; or in other words, I subsume the pretended truth of the story under the pretence of truthful telling. Thus I dodge Kripke's objection that the story might come true by accident, yet be as fictional as ever. For the part about the deeds of Holmes might come true by accident, but not the part about the historical origins of the stories we were told.

I thought this an artificial dodge to meet a technical difficulty. But Kendall Walton's papers on fiction[14] have persuaded me, first, that it is not at all artificial; and second, that the storyteller's pretence of truth and knowledge is only the tip of the iceberg. There is a cooperative game of make-believe, governed by conventional understandings, with players in (at least) two roles. The storytellers pretend to pass on historical information to their audience; the audience pretends to learn from their words, and to respond accordingly.

Attention to this broader game of make-believe ties up some of the loose ends. The audience may make-believedly learn their history from several different storytellers. They make-believedly do what real students of history really do: they combine information from several sources. Consider the worlds where all our accumulated make-believe learning about the doings of dragons is honest history: in the closest of these, Scrulch the dragon breathes fire. (Or better, some where he does are closer than any where he doesn't.) It doesn't matter how much about fire-breathing we get from the tale of Scrulch, how much from other stories in the same game. Likewise, take the worlds where we learn the true history of famous mysteries partly from Conan Doyle and Christie, and partly from the newspapers. (The fact that we really do trust the newspapers need not stop us from putting them to use in this game.) In the closest of these worlds, arguably, Holmes could have solved the A.B.C. murders sooner than Poirot, and he would not have needed tapes to get the goods on Nixon.

B. Impossible Fictions

An inconsistent fiction is not to be treated directly, else everything comes out true in it indiscriminately. But where we have an inconsistent fiction, there also we have several consistent fictions that may be extracted from it. (Perhaps not in the very hardest cases—but I think those cases are *meant* to defy our efforts to figure out what's true in the story.) I spoke of the consistent corrections of the original fiction. But perhaps it will be enough to consider *fragments*: corrections by deletion, with nothing written in to replace the deleted bits.

Perhaps we should take the maximal consistent fragments, obtained by deleting the bare minimum that will give us consistency. But I think it might be better to respect the salient divisions of the story into parts, even if that means taking less-than-maximal consistent fragments. I believe that Isaac Asimov's *The End of Eternity*[15] falls into inconsistency by changing its conception of time travel part way through. If so, perhaps the book less its final chapters would make a salient consistent fragment, even if we leave out scattered bits from the final chapters that could consistently have been left in.

Be that as it may, what do we do with our several consistent fragments (or corrections) when we have them? See what is true in each according to my analysis of non-vacuous truth in fiction (in whichever version seems called for). Then what?

I suggested this *method of intersection*: ϕ is true in the original fiction iff ϕ is true in every fragment. Now I would favor instead this *method of union*: ϕ is true in the original fiction iff ϕ is true in some fragment. (Not that we need choose once and for all—we can have both methods, distinguishing two senses of truth in inconsistent fiction.)

Intersection is the conservative method. Even if the fiction was inconsistent, what's true in it will still comprise a consistent theory, fully closed under implication. (I mean, to speak redundantly, *classical* implication.) But we pay a price: some of what's explicit in the fiction gets lost. That price now seems to me too high.

The method of union gives us all the truth in inconsistent fiction that the method of intersection does, and more besides. What's explicit will not get lost, for presumably it will be true in its own fragment. But we lose consistency and we lose closure under implication. Suppose two fragments disagree: ϕ is true in one, not-ϕ in the other. Then ϕ and not-ϕ both are true in the fiction as a whole. But their inconsistent conjunction is not, though they jointly imply it. Likewise many other things are not true in the fiction, though every one of them is implied jointly by two premises both true in the fiction.

All this is as it should be. If we deny that contradictory pairs are true in inconsistent fiction, we deny its distinctive peculiarity. Then we must not close under implication, on pain of obliterating the distinction between what's true in the story and what isn't. We should not even close under the most obvious and uncontroversial sort of implication: the inference from conjuncts to conjunction. (Here is where the relevantists go wrong, seduced by their hope that truth in inconsistent fiction might after all be closed under some relation that might colorably bear the name of implication.) It is true in the Holmes stories that Watson was wounded in the shoulder; it is true in the stories that he was wounded in the leg. It is simply not true in the stories that he was wounded in the shoulder and the leg both—he had only *one* wound, despite the discrepancy over its location.[16]

C. Fiction in the Service of Truth

There are some who value fiction mostly as a means for the discovery of truth, or for the communication of truth. "Truth in Fiction" had nothing to say about fiction as a means to truth. But the topics can indeed be connected.

Most simply, there may be an understanding between the author and his readers to the effect that what is true in his fiction, on general questions if not on particulars, is not to depart from what he takes to be the truth. (Indeed, such an understanding might extend to particular matters as well. Imagine a scandalous political exposé, by an insider, with characters called "Nicksen," "Hague," "Wagoner," "Bondsman,". . . .) Then the audience, if they know that the author is well informed, could learn the truth by figuring out what is true in his fictions. Further, the author might discover some truth in the course of trying to keep his side of the bargain.—Doubtless this is not quite what people have in mind when they speak of the cognitive value of literature! Let us find something a bit loftier for them to mean.

Fiction might serve as a means for discovery of modal truth. I find it very hard to tell whether there could possibly be such a thing as a dignified beggar. If there could be, a story could prove it. The author of a story in which it is true that there is a dignified beggar would both discover and demonstrate that there does exist such a possibility. An actor or a painter might accomplish the same. Here the fiction serves the same purpose as an example in philosophy, though it will not work unless the story of the dignified beggar is more fully worked out than our usual examples. Conversely, note that the philosophical example is just a concise bit of fiction.

More importantly, fiction can offer us contingent truths about this world. It cannot take the place of nonfictional evidence, to be sure. But sometimes evidence is not lacking. We who have lived in the world for a while have plenty of evidence, but we may not have learned as much from it as we could have done. This evidence bears on a certain proposition. If only that proposition is formulated, straightway it will be apparent that we have very good evidence for it. If not, we will continue not to know it. Here, fiction can help us. If we are given a fiction such that the proposition is obviously true in it, we are led to ask: and is it also true *simpliciter?* And sometimes, when we have plenty of unappreciated evidence, to ask the question is to know the answer. Then the author of the fiction has made a discovery, and he gives his readers the means to make that same discovery for themselves.

Sometimes the proposition learned may be one that we could formulate, once we have it in mind, without reference to the fiction that drew our attention to it. Not so in general. Sometimes reference to a fiction is the only way we have, in practice if not in principle, to formulate the truths that the fiction has called to our attention. A schlemiel is someone such that what is true of him strikingly resembles what is true in a certain fiction of a certain character therein, Schlemiel by name. Temporarily or permanently, first for those who know the story and then for others (like myself) who don't, the word "schlemiel" is indispensable in stating various truths.

So fiction can indeed serve truth. But we must beware, for also it can spread error. (1) Whatever understandings to the contrary might prevail, what is true in an author's fiction might not be true, either because the author is mistaken or because he wishes to deceive those who rely on the supposed understanding. (2) Under the method of union, several things might be true together in a fiction, but not really compossible. Then the fiction might persuade us of a modal falsehood, leading us to believe in a possibility that doesn't really exist. (3) If we have plenty of misleading evidence stored up, there may well be falsehoods that need only be stated to be believed.

D. The Puzzle of the Flash Stockman

The singer sings this song.

> I'm a stockman to my trade, and they call me Ugly Dave.
> I'm old and grey and only got one eye.
> In a yard I'm good, of course, but just put me on a horse,
> And I'll go where lots of young-'uns daren't try.

The boasting gets ever steeper: riding, whipping, branding, shearing, ...

> In fact, I'm duke of every blasted thing.

Plainly, this is fiction. What is true in it?

The answer should be that in the fiction a stockman called Ugly Dave tells a boastful pack of lies.[17] And that is indeed the answer we get if we take the closest worlds where the storyteller really is doing what he here pretends to be doing. For this is one of those exceptional cases, covered briefly in my footnote 7, in which the storyteller does not pretend to be telling the truth about matters whereof he has knowledge. The singer makes believe that he is Ugly Dave telling boastful lies.

There is a fiction in the fiction: Ugly Dave's lies are themselves a fiction, and his boasting is make-believe truthtelling. In the fiction in the fiction, he really is duke of everything. In the outer fiction he is not, but only claims to be. This iteration, in itself, is not a problem.

But there is a real problem nearby, and I have no solution to offer. Why doesn't the iteration collapse? When the singer pretends to be Ugly Dave pretending to tell the truth about himself, how does this differ from pretending to be Ugly Dave *really* telling the truth about himself? It must be the former, not the latter; else we should conclude that there is no inner fiction and that what is true in the outer fiction—now the only fiction—is that Ugly Dave is duke of everything and tells us so. That would be to miss the point entirely. We must distinguish pretending to pretend from really pretending. Intuitively it seems that we can make this distinction, but how is it to be analyzed?

Acknowledgments

I thank the many friends and colleagues who have given me helpful comments on a previous version of this paper, and I thank the American Council of Learned Societies for research support. Special thanks are due to John G. Bennett and Saul Kripke for valuable discussions.

Notes

1 In "A Prolegomenon to Meinongian Semantics," *Journal of Philosophy* 71 (1974): 561–80, and in "A Meinongian Analysis of Fictional Objects," *Grazer Philosophische Studien* 1 (1975): 73–86.

2 I have also been told that there has never been any building at that address. It doesn't matter which is correct.

3 For instance, the system given in Dana Scott, "Existence and Description in Formal Logic," in *Bertrand Russell: Philosopher of the Century*, ed. by Ralph Schoenman (London: Allen & Unwin, 1967).

4 Thus far, the account I have given closely follows that of John Heintz, "Reference and Inference in Fiction." *Poetics* 8 (1979).

5 Briefly stated in his addenda to "Naming and Necessity," in *Semantics of Natural Language*, ed. by Gilbert Harman and Donald Davidson (Dordrecht: Reidel, 1972); and discussed at greater length in an unpublished lecture given at a conference held at the University of Western Ontario in 1973 and on other occasions. My views and Kripke's overlap to some extent. He also stresses what I have called the ambiguity of prefixing and regards the storyteller as engaged in pretence. The conclusions he draws from the present observation, however, differ greatly from mine.

6 Jorge Luis Borges, "Pierre Menard, Author of the *Quixote*" in *Ficciones* (Buenos Aires, 1944; English translation, New York: Grove, 1962).

7 There are exceptions. Sometimes the storyteller purports to be uttering a mixture of truth and lies about matters whereof he has knowledge, or ravings giving a distorted reflection of the events, or the like. Tolkien explicitly purports to be the translator and editor of the Red Book of Westmarch, an ancient book that has somehow come into his possession and that he somehow knows to be a reliable record of the events. He does not purport to be its author, else he would nor write in English. (Indeed, the composition of the Red Book by several hobbits is recorded in the Red Book itself.) I should say the same about a first-person historical novel written in English in which the narrator is an ancient Greek. The author does not pretend to be the truthful narrator himself, but rather pretends to be someone of our time who somehow has obtained the Greek narrator's story, knows it to be true, and passes it on to us in translation. In these exceptional cases also, the thing to do is to consider those worlds where the act of storytelling really is whatever it purports to be—ravings, reliable translation of a reliable source, or whatever—here at our world. I shall omit mention of these exceptional cases in the remainder of this paper.

8 A rather similar treatment of fictional names, different from mine in that it allows the actual and purported meanings of "Sherlock Holmes" to be the same, is given in Robert Stalnaker, "Assertion" in *Syntax and Semantics* 9, ed. by Peter Cole, (New York: Academic Press, 1978).

9 Many of us have never read the stories, could not produce the descriptions that largely govern the non-rigid sense of "Sherlock Holmes," yet use this name in just the same sense as the most expert Baker Street Irregular. There is no problem here. Kripke's causal picture of the contagion of meaning, in "Naming and Necessity," (*op. cit.*), will do as well for non-rigid senses, as for rigid ones. The ignoramus uses "Sherlock Holmes" in its standard non-rigid sense if he has picked it up (in the right way) from someone who knew the governing descriptions, or who picked it up from someone else who knew them, or . . . Kripke's doctrines of rigidity could not be defended without the aid of his doctrine of contagion of meaning; contagion without rigidity, on the other hand, seems unproblematic.

10 Given in *Counterfactuals* (Oxford: Blackwell, 1973).

11 Heintz (op. cit.) disagrees; he supposes that for each fiction there is a single world to be considered, but a world that is in some respects indeterminate. I do not know what to make of an indeterminate world, unless I regard it as a superposition of all possible ways of resolving the indeterminacy—or, in plainer language, as a set of determinate worlds that differ in the respects in question.

12 Carl Gans, "How Snakes Move," Scientific American, 222 (1970): 93.

13 A better definition of overt belief, under the name of "common knowledge," may be found in my Convention (Cambridge, Mass.: Harvard University Press, 1969), pp. 52–60. That name was unfortunate, since there is no assurance that it will be knowledge, or even that it will be true. See also the discussion of "mutual knowledge*" in Stephen Schiffer, Meaning (Oxford: Oxford University Press, 1972), pp. 30–42.

14 In particular, his "On Fearing Fictions," Journal of Philosophy 75 (1978): 5–27, and others cited therein.

15 (New York: Fawcett, 1955).

16 The method of union goes back to Stanisław Jaśkowski, "Propositional Calculus for Contradictory Deductive Systems," Studia Logica 24 (1969): 143–57, and has been revived in several recent discussions of how to tolerate inconsistency. See my "Logic for Equivocators," Noûs 16 (1982): 431–441, and works there cited.

17 Or, at least, it is not true in the fiction that he is telling the truth. Even that would be enough to serve my purpose here. But it is simpler, and credible enough, to stick with the stronger answer.

Chapter 8

Peter Unger

I DO NOT EXIST

It seems utterly obvious that the question 'Do I exist?' may be correctly answered only in the affirmative; of course the answer must be 'Yes.' Descartes, it may be said, made this idea the keystone of his philosophy, he found it so compelling. Hume, however, in his characteristically sceptical style, at least at times questioned the propriety of an affirmative reply. My teacher, Professor Sir Alfred Jules Ayer, to whom this essay is dedicated, customarily expressed himself in a conditional manner, which I find quite congenial:

> The sentence 'I exist', in this usage, may be allowed to express a statement which like other statements is capable of being either true or false. It differs, however, from most other statements in that if it is false it can not actually be made. Consequently, no one who uses these words intelligently and correctly can use them to make a statement which he knows to be false. If he succeeds in making the statement, it must be true.[1]

Of course Ayer is right in pointing to the absurdity of a person's trying to deny his own existence. Prepared to pay this price, in this brief essay I mean to deny my own putative existence, a position which I take to be even more radical than Hume's. This is owing not to a desire to be more perverse than any of my predecessors, but, rather, to certain arguments which have occurred to me, and which seem quite far from any of their thoughts. As may be expected of a student of Ayer's, and as I have indicated, I appreciate the utterly paradoxical position into which these arguments lead me. But I venture to suppose that this does not reflect badly on my reasonings in any relevant regard. Rather, it may show their great scope, thus highlighting obscure defects in prevalent conceptions. With this understanding, I mean to present herein the main lines of reasoning against my own existence.

I offer my arguments as a challenge to any others that there may be, so that they may dissuade me from the path of extreme nihilism that reason appears to require. Accordingly. I shall present my ideas as forcefully as possible, not to indicate any enormous confidence on my part, but rather to provoke others to reply most promptly and effectively. For my own part, I can find nothing importantly wrong with the uncomfortable thoughts I shall thus boldly put forth. The more I reflect upon them, the more I become convinced of their essential truth or justice, for any errors I ever find are superficial mistakes, requiring at most only minor changes in formulation. As a consequence, there appears to be growing within me an inclination to expend much effort toward developing the required nihilism in great detail, no matter how painfully laborious the attempt may be. Perhaps this growth had best be stopped, but then only by an appropriate rational argument.

To compound my dilemma, I notice that, in general outline, the same view lately has been conjectured by another writer, Samuel Wheeler, or so it appears. In a pioneering paper, 'Reference and Vagueness', Wheeler conjectured that there may not be any people; I should suppose he meant to include himself.[2] While he does not offer a positive argument for the nihilistic surmise, he does disarm prevalent ideas which would point the other way. Appearing to find a similar current in another, but no adequate compelling force in the opposite direction, the situation encourages my thoughts to move, however slowly and painfully, toward their properly destructive denial. Perhaps a response to my challenge may save me from the ultimately fruitless labours I seem required to undertake.

The challenging position is this: I do not exist and neither do you. The scientific perspective, especially as developed over the last few centuries, compels this result. Now, there is nothing especially unfortunate in this as regards the human condition. For, as regards almost everything which is commonly alleged to exist, it may be argued, in like manner, that it in fact does not. There are, then, no tables or chairs, nor rocks or stones or ordinary stars. Neither are there any plants or animals. No finite persons or conscious beings exist, including myself Peter Unger: I do not exist. So much for this challenging position. To the main arguments for it, rather briefly presented, I now turn.

I. The Sorites of Decomposition

Tables, as well as chairs, have often been believed to be paradigms of existing things or entities, but I shall argue that they do not exist at all. They are, if you will, only fictions, though nothing whatever depends on my use of such a term of convenience. My argument will be in the form of an indirect proof, wherein I reduce to absurdity the supposition of their existence.

According to our modern scientific view,

if there are any tables, then each of them is constituted of, or is composed of, or comprises, or consists of, or whatever, many atoms, and still more 'elementary particles', but only a finite number of each. Now, nothing here depends on the expression 'is constituted of', or on any similar expression. Baldly put, the point is this: where and when there are no atoms present, there and then there is no table. This idea is not crucial to the argument; a 'less scientific' analogue will work as well, so far as the purer logical features go. But it is good to have nature apparently so co-operative.

Now, at the same time, according to our common-sense view of the matter, which for something like a *table* is, of course, all but definitive, one atom, or only a few, removed, or added, quite innocuously, will not make a relevant difference. If you have a table at the start, then, after an atom has been gently ticked off the edge somewhere, there will still be a table present. These simple ideas, when brought into combination, leave nothing for reason but to conclude that there really are no tables. It takes no great acumen to see this, as the reasoning is utterly simple, and most just and suitable to the subject before us.

For, if there is a table there, then it has only a finite number of atoms—say, a billion billion; it does not matter. The net removal of one, then, leaves us with a supposed table of a billion billion minus one atoms; after two are removed, the supposed table has a billion billion minus two; and so on. After a billion billion atoms have been removed, we have a table consisting of no atoms at all. In this simple fashion, I suggest, we have reduced to an absurdity the supposition that the table in question exists, or ever did exist. As this argument may be most readily generalised, we may conclude that there really are no such things as tables.

To advance discussion, it may be helpful if I give the argument just presented something like a formal shape or presentation. We begin with a supposition of existence:

(1)   There exists at least one table.

But, from our scientific perspective, we may add this second premiss:

(2)   For anything there may be, if it is a table, then it consists of many atoms, but only a finite number.

From these two premisses, we may deduce that there is at least one table which consists of many atoms, but a finite number of them. The crux and bite of my argument, however, may be supposed to come with a third and final premiss:

(3)   For anything there may be, if it is a table (which consists of many atoms, but a finite number), then the net removal of one atom, or only a few, in a way which is most innocuous and favourable, will not mean the difference as to whether there is a table in the situation.

These three premisses, I take it, are inconsistent. The assessment of this inconsistency, I submit, leads one to reject, and to deny, the first premiss, whatever one may subsequently think of the remaining two propositions.

Discounting minor matters of formulation, I doubt that many would deny our second premiss. Many more, I imagine, are liable to deny our third and final proposition. It has, I must admit, been stated in a way which leaves matters less than completely clear and evident. Accordingly, I shall try to provide some clarificatory interpretation, to the extent that this seems merited even in a very brief treatment.

I have said that an atom is to be removed in a way which is most innocuous and favourable. What do I mean by such a way? First, I mean for the removal to be *net*, of course, and in the fullest way. The process which removes an atom does not put something else in its place, or in anywhere else; nor does such a thing happen in any other way. And, what is removed is randomly

cast aside, so to speak. Secondly, I mean for the net removal to take place with as little disruptive effect as possible on what remains, especially as regards the question, if it really has any substance, as to whether or not any table remains. In other words, we might say, it is most unlikely that an atom will ever be blasted out of a central position; rather, one will be gently dislodged from an outside spot. Additionally, we are to conceive of the most favourable, or least disruptive, conditions, as regards temperature, pressure, electricity, magnetism, and so on. Further, if an occasion arises where, vary conditions as we may, a single atom cannot be removed without substantial relevant disruption, then we remove as few as possible, balanced against a disruptive effect. Finally, I close this interpretation with a remark on the alleged matter of whether an entity may be *as much as possible*, or be *as well off toward being, a table*. I am supposing this matter to have substance, of course, but only on way toward exposing its absurdity. This is an indirect argument.

Thus clarified, perhaps we may profitably divide what our premiss is saying under two heads. First, it makes a 'causal' claim: there is no relevant breaking point where, no matter what is done to be gentle and to retain things, the whole business, or a substantial portion thereof, collapses, or turns into an apparent donkey, or disappears, or whatever. Rather, things are relevantly quite gradual. To deny this, I believe, is to cast aside science, and even common sense as well. And, secondly, our premiss claims that, in this rather gradual way of things, the difference made by the small removals encountered, by one atom, more or less, is never nearly so much as the difference, merely alleged as it may be, between a table's being there and not being there. To deny this premiss, then, is as much as to affirm that there comes a place where, by taking away an atom or so, presumably *any one or few of millions* still, one makes a table cease to exist. And this, I suggest, is as much as to expect a miracle.

Now, as it is stated, of course, our final premiss points to conditions, and a way, that are quite ideal. That is no fault. It may make one think, however, that the whole argument has an 'airy-fairy' character, and is quite unrealistic. But conditions close enough to those which are most favourable do occur almost all the time. And, very small bits, if not nearly so small as an atom, can be removed in stepwise fashion, for an argument to similar effect. Whatever 'airy-fairy' features are there, then, cannot be basic to the argument.

Within fine points of formulation, our third premiss thus fairly compels belief. As a move to escape our just but uncomfortable conclusion, it remains only to deny the reasoning employed. In this vein, some may object that 'the logic' I have used is what is at fault. If some 'alternative logic' is chosen, they may respond, instead of the system of rules and formulae I have employed, the integrity of our tables may be secured. But I do not believe that good reasoning can ever be captured or frozen into any such system, or that the matter is really one of choosing one or another optional pieces of logical apparatus, like so many hammers or wrenches. There is not, I suggest, here a question of this logic or that one. Without my now being less than sceptical, it is a question of whether my reasoning has been sound, and has been just and appropriate to the topic before us. Now, if I have been in error in my reasoning, or unjust to my subject matter, then such an error or injustice should be made manifest. But, excepting small points of formulation, and with a proper sceptical hesitancy, I doubt that this will be done. Of course, I am no mathematician. But, I think that a fair appraisal of the matter by those more mathematically inclined will find them to view things in much the way that I here recommend.

In a somewhat deeper vein, perhaps, it should be re-emphasised that my argument is not dependent upon the existence of atoms, at least not in any fundamental way. Perhaps there are no atoms, and in 'removing an atom' what really happens is something involving, say, an underlying plenum, which is the only existing (physical) reality. If so, then perhaps the argument presented is acceptable only provisionally; perhaps it operates only on a superficial level. But, whatever changes or profundities may be compellingly envisioned, I hardly think that the reinstatement of tables is among them.

As a related, already anticipated point, while the gradual nature of things is needed for my argument, no deep theories about material reality are important. While it is nice to have ready-made units there to remove—molecules, atoms and particles—the slightest contrivance will work about as well. Thus, from an alleged table, one may remove a tiny chip or splinter, until not a single one remains.

In the manner of G. E. Moore, some will object to my argument along the following lines. First, they will claim to be *more certain* of the existence of tables than of *anything* which I am bringing to bear against such alleged existence. And, then, they will say, with apparent caution and modesty, that, while they are *not sure which of the* things I advance is in error, there *must be at least one* weak link, or fault, in my reasoning. Now, it well may be that this Moorian reply is often, or even usually, a proper answer to a philosophical attack on common sense. But, is it *always* proper, appropriate or correct? Is common sense *always* to be believed, while philosophy, along with science, is *always* to yield? I cannot believe that this is so, and that *no exceptions* can be made to this popular Moorian doctrine. What of the *present case*, then: may not *that* be just such an exception? We have seen, I suggest, that to deny my argument amounts to supposing a miracle: the gentle, innocuous removal of a single atom, or only a few, *which is not even perceptible to the unaided senses*, takes us from a situation where a table is present to one where there is no table at all. Indeed, the removal of *any one*, or *any few*, of *millions* of removable atoms or groups, will be enough to work the trick. This is, after all, where the issue does lie. Can common sense be so powerful as to sustain such a miraculous supposition as this? I do not think so.

In contrast to its employment with tables and chairs, our argument does not seem nearly so compelling, if at all, against *physical objects*. Intuitively, we have the idea that if we consider a biggish physical object, consisting of many atoms, as we take one away and then another, and so on, what we have left is always a physical object, so long as any object at all remains. The last atom, particle or whatever, it may be supposed, is as well off toward being a physical object as is the biggish thing at the start.

Let us be a bit particular as regards the differences between our sorites against tables, or any other ordinary things, and a similar attempt against physical objects. In the first place, we cannot say, in parallel with (2), that, for anything there may be, if it is a physical object, then it consists of many atoms but only a finite number. For an atom itself is a physical object and it does not consist of atoms, let alone many of them. Nor will matters improve if we look for a finer component than atoms, for what we find may also be regarded, I suppose, as a physical object if it is any proper component at all. Nor can a parallel with (3) be accepted readily. Unlike with a table, if you have a physical object and remove an atom, you may have left no physical object at all. For that atom, now removed, may have been the only physical object there to be removed. Now, none of this is to suppose that physical objects do exist. But, as the present argument does not compellingly disprove their existence, they appear to be a somewhat extraordinary thing, whether truly existent or only alleged for all that.

All in all, it may be said, I hope, that the argument I have employed is a rather *simple* piece of reasoning. I call this sort of argument the *sorites of decomposition*. A parallel argument, going the other way, suggests itself, *the sorites of accumulation*, as well as variations upon, and combinations of, both of these forms of reasoning. In particular, counter-

factual variations should be of interest to many contemporary writers.

We employed our argument against tables, which, if they exist at all, have certain more or less special features. They are in some sense functional things; they are typically man-made; and so on. But none of this, it will be easily recognised, has anything to do with the matter at hand. Our argument may be employed equally well to deny the existence of such alleged things as sticks and stones, mountains and lakes, planets, (ordinary) stars and galaxies, ships and carriages, pieces of hair and of money, bodies of horses and of generals, and so on, and so forth. Such things as are not susceptible to decomposition withstand this form of argument: certain sub-atomic particles may provide an example. More importantly, decomposible things which are in a relevant way 'defined with precision' escape the present reasonings. Accordingly, I shall not now deny the existence of most molecules, even some 'quite large' ones, nor, perhaps, even certain crystal structures. However, something such as a blue 1968 Chevrolet four-door sedan, while according to most accounts not something vaguely described, will fall prey to our sorites. While much of physics and chemistry thus *might* remain relatively unscathed, biological entities, above the molecular level, appear to be nothing but fictions. I deny, then, not only the bodies of animals, including human beings, but also their organs, such as livers, hearts and brains, their tissues, and even individual cells, such as neurons.

Similar decomposition arguments make it clear, as well, that many alleged substances in fact do not exist at all. Unlike water and gold, which may be real, but which do not come in drops or hunks, juice and brass are only fictions. Also among the sorts of stuff that do not exist are, I should think, air and earth, meat and flesh, wood and rock, cloth and paper, and so on.

None of the things so far placed in the range of our reasonings, however, is of nearly so great an interest, I imagine, as we ourselves.

Accordingly, I now turn-to begin a new section, devoted to this topic, wherein I explicitly reason to deny, not without paradox, but perhaps with success, the very thing that Descartes would have me consider *certain*: my own present existence.

II. A Disproof of My Own Existence

The developing scientific perspective, especially owing to gains in biology and chemistry over the last few centuries, renders it exceedingly likely, at least, that no finite people or beings exist. In particular, and more conservatively, this perspective indicates that I myself do not exist; that I never have and never shall.

To achieve this paradoxical result, I shall again employ the sorties of decomposition. Now, the 'normal growth of the human being from conception' also provides, I believe, a sound sorites of accumulation. That sorites is naturally instanced, we might say, even though, with cellular growth not being clearly arthmetic, a unit of increment may have to be contrived: what happens during the first second; what happens during the next; and so on. But, the very artificiality of a gradual decomposition may better jar the mind. Thus, it may increase the chances for acceptance of the uncomfortable conclusion. Now, the most compelling decompositions are not yet attainable. We cannot remove, for example, one cell at a time, while keeping the remainder alive and functioning impressively. While it is not strictly relevant, I should think that this ability is not too far off for us, perhaps no more than a few centuries. In any case, if and when it can be done, I hope that it will not be. What is most relevant is that nature allow for the decompositions herein to be imagined.

As I have indicated, the unit of decrement which I shall choose is the cell. It is instructive for us now to argue at this level. As a cell consists of millions of atoms, a sorites of decomposition based on the atom can show that cells do not exist. Thus, the success of an argument against myself, or even my body, based on the cell,

makes it quite clear that, in our argument against tables, the reliance on atoms was far from fundamental.

To mirror our previous argument, against tables, I now display the following three premisses:

(1) I exist.
(2) If I exist, then I consist of many cells, but a finite number.
(3) If I exist (and consist of many cells, but a finite number), then the net removal of one cell, or only a few, in a way which is most innocuous and favourable, will not mean the difference as to whether I exist.

As before, these three propositions form an inconsistent set. They have it that I am still there with no cells at all, even while my existence depends on cells. To escape this inconsistency realistically, we must suppose this. Even under conditions most favourable to me, the removal of a single cell, or only a few, *any* one or few of those in the situation, will mean the difference between my existence and no me at all. But, if I do exist, can my existence really be that tenous? I think not. Therefore, I do not exist.

A bit more informally, the idea is this. One cell, more or less, will not mean the difference between my being there and not. So, take one away, and I am still there. Take another away; again, no problem. But after a while there are no cells at all. Indeed, as they have been replaced by nothing, in the relevant structures, it is unclear what will be there: perhaps, some salty water. Supposedly, I am still there. But given anything like the developed perspective of science, this is really quite absurd. Thus, the supposition of my existence has been reduced to an absurdity.

As before, it is important to discuss our third and final premiss. Because of the previous parallel discussion, various points may now be safely passed over. But a few new things arise in the present context which, even in a brief essay, are worthy of some consideration.

In the first place, it should be noted that, in the previous reasoning, about tables, we did not become involved in matters of identity, or persistence. There, I argued that *no* table, the same or any other, survived the decremental changes, and so *no* table existed in the first place. In contrast, the present argument does involve identity and, except for its counterfactual form, even persistence through time: I myself must survive. No new problems of importance are, I suggest, thus introduced for us. Indeed, we may abandon questions of identity entirely, and construct a general argument, upon the alleged existence of finite persons or beings, to parallel more completely our argument about tables. To play it safe with respect to such various forms as there may be of 'extra-terrestrial beings', we should then make our unit the atom, or even the particle, instead of the cell. It was to honour Descartes, so to say, and to pack the punch of particularity, that I focused the argument on myself, quite directly, thus becoming involved with identity. But that involvement is not essential.

In the second place, it will be maintained, I suppose, that my argument about tables did not involve considerations of life, or of consciousness. Let us grant this point. But how might such involvements as are now upon us serve to promote my own existence, or that of any finite being? I think there is no realistic way. Let us try to interpret our third premiss quite graphically, now, to clarify its import. On its most relevant interpretation, I suggest, life and consciousness, as well as the 'capacity' for them, will be present for as long as anyone might need to appreciate our argument's point. For it is supposed, in our third premiss, that the 'way' in which a cell is removed is one which is most innocuous and favourable—that is, with respect to me, or to my own identity. How might that happen?

At the present level of reasoning, the following scenario, I suggest, is more or less appropriate. At a certain stage in the decremental process, not very far along, it seems clear, life-support systems will be brought in to keep me going as well as possible. I shall be placed *in vitro*; nourishing fluids will be pumped into me; electrical stimulation will be provided, but not in such a way that any apparatus 'does my experiencing or thinking for me'; and so on. Cell after cell is pulled away. The remaining ones are kept alive, and kept functioning 'at the highest level of achievement of which they are capable'. The added apparatus has not, in the case here described, replaced the removed cells as part of me. In this present case, an electric wire will only be a means of support, much as a cardiac pacemaker serves even now. While *other cases* may be construed as involving the replacement of natural parts by synthetic ones, this present one is not correctly understood in such terms. Sticking to what might here most plausibly be considered myself, then, at a certain point we are down to a brain in a vat and, then, half a brain. So far, so good; but then we get down to a third of a brain, then a sixteenth. Still later, there are only fifty-three neurons in living combination. Where at the end, there is but one living nerve cell, and then it too is gone. Where will I disappear from the scene? Realistically, now, will the removal of a single cell ever, under such favourable conditions, mean my disappearance from reality? While that may be a 'logical possibility', it does not compel belief. The conclusion of our argument, in contrast, is quite compelling: I do not disappear at any time, because I was never around in the first place.

We may agree that at one time it may have been a very compelling thought that there were souls, or individual essences, one for each person. Many people even now believe in such things, and in minds, a life force, if not entelechies, ghosts, spirits, and so on. Many of these believers, I imagine, think that a person is not only real, but an immaterial, indivisible entity. Thus, I expect, they lay the ground for a hope in survival of bodily death, and perhaps even immortality. At the time of Descartes, for example, it may be that all of these suppositions fairly demanded or compelled credence. But they do not sit well, I suggest, with our developed scientific perspective. For that reason, I believe, they offer no compelling alternative now to the bleak conclusions drawn herein.

My sorites of decomposition, against my own existence, has, to be sure, required some speculative effort. But such speculation as there may be is, I submit, far from wild. Further, it does jar the mind, and lets us look anew at the process of cellular development. We may reason justly, then, about the embryo growing from a fertilised egg, and we may conclude again, less speculatively, that, just like you, I do not exist. Against this more 'natural' argument, some would object, I suppose, that I myself was once nothing but a fertilised egg. Now, while I admire attempts to be consistent, I think that, in the present case, the attempt has little to recommend it, and is in any case erroneous. If someone persists in such a thought, however, I should bid him consider whether even a sperm, or an egg, was any existing entity, much less a fertilised egg. Accumulation and decomposition arguments, it seems, may also be used to refute the supposed existence of any of them.

III. The Substance of the Argument and the Irrelevance of Logical Inventions

The main thrust of this argument is, in light of our scientific perspective, the same in my own case and in those of a table, a stone and, for that matter, even of a yo-yo. Let us reconsider the matter, then, with respect to alleged yo-yos, for they give us an example which is refreshingly light and calmly unemotional. Again the main issues seem to turn on a suitable third premiss:

For anything there may be, if it is a yo-yo (which consists of many atoms, but a finite number), then the net removal of one atom, or only a few, in a way which is most innocuous and favorable, will not mean the

difference as to whether there is a yo-yo in the situation.

Now, how could such a premiss as this be false, and untrue, and inaccurate and unacceptable? Apart from minor matters of formulation, there are, it seems clear, only two ways in which things might go wrong for it.

First, and more on 'the side of things in the world', it might be that nature protected yo-yos, or at least one of them, by giving it a place of its own in the world, set apart from other things, an essence if you please. But how might anything like this actually obtain? The matter is, I think, very important, so, even if we repeat some of our previous words, let us try to outline the possibilities. First, yo-yos would be protected if, either at the start or at some later point, we just could not take out any atoms from them. Or, being realistic, and supposing that that way is not available, they might still be saved if new atoms were to rush in whenever crucial old ones were extracted. Or if that is out, as it surely appears to be, it might be that at some point, even under the most favourable conditions for relevant gradualness, a spontaneous explosion should take place, a yo-yo's previous existence thus being preserved by such sudden destruction. Or, failing that, which does seem more in line with any actual experience of the world, a god on high, or a suitable natural law, might turn an endangered dwindling yo-yo into a sousaphone, perhaps upon the removal of the four million and twelfth atom, so that our concepts themselves would never have to be tested on its behalf. And so on; and so forth. There are, then, many logical possibilities for nature to conspire, as it were, so that things would fit our term 'yo-yo'. But we are confident that none of them actually obtain. To think otherwise, I should say, is to expect a miracle: if you will, a *miracle of metaphysical illusion*.

With the world being so unfavourable for them, as it surely seems to be, the only chance for yo-yos lies on 'the side of our terms and concepts'. But what can be expected here? At the very least, we need the concept of a yo-yo to be atomically precise. Certain concepts of molecules seem to be thus precise: when you snip a hydrogen atom off the end somewhere, and do not replace it, you no longer have in the situation a molecule of that original kind. But is the concept of a yo-yo relevantly like that? I think we ask too much of ourselves if we expect ourselves to be working here in such a precise manner. Accordingly, to suppose this much for ourselves and 'yo-yo' is to expect another miracle, perhaps a *miracle of conceptual comprehension*. On either hand, then, yo-yos require a miracle; for any who do not believe in miracles, there is no rational belief in yo-yos.

Our reasonings turn up for us an implicit contradiction in our beliefs. To strive to be reasonable we must give up one at least. To deny a suitable second premiss is to have yo-yos floating around with no atoms at all, nor any matter in the situation, and that is yet more miraculous than the two apparent wonders we have just considered. The only path to consistency, then, which is even remotely reasonable or realistic is to deny existence for alleged yo-yos, for we have just covered the whole story as to what wonders a commitment to them means. If this is appreciated we may see the irrelevance of remarks about clear cases, paradigms, family resemblances, and other soothing remedies, lately influential but now happily well on the wane. Perhaps more importantly, in these more technical times, we may also thus see the emptiness in the suggestion, currently favoured by certain philosophers, that we escape the argument by assigning to relevant sentences truth values other than truth and falsity.[3] For, whatever these values may be, they do not reduce one bit the miracles that yo-yos require; at most they occasion only a mildly different description of them.

Let us suppose we have before us a yo-yo. As atoms are removed one at a time, without replacement, we keep considering singular propositions each to the effect that at the appropriate new time a yo-yo is before us. We begin, as in any *reductio*, by assigning truth. As things progress, at some particular point, atomically counted, we are for the first time no longer to assign truth! Instead, when some peripheral atom is gently removed, and there would appear to be at least virtually no significant difference in what is before us, we are for the first time to depart from our initial kind of assignment, and to assign *some other* value. Perhaps the new value will not be falsity; it may be indefiniteness, or some numerical value just a shade less than unity, say 0.999, or some other newly invented candidate. But whatever else it is, there will be just as much of a miracle for us to expect. For, given that we have no miracle of metaphysical illusion to help us—that is, the world is indeed relevantly gradual—it will take a miraculous sensitivity on the part of 'yo-yo' to generate the difference, however, we should choose to label such a wonderful discrimination. So sensitive is our concept of a yo-yo that, as a single atom goes away at the periphery, truth or unity or whatever is suddenly left behind! To expect that is, I submit, still to expect a miracle of conceptual comprehension. Hence, any new values, as well as the logical inventiveness they may occasion, are utterly irrelevant to the issues here.

Nor will it help matters to invoke a distinction between propositions and sentences, which may express or fail to express relevant propositions. Let us focus on the sentence 'There is a yo-yo before us now.' We may begin as before, with a putative paradigm yo-yo, and may then judge that our sentence expresses a proposition which is true. We then take off peripheral atoms, one at a time, and ask whether the sentence does something else, for the first time, with the removal of each single one. The supposition that with a single atom something else is for the first time done appears quite incredible, as well it should; it is but another form of our miracle of conceptual comprehension. But if this miracle may not be expected, then, if the sentence is not to express a truth with no atoms before us, we must conclude that our sentence never expresses a truth.[4]

Concerning the question of our putative yo-yos, then, it appears that only two responses are relevant: a belief in the miraculous or else an acceptance of nihilism. And the same choice, I submit, is there with alleged tables, and stones, and even my very own self. No matter how it is looked at, there is not much of a choice here. Habit and emotion appear on one side, while reason seems to be on quite the other.

IV. The Scope of these Problems

The argument I have employed derives, of course, from 'the paradox of the heap', an ancient problem devised by Eubulides, the great Megarian thinker. In way of reconstruction, we might say that Eubuildes showed that there were and are no heaps. First, we may suppose the existence of heaps. Secondly, we note that, if any heap exists, it consists of various other entities—of grains of sand, or of beans, for example. Finally, we note that, if one bean is removed without replacement, and this is done most favourably and innocuously, what remains will be a heap. Thus, given anything like our view of reality, heaps, which many suppose to be ordinary existing things, are only fictions: there are no heaps.

I shall not here bother to detail the differences and similarities between Eubulides's original argument and my own variations upon it. So far as the compelling force goes, though, suffice it to say that our modern scientific perspective means that there is little difference between a heap and almost anything else, so to say, including myself. As far as repercussions or consequences are concerned, however, my own arguments are of course enormously more effective than the original version. While this is rather obvious, the details may be worth some presentation.

First, virtually all of our common-sense beliefs are untrue, and even as to nothing.

Moreover, most of our learned studies are similarly unfortunate, at least in anything like their present formulations. Samuel Wheeler begins to put the point in a manner which is conjectural, and perhaps somewhat ironic: 'If there is no objective difference between possible persons and possible non-persons, much of what we believe about morality, psychology, etc., is in trouble.'[5] We may say, now, that the matter is not very conjectural, and that all of moral reasoning, as well as psychological understanding, looks to be in deep trouble indeed. This holds as well, of course, for the other studies concerning man. History, law and medicine are all a tissue of fictions, as are economics, linguistics and politics. Various related areas of philosophy, such as epistemology, the philosophy of language and the philosophy of mind, can contain nothing sound and true. Unless mathematics is clearly severed from connections with human beings, it too must fall prey to our sorites. Various other studies look to fare poorly. Biology, for example, is a tissue of nonentities and untruth, except as it becomes biochemistry perhaps, or something much of that sort. Astronomy too, except as it becomes astrophysics, or something similar, looks to be about anything but our universe.

Under a second head, we may notice that, while they may in some respects involve language importantly, our sorites arguments undermine all natural languages, while the argument of Eubulides hardly begins to do anything here. In the first place, as there are no human beings, there is no human language or thought. Waiving that basic point, and supposing the opposite, we shall notice that our existing expressions, at least by and large, fail to make any contact with whatever is there. For example, the proper names so far given do not refer to anything real. We may confirm this by a sorites argument directly involving such famous nonentities as Cicero, Descartes, Venus, Everest, and so on. Should someone name an individual atom 'Adam', things might be different on this score. The personal pronouns, we have seen, fare little better. Except for atoms, and so on, none of our referential devices look to be of much distinction.

But then, too, the picture looks bleak for the question of whether atoms exist, and so for any other things. For we cannot, in good faith, long waive the point that there is no human language or thought, nor even any human or other finite beings. And from such a standpoint even simple arithmetic looks to be beyond comprehension, there being none of us to grasp any realities or truth which might be there. Finally, the existence of any sorites arguments themselves cannot be relevantly affirmed, there being not a one of us ever to consider any such piece of reasoning. The chain of nihilistic propositions appears to come full circle.

This undeniable absurdity is, I suggest, no blameworthy fault of our Eubulidean reasonings. On the contrary, by such means, our sorites arguments allow us to perceive the truly thoroughgoing inconsistencies in our available language and thought. Continuing to speak in the paradoxical manner they expose, we might say this. For anything like truth's sake, these arguments counsel us to begin a radical reconstruction of our means of thought and expression. No available earthly means, which is sufficiently rich for many of our purposes, fares any better than does English. I have been disclosing no peculiar subtleties of our language which may be absent in Chinese, or in ancient Greek. But what steps should we take to make things better?

With something like a heap, and sticking to Eubulides's original level of argument, moderately good steps can be taken quickly and easily. For, if there are no heaps, we can define the word 'hoap', for example, so that a hoap may consist, minimally, of two items: for example, beans or grains of sand, touching each other. But, if there are no tables, trees or cats, what are we supposed to define, and, even very roughly, what is to be the definition of it? If I do not exist, then what does exist in which, so to speak, I should have an

appropriate and rather intense interest? If you do not exist, as is here argued, what does exist over there which must not be inappropriately interfered with, or harmed? I am truly in darkness on these momentous matters, with no light at all to guide me.

These problems are, I believe, of the first importance for any who value philosophy and the traditional quest after truth. But I am far from sanguine that my challenge, from which they flow, will be met with an attempt to reply which is properly serious, let alone rationally effective. For it is easiest to shun the most pervasive difficulties in philosophy, to leave it to others, in times long to come, to explain their solutions. It is easiest to presume we know in advance, without knowing the details, which way the answer must go, letting the social acceptance of others serve as our assurance and even foundation, rather than anything like the light of one's own reason. But I am hopeful that one or two thoughtful souls may break the common easy pattern. Perhaps they will allow me to avoid the labours, apparently painful and fruitless, involved in developing an adequate philosophy of nihilism, which it now appears is the only adequate philosophy there can be. Or perhaps, on the contrary, they will provide me with further reason for thinking that this challenge is too powerful to be met adequately, and that there is no rational hope at all for the thought that anyone might be real. That might not be cheerful, but at least it would be something. Either way, I doubt that Eubulides ever had it so good.[6]

Notes

1   A. J. Ayer, *The Problem of Knowledge* (London: Macmillan, 1956) p. 50.

2   Samuel C. Wheeler III, 'Reference and Vagueness', *Synthèse*, xxx (1967) no. 3–4 367–79.

3   A recent example of a philosopher who would treat of vagueness by means of exotic truth values is

David H. Sanford in his 'Borderline Logic', *American Philosophical Quarterly*, XII, (1975) no. 1, 29–39. Sanford provides references to other writers of a similar persuasion.

4   On these matters, I am indebted to discussion with David Sanford:

5   Wheeler, in *Synthese*, xxx (1967), no. 3–4, 371.

6   I have been helped in writing this paper by discussion with various people; Ralph Silverman and Samuel Wheeler deserve special thanks.

For a discussion of related matters, I refer the reader to my paper, 'There are No Ordinary Things', *Synthese*, xli (1979), 117–54. For a detailed analysis of sorites arguments, see my 'Why There are No People', *Midwest Studies in Philosophy*, vol. IV: *Studies in Metaphysics*. And, for a discussion of relations between the nihilistic approach of this present paper and the sceptical approach in epistemology, see my 'Skepticism and Nihilism', *Noûs*, xiv (1980), 517–45.

PART 2

Time and Time Travel

INTRODUCTION TO PART 2

TIME AND TEMPORAL PASSAGE pose a number of serious philosophical problems. One question in the philosophy of time concerns the existence of non-present times, objects, and events. Are there such things? On the one hand, it is hard to believe that times and events in the past and the future—your birth, your death, the age of the dinosaurs, and so on—are somehow "just as real" as the present. Where, after all, would such things be? St. Augustine reasons as follows:

> If future and past events exist, I want to know where they are. If I have not the strength to discover the answer, at least I know that wherever they are, they are not there as future or past, but as present. For if there also they are future, they will not yet be there. If there also they are past, they are no longer there. Therefore, wherever they are, whatever they are, they do not exist except in the present.
>
> (St. Augustine, *Confessions* XI. xviii (23), trans. by H. Chadwick, Oxford:
> Oxford University Press 1991, pp. 233–34)

So it is tempting to endorse *presentism*—the view, roughly, that it always has been and always will be the case that there are no objects or events other than present objects and events. On the other hand, it is hard to see how we can refer to and stand in relations (causal relations, for example) with objects and persons in the past (and future) unless such things exist. How can I admire J. R. R. Tolkien, for example, if there *is* no such person as Tolkien to be the object of my admiration? How can I remember my late grandfather—remember *him*, the *man himself*—if he does not exist and therefore cannot be the object of any memory? Thus, one might also find it tempting to endorse some version of *four-dimensionalism*, the denial of presentism. Four-dimensionalism is currently the majority view among those writing in the field, in no small part because it is the view that seems to fit best with our most successful theories in physics. Moreover, most four-dimensionalists endorse a view known as *eternalism*—roughly, the claim that everything that ever did exist or ever will exist *does* exist.[1]

Another important question concerns the *flow* of time. Initially, it is hard to see what the passage of time could amount to. Intuitively, temporal *passage* is a kind of movement—perhaps the movement of "presentness" along a timeline, or perhaps the absolute generation of new times and subsequent destruction of old times. (The former conception is sometimes referred to as the "moving spotlight" theory of time. The latter conception is roughly what the passage of time would be if presentism were true.) But how could *time itself* move? One wants to say that something moves if, and only if, it is at one place at one time and at another place at another time. Likewise, one wants to say that something is generated if it doesn't exist at one time and does exist at another. So it would appear that time passes if, and only if, there is a pair of times T1 and T2, such that a certain time *t* is present at T1 but not at T2. But what could T1 and T2 possibly be? At first glance, it seems that they would have to be times in some sort of higher-level time series. In other words, it appears that, in order to make sense of the passage of time, we have to believe not only in *our* time-series (call it "the *t*-series") but also in another time-series (the T-series) in which t-times come into and pass out of existence, or gain and lose the property of presentness. But now we just face more questions: Do times in the T-series come into and pass out of existence? Is there T-passage, just like there is t-passage? And if not, then is it really important to believe in temporal passage at all? These are hard questions.

Our two main questions about the ontology of time are related to one another. If temporal passage is impossible, then presentism cannot be true. Thus, arguments against the possibility of temporal passage are ultimately also arguments against the truth of presentism. The first six readings in this part of the book focus on these issues. The selection by Wells describes the eternalist view about the reality of past and future times; the selection by Lightman describes a variety of other ways of thinking about time and related notions. The selections by Markosian and Prior present considerations on behalf of presentism; and the selections by Horwich and Williams discuss reasons for rejecting temporal passage (and, by extension, presentism as well).

The remaining selections in this part take up the topic of time travel. Time travel is a staple of contemporary science fiction, and the philosophically puzzling features of time travel are precisely those features that make for the most interesting science fiction stories. Thus, for example, if time travel to the past is possible, then it seems in principle possible for a person to travel in time to kill one of her ancestors before that ancestor ever manages to become a parent. But the ancestor *must* become a parent in order for the time traveler to exist and make the journey to kill him or her. Thus, it seems that there is a perfectly good sense in which the time traveler cannot kill her ancestor. But what explains the impossibility? This and a variety of other time travel paradoxes are discussed in the essay by David Lewis.

Moreover, time travel seems to imply the possibility of causal loops. A causal loop is a series of events such that each event in the series lies in its own causal history: each event in a loop helps to cause *itself*. Indeed, some of the most interesting time travel stories present us with *objects* whose very existence is loopy: the object has no beginning in time and no end, and each "stage" of the object's career lies in its own causal history. In the story by Robert Silverberg, we find a time machine whose career is a causal loop; and in the story by Robert Heinlein, it is a person who exists as a causal loop. Causal loops are deeply puzzling; many think that they are impossible and that their impossibility is a reason to believe that time travel is impossible. In the final essay in this section, Richard Hanley takes a careful look at this sort of argument against time travel and ultimately defends the conclusion that causal loops are possible after all.

Note

1   There are other versions of four-dimensionalism too, however. For example, the *growing block* view maintains that all and only past and present objects are real—merely future things do not exist. The *shrinking block* view maintains that only present and future things are real—merely past things do not exist. And there are still other views. For more detailed treatment of the topic of four-dimensionalism, see my "Four Dimensionalism," in Michael J. Loux and Dean Zimmerman (eds.), *The Oxford Handbook of Metaphysics* (Oxford: Oxford University Press, 2002).

Chapter 9

H. G. Wells

THE TIME TRAVELLER'S SPEECH

The Time Traveller (for so it will be conveni-ent to speak of him) was expounding a recondite matter to us. His grey eyes shone and twinkled, and his usually pale face was flushed and animated. The fire burned brightly, and the soft radiance of the incandescent lights in the lilies of silver caught the bubbles that flashed and passed in our glasses. Our chairs, being his patents, embraced and caressed us rather than submitted to be sat upon, and there was that luxurious after-dinner atmosphere, when thought runs gracefully free of the tram-mels of precision. And he put it to us in this way—marking the points with lean forefinger—as we sat and lazily admired his earnestness over this new paradox (as we thought it) and his fecundity.

'You must follow me carefully. I shall have to controvert one or two ideas that are almost uni-versally accepted. The geometry, for instance, they taught you at school is founded on a misconception.'

'Is not that rather a large thing to expect us to begin upon?' said Filby, an argumentative per-son with red hair.

'I do not mean to ask you to accept anything without reasonable ground for it. You will soon admit as much as I need from you. You know of course that a mathematical line, a line of thick-ness nil, has no real existence. They taught you that? Neither has a mathematical plane. These things are mere abstractions.'

'That is all right,' said the Psychologist.

'Nor, having only length, breadth, and thick-ness, can a cube have a real existence.'

'There I object,' said Filby. 'Of course a solid body may exist. All real things——'.

'So most people think. But wait a moment. Can an *instantaneous* cube exist?'

'Don't follow you,' said Filby.

'Can a cube that does not last for any time at all, have a real existence?'

Filby became pensive. 'Clearly,' the Time Traveller proceeded, 'any real body must have extension in four directions: it must have Length, Breadth, Thickness, and—Duration. But through a natural infirmity of the flesh, which I will explain to you in a moment, we incline to over-look this fact. There are really four dimensions, three which we call the three planes of Space, and a fourth, Time. There is, however, a tendency to draw an unreal distinction between the for-mer three dimensions and the latter, because it happens that our consciousness moves intermit-tently in one direction along the latter from the beginning to the end of our lives.'

'That,' said a very young man, making spasmodic efforts to relight his cigar over the lamp; 'that . . . very clear indeed.'

'Now, it is very remarkable that this is so extensively overlooked,' continued the Time Traveller, with a slight accession of cheerfulness. 'Really this is what is meant by the Fourth Dimension, though some people who talk about the Fourth Dimension do not know they mean it. It is only another way of looking at Time. *There is no difference between Time and any of the three dimensions of Space except that our consciousness moves along it.* But some foolish people have got hold of the wrong side of that idea. You have all heard what they have to say about this Fourth Dimension?'

'I have not,' said the Provincial Mayor.

'It is simply this. That Space, as our mathematicians have it, is spoken of as having three dimensions, which one may call Length, Breadth, and Thickness, and is always definable by reference to three planes, each at right angles to the others. But some philosophical people have been asking why *three* dimensions particularly—why not another direction at right angles to the other three? and have even tried to construct a Four-Dimensional geometry. Professor Simon Newcomb was expounding this to the New York Mathematical Society only a month or so ago. You know how on a flat surface, which has only two dimensions, we can represent a figure of a three-dimensional solid, and similarly they think that by models of three dimensions they could represent one of four—if they could master the perspective of the thing. See?'

'I think so,' murmured the Provincial Mayor; and, knitting his brows, he lapsed into an introspective state, his lips moving as one who repeats mystic words. 'Yes, I think I see it now,' he said after some time, brightening in a quite transitory manner.

'Well. I do not mind telling you I have been at work upon this geometry of Four Dimensions for some time. Some of my results are curious. For instance, here is a portrait of a man at eight years old, another at fifteen, another at seventeen, another at twenty-three, and so on. All these are evidently sections, as it were, Three-Dimensional representations of his Four-Dimensioned being, which is a fixed and unalterable thing.'

'Scientific people,' proceeded the Time Traveller, after the pause required for the proper assimilation of this, 'know very well that Time is only a kind of Space. Here is a popular scientific diagram, a weather record. This line I trace with my finger shows the movement of the barometer. Yesterday it was so high, yesterday night it fell, then this morning it rose again, and so gently upward to here. Surely the mercury did not trace this line in any of the dimensions of Space generally recognised? But certainly it traced such a line, and that line, therefore, we must conclude was along the Time-Dimension.'

'But,' said the Medical Man, staring hard at a coal in the fire, 'if Time is really only a fourth dimension of Space, why is it, and why has it always been, regarded as something different? And why cannot we move in Time as we move about in the other dimensions of Space?'

The Time Traveller smiled. 'Are you so sure we can move freely in Space? Right and left we can go, backward and forward freely enough, and men always have done so. I admit we move freely in two dimensions. But how about up and down? Gravitation limits us there.'

'Not exactly,' said the Medical Man. 'There are balloons.'

'But before the balloons, save for spasmodic jumping and the inequalities of the surface, man had no freedom of vertical movement.'

'Still, they could move a little up and down,' said the Medical Man.

'Easier, far easier down than up.'

'And you cannot move at all in Time, you cannot get away from the present moment.'

'My dear sir, that is just where you are wrong. That is just where the whole world has gone wrong. We are always getting away from the present moment. Our mental existences, which are immaterial and have no dimensions, are passing along the Time-Dimension with a uniform velocity from the cradle to the grave. Just as we should travel *down* if we began our existence fifty miles above the earth's surface.'

'But the great difficulty is this,' interrupted the Psychologist. 'You *can* move about in all directions of Space, but you cannot move about in Time.'

'That is the germ of my great discovery. But

you are wrong to say that we cannot move about in Time. For instance, if I am recalling an incident very vividly I go back to the instant of its occurrence: I become absent-minded, as you say. I jump back for a moment. Of course we have no means of staying back for any length of Time, any more than a savage or an animal has of staying six feet above the ground. But a civilised man is better off than the savage in this respect. He can go up against gravitation in a balloon, and why should he not hope that ultimately he may be able to stop or accelerate his drift along the Time-Dimension, or even turn about and travel the other way?'

'Oh, this,' began Filby, 'is all——'

'Why not?' said the Time Traveller.

'It's against reason,' said Filby.

'What reason?' said the Time Traveller.

'You can show black is white by argument,' said Filby, 'but you will never convince me.'

'Possibly not,' said the Time Traveller. 'But now you begin to see the object of my investigations into the geometry of Four Dimensions. Long ago I had a vague inkling of a machine——'

'To travel through Time!' exclaimed the Very Young Man.

'That shall travel indifferently in any direction of Space and Time, as the driver determines.'

Filby contented himself with laughter. [. . .]

Chapter 10

Alan Lightman

EINSTEIN'S DREAMS

Prologue

In some distant arcade, a clock tower calls out six times and then stops. The young man slumps at his desk. He has come to the office at dawn, after another upheaval. His hair is uncombed and his trousers are too big. In his hand he holds twenty crumpled pages, his new theory of time, which he will mail today to the German journal of physics.

Tiny sounds from the city drift through the room. A milk bottle clinks on a stone. An awning is cranked in a shop on Marktgasse. A vegetable cart moves slowly through a street. A man and woman talk in hushed tones in an apartment nearby.

In the dim light that seeps through the room, the desks appear shadowy and soft, like large sleeping animals. Except for the young man's desk, which is cluttered with half-opened books, the twelve oak desks are all neatly covered with documents, left from the previous day. Upon arriving in two hours, each clerk will know precisely where to begin. But at this moment, in this dim light, the documents on the desks are no more visible than the clock in the corner or the secretary's stool near the door. All that can be seen at this moment are the shadowy shapes of the desks and the hunched form of the young man.

Ten minutes past six, by the invisible clock on the wall. Minute by minute, new objects gain form. Here, a brass wastebasket appears. There, a calendar on a wall. Here, a family photograph, a box of paperclips, an inkwell, a pen. There, a typewriter, a jacket folded on a chair. In time, the ubiquitous bookshelves emerge from the night mist that hangs on the walls. The bookshelves hold notebooks of patents. One patent concerns a new drilling gear with teeth curved in a pattern to minimize friction. Another proposes an electrical transformer that holds constant voltage when the power supply varies. Another describes a typewriter with a low-velocity typebar that eliminates noise. It is a room full of practical ideas.

Outside, the tops of the Alps start to glow from the sun. It is late June. A boatman on the Aare unties his small skiff and pushes off, letting the current take him along Aarstrasse to Gerberngasse, where he will deliver his summer apples and berries. The baker arrives at his store on Marktgasse, fires his coal oven, begins mixing flour and yeast. Two lovers embrace on the Nydegg Bridge, gaze wistfully into the river below. A man stands on his balcony on Schifflaube, studies the pink sky. A woman who cannot sleep walks slowly down Kramgasse, peering into each dark arcade, reading the posters in half-light.

In the long, narrow office on Speichergasse, the room full of practical ideas, the young patent clerk still sprawls in his chair, head down on his desk. For the past several months, since the middle of April, he has dreamed many dreams about time. His dreams have taken hold of his research. His dreams have worn him out, exhausted him so that he sometimes cannot tell whether he is awake or asleep. But the dreaming is finished. Out of many possible natures of time, imagined in as many nights, one seems compelling. Not that the others are impossible. The others might exist in other worlds.

The young man shifts in his chair, waiting for the typist to come, and softly hums from Beethoven's *Moonlight* Sonata.

14 April 1905

Suppose time is a circle, bending back on itself. The world repeats itself, precisely, endlessly.

For the most part, people do not know they will live their lives over. Traders do not know that they will make the same bargain again and again. Politicians do not know that they will shout from the same lectern an infinite number of times in the cycles of time. Parents treasure the first laugh from their child as if they will not hear it again. Lovers making love the first time undress shyly, show surprise at the supple thigh, the fragile nipple. How would they know that each secret glimpse, each touch, will be repeated again and again and again, exactly as before?

On Marktgasse, it is the same. How could the shopkeepers know that each handmade sweater, each embroidered handkerchief, each chocolate candy, each intricate compass and watch will return to their stalls? At dusk, the shopkeepers go home to their families or drink beer in the taverns, calling happily to friends down the vaulted alleys, caressing each moment as an emerald on temporary consignment. How could they know that nothing is temporary, that all will happen again? No more than an ant crawling round the rim of a crystal chandelier knows that it will return to where it began.

In the hospital on Gerberngasse, a woman says goodbye to her husband. He lies in bed and stares at her emptily. In the last two months, his cancer has spread from his throat to his liver, his pancreas, his brain. His two young children sit on one chair in the corner of the room, frightened to look at their father, his sunken cheeks, the withered skin of an old man. The wife comes to the bed and kisses her husband softly on the forehead, whispers goodbye, and quickly leaves with the children. She is certain that this was the last kiss. How could she know that time will begin again, that she will be born again, will study at the gymnasium again, will show her paintings at the gallery in Zürich, will again meet her husband in the small library in Fribourg, will again go sailing with him in Thun Lake on a warm day in July, will give birth again, that her husband will again work for eight years at the pharmaceutical and come home one evening with a lump in his throat, will again throw up and get weak and end up in this hospital, this room, this bed, this moment. How could she know?

In the world in which time is a circle, every handshake, every kiss, every birth, every word, will be repeated precisely. So too every moment that two friends stop becoming friends, every time that a family is broken because of money, every vicious remark in an argument between spouses, every opportunity denied because of a superior's jealousy, every promise not kept.

And just as all things will be repeated in the future, all things now happening happened a million times before. Some few people in every town, in their dreams, are vaguely aware that all has occurred in the past. These are the people with unhappy lives, and they sense that their misjudgments and wrong deeds and bad luck have all taken place in the previous loop of time. In the dead of night these cursed citizens wrestle with their bedsheets, unable to rest, stricken with the knowledge that they cannot change a single action, a single gesture. Their mistakes will be repeated precisely in this life as in the life before. And it is these double unfortunates who give the only sign that time is a circle. For in each town, late at night, the vacant streets and balconies fill up with their moans.[. . .]

19 April 1905

It is a cold morning in November and the first snow has fallen. A man in a long leather coat stands on his fourth-floor balcony on Kramgasse overlooking the Zähringer Fountain and the white street below. To the east, he can see the fragile steeple of St. Vincent's Cathedral, to the west, the curved roof of the Zytgloggeturm. But the man is not looking east or west. He is staring down at a tiny red hat left in the snow below, and he is thinking. Should he go to the woman's house in Fribourg? His hands grip the metal balustrade, let go, grip again. Should he visit her? Should he visit her?

He decides not to see her again. She is manipulative and judgmental, and she could make his life miserable. Perhaps she would not be interested in him anyway. So he decides not to see her again. Instead, he keeps to the company of men. He works hard at the pharmaceutical, where he hardly notices the female assistant manager. He goes to the brasserie on Kochergasse in the evenings with his friends and drinks beer, he learns to make fondue. Then, in three years, he meets another woman in a clothing shop in Neuchâtel. She is nice. She makes love to him very very slowly, over a period of months. After a year, she comes to live with him in Berne. They live quietly, take walks together along the Aare, are companions to each other, grow old and contented.

In the second world, the man in the long leather coat decides that he must see the Fribourg woman again. He hardly knows her, she could be manipulative, and her movements hint at volatility, but that way her face softens when she smiles, that laugh, that clever use of words. Yes, he must see her again. He goes to her house in Fribourg, sits on the couch with her, within moments feels his heart pounding, grows weak at the sight of the white of her arms. They make

love, loudly and with passion. She persuades him to move to Fribourg. He leaves his job in Berne and begins work at the Fribourg Post Bureau. He burns with his love for her. Every day he comes home at noon. They eat, they make love, they argue, she complains that she needs more money, he pleads with her, she throws pots at him, they make love again, he returns to the Post Bureau. She threatens to leave him, but she does not leave him. He lives for her, and he is happy with his anguish.

In the third world, he also decides that he must see her again. He hardly knows her, she could be manipulative, and her movements hint at volatility, but that smile, that laugh, that clever use of words. Yes, he must see her again. He goes to her house in Fribourg, meets her at the door, has tea with her at her kitchen table. They talk of her work at the library, his job at the pharmaceutical. After an hour, she says that she must leave to help a friend, she says goodbye to him, they shake hands. He travels the thirty kilometers back to Berne, feels empty during the train ride home, goes to his fourth-floor apartment on Kramgasse, stands on the balcony and stares down at the tiny red hat left in the snow.

These three chains of events all indeed happen, simultaneously. For in this world, time has three dimensions, like space. Just as an object may move in three perpendicular directions, corresponding to horizontal, vertical, and longitudinal, so an object may participate in three perpendicular futures. Each future moves in a different direction of time. Each future is real. At every point of decision, whether to visit a woman in Fribourg or to buy a new coat, the world splits into three worlds, each with the same people but with different fates for those people. In time, there are an infinity of worlds.

Some make light of decisions, arguing that all possible decisions will occur. In such a world, how could one be responsible for his actions? Others hold that each decision must be considered and committed to, that without commitment there is chaos. Such people are content to live in contradictory worlds, so long as they know the reason for each. [. . .]

2 June 1905

A mushy, brown peach is lifted from the garbage and placed on the table to pinken. It pinkens, it turns hard, it is carried in a shopping sack to the grocer's, put on a shelf, removed and crated, returned to the tree with pink blossoms. In this world, time flows backward.

A withered woman sits in a chair hardly moving, her face red and swollen, her eyesight almost gone, her hearing gone, her breathing scratchy like the rustle of dead leaves on stones. Years pass. There are few visitors. Gradually, the woman gains strength, eats more, loses the heavy lines in her face. She hears voices, music. Vague shadows gather themselves into light and lines and images of tables, chairs, people's faces. The woman makes excursions from her small house, goes to the market, occasionally visits a friend, drinks tea at cafés in good weather. She takes needles and yarn from the bottom drawer of her dresser and crochets. She smiles when she likes her work. One day her husband, with whitened face, is carried into her house. In hours, his cheeks become pink, he stands stooped over, straightens out, speaks to her. Her house becomes their house. They eat meals together, tell jokes, laugh. They travel through the country, visit friends. Her white hair darkens with brown streaks, her voice resonates with new tones. She goes to a retirement party at the gymnasium, begins teaching history. She loves her students, argues with them after class. She reads during her lunch hour and at night. She meets friends and discusses history and current events. She helps her husband with the accounts at his chemist's store, walks with him at the foot of the mountains, makes love to him. Her skin becomes soft, her hair long and brown, her breasts firm. She sees her husband for the first time in the library of the university, returns his glances.

She attends classes. She graduates from the gymnasium, with her parents and sister crying tears of happiness. She lives at home with her parents, spends hours with her mother walking through the woods by their house, helps with the dishes. She tells stories to her younger sister, is read to at night before bed, grows smaller. She crawls. She nurses.

A middle-aged man walks from the stage of an auditorium in Stockholm, holding a medal. He shakes hands with the president of the Swedish Academy of Sciences, receives the Nobel Prize for physics, listens to the glorious citation. The man thinks briefly about the award he is to receive. His thoughts quickly shift twenty years to the future, when he will work alone in a small room with only pencil and paper. Day and night he will work, making many false starts, filling the trash basket with unsuccessful chains of equations and logical sequences. But some evenings he will return to his desk knowing he has learned things about Nature that no one has ever known, ventured into the forest and found light, gotten hold of precious secrets. On those evenings, his heart will pound as if he were in love. The anticipation of that rush of the blood, that time when he will be young and unknown and unafraid of mistakes, overpowers him now as he sits in his chair in the auditorium in Stockholm, at great distance from the tiny voice of the president announcing his name.

A man stands at the graveside of his friend, throws a handful of dirt on the coffin, feels the cold April rain on his face. But he does not weep. He looks ahead to the day when his friend's lungs will be strong, when his friend will be out of his bed and laughing, when the two of them will drink ale together, go sailing, talk. He does not weep. He waits longingly for a particular day he remembers in the future when he and his friend will have sandwiches on a low flat table, when he will describe his fear of growing old and unloved and his friend will nod gently, when the rain will slide down the glass of the window. [. . .]

22 June 1905

It is graduation day at Agassiz Gymnasium. One hundred twenty-nine boys in white shirts and brown ties stand on marble steps and fidget in the sun while the headmaster reads out their names. On the front lawn, parents and relatives listen halfheartedly, stare at the ground, doze in their chairs. The valedictorian delivers his address in a monotone. He smiles weakly when handed his medal and drops it in a bush after the ceremony. No one congratulates him. The boys, their mothers, fathers, sisters walk listlessly to houses on Amthausgasse and Aarstrasse, or to the waiting benches near the Bahnhofplatz, sit after the noon meal, play cards to pass time, nap. Dress clothes are folded and put away for another occasion. At the end of the summer, some of the boys go to university in Berne or in Zürich, some work in their fathers' businesses, some travel to Germany or France in search of a job. These passages take place indifferently, mechanically, like the back-and-forth swing of a pendulum, like a chess game in which each move is forced. For in this world, the future is fixed.

This is a world in which time is not fluid, parting to make way for events. Instead, time is a rigid, bonelike structure, extending infinitely ahead and behind, fossilizing the future as well as the past. Every action, every thought, every breath of wind, every flight of birds is completely determined, forever.

In the performing hall of the Stadttheater, a ballerina moves across the stage and takes to the air. She hangs for a moment and then alights on the floor. *Saut, batterie, saut.* Legs cross and flutter, arms unfold into an open arch. Now she prepares for a *pirouette*, right leg moving back to fourth position, pushing off on one foot, arms coming in to speed the turn. She is precision. She is a clock. In her mind, while she dances, she thinks she should have floated a little on one leap, but she cannot float because her movements are not hers. Every interaction of her body with floor or with space is predetermined to a

billionth of an inch. There is no room to float. To float would indicate a slight uncertainty, while there is no uncertainty. And so she moves around the stage with clocklike inevitability, makes no unexpected leaps or dares, touches down precisely on the chalk, does not dream of unplanned *cabrioles.*

In a world of fixed future, life is an infinite corridor of rooms, one room lit at each moment, the next room dark but prepared. We walk from room to room, look into the room that is lit, the present moment, then walk on. We do not know the rooms ahead, but we know we cannot change them. We are spectators of our lives.

The chemist who works at the pharmaceutical on Kochergasse walks through the town on his afternoon break. He stops at the shop selling clocks on Marktgasse, buys a sandwich at the bakery next door, continues toward the woods and the river. He owes his friend money but prefers to buy himself presents. As he walks, admiring his new coat, he decides he can pay his friend back the next year, or perhaps never at all. And who can blame him? In a world of fixed future, there can be no right or wrong. Right and wrong demand freedom of choice, but if each action is already chosen, there can be no freedom of choice. In a world of fixed future, no person is responsible. The rooms are already arranged. The chemist thinks all these thoughts as he steps along the path through the Brunngasshalde and breathes the moist air of the forest. He almost permits himself a smile, so pleased is he at his decision. He breathes the moist air and feels oddly free to do as he pleases, free in a world without freedom. [. . .]

27 June 1905

Every Tuesday, a middle-aged man brings stones from the quarry east of Berne to the masonry on Hodlerstrasse. He has a wife, two children grown and gone, a tubercular brother who lives in Berlin. He wears a gray wool coat in all seasons, works in the quarry until after dark, has dinner with his wife and goes to bed, tends his garden on Sundays. And on Tuesday mornings, he loads his truck with stones and comes to town.

When he comes, he stops on Marktgasse to purchase flour and sugar. He spends a half-hour sitting quietly in the back pew of St. Vincent's. He stops at the Post Bureau to send a letter to Berlin. And as he passes people on the street, his eyes are on the ground. Some people know him, try to catch his eye or say hello. He mumbles and walks on. Even when he delivers his stones to Hodlerstrasse, he cannot look the mason in the eye. Instead, he looks aside, he talks to the wall in answer to the mason's friendly chatter, he stands in a corner while his stones are weighed.

Forty years ago in school, one afternoon in March, he urinated in class. He could not hold it in. Afterwards, he tried to stay in his chair, but the other boys saw the puddle and made him walk around the room, round and round. They pointed at the wet spot on his pants and howled. That day the sunlight looked like streams of milk as it poured whitely through the windows and spilled onto the floorboards of the room. Two dozen jackets hung from hooks beside the door. Chalk marks stretched across the blackboard, the names of Europe's capitals. The desks had swivel tops and drawers. His had "Johann" carved in the upper right. The air was moist and close from the steam pipes. A clock with big red hands read 2:15. And the boys hooted at him, hooted at him as they chased him around the room, with the wet spot on his pants. They hooted and called him "bladder baby, bladder baby, bladder baby."

That memory has become his life. When he wakes up in the morning, he is the boy who urinated in his pants. When he passes people on the street, he knows they see the wet spot on his pants. He glances at his pants and looks away. When his children visit, he stays within his room

and talks to them through the door. He is the boy who could not hold it in.

But what is the past? Could it be, the firmness of the past is just illusion? Could the past be a kaleidoscope, a pattern of images that shift with each disturbance of a sudden breeze, a laugh, a thought? And if the shift is everywhere, how would we know?

In a world of shifting past, one morning the quarryman awakes and is no more the boy who could not hold it in. That afternoon in March long gone was just another afternoon. On that afternoon forgotten, he sat in class, recited when the teacher called him, went skating with the other boys after school. Now he owns a quarry. He has nine suits of clothes. He buys fine pottery for his wife and takes long walks with her on Sunday afternoons. He visits friends on Amthausgasse and Aarstrasse, smiles at them and shakes their hand. He sponsors concerts at the Casino.

One morning he wakes up and . . .

As the sun rises over the city, ten thousand people yawn and take their toast and coffee. Ten thousand fill the arcades of Kramgasse or go to work on Speichergasse or take their children to the park. Each has memories: a father who could not love his child, a brother who always won, a lover with a delicious kiss, a moment of cheating on a school examination, the stillness spreading from a fresh snowfall, the publication of a poem. In a world of shifting past, these memories are wheat in wind, fleeting dreams, shapes in clouds. Events, once happened, lose reality, alter with a glance, a storm, a night. In time, the past never happened. But who could know? Who could know that the past is not as solid as this instant, when the sun streams over the Bernese Alps and the shopkeepers sing as they raise their awnings and the quarryman begins to load his truck.

Chapter 11

A. N. Prior

THANK GOODNESS THAT'S OVER

In a pair of very important papers, namely "Space, Time and Individuals" (STI) in the *Journal of Philosophy* for October 1955 and "The Indestructibility and Immutability of Substances" (IIS) in *Philosophical Studies* for April 1956, Professor N. L. Wilson began something which badly needed beginning, namely the construction of a logically rigorous "substance-language" in which we talk about enduring and changing individuals as we do in common speech, as opposed to the "space-time" language favoured by very many mathematical logicians, perhaps most notably by Quine. This enterprise of Wilson's is one with which I could hardly sympathize more heartily than I do; and one wishes for this logically rigorous "substance-language" not only when one is reading Quine but also when one is reading many other people. How fantastic it is, for instance, that Kotarbinski[1] should call his metaphysics "Reism" when the very last kind of entity it has room for is *things*—instead of them it just has the world-lines or life-histories of things; "four-dimensional worms", as Wilson says. Wilson, moreover, has at least one point of superiority to another rebel against space-time talk, P. F. Strawson; namely he (Wilson) does seriously attempt to meet formalism with formalism—to show that logical rigour is not a monopoly of the other side. At another point, however, Strawson seems to me to see further than Wilson; he (Strawson) is aware that substance-talk cannot be carried on without

tenses, whereas Wilson tries (vainly, as I hope to show) to do without them. Wilson, in short, has indeed brought us out of Egypt; but as yet has us still wandering about the Sinai Peninsula; the Promised Land is a little further on than he has taken us.

From this point on, then, I shall be quarrelling with Wilson, but from what has just been said I hope it will be clear that this is a dispute between allies—I want Wilson (with any Wilsonians there may be) to go further in a direction in which he has already started to go, for I do not think the place where he has left us is or can be a real resting-place. From such a place as that, we must either go forwards or go back.[2]

First let me sketch Wilson's position more fully, and mainly in his own words. Early (p. 592) in the paper STI, he says that when we pass from a space-time language to a substance-language, "the time determinant is shifted across the copula of empirical sentences from subject to predicate". Later (p. 594) he explains what he means by this. "In our S-T language", he says, "we might record a simple matter of fact in a sentence like the following:" (here he gives the Russellian for "The x such that x occupies u_1, u_1, u_1, t_1, is blue"). "In substance-language we might say:

"a is blue at (time) t_1, where the copula 'is' is used tenselessly". And again (p. 597) he says that "the simplest kind of empirical statement in substance-language" is one of the form "a has the quality Q_1 at time t_1". "It is so obvious, so necessary", he goes on, "that if Philip is drunk, Philip is drunk *at some time*, that if Scott wrote *Waverley*, he wrote it *during some period*—it is so obvious and necessary, that in ordinary language we generally drop the 'at some time' and are left with the simple, the *too* simple, noun-copula-adjective form of sentence". ("Perfidious ordinary language!" he adds in parentheses at this point). Much of this is repeated in IIS. At the end of this (p. 48) Wilson says that although it may be true that a thing "changes qualitatively and is numerically the same", e.g. "if a leaf is green in August and red in September it is still *that* leaf", yet nevertheless "a 'complete' property of an individual is a compound, temporalized (or dated) property, like *being green in August* 1955 or *being born in* 1769, and there is no question of an individual changing in the sense of once having and later lacking one of these compound properties."

This last conclusion should in itself have been enough to frighten him. From this leaf whose "complete" properties never change, to the pure "four-dimensional worm" of Quine, Kotarbinski, etc., is surely a very short step indeed. And this "substance-language" goes wrong at the end because it goes wrong at the start. Wilson's basic sentence-form is "S is P", and his idea appears to be that you get from a space-time language to a substance-language by exchanging "S-at-t is P" for "S is P-at-t"; in this way the "t" "crosses the copula", which is thought of as a sort of bridge between S and P. But if the "is" in these two forms is tenseless, as Wilson explicitly says that it is, I cannot see what the difference between them amounts to. "S-at-t is P" presumably means that that part of the four-dimensional worm S which has the time co-ordinate t, is P; what else "S is P-at-t" could mean, i.e. what it means if it does not mean that S is P in the stretch of it specified by t, I cannot imagine. I can, indeed, see something different in the form "S *was* P at t", e.g. "The leaf was green in August"; but here "In August" is only

intelligible as an answer to the question "*When was* the leaf green?", not as an answer to the question "In what way is (was) it green?", "What sort of green is (was) it?". The thing then means, not "The leaf was green-in-August" but "The leaf was-in-August green". The t in fact has not "crossed the copula" but stopped *at* the copula; though it seems to me that this bridge theory of the copula is wrong anyway. Write "The leaf is green" in the modern way as "ϕx"; here "x" denotes the leaf, "ϕ" means "is-green", and there is no copula needed, but if we want one we can put "S" for "It is the case that—" before the whole, i.e. in the place where we would put "N" or a tilde for "It is not the case that——" if we wanted to construct a negative proposition. Then we can think of "at t" as neither moving across the copula to the predicate nor staying with the copula on the way to the predicate, but as moving across the predicate to the copula, and changing "It is the case that——" to "It was the case in August that——".

A parallel case will, I think, make the matter clear. A person, call him Owen, who is colourblind, might see this leaf as green when it is in fact red. The leaf, we might than say, looks green to Owen; i.e. though it is not the case that, it does appear to Owen that, the leaf is green. And some philosophers would want to replace this by "is green-to-Owen", abolishing the explicit reference to looking or seeming in the same way as Wilson abolishes the explicit tense. But as in the other case, the supposed abolition is only a disguise. "To Owen" is intelligible as an answer to the question "To whom does it look green?"; as a description of the kind of green the leaf is, or of the kind of green leaf it is, "green-to-Owen" is just nothing at all. Unless, indeed, we mean by calling it "green-to-Owen" that the leaf is green where it is turned *towards* Owen—green on that side of it. And we might give "green-in-August" a similar sense—we might mean that that part of the leaf which is in August (like "that part of it which faces Owen") is green; but then it cannot be really a *leaf* that we are talking about, for it is not leaves but their world-lines that have parts of that sort. We are, in short, back in Pharaoh's House, with S-at-t being P.

I do not, however, want to make a difference where there is none; and in particular I do not wish to deny that there is such a property as that of *having been green in August* as well as the property of *being green*, i.e. being green now; nor even, for that matter, that there is such a property as *looking green to Owen* as well as that of *being green*, i.e. being green really. I only insist (*a*) that what is now in question with this leaf is not a property of *being green in August* which attaches to it tenselessly, but a property of *having been* green in August which attaches to it *now*; and (*b*) that having been green in August is not a way of being green now (I am not writing in August); (*c*) that neither is it a way of being green timelessly—there is in fact *no* way of being green timelessly (as Wilson very truly says, Philip cannot be drunk without being drunk at some time; and neither can a leaf be green without being green at some time); and (*d*) that the *internal* punctuation of "having been green in August" is "having-in-August been green", not "having been green-in-August". Putting it yet another way: A leaf that was green in August is one sort of formerly-green leaf (because "in August" is one sort of "formerly"); but a formerly-green leaf is not one sort of green leaf. Indeed in common parlance being formerly-green and being green are often *inconsistent*—the "formerly green" is precisely that which *is not* green but *was* green, just as a *soi-disant* philosopher is precisely someone who *is not* a philosopher but *says he is* one. And, of course, a leaf which is merely "green-to-Owen" is precisely one which *is not* green but seems to that person to be so.[3]

This is perhaps the most suitable point at which to consider a very strange argument put forward by Wilson in IIS, p. 47 on the subject of identity: "When we say that the individual who wrote *Marmion* in 1807 is identical with the individual who wrote *Waverley* in 1814, we are not saying that the individuals are identical in 1807

or in 1814. They are identical outside of time, as it were. *Dates cannot be significantly associated with the identity sign*". (Italics Wilson's.) In this passage perhaps more than any other we see the incompleteness of Wilson's emancipation from space-time language. Certainly to say in 1955 or 6 that *X* and *Y* (not "were" but) "are" identical in 1807, is to say something that grates upon the ear and the mind intolerably; but that is not what Wilson means, for it is clear from his conclusion that he would object equally to the result of repairing his syntax by due attention to tenses. If we do this, we will say that the individual who wrote *Marmion* in 1807 was not then identical with the individual who had written *Waverley* in 1814 because at that time (1807) nobody at all had written *Waverley*, or done either that or anything else in 1814. Was he identical, then, with the individual who *was going to* write *Waverley* in 1814? This, I admit, is a tricky one, but only because indeterminism makes me wonder whether there was yet any such individual; the question is not actually improper. Leaving that for the other date: the individual who had written *Marmion* in 1807 was certainly identical in 1814 with the individual who was then writing *Waverley*, and after that with the individual who had written *Waverley*. But Wilson does not want to say any of these things: he wants to say that the author of *Marmion* and the author of *Waverley* are "identical outside of time", whatever that might be.

I cannot help thinking that Wilson is worried here about the relation between Scott-in-1807 and Scott-in-1814—there they are, separated for ever by seven years, and yet somehow the same person; but *when* can they be the same person?— clearly nowhen. But of course Scott-in-1807 and Scott-in-1814 aren't persons at all; they are year-thick slices of a four-dimensional worm (as Wilson says, "S-at-t" is a description from the space-time language, not from substance-language); and as they are distinct slices, there is no time whatever at which they are identical. Had he really left these 4-D worms behind—Scott-in-1807, Scott-in-1814, *and* Scott-from-his-birth-to-his-death (equally a no-person, a by-product of mispunctuating sentences like "Scott, from his birth to his death, lived in the Northern Hemisphere")—and learnt again to talk simply about Scott, it is hard to see how this strange talk of identity-outside-time, in an enduring object, could have arisen.

Wilson also says on p. 47 of IIS that existence is not datable, but is "a simple something or other which Napoleon simply has and Pegasus (for example) simply lacks". This will surely not do; but before saying anything more about it let me interpose a *peccavi*. I have suggested elsewhere that just as there were no facts about me before I existed (not even this fact of there being no facts about me; though of course there is *now* the past-tense fact of there having been none then), so there will be no facts about me after my existence ends (if it does end). And my ground for saying this was the very weak one that if some facts about a thing imply that it still exists and some do not, nobody can state with any precision where to draw the line between these two classes of facts.[4]

This situation is not in fact anything like as hard for the logician as I made out. For he can use special variables f, g, etc. for predicates entailing existence (call them E-predicates) without committing himself as to what these predicates are; and he can lay it down that E-predicates are predicates, substitutable for the usual predicate-variables ϕ, ψ, etc., and functions of E-predicates like Nf ("—does not f") and Pf ("—has f'd in the past") are likewise predicates, substitutable for ϕ, ψ, etc., but these last (Nf, Pf, etc.) are not themselves E-predicates, substitutable for f, g, etc. Then we can say that there are facts about Napoleon still, e.g. the fact that no E-predicates apply to him now; and this not being itself an E-predicate, there is no contradiction in so speaking.[5]

So there is indeed a sort of "being" that Napoleon has even after having ceased to "exist"; he is at least a subject of predicates still, and cannot now ever cease to be that. But there is nothing

timeless about this. For one thing, even this "being" of Napoleon, i.e. there being facts about him, is something that had a beginning (when *he* had a beginning).[6] And for another thing, even now this fact that there are facts about Napoleon is not a timeless but a present (and abiding) one.

Turning now to a fundamental: I'm a symbol-man rather than an ordinary-speech man myself, but I can see what the ordinary-speech men are worried about when I find Wilson crying "Perfidy!" at locutions which in fact constitute a more coherent and smoothed-out substance-language than his own. His chief quarrel with ordinary speech is, as he says, that it omits dates; but it is misleading to treat this as pretending to do without a time-reference. I do not know how it is with Wilson, but half the time I personally have forgotten what the date is, and have to look it up or ask somebody when I need it for writing cheques, etc.; yet even in this perpetual dateless haze one somehow communicates, one makes oneself understood, and with time-references too. One says, e.g. "Thank goodness that's over!", and not only is this, when said, quite clear without any date appended, but it says something which it is impossible that any use of a tenseless copula with a date should convey. It certainly doesn't mean the same as, e.g. "Thank goodness the date of the conclusion of that thing is Friday, June 15, 1954", even if it be said then. (Nor, for that matter, does it mean "Thank goodness the conclusion of that thing is contemporaneous with this utterance". Why should anyone thank goodness for that?)

Wilson seems to have the notion that a tensed copula is analysable into a tenseless one plus a date (which once obtained can be transferred to any other part of the proposition that we fancy); but the above example is sufficient to refute this assumption. The fact is that propositions with dates are just *not* "the simplest empirical propositions", but are highly sophisticated propositions; well, medium sophisticated—an essential prelude, though only a prelude, to space-time talk. Just the bricks, in fact, for building half-way houses.

Notes

1 T. Kotarbinski, "The Fundamental Ideas of Pansomatism", *Mind*, October 1955, p. 488. Cf. also C. Lejewski, "Proper Names", Arist. Soc. Supp. Vol. XXXI (1957), pp. 253–4, and papers there cited.

2 In thus asking for consistency above all else, I am consciously echoing J. J. C. Smart's note on "Spatializing Time" in *Mind* for April 1955. Smart's strictures upon those on his own side—the Quine-Kotarbinski side—who talk about "consciousness crawling up world-lines" may be compared with what is said here.

3 Cf. P. T. Geach on *alienans* adjectives in "Good and Evil", *Analysis*, December 1956, p. 33.

4 A. N. Prior, *Time and Modality* (1957), p. 31. My present modification of the position there stated owes much to P. T. Geach's criticism in the *Cambridge Review*, May 4, 1957, p. 543.

5 There is an instructive discussion of E-predicates and others in Walter Burleigh's *De Puritate Artis Logicae Tractatus Longior*, Franciscan Institute edition (1955), pp. 57–8.

6 I'm not taking that part back; nor the view that some statements have not always been statable. Nothing can be surer than that whereof we cannot speak thereof we must be silent; but this does not mean that whereof we could not have spoken yesterday thereof we must be silent today.

Chapter 12

Ned Markosian

A DEFENSE OF PRESENTISM

1. Introduction

Presentism is the view that only present objects exist.[1] According to Presentism, if we were to make an accurate list of all the things that exist—i.e. a list of all the things that our most unrestricted quantifiers range over—there would be not a single non-present object on the list. Thus, you and I and the Taj Mahal would be on the list, but neither Socrates nor any future grandchildren of mine would be included.[2] And it's not just Socrates and my future grandchildren—the same goes for any other putative object that lacks the property of being present. All such objects are unreal, according to Presentism. According to Non-presentism, on the other hand, non-present objects like Socrates and my future grandchildren exist right now, even though they are not currently present.[3] We may not be able to see them at the moment, on this view, and they may not be in the same space–time vicinity that we find ourselves in right now, but they should nevertheless be on the list of all existing things.

I endorse Presentism, which, it seems to me, is the "common sense" view, i.e. the one that the average person on the street would accept. But there are some serious problems facing Presentism. In particular, there are certain embarrassingly obvious objections to the view that are not easily gotten around. The aims of this paper are (i) to spell out the most obvious objections that can be raised against Presentism, and (ii) to show that these objections are not fatal to the view. In section 2 I will spell out the embarrassing problems facing Presentism that I will be concerned with, and in Section 3 I will consider various possible solutions to those problems, rejecting some but endorsing others.

2. Problems for Presentism

2.1 Singular Propositions and Non-present Objects

One of the most obvious problems facing Presentism concerns singular propositions about non-present objects.[4] A singular proposition depends for its existence on the individual object(s) it is about. Thus, Presentism entails that there are no singular propositions about non-present objects.[5]

This is a very counterintuitive consequence. Most of us would have thought that there are many propositions about specific non-present objects (like Socrates, for example). And it seems clear that a proposition that is specifically about a non-present object would count as a singular proposition about the object. Thus, it is natural to think that sentence (1), for example, expresses a singular proposition about Socrates:

(1) Socrates was a philosopher.

Similarly, most of us would have thought that we often believe singular propositions about non-present objects, like the proposition that is apparently expressed by (1).

But according to Presentism, there are never any singular propositions about non-present objects, and hence no sentence ever expresses any such proposition, and no person ever believes any such proposition. This is surely a strange consequence of Presentism.[6]

Here is a variation on the same problem. Consider the time when Socrates ceased to be present. According to Presentism, Socrates went out of existence at that time. Thus, according to Presentism, all singular propositions about Socrates also went out of existence at that time. Now consider someone—Glaucon, say—who knew Socrates, and believed various singular propositions about him in the period right before Socrates ceased to be present, but who was unaware of Socrates's unfortunate demise. When Socrates ceased to be present and thereby popped out of existence, according to Presentism, all of those singular propositions about him also popped out of existence. But there was poor Glaucon, who we can suppose did not change in any important intrinsic way when Socrates ceased to be present. According to Presentism, although Glaucon did not change in any significant intrinsic way when Socrates ceased to be present, he nevertheless did undergo a very important change right at that moment: Glaucon all of a sudden went from believing all of those singular propositions about Socrates to not believing any of them—through no fault of his own, and without any knowledge that his beliefs were changing in such a dramatic way! Isn't that a strange and absurd consequence of the view?

2.2 Relations between Present and Non-present Objects

There is more. If there are no non-present objects, then no one can now stand in any relation to any non-present object. Thus, for example, you cannot now stand in the *admires* relation to Socrates; I cannot now stand in the *grandson* relation to my paternal grandfather; and no event today can stand in any causal relation to George Washington's crossing the Delaware. These are all fairly counterintuitive consequences of Presentism, and it must be acknowledged that they pose serious problems for the view.[7]

2.3 Presentism and Special Relativity

A third challenge for Presentism comes from an empirical theory in physics, namely, the Special Theory of Relativity. It is apparently a consequence of that theory that there is no such thing as absolute simultaneity, and this suggests that which things are *present* is a relativistic matter that can vary from one reference frame to another. This in turn suggests that the Presentist is committed to the claim that what *exists* is a relativistic matter, so that it may well be the case that Socrates exists relative to your frame of reference but does not exist relative to my frame of reference. This would surely be an untenable consequence of the view.

2.4 Past and Future Times

Here is the fourth embarrassing problem for Presentism that I will discuss in this paper. It is very natural to talk about times. We often speak as if times are genuine entities, and we often appear to express propositions about times. But Presentism seems to entail that there is no time except the present time. Thus, Presentism also seems to entail that there are no propositions about any non-present times, and that we never say anything about any such times. These would be very odd consequences of Presentism, to say the least. If they are indeed consequences of the view, then some account of why they are not completely unacceptable is needed. And if they are not consequences of the view, then some explanation of this fact is required.

3. Presentist Solutions to These Problems

3.1 Non-existent Objects that Have Properties and Stand in Relations

Let me begin my discussion of responses to these problems by mentioning some possible solutions that I do not endorse. One response available to the Presentist for dealing with both the problem of singular propositions about non-present objects and the problem of relations between present and non-present objects (and perhaps the problem of past and future times as well) involves a view that has been advocated by Mark Hinchliff.[8] Hinchliff distinguishes between *Serious Presentism* and *Unrestricted Presentism*. Serious Presentism is the conjunction of Presentism with the claim that an object can have properties, and stand in relations, only when it exists, while Unrestricted Presentism is the conjunction of Presentism with the claim that an object can have properties, and stand in relations, even at times when it does not exist.

Thus, according to Unrestricted Presentism, Socrates can now have properties like *having been a philosopher*, and can stand in the *admired by* relation to me, even though he no longer exists. Moreover, according to Unrestricted Presentism, we can now express singular propositions about Socrates (such as the proposition expressed by (1)), even though Socrates does not exist.

There is a great deal to be said for this response to our problems. But the response comes with a price—namely, accepting the claim that an object can have properties, and can stand in relations, at a time when it does not exist—that I personally am not willing to pay. That is, my pre-philosophical intuitions commit me not only to Presentism but also to Serious Presentism. This is of course not meant to be an argument against Unrestricted Presentism. But it does mean that the response to these two problems that is available to the Unrestricted Presentist is not available to me.

3.2 No Singular Propositions

Another solution available to the Presentist for dealing with the problem of singular propositions about non-present objects would be simply to deny that there are any singular propositions about concrete objects in the first place. I don't know of any Presentist who adopts this position specifically for the purpose of defending Presentism, but the view that there are no singular propositions about concrete objects has been discussed by Chisholm (who was in fact a Presentist) and various others.[9] One who says that there are no singular propositions about concrete objects at all will have to give an account of sentences that seem to express singular propositions about such objects, like the following.

(2)   Peter van Inwagen is a philosopher.

For example, such a person could say that (2) expresses the same general proposition as

(2a) $(\exists x)$ (x is the referent of "Peter van Inwagen" and x is a philosopher).

Instead of involving van Inwagen himself, or referring directly to him, this proposition involves the property of being the referent of "Peter van Inwagen" (as well as the property of being a philosopher and the relation of coinstantiation).

If the Presentist insists that there are no singular propositions about concrete objects at all, not even singular propositions about present concrete objects, then he or she can say that there is nothing peculiar about maintaining that sentences that appear to express singular propositions about past or future concrete objects really express general propositions about the way things were or will be. For on this view, even when Socrates was present the sentence

(3)   Socrates is a philosopher

did not express any singular proposition about

Socrates. Instead, it expressed some general proposition, such as the one expressed by the following sentence.

(3a) (∃x) (x is the referent of "Socrates" and x is a philosopher).

Thus, there is nothing odd about saying that (1) does not now express a singular proposition about Socrates. Instead, the Presentist might say, what (1) really expresses is the past-tensed version of the proposition expressed by (3a), which proposition can be more perspicuously expressed by the following sentence (in which "P" is the past-tense sentential operator, short for "it has been the case that").

(1a) P(∃x) (x is the referent of "Socrates" and x is a philosopher).

Similarly, a Presentist who does not believe in singular propositions about concrete objects in the first place will say that there was no immediate change in Glaucon's beliefs brought about by Socrates's ceasing to be present, since all of Glaucon's beliefs "about" Socrates involved purely general propositions all along.

Unfortunately, however, this no-singular-propositions-about-concrete-objects strategy is not appealing to me, for one main reason: it presupposes a controversial thesis—that there are no singular propositions about concrete objects—that I am not willing to endorse. It seems pretty clear to me that there are in fact singular propositions about existing concrete objects (such as the singular propositions that Peter van Inwagen is a philosopher), that many sentences express such propositions, and that many of us often believe such propositions.

3.3 Singular Propositions with Blanks

Another response to the problem of singular propositions about non-present objects would involve appealing to a view about empty names

that has been developed by Kaplan, Adams and Stecker, Braun, Salmon, and Oppy.[10] I cannot do justice to the view in question in the limited space I have here, but the basic idea is that a sentence with an empty name in it, like "Harry Potter wears glasses", expresses just the kind of singular proposition that a similar sentence with a normal name (such as "Woody Allen wears glasses") expresses, except that the singular proposition expressed by the sentence with the empty name contains a blank where the other singular proposition contains an individual.[11] A Presentist who took this line could say that sentences like (1) do indeed express singular propositions, albeit singular propositions with blanks in them rather than ordinary singular propositions.

Although I think that there is a lot to be said for the singular-propositions-with-blanks view as a theory about empty names, I do not think that the view is of much use to the Presentist when it comes to our current problem. The reason is that combining Presentism with the singular-propositions-with-blanks view yields the result that the sentences "Socrates was a philosopher" and "Beethoven was a philosopher" express the same singular proposition (namely, the singular proposition that _____ was a philosopher). And if the goal of the Presentist is to give some account of sentences like (1) that has plausible consequences regarding the meanings and truth values of those sentences, this result will clearly not do.

3.4 Haecceities to the Rescue?

A fourth strategy for dealing with the problem of singular propositions about non-present objects would be to appeal to unexemplified *haecceities*. Haecceities are supposed to be properties like the property of being identical to Socrates, each of which can be exemplified only by one unique object. Those who believe in haecceities typically believe that a haecceity comes into existence with its object, and continues to exist as long as it is exemplified by that object. That much is relatively uncontroversial. But some Presentists also believe that a haecceity continues to exist even after its object ceases to exist. On this view, which has been defended by Robert Adams, there is a property—Socrates's haecceity, which we might call "Socraticity"—that came into existence with Socrates and was uniquely exemplified by Socrates, and that continues to exist today, even though it is no longer exemplified.[12] Thus, according to Adams, sentences like (1) do express singular propositions about the relevant concrete objects after all, even though those concrete objects no longer exist. The idea is that a sentence like (1) now expresses the proposition that there was a unique x who exemplified Socraticity and who was a philosopher, and that this proposition somehow involves or directly refers to Socrates, in virtue of having Socraticity as a constituent. (It is worth noting here that Adams believes in unexemplified haecceities of past objects, but not of future objects. Thus, Adams's version of the haecceity approach purports to solve the problem of singular propositions about non-present objects for the case of past objects but not for the case of future objects. On his view, there are no singular propositions about future objects.)

Unfortunately, there are several problems with the haecceity approach. One problem with the approach, at least as it is defended by Adams, is that, although it allows us to say that there are now singular propositions about past objects, like Socrates, it does not allow us to say that there are now any singular propositions about future objects, like my first grandson.[13] Thus, Adams's version of the haecceity approach to the problem of singular propositions about non-present objects involves an important asymmetry between the past and the future. And it seems to me that any adequate Presentist solution to the problem should treat the past and the future as perfectly analogous.[14]

A second, and more serious, problem with the haecceity approach is that it requires an ontological commitment to the haecceities of non-existent objects, and the claim that there are such things is a controversial claim that many Presentists, including myself, are not willing to accept. If we are to understand Socraticity as the property of being identical to Socrates, for example, then it seems that Socrates must be a constituent of Socraticity. But in that case, it's hard to see how Socraticity could continue to exist after Socrates goes out of existence.[15]

A third problem facing the haecceity approach is that it is not at all clear that the proposition that there was a unique x that exemplified Socraticity and that was a philosopher is really a singular proposition about Socrates. That is, it's not clear that this proposition involves or refers to Socrates directly. Consider the proposition that there was a unique x that was Plato's best teacher and that was a philosopher. That proposition is not a singular proposition about Socrates. And it seems to me that these two propositions are alike in this respect, so that if the one is not a singular proposition about Socrates then neither is the other. After all, what is the difference between Socraticity and the property of being Plato's best teacher in virtue of which a proposition containing the former property is a singular proposition about Socrates while a proposition containing the latter property is not?

Finally, there is a fourth problem with this approach which combines the second and third problems to generate a dilemma for the haecceity approach. Either the proposition that there was a unique x that exemplified Socraticity and that was a philosopher is really a singular proposition about Socrates, or it is not. If it is not, then the haecceity approach has not given us a singular proposition about Socrates. And if it is, then that must be because there is something special about Socraticity in virtue of which propositions containing it are singular propositions about Socrates, whereas propositions containing the property of being Plato's best teacher are not. But it seems like the only feature that Socraticity could have to give it this distinction is having

Socrates himself as a constituent. And in that case, it looks like Socraticity cannot exist without Socrates after all.

3.5 Paraphrasing

Accepting (i) the view that there can be singular propositions about non-existent objects, or (ii) the view that there are no singular propositions at all, or (iii) the singular-propositions-with-blanks view, or (iv) the view that there are unexemplified haecceities that can "stand in" for non-present, concrete objects in singular propositions about those objects would allow the Presentist to solve the problem of singular propositions about non-present objects in a more or less straightforward way.[16] But as I have said, none of these strategies will work for me. A fifth strategy for dealing with the problem of singular propositions about non-present objects involves the technique of paraphrasing sentences that seem to be about non-present objects into purely general past-and future-tensed sentences.[17] We have already encountered this technique above, when we considered paraphrasing

(1)   Socrates was a philosopher

as

(1a)   P($\exists$x)(x is the referent of "Socrates" and x is a philosopher).

The idea is that, once Socrates ceases to be present and thereby goes out of existence, according to Presentism, (1) has the same meaning as (1a). That is, once Socrates ceases to be present, (1) ceases to express a singular proposition about Socrates. Instead, according to this line of thought, (1) begins at that point to express the general proposition expressed by (1a).

This paraphrasing approach differs from the no-singular-propositions approach in that, on the paraphrasing approach, it is admitted that there are singular propositions about present objects; the claim on this approach is that, once an object ceases to be present, all singular propositions about it go out of existence, so that sentences about it—like (1) in the case of Socrates—must then be understood in some other way, as suggested by (1a). The paraphrasing approach also differs from the haecceity approach in that it does not entail the existence of any controversial items such as unexemplified haecceities.

But the paraphrasing approach is not without its own problems.[18] Perhaps the main difficulty with this approach is that the relevant paraphrases just don't seem to have the same meanings as the originals. For example, (1) seems to be about a man, while (1a) seems to be about a name. Also, (1) has the form of a sentence that expresses a singular proposition, while (1a) has the form of a sentence that expresses a general proposition. Moreover, it seems pretty clear that (1) did not have the same meaning as (1a) back when Socrates was still present,[19] and it would be strange to say that the two sentences differed in meaning at one time and then had exactly the same meaning at a later time, even though (we can assume) there were no changes in the interpretation of the relevant language between those two times.[20]

3.6 Indirect Relations Between Present and Non-present Objects

We will return to the problem of singular propositions about non-present objects, and consider a variation on the paraphrasing strategy, below. First, however, let us consider two strategies that I want to endorse for dealing with the problem of relations between present and non-present objects. The first strategy I have in mind involves insisting that there never really are relations between objects that are not contemporaneous, but trying to accommodate our intuition that there are by appealing to various other truths that are "in the ballpark". The strategy will also involve pointing out that the fact that there cannot be direct relations between two objects at a time when one of those objects is not present, and hence does not exist, is an instance of a more general phenomenon. The more general phenomenon occurs whenever we are inclined to say that two things stand in some relation to one another even though they do not both exist.

For example, we are inclined to say that Chelsea Clinton stands in the *sibling* relation to her possible brother, who does not exist.[21] Since there really is no possible brother for Chelsea to be related to, it is not literally true that she stands in the sibling relation to any such person. But we can capture what is true about this case with a sentence in which the relevant existential quantifier lies within the scope of a modal operator, like the following (where the diamond is the modal operator standing for "it is possible that"):

(4) $\Diamond(\exists x)$(x is a brother of Chelsea).

Because the existential quantifier in (4) lies within the scope of a modal operator, (4) does not entail the actual existence of any possible brother of Chelsea. For this reason, (4) is acceptable even to the Actualist, who can say that, although it is not literally true that Chelsea stands in the sibling relation to her possible brother, there is nevertheless a literal truth in the ballpark that we can point to in order to justify our intuition that Chelsea does stand in that relation to some possible brother.

Similarly, the Presentist can maintain, when we are inclined to say that a present object stands in some relation to a non-present object, as in the case of my grandfather and myself, that the thing we are inclined to say is not literally true. But in such a case, the Presentist can maintain, there is nevertheless a general truth in the ballpark that is literally true, and that we can point to in justifying our intuition. In the case of my grandfather, we can express this general truth with a sentence in which the relevant existential

quantifier lies within the scope of a tense operator, like the following:

(5) $P(\exists x)$(x is the grandfather of Ned).

A similar technique will work even in a case in which the two objects in question never existed at the same time. For example, when we are inclined to say that I stand in the *great-great-grandson of* relation to my great-great-grandfather, the Presentist can appeal to the following sentence, which is literally true:

(6) $P(\exists x)$[x is the grandfather of Ned and $P(\exists y)$(y is the grandfather of x)].[22]

The matter is more complicated in the case of *causal* relations among entities that are never contemporaneous, but I see no reason not to think that the same basic strategy will work even in such cases. Here is a very brief sketch of one way in which the indirect relations approach could be applied to the case of causal relations among non-contemporaneous events. It is natural to think that events generally take some time to occur, and also that direct causal relations between events always involve events that are contemporaneous for at least some period of time. If we grant these assumptions, then it will turn out that, whenever we want to say that one event, e_1, causes another, much later event, e_{23}, there will be a causal chain of linking events connecting e_1 and e_{23}, such that each adjacent pair of events in the chain will be contemporaneous for at least some period of time.[23]

3.7 Similarities between Time and Modality; Differences between Time and Space

Some may feel that this approach still leaves something to be desired, however, since it remains true, even according to the Presentist who takes this line, that there is still no direct relation between me and my grandfather. Also, it looks as if the type of account exemplified by (6) won't work when we want to say that I stand in the *admires* relation to Socrates. This is where the second strategy that I want to endorse for dealing with the problem of relations between present and non-present objects comes in. The second strategy involves emphasizing fundamental similarities between time and modality while at the same time emphasizing fundamental differences between time and space. The claim that putative objects like Socrates, my grandfather, and my future grandchildren do not really exist, and can neither feature in singular propositions nor stand in direct relations to existing objects, is much less counterintuitive on the assumption that time is fundamentally like modality and fundamentally unlike the dimensions of space. But it can be plausibly argued that this is in fact the case. In fact, Prior and others have argued for the first part of this claim (time's fundamental similarity to modality);[24] and Prior, myself, and others have argued for the second part (time's fundamental dissimilarity to the dimensions of space).[25] Thus, according to this line of thought, putative non-present objects like Socrates and the others have more in common with putative non-actual objects like Santa Claus than they have in common with objects that are located elsewhere in space, like Alpha Centauri. It's very plausible to say that, although Alpha Centauri is located far away from us in space, it is no less real because of that. And similarly, it is very plausible to say that Santa Claus *is* less real in virtue of being non-actual. The question, then, is whether putative non-present objects like Socrates are in the same boat as Alpha Centauri in this regard or, instead, in the same boat as Santa Claus. And once it is accepted that time is fundamentally similar to modality, and fundamentally different from space, then the natural answer to this question is that Socrates is in the same boat as Santa Claus.

Someone might object at this point by saying something like the following. "You're overlooking an important fact about Socrates: he was once real. For that reason, it is a big mistake to lump him together with Santa Claus, who never was real and never will be real. Socrates ought to be in the same boat as Alpha Centauri, not in the same boat as Santa Claus."

My reply to this objection is that it misses the point about the fundamental similarity between time and modality and the fundamental difference between time and space. Given the fundamental similarity between time and modality, being formerly real is analogous to being possibly real. And given the fundamental difference between time and space, there is no reason to think that being real at a remote temporal location is analogous to being real at a remote spatial location. So, although I admit that it might seem a little counterintuitive, I think it is actually a desirable consequence of Presentism that I cannot now stand in any direct relations to Socrates, or my grandfather, or any other non-present object, just as I cannot stand in any direct relations to Santa Claus, or my possible sister, or any other non-actual object.

What about admiring Socrates, then? The problem, it will be recalled, is that it would be natural to say that I stand in the *admires* relation to Socrates, but according to Presentism I cannot do so, since Socrates does not now exist. What I want to say in response to this problem is that there is an exactly analogous problem with non-actual objects, and that the solution to the modal case will also work for the temporal case.

Consider Sherlock Holmes, for example. I admire him too, almost as much as I admire Socrates. Or anyway, I am inclined, when speaking loosely, to say that I admire Sherlock Holmes. But of course I can't really stand in the *admires* relation to Sherlock Holmes if, as I am assuming, Actualism is true and Sherlock Holmes doesn't really exist.[26] What truth is there, then, in the intuitive idea that I admire Sherlock Holmes? Surely the correct answer will involve an analysis roughly along these lines:

(7)   There are various properties, p_1–p_n, such that (i) I associate p_1–p_n with the name

"Sherlock Holmes" and (ii) thoughts of either p_1–p_n or the name "Sherlock Holmes" evoke in me the characteristic feeling of admiration.

Note that (7) can be true even though it's also true that, when the characteristic feeling of admiration is evoked in me by the relevant thoughts, the feeling is not directed *at* any particular object. Thus, (7) captures what is true in the claim that I admire Sherlock Holmes, without requiring that there actually *be* such a person as Sherlock Holmes.

Note also that (7) is consistent with the truth of this claim:

(7a) There are various properties, p_1–p_n, such that (i) I associate p_1–p_n with the name "Sherlock Holmes", (ii) thoughts of either p_1–p_n or the name "Sherlock Holmes" evoke in me the characteristic feeling of admiration, and (iii) according to the Conan Doyle story, $(\exists x)(x$ has p_1–p_n and x is the referent of "Sherlock Holmes").

Thus, it can be true that (loosely speaking) I admire Sherlock Holmes, and also true that my admiration is connected with the actual story.

If this is right, then we can say a similar thing about my admiration of Socrates: namely,

(8) There are various properties, p_1–p_n, such that (i) I associate p_1–p_n with the name "Socrates", and (ii) thoughts of either p_1–p_n or the name "Socrates" evoke in me the characteristic feeling of admiration.

And (8), like (7), can be true even though it's also true that, when the characteristic feeling of admiration is evoked in me by the relevant thoughts, the feeling is not directed *at* any particular object. Thus, (8) captures what is true in the claim that I admire Socrates, without requiring that there presently *be* such a person as Socrates.

Now, (8) is consistent with the truth of this additional claim:

(8a) There are various properties, p_1–p_n, such that (i) I associate p_1–p_n with the name "Socrates", (ii) thoughts of either p_1–p_n or the name "Socrates" evoke in me the characteristic feeling of admiration, and (iii) $P(\exists x)(x$ has p_1–p_n and x is the referent of "Socrates").

Thus, it can be true that (loosely speaking) I admire Socrates, and also true that my admiration is connected with the actual course of history in such a way that I am indirectly related to Socrates.[27]

Time's alleged similarity with modality and alleged dissimilarity with space are relevant here. For the plausibility of (8) as an analysis of what is correct about the intuitive idea that I am an admirer of Socrates depends on the claim that the case of Socrates is similar to the case of a non-actual object like Sherlock Holmes, and not similar to a case involving someone who is (temporally) present but very far away.

Here is a related point. As a way of developing the objection to Presentism involving Glaucon and the sudden change in his beliefs when Socrates ceased to be present, the Non-presentist might say something like the following:

Consider the time right before Socrates suddenly ceased to be present and the time right after. And consider the states Glaucon was in at these two times. If you just look at Glaucon, there is virtually no difference between how he is at the first of these times and how he is at the second (since we are assuming that Glaucon did not change in any important intrinsic way when Socrates ceased to be present). How is it possible, then, that there is such a big difference between Glaucon before Socrates ceased to be present and Glaucon after Socrates ceased to be present? How is it possible that the earlier

Glaucon believes the singular proposition that Socrates is a philosopher and the later Glaucon does not believe that proposition, when the two Glaucons are so similar?

And here is my reply to this objection. Imagine someone arguing as follows:

Consider two possible worlds: the actual world, in which George W. Bush really exists, and a merely possible world—call it "w_1"—in which some very powerful being is playing an elaborate trick on all of us by making it seem as if there is a man named "George W. Bush" when in fact there is not. Let the two versions of me in the two worlds have exactly the same intrinsic properties, and let my experinces in the two worlds be exactly alike, so that, whenever I experience a television image of Bush in the actual world, I experience a qualitatively identical television image of (what appears to be) Bush in w_1. Now, if you just look at my intrinsic properties, there is no difference between how I am in the actual world and how I am in w_1. How is it possible, then, that there is such a big difference between me in the actual world and me in w_1? How is it possible that the actual me believes the singular proposition that Bush is president and the me in w_1 does not believe that proposition, when the two versions of me are so similar?

The correct response to someone who argues like this would be that the me in w_1 cannot believe any singular proposition about Bush, for the simple reason that Bush does not exist in that world. No object, no singular proposition; and no singular proposition, no belief in that singular proposition. That's how there can be such a big difference between the two versions of me even though they are so similar. And, I am suggesting, it is the same with poor Glaucon and the time after Socrates has ceased to be present. He cannot believe any singular proposition about

Socrates at that time for the simple reason that Socrates does not exist at that time. No object, no singular proposition; and no singular proposition, no belief in that singular proposition. That's how there can be such a big difference between Glaucon before Socrates has passed out of existence and Glaucon after Socrates has passed out of existence.[28]

3.8 *A Variation on the Paraphrasing Strategy*

Emphasizing the similarities between time and modality can also help the Presentist to deal with the problem of singular propositions about non-present objects by employing a variation on the paraphrasing strategy discussed above. Recall that, on that strategy, the claim was that

(1)   Socrates was a philosopher

now has the same meaning as

(1a) $P(\exists x)(x$ is the referent of "Socrates" and x is a philosopher).

This approach was rejected because, upon reflection, it seems pretty clear that (1) and (1a) do not really have the same meaning at all.

But now consider the case of the two worlds discussed in the above example: the actual world, in which George W. Bush exists, and w_1, in which a very powerful being is playing a trick on all of us by making it seem as if there is a guy named "George W. Bush" when there really is no such person. We surely don't want to say that in w_1 the sentence

(9)   George W. Bush is president of the US

expresses a singular proposition about Bush, even though (9) does have the form of a sentence that expresses a singular proposition about a man named "George W. Bush". And the reason we don't want to say that (9) expresses a singular proposition in w_1 is that there is no such man in that world, so that there can be no such singular proposition there. But this doesn't mean that we have to say that (9) is utterly meaningless in w_1.

The way to say that (9) has some meaning in w_1, even though it doesn't there express a singular proposition about Bush, is to distinguish between two different kinds of meaning that a declarative sentence can have. One type of meaning that a declarative sentence can have is simply the proposition (if any) expressed by that sentence. Let's call this the *propositional content* of the sentence.[29] Sentence (9) has no propositional content in w_1.[30] But another type of meaning that a declarative sentence can have is the meaning associated with the truth and falsity conditions for the sentence. I'll follow Greg Fitch in calling this the *linguistic meaning* of the sentence.[31]

Acknowledging the distinction between the propositional content and the linguistic meaning of a sentence allows us to say that, although (9) has no propositional content in w_1, it nevertheless has linguistic meaning in that world. For in w_1, just as in the actual world, (9) will have the following truth condition.

(TC9) "George W. Bush is president of the US" is true iff $(\exists x)$ (x is the referent of "George W. Bush" and x is president of the US).

(TC9) tells us, in effect, that if the name "George W. Bush" picks someone out, and if that individual happens to be president of the US, then (9) is true. Otherwise, according to (TC9), the sentence is not true. In w_1, then, where "George W. Bush" fails to refer to anything, (9) fails to express a proposition, and thus has no propositional content. That's why it is not true there, and that's why (TC9) gets the correct result in this case.[32]

Notice that all of this is consistent with the denizens of w_1 being utterly convinced that (9) really does express a true proposition (in their world). But since we know something important about their world that they do not know

(namely, that there is no referent of "George W. Bush" in w_1), we are in a position to say, "Poor folks—they think they are expressing a true proposition when they utter (9), when really they are not. All they are doing instead is uttering a sentence with a linguistic meaning but with no propositional content; and on top of that, it's not even a sentence that happens to be true (for according to the correct truth and falsity conditions for (9), it is neither true nor false in w_1)."

Returning to our original sentence,

(1) Socrates was a philosopher,

what I want to say about its situation at the present time is analogous to what I have just said about (9) in w_1. Sentence (1) currently has no propositional content, because it is "trying" to express a singular proposition about the referent of "Socrates", and there is no such thing. But it doesn't follow that (1) is utterly meaningless. For it has a linguistic meaning. And in fact, as I will argue below, the correct truth condition for (1) is the following:

(TC1$_g$) "Socrates was a philosopher" is true iff $(\exists x)[x$ is the referent of "Socrates" and $P(x$ is a philosopher$)]$.[33]

At this point the Non-presentist might say, "Fine. If you're willing to outSmart us on the question of whether (1) expresses any proposition, by happily biting the bullet and denying that it does, there's nothing we can do about that. But what about the fact that the majority of English speakers will want to say that (1) happens to be *true*? How do you account for that fact if, as you insist, the sentence does not express any proposition at all?"

Here is my response. I agree that many English speakers will be inclined to say that (1) is true. But I think that there are three main reasons for this, all of which are consistent with the truth of Presentism. The first reason is that some English speakers are at least sometimes inclined toward Non-presentism. Those people are likely to think (sometimes, at least) that (1) expresses something like a true, singular proposition about Socrates.[34] They're making a mistake, but still, this explains why they think (1) is true.[35]

The second reason why so many English speakers are inclined to say that (1) is true is that even those of us who are confirmed Presentists sometimes prefer not to focus on the Presentism/Non-presentism dispute in our everyday lives. As a purely practical matter, it turns out that you can't be doing serious ontology all the time. But here something like Ted Sider's notion of *quasi-truth* comes in handy.[36] The idea is roughly this. Presentists and Non-presentists disagree over a philosophical matter, but we don't necessarily disagree over any non-philosophical matter regarding some empirical fact about the current state of the world. In particular, we Presentists think that the current state of the world is qualitatively indiscernible from the way it would be if Non-presentism and (1) were both true. And that is good enough to make us want to assent to (1), in everyday circumstances, even if we don't really think it is literally true.[37]

The following technical term can be used to describe the situation:

S is *quasi-true* = df S is not literally true, but only in virtue of certain non-empirical or philosophical facts.

Now the point can be put this way: Presentists and Non-presentists alike, not to mention people who don't have a view on the Presentism/Non-presentism dispute, all assent to (1), in everyday circumstances, because we all think it is at least quasi-true.

The third reason for the fact that a majority of people will want to say that (1) is true has to do with a very understandable mistake that people tend to make regarding the truth conditions for sentences like (1). The mistake involves blurring a distinction between two kinds of

truth condition for sentences that combine names with certain modal operators.[38] The distinction I have in mind can be illustrated by a difference between two different possible truth conditions that we could assign to (1). One truth condition we could assign to (1) is $(TC1_g)$, which we have already considered above, and which goes as follows:

$(TC1_g)$ "Socrates was a philosopher" is true iff $(\exists x)$ [x is the referent of "Socrates" and P(x is a philosopher)].

The other truth condition we could assign to (1) is the following:

$(TC1_s)$ "Socrates was a philosopher" is true iff $P(\exists x)$(x is the referent of "Socrates" and x is a philosopher).[39]

The difference between $(TC1_g)$ and $(TC1_s)$ has to do with the scope of the past-tense operator on the right-hand side of the biconditional. In $(TC1_g)$ the past-tense operator has narrow scope, while in $(TC1_s)$ it has wide scope. $(TC1_g)$ tells us, in effect, to grab the thing that is now the referent of "Socrates", and then to go back to see whether there is some past time at which that thing is a philosopher. $(TC1_s)$, on the other hand, tells us, in effect, to go back to past times, and to search for a thing that is the referent of "Socrates" and that is a philosopher. Thus, the difference between $(TC1_g)$ and $(TC1_s)$ illustrates a difference between what we might call *grabby truth conditions* and what we might call *searchy truth conditions* for sentences combining names with modal operators.[40]

It should be clear that, if we apply $(TC1_s)$ to (1), then, even assuming Presentism, (1) may well turn out to be true. For it may well be the case that there *was* a person who was the referent of "Socrates" and who was a philosopher.[41] But if we take $(TC1_g)$ to be the correct truth condition for (1), on the other hand, then (again assuming Presentism) (1) turns out not to be true (which means that it is either false or without a truth value).

So which kind of truth condition should we apply to (1)? I think there is good evidence that, given the way such sentences are understood in English, the answer is that we should apply the grabby truth condition to (1). For consider this sentence

(16) Joe Montana was a quarterback.

The current truth of (16) should depend on how things have been with the guy who is currently the referent of "Joe Montana". But if (16) had a searchy truth condition, such as

(TC16_s) "Joe Montana was a quarterback" is true iff $P(\exists x)(x$ is the referent of "Joe Montana" and x is a quarterback),

then (16) could be true now in virtue of the fact that someone else was formerly both the referent of "Joe Montana" and a quarterback, even if our current Joe Montana never was a quarterback. And that would be the wrong result. So I think it's clear that (16) now has the following grabby truth condition:

(TC16_g) "Joe Montana was a quarterback" is true iff $(\exists x)[x$ is the referent of "Joe Montana" and $P(x$ is a quarterback$)]$.

Moreover, I think that, even when (16) loses its propositional content, as a result of Montana's going out of existence, the sentence will not then suddenly come to have a different linguistic meaning; which means that (16) will continue to have the same grabby truth condition it now has even after Montana ceases to exist.

These considerations suggest that the conventions of English are such that two things will normally be true of any standard sentence combining a name and a past-tense operator: (i) like other sentences containing standard uses of names, that sentence will express a singular

proposition about the referent of that name, if it expresses any proposition at all; and (ii) that sentence will have a grabby truth condition.[42]

If I am right about the second part of this claim, then (TC1_g) is the correct truth condition for (1). Which means (again, assuming Presentism) that (1) is not true. But still, even if I am right about the correct truth condition for (1), it is quite natural that we sometimes think "True" when we think of (1), for the simple reason that the difference between grabby truth conditions and searchy truth conditions is a fairly subtle difference. I mean, it's really not surprising that the average English speaker would confuse (TC1_g) and (TC1_s). I can barely tell them apart myself.

If the reader still has doubts about my claim that (TC1_g) is the correct truth condition for (1), here is a little empirical test that is easy to do. Go out and corral a typical English speaker on the street. As her to consider sentence (1), and to tell you whether it is true. She will most likely say "Yes". Then ask her this question: "Do you think this sentence is true because there *is* a guy called 'Socrates' who was a philosopher, or do you think it is true because there *was* a guy called 'Socrates' who was a philosopher?" I'm willing to bet five dollars that, if you can get her to take this last question seriously, she will opt for the second alternative (the one that corresponds to (TC1_s)). And what I think this shows is that, even though the correct truth condition for (1) is (TC1_g), the grabby truth condition, the average person on the street is likely to think (mistakenly) that the correct truth condition for (1) is something like (TC1_s), the searchy truth condition.

Now, I have argued above that (TC1_g) rather than (TC1_s) is the correct truth condition for (1). But there is always the possibility that I am wrong about this. If (TC1_s) is actually the right truth condition for (1), then the explanation for our inclination to think that (1) is true is even simpler. The explanation is that we think (1) is true because it is (since, presumably, it has been the case that there is a guy called "Socrates" who is a philosopher).[43] But notice that, if we say that (TC1$_s$) is the appropriate truth condition for (1), then we must say either (*a*) that (1) is true even though it fails to express a proposition, or else (*b*) that (1) expresses a general proposition, such as the one expressed by this sentence:

(1a) P($\exists$x)(x is the referent of "Socrates" and x is a philosopher).

And I don't think either of these alternatives is at all tenable.

On the strategy that I am endorsing, then, the claim is not that (1a) has the same meaning (in any sense of "meaning") as (1). Nor am I claiming that the right-hand side of (TC1$_g$) expresses the same proposition as (1). Rather, the claim is that (1) fails to express any proposition at all, but nevertheless has the linguistic meaning that is captured by (TC1$_g$).[44] In addition, I am admitting that the majority of English speakers would be inclined to say that (1) is true, but I am suggesting that there are three main reasons for this that are all consistent with Presentism: (i) some English speakers are occasional Non-presentists; (ii) Presentists, Non-presentists, and agnostics with respect to the Presentism/Non-presentism dispute are all happy to say that (1) is true, because we all think it is at least quasi-true; and (iii) many English speakers are confused about the correct truth conditions for sentences like (1), mistakenly thinking that they are searchy truth conditions that happen to be satisfied rather than grabby truth conditions that are not satisfied.

3.9 Presentism and Special Relativity

What about the argument from the Special Theory of Relativity (STR) against Presentism? In order to discuss the best Presentist response to it, let's first get clear on exactly how the argument is supposed to go. As I understand it, the argument goes something like this:

The Argument from Relativity

(1) STR is true.

(2) STR entails that there is no such relation as absolute simultaneity.

(3) If there is no such relation as absolute simultaneity, then there is no such property as absolute presentness.

(4) Presentism entails that there is such a property as absolute presentness.

———

(5) Presentism is false.

The rationale for premise (1) is whatever empirical evidence supports STR. The rationale for premise (2) is that STR apparently entails that the relation of simultaneity never holds between two objects or events *absolutely*, but instead only *relative to a particular frame of reference.* The rationale for premise (3) is that, if there were such a property as absolute presentness, then whatever objects or events possessed it would be absolutely simultaneous with one another. And the rationale for premise (4) is that, if Presentism allowed what is present to be a relativistic matter, then Presentism would entail that what exists is a relativistic matter, which would be an unacceptable consequence.[45]

My response to this argument requires a small digression on a general matter concerning philosophical method. It is fashionable nowadays to give arguments from scientific theories to philosophical conclusions. I don't have a problem with this approach in general. But I think it is a seldom-observed fact that, when people give arguments from scientific theories to philosophical conclusions, there is usually a good deal of philosophy built into the relevant scientific theories. I don't have a problem with this, either. Scientists, especially in areas like theoretical physics, cannot be expected to do science without sometimes appealing to philosophical principles.

Still, I think it is important, when evaluating an argument from some scientific theory to a philosophical conclusion, to be aware of the fact that there is likely to be some philosophy built into the relevant scientific theory. Otherwise there is the danger of mistakenly thinking that the argument in question involves a clear-cut case of science versus philosophy. And I think it very rarely happens that we are presented with a genuine case of science versus philosophy.

The reason I raise this methodological point here is that how I want to respond to the Argument from Relativity depends on how philosophically rich we understand STR to be. Does STR have enough philosophical baggage built into it to make it either literally contain or at least entail that there is no such relation as absolute simultaneity?

I don't have a view about the correct answer to this question. But I do know that there are two ways of answering it (Yes and No). So let us consider two different versions of STR, which we can characterize as follows:

STR⁺ = A philosophically robust version of STR that has enough philosophical baggage built into it to make it either literally contain or at least entail the proposition that there is no such relation as absolute simultaneity.

STR⁻ = A philosophically austere version of STR that is empirically equivalent to STR⁺ but does not have enough philosophical baggage built into it to make it either literally contain or even entail the proposition that there is no such relation as absolute simultaneity.

Suppose we understand the Argument from Relativity to be concerned with STR⁺. Then I think premise (1) of the argument is false, because STR⁺ is false. Although I agree that there seems to be a great deal of empirical evidence supporting the theory, I think it is notable that the same empirical evidence supports STR⁻ equally well. And since I believe there is good *a priori* evidence favoring STR⁻ over STR⁺, I conclude that STR⁻ is true and that STR⁺ is false.

Suppose, on the other hand, that we understand the Argument from Relativity to be concerned with STR⁻. Then I reject premise (2) of the argument. STR⁻ will entail, among other things, that, while it is physically possible to determine whether two objects or events are simultaneous relative to a particular frame of reference, it is not physically possible to determine whether two objects or events are absolutely simultaneous. But this is consistent with there being such a relation as absolute simultaneity. And it is also consistent with there being such a property as absolute presentness.[46]

3.10 Presentism and Past and Future Times

All of this is well and good, but what about the problem of non-present times? Here are two questions that are crucial to this topic:

(Q1) What are times?
(Q2) Are there any non-present times?

And here are the answers to these questions that I want to endorse:

(A1) Times are like worlds.[47]
(A2) In one sense there are many non-present times, while in another sense there are none.

Here's how times are like worlds. Consider the actual world. There are really two of them. There is the abstract actual world, which is a maximal, consistent proposition.[48] There are many things that are similar to the abstract actual world in being maximal, consistent propositions. Each one is a possible world. The abstract actual world is the only one of all of these possible worlds that happens to be true. And then there is the concrete actual world, which is the sum total of all actual facts.[49] The concrete actual world is the only concrete world that exists, and it is what makes the abstract actual world true.

The Presentist can say that it is the same with

the present time. There are really two of them. There is the abstract present time, which is a maximal, consistent proposition. There are many things that are similar to the abstract present time in being maximal, consistent propositions that either will be true, are true, or have been true. Each one is a time.[50] The abstract present time is the only one of all of these abstract times that happens to be true right now. And then there is the concrete present time, which is the sum total of all present facts. It is the only concrete time that exists, and it is what makes the abstract present time true. Talk about non-present times can be understood as talk about maximal, consistent propositions that have been or will be true. For example, the time ten years from now can be identified with the maximal, consistent proposition that will be true in ten years.

It might be objected that there is an undesirable consequence of what I have just said, namely that if history were cyclical, repeating itself every 100 years, say, then the time 100 years from now would be identical to the time 200 years from now. In general, it might be objected, the view about times I have endorsed entails that it is impossible for history to be cyclical without time's being closed.[51]

Here is my reply to this objection. On the view I am endorsing, 100 years from now there will be two items that deserve the name "the present time". One will be the concrete present time, i.e. the sum total of all facts then obtaining. The other will be the abstract present time, i.e. the maximal, consistent proposition that will then be true. The latter will be identical to the time 200 years from now, but the former will not.[52] So all that follows from the combination of the view about times I am endorsing with the assumption that history repeats itself every 100 years is that the thing that will be the abstract present time in 100 years is identical to the thing that will be the abstract present time in 200 years.

Here a small digression on the nature of possible worlds may be helpful. It is important to

remember when talking about abstract possible worlds that they are not really *worlds*, in the robust sense of the word. They are not composed of stars and planets and flesh-and-blood beings (the way the concrete actual world is). They are not even composed of matter. They are just abstract objects that play a certain role in philosophers' talk about modality. They are ways things could be. That's why there are no two abstract possible worlds that are qualitatively identical. If w_1 is a way things could be, and w_2 is also a way things could be, and w_2 is just like w_1 in every detail, then w_2 is identical to w_1.

Similar remarks can be made about abstract times on the view I am endorsing. It is important to remember when talking about these abstract times that they are just abstract objects that play a certain role in philosophers' talk about temporal matters. They are ways things are, or have been, or will be. That's why there are no two abstract times that are qualitatively identical. If t_1 is a way things are, or have been, or will be, and t_2 is also a way things are, or have been, or will be, and t_2 is just like t_1 in every detail, then t_2 is identical to t_1.

For that reason, I don't find the relevant consequence of my view about times to be undesirable. In fact, I find it highly desirable. Of course, it *would* be a strike against it if the view entailed that the concrete present time that will obtain in 100 years was identical to the concrete present time that will obtain in 200 years (on the assumption of cyclical history, that is). For in that case, the view would come with an extra commitment—namely, the impossibility of cyclical history without closed time—that some philosophers would find undesirable. But as I have said, this is in fact not a consequence of the view.

Meanwhile, talk about the passage of time— the process by which times become less and less future, and then present, and then more and more past—can also be understood as talk about maximal, consistent propositions. For example, I have said that the time ten years from now can be identified with a certain maximal, consistent proposition. Call that proposition "T". T is false right now, but will be true ten years hence. In other words, the future-tensed proposition *that it will be the case in ten years that* T is true right now. In one year's time the future-tensed proposition *that it will be the case in nine years that* T will be true, and then a year later the future-tensed proposition *that it will be the case in eight years that* T will be true, and so on. To put the point a different way: T will go from instantiating *will-be-true-in-ten-years* to instantiating *will-be-true-in-nine-years* and then *will-be-true-in-eight-years*, and so on. And the process by which T goes from instantiating *will-be-true-in-ten-years* to instantiating *will-be-true-in-nine-years*, and so on, can be identified with the process by which that time—T—becomes less and less future. In a similar way, it will eventually recede further and further into the past. Thus, what appears to be talk about a non-present time's becoming less and less future can be understood as talk about a maximal, consistent proposition's instantiating a succession of properties like *will-be-true-in-ten-years*.

Here, then, is the sense in which there are some non-present times: there are some maximal, consistent propositions that will be true or have been true, but are not presently true. (This is analogous to the sense in which there are some non-actual worlds: there are some maximal, consistent propositions that are not actually true.)

And here is the sense in which there are no non-present times: there is only one concrete time, and it is the present time, i.e. the sum total of all present facts. (This is analogous to the sense in which there are no non-actual worlds: there is only one concrete world, and it is the actual world, i.e. the sum total of all actual facts.)

An Actualist who is also a Presentist (such as myself) can say that the concrete actual world is identical to the concrete present time. It is the sum total of all current facts. Similarly, such a person can say that the abstract actual world is identical to the abstract present time. It is the one

maximal, consistent proposition that is actually and presently true.

Acknowledgments

Apologies to Mark Hinchliff for stealing the title of his dissertation (see Hinchliff, *A Defense of Presentism*). As it turns out, however, the version of Presentism defended here is different from the version defended by Hinchliff: see Section 3.1 below. I'm grateful to West Virginia University for a research grant that helped support the writing of an earlier draft of this paper. And although they didn't give me any money, I'm even more grateful to Stuart Brock, Matthew Davidson, Greg Fitch, Geoffrey Goddu, Mark Heller, Hud Hudson, Aleksandar Jokic, Trenton Merricks, Bradley Monton, Joshua Parsons, Laurie Paul, Sharon Ryan, Steven Savitt, Ted Sider, Quentin Smith, and Dean Zimmerman for helpful comments on earlier versions of the paper, and to Greg Fitch, Tom Ryckman, and Ted Sider for many helpful discussions of these topics.

Notes

1 More precisely, it is the view that, necessarily, it is always true that only present objects exist. At least, that is how I am using the name "Presentism". Quentin Smith has used the name to refer to a different view; see his *Language and Time*. Note that, unless otherwise indicated, what I mean by "present" is *temporally present*, as opposed to *spatially present*. For discussions of Presentism and Non-presentism, see R. M. Adams, "Time and Thisness"; Augustine; *Confessions*; Bigelow, "Presentism and Properties"; Brogaard, "Presentist Four-Dimensionalism"; Chisholm, *On Metaphysics*; Chisholm, "Referring to Things that No Longer Exist"; Christensen, *Space-Like Time*; Fine, "Prior on the Construction of Possible Worlds and Instants"; Fitch, "Does Socrates Exist?"; Fitch, "Singular Propositions in Time"; Hinchliff, *A Defense of Presentism*; Hinchliff, "The Puzzle of Change"; Keller and Nelson, "Presentists Should Believe in Time Travel"; Long and Sedley, *The Hellenistic Philosophers*,

Vol. 1, *Translations of the Principal Sources with Philosophical Commentary* (especially the writings of Sextus Empiricus); Lucretius, *On the Nature of the Universe*; Markosian, "The 3D/4D Controversy and Non-present Objects"; McCall, *A Model of the Universe*; Merricks, "On the Incompatibility of Enduring and Perduring Entities"; Monton, "Presentism and Spacetime Physics"; Prior, "Changes in Events and Changes in Things"; Prior, "The Notion of the Present"; Prior, *Papers on Time and tense*; Prior, *Past, Present and Future*; Prior, "Some Free Thinking About Time"; Prior, "A Statement of Temporal Realism"; Prior, *Time and Modality*; Prior and Fine, *Worlds, Times and Selves*; Sextus Empiricus, *Against the Physicists*; Sider, "Presentism and Ontological Commitment"; Sider, *Four-Dimensionalism*; Smith, *Language and Time*; Smith, "Reference to the Past and Future"; Tooley, *Time, Tense, and Causation*; Wolterstorff, "Can Ontology Do without Events?"; and Zimmerman, "Persistence and Presentism".

2 I am assuming that each person is identical to his or her body, and that Socrates's body ceased to be present—thereby going out of existence, according to Presentism—shortly after he died. Those philosophers who reject the first of these assumptions should simply replace the examples in this paper involving allegedly non-present people with appropriate examples involving the non-present bodies of those people.

3 Let us distinguish between two senses of "x exists now". In one sense, which we can call the *temporal location* sense, this expression is synonymous with "x is present". The Non-presentist will admit that, in the temporal location sense of "x exists now", it is true that no non-present objects exist right now. But in the other sense of "x exists now", which we can call the *ontological* sense, to say that x exists now is just to say that x is now in the domain of our most unrestricted quantifiers, whether it happens to be present, like you and me, or non-present, like Socrates. When I attribute to Non-presentists the claim that non-present objects like Socrates exist right now, I mean to commit the Non-presentist only to the claim that these non-present objects exist now in the ontological sense (the one involving the most unrestricted quantifiers).

4 In what follows I'll adopt Robert Adams's

definition of "singular proposition", according to which "a singular proposition about an individual x is a proposition that involves or refers to x directly, perhaps by having x or the thisness of x as a constituent, and not merely by way of x's qualitative properties or relations to other individuals" (Adams, "Time and Thisness", p. 315). By the "thisness" of x, Adams means "the property of being x, or the property of being identical with x". I will refer to such a property below as x's *haecceity*.

5 Adams would disagree; he maintains that there are singular propositions about past objects even though those past objects no longer exist. See Section 3.4 below.

6 Greg W. Fitch is an example of someone who rejects Presentism for this reason. See Fitch, "Singular Propositions in Time".

7 W. V. Quine is an example of a philosopher who rejects Presentism because of the problem of relations between present and non-present objects; see his *Quiddities*, pp. 197–8.

For discussions of the special version this problem that has to do with causation, see Bigelow, "Presentism and Properties"; Tooley, *Time, Tense, and Causation*; and Zimmerman, "Chisholm and the Essences of Events". Tooley rejects Presentism because of the causal version of the problem, while Bigelow and Zimmerman propose solutions to the causal version of the problem that are inspired by the writings of Lucretius and the Stoics (see Lucretius, *On the Nature of the Universe*; Sextus Empiricus, *Against the Physicists*; and Long and Sedley, *The Hellenistic Philosophers*, vol. 1, *Translations of the Principal Sources with Philosophical Commentary*, especially the writings of Sextus Empiricus). (It should be noted, however, that Bigelow's proposed solution to the causal version of the problem seems to require the existence of singular propositions about non-present objects.)

8 See Hinchliff, *A Defense of Presentism*, ch. 2 and 3, and "The Puzzle of Change", pp. 124–6.

9 See e.g. Chisholm, *The First Person*.

10 See Kaplan, "Demonstratives"; Adams and Stecker, "Vacuous Singular Terms"; Braun, "Empty Names"; Salmon, "Nonexistence"; and Oppy, "The Philosophical Insignificance of Gödel's Slingshot".

11 For the sake of simplicity, I am now talking as

if singular propositions literally contained the individuals they are about, as opposed to merely referring to them directly in some way.

12 See R. M. Adams, "Time and Thisness".

13 Since Adams doesn't believe in haecceities of future individuals.

14 Adams responds to this objection in "Time and Thisness": see pp. 319–20.

15 Adams suggests that individuals are not constituents of their haecceities (see "Time and Thisness", p. 320.) But I have a hard time understanding how Socrates could fail to be a constituent of Socraticity, although, admittedly, what we say about this matter depends partly on what we say about the tricky subject of the nature of constituency. In any case, whatever we say about the nature of constituency, it seems clear to me that this principle will be true: *The property of being identical with x exists only if x itself exists.* For it seems to me that, for any relation and for any object, the property of standing in that relation to that object will exist only if the object exists.

16 I say "in a more or less straightforward way" partly because, as I noted above, Adams's version of the haecceity approach purports to solve the problem of singular propositions about non-present objects for the case of past objects but not for the case of future objects.

17 Something like this strategy is tentatively suggested by Prior in "Changes in Events and Changes in Things" (see pp. 12–14). The paraphrasing strategy is explicitly endorsed by Wolterstorff in "Can Ontology Do without Events?" (see pp. 190 ff).

18 For a discussion of further problems for the paraphrasing approach, see Smith, *Language and Time*, pp. 162 ff.

19 Let's pretend, for simplicity's sake, that English existed in its present form back then. For arguments that seem to show that (1) did not have the same meaning as (1a) back when Socrates was present, see Kripke, *Naming and Necessity*.

20 I'm grateful to Greg Fitch for making this point in correspondence.

21 For the remainder of this paper I will be assuming that Actualism is true, i.e. that there are no non-actual objects. This is because I am offering a defense of Presentism, and Presentists tend to be Actualists as well. (In fact, I do not know of a single Presentist who is not also an Actualist.) But all of the points I make based on this assumption could be made—although in a much more cumbersome way—without assuming that Actualism is true.

22 There is a further assumption that is required for this approach to work. It is the assumption that, in every case in which there is some truth to the claim that a certain present object stands in some relation to a putative non-present object, there will be sufficient "linking objects" that will connect the present object to the putative non-present object, the way my grandfather links me to my great-great-grandfather. I am inclined to accept this assumption, although I won't attempt to defend it here.

23 A great deal more space than I have here would be required to do justice to the causal version of the problem of relations between non-contemporaneous entities. For more extended discussions of the problem, see Bigelow, "Presentism and Properties"; Lucretius, *On the Nature of the Universe*; Sextus Empiricus, *Against the Physicists*; Sider, *Four-Dimensionalism*; the writings of the Stoics in Long and Sedley, *The Hellenistic Philosophers*, vol. 1, *Translations of the Principal Sources with Philosophical Commentary*; Tooley, *Time, Tense, and Causation*; and Zimmerman, "Chisholm and the Essences of Events".

It is worth noting that at least some Presentists are reductionists about events, insisting that all talk that appears to be about events is really talk about things (see e.g. Prior, "Changes in Events and Changes in Things"). Such Presentists will perhaps have an easier time than others of dealing with the problem of causal relations between non-contemporaneous events, since for them the problem will turn out more or less straightforwardly to be just a special case of the general problem of relations between present and non-present objects.

24 See Prior, "The Notion of the Present"; Prior, *Time and Modality*; Prior and Fine, *Worlds, Times and Selves*; Fine, "Prior on the Construction of Possible Worlds and Instants"; and Zalta, "On the Structural Similarities between Worlds and Times". One of the main similarities between time and modality has to do with the similarities between modal logic and tense logic, and in particular the way

the tense operators function just like modal operators. Another main similarity between time and modality involves similarities between worlds (construed as abstract objects) and times (construed as abstract objects). A third similarity between time and modality, at least according to the Presentist, has to do with ontology, and the fact that the past and the future are as unreal as the merely possible.

25 See Prior, *Past, Present, and Future*; Prior, "Thank Goodness That's Over"; Prior, *Time and Modality*; Markosian, "On Language and the Passage of Time"; Markosian, "How Fast Does Time Pass?"; Markosian, "The 3D/4D Controversy and Non-present Objects"; and Markosian, "What Are Physical Objects?". Here are some of the main ways in which it is claimed that time is unlike the dimensions of space. (1) Propositions have truth-values at times, and a single proposition can have different truth-values at different times, but the corresponding things are not true about space. (2) The so-called "A-properties" (putative properties like pastness, presentness, and futurity) are genuine, monadic properties that cannot be analyzed purely in terms of "B-relations" (binary, temporal relations such as earlier-than and simultaneous-with), but there are no genuine spatial properties analogous to the A-properties. (3) Time passes—that is, times and events are constantly and inexorably changing from being future to being present and then on to being more and more remotely past—but nothing analogous is true of any dimension of space.

26 This is perhaps an oversimplification. Some people would say that Actualism is true and that Sherlock Holmes *does* really exist. For some people believe that fictional characters are abstract, actual objects (like sets of properties); see e.g. van Inwagen, "Creatures of Fiction"; Howell, "Fictional Objects: How They Are and How They Aren't"; Emt, "On the Nature of Fictional Entities"; Levinson, "Making Believe"; and Salmon, "Nonexistence". For the sake of simplicity, I will ignore this point in what follows.

27 I mentioned (in n. 22) that the indirect relations strategy is based on the assumption that there will in general be sufficient "linking objects" to generate the requisite truths. Notice that, in the case of

the truth about my admiring Socrates that is captured by sentence (8a), it is the name and the properties in question that do the linking.

28 It is worth mentioning here that the Presentist line I am defending on beliefs about non-present objects commits me to at least one version of "externalism" about beliefs: namely, the thesis that which propositions one believes is not determined solely by one's intrinsic properties, but rather is partly determined by features of the external world, such as whether there is an object for the relevant belief to be about. This is what makes it possible for Glaucon to go from believing various singular propositions about Socrates to not believing any such propositions, even though he doesn't change in any intrinsic way. (I am grateful to Ted Sider for making this point in correspondence.)

29 The propositional content of a sentence is, strictly speaking, a feature of individual tokens of the sentence rather than a feature of the sentence type itself (since it is, strictly speaking, sentence tokens that express propositions, rather than sentence types). But I will for the most part talk loosely here, as if propositional content were somehow a feature of sentence types.

30 That is, tokens of (9) that occur in w_1 do not express any proposition. This claim is consistent with the claim that tokens of (9) in the actual world do express a (singular) proposition, and also with the claim that tokens in the actual world of the sentence

(9a) In w_1, George W. Bush is president of the US

express a (false, singular) proposition. (Since, after all, George W. Bush does exist in the actual world, and so does the proposition that he is president of the US in w_1.)

31 See Fitch, "Non Denoting". As I see it, linguistic meaning will be primarily a feature of sentence types (although it also makes sense to ascribe to a sentence token the linguistic meaning associated with its type). Thus, for example, we can say that the following sentence (type),

(2) Peter van Inwagen is a philosopher,

has this truth condition:

(TC2) "Peter van Inwagen is a philosopher" is true iff (∃x)(x is the referent of "Peter van Inwagen" and x is a philosopher).

But if need be, we can make it explicit that (TC2) should be understood as saying that a given token of "Peter van Inwagen is a philosopher" is true iff (∃x)(x is the referent of the relevant occurrence of "Peter van Inwagen" and x is a philosopher).

32 But notice that (9) is not false in w_1, either. For, as we have noted, (9) has no propositional content in w_1. (TC9) entails that (9) is not true in w_1, but it does not entail that (9) is also not false in that world. In order to guarantee that result, we will need to accept the following falsity condition for (9).

(FC9) "George W. Bush is president of the US" is false iff (∃x)(x is the referent of "George W. Bush" and it's not the case that x is president of the US).

What this shows is that the linguistic meaning of a sentence should be identified not simply with the truth condition for that sentence, but rather with the combination of the truth and falsity conditions for the sentence. (I will sometimes gloss over this point in what follows.)

33 The relevance of the subscript in the name "$(TC1_g)$" will be clear shortly.

34 I say "something like a true, singular proposition about Socrates" because I don't suppose that typical non-philosophers have any view about the existence of singular propositions. But in any case, to the extent that some people have Non-presentist leanings, they will think that (1) is currently true, because they will think that it satisfies the above truth condition.

35 If I became convinced that there were enough of such people, I would have to give up my claim (from Section 1) that Presentism is the view of the average person on the street.

36 See Sider, "Presentism and Ontological Commitment". What I describe in the text is a variation on Sider's actual notion of quasi-truth.

37 Similarly, we think that the current state of the world is qualitatively indiscernible from the way it would be if Non-presentism were true and "Socrates was a plumber" were false; and that is good

enough to make us want to say (when we are not obsessing about philosophical issues) that "Socrates was a plumber" is false.

38 Following Prior and others, I am counting tense operators as a species of modal operator.

39 Technical point: in order to accommodate the possibility that Socrates was not named "Socrates" way back when, we may instead want the "searchy" truth condition for (1) (see explanation below) to say something like the following (in which "F" is the future-tense sentential operator, short for "it will be the case that").

(TC1$_s'$) "Socrates was a philosopher" is true iff P(∃x)[F(x is the referent of "Socrates") and x is a philosopher].

40 I am grateful to Tom Ryckman for suggesting the terms "searchy" and "grabby".

41 If we take (TC1$_s'$) (see no. 39) to be the correct truth condition for (1), then the point here is that it may well be the case that there *was* a person who *would be* the referent of later occurrences of "Socrates", and who was a philosopher.

42 Similar remarks apply to sentences containing names and alethic modal operators: they also are meant to express singular propositions about the things named, and they also have grabby rather than searchy truth conditions. For example, the sentence

(17) Joe Montana might have been a plumber

expresses a singular proposition about Joe Montana, and it has the following grabby truth condition:

(TC17$_g$) "Joe Montana might have been a plumber" is true iff (∃x)(x is the referent of "Joe Montana" and ◇(x is a plumber)).

That is, the correct truth condition for (17) tells us to grab the thing named "Joe Montana" and to check other possible worlds to see whether *that thing* is a plumber in any of them (rather than telling us to go to other possible worlds and search around for a thing that is both named "Joe Montana" and a plumber).

43 Better yet (again taking into account the possibility

that Socrates was not called "Socrates" in his time): If (TC1$_s$') (see n. 39) is the correct truth condition for (1), then the explanation for our inclination to think (1) is true is simply that it is, since, presumably, it has been the case that there is a guy whom we will later call "Socrates" and who is a philosopher.

44 Together with the corresponding falsity condition.

45 A similar argument from STR can be used against the A Theory of time.

46 For more discussions of STR and the A Theory and/or Presentism, see Prior, "The Notion of the Present"; Putnam, "Time and Physical Geometry"; Maxwell, "Are Probabilism and Special Relativity Incompatible?", and Monton, "Presentism and Spacetime Physics".

47 Cf. Prior and Fine, *Worlds, Times and Selves*; Fine, "Prior on the Construction of Possible Worlds and Instants"; and Zalta, "On the structural Similarities Between Worlds and Times".

48 As before, I am assuming that Actualism is true. There are alternative "ersatzist" accounts that the Actualist can give of possible worlds. See Lewis, *On the Plurality of Worlds*. For our purposes it won't matter what specific account the Actualist gives.

49 I understand facts to be complex entities, each one consisting of the instantiation of some universal by some thing (in the case of a property) or things (in the case of a relation).

50 For reasons that have to do with what I will say below about the passage of time, the propositions that I am identifying with abstract times will have to be maximal, consistent, *purely qualitative* propositions.

51 For a detailed discussion of the possibility of history's being cyclical while time is closed, see Newton-Smith, *The Structure of Time*, pp. 57–78.

52 Or at least, the view I am endorsing does not entail that, on our assumption about history's being cyclical, the concrete present time in 100 years will be identical to the concrete present time in 200 years. That's because the view does not entail that the objects existing in 100 years will be identical to their counterparts in 200 years, and hence the view also does not entail that the facts containing those objects as constituents will be identical.

References

Adams, Fred, and Stecker, Robert, "Vacuous Singular Terms", *Mind and Language*, **9** (1994), pp. 387–401.

Adams, Robert M., "Actualism and Possible Worlds", *Synthese*, **49** (1981), pp. 3–41.

Adams, Robert M., "Time and Thisness", in Peter A., French, Theodore E., Uehling, and Howard Wettstein (eds.), *Midwest Studies in Philosophy*, vol. XI (Minneapolis: University of Minnesota Press, 1986), pp. 315–29.

Augustine, *Confessions* (New York: Modern Library, 1949).

Bigelow, John, "Presentism and Properties", *Philosophical Perspectives*, **10** (1996), pp. 35–52.

Braun, David, "Empty Names", *Noûs*, **27** (1993), pp. 449–69.

Brogaard, Berit, "Presentist Four-Dimensionalism", *The Monist*, **83** (2000), 341–56.

Chisholm, Roderick M., *The First Person* (Minneapolis: University of Minnesota Press, 1981).

Chisholm, Roderick M., *On Metaphysics* (Minneapolis: University of Minnesota Press, 1989).

Chisholm, Roderick M., "Referring to Things that No Longer Exist", *Philosophical Perspectives*, **4** (1990), pp. 546–56.

Christensen, Ferrel M., *Space-Like Time* (Toronto: University of Toronto Press, 1993).

Emt, Jeanette, "On the Nature of Fictional Entities", in Jeanette Emt and Goran Hermerén (eds.), *Understanding the Arts: Contemporary Scandinavian Æsthetics* (Lund: Lund University Press, 1992), pp. 149–76.

Fine Kit, "Prior on the Construction of Possible Worlds and Instants", in Arthur N. Prior and Kit Fine, *Worlds, Times and Selves* (Amherst, MA: University of Massachusetts Press, 1977), pp. 116–61.

Fitch, Greg W., "Does Socrates Exist?", unpublished paper, 2002.

Fitch, Greg W., "Non Denoting", *Philosophical Perspectives*, **7** (1993), pp. 461–86.

Fitch, Greg W., "Singular Propositions in Time", *Philosophical Studies*, **73** (1994), pp. 181–7.

Forbes, Graeme, *The Metaphysics of Modality* (Oxford: Oxford University Press, 1983).

Frege, Gottlob, "On Sense and Meaning", in Peter Geach and Max Black (eds.), *Translations from the Philosophical Writings of Gottlob Frege*, 3rd edn (Totowa, NJ: Rowman & Littlefield, 1980), pp. 56–78.

Hinchliff, Mark, *A Defense of Presentism* (doctoral dissertation, Princeton University, 1988).

Hinchliff, Mark, "The Puzzle of Change", in James Tomberlin (ed.), *Philosophical Perspectives*, vol. 10, *Metaphysics* (Cambridge, MA: Blackwell, 1996), pp. 119–36.

Howell, Robert, "Fictional Objects: How They Are and How They Aren't", *Poetics*, **8** (1979), pp. 129–77.

Kaplan, David, "Demonstratives", in Joseph Almog, John Perry, and Howard Wettstein (eds.), *Themes from Kaplan* (New York: Oxford University Press, 1989), pp. 481–564.

Keller, Simon and Nelson, Michael, "Presentists Should Believe in Time Travel", *Australasian Journal of Philosophy*, **79** (2001), pp. 333–45.

Kripke, Saul, *Naming and Necessity* (Cambridge, MA: Harvard University Press, 1972).

Levinson, Jerrold, "Making Believe", *Dialogue*, **32** (1993), pp. 359–74.

Lewis, David, *On the Plurality of Worlds* (Oxford: Basil Blackwell, 1986).

Long, A. A., and Sedley, D. N., *The Hellenistic Philosophers*, vol. 1, *Translations of the Principal Sources with Philosophical Commentary* (Cambridge: Cambridge University Press, 1987).

Lucretius, *On the Nature of the Universe* (R. Latham, trans.) (Baltimore: Penguin Books, 1951).

Markosian, Ned, "On Language and the Passage of Time", *Philosophical Studies*, **66** (1992), pp. 1–26.

Markosian, Ned, "How Fast Does Time Pass?" *Philosophy and Phenomenological Research*, **53** (1993), pp. 829–44.

Markosian, Ned, "The 3D/4D Controversy and Non-present Objects", *Philosophical Papers*, **23** (1994), pp. 243–9.

Markosian, Ned, "What Are Physical Objects?" *Philosophy and Phenomenological Research*, **61** (2000), pp. 375–95.

Maxwell, Nicholas, "Are Probabilism and Special Relativity Incompatible?" *Philosophy of Science*, **52** (1985), pp. 23–43.

McCall, Storrs, *A Model of the Universe* (Oxford: Clarendon Press, 1994).

Merricks, Trenton, "On the Incompatibility of Enduring and Perduring Entities", *Mind*, **104** (1995), pp. 523–31.

Monton, Bradley, "Presentism and Spacetime Physics", unpublished paper, 2000.

Newton-Smith, W. H., *The Structure of Time* (London: Routledge & Kegan Paul, 1980).

Oppy, Graham, "The Philosophical Insignificance of Gödel's Slingshot", *Mind*, **106** (1997), pp. 121–41.

Plantinga, Alvin, *The Nature of Necessity* (Oxford: Oxford University Press, 1974).

Plantinga, Alvin, "Actualism and Possible Worlds", *Theoria*, **42** (1976); reprinted in Michael J. Loux (ed.), *The Possible and the Actual* (Ithaca, NY: Cornell University Press, 1979), pp. 253–73.

Prior, Arthur N., *Time and Modality* (Oxford: Oxford University Press, 1957).

Prior, Arthur N., *Past, Present and Future* (Oxford: Oxford University Press, 1967).

Prior, Arthur N., *Papers on Time and Tense* (Oxford: Oxford University Press, 1968).

Prior, Arthur N., "Changes in Events and Changes in Things", in Arthur N. Prior, *Papers on Time and Tense* (Oxford: Oxford University Press, 1968), pp. 1–14.

Prior, Arthur N., "The Notion of the Present", *Stadium Generale*, **23** (1970), pp. 245–8.

Prior, Arthur N., "Thank Goodness That's Over", in Arthur N. Prior, *Papers in Logic and Ethics* (London: Duckworth, 1976), pp. 78–84.

Prior, Arthur N., "Some Free Thinking about Time", in Jack Copeland (ed.), *Logic and Reality: Essays on the Legacy of Arthur Prior* (Oxford: Clarendon Press, 1996), pp. 47–51.

Prior, Arthur N., "A Statement of Temporal Realism", in Jack Copeland (ed.), *Logic and Reality: Essays on the Legacy of Arthur Prior* (Oxford: Clarendon Press, 1996), pp. 45–46.

Prior, Arthur N., and Fine, Kit, *Worlds, Times and Selves* (Amherst, MA: University of Massachusetts Press, 1977).

Putnam, Hilary, "Time and Physical Geometry", *Journal of Philosophy*, **64** (1967), pp. 240–7.

Quine, W. V., *Quiddities* (Cambridge, MA: Harvard University Press, 1987).

Salmon, Nathan, "Nonexistence", *Noûs*, **32** (1998), pp. 277–319.

Sextus Empiricus, *Against the Physicists*, vol. 3 (R. G. Bury, trans.) (Cambridge, MA: Harvard University Press, 1960).

Sider, Ted, "Presentism and Ontological Commitment", *Journal of Philosophy*, **96** (1999), pp. 325–47.

Sider, Ted, *Four-Dimensionalism: An Ontology of Persistence and Time* (Oxford: Clarendon Press, 2001).

Smith, Quentin, *Language and Time* (Oxford: Oxford University Press, 1993).

Smith, Quentin, "Reference to the Past and Future", in Q. Smith and A. Jokic (eds.), *Time, Tense and Reference* (Cambridge, MA: MIT Press, 2002).

Tooley, Michael, *Time, Tense, and Causation* (Oxford: Oxford University Press, 1997).

Van Inwagen, Peter, "Creatures of Fiction", *American Philosophical Quarterly*, **24** (1977), pp. 299–308.

Wolterstorff, Nicholas, "Can Ontology Do without Events?" in Ernest Sosa (ed.), *Essays on the Philosophy of Roderick Chisholm* (Amsterdam: Rodopi, 1979).

Zalta, Edward N., "On the Structural Similarities between Worlds and Times", *Philosophical Studies*, **51** (1987), pp. 213–39.

Zimmerman, Dean, "Persistence and Presentism", *Philosophical Papers*, **35** (1996), pp. 115–26.

Zimmerman, Dean, "Chisholm and the Essences of Events", in Lewis E. Hahn (ed.), *The Philosophy of Roderick M. Chisholm* (Chicago: Open-Court, 1997).

Chapter 13

Paul Horwich

THE METAPHYSICS OF *NOW*

1. The 'Moving Now' Conception of Time

The quintessential property of time, it may seem, is the difference between the past and the future. And here I don't just mean that the past and the future are separate regions, or that the past and future directions along the continuum of instants are opposite to one another, but rather that these two directions are somehow fundamentally unalike. This idea is fostered by the desire to explain pervasive temporally asymmetric phenomena, such as causation, knowledge, decay, and the phenomenological feeling of 'moving into the future'. And it is reflected in the use of such phrases as "time's arrow" and in our inclination to say that time "goes" in one direction and not the other. Despite the fact that these expressions have an air of metaphor about them, they clearly imply *anisotropy*—that is, a significant lack of symmetry between the two directions of the temporal continuum. We tend to believe, in short, that time *itself* is temporally asymmetric.

This view of time contrasts with our attitude towards space. We can pick any straight line and define two opposite directions along it. Although the directions are numerically distinct from one another, we would regard them as essentially similar. We wouldn't expect the result of an experiment to depend on the direction in which our apparatus is pointing. Thus we suppose that space is isotropic. Not that this supposition is taken to be *necessarily* true. Aristotelian space, for example, is anisotropic in that directions toward and away from the center of the universe are ascribed quite different causal properties: fire naturally goes one way, and earth another. Similarly it should not be surprising if the question of time's anisotropy proves to be an empirical, contingent matter.

Often, however, those who proclaim the anisotropy of time are not motivated by scientific considerations but are gripped by a certain metaphysical picture. They have in mind that time is more than just a fixed sequence of events ordered by such relations as *later than* and *simultaneous with*, but that it also contains a peculiar property—being *now*—which moves gradually along the array in the direction from past to future. This idea is sometimes combined with a further metaphysical doctrine: namely, that there is an ontological distinction between the past and the future—a distinction that can be represented in a tree model of reality, in which the past consists of a fixed, definite course of events and the future contains nothing but a manifold of branching possibilities. These alleged aspects of time—which I shall describe in more detail as we proceed—are thought to especially distinguish it from space, which possesses no such features. Recent advocates of this sort of view include Broad (1938), Gale (1968), Geach (1972), and Schliesinger (1980). On the other hand, there are many philosophers—for example, Russell (1903), Williams (1951), Smart (1955), and Grünbaum (1963)—who reject the 'moving *now*' conception and think that the past and future have exactly the same ontological status. The maintain that the word "now" is an indexical expression (on a par with "here" and "I") whose special function is to designate whatever time happens be the time at which the word-token is uttered. On this account, the thought that an event E is first in the future, will become present, and then fade into the past does not presuppose a 'moving *now*', but it implies merely that E is later than the time at which that thought is entertained, simultaneous with some subsequent time, and earlier than times after that.

Our job in this chapter will be to try to settle these issues—that is, to decide whether there really is any objective feature of the world that corresponds to the idea of a 'moving *now*' and to assess the merits of the tree model. To this end I shall begin by describing and defending McTaggart's (1908) notorious proof that there is no such thing as the 'moving *now*'. But I won't endorse his entire line of thought. McTaggart argues that the 'moving property' theory of *now* is self-contradictory, but he thinks that this conception is nevertheless essential to time. He concludes therefore that time does not exist and that, though "now" indeed functions as an indexical, it refers not to times but rather to other entities that are somewhat like instants of time but only pale substitutes for them. I shall support McTaggart's rejection of the 'moving *now*' but not his further claim that genuine time could not exist without it. We shall see that the best defense against McTaggart's attack on the 'moving *now*' involves a commitment to the tree model of reality. Therefore, in exposing and undermining the antifatalistic and the verificationist motivations for that ontological picture, I hope to reinforce McTaggart's criticism of the 'moving *now*'.

After reaching these conclusions, I shall try to explain why we are nevertheless so captivated by

the 'moving *now*' conception. And in the next chapter we shall see that the metaphysical asymmetries suggested by the 'moving *now*' and the tree model are not needed for time to be anisotropic. Even if those ideas are wholly incorrect, there remains the possibility that time is intrinsically asymmetric in virtue of some purely physical, empirical phenomenon.

To begin with, it is worth a moment's digression to note that although McTaggart follows Leibniz (the Leibniz/Clarke correspondance; see Alexander 1956) in trying to prove *a priori* that time does not exist, their two arguments are totally unrelated. This is because Leibniz and McTaggart disagree radically about the sort of thing time would have to be, in order to be real. For Leibniz, real time would be a substance—a Newtonian continuum of thinglike instants at which events are located, ordered by the relation *later than*. But according to McTaggart, something quite different would have to be involved for time to exist: namely, a property, *being now*, which glides along the continuum of instants in the future direction. Moreover there is no need, in his view, for substantial instants. It would suffice if there were merely states of the world ordered by the relation, *later than*, just so long as the property, *now*, moves through these states, singling out progressively later and later ones, as shown in figure 13.1.

In McTaggart's terminology temporal locations may be specified in terms of two alternative systems of coordinates: the *A*-series, which locates an event relative to *now* (as being in the distant past, the recent past, the present, tomorrow, etc.), and the *B*-series, which locates an event relative to other events (as earlier than F, or simultaneous with G, etc.). His view is that time requires that there be a *B*-series, which in turn requires an *A*-series; but that the *A*-series is self-contradictory. Thus Leibniz and McTaggart are arguing against the instantiation of different conceptions of time. Leibniz tries to show that a continuum of instants cannot exist because it would violate the principles of Sufficient Reason

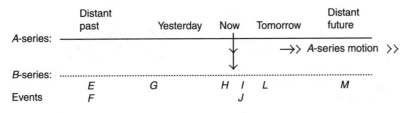

Figure 13.1

and Identity of Indiscernibles. McTaggart contends that the 'moving *now*' model of time is indispensible yet incoherent.

2. McTaggart's Argument for the Unreality of Time

The outline of McTaggart's proof is as follows:

1.   Events are located in a B-series (ordered with respect to *later than*), only if time exists.
2.   Time exists, only if there is genuine change.
3.   There is genuine change in the world, only if events are located in a real *A*-series.

THEREFORE:

i. Events are ordered with respect to *later than*, only if they are located in a real *A*-series.

4.   If events are located in a real *A*-series, then each event acquires the absolute properties *past, now*, and *future*.
5.   There is a contradiction in supposing that any event has any two of these absolute properties.

THEREFORE:

ii. A real *A*-series cannot exist.

THEREFORE:

(M) Events are not ordered with respect to *later than*.

Evidently this is a perfectly valid argument: there is nothing wrong with the deductive reasoning by which the preliminary conclusions, i and ii, are derived from their respective premises, and by which McTaggart's final conclusion, (M), is then drawn. It remains, however, to justify these premises. Let us consider what may be said on their behalf.

2.1. Events are Located in a B-series, Only if Time Exists

In order to see that McTaggart's first premise is correct, one must remember that it is not time in the Newtonian sense—an array of thinglike instants—whose reality is in question. Rather, the consequent of (1)—time exists—is supposed to be construed in a very broad way, as something like 'the world exhibits temporality'. And in that case, premise 1 becomes a trivial truth.

2.2. Time Exists, Only if there is Genuine Change

It might seem as though there could be time without change. For consider the scenarios schematized in figure 13.2. Cases like these are good candidates for time without change, and many philosophers who believe there could be time without change (e.g., Shoemaker 1969) have thought that it would suffice to show that worlds like those can occur. Such possibilities, however, are not what McTaggart is intent to deny. His view is that even in those cases there is still, contrary to first appearances, change of a

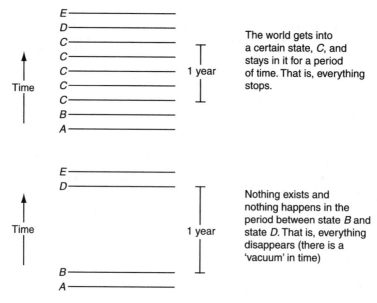

Figure 13.2

certain kind taking place: namely, states *A* and *B* are receding further and further into the past, and *D* is approaching the present. The *now* is in motion.

According to McTaggart, this sort of change is not only necessarily present if time passes, but also it is the only sort of *genuine* change that there could be. Consider, for example, a hot poker, which gradually cools in the period from t1 to t2. McTaggart denies that its being hot at t1 and cold at t2 constitutes a genuine change. For, he says, it was and will be true throughout the history of the universe that this poker is hot at t1 and cold at t2. Those facts are eternal; they always were, and always will obtain. That kind of variation with respect to time no more qualifies as genuine change than a variation of the temperature along the poker's length. What is required for genuine change, on the other hand, is that the sum total of facts at one time be not the same as the sum total of facts at another time.

Here, by the way, is the place at which I would quarrel with Mc-Taggart's proof, although the rationale for digging in at exactly this point will become clear only in retrospect.

When we see what he has in mind by "genuine change", this will undermine whatever initial inclination we may have had to agree that the reality of time requires such a thing. In other words, McTaggart's demonstration, in the second part of his argument, that 'genuine change' is self-contradictory should not persuade us that time is unreal but, rather, should force us to acknowledge that time does not require 'genuine change' after all.

2.3. There is Genuine Change in the World, Only if Events are Located in a Real A-series

A variation in the facts would not occur if time consisted in the B-series alone. For the B-series is a fixed ordering of events with respect to one another (and with respect to instants of time, if there are such entities). Therefore the B-series provides only for temporal facts like 'the poker is hot at t1', which, if it obtains at all, obtains forever. Genuine change can come about only in virtue of the relative motion of the A- and the B-series, in which the *now* moves gradually in the direction from earlier to later. This generates genuine changes of the following kind: E is in the distant future, E is in the near future, E is now, E is in the past, and so on.

Note that there are certain metaphysically innocuous construals of the terms "past", "now", and "future" that must be rejected by Mc-Taggart, since they would not imply a real A-series. Consider, for example, the use of "now" in sentences such as "E is now (present) at t". This usually means "E occurs at t", which is a B-series fact. Similarly "E is past at t", means "E is earlier than t", and "E is future at t" means "E is later than t". Past, present, and future have become *relative* properties, whose exemplification is accommodated by the B-series.

Alternatively, suppose that "now" is an indexical expression, like "here" and "I", whose referent depends on the context of utterance. In particular, "now" would rigidly pick out the time, whatever it happens to be, at which the word is used. And suppose that at t1 I truthfully say "E is now", and at t2 I say "E is not now". Each of these utterances expresses facts, and each of the facts obtains throughout all time. One might be tempted to dispute this claim. One might doubt that "E is now", said at t1, expresses a fact that obtains at t2, since that sentence uttered at t2 would be false. But this would be a non sequitur because the sentence does not say the same thing at the two different times. The word "now", used at t1, simply provides a way of referring to the time t1. And the fact expressed by the first remark—though perhaps not the same as the fact expressed by "E is at t1"—is just as permanent. Consequently McTaggart holds that for there to be genuine change and a real A-series, "past", "present", and "future" can be neither relational predicates nor indexicals.

So far McTaggart has tried to show that time requires the existence of a genuinely moving *now*. And, as I have already said, this preliminary conclusion may be resisted. The remainder of his argument is a demonstration that the 'moving *now*' conception is self-contradictory. This is part of his reasoning that I believe is correct and important.

2.4. If Events are Located in a Real A-series, then Each Event Acquires the Absolute Properties Past, Now, and Future

A real A-series entails that for every event such as E, there is a fact, included in the totality of facts that constitutes the universe, consisting of E's having the quality of *presentness*, that is,

E is   (or, E is now)

but also the universe must contain the facts

E will be   (or, E is future)

and

E was   (or, E is past)

Given what is meant by "a real A-series," such facts are not relations between events and times. They are not, in other words, the exemplification of merely *relative* properties, which can both apply and fail to apply to the same event relative to different frames of reference. Rather, such facts consist in the exemplification by events of absolute properties.

2.5. There is a Contradiction in Supposing that Any Event Possesses Any Two of these Absolute Properties

Past, present, and future (which are equivalent to 'earlier than now', 'now', and 'later than now') are incompatible attributes. Therefore the supposition that one event has them all involves a contradiction. That is to say, it is impossible that the history of the universe contain the three facts: E is past, E is now, E is future.

One will be tempted to object, as follows. There is a contradiction only if the A-series qualities are attributed *simultaneously* to E; but such simultaneous attribution is not required by the existence of the A-series; rather, its existence entails only that each of the A-series qualities apply to E at some time or other. That is to say, McTaggart's premise 4 will be satisfied even if the A-series determinations are acquired *successively*, and in that case no contradiction arises. In other words, the requirement described in premise 4 may be met by the existence of the facts

E is future at t1
E is present at t2
E is past at t3

which are quite compatible. There is no need to take premise 4 to imply that all the A-series determinations would have to apply at the same time.

However, one must beware of resolving the contradiction in ways that involve eliminating any real A-series. And this is exactly what has just happened. For the meanings of "future", "present", and "past" in the preceding sentences are "later than", "simultaneous with", and "earlier than". The facts described are generated by the B-series. Genuine change has been lost in the reformulation. To preserve genuine change—to have a real A-series—it is not enough that there be a variation in *relative* presentness from one time to another (like the variation in the velocity of an object relative to different reference frames). Rather, there must be variation of facts. Thus it is necessary to construe premise 4 in such a way that the transitions from 'E will be' to 'E is' to 'E was' are transitions between mutually exclusive, absolute states.

At this point McTaggart's opponent might well complain that revealing such a variation of facts was precisely the intention behind his reformulation of premise 4. The idea, he says, was *not* to transform *past*, *present*, and *future* into mere relations (which admittedly only succeeds in eliminating the A-series) but rather to suggest that the facts "E is past", and so on, might themselves obtain only relative to a temporal perspective. In other words, the premise 4 should have been formulated more perspicuously with the following sentences:

The fact that E is *future* obtains at t1
The fact that E is *present* obtains at t2
The fact that E is *past* obtains at t3

Thus there is, after all, a variation, from one time to another, as to which facts obtain.

In response to this suggestion, however, we are justified in resisting the crucial assumption that the italicized internal sentences express facts. For a strong case can be made that this latest formulation of premise 4 trades on an idiosyncratic and unmotivated conception of *fact*. After all, we do not regard

X is to the left of Y

and

X is not to the left of Y

as explicit descriptions of facts. Rather, we suppose that whenever such claims are true, they are partial accounts of facts whose explicit descriptions take the form

X is to the left of Y relative to Z

and

X is not to the left of Y relative to W

Similarly one does not say that the facts, fully articulated, include

It is raining

and

It is not raining

But rather, for example,

It is raining in Manchester

and

It is not raining in Florida

The general point is that we reserve the term "fact" for those aspects of reality whose explicit descriptions are sentences that are true *simpliciter*—and not merely true relative to some context or point of view, and false relative to others. Consequently, if we are going to say that "E is past" is sometimes true and sometimes false, then unless some good reason is given to depart from our usual conception of fact, we should not countenance this sentence as an explicit characterization of a fact. The real facts, as we said initially, are described by sentences of the form "E is past at t", in which pastness has been transformed into a relation.

These remarks do not absolutely preclude the idea that facts may be relative: that is, dependent on a frame of reference. The point is, rather, that such a perspectival view of reality would require a radical change in our conception of fact, and that any such revision would call for some independent motivation. So far, in our discussion of this problem, no reason to abandon the usual notion of fact has been offered. And this is why the response to McTaggart that we are now considering is inadequate as it stands. However, that is not to say that no such argument for perspectivalism *could* be given. Indeed, a strategy to that end, based on verificationist considerations, is suggested by Dummett (1960). I shall take it up in the next section, in connection with Aristotle's tree model of reality.

I have been arguing that McTaggart's contradiction is not avoided by the supposition that the futurity, presentness, and pastness of E obtain relative to three times, t1, t2, and t3. Notice that it is equally futile to try to escape his conclusion by rendering the facts as follows:

E is future, in the past
E is now, in the present
E is past, in the future

In the first place, this strategy is subject to the same criticism as before: the initial occurrences of "future", "present", and "past" have been transformed into relative properties. So these sentences can be reformulated as

E is later than past times
E is simultaneous with the present time
E is earlier than future times

which do not entail the existence of the facts required by a real *A*-series. And in the second place, such second-order temporal attributions are just as problematic, from McTaggart's point of view, as the first-order ones. For they are compatible with one another only if we assume that the *past*, *present*, and *future* are disjoint regions of time (or of events). And that assumption is contrary to his requirement: that every event and time has the qualities of *past*, *present*, and *future*. This being so, we can derive from the first statement (supposing that "past" and "present" are coextensive)

E is future, in the present

which conflicts with the second statement. Therefore the contradiction is not avoided by introducing second-order temporal attributions. This is because, from the fact that each of the first-order attributions must hold, it follows that each of the second-order attributions must hold. And they conflict just as blatantly as the first-order attributions.

The most common criticism of McTaggart's argument (e.g., Broad 1938; Prior 1967) is exactly the point just dealt with: to claim that consistency may be achieved by a reformulation in terms of higher-order temporal attributions. It is not appreciated that McTaggart himself considers and refutes this strategy. To repeat, he denies that his requirement that the world contain the facts

E is past
E is present

E is future

is misstated when construed literally, in which case the facts are mutually inconsistent with one another; and therefore he denies that the required facts are accurately represented by, for example,

E is past, in the future
E is now, in the present
E is future, in the past

For the operative occurrences of "past", "present", and "future" have been turned into relations. Therefore McTaggart denies that the initial contradiction is treated by introducing second-order attributions. Nevertheless he is quite happy to conduct the argument at the second level. For, from his first-order requirement, it follows that *every* second-order attribution must hold—and this is also a contradiction.

Thus McTaggart shows that a certain very tempting, 'moving *now*' conception of time is not actualized. But he does not succeed in proving that time is unreal, because the first part of his argument is not persuasive (Mellor 1981). In other words, we need not agree with him (premise 2) that it is essential to the reality of time that there be 'genuine change', in his sense. This claim is implausible and never really substantiated. If we are persuaded, as I think we should be, by the second part of his argument, we will conclude that there can be no 'real A-series' or 'genuine change'. Rather, change is always variation in one thing with respect to another, the totality of absolute facts about those functional relations remaining forever constant.

3.   The Tree Model of Reality

Affiliated with the 'moving *now*' conception of time is another unorthodox metaphysical theory—roughly speaking, that only past and present events exist, and future ones do not. Reality, in this view, is thought to resemble an unlimited tree: from any point, there is a single definite path downward (history is fixed) but above each point we encounter a proliferation of many possible branches (the future is open). Thus statements about the past and present are, right now, determinately true or false, unlike current claims about the future, which do not attain a truth value until the predicted events either occur or fail to occur. Only the advance of the *now* settles which path through the tree is taken and which predictions are true.

In figure 13.3, N represents the present state of the world. The chain of stars represents the fixed past. (Note that there is just one way down the tree from N.) And the branches growing up from N represent the many things that might happen later; thus the future is open. The only statements about the future that hold at N are those that are obtain in all of the branches that stem from N. If something—for example, a sea battle tomorrow—occurs in some branches but not in others, then from the perspective of N, there is no fact of the matter as to whether there will be a sea battle tomorrow.

Aristotle, with whom this sort of view is often credited, was not the first philosopher to deal with time; but he was the first to offer more than provocative aphorisms and to try, in a scientific spirit, to clarify and demystify our conception of temporality. And he reached the conclusion that time is *doubly* asymmetrical. In the *Physics* (Book IV) he endorses the 'moving *now*', and in *De Interpretatione*—according to one natural construal of it—he advocates a truth-value asymmetry as the only way to avoid fatalism.

I am going to argue, on the contrary, that there is no ontological asymmetry between past and future and that the threat of fatalism can be averted without radical measures of this sort. To begin with, however, I want to explore the relationship between the tree model of reality and the 'moving *now*' conception of time. We shall see that although advocates of the 'moving *now*' can base a defense against McTaggart on the tree model, there is, on the other hand, no incentive

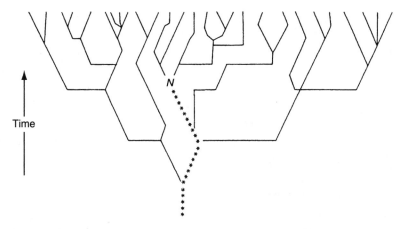

Figure 13.3

for advocates of the tree model to endorse the 'moving *now*' conception of time.

On the latter point, notice that the tree model does not preclude an indexical construal of "now"; and so there is no compulsion to hold that reality contains not merely the tree but also a quality—*now*—that moves up the tree, selecting which branches are to be actual. To see more vividly why this addition to the tree model is not needed, suppose that the past, as well as the future, were not determined by the present. Suppose, in other words, that more than one possible course of history were compatible with the current state of the world. Then a network of possibilities would branch out into the past. And in that case both the past and the future would be open. One would think that if the openness of the future called for a future-directed *now*, then the openness of the past would similarly entail a past-directed *now*. Yet there surely would be no philosopher who would go quite so far as to postulate a *pair* of oppositely moving *nows*. (When would they meet?) This suggests that a fondness for the tree model does not produce a taste for the 'moving *now*' conception of time.

On the other hand, one can quite understand why advocates of a 'moving *now*' would be inclined to sympathize with the tree model. McTaggart's argument that the 'moving *now*'

does not exist depends on exposing a contradiction between facts "E is past", "E is present", and "E is future", all of which must, given a genuinely moving *now*, belong to the totality of absolute facts in the world. However, as Dummett (1960) has observed, this argument requires the assumption (which, as we shall see in a minute, is questionable) that there *is* such a totality of facts. If there is no such thing—if the facts change from one temporal perspective to another—then the only troublesome contradictions are contradictions from a particular temporal perspective. But a 'moving *now*' does not require that E be past, present, and future from a single temporal perspective. So if there is no time-neutral body of absolute facts, there is no contradiction. Thus, by denying the assumption of this totality, McTaggart's objection can be sidestepped.

But only at substantial cost. For the crucial move—denying the assumption that there is a totality of facts—seems quite bizarre, unless it is independently motivated. As we saw in our discussion of McTaggart's proof, it looks simply ad hoc, and contrary to our usual conception of fact, to say

The fact that E *is future* obtains at t1

rather than

E is the future at t1

or, in other words

E is later than t1

Thus there might seem to be no reason to countenance facts that obtain at some times and not at others. The attraction of the tree model of reality is precisely its ability to supply this rationale. For the tree model purports to show, independently of anything to do with *now*, that there is no complete, time-neutral body of facts. At any point the facts consist of a certain course of history, plus the present state and whatever is in every future branch. But this body of facts changes. And there is no summing up, from a temporally neutral point of view, to obtain an overall picture of reality. Thus defenders of the 'moving *now*' will be happy to embrace the tree model. For, in the context of that model, their best reply to McTaggart is not ad hoc: genuine change can be achieved without contradiction. By the same token a thorough criticism of the 'moving *now*' conception must eventually deal with the tree model of reality. Let us therefore examine the reason that, following Aristotle, is most often cited as motivating this ontological asymmetry: the avoidance of fatalism.

4. Fatalism

The case for fatalism goes something like this. What was true in the past logically determines what will be true in the future; therefore, since the past is over and done with and beyond our control, the future must also be beyond our control; consequently, there is no point in worrying, planning, and taking pains to influence what will happen.

The fatalist's assumption that the future is already logically determined derives from his supposition that if some sentence, such as "A sea battle is occurring", would be true if asserted at a future time, say, on January 1, 1999, then it

would always have been correct to predict that a sea battle will occur on that date. In particular, on January 1, 1000, it was the case that a sea battle will occur on January 1, 1999. But this past fact—namely, "On January 1, 1000, it was the case that there will be a sea battle on January 1, 1999"—logically entails "A sea battle will occur on January 1, 1999". This is the rationale for the fatalist's assumption of logical determinism of the future by the past. Aristotle's idea is to avoid fatalism by rejecting this deterministic thesis. He undermines its rationale by maintaining that contingent statements about the future are presently neither true nor false.

More precisely, the argument for fatalism proceeds as follows. Let f refer to an arbitrary future time and p to an arbitrary past time; let capital letters stand for statements that are about free actions, and $\Box$ . . . stand for "It is now determined, and beyond our ability to influence the fact, that . . ."; and let, for example, Qp mean "Q was true at past time p", and Sfp mean "It was the case at past time p that S will be true at future time f".

We begin with a premise intended to express the idea that due to the future orientation of causation, the past is fixed and beyond our control:

$$Qp \rightarrow \Box(Qp) \tag{1}$$

Then we substitute for Q the statement, "S will be true at future time f" and obtain

$$Sfp \rightarrow \Box(Sfp) \tag{2}$$

But Sfp necessarily has the same truth value as Sf, and if one of these facts is beyond our control, then so is the other. Therefore we can replace the antecedent of (2) with Sf, and its consequent with $\Box$ (Sf), to get

$$Sf \rightarrow \Box(Sf) \tag{3}$$

If we can assume that there is now a definite fact

about whether some act, described by R, will or will not occur in the future, then we can say

$$Rf \vee (-R)f \qquad (4)$$

But now we may substitute, first R, and then –R, for S, and obtain

$$\Box\, (Rf) \vee \Box((-R)\, f) \qquad (5)$$

which says that either R's future truth is now fixed and beyond our control, or R's future falsity is fixed and beyond our control.

It seems clear that the reasoning involved in this argument is perfectly valid. And if so, then our options are as follows:

i. Abandon the plausible sounding view that the past is already determined and beyond our control—that is, deny (1).
ii. Follow Aristotle by giving up the idea that all statements about the future have a present truth value—that is, deny (4).
iii. Invite fatalism by agreeing that even future events are presently beyond our control—that is, accept (5).

None of these alternatives looks attractive. However, some are clearly worse then others. In particular, the practical consequences of fatalism make that doctrine literally impossible to accept, and therefore make it impossible for us to accept statement (5). Moreover, the Aristotelian renunciation of facts about the future runs counter to logical principles (e.g., that every statement is either true or false) and a conception of time that are extremely plausible and have been pillars of science and common sense. So we would very much like to avoid options ii and iii. Why then resist the first option? Why not agree that, in some sense, the past is not beyond our control? Is it so paradoxical to allow, for example, that I can now decide whether or not it was true last week that I would scratch my head today?

No sooner is it formulated, than this escape from the paradox seems obviously right. But why wasn't this clear from the beginning? Why did we find premise (1) so plausible? The answer is that there is a definite sense in which the past is beyond our control. We would doubt the sanity of anyone who announced his intention to do something now in order to bring about some past event. So, at first sight, there is a conflict between our way out of the choice between fatalism or Aristotelianism and our respect for the fact that effects do not precede their causes.

But of course there really is no such conflict. The way to reconcile our influence over the past with the direction of causation is to recognize that S may be true at time p without there being any concrete event or state of affairs at p that makes S true at that time. It is a failure to notice this simple point that is responsible for the paradox. Consider:

The wheel was invented several thousand years ago in Egypt

Suppose this is true. There need be nothing now (or here, for that matter)—no present occurrences—that make it true. What makes it true, if it is true, are certain events that took place in Egypt thousands of years ago. Similarly, even though it was true last week that I would now scratch my head, there was no event or state of affairs last week that made it true.

Therefore, although my present decision does, in some sense, influence the past—since it was responsible for making it true in the past that I would scratch my head—my decision did not bring about any past event, and so there is no conflict with the principle that events never precede their causes. Therefore we can happily deny premise (1) of the fatalist's reasoning. Thus Aristotle's argument for an ontological time asymmetry is unconvincing. It derives, I have suggested, from mistakenly supposing that premise (1) is justified by the direction of causation—a mistake that derives in turn from a confounding of facts with events, or, more accurately, from confusing a proposition's being true at a given time with the existence of concrete circumstances at that time in virtue of which the proposition is true.

5. Verificationist Roots of the Tree Model

But is this conclusion really fair to Aristotle and his sympathizers? Perhaps he was not at all confused on this point? Perhaps one might maintain, quite deliberately, that a fact obtains at a time only in virtue of something going on at that time? If so, then premise (1) will be justified, the tree model will begin to look much more attractive, and one will be in a position to defend the 'moving *now*' against McTaggart's objection, as we saw earlier, by denying the existence of an absolute totality of facts. Let us explore this possibility.

Aristotle seems to think that the state of the world at any given time contains determinants of every past event but does not determine everything (e.g., free actions) that will happen later. In other words, he holds that the relation of physical determination is time-asymmetric. . . . Such an asymmetry will suggest, perhaps even entail, that time itself is asymmetric (or anisotropic). However, there is no immediate implication that future events do not enjoy exactly the same ontological status as past events—namely, the status of existing at some moment of time or other. One can, it seems, endorse a tree model of *possibility*, thereby avoiding fatalism, without being committed to a tree model of *actuality*.

Thus the tree diagrammed in figure 13.3 may be taken to represent an Aristotelian world in which relations of physical possibility are asymmetrical in time. The laws of nature in this world are indeterministic in such a manner that given the state of things at any time, there is only one course of history that could have led up to that state but there are many alternative ways that the future could go. However, unlike Aristotle, it

would seem that one might perfectly well claim that only one of these ways will be actual and that future reality (which could be represented by a continuing chain of stars) is quite definite. From the point of view of the present state of affairs, N, the future is not determined and not predictable, as the past is—but it is no less real.

Aristotle's position, however, is that no particular future path is singled out as actual—there should be no stars above the N in figure 13.3. He can agree there are *some* truths about the future. It will be the case that either a sea battle takes place tomorrow or it doesn't; for that disjunction is true in every branch. But he must deny that the battle either will or will not take place; for a battle occurs tomorrow in some branches but not in others, and no particular branch is especially relevant to the question of what the future holds.

It will be conceded by proponents of the Aristotelian position that most of us implicitly reject their view. We might be persuaded that the avoidence of fatalism calls for a tree model of possibility. But we do not suppose that a fact may obtain at a time, only if there are concrete events at that time to make it hold. Therefore we see no reason to go so far as a tree model of actuality. On the contrary, most of us do believe that some definite course of future events will occur whether determined or not. We naively make a distinction between what *will* happen and what *must* happen. And such a distinction is recognized in practical affairs when we give credit (e.g., by paying off bets) for correct predictions. So the question arises: What could possibly count against our ordinary way of thinking, and in favor of the counterintuitive Aristotelian position?

Antirealist theses are typically motivated by verificationism—by the thought that we can understand a sentence only to the extent that we know how to recognize if it is true (Dummett 1978). This is the route to intuitionism in mathematics and behaviorism in psychology, and the domain at issue here is no exception. According to our antirealist regarding the future, we now understand a prediction that some event will occur tomorrow only if we are now able to tell whether such a prediction is correct or not. And we can do this only if there exist present determinants of the truth, or the falsity, of the prediction. But usually there are no such determinants. So, in those cases, there is no sense to the idea that the prediction is true. Therefore, claims the antirealist, the elements of our linguistic practice that presuppose a definite future are incoherent and unintelligible. We are mistaken in thinking that we truly understand such talk of the future.

Thus extraordinarily strict standards of intelligibility are presupposed by the antirealist; and the plausibility of his tree model hangs precisely on the question of whether those standards should in fact be adopted. Can we be satisfied with ordinary understanding as revealed by a facility with a stable, useful, linguistic practice? Or should we insist on the sort of super '*understanding*' provided by strict verificationist standards? I myself am not moved by a desire to streamline language along verificationist lines and, in particular, see nothing unfortunate or ontologically significant in the fact that statements about the future are not often verifiable in advance. But clearly a proper discussion of verificationism would take us too far afield. In its absence we can perhaps make do with the following uncontentious conclusion. '*Reality*'—defined in terms of what we '*understand*'—conforms to the tree model; but common or garden reality, described by means of what we ordinarily take ourselves to understand, does not. In other words, let us grant the verificationist his special, sanitized conceptions of *meaning, truth,* and so on; allow that certain instances of "*p* or not *p*" are *false,* in his sense; but proceed to operate with our own convenient notions, without regard for the standards of verifiability that they fail to meet. Insofar as this attitude is legitimate, we will have no use for the tree model and, therefore, no perspective from which to rescue the 'moving *now*' from McTaggart's refutation.

6. Our Sense of Passage

If the 'moving *now*' conception of time is wrong, then why is it so compelling? A neat answer to this question (Grünbaum 1963) is that because the word "now" functions somewhat like a noun, we are seduced into regarding it as standing for a single entity whose varying locations are instants of time. But the direction of motion of any object is, by definition, the set of its locations ordered according to the times at which it possesses them. In this way we evolve a picture of a mysterious entity, *now*, gliding inexorably into the future.

Thus the asymmetry involved in regarding the future, rather than the past, as *the* direction of time, seems to stem entirely from the time bias built into the meaning we have given to the expression "*the* direction of change" and does not arise from any asymmetry within the temporal continuum itself. Indeed, our temptation to recognize such a 'substantial' asymmetry gives every indication of being a good example of what Wittgenstein constantly warned against: the derivation of misleading metaphysical conceptions from structures in language:

> In our failure to understand the use of a word we take it as the expression of a queer *process.* (As we think of time as a queer medium, of the mind as a queer kind of being.) (1953, sec. 196)

However, one cannot be fully satisfied with this sort of answer until the '*feeling*' of time flow has been explained. There appears to be something about the structure of our awareness of things that makes it very natural for us to characterize ourselves as "moving into the future", or as "perceiving the passage of events as if they were floating on a river that flows past us". But what are the aspects of experience that produce our sense that time passes? And how do these phenomenological features contribute to the attractiveness of the 'moving *now*' conception?

Let us consider, therefore, the temporal structure of a typical experience. (The following account is derived from Izchak Miller's (1984) elucidation of Husserl's *Phenomenology of Internal Time-Consciousness* (1928)). In the first place, it is significant that a normal experience is a complex entity made up of, among other things, memories of the distant past, more recent recollections, sensations, and anticipations projected for various times in the future. Moreover some of the memories and anticipations are of experiences that themselves contain just those sorts of constituents. Thus, each normal experience involves not only an awareness of variation in the physical world but also an awareness of the fact that there has been, and will be, a sequence of experiences in which what is anticipated will be sensed and subsequently remembered. In other words, an experience represents both a set of events strung out in time and a set of experiences, each of which represents, from different perspectives, the same string of events.

In figure 13.4 the central vertical line stands for my experience at a given time, and the rest of the diagram pictures part of the intensional content of that experience. The points in the bottom half of the line are memories, the central point is a sensation, and the upper points are anticipations. The horizontal line stands for the stream of events in time that are represented by these various components of my experience. The intensional content of each component is indicated by the arrow leading from it. Thus each component (memory, sensation, or anticipation) attributes a particular distance from *now* (respectively, negative, zero or positive) to a specific event and also attributes experiences (shown by vertical dashed lines) to those times. The components of these experiences bear a systematic relationship to the experience I am now having. Thus I anticipate that things I now remember will at some later time be remembered as having occurred even further in the past, that the things I now sense will be remembered, and that some things I now anticipate will then be expected to happen not so

far in the future. And I remember that many of the things I now remember were once remembered as not having happened so far in the past, that the things I now sense were once anticipated, and that things I now anticipate were then expected to happen even further in the future than they now are.

In virtue of the phenomenological difference between memory and anticipation, this picture of our experience is asymmetrical. It is therefore able to accommodate certain elements in our conception of time, such as the phenomenological difference between past and future orientations. But it remains unclear why there should be a sense of 'movement' through time.

Some philosophers have been inclined to attribute this feeling of time flow to the fact that memories are taken to be more reliable than anticipations, so that we are conscious of a continual accumulation of perceptual knowledge. But this does not help to account for a sense of motion (Smart 1980). In the first place, it is left unexplained why we should seem to move through time in the direction of *increasing* knowledge, rather than in the opposition direction of *decreasing* knowledge. And second, one can imagine there being a limit to memory, so that every experience is automatically forgotten after, say, five seconds (as in the case of those who suffer from Korsakoff's syndrome). In such circumstances there would be no change in our total quantity of perceptual knowledge and yet we would still experience the passage of time.

What then is capable of transforming our awareness of the variation in experience across time into a sense of time flow? I think that the answer is suggested in what I said initially about the so-called motion of *now*. That is, all we mean by "the direction of change" of any process is the direction from the earlier states of the process *to* the later states. In particular, the direction of motion of an object in space is, by definition, from its earlier locations *toward* its later locations. Now, as I have just described, we are aware of a succession of complex experiences. Each has the

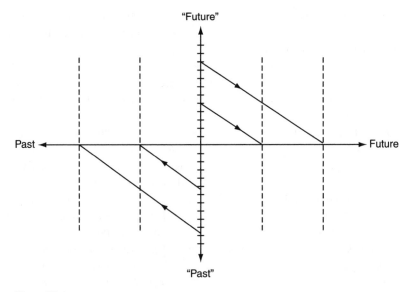

Figure 13.4

same structure consisting of a present sensation, anticipations with various degrees of projected futurity, and recollections of various types. And each has roughly the same content—a set of phenomena strung out in time. The difference between them is that the later that an experience is represented as occurring, the more pastness and less futurity it attributes to any given event. Thus we are conscious of the same experiential framework being filled with the same contents from different temporal perspectives. Therefore it seems to us as if a single entity—the structure of experience—is undergoing these changes. However, as I have been emphasizing, the direction of a change is from its earlier to its later states. Thus we obtain a sense of our consciousness in motion relative to the world—either crawling into the future or else interacting briefly with events as they rush into the past.

In summary, I explain our 'sense of the passage of time' as the product of two factors: phenomenological and linguistic. In the first place, the framework of a single experience contains elements of anticipation and recollection that picture time as a one-dimensional continuum, distinguish the two directions along that continuum, locate a string of physical and mental events in it, and also locate an array of various states of awareness of those same events, each from a different vantage point. This is the substantive phenomenological component in our awareness of time flow. In the second place, our conventions concerning the concepts of 'motion' and 'direction' lead to a particular way of describing the array of states of mind that is pictured in any single experience. Since each state consists in our experiential framework, located at a given phenomenological time and filled with the content that is appropriate for that vantage point on the string of events, the change of state that we are aware of is a variation in the temporal *location* of our experiential framework. Thus we describe this change as "movement through time". And since, by convention, we suppose that the direction of any process is from earlier to later stages in the process, so we come to say that our experience involves a sense of motion into the future.

References

Alexander, H. G. (ed.). 1956. *The Leibniz-Clarke Correspondence*. Manchester: Manchester University Press.

Broad, C. D. 1938. *Examination of McTaggart's Philosophy*,

vol. 2, part 1. Cambridge: Cambridge University Press.

Dummett, Michael. 1960. "A Defense of McTaggart's Proof of the Unreality of Time." *Philosophical Review* 69: 497–504.

Dummett, Michael. 1978. *Truth and Other Enigmas.* Oxford: Clarendon Press.

Gale, Richard. 1968. *The Language of Time.* London: Routledge & Kegan Paul.

Geach, P. T. 1972. *Logic Matters.* Berkeley: University of California Press.

Grünbaum, Adolf. 1963. *Philosophical Problems of Space and Time.* New York: Alfred A. Knopf.

Husserl, E. 1928. *The Phenomenology of Internal Time Consciousness.* Translated by J. S. Churchill. Bloomington: University of Indiana Press.

McTaggart, J. M. E. 1908. "The Unreality of Time." *Mind* 18: 457–84.

Mellor, D. H. 1981. *Real Time.* Cambridge: Cambridge University Press.

Miller, I. 1984. *Husserl, Perception, and the Awareness of Time.* Cambridge, Mass.: MIT Press. A Bradford Book.

Prior, A. N. 1967. *Past, Present, and Future.* Oxford: Clarendon Press.

Russell, B. 1903. *The Principles of Mathematics.* New York: Norton.

Schliesinger, G. 1980. *Aspects of Time.* Indianapolis, IN: Hackett Publishing Company.

Shoemaker, S. S. 1969. "Time Without Change." *Journal of Philosophy* 66: 363–81.

Smart, J. J. C. 1955. "Spatializing Time." Reprinted in *The Philosophy of Time*, edited by R. Gale. New York: Anchor Books, 1967.

Smart, J. J. C. 1980. "Time and Becoming." In *Time and Cause*, edited by P. van Inwagen. Dordrecht: Reidel.

Williams, D. C. 1951. "The Myth of Passage." Reprinted in the present volume as Chapter 14.

Wittgenstein, L. 1953. *Philosophical Investigations.* Oxford: Oxford University Press.

Donald C. Williams

THE MYTH OF PASSAGE[1]

At every moment each of us finds himself the apparent center of the world, enjoying a little foreground of the here and now, while around him there looms, thing beyond thing, event beyond event, the plethora of a universe. Linking the furniture of the foreground are sets of relations which he supposes also to bind the things beyond and to bind the foreground with the rest. Noteworthy among them are those queerly obvious relations, peculiarly external to their terms, which compose the systems of space and time, modes of connection exhaustively specifiable in a scheme of four dimensions at right angles to one another. Within this manifold, for all that it is so firmly integrated, we are immediately struck by a disparity between the three-dimensional spread of space and the one dimension of time. The spatial dimensions are in a literal and precise sense perpendicular to one another, and the sub-manifold which they compose is isotropic, the same in all directions. The one dimension of time, on the other hand, although it has the same formal properties as each of the other three, is at least sensuously different from them as they are not from one another, and the total manifold is apparently not isotropic. Whereas an object can preserve the same shape while it is so shifted that its height becomes its breadth, we can not easily conceive how it could do so while being shifted so that its breadth becomes its duration.

The theory of the manifold, I think, is the one model on which we can describe and explain the foreground of experience, or can intelligibly and credibly construct our account of the rest of the world, and this is so because in fact the universe is spread out in those dimensions. There may be Platonic entities which are foreign to both space and time; there may be Cartesian spirits which are foreign to space; but the homely realm of natural existence, the total of world history, is a spatio-temporal volume, of somewhat uncertain magnitude, chockablock with things and events. Logic, with its law of excluded middle and its tenseless operators, and natural science, with its secular world charts, concur inexorably with the vision of metaphysics and high religion that truth and fact are thus eternal.

I believe that the universe consists, without residue, of the spread of events in space-time, and that if we thus accept realistically the four-dimensional fabric of juxtaposed actualities we can dispense with all those dim non-factual categories which have so bedevilled our race: the potential, the subsistential, and the influential, the noumenal, the numinous, and the non-natural. But I am arguing here, not that there is nothing outside the natural world of events, but that the theory of the manifold is anyhow literally true and adequate to that world.

The chink in the armor of the theory is supposed to be on the side of time. Sir James Jeans regretted that time is mathematically attached to space by so "weird" a function as the square root of minus one,[2] and the very word "weird," being cognate with *"werden," to become*, is a monument to the uncanniness of our fourth dimension. Perhaps there exists an intellectualistic solipsist who grants the propriety of conceiving a temporal stretch of events, to wit, his own whole inner biography, while denying that the spatial scheme is a literal truth about anything. Most of the disparagers of the manifold, however, are of opposite bias. Often ready enough to take literally the spatial extension of the world, they dispute the codicil which rounds it out in the dimension of time. They do not intend this as a disparagement of time. On the contrary, they are what Wyndham Lewis (in *Time and Western Man*) called "time snobs." They plume themselves that by refusing to time the dimensional status they alone are "taking time seriously."

The partisans of time often take it with such Spartan seriousness that they deny existence to virtually all of it—to all of it, in short, but the infinitesimal pulse of the present. If we may interpret strictly some characteristic statements of Schopenhauer and the late Professor Mead,[3] for example, they would have it that the totality of being consists of the set of events which are simultaneous with the utterance "*now*," and most of the schools which are loosely called "romantic" would seem committed at heart to the same conclusion. This, of course, is incredible in point of psychology, for nobody can help believing at any moment that it has predecessors and successors. Also, it is incredible in point of logic, not just because induction tells us the contrary, but deductively, because a concrete object can no more exist with zero duration than with zero breadth and length.

One motive for the paradoxical philosophy of the present is the general romantic polemic against logic and the competence of concepts. The theory of the manifold is the logical account of events *par excellence*, the teeth by which the jaws of the intellect grip the flesh of occurrence. The Bergsonian, who thinks that concepts cannot convey the reality of time because they are "static," and the Marxist who thinks that process defies the cadres of two-valued logic, have thus an incentive for denying, in effect, all of the temporal universe except the present flash and urge. To counter their attack, it is a nice and tempting question whether and how concepts are "static," and whether and how, in any case, a true concept must be similar to its object. But we cannot here undertake the whole defense of the intellect against its most radical critics. We shall rather notice those two main motives for trimming down the time system which affect to utilize conceptual analysis and do not outright condemn it. One of them is an extreme sharpening of the positivistic argument from the egocentric predicament. For if it is impossible for my concepts to transcend experience in general, it may well be impossible for them to transcend the momentary experience in which they are entertained. Conversely, however, anybody who rejects the arguments for instantaneous solipsism, as most people do, must reject this argument for diminishing the manifold. The remaining motive is the finding of an intolerable anomaly in the statement that what was but has ceased, or what will be but has not begun, nevertheless *is*. Although equally cogent against the past and the future, this sort of reflection has generally been used, as by Aristotle, by certain neo-scholastics, by C. D. Broad, and by Professors Weiss and Hartshorne, to deny the reality only of the future, while preserving the past. I have contended elsewhere[4] that the argument is in any case invalid, because it mistakes for an ontological absolute the semantical accident that the significance of Indo-European verbs is generally complicated by *tenses*. Thus when I replace the colloquial "There will be a sea fight tomorrow" with the logically proper "There is a sea fight tomorrow," I seem to be making, not the innocuous assertion that there is a sea fight and it is located in the world manifold one day later than the utterance, but the contradiction that it is both on the same day with the utterance and on the latter day. Strictly, of course, the statement today that there is a sea fight tomorrow no more means that tomorrow's sea fight is today than the statement, in New York, that there are pyramids in Egypt, means that the pyramids are in New York.

Let us assume now provisionally that the theory of the manifold is at least true as far as it goes. The temporalist must shorten his lines, then, and insist that, even so, it is not adequate: the time axis is not the whole story, is not "real time" not "the genuine creative flux." If he means by this that the theory of temporal extension, along with the spatial models provided by calendars, kymographs, and statistical time charts, is in the last analysis fictitious, corresponding to nothing in the facts, he is reverting, under a thin cloak of dissimulation, to the mere rejection which we have agreed to leave aside. If he means, at the other extreme, no more than that the theory and the models themselves are not identical, either numerically or qualitatively, with the actual temporal succession which they represent, he is uttering a triviality which is true of every theory or representation. If he means that the temporal spread, though real and formally similar to a spatial spread, is qualitatively or intuitively very different from it, or lies in a palpably and absolutely unique direction, he says something plausible and important but not at all incompatible with the philosophy of the manifold. He is most likely to mean, however, another proposition which is never more than vaguely expressed: that over and above the sheer spread of events, with their several qualities, along the time axis, which is analogous enough to the spread of space, there is something extra, something active and dynamic, which is often and perhaps best described as "passage." This something extra I think is a myth: not one of those myths which foreshadow a difficult truth in a metaphorical way, but one which is fundamentally false, deceiving us about the facts, and blocking our understanding of them.

The literature of "passage" is immense, but it is naturally not very exact and lucid, and we can not be sure of distinguishing in it between mere harmless metaphorical phenomenology and the special metaphysical declaration which I criticize. But "passage," it would seem, is a character supposed to inhabit and glorify the present, "the passing present,"[5] "the moving present,"[6] the "travelling now."[7] It is "the passage of time as actual . . . given now with the jerky or whooshy quality of transience."[8] It is James's "passing moment."[9] It is what Broad calls "the transitory aspect" of time, in contrast with the "extensive."[10] It is Bergson's living felt duration. It is Heidegger's *Zeitlichkeit*. It is Tillich's "moment that is creation and fate."[11] It is "the act of becoming," the mode of potency and generation, which Mr. Hugh King finds properly appreciated only by Aristotle and Whitehead.[12] It is Eddington's "ongoing" and "the formality of taking place,"[13] and Dennes's "surge of process."[14] It is the dynamic essence which Professor Ushenko believes that Einstein omits from the world.[15] It is the mainspring of McTaggart's "A-series" which puts movement in time,[16] and it is Broad's pure becoming.[17] Withal it is the flow and go of very existence, nearer to us than breathing, closer than hands and feet.

So far as one can interpret these expressions into a theory, they have the same purport as all the immemorial turns of speech by which we describe time as *moving*, with respect to the present or with respect to our minds. Time flows or flies or marches, years roll, hours pass. More explicitly we may speak as if the perceiving mind were stationary while time flows by like a river, with the flotsam of events upon it; or as if presentness were a fixed pointer under which the tape of happenings slides; or as if the time sequence were a moving-picture film, unwinding from the dark reel of the future, projected briefly on the screen of the present, and rewound into the dark can of the past. Sometimes, again, we speak as if the time sequence were a stationary plain or ocean on which we voyage, or a variegated river gorge down which we drift; or, in Broad's analogy, as if it were a row of housefronts along which the spotlight of the present plays. "The essence of nowness," Santayana says, "runs like fire along the fuse of time."[18] Augustine pictures the present passing into the past, where the modern pictures the present as invading the future,[19] but these do not conflict, for Augustine means that the *events* which were present become past, while the modern means that *presentness* encroaches on what was previously the future. Sometimes the surge of presentness is conceived as a mere moving illumination by consciousness, sometimes as a sort of vivification and heightening, like an ocean wave heaving along beneath a stagnant expanse of floating seaweed, sometimes as no less than the boon of existence itself, reifying minute by minute a limbo of unthings.

The doctrine of the moving present has some startling applications, notably in the idea of a time machine. The theory of the four-dimensional manifold seemed already an invitation to the notion of time travel, and the additional idea that we move with respect to time confirms it. For if I normally voyage through time in a single direction at a fixed rate, I can hope to make a machine which will enable me to voyage slower or faster or backward.

Now, the most remarkable feature of all this is that while the modes of speech and thought which enshrine the idea of passage are universal and perhaps ineradicable, the instant one thinks about them one feels uneasy, and the most laborious effort can not construct an intelligible theory which admits the literal truth of any of them. McTaggart was driven to deny the reality of time because he believed that while time must combine the dimensional spread with the fact of passage, the B-series with the A-series, every attempt to reconcile the two ended in absurdity. Broad can only cling to the hope that a better reconciliation may yet be found. My present thesis would resolve the antinomy by rejecting the extra idea of passage as spurious altogether.

The obvious and notorious fault of the idea, as we have now localized it, is this. Motion is already defined and explained in the dimensional manifold as consisting of the presence of the same individual in different places at different times. It consists of bends or quirks in the world lines, or the space-time worm, which is the four-dimensioned totality of the individual's existence. This is motion in space, if you like; but we can readily define a corresponding "motion in time." It comes out as nothing more dramatic than an exact equivalent: "motion in time" consists of being at different times in different places. True motion then is motion at once in time and space. Nothing can "move" in time alone any more than in space alone, and time itself cannot "move" any more than space itself. "Does this road go anywhere?" asks the city tourist. "No, it stays right along here," replies the countryman. Time "flows" only in the sense in which a line flows or a landscape "recedes into the west." That is, it is an ordered extension. And each of us proceeds through time only as a fence proceeds across a farm: that is, parts of our being, and the fence's, occupy successive instants and points, respectively. There is passage, but it is nothing extra. It is the mere happening of things, their strung-along-ness in the manifold. The term "the present" is the conventional way of designating the cross-section of events which are simultaneous with the uttering of the phrase, and "the present moves" only in that when similar words occur at successively different moments, they denote, by a twist of language, different cross-sections of the manifold. Time travel, then, is analyzable either as the banality that at each different moment we occupy a different moment from the one we occupied before, or the contradiction that at each different moment we occupy a different moment from the one which we are then occupying—that five minutes from now, for example, I may be a hundred years from now.[20]

The tragedy then of the extra idea of passage or absolute becoming, as a philosophical principle, is that it incomprehensibly doubles its world by re-introducing terms like "moving" and "becoming" in a sense which both requires and forbids interpretation in the preceding ways. For as soon as we say that time or the present or we move in the odd extra way which the doctrine of passage requires, we have no recourse but to suppose that this movement in turn takes time of a special sort: time$_1$ move at a certain rate in time$_2$, perhaps one second$_1$ per one second$_2$, perhaps slower, perhaps faster. Or, conversely, the moving present slides over so many seconds of time$_1$ in so many seconds of time$_2$. The history of the new moving present, in time$_2$, then composes a new and higher time dimension again, which cries to be vitalized by a new level of passage, and so on forever.

We hardly needed to point out the unhappy regress to which the idea of time's motion commits us, for any candid philosopher, as soon as he looks hard at the idea, must *see* that it is preposterous. "Taking place" is not a formality to which an event incidentally submits—it is the event's very being. World history consists of actual concrete happenings in a temporal sequence; it is not necessary or possible that happening should happen to them all over again. The system of the manifold is thus "complete" in something like the technical logical sense, and any attempted addition to it is bound to be either contradictory or supererogatory.

Bergson, Broad, and some of the followers of Whitehead[21] have tried to soften the paradoxes of passage by supposing that the present does not move across the total time level, but that it is the very fountain where the river of time gushes out of nothingness (or out of the power of God). The past, then, having swum into being and floated away, is eternally real, but the future has no existence at all. This may be a more appealing figure, but logically it involves the same anomalies of meta-happening and meta-time which we observed in the other version.

What, then, we must ask, were the motives which drove men to the staggering philosophy of passage? One of them, I believe, we can dispose of at once. It is the innocent vertigo which inevitably besets a creature whose thinking is strung out in time, as soon as he tries to think of the time dimension itself. He finds it easiest to conceive and understand purely geometrical structures. Motion is more difficult, and generally remains vague, while time *per se* is very difficult indeed, but being now identified as the principle which imports motion into space, it is put down as a kind of quintessential motion itself. The process is helped by the fact that the mere further-along-ness of successive segments, either of a spatial or of a temporal stretch, can quite logically be conceived as a degenerate sort of change, as when we speak of the flow of a line or say that the scenery changes along the Union Pacific.

A rather more serious excuse for the idea of passage is that it is supposed necessary and sufficient for adding to the temporal dimension that intrinsic *sense*, from earlier to later, in which it is supposed to differ radically from any dimension of space.[22] A meridian of longitude has only a direction, but a river has a "sense," and time is in this like the river. It is, as the saying goes, irreversible and irrevocable. It has a "directed tension."[23] The mere dimension of time, on the other hand, would seem to be symmetrical. The principle of absolute passage is bidden to rectify this symmetry with what Eddington called "time's arrow."

It might be replied that science does not supply an arrow for time because it has no need of it. But I think it plain that time does have a sense, from early to late. I only think that it can be taken care of on much less draconian principles than absolute passage. There is nothing in the dimensional view of time to preclude its being generated by a uniquely asymmetrical relation, and experience suggests powerfully that it is so generated. But the fact is that every real series has a "sense" anyhow. This is provided, if by nothing else, than by the sheer numerical identity and diversity of terms. In the line of individual things or events, $a, b, c, \ldots z$, whether in space or in time, the "sense" from a to z is *ipso facto* other than the "sense" from *z* to *a*. Only because there is a difference between the ordered couple *a; z* and the couple *a; z* can we define the difference between a symmetrical and an asymmetrical relation. Only because there are already two distinguishable "ways" on a street, determined by its individual ends, can we decide to permit traffic to move one way and prohibit it the other. But a sufficient difference of sense, finally, would appear to be constituted, if nothing else offered, by the inevitably asymmetrical distribution of properties along the temporal line (or any other). The time-extended organization of living and conscious beings, in particular, has a special and asymmetrical "run," fore and aft. Eddington suggested that the arrow could be provided for the cosmos by the principle of entropy.[24] As for the irrevocability of past time, it seems to be no more than the trivial fact that the particular events of 1902, let us say, can not also be the events of 1952. Very similar events might be so, however, and if very few of them are, this is the fault of the concrete nature of things and not of any grudge on the part of time.[25]

The final motive for the attempt to consummate the fourth dimension of the manifold with the special perfection of passage is the vaguest but the most substantial and incorrigible. It is simply that we *find* passage, that we are immediately and poignantly involved in the jerk and whoosh of process, the felt flow of one moment into the next. Here is the focus of being. Here is the shore whence the youngster watches the golden mornings swing toward him like serried bright breakers from the ocean of the future. Here is the flood on which the oldster wakes in the night to shudder at its swollen black torrent cascading him into the abyss.

It would be futile to try to deny these experiences, but their correct description is another matter. If they are in fact consistent with our theory, they are no evidence against it; and if they are entailed by it, they are evidence in its favor. Since the theory was originally constructed to take account of them, it would be odd if they

were inconsistent with it or even irrelevant to it. I believe that in fact they are neither, and that the theory of the manifold provides the true and literal description of what the enthusiastic metaphors of passage have deceptively garbled.

The principal reason why we are troubled to accommodate our experience of time to the intellectual theory of time goes very deep in the philosophy of philosophy. It is that we must here scrutinize the undoctored fact of perception, on the one hand, and must imagine our way into a conceptual scheme, and envisage the true intrinsic being of its objects, on the other hand, and then pronounce on the numerical identity of the first with the second. This is a very rare requirement. Even such apt ideas as those of space and of physical objects, as soon as we contemplate them realistically, begin to embarrass us, so that we slip into the assumption that the real objects of the conceptions, if they exist at all, exist on a different plane or in a different realm from the sensuous spread and lumpiness of experience. The ideas of time and of the mind, however, do not permit of such evasion. Those beings are given in their own right and person, filling the foreground. Here for once we must fit the fact directly into the intellectual form, without benefit of precedent or accustomed criteria. First off, then, comparing the calm conceptual scheme with the turbid event itself, we may be repelled by the former, not because it is not true to the latter, but because it is not the latter. When we see that this kind of diversity is inevitable to every concept and its object, and hence is irrelevant to the validity of any, we demur because the conceptual scheme is indifferently flat and third-personal, like a map, while the experienced reality is centripetal and perspectival, piled up and palpitating where we are, gray and retiring elsewhere. But this, of course, affecting the spread of time no more than that of space, is only because every occasion on which we compare the world map with experience has itself a single specific location, confronting part of the world, remote from the rest. The perspectivity of the view is exactly predictable from the map. The deception with respect to time is worse than with respect to space because our memories and desires run time-wise and not space-wise. The jerk and whoosh of this moment, which are simply the real occurrence of one particular batch of events, are no different from the whoosh and being of any other patch of events up and down the eternal time-stretch. Remembering some of the latter, however, and anticipating more, and bearing in mind that while they happen they are all called "the present," we mistakenly hypostatize the Present as a single surge of bigness which rolls along the time-axis. There is in fact no more a single rolling Now than there is a single rolling Here along a spatial line—a standing line of soldiers, for example, though each of them has his vivid presentment of his own Here.

Let us hug to us as closely as we like that there is real succession, that rivers flow and winds blow, that things burn and burst, that men strive and guess and die. All this is the concrete stuff of the manifold, the reality of serial happening, one event after another, in exactly the time spread which we have been at pains to diagram. What does the theory allege except what we find, and what do we find that is not accepted and asserted by the theory? Suppose a pure intelligence, bred outside of time, instructed in the nature of the manifold and the design of the human space-time worm, with its mnemic organization and the strands of world history which flank it, and suppose him incarnated among us: what could he have expected the temporal experience to be like except just about what he actually discovers it to be? How, in brief, could processes which endure and succeed each other along the time line appear as anything other than enduring and successive processes?

The theory of the manifold leaves abundant room for the sensitive observer to record any describable difference he may find, in intrinsic quality, relational texture, or absolute direction, between the temporal dimension and the spatial ones. He is welcome to mark it so on the map.

The very singleness of the time dimension, over against the amalgamated three dimensions of space, may be an idiosyncrasy with momentous effects; its *fourthness*, so to speak, so oddly and immensely multiplying the degrees of freedom embodied in the familiar spatial complex, was bound to seem momentous too. The theory of the manifold has generally conceded or emphasized that time is unique in these and other respects, and I have been assuming that it was right to do so. In the working out of this essay, however, I have come a little uneasily to the surmise that the idea of an absolute or intrinsic difference of texture of orientation is superfluous. For, regardless of whether there is such an underlying absolute disparity, it is plain that things, persons, and events, as a matter of natural fact, are strung along with respect to the time axis in patterns notably different from those in which they are deployed in space. The very concept of "things" or "individual substances" derives from a peculiar kind of coherence and elongation of clumps of events in the time direction. Living bodies in particular have a special organized trend timewise, a *conatus sese conservandi*, which nothing has in spatial section. Characteristic themes of causation run in the same direction, and paralleling all these, and accounting for their importance and obviousness to us, is the pattern of mental events, the stream of consciousness, with its mnemic cumulation and that sad anxiety to *keep going* futureward which contrasts strangely with our comparative indifference to our spatial girth. An easy interpretation would be that the world content is uniquely organized in the time direction because the time direction itself is aboriginally unique. Modern philosophical wisdom, however, consists mostly of trying the cart before the horse, and I find myself more than half convinced by the oddly repellent hypothesis that the peculiarity of the time dimension is not thus primitive but is wholly a resultant of those differences in the mere *de facto* run and order of the world's filling. It is then conceivable, though doubtless physically impossible, that one four-dimensional area of the manifold be slewed around at right angles to the rest, so that the time order of that area, as composed by its interior lines of strain and structure, runs parallel with a spatial order in its environment. It is conceivable, indeed, that a single whole human life should lie thwartwise of the manifold, with its belly plump in time, its birth at the east and its death in the west, and its conscious stream perhaps running alongside somebody's garden path.[26] It is part of the same proposal, I think, that the "sense" of time be similarly composed. It is conceivable too then that a human life be twisted, not 90° but 180°, from the normal temporal grain of the world. F. Scott Fitzgerald tells the story of Benjamin Button who was born in the last stages of senility and got younger all his life till he died a dwindling embryo.[27] Fitzgerald imagined the reversal to be so imperfect that Benjamin's stream of consciousness ran, not backward with his body's gross development, but in the common clockwise manner. We might better conceive a reversal of every cell twitch and electron whirl, and hence suppose that he experienced his own life stages in the same order as we do ours, but that he observed everyone around him moving backward from the grave to the cradle. I may be overbold to unveil such speculations, since to some they will seem a warning of the dangers of any dimensional view. The more reasonable reflection, however, is that if even this extravagant version, a completely isotropic theory of space-time, can be squared pretty well with the experience and idea of passage, there can be no serious doubt of the adequacy of the more moderate theory which neither asserts nor denies that the manifold is isotropic.

The same fact of the grain and configuration of events which, if it does not constitute, certainly accompanies and underlines the "senses" of space and time, has other virtues which help to naturalize experience in the manifold. I think that it accounts for the apparent *rate* of happening, for example; for the span of the specious

present; and for the way in which the future is comparatively malleable to our present efforts and correspondingly dark to our present knowledge.

As the dimensional theory accommodates what is true in the notion of passage, that is, the occurrence of events, in contrast with a mythical rearing and charging of time itself, so it accounts for what is true in the notions of "flux," "becoming," "emergence," "creative advance," and the rest. Having learned the trick of mutual translation between theory and experience, we see where the utter misrepresentation lies in the accusation that the dimensional theory denies that time is "real," or that it substitutes a safe and static world, a block universe, a petrified *fait accompli*, a *totum simul*, for the actuality of risk and change. Taking time with the truest seriousness, on the contrary, it calmly diagnoses "novelty" or "becoming," for example, as the occurrence of an entity, or kind of entity, at one time in the world continuum which does not occur at any previous time. No other sort of novelty than this, I earnestly submit, is discoverable or conceivable—or desirable. In practice, the modern sciences of the manifold have depicted it as a veritable caldron of force and action. Although the theory entails that it is true at every time that events occur at other times, it emphatically does not entail that all events happen at the same time or at every time, or at no time. It does not assert, therefore, that future things "already" exist or exist "forever." Emphatically also it does not, as is frequently charged, "make time a dimension of space,"[28] any more than it makes space a dimension of time.

The theory of the manifold, which is thus neutral with respect to the amount of change and permanence in the world, is surprisingly neutral also toward many other topics often broached as though they could be crucial between it and the extra idea of passage. It is neutral, so far, toward whether space and time are absolute and substantival in the Democritean and Newtonian way, or relative and adjectival in

Spencer's and Whitehead's way, or further relativistic in Einstein's way. The theory of space does not, as Bergson pretended, have any preference for discontinuity over continuity, and the philosophy of the manifold is quite prepared to accept any verdict on whether space or time or both are continuous or discrete, as it is also on whether they are finite or infinite. Instead of "denying history," it preserves it, and is equally hospitable to all philosophies of history except such as themselves deny history by disputing the objectivity and irrevocability of historical truth. It does not care whether events eternally recur, or run along forever on the dead level as Aristotle thought, or enact the ringing brief drama of the Christian episode, or strive into the Faustian boundless. It is similarly neutral toward theories of causation and of knowledge. The world manifold of occurrences, each eternally determinate at its own place and date, may and may not be so determined in its texture that what occurs at one juncture has its sufficient reason at others. If it does evince such causal connections, these may be either efficient (as apparently they are) or final (as apparently they are not). The core of the causal nexus itself may be, so far as the manifold is concerned, either a real connection of Spinoza's sort, or Whitehead's, or the scholastics', or the mere regular succession admitted by Hume and Russell. It was as much a mistake for Spinoza to infer, if he did, that the eternal manifold and strict causation entail one another, as it is for Whitehead, the scholastics, and Professors Ushenko and Weiss to infer the opposite (as they seem to), that "real time" and "real causation" entail one another.[29] The theory is similarly noncommittal toward metaphysical accounts of individual substances, which it can allow to be compounds of form and matter or mere sheaves of properties.

The theory of the manifold makes a man at home in the world to the extent that it guarantees that intelligence is not affronted at its first step into reality. Beyond that, the cosmos is as it is. If there is moral responsibility, if the will is free, if there is reasonableness in regret and hope in decision, these must be ascertained by more particular observations and hypotheses than the doctrine of the manifold. It makes no difference to our theory whether we are locked in an icepack of fate, or whirled in a tornado of chance, or are firm-footed makers of destiny. It will accept benignly either the Christian Creator, or the organic and perfect Absolute, or Hume's sandpile of sensation, or the fluid melée of contextualism, or the structured world process of materialism.

The service which the theory performs with respect to all these problems is other than dictating solutions of them. It is the provision of a lucent frame or arena where they and their solutions can be laid out and clearheadedly appraised in view of their special classes of evidence. Once under this kind of observation, for example, the theories of change which describe becoming as a marriage of being and not-being, or an interpenetration of the present with the future and the past, become repulsive, not because they conflict especially with the philosophy of the manifold, but because they plainly contradict themselves. When we see that the problem how Achilles can overtake the tortoise is essentially the same as the problem how two lines can intersect one another obliquely, we are likely to be content with the simple mathematical intelligibility of both. When we see that the "change" of a leaf's color from day to day is of the same denomination as its "change" from inch to inch of its surface, we are less likely to hope that mysterious formulas about the actualization of the potential and the perdurance of a substratum are of any use in accounting for either of them.

If there is some appearance of didactic self-righteousness in my effort here to save the pure theory of the manifold from being either displaced or amended by what I think is the disastrous myth of passage, this is because I believe that the theory of the manifold is the very paradigm of philosophic understanding. This is so with respect to its content, since it grasps with a strong but delicate logic the most crucial and richest facts. It is so also with respect to its method, which is that of clarifying the obscure and assimilating the apparently diverse. Most of the effect of the prophets of passage, on the other hand, is to melt back into the primitive magma of confusion and plurality the best and sharpest instruments which the mind has forged. Some of those who do this have a deliberate preference for the melting pot of mystery as an end in itself. The others hope eventually to cast from it, no doubt, a finer metal and to forge a sharper point. I suggest to them, however, that if a tithe of the genius and industry which they spend on that ill-omened enterprise were spent on the refinement and imaginative use of the instrument we have, whatever difficulties still attend it would soon be dissipated.

Notes

1   Read at a meeting of the Metaphysical Society of America, Barnard College, New York, February 24, 1951.

2   The Mysterious Universe, New York, 1930, p. 118.

3   Die Welt als Wille und Vorstellung, Bk. 4, Sect. 54; The Philosophy of the Present, Chicago, 1932.

4   "The Sea Fight Tomorrow," in Structure, Method, and Meaning: Essays in Honor of Henry M. Sheffer, New York, 1951. The argument there is mainly that the world of natural events anyhow embraces no less than the eternal manifold; my argument below is mainly that it involves no more.

5   William Dennes, "Time as Datum and as Construction," in The Problem of Time, Berkeley, 1935, p. 103.

6   Isabel Stearns, "Time and the Timeless," Review of Metaphysics, Vol. 4 (1950), p. 198.

7   George Santayana, Realms of Being, New York, 1942, p. 258.

8   Clarence Lewis, An Analysis of Knowledge and Valuation, La Salle, 1946, p. 19. This is pretty surely phenomenology, not metaphysics, but it is too good to omit.

9   A Pluralistic Universe, New York, 1928, p. 254.

10   Examination of McTaggart's Philosophy, Cambridge, 1938, Vol. II, Pt. I, p. 271.

11   Paul Tillich, The Interpretation of History, New York, 1936, p. 129.

12   Hugh R. King, "Aristotle and the Paradoxes of Zeno," this JOURNAL, Vol. XLVI (1949), pp. 657–670. This is an exceptionally ingenious, serious, and explicit statement of the philosophy which I am opposing.

13   Space, Time, and Gravitation, 1920, p. 51; The Nature of the Physical World, 1928, p. 68.

14   "Time as Datum and as Construction," pp. 91, 93.

15   A. P. Ushenko, Power and Events, Princeton, 1949, p. 146.

16   The Nature of Existence, Vol. II, Book v, Chap. 33.

17   Scientific Thought, 1923, p. 67; Examination of McTaggart, p. 277.

18   Realms of Being, p. 491.

19   Augustine, Confessions, Book XI, Chap. 14; cf. E. B. McGilvary, "Time and the Experience of Time," in An Anthology of Recent Philosophy, ed. Robinson, New York, 1929.

20   "He may even now—if I may use the phrase—be wandering on some plesiosaurus-haunted oolitic coral reef, or beside the lonely saline seas of the Triassic Age"—H. G. Wells, The Time Machine, epilogue. This book, perhaps the best yarn ever written, contains such early and excellent accounts of the theory of the manifold that it has been quoted and re-quoted by scientific writers.

21   Bergson's theory of the snowball of time may be thus understood: the past abides in the center while ever new presents accrete around it. For Broad, see Scientific Thought, p. 66, and on Whitehead see King, loc. cit., esp. p. 663.

22   See, for example, Broad, Scientific Thought, p. 57.

23   Tillich, op. cit., p. 245.

24   The Nature of the Physical World, Chap. 3. See Russell too. An Inquiry Into Meaning and Truth, New York, 1942, p. 122.

25   Dennes argues thus, loc. cit. The root of the tragedy is that our wills and feelings are pointed forward in time. We want a plethoric and repetitive future, while we seldom bemoan the deficiencies of the past or the southeast.

26   I should expect the impact of the environment on such a being to be so wildly queer and out of step with the way he is put together, that his mental life must be a dragged-out monstrous delirium. Professor George Burch has suggested to me that it

might be the mystic's timeless illumination. Whether these diagnoses are different I shall not attempt to say.

27 "The Curious Case of Benjamin Button," reprinted in *Pause to Wonder*, ed. Fischer and Humphries, New York, 1944, pp. 16–41.

28 This is asserted, perhaps not with literal intent, by Charles Hartshorne, *Man's Vision of God*, p. 140, and Paul Tillich, *op. cit.*, pp. 132, 248. It is close kin to Bergson's allegation that the principle of the manifold "spatializes" time.

29 See, for example, Whitehead, *Process and Reality*, New York, p. 363; Paul Weiss, *Nature and Man*, New York, 1947.

Chapter 15

Robert Heinlein

" —ALL YOU ZOMBIES— "

2217 Time Zone V (EST) 7 Nov 1970 NYC—"Pop's Place": I was polishing a brandy snifter when the Unmarried Mother came in. I noted the time—10.17 P.M. zone five or eastern time November 7th, 1970. Temporal agents always notice time & date; we must.

The Unmarried Mother was a man twenty-five years old, no taller than I am, immature features and a touchy temper. I didn't like his looks—I never had—but he was a lad I was here to recruit, he was my boy. I gave him my best barkeep's smile.

Maybe I'm too critical. He wasn't swish; his nickname came from what he always said when some nosy type asked him his line: "I'm an unmarried mother." If he felt less than murderous he would add: "—at four cents a word. I write confession stories."

If he felt nasty, he would wait for somebody to make something of it. He had a lethal style of in-fighting, like a female cop—one reason I wanted him. Not the only one.

He had a load on and his face showed that he despised people more than usual. Silently I poured a double shot of Old Underwear and left the bottle. He drank, poured another.

I wiped the bar top. "How's the 'Unmarried Mother' racket?"

His fingers tightened on the glass and he seemed about to throw it at me; I felt for the sap under the bar. In temporal manipulation you try to figure everything, but there are so many factors that you never take needless risks.

I saw him relax that tiny amount they teach you to watch for in the Bureau's training school. "Sorry," I said. "Just asking, 'How's business?' Make it 'How's the weather?'"

He looked sour. "Business is okay. I write 'em, they print 'em, I eat."

I poured myself one, leaned toward him, "Matter of fact," I said, "you write a nice stick—I've sampled a few. You have an amazingly sure touch with the woman's angle."

It was a slip I had to risk; he never admitted what pennames he used. But he was boiled enough to pick up only the last. "'Woman's angle!'" he repeated with a snort. "Yeah, I know the woman's angle. I should."

"So?" I said doubtfully. "Sisters?"

"No. You wouldn't believe me if I told you."

"Now, now," I answered mildly, "bartenders and psychiatrists learn that nothing is stranger than the truth. Why, son, if you heard the stories I do—well, you'd make yourself rich. Incredible."

"You don't know what 'incredible' means!"

"So? Nothing astonishes me. I've always heard worse."

He snorted again. "Want to bet the rest of the bottle?"

"I'll bet a full bottle." I placed one on the bar.

"Well—" I signaled my other bartender to handle the trade. We were at the far end, a single-stool space that I kept private by loading the bar top by it with jars of pickled eggs and other clutter. A few were at the other end watching the fights and somebody was playing the juke box—private as a bed where we were.

"Okay," he began, "to start with, I'm a bastard."

"No distinction around here," I said.

"I mean it," he snapped. "My parents weren't married."

"Still no distinction," I insisted. "Neither were mine."

"When——" He stopped, gave me the first warm look I ever saw on him. "You mean that?"

"I do. A one-hundred-percent bastard. In fact," I added, "No one in my family ever marries. All bastards."

"Don't try to top me—*you're* married." He pointed at my ring.

"Oh that." I showed it to him. "It just looks like a wedding ring; I wear it to keep women off." That ring is an antique I bought in 1985 from a fellow operative—he had fetched it from pre-Christian Crete. "The Worm Ouroboros . . . the World Snake that eats its own tail, forever without end. A symbol of the Great Paradox."

He barely glanced at it. "If you're really a bastard, you know how it feels. When I was a little girl——"

"Wups!" I said. "Did I hear you correctly?"

"Who's telling this story? When I was a little girl—Look, every hear of Christine Jorgenson? Or Roberta Cowell?"

"Uh, sex change cases. You're trying to tell me——"

"Don't interrupt or swelp me, I won't talk. I was a foundling, left at an orphanage in Cleveland in 1945 when I was a month old. When I was a little girl, I envied kids with parents. Then, when I learned about sex—and, believe me, Pop, you learn fast in an orphanage——"

"I know."

"——I made a solemn vow that any kid of mine would have both a pop and a mom. I kept me 'pure,' quite a feat in that vicinity—I had to learn to fight to manage it. Then I got older and realized I stood darned little chance of getting married—for the same reason I hadn't been adopted." He scowled. "I was horse-faced and buck-toothed, flat-chested and straight-haired."

"You don't look any worse than I do."

"Who cares how a barkeep looks? Or a writer? But people wanting to adopt pick little blue-eyed golden-haired morons. Later on, the boys want bulging breasts, a cute face, and an Oh-you-wonderful-male manner." He shrugged. "I couldn't compete. So I decided to join the W.E.N.C.H.E.S."

"Eh?"

"Women's Emergency National Corps, Hospitality & Entertainment Section, what they now call 'Space Angels'—Auxiliary Nursing Group, Extraterrestrial Legions."

I knew both terms, once I had them chronized. Although we now use still a third name; it's that elite military service corps; Women's Hospitality Order Refortifying & Encouraging Spacemen. Vocabulary shift is the worst hurdle in time-jumps—did you know that "service station" once meant a dispensary for petroleum fractions? Once on an assignment in the Churchill Era a woman said to me, "Meet me at the service station next door"—which is *not* what it sounds; a "service station" (then) wouldn't have a bed in it.

He went on: "It was when they first admitted you can't send men into space for months and years and not relieve the tension. You remember how the wowsers screamed?—that improved my chances, volunteers were scarce. A gal had to be respectable, preferably virgin (they liked to train them from scratch), above average mentally, and stable emotionally. But most volunteers were old hookers, or neurotics who would crack up ten days off Earth. So I didn't need looks; if they accepted me, they would fix my buck teeth, put a wave in my hair, teach me to walk and dance and how to listen to a man pleasingly, and everything else—plus training for the prime duties. They would even use plastic surgery if it would help—nothing too good for Our Boys.

"Best yet, they made sure you didn't get pregnant during your enlistment—and you were almost certain to marry at the end of your hitch. Same way today, A.N.G.E.L.S. marry spacers—they talk the language.

"When I was eighteen I was placed as a 'mother's helper.' This family simply wanted a cheap servant but I didn't mind as I couldn't enlist till I was twenty-one. I did housework and went to night school—pretending to continue my high school typing and shorthand but going to charm class instead, to better my chances for enlistment.

"Then I met this city slicker with his hundred dollar bills." He scowled. "The no-good actually did have a wad of hundred dollar bills. He showed me one night, told me to help myself.

"But I didn't. I liked him. He was the first man I ever met who was nice to me without trying to take my pants off. I quit night school to see him oftener. It was the happiest time of my life.

"Then one night in the park my pants did come off:" He stopped. I said, "And then?"

"And then *nothing!* I never saw him again. He walked me home and told me he loved me—and kissed me good-night and never came back." He looked grim. "If I could find him, I'd kill him!"

"Well," I sympathized, "I know how you feel, but killing him—just for doing what comes naturally—hmm . . . Did you struggle?"

"Huh? What's that got to do with it?"

"Quite a bit. Maybe he deserves a couple of broken arms for running out on you, but—"

"He deserves worse than that! Wait till you hear. Somehow I kept anyone from suspecting and decided it was all for the best. I hadn't really loved him and probably would never love anybody—and I was more eager to join the W.E.N.C.H.E.S. than ever. I wasn't disqualified, they didn't insist on virgins. I cheered up.

"It wasn't until my skirts got tight that I realized."

"Pregnant?"

"The bastard had me higher 'n a kite! Those skinflints I lived with ignored it as long as I could

work—then kicked me out and the orphanage wouldn't take me back. I landed in a charity ward surrounded by other big bellies and trotted bedpans until my time came.

"One night I found myself on an operating table, with a nurse saying, 'Relax. Now breathe deeply.'

"I woke up in bed, numb from the chest down. My surgeon came in. 'How do you feel?' he says cheerfully.

" 'Like a mummy.'

" 'Naturally. You're wrapped like one and full of dope to keep you numb. You'll get well—but a Caesarian isn't a hangnail.'

" ' "Caesarian?" ' I said. 'Doc—*did I lose the baby?*'

" 'Oh, no. Your baby's fine.'

" 'Oh. Boy or girl?'

" 'A healthy little girl. Five pounds, three ounces.'

"I relaxed. It's something, to have made a baby. I told myself I would go somewhere and tack 'Mrs.' on my name and let the kid think her papa was dead—no orphanage for my kid!

"But the surgeon was talking. 'Tell me, uh—' He avoided my name. '—did you ever think your glandular setup was odd?'

"I said, 'Huh? Of course not. What are you driving at?'

"He hesitated. 'I'll give you this in one dose, then a hypo to let you sleep off your jitters. You'll have 'em.'

" 'Why?' I demanded.

" 'Ever hear of that Scottish physician who was female until she was thirty-five?—then had surgery and became legally and medically a man? Got married. All okay.'

" 'What's that got to do with me?'

" 'That's what I'm saying. You're a man.'

"I tried to sit up. '*What?*'

" 'Take it easy. When I opened you, I found a mess. I sent for the Chief of Surgery while I got the baby out, then we held a consultation with you on the table—and worked for hours to salvage what we could. You had two full sets of organs, both immature, but with the female set well enough developed that you had a baby. They could never be any use to you again, so we took them out and rearranged things so that you can develop properly as a man.' He put a hand on me. 'Don't worry. You're young, your bones will readjust, we'll watch your glandular balance— and make a fine young man out of you.'

"I started to cry. 'What about my *baby?*'

"'Well, you can't nurse her, you haven't milk enough for a kitten. If I were you, I wouldn't see her—put her up for adoption.'

"'No!'

"He shrugged. 'The choice is yours; you're her mother—well, her parent. But don't worry now; we'll get you well first.'

"Next day they let me see the kid and I saw her daily—trying to get used to her. I had never seen a brand-new baby and had no idea how awful they look—my daughter looked like an orange monkey. My feeling changed to cold determination to do right by her. But four weeks later that didn't mean anything."

"Eh?"

"She was snatched."

"'Snatched?'"

The Unmarried Mother almost knocked over the bottle we had bet. "Kidnapped—stolen from the hospital nursery!" He breathed hard. "How's that for taking the last thing a man's got to live for?"

"A bad deal," I agreed. "Let's pour you another. No clues?"

"Nothing the police could trace. Somebody came to see her, claimed to be her uncle. While the nurse had her back turned, he walked out with her."

"Description?"

"Just a man, with a face-shaped face, like yours or mine." He frowned. "I think it was the baby's father. The nurse swore it was an older man but he probably used makeup. Who else would swipe my baby? Childless women pull such stunts—but whoever heard of a man doing it?"

"What happened to you then?"

"Eleven more months of that grim place and three operations. In four months I started to grow a beard; before I was out I was shaving regularly . . . and no longer doubted that I was male." He grinned wryly. "I was staring down nurses' necklines."

"Well," I said, "seems to me you came through okay. Here you are, a normal man, making good money, no real troubles. And the life of a female is not an easy one."

He glared at me. "A lot you know about it!"

"So?"

"Ever hear the expression 'a ruined woman'?"

"Mmm, years ago. Doesn't mean much today."

"I was as ruined as a woman can be; that bastard *really* ruined me—I was no longer a woman . . . and I didn't know *how* to be a man."

"Takes getting used to, I suppose."

"You have no idea. I don't mean learning how to dress, or not walking into the wrong rest room; I learned those in the hospital. But how could I *live?* What job could I get? Hell, I couldn't even drive a car. I didn't know a trade; I couldn't do manual labor—too much scar tissue, too tender.

"I hated him for having ruined me for the W.E.N.C.H.E.S., too, but I didn't know how much until I tried to join the Space Corps instead. One look at my belly and I was marked unfit for military service. The medical officer spent time on me just from curiosity; he had read about my case.

"So I changed my name and came to New York. I got by as a fry cook, then rented a typewriter and set myself up as a public stenographer—what a laugh! In four months I typed four letters and one manuscript. The manuscript was for *Real Life Tales* and a waste of paper, but the goof who wrote it, sold it. Which gave me an idea; I bought a stack of confession magazines and studied them." He looked cynical. "Now you know how I get the authentic woman's angle on an unmarried-mother story . . . through the only version I haven't sold—the true one. Do I win the bottle?"

I pushed it toward him. I was upset myself, but there was work to do. I siad, "Son, you still want to lay hands on that so-and-so?"

His eyes lighted up—a feral gleam.

"Hold it!" I said. "You wouldn't kill him?"

He chuckled nastily. "Try me."

"Take it easy. I know more about it than you think I do. I can help you. I know where he is."

He reached across the bar. "*Where is he?*"

I said softly, "Let go my shirt, sonny—or you'll land in the alley and we'll tell the cops you fainted." I showed him the sap.

He let go. "Sorry, but where is he?" He looked at me. "And how do you know so much?"

"All in good time. There are records— hospital records, orphanage records, medical records. The matron of your orphanage was Mrs. Fetherage—right? She was followed by Mrs. Gruenstein—right? Your name, as a girl, was 'Jane'—right? And you didn't tell me any of this—right?"

I had him baffled and a bit scared. "What's this? You trying to make trouble for me?"

"No indeed. I've your welfare at heart. I can put this character in your lap. You do to him as you see fit—and I guarantee that you'll get away with it. But I don't think you'll kill him. You'd be nuts to—and you aren't nuts. Not quite."

He brushed it aside. "Cut the noise. *Where is he?*"

I poured him a short one; he was drunk but anger was offsetting it. "Not so fast, I do something for you—you do something for me."

"Uh . . . what?"

"You don't like your work. What would you say to high pay, steady work, unlimited expense account, your own boss on the job, and lots of variety and adventure?"

He stared. "I'd say, 'Get those goddam reindeer off my roof!' Shove it, Pop—there's no such job."

"Okay, put it this way: I hand him to you, you

settle with him, then try my job. If it's not all I claim—well, I can't hold you."

He was wavering; the last drink did it. "When d'yuh d'liver 'im?" he said thickly.

"If it's a deal—*right now!*"

He shoved out his hand. "It's a deal!"

I nodded to my assistant to watch both ends, noted the time—2300—started to duck through the gate under the bar—when the juke box blared out: "*I'm My Own Granpaw!*" The service man had orders to load it with old Americana and classics because I couldn't stomach the "music" of 1970, but I hadn't known that tape was in it. I called out, "Shut that off! Give the customer his money back." I added, "Storeroom, back in a moment," and headed there with my Unmarried Mother following.

It was down the passage across from the johns, a steel door to which no one but my day manager and myself had a key; inside was a door to an inner room to which only I had a key. We went there.

He looked blearily around at windowless walls. "Where is 'e?"

"Right away." I opened a case, the only thing in the room; it was a U.S.F.F. Co-ordinates Trans-former Field Kit, series 1992, Mod. II—a beauty, no moving parts, weight twenty-three kilos fully charged, and shaped to pass as a suitcase. I had adjusted it precisely earlier that day; all I had to do was to shake out the metal net which limits the transformation field.

Which I did. "Wha's that?" he demanded.

"Time machine," I said and tossed the net over us.

"Hey!" he yelled and stepped back. There is a technique to this; the net has to be thrown so that the subject will instinctively step back *onto* the metal mesh, then you close the net with both of you inside completely—else you might leave shoe soles behind or a piece of foot, or scoop up a slice of floor. But that's all the skill it takes. Some agents con a subject into the net; I tell the truth and use that instant of utter astonishment to flip the switch. Which I did.

1030-V-3 April 1963-Cleveland, Ohio-Apex Bldg.: "Hey!" he repeated "Take this damn thing off!"

"Sorry," I apologized and did so, stuffed the net into the case, closed it. "You said you wanted to find him."

"But—You said that was a time machine!"

I pointed out a window. "Does that look like November? Or New York?" While he was gawking at new buds and spring weather, I reopened the case, took out a packet of hundred dollar bills, checked that the numbers and signatures were compatible with 1963. The Temporal Bureau doesn't care how much you spend (it costs nothing) but they don't like unnecessary anachronisms. Too many mistakes and a general court martial will exile you for a year in a nasty period, say 1974 with its strict rationing and forced labor. I never make such mistakes, the money was okay. He turned around and said, "What happened?"

"He's here. Go outside and take him. Here's expense money." I shoved it at him and added, "Settle him, then I'll pick you up."

Hundred dollar bills have a hypnotic effect on a person not used to them. He was thumbing them unbelievingly as I eased him into the hall, locked him out. The next jump was easy, a small shift in era.

1700-V-10 March 1964-Cleveland-Apex Bldg.: There was a notice under the door saying that my lease expired next week; otherwise the room looked as it had a moment before. Outside, trees were bare and snow threatened; I hurried, stopping only for contemporary money and a coat, hat and topcoat I had left there when I leased the room. I hired a car, went to the hospital. It took twenty minutes to bore the nursery attendant to the point where I could swipe the baby without being noticed; we went back to the Apex Building. This dial setting was more involved as the building did not yet exist in 1945. But I had precalculated it.

0100-V-20 Sept 1945-Cleveland-Skyview Motel: Field kit, baby, and I arrived in a motel outside town. Earlier I had registered as "Gregory Johnson, Warren, Ohio," so we arrived in a room with curtains closed, windows locked, and doors bolted, and the floor cleared to allow for waver as the machine hunts. You can get a nasty bruise from a chair where it shouldn't be—not the chair of course, but backlash from the field.

No trouble. Jane was sleeping soundly; I carried her out, put her in a grocery box on the seat of a car I had provided earlier, drove to the orphanage, put her on the steps, drove two blocks to a "service station" (the petroleum products sort) and phoned the orphanage, drove back in time to see them taking the box inside, kept going and abandoned the car near the motel—walked to it and jumped forward to the Apex Building in 1963.

2200-V-24 April 1963-Cleveland-Apex Bldg.: I had cut the time rather fine—temporal accuracy depends on span, except on return to zero. If I had it right, Jane was discovering, out in the park this balmy spring night, that she wasn't quite as "nice" a girl as she had thought. I grabbed a taxi to the home of those skinflints, had the hackie wait around a corner while I lurked in shadows.

Presently I spotted them down the street, arms around each other. He took her up on the porch and made a long job of kissing her goodnight—longer than I had thought. Then she went in and he came down the walk, turned away. I slid into step and hooked an arm in his. "That's all, son," I announced quietly. "I'm back to pick you up."

"*You!*" He gasped and caught his breath.

"Me. Now you know who *he* is—and after you think it over you'll know who *you* are . . . and if you think hard enough, you'll figure out who the baby is . . . and who I am."

He didn't answer, he was badly shaken. It's a shock to have it proved to you that you can't resist seducing yourself. I took him to the Apex Building and we jumped again.

2300-VII-12 Aug 1985-Sub Rockies Base: I woke the duty sergeant, showed my I.D., told the sergeant to bed him down with a happy pill and recruit him in the morning. The sergeant looked sour but rank is rank, regardless of era; he did what I said—thinking, no doubt, that the next time we met he might be the colonel and I the sergeant. Which can happen in our corps. "What name?" he asked.

I wrote it out. He raised his eyebrows. "Like so, eh? Hmm—"

"You just do your job, Sergeant." I turned to my companion. "Son, your troubles are over. You're about to start the best job a man ever held—and you'll do well. I *know*."

"But—"

" 'But' nothing. Get a night's sleep, then look over the proposition. You'll like it."

"That you will!" agreed the sergeant. "Look at me—born in 1917—still around, still young, still enjoying life." I went back to the jump room, set everything on preselected zero.

2301-V-7 Nov 1970-NYC-"Pop's Place": I came out of the storeroom carrying a fifth of Drambuie to account for the minute I had been gone. My assistant was arguing with the customer who had been playing "*I'm My Own Granpaw!*" I said, "Oh, let him play it, then unplug it." I was very tired.

It's rough, but somebody must do it and it's very hard to recruit anyone in the later years, since the Mistake of 1972. Can you think of a better source than to pick people all fouled up where they are and give them well-paid, interesting (even though dangerous) work in a necessary cause? Everybody knows now why the Fizzle War of 1963 fizzled. The bomb with New York's number on it didn't go off, a hundred other things didn't go as planned—all arranged by the likes of me.

But not the Mistake of '72; that one is not our fault—and can't be undone; there's no paradox to resolve. A thing either is, or it isn't, now and forever amen. But there won't be another like

it; an order dated "1992" takes precedence any year.

I closed five minutes early, leaving a letter in the cash register telling my day manager that I was accepting his offer, so see my lawyer as I was leaving on a long vacation. The Bureau might or might not pick up his payments, but they want things left tidy. I went to the room back of the storeroom and forward to 1993.

2200-VII-12 Jan 1993-Sub Rockies Annex-HQ Temporal DOL: I checked in with the duty officer and went to my quarters, intending to sleep for a week. I had fetched the bottle we bet (after all, I won it) and took a drink before I wrote my report. It tasted foul and I wondered why I had ever liked Old Underwear. But it was better than nothing; I don't like to be cold sober, I think too much. But I don't really hit the bottle either; other people have snakes—I have people.

I dictated my report: forty recruitments all okayed by the Psych Bureau—counting my own, which I knew would be okayed. I was here, wasn't I? Then I taped a request for assignment to operations; I was sick of recruiting. I dropped both in the slot and headed for bed.

My eye fell on "The By-Laws of Time," over my bed:

Never Do Yesterday What Should Be Done Tomorrow.
If At Last You Do Succeed, Never Try Again.
A Stitch in Time Saves Nine Billion.
A Paradox May be Paradoctored.
It is Earlier When You Think.
Ancestors Are Just People.
Even Jove Nods.

They didn't inspire me the way they had when I was a recruit; thirty subjective-years of time-jumping wears you down. I undressed and when I got down to the hide I looked at my belly. A Caesarian leaves a big scar but I'm so hairy now that I don't notice it unless I look for it.

Then I glanced at the ring on my finger.

The Snake That Eats Its Own Tail, Forever and

Ever . . . I *know* where I came from—but *where did all you zombies come from?*

I felt a headache coming on, but a headache powder is one thing I do not take. I did once— and you all went away.

So I crawled into bed and whistled out the light.

You aren't really there at all. There isn't anybody but me—Jane—here alone in the dark.

I miss you dreadfully!

Chapter 16

Robert Silverberg

ABSOLUTELY INFLEXIBLE

The detector over in one corner of Mahler's little office gleamed a soft red. He indicated it with a weary gesture of his hand to the sad-eyed time-jumper who sat slouched glumly across the desk from him, looking cramped and uncomfortable in the bulky space suit he was compelled to wear.

"You see," Mahler said, tapping his desk. "They've just found another one. We're constantly bombarded with you people. When you get to the Moon, you'll find a whole Dome full of them. I've sent over four thousand there myself since I took over the Bureau. And that was eight years ago—in 2776. An average of five hundred a year. Hardly a day goes by without someone dropping in on us."

"And not one has been set free," the time-jumper said. "Every time-traveler who's come here has been packed off to the Moon immediately. Every one."

"Every one," Mahler said. He peered through the thick shielding, trying to see what sort of man was hidden inside the space suit. Mahler often wondered about the men he condemned so easily to the Moon. This one was small of stature, with wispy locks of white hair pasted to his high forehead by perspiration. Evidently he had been a scientist, a respected man of his time, perhaps a happy father (although very few of the time-jumpers were family men). Perhaps he possessed some bit of scientific knowledge which would be invaluable to the twenty-eighth

century; perhaps not. It did not matter. Like all the rest, he would have to be sent to the Moon, to live out his remaining days under the grueling, primitive conditions of the Dome.

"Don't you think that's a little cruel?" the other asked. "I came here with no malice, no intent to harm whatsoever. I'm simply a scientific observer from the past. Driven by curiosity, I took the Jump. I never expected that I'd be walking into life imprisonment."

"I'm sorry," Mahler said, getting up. He decided to end the interview; he had to get rid of this jumper because there was another coming right up. Some days they came thick and fast, and this looked like one of them. But the efficient mechanical tracers never missed one.

"But can't I live on Earth and stay in this space suit?" the time-jumper asked, panicky now that he saw his interview with Mahler was coming to an end. "That way I'd be sealed off from contact at all times."

"Please don't make this any harder for me," Mahler said. "I've explained to you why we must be absolutely inflexible about this. There cannot—must not—be any exceptions. It's two centuries since last there was any occurrence of disease on Earth. In all this time we've lost most of the resistance acquired over the previous countless generations of disease. I'm risking my life coming so close to you, even with the space suit sealing you off."

Mahler signaled to the tall, powerful guards

waiting in the corridor, grim in the casings that protected them from infection. This was always the worst moment.

"Look," Mahler said, frowning with impatience. "You're a walking death trap. You probably carry enough disease germs to kill half the world. Even a cold, a common cold, would wipe out millions now. Resistance to disease has simply vanished over the past two centuries; it isn't needed, with all diseases conquered. But you time-travelers show up loaded with potentialities for all the diseases the world used to have. And we can't risk having you stay here with them."

"But I'd—"

"I know. You'd swear by all that's holy to you or to me that you'd never leave the confines of the space suit. Sorry. The word of the most honorable man doesn't carry any weight against the safety of the lives of Earth's billions. We can't take the slightest risk by letting you stay on Earth. It's unfair, it's cruel, it's everything else. You had no idea you would walk into something like this. Well, it's too bad for you. But you knew you were going on a one-way trip to the future, and you're subject to whatever that future wants to do with you, since there's no way of getting back."

Mahler began to tidy up the papers on his desk in a way that signaled finality. "I'm terribly sorry, but you'll just have to see our way of thinking about it. We're frightened to death at your very presence here. We can't allow you to roam Earth, even in a space suit. No; there's nothing for you but the Moon. I have to be absolutely inflexible. Take him away," he said, gesturing to the guards. They advanced on the little man and began gently to ease him out of Mahler's office.

Mahler sank gratefully into the pneumochair and sprayed his throat with laryngogel. These long speeches always left him exhausted, his throat feeling raw and scraped. Someday I'll get throat cancer from all this talking, Mahler thought. And that'll mean the nuisance of an operation. But if I don't do this job, someone else will have to.

Mahler heard the protesting screams of the time-jumper impassively. In the beginning he had been ready to resign when he first witnessed the inevitable frenzied reaction of jumper after jumper as the guards dragged them away, but eight years had hardened him.

They had given him the job because he was hard, in the first place. It was a job that called for a hard man. Condrin, his predecessor, had not been the same sort of man Mahler was, and for that reason Condrin was now himself on the Moon. He had weakened after heading the Bureau a year, and had let a jumper go; the jumper had promised to secret himself at the tip of Antarctica, and Condrin, thinking that Antarctica was as safe as the Moon, had foolishly released him. That was when they called Mahler in. In eight years Mahler had sent four thousand men to the Moon. (The first was the runaway jumper, intercepted in Buenos Aires after he had left a trail of disease down the hemisphere from Appalachia to the Argentine Protectorate. The second was Condrin.)

It was getting to be a tiresome job Mahler thought. But he was proud to hold it. It took a strong man to do what he was doing. He leaned back and awaited the arrival of the next jumper.

The door slid smoothly open as the burly body of Dr. Fournet, the Bureau's chief medical man, broke the photoelectronic beam. Mahler glanced up. Fournet carried a time-rig dangling from one hand.

"Took this away from our latest customer," Fournet said. "He told the medic who examined him that it was a two-way rig, and I thought I'd bring it to show you."

Mahler came to full attention quickly. A two-way rig? Unlikely, he thought. But it would mean the end of the dreary jumper prison on the Moon if it were true. Only how could a two-way rig exist?

He reached out and took it from Fournet. "It seems to be a conventional twenty-fourth-century type," he said.

"But notice the extra dial here," Fournet said, pointing. Mahler peered and nodded.

"Yes. It *seems* to be a two-way rig. But how can we test it? And it's not really very probable," Mahler said. "Why should a two-way rig suddenly show up from the twenty-fourth century, when no other traveler's had one? We don't even have two-way time-travel ourselves, and our scientists don't think it's possible. Still," he mused, "it's a nice thing to dream about. We'll have to study this a little more closely. But I don't seriously think it'll work. Bring him in, will you?"

As Fournet turned to signal the guards, Mahler asked him, "What's his medical report, by the way?"

"From here to here," Fournet said somberly. "You name it, he's carrying it. Better get him shipped off to the Moon as soon as possible. I won't feel safe until he's off this planet." The big medic waved to the guards.

Mahler smiled. Fournet's overcautiousness was proverbial in the Bureau. Even if a jumper were to show up completely free from disease, Fournet would probably insist that he was carrying everything from asthma to leprosy.

The guards brought the jumper into Mahler's office. He was fairly tall, Mahler saw, and young. It was difficult to see his face clearly through the dim plate of the protective space suit all jumpers were compelled to wear, but Mahler could tell that the young time-jumper's face had much of the lean, hard look of Mahler's own. It seemed that the jumper's eyes had widened in surprise as he entered the office, but Mahler was not sure.

"I never dreamed I'd find you here," the jumper said. The transmitter of the space suit brought his voice over deeply and resonantly. "Your name is Mahler, isn't it?"

"That's right," Mahler agreed.

"To go all these years—and find you. Talk about improbabilities!"

Mahler ignored him, declining to take up the gambit. He had found it was good practice never to let a captured jumper get the upper hand in conversation. His standard procedure was firmly to explain to the jumper the reasons why it was imperative that he be sent to the Moon, and then send him, as quickly as possible.

"You say this is a two-way time-rig?" Mahler asked, holding up the flimsy-looking piece of equipment.

"That's right," the other agreed. "Works both ways. If you pressed the button you'd go straight back to 2360 or thereabouts."

"Did you build it?"

"Me? No, hardly," said the jumper. "I found it. It's a long story, and I don't have time to tell it. In fact, if I tried to tell it, I'd only make things ten times worse than they are, if that's possible. No. Let's get this over with, shall we? I know I don't stand much of a chance with you, and I'd just as soon make it quick."

"You know, of course, that this is a world without disease—" Mahler began sonorously.

"And that you think I'm carrying enough germs of different sorts to wipe out the whole world. And therefore you have to be absolutely inflexible with me. All right. I won't try to argue with you. Which way is the Moon?"

Absolutely inflexible. The phrase Mahler had used so many times, the phrase that summed him up so neatly. He chuckled to himself; some of the younger technicians must have tipped the jumper off about the usual procedure, and the jumper was resigned to going peacefully, without bothering to plead. It was just as well.

Absolutely inflexible.

Yes, Mahler thought, the words fit him well. He was becoming a stereotype in the Bureau. Perhaps he was the only Bureau chief who had never relented and let a jumper go. Probably all the others, bowed under the weight of the hordes of curious men flooding in from the past, had finally cracked and taken the risk. But not Mahler; not Absolutely Inflexible Mahler. He knew the deep responsibility that rode on his shoulders, and he had no intention of failing what amounted to a sacred trust. His job was to find the jumpers and get them off Earth as quickly and as efficiently as possible. Every one. It was a task that required unsoftening inflexibility.

"This makes my job much easier," Mahler said. "I'm glad I won't have to convince you of the necessity of my duty."

"Not at all," the other agreed. "I understand. I won't even waste my breath. You have good reasons for what you're doing, and nothing I say can alter them." He turned to the guards. "I'm ready. Take me away."

Mahler gestured to them, and they led the jumper away. Amazed, Mahler watched the retreating figure, studying him until he could no longer be seen.

If they were all like that, Mahler thought.

I could have gotten to like that one. That was a sensible man—one of the few. He knew he was beaten, and he didn't try to argue in the face of absolute necessity. It's too bad he had to go; he's the kind of man I'd like to find more often these days.

But I mustn't feel sympathy, Mahler told himself.

He had performed his job so well so long because he had managed to suppress any sympathy for the unfortunates he had to condemn. Had there been someplace else to send them— back to their own time, preferably—he would have been the first to urge abolition of the Moon prison. But, with no place else to send them, he performed his job efficiently and automatically.

He picked up the jumper's time-rig and examined it. A two-way rig would be the solution, of course. As soon as the jumper arrives, turn him around and send him back. They'd get the idea soon enough. Mahler found himself wishing it were so: he often wondered what the jumpers stranded on the Moon must think of him.

A two-way rig could change the world completely; its implications were staggering. With men able to move with ease backward and forward in time, past, present, and future would blend into one mind-numbing new entity. It was impossible to conceive of the world as it would be, with free passage in either direction.

But even as Mahler fondled the confiscated time-rig he realized something was wrong. In the six centuries since the development of time-travel, no one had yet developed a known two-way rig. And, more important, there were no documented reports of visitors from the future. Presumably, if a two-way rig existed, such visitors would have been commonplace.

So the jumper had been lying, Mahler thought with regret. The two-way rig was an impossibility. He had merely been playing a game with his captors. This *couldn't* be a two-way rig, because the past held no record of anyone's going back.

Mahler examined the rig. There were two dials on it, one the conventional forward dial and the other indicating backward travel. Whoever had prepared this hoax had gone to considerable extent to document it. *Why?*

Could it be that the jumper had told the truth? Mahler wished he could somehow test the rig in his hands; there was always that one chance that it might actually work, that he would no longer have to be the rigid dispenser of justice, Absolutely Inflexible Mahler.

He looked at it. As a time machine, it was fairly crude. It made use of the standard distorter pattern, but the dial was the clumsy wide-range twenty-fourth-century one; the vernier system, Mahler reflected, had not been introduced until the twenty-fifth.

Mahler peered closer to read the instruction label. PLACE LEFT HAND HERE, it said. He studied it carefully. The ghost of a thought wandered into his mind; he pushed it aside in horror, but it recurred. It would be so simple. What if—?

No.

But—

PLACE LEFT HAND HERE.

He reached out tentatively with his left hand.

Just a bit—

No.

PLACE LEFT HAND HERE.

He touched his hand gingerly to the indicated place. There was a little crackle of electricity. He let go, quickly, and started to replace the time-rig on his desk when the desk abruptly faded out from under him.

The air was foul and grimy. Mahler wondered what had happened to the Conditioner. Then he looked around.

Huge grotesque ugly buildings raised to the sky. Black, despairing clouds of smoke overhead. The harsh screech of an industrial society.

He was in the middle of an immense city, with streams of people rushing past him on the street at a furious pace. They were all small, stunted creatures, angry-looking, their faces harried, neurotic. It was the same black, frightened expression Mahler had seen so many times on the faces of jumpers escaping to what they hoped might be a more congenial future.

He looked at the time-rig clutched in one hand, and knew what had happened.

The two-way rig.

It meant the end of the Moon prisons. It meant a complete revolution in civilization. But he had no further business back in this age of nightmare. He reached down to activate the time-rig.

Abruptly someone jolted him from behind. The current of the crowd swept him along, as he struggled to regain his control over himself. Suddenly a hand reached out and grabbed the back of his neck.

"Got a card, Hump?"

He whirled to face an ugly, squinting-eyed man in a dull-brown uniform with a row of metallic buttons.

"Hear me? Where's your card, Hump? Talk up or you get Spotted."

Mahler twisted out of the man's grasp and started to jostle his way quickly through the crowd, desiring nothing more than a moment to set the time-rig and get out of this disease-ridden squalid era. As he shoved people out of his way, they shouted angrily at him.

"There's a Hump!" someone called. "Spot him!"

The cry became a roar. "Spot him! Spot him!"

Wherever—whenever—he was, it was no place to stay in long. He turned left and went pounding down a side street, and now it was a full-fledged mob that dashed after him, shouting wildly.

"Send for the Crimers!" a deep voice boomed. "They'll Spot him!"

Some one caught up to him, and without looking Mahler reached behind and hit out, hard. He heard a dull grunt of pain, and continued running. The unaccustomed exercise was tiring him rapidly.

An open door beckoned. He stepped inside, finding himself inside a machine store of sorts, and slammed the door shut. They still had manual doors, a remote part of his mind observed coldly.

A salesman came toward him. "Can I help you, sir? The latest models, right here."

"Just leave me alone," Mahler panted, squinting at the time-rig. The salesman watched uncomprehendingly as Mahler fumbled with the little dial.

There was no vernier. He'd have to chance it and hope he hit the right year. The salesman suddenly screamed and came to life, for reasons Mahler would never understand. Mahler averted him and punched the stud viciously.

It was wonderful to step back into the serenity of twenty-eighth-century Appalachia. Small wonder so many time-jumpers come here, Mahler reflected, as he waited for his over-worked heart to calm down. Almost anything would be preferable to then.

He looked around the quiet street for a Convenience where he could repair the scratches and bruises he had acquired during his brief stay in the past. They would scarcely be able to recognize him at the Bureau in his present battered condition, with one eye nearly closed, a great livid welt on his cheek, and his clothing hanging in tatters.

He sighted a Convenience and started down the street, pausing at the sound of a familiar soft mechanical whining. He looked around to see one of the low-running mechanical tracers of the Bureau purring up the street toward him, closely followed by two Bureau guards, clad in their protective casings.

Of course. He had arrived from the past, and the detectors had recorded his arrival, as they would that of any time-traveler. They never missed.

He turned and walked toward the guards. He failed to recognize either one, but this did not surprise him; the Bureau was a vast and wide-ranging organization, and he knew only a handful of the many guards who accompanied the tracers. It was a pleasant relief to see the tracer; the use of tracers had been instituted during his administration, so at least he knew he hadn't returned too early along the time stream.

"Good to see you," he called to the approaching guards. "I had a little accident in the office."

They ignored him and methodically unpacked a space suit from the storage trunk of the mechanical tracer. "Never mind talking," one said, "Get into this."

He paled. "But I'm no jumper," he said. "Hold on a moment, fellows. This is all a mistake. I'm Mahler—head of the Bureau. Your boss."

"Don't play games with us, fellow," the taller guard said, while the other forced the space suit down over Mahler. To his horror, Mahler saw that they did not recognize him at all.

"If you'll just come peacefully and let the Chief explain everything to you, without any trouble—" the short guard said.

"But I *am* the Chief," Mahler protested. "I was examining a two-day time-rig in my office and accidentally sent myself back to the past. Take this thing off me and I'll show you my identification card; that should convince you."

"Look, fellow, we don't want to be convinced of anything. Tell it to the Chief if you want. Now, are you coming, or do we bring you?"

There was no point, Mahler decided, in trying to prove his identity to the clean-faced young medic who examined him at the Bureau office.

That would only add more complications, he realized. No; he would wait until he reached the office of the Chief.

He saw now what had happened: apparently he had landed somewhere in his own future, shortly after his own death. Someone else had taken over the Bureau, and he, Mahler, was forgotten. (Mahler suddenly realized with a little shock that at this very moment his ashes were probably reposing in an urn at the Appalachia Crematorium.)

When he got to the Chief of the Bureau, he would simply and calmly explain his identity and ask for permission to go back the ten or twenty or thirty years to the time in which he belonged, and where he could turn the two-way rig over to the proper authorities and resume his life from his point of departure. And when that happened, the jumpers would no longer be sent to the Moon, and there would be no further need for Absolutely Inflexible Mahler.

But, he realized, if I've already done this then why is there still a Bureau now? An uneasy fear began to grow in him.

"Hurry up and finish that report," Mahler told the medic.

"I don't know what the rush is," the medic said. "Unless you like it on the Moon."

"Don't worry about me," Mahler said confidently. "If I told you who I am, you'd think twice about—"

"Is this thing your time-rig?" the medic asked boredly, interrupting.

"Not really. I mean—yes, yes it is," Mahler said. "And be careful with it. It's the world's only two-way rig."

"Really, now?" said the medic. "Two ways, eh?"

"Yes. And if you'll take me in to your Chief—"

"Just a minute. I'd like to show this to the Head Medic."

In a few moments the medic returned. "All right, let's go to the Chief now. I'd advise you not to bother arguing; you can't win. You should have stayed where you came from."

Two guards appeared and jostled Mahler down the familiar corridor to the brightly-lit little office where he had spent eight years. Eight years on the other side of the fence.

As he approached the door of what had once been his office, he carefully planned what he would say to his successor. He would explain the accident, demonstrate his identity as Mahler, and request permission to use the two-way rig to return to his own time. The Chief would probably be belligerent at first, then curious, finally amused at the chain of events that had ensnarled Mahler. And, of course, he would let him go, after they had exchanged anecdotes about their job, the job they both held at the same time and across a gap of years. Mahler swore never again to touch a time machine, once he got back. He would let others undergo the huge job of transmitting the jumpers back to their own eras.

He moved forward and broke the photoelectronic beam. The door to the Bureau Chief's office slid open. Behind the desk sat a tall, powerful-looking man, lean, hard.

Me.

Through the dim plate of the space suit into which he had been stuffed, Mahler saw the man behind the desk. Himself. Absolutely Inflexible Mahler. The man who had sent four thousand men to the Moon, without exception, in the unbending pursuit of his duty.

And if he's Mahler—

Who am I?

Suddenly Mahler saw the insane circle complete. He recalled the jumper, the firm, deep-voiced, unafraid time jumper who had arrived claiming to have a two-way rig and who had marched off to the Moon without arguing. Now Mahler knew who that jumper was.

But how did the cycle start? Where did the two-way rig come from in the first place? He had gone to the past to bring it to the present to take it to the past to—

His head swam. There was no way out. He looked at the man behind the desk and began to walk toward him, feeling a wall of circumstance growing around him, while he, in frustration, tried impotently to beat his way out.

It was utterly pointless to argue. Not with Absolutely Inflexible Mahler. It would just be a waste of breath. The wheel had come full circle, and he was as good as on the Moon. He looked at the man behind the desk with a new, strange light in his eyes.

"I never dreamed I'd find you here," the jumper said. The transmitter of the space suit brought his voice over deeply and resonantly.

Chapter 17

David Lewis

THE PARADOXES OF TIME TRAVEL

Time travel, I maintain, is possible. The paradoxes of time travel are oddities, not impossibilities. They prove only this much, which few would have doubted: that a possible world where time travel took place would be a most strange world, different in fundamental ways from the world we think is ours.

I shall be concerned here with the sort of time travel that is recounted in science fiction. Not all science fiction writers are clear-headed, to be sure, and inconsistent time travel stories have often been written. But some writers have thought the problems through with great care, and their stories are perfectly consistent.[1]

If I can defend the consistency of some science fiction stories of time travel, then I suppose parallel defenses might be given of some controversial physical hypotheses, such as the hypothesis that time is circular or the hypothesis that there are particles that travel faster than light. But I shall not explore these parallels here.

What is time travel? Inevitably, it involves a discrepancy between time and time. Any traveler departs and then arrives at his destination; the time elapsed from departure to arrival (positive, or perhaps zero) is the duration of the journey. But if he is a time traveler, the separation in time between departure and arrival does not equal the duration of his journey. He departs; he travels for an hour, let us say; then he arrives. The time he reaches is not the time one hour after his departure. It is later, if he has traveled toward the future; earlier, if he has traveled toward the past. If he has traveled far toward the past, it is earlier even than his departure. How can it be that the same two events, his departure and his arrival, are separated by two unequal amounts of time?

It is tempting to reply that there must be two independent time dimensions; that for time travel to be possible, time must be not a line but a plane.[2] Then a pair of events may have two unequal separations if they are separated more in one of the time dimensions than in the other. The lives of common people occupy straight diagonal lines across the plane of time, sloping at a rate of exactly one hour of time$_1$ per hour of time$_2$. The life of the time traveler occupies a bent path, of varying slope.

On closer inspection, however, this account seems not to give us time travel as we know it from the stories. When the traveler revisits the days of his childhood, will his playmates be there to meet him? No; he has not reached the part of the plane of time where they are. He is no longer separated from them along one of the two dimensions of time, but he is still separated from them along the other. I do not say that two-dimensional time is impossible, or that there is no way to square it with the usual conception of what time travel would be like. Nevertheless I shall say no more about two-dimensional time. Let us set it aside, and see how time travel is possible even in one-dimensional time.

The world—the time traveler's world, or

ours—is a four-dimensional manifold of events. Time is one dimension of the four, like the spatial dimensions except that the prevailing laws of nature discriminate between time and the others—or rather, perhaps, between various timelike dimensions and various spacelike dimensions. (Time remains one-dimensional, since no two timelike dimensions are orthogonal.) Enduring things are timelike streaks: wholes composed of temporal parts, or *stages*, located at various times and places. Change is qualitative difference between different stages—different temporal parts—of some enduring thing, just as a "change" in scenery from east to west is a qualitative difference between the eastern and western spatial parts of the landscape. If this paper should change your mind about the possibility of time travel, there will be a difference of opinion between two different temporal parts of you, the stage that started reading and the subsequent stage that finishes.

If change is qualitative difference between temporal parts of something, then what doesn't have temporal parts can't change. For instance, numbers can't change; nor can the events of any moment of time, since they cannot be subdivided into dissimilar temporal parts. (We have set aside the case of two-dimensional time, and hence the possibility that an event might be momentary along one time dimension but divisible along the other.) It is essential to distinguish change from "Cambridge change," which can befall anything. Even a number can "change" from being to not being the rate of exchange between pounds and dollars. Even a momentary event can "change" from being a year ago to being a year and a day ago, or from being forgotten to being remembered. But these are not genuine changes. Not just any old reversal in truth value of a time-sensitive sentence about something makes a change in the thing itself.

A time traveler, like anyone else, is a streak through the manifold of space-time, a whole composed of stages located at various times and places. But he is not a streak like other streaks. If

he travels toward the past he is a zig-zag streak, doubling back on himself. If he travels toward the future, he is a stretched-out streak. And if he travels either way instantaneously, so that there are no intermediate stages between the stage that departs and the stage that arrives and his journey has zero duration, then he is a broken streak.

I asked how it could be that the same two events were separated by two unequal amounts of time, and I set aside the reply that time might have two independent dimensions. Instead I reply by distinguishing time itself, *external time* as I shall also call it, from the *personal time* of a particular time traveler: roughly, that which is measured by his wristwatch. His journey takes an hour of his personal time, let us say; his wristwatch reads an hour later at arrival than at departure. But the arrival is more than an hour after the departure in external time, if he travels toward the future; or the arrival is before the departure in external time (or less than an hour after), if he travels toward the past.

That is only rough. I do not wish to define personal time operationally, making wristwatches infallible by definition. That which is measured by my own wristwatch often disagrees with external time, yet I am no time traveler; what my misregulated wristwatch measures is neither time itself nor my personal time. Instead of an operational definition, we need a functional definition of personal time: it is that which occupies a certain role in the pattern of events that comprise the time traveler's life. If you take the stages of a common person, they manifest certain regularities with respect to external time. Properties change continuously as you go along, for the most part, and in familiar ways. First come infantile stages. Last come senile ones. Memories accumulate. Food digests. Hair grows. Wristwatch hands move. If you take the stages of a time traveler instead, they do not manifest the common regularities with respect to external time. But there is one way to assign coordinates to the time traveler's stages, and one way only (apart from the arbitrary choice of a zero point), so that the regularities that hold with respect to this assignment match those that commonly hold with respect to external time. With respect to the correct assignment properties change continuously as you go along, for the most part, and in familiar ways. First come infantile stages. Last come senile ones. Memories accumulate. Food digests. Hair grows. Wristwatch hands move. The assignment of coordinates that yields this match is the time traveler's personal time. It isn't really time, but it plays the role in his life that time plays in the life of a common person. It's enough like time so that we can—with due caution—transplant our temporal vocabulary to it in discussing his affairs. We can say without contradiction, as the time traveler prepares to set out, "Soon he will be in the past." We mean that a stage of him is slightly later in his personal time, but much earlier in external time, than the stage of him that is present as we say the sentence.

We may assign locations in the time traveler's personal time not only to his stages themselves but also to the events that go on around him. Soon Caesar will die, long ago; that is, a stage slightly later in the time traveler's personal time than his present stage, but long ago in external time, is simultaneous with Caesar's death. We could even extend the assignment of personal time to events that are not part of the time traveler's life, and not simultaneous with any of his stages. If his funeral in ancient Egypt is separated from his death by three days of external time and his death is separated from his birth by three score years and ten of his personal time, then we may add the two intervals and say that his funeral follows his birth by three score years and ten and three days of *extended personal time*. Likewise a bystander might truly say, three years after the last departure of another famous time traveler, that "he may even now—if I may use the phrase—be wandering on some plesiosaurus-haunted oolitic coral reef, or beside the lonely saline seas of the Triassic Age."[3] If the time traveler does wander on an oolitic coral reef three

years after his departure in his personal time, then it is no mistake to say with respect to his extended personal time that the wandering is taking place "even now".

We may liken intervals of external time to distances as the crow flies, and intervals of personal time to distances along a winding path. The time traveler's life is like a mountain railway. The place two miles due east of here may also be nine miles down the line, in the west-bound direction. Clearly we are not dealing here with two independent dimensions. Just as distance along the railway is not a fourth spatial dimension, so a time traveler's personal time is not a second dimension of time. How far down the line some place is depends on its location in three-dimensional space, and likewise the location of events in personal time depend on their locations in one-dimensional external time.

Five miles down the line from here is a place where the line goes under a trestle; two miles further is a place where the line goes over a trestle; these places are one and the same. The trestle by which the line crosses over itself has two different locations along the line, five miles down from here and also seven. In the same way, an event in a time traveler's life may have more than one location in his personal time. If he doubles back toward the past, but not too far, he may be able to talk to himself. The conversation involves two of his stages, separated in his personal time but simultaneous in external time. The location of the conversation in personal time should be the location of the stage involved in it. But there are two such stages; to share the locations of both, the conversation must be assigned two different locations in personal time.

The more we extend the assignment of personal time outwards from the time traveler's stages to the surrounding events, the more will such events acquire multiple locations. It may happen also, as we have already seen, that events that are not simultaneous in external time will be assigned the same location in personal time—or rather, that at least one of the locations of one will be the same as at least one of the locations of the other. So extension must not be carried too far, lest the location of events in extended personal time lose its utility as a means of keeping track of their roles in the time traveler's history.

A time traveler who talks to himself, on the telephone perhaps, looks for all the world like two different people talking to each other. It isn't quite right to say that the whole of him is in two places at once, since neither of the two stages involved in the conversation is the whole of him, or even the whole of the part of him that is located at the (external) time of the conversation. What's true is that he, unlike the rest of us, has two different complete stages located at the same time at different places. What reason have I, then, to regard him as one person and not two? What unites his stages, including the simultaneous ones, into a single person? The problem of personal identity is especially acute if he is the sort of time traveler whose journeys are instantaneous, a broken streak consisting of several unconnected segments. Then the natural way to regard him as more than one person is to take each segment as a different person. No one of them is a time traveler, and the peculiarity of the situation comes to this: all but one of these several people vanish into thin air, all but another one appear out of thin air, and there are remarkable resemblances between one at his appearance and another at his vanishing. Why isn't that at least as good a description as the one I gave, on which the several segments are all parts of one time traveler?

I answer that what unites the stages (or segments) of a time traveler is the same sort of mental, or mostly mental, continuity and connectedness that unites anyone else. The only difference is that whereas a common person is connected and continuous with respect to external time, the time traveler is connected and continuous only with respect to his own personal time. Taking the stages in order, mental (and bodily) change is mostly gradual rather than sudden, and at no point is there sudden change in too many different respects all at once. (We can include position in external time among the respects we keep track of, if we like. It may change discontinuously with respect to personal time if not too much else changes discontinuously along with it.) Moreover, there is not too much change altogether. Plenty of traits and traces last a lifetime. Finally, the connectedness and the continuity are not accidental. They are explicable; and further, they are explained by the fact that the properties of each stage depend causally on those of the stages just before in personal time, the dependence being such as tends to keep things the same.[4]

To see the purpose of my final requirement of causal continuity, let us see how it excludes a case of counterfeit time travel. Fred was created out of thin air, as if in the midst of life; he lived a while, then died. He was created by a demon, and the demon had chosen at random what Fred was to be like at the moment of his creation. Much later someone else, Sam, came to resemble Fred as he was when first created. At the very moment when the resemblance became perfect, the demon destroyed Sam. Fred and Sam together are very much like a single person: a time traveler whose personal time starts at Sam's birth, goes on to Sam's destruction and Fred's creation, and goes on from there to Fred's death. Taken in this order, the stages of Fred-cum-Sam have the proper connectedness and continuity. But they lack causal continuity, so Fred-cum-Sam is not one person and not a time traveler. Perhaps it was pure coincidence that Fred at his creation and Sam at his destruction were exactly alike; then the connectedness and continuity of Fred-cum-Sam across the crucial point are accidental. Perhaps instead the demon remembered what Fred was like, guided Sam toward perfect resemblance, watched his progress, and destroyed him at the right moment. Then the connectedness and continuity of Fred-cum-Sam has a causal explanation, but of the wrong sort. Either way, Fred's first stages do not depend causally for their properties on Sam's last stages. So the case of Fred and Sam is rightly disqualified as a case of personal identity and as a case of time travel.

We might expect that when a time traveler visits the past there will be reversals of causation. You may punch his face before he leaves, causing his eye to blacken centuries ago. Indeed, travel into the past necessarily involves reversed causation. For time travel requires personal identity—he who arrives must be the same person who departed. That requires causal continuity, in which causation runs from earlier to later stages in the order of personal time. But the orders of personal and external time disagree at some point, and there we have causation that runs from later to earlier stages in the order of external time. Elsewhere I have given an analysis of causation in terms of chains of counterfactual dependence, and I took care that my analysis would not rule out causal reversal *a priori*.[5] I think I can argue (but not here) that under my analysis the direction of counterfactual dependence and causation is governed by the direction of other *de facto* asymmetries of time. If so, then reversed causation and time travel are not excluded altogether, but can occur only where there are local exceptions to these asymmetries. As I said at the outset, the time traveler's world would be a most strange one.

Stranger still, if there are local—but only local—casual reversals, then there may also be causal loops: closed causal chains in which some of the causal links are normal in direction and others are reversed. (Perhaps there must be loops if there is reversal; I am not sure.) Each event on the loop has a causal explanation, being caused by events elsewhere on the loop. That is not to say that the loop as a whole is caused or explicable. It may not be. Its inexplicability is especially remarkable if it is made up of the sort of causal processes that transmit information. Recall the time traveler who talked to himself. He talked to himself about time travel, and in the course of the conversation his older self told his younger self how to build a time machine. That information was available in no other way. His older self

knew how because his younger self had been told and the information had been preserved by the causal processes that constitute recording, storage, and retrieval of memory traces. His younger self knew, after the conversation, because his older self had known and the information had been preserved by the causal processes that constitute telling. But where did the information come from in the first place? Why did the whole affair happen? There is simply no answer. The parts of the loop are explicable, the whole of it is not. Strange! But not impossible, and not too different from inexplicabilities we are already inured to. Almost everyone agrees that God, or the Big Bang, or the entire infinite past of the universe or the decay of a tritium atom, is uncaused and inexplicable. Then if these are possible, why not also the inexplicable causal loops that arise in time travel?

I have committed a circularity in order not to talk about too much at once, and this is a good place to set it right. In explaining personal time, I presupposed that we were entitled to regard certain stages as comprising a single person. Then in explaining what united the stages into a single person, I presupposed that we were given a personal time order for them. The proper way to proceed is to define personhood and personal time simultaneously, as follows. Suppose given a pair of an aggregate of person-stages, regarded as a candidate for personhood, and an assignment of coordinates to those stages, regarded as a candidate for his personal time. Iff the stages satisfy the conditions given in my circular explanation with respect to the assignment of coordinates, then both candidates succeed: the stages do comprise a person and the assignment is his personal time.

I have argued so far that what goes on in a time travel story may be a possible pattern of events in four-dimensional space-time with no extra time dimension; that it may be correct to regard the scattered stages of the alleged time traveler as comprising a single person; and that we may legitimately assign to those stages and their surroundings a personal time order that disagrees sometimes with their order in external time. Some might concede all this, but protest that the impossibility of time travel is revealed after all when we ask not what the time traveler *does*, but what he *could do*. Could a time traveler change the past? It seems not: the events of a past moment could no more change than numbers could. Yet it seems that he would be as able as anyone to do things that would change the past if he did them. If a time traveler visiting the past both could and couldn't do something that would change it, then there cannot possibly be such a time traveler.

Consider Tim. He detests his grandfather, whose success in the munitions trade built the family fortune that paid for Tim's time machine. Tim would like nothing so much as to kill Grandfather, but alas he is too late. Grandfather died in his bed in 1957, while Tim was a young boy. But when Tim has built his time machine and traveled to 1920, suddenly he realizes that he is not too late after all. He buys a rifle; he spends long hours in target practice; he shadows Grandfather to learn the route of his daily walk to the munitions works; he rents a room along the route; and there he lurks, one winter day in 1921, rifle loaded, hate in his heart, as Grandfather walks closer, closer, . . .

Tim can kill Grandfather. He has what it takes. Conditions are perfect in every way: the best rifle money could buy, Grandfather an easy target only twenty yards away, not a breeze, door securely locked against intruders, Tim a good shot to begin with and now at the peak of training, and so on. What's to stop him? The forces of logic will not stay his hand! No powerful chaperone stands by to defend the past from interference. (To imagine such a chaperone, as some authors do, is a boring evasion, not needed to make Tim's story consistent.) In short, Tim is as much able to kill Grandfather as anyone ever is to kill anyone. Suppose that down the street another sniper, Tom, lurks waiting for another victim, Grandfather's partner. Tom is not a time traveler, but otherwise he is just like Tim: same make of rifle, same murderous intent, same everything. We can even suppose that Tom, like Tim, believes himself to be a time traveler. Someone has gone to a lot of trouble to deceive Tom into thinking so. There's no doubt that Tom can kill his victim; and Tim has everything going for him that Tom does. By any ordinary standards of ability, Tim can kill Grandfather.

Tim cannot kill grandfather. Grandfather lived, so to kill him would be to change the past. But the events of a past moment are not subdivisible into temporal parts and therefore cannot change. Either the events of 1921 timelessly do include Tim's killing of Grandfather, or else they timelessly don't. We may be tempted to speak of the "original" 1921 that lies in Tim's personal past, many years before his birth, in which Grandfather lived; and of the "new" 1921 in which Tim now finds himself waiting in ambush to kill Grandfather. But if we do speak so, we merely confer two names on one thing. The events of 1921 are doubly located in Tim's (extended) personal time, like the trestle on the railway, but the "original" 1921 and the "new" 1921 are one and the same. If Tim did not kill Grandfather in the "original" 1921, then if he does kill Grandfather in the "new" 1921, he must both kill and not kill Grandfather in 1921—in the one and only 1921, which is both the "new" and the "original" 1921. It is logically impossible that Tim should change the past by killing Grandfather in 1921. So Tim cannot kill Grandfather.

Not that past moments are special; no more can anyone change the present or the future. Present and future momentary events no more have temporal parts than past ones do. You cannot change a present or future event from what it was originally to what it is after you change it. What you *can* do is to change the present or the future from the unactualized way they would have been without some action of yours to the way they actually are. But that is not an actual change: not a difference between two successive actualities. And Tim can certainly do as much; he changes the past from the unactualized way it would have been without him to the one and only way it actually is. To "change" the past in this way, Tim need not do anything momentous; it is enough just to be there, however unobtrusively.

You know, of course, roughly how the story of Tim must go on if it is to be consistent: he somehow fails. Since Tim didn't kill Grandfather in the "original" 1921, consistency demands that neither does he kill Grandfather in the "new" 1921. Why not? For some commonplace reason. Perhaps some noise distracts him at the last moment, perhaps he misses despite all his target practice, perhaps his nerve fails, perhaps he even feels a pang of unaccustomed mercy. His failure by no means proves that he was not really able to kill Grandfather. We often try and fail to do what we are able to do. Success at some tasks requires not only ability but also luck, and lack of luck is not a temporary lack of ability. Suppose our other sniper, Tom, fails to kill Grandfather's partner for the same reason, whatever it is, that Tim fails to kill Grandfather. It does not follow that Tom was unable to. No more does it follow in Tim's case that he was unable to do what he did not succeed in doing.

We have this seeming contradiction: "Tim doesn't, but can, because he has what it takes" versus "Tim doesn't, and can't, because it's logically impossible to change the past." I reply that there is no contradiction. Both conclusions are true, and for the reasons given. They are compatible because "can" is equivocal.

To say that something can happen means that its happening is compossible with certain facts. Which facts? That is determined, but sometimes not determined well enough, by context. An ape can't speak a human language—say, Finnish—but I can. Facts about the anatomy and operation of the ape's larynx and nervous system are not compossible with his speaking Finnish. The corresponding facts about my larynx and nervous system are compossible with my speaking

Finnish. But don't take me along to Helsinki as your interpreter: I can't speak Finnish. My speaking Finnish is compossible with the facts considered so far, but not with further facts about my lack of training. What I can do, relative to one set of facts, I cannot do, relative to another, more inclusive, set. Whenever the context leaves it open which facts are to count as relevant, it is possible to equivocate about whether I can speak Finnish. It is likewise possible to equivocate about whether it is possible for me to speak Finnish, or whether I am able to, or whether I have the ability or capacity or power or potentiality to. Our many words for much the same thing are little help since they do not seem to correspond to different fixed delineations of the relevant facts.

Tim's killing Grandfather that day in 1921 is compossible with a fairly rich set of facts: the facts about his rifle, his skill and training, the unobstructed line of fire, the locked door and the absence of any chaperone to defend the past, and so on. Indeed it is compossible with all the facts of the sorts we would ordinarily count as relevant in saying what someone can do. It is compossible with all the facts corresponding to those we deem relevant in Tom's case. Relative to these facts, Tim can kill Grandfather. But his killing Grandfather is not compossible with another, more inclusive set of facts. There is the simple fact that Grandfather was not killed. Also there are various other facts about Grandfather's doings after 1921 and their effects: Grandfather begat Father in 1922 and Father begat Tim in 1949. Relative to these facts, Tim cannot kill Grandfather. He can and he can't, but under different delineations of the relevant facts. You can reasonably choose the narrower delineation, and say that he can; or the wider delineation, and say that he can't. But choose. What you mustn't do is waver, say in the same breath that he both can and can't, and then claim that this contradiction proves that time travel is impossible.

Exactly the same goes for Tom's parallel failure. For Tom to kill Grandfather's partner also is compossible with all facts of the sorts we ordinarily count as relevant, but not compossible with a larger set including, for instance, the fact that the intended victim lived until 1934. In Tom's case we are not puzzled. We say without hesitation that he can do it, because we see at once that the facts that are not compossible with his success are facts about the future of the time in question and therefore not the sort of facts we count as relevant in saying what Tom can do.

In Tim's case it is harder to keep track of which facts are relevant. We are accustomed to exclude facts about the future of the time in question, but to include some facts about its past. Our standards do not apply unequivocally to the crucial facts in this special case: Tim's failure, Grandfather's survival, and his subsequent doings. If we have foremost in mind that they lie in the external future of that moment in 1921 when Tim is almost ready to shoot, then we exclude them just as we exclude the parallel facts in Tom's case. But if we have foremost in mind that they precede that moment in Tim's extended personal time, then we tend to include them. To make the latter be foremost in your mind, I chose to tell Tim's story in the order of his personal time, rather than in the order of external time. The fact of Grandfather's survival until 1957 had already been told before I got to the part of the story about Tim lurking in ambush to kill him in 1921. We must decide, if we can, whether to treat these personally past and externally future facts as if they were straightforwardly past or as if they were straightforwardly future.

Fatalists—the best of them—are philosophers who take facts we count as irrelevant in saying what someone can do, disguise them somehow as facts of a different sort that we count as relevant, and thereby argue that we can do less than we think—indeed, that there is nothing at all that we don't do but can. I am not going to vote Republican next fall. The fatalist argues that, strange to say, I not only won't but can't; for my voting Republican is not compossible with the fact that it was true already in the year 1548 that I was not going to vote Republican 428 years later. My rejoinder is that this is a fact, sure enough; however, it is an irrelevant fact about the future masquerading as a relevant fact about the past, and so should be left out of account in saying what, in any ordinary sense, I can do. We are unlikely to be fooled by the fatalist's methods of disguise in this case, or other ordinary cases. But in cases of time travel, precognition, or the like, we're on less familiar ground, so it may take less of a disguise to fool us. Also, new methods of disguise are available, thanks to the device of personal time.

Here's another bit of fatalist trickery. Tim, as he lurks, already knows that he will fail. At least he has the wherewithal to know it if he thinks, he knows it implicitly. For he remembers that Grandfather was alive when he was a boy, he knows that those who are killed are thereafter not alive, he knows (let us suppose) that he is a time traveler who has reached the same 1921 that lies in his personal past, and he ought to understand—as we do—why a time traveler cannot change the past. What is known cannot be false. So his success is not only not compossible with facts that belong to the external future and his personal past, but also is not compossible with the present fact of his knowledge that he will fail. I reply that the fact of his foreknowledge, at the moment while he waits to shoot, is not a fact entirely about that moment. It may be divided into two parts. There is the fact that he then believes (perhaps only implicitly) that he will fail; and there is the further fact that his belief is correct, and correct not at all by accident, and hence qualifies as an item of knowledge. It is only the latter fact that is not compossible with his success, but it is only the former that is entirely about the moment in question. In calling Tim's state at that moment knowledge, not just belief, facts about personally earlier but externally later moments were smuggled into consideration.

I have argued that Tim's case and Tom's are alike, except that in Tim's case we are more tempted than usual—and with reason—to opt for a semi-fatalist mode of speech. But perhaps they differ in another way. In Tom's case, we can expect a perfectly consistent answer to the counterfactual question: what if Tom had killed Grandfather's partner? Tim's case is more difficult. If Tim had killed Grandfather, it seems offhand that contradictions would have been true. The killing both would and wouldn't have occurred. No Grandfather, no Father; no Father, no Tim; no Tim, no killing. And for good measure: no Grandfather, no family fortune; no fortune, no time machine; no time machine, no killing. So the supposition that Tim killed Grandfather seems impossible in more than the semi-fatalistic sense already granted.

If you suppose Tim to kill Grandfather and hold all the rest of his story fixed, of course you get a contradiction. But likewise if you suppose Tom to kill Grandfather's partner and hold the rest of his story fixed—including the part that told of his failure—you get a contradiction. If you make *any* counterfactual supposition and hold all else fixed you get a contradiction. The thing to do is rather to make the counterfactual supposition and hold all else as close to fixed as you consistently can. That procedure will yield perfectly consistent answers to the question: what if Tim had not killed Grandfather? In that case, some of the story I told would not have been true. Perhaps Tim might have been the time-traveling grandson of someone else. Perhaps he might have been the grandson of a man killed in 1921 and miraculously resurrected. Perhaps he might have been not a time traveler at all, but rather someone created out of nothing in 1920 equipped with false memories of a personal past that never was. It is hard to say what is the least revision of Tim's story to make it true that Tim kills Grandfather, but certainly the contradictory story in which the killing both does and doesn't occur is not the least revision. Hence it is false (according to the unrevised story) that if Tim had killed Grandfather then contradictions would have been true.

What difference would it make if Tim travels in branching time? Suppose that at the possible world of Tim's story the space-time manifold branches; the branches are separated not in time, and not in space, but in some other way. Tim travels not only in time but also from one branch to another. In one branch Tim is absent from the events of 1921; Grandfather lives; Tim is born, grows up, and vanishes in his time machine. The other branch diverges from the first when Tim turns up in 1921; there Tim kills Grandfather and Grandfather leaves no descendants and no fortune; the events of the two branches differ more and more from that time on. Certainly this is a consistent story; it is a story in which Grandfather both is and isn't killed in 1921 (in the different branches); and it is a story in which Tim, by killing Grandfather, succeeds in preventing his own birth (in one of the branches). But it is not a story in which Tim's killing of Grandfather both does occur and doesn't: it simply does, though it is located in one branch and not in the other. And it is not a story in which Tim changes the past. 1921 and later years contain the events of both branches, coexisting somehow without interaction. It remains true at all the personal times of Tim's life, even after the killing, that Grandfather lives in one branch and dies in the other.[6]

Notes

1 I have particularly in mind two of the time travel stories of Robert A. Heinlein: "By His Bootstraps," in R. A. Heinlein, *The Menace from Earth* (Hicksville, N.Y., 1959), and "—All you Zombies—," in R. A. Heinlein, *The Unpleasant Profession of Jonathan Hoag* (Hicksville, N.Y., 1959).

2 Accounts of time travel in two-dimensional time are found in Jack W. Meiland, "A Two-Dimensional Passage Model of Time for Time Travel," *Philosophical Studies*, vol. 26 (1974), pp. 153–173; and in the initial chapters of Isaac Asimov, *The End of Eternity* (Garden City, N.Y., 1955). Asimov's denouement, however, seems to require some different conception of time travel.

3   H. G. Wells, *The Time Machine, An Invention* (London 1895), epilogue. The passage is criticized as contradictory in Donald C. Williams, "The Myth of Passage," *The Journal of Philosophy*, vol. 48 (1951), p. 463.

4   I discuss the relation between personal identity and mental connectedness and continuity at greater length in "Survival and Identity" in *The Identities of Persons*, ed. by Amélie Rorty (Berkeley and Los Angeles, 1976).

5   "Causation," *The Journal of Philosophy*, vol. 70 (1973), pp. 556–567; the analysis relies on the analysis of counterfactuals given in my *Counterfactuals* (Oxford, 1973).

6   The present paper summarizes a series of lectures of the same title, given as the Gavin David Young Lectures in Philosophy at the University of Adelaide in July, 1971. I thank the Australian-American Educational Foundation and the American Council of Learned Societies for research support. I am grateful to many friends for comments on earlier versions of this paper; especially Philip Kitcher, William Newton-Smith, J. J. C. Smart, and Donald Williams.

Chapter 18

Richard Hanley

NO END IN SIGHT
Causal Loops in Philosophy, Physics and Fiction*

1. Introduction

Time travel, I maintain, is logically, physically, and epistemically possible.[1] But I am not concerned to argue directly for these claims here. It seems to me that, despite the widespread failure to notice it (amongst philosophers and non-philosophers alike), several issues concerning time travel have effectively been laid to rest.[2] Bugbears remain, however. *Reverse causation* is a causal relationship between events in which effect precedes cause. And in David Lewis's characterization, *causal loops* are "closed causal chains in which some of the causal links are normal in direction and others are reversed" (1986, 74). Given these characterizations, here is the *No Loops Argument* against the possibility of time travel:

P1. If time travel is possible, then time travel to the past is possible.
P2. Time travel to the past requires reverse causation.
P3. Reverse causation requires causal loops.
P4. Causal loops are not possible.
∴ C. Time travel is not possible.

For the purposes of this paper at least. I grant P1 and P2. Since Lewis (1986, 74) conjectures (noncommittally) that causal loops must obtain if reverse causation does, I shall call P3 'Lewis's conjecture'. I'll argue in Section 3 that we have no compelling reason to believe it. The

No Loops 'argument' is really a schema for an argument, of course, since the modality in P4 can be interpreted in different ways. The instances we'll examine involve logical and physical possibility. In what follows, I claim that we have no compelling reason to believe either instance of P4.

But that is not my main aim in this paper. With impossibility arguments out of the way, I will undertake a survey of causal loop possibilities, and make three interrelated claims about them. First, I will argue that although many possible causal loops are intuitively bizarre, philosophers have yet to give the proper diagnosis of the bizarreness. Second, I will argue that when we attend to the variety of possible causal loops, we see that it is a mistake to think that they *necessarily* are bizarre – indeed, I think that many loops are less objectionable than even the friends of time travel might have thought. Third, I conjecture that the best candidates for the least bizarre are causal loops mediated by human intention. This last would be ironic, since the literature in philosophy, physics and science fiction has tended to ignore the possibilities for the role of human intention in time travel.

2. Untangling the Concept of a Loop

According to Lewis's characterization, causal loops are "closed causal chains in which some of the causal links are normal in direction and others are reversed". A simple example would be if event E_1 causes event E_2, which causes event E_1. As we shall see, there are several very puzzling aspects of causal loops. But often the notion is more mysterious than it need be, because of misconceptions. So before we attempt to untangle the real puzzles, it behooves us to dispose of merely apparent ones.[3] A depressingly common fallacy is that of supposing that any effect on the past *changes* it. A second, and possibly related, misconception is to think of a causal loop as 'repeating endlessly'. If this meant just that there is strictly no beginning and no end to the sequence of events, then it would be harmless enough. But it is apparently very tempting to think that each event in a causal loop occurs *more than once*. This is a conceptual impossibility, however. Each event is an individual, uniquely located in space-time. There is no inconsistency in supposing that type-identical events can actually recur, but token events can actually occur only once.[4]

Third, note that there are in fact two distinct conditions in Lewis's characterization: a causal loop is a causal chain that is closed, *and* involves both 'normal' and reverse causation. This may or may not be redundant, and matters to terminological choices. If Lewis's conjecture (P3) is incorrect, then it's possible for there to be chains in which both 'normal' and reverse causation obtain, and yet the chain is *not* closed; sometimes 'causal loop' is used to refer to such chains.[5] The closure condition is captured by Lewis's observation (1986, 74), 'Each event on the loop has a causal explanation, being caused by events elsewhere on the loop'. But if simultaneous causation is possible, then a causal chain might meet the closure condition in the absence of reverse causation.[6] We should not ignore the possibility (if it is a possibility) of simultaneous closed causal chains, even though it is completely independent of the possibility of time travel, for precisely the reason that it may turn out that objections to causal loops are directed at the closure condition and not at the fact

that reverse causation is involved. To avoid confusion, I shall stick strictly to Lewis's usage. (So the common locution 'closed causal loop' is redundant.)

Third, I shall also stick strictly to understanding closure in a causal chain to entail that every event is an effect of an event on the loop. If causation is transitive (as Lewis has maintained elsewhere), then something much stronger is entailed: namely that every event on the loop is both a cause and an effect of every event on the loop, including itself. But I wish wherever possible to remain neutral on the transitivity issue, especially in the light of several recent putative counterexamples.[7]

Fourth, there is no reason whatsoever to suppose that a causal loop must be 'detached' from the rest of the world.[8] Take the simple loop I described earlier. E_1 need not be the only cause of E_2, and E_2 need not be the only cause of E_1. Whether or not 'detached' loops—in which the only causes of events on the loop are events on the loop—are possible (and I make no judgment on this), we must take care not to dismiss causal loops in general on grounds that would apply only to 'detached' ones.

Fifth, sometimes included in 'causal loops' are putative arrangements that are straightforward logical impossibilities. An example is the inaptly named 'Möbius' loop which is sometimes offered as a solution to time travel paradoxes.[9] Here is an informal description, using the example of Tim: Tim goes back in time and kills his paternal grandfather, Ed. No Ed, No Dad. No Dad, no Tim. But no Tim, and Ed lives. So Dad lives, and Tim lives. Tim goes back in time, and kills Ed. . . . The result can be represented in a figure eight, as in Figure 18.1.

Such a 'solution' is incoherent, even when it does not illegitimately suppose that the sequence occurs more than once. It is a special case of the fallacy of supposing that the past can be changed. More interestingly, the pseudo-Möbius solution appears to conflate logical consequence with *causal* consequence, and we do well to be on the

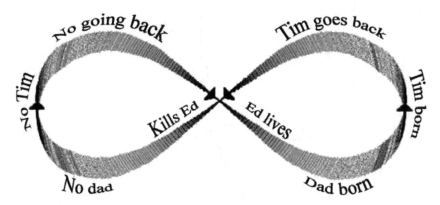

Figure 18.1

lookout for such conflation more generally. For instance, a prevalent thesis (especially in response to bilking paradoxes) is that there must be special provision in the laws of nature—a 'temporal censor'—to prevent changes to the past that might otherwise occur if reverse causation obtains. Some proponents of a temporal censor have an odd idea of its operation: they imagine that a contradiction obtains, and that the universe must then actively eliminate it.[10] The pseudo-Möbius loop might be seen as a rather special case of this allegedly possible phenomenon. But causal loops, if they exist, cannot involve such contradictions.

A good illustration of the difference between a logically possible loop and an impossible pseudo-Möbius loop concerns a thought experiment published in 1949 by John Wheeler and Richard Feynman (1949). The example is complicated, but will again be useful in Section 7. The experimental arrangement illustrated in Figure 18.2 has been called a 'logically pernicious self-inhibitor', and gives rise to what Wheeler and Feynman call the 'paradox of advanced actions'. There are two charged particles, A and B, and a mechanism by means of which a shutter's movement is controlled by A's acceleration. A's acceleration in turn is determined by whether or not it is impacted by a pellet. Finally, the acceleration of A and of B are in a causal loop: each is a cause and effect of the other, separated by 5 light-hours in each

direction, and so, by Wheeler and Feynman's hypothesis (which we shall not discuss here) by a 5-hour causal lag. More specifically, any change in A's acceleration affects B's acceleration both 5 hours after *and* 5 hours before, and vice versa.

The paradox is generated this way: suppose that the pellet strikes A at 6 pm. Then A's acceleration will affect B's acceleration at 11 pm, but also at 1 pm the same day. The change in B's acceleration at both these times causes changes in A's acceleration at both 6 pm and 8 am, earlier that day. But the control mechanism is set up so that changes in A's acceleration cause the shutter to close. So when A's acceleration changes at 8 am, that causes the shutter to be closed at 6 pm, which will prevent the pellet from striking A. A will be struck by the pellet iff A is not struck by the pellet.

Wheeler and Feynman argued (contentiously, but correctly), that the paradox could be resolved if the forces in nature are continuous (so that, for instance, the speed of the shutter varies continuously with A's acceleration). This permits a kind of attenuation of the causation in the loop. It is not a matter of A being either struck in one way, or not being struck at all; a 'glancing' blow will impart less acceleration to A, and will result in less movement in the shutter. The attenuated, consistent, solution is one where the shutter merely deflects the pellet, which glances off A, causing the shutter to move just enough to deflect the pellet.

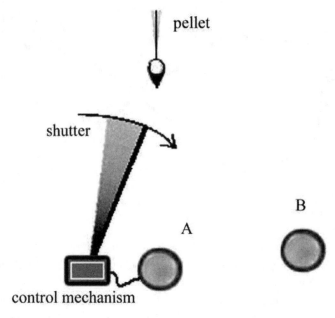

Figure 18.2

There is a right way and a wrong way to understand this solution, however. Riggs (1997, 62), after a summary discussion of the example, draws three morals from it.

> their solution of the paradox serves to high-light some important features of closed causal processes:
>
> (i)   causal influences need not act in a discontinuous fashion;
> (ii) causal influences propagating around a closed causal chain need not remain at fixed strength or intensity, but may be subject to attenuation;
> (iii) the events comprising the chain are not individually distinguishable as either causes or effects.

(iii) seems to me overstated, but my present concern is (ii), which is at best misleading, and most likely outright false. It encourages thinking of the solution in a pseudo-Möbius fashion, as though it is the continued mutual influence of the forces over time that brings about an attenuated solution.[11] Rather, we arrive at the attenuated

solution by reasoning; by considering a welter of counterfactuals. For instance, Riggs correctly observes that, on account of being struck a glancing blow:

> Particle A will have a smaller movement in the morning than it would otherwise have had, resulting in the shutter only partly blocking the pellet's path. (1997, 62)

But it is certainly not the case that any causal influences in the causal loop can actually *change*, as even a generous reading of (ii) would have it.

Sixth, in the physics literature the issues we are considering arise in connection with the postulation of 'closed timelike curves', or 'CTCs'. But the notion of a CTC is unfortunately imprecise when it comes to metaphysical interpretation. In particular, it is unclear whether or not CTCs are to be understood concretely or abstractly (cf. note 20); so it is unclear whether or not the existence of CTCs entails the existence of causal loops. It suffices here, though, to say that physicists concerned about whether or not to admit CTCs are concerned ultimately either about reverse causation or about causal loops.

Finally, I want to emphasize that by *reverse causation* I mean just a cause and effect relation where effect precedes cause. (More precisely, given Special Relativity, where effect precedes cause in some privileged frame of reference – see note 6.) It should not be confused with a rather different notion that also goes under the name of 'reverse' or 'backwards' or 'retro' causation. For instance, Jan Faye (2001) writes that 'The idea of backward causation should not be confused with that of time travel'. But a better name for what Faye has in mind is *temporal reversal*. The laws of physics are apparently time-invariant (cf. Price, 1996). A complete physical description of a certain process, like the water draining out of a bathtub from t_1 and t_2, could equally well be described mathematically as a process of a bath filling (upwards, from the drain) from t_2 and t_1. If we include an ordinary clock as part of the system being described, then we can apparently say that, from the mathematical point of view, the clock might as well be running backwards as forwards. Let's suppose this is correct. Then if the clock is *really* running forwards and not backwards, there must be *something* (an 'extra' so to speak) that makes it so. Now suppose the opposite, the presence of an extra condition that reverses the usual arrow of time, so that the clock *really* runs backwards. This is what Faye means by 'backwards causation'. This *temporal reversal* notion (assuming it is coherent) describes something that entails, but is not entailed by, reverse causation as I have defined it.

3. Lewis's Conjecture (P3)

MacBeath (1982, 417) provisionally argues against Lewis's conjecture that reverse causation entails causal loops. After quoting Lewis, he writes:

In the absence of any argument to support this suggestion, I shall assume that stories of

time travel into the past are not bound to contain loops.

Lewis tells a very simple story of a time traveler who talks to his younger self, thereby communicating the plans to build the time machine.[12] The older man gives the plans to the younger man, and gets them from him in turn, via the aging process. MacBeath tells a different story, where the hero 'discovers the principles of time-machine construction at a university', implying that his story thereby contains no causal loops. But upon further examination of his own story, MacBeath concludes:

Anyone who writes stories of time travel into the past will find it difficult to avoid telling loopy stories. Indeed, perhaps Lewis is right in his suggestion that the task might be impossible. (428)

It should be noted, though, that MacBeath's own story is one in which the main character is his own father, brings himself up, kills himself, and eats himself. It is not surprising that causal loops abound in such a story.

Is Lewis's conjecture correct? Following MacBeath, we can ask whether or not it is possible to tell a consistent, loopless, story. Such proof as there is will be in the counterfactuals we take to be true in the story. Note first that our counterfactual thinking seems not to endorse the global thesis that every event temporally prior to event E is thereby a cause of E (contrary to Mellor 1981, 175–176; otherwise Lewis's conjecture follows easily). Even if it's true that every past event has a trace in the present, it doesn't seem plausible to suppose that every present event is an effect of every past event.

Here's one story. Suppose that Max, who was born in Sydney in 1970, living there continuously up until 2000, and whose ancestors are Australian going back 200 years, time travels from 2000 to 1900, arriving in New York City. He does not father any children, and has little impact of any sort in the 7 days he is in New York before accidentally drowning himself in the East River; and his body is never recovered. No missing persons report, indeed, no official document of any kind records his presence in 1990. Suppose further that Max didn't travel by time machine. Or, if he did, the machine immediately combusted, unobserved, leaving no unusual traces. Undoubtedly, events in 2000 in Sydney are amongst the causes of events in New York in 1900. So this is a story in which reverse causation obtains. But are any of the latter events causes of any of the former? This is doubtful. I accept that there can be causation by prevention. So is it true that had Max not drowned, he would have lived quite a time, and left traces which would have had effects on his life from 1970–2000? I see no reason to suppose so.[13] It might after all be difficult to tell an *interesting*, loopless story about time travel to the past, but not difficult to tell a story that is loopless simpliciter.

What does this show? Well, that depends in part on what sort of theory of causation one holds. I have none to offer here, in part because I wish to maintain that causal loops are compatible with any plausible account. But I will make the minimal claim that there is a close connection between causation and counterfactual dependence. Hence, lack of counterfactual dependence of event E_1 on event E is good, though perhaps defeasible, evidence that there is no causal dependence of E_1 on E. We can shore this up a little by noting that standard putative counterexamples to an exceptionless generalization here involve cases of overdetermination. But overdetermination seems not a factor in the case I have described.

I'm inclined to think, on balance, that Lewis's conjecture is probably false. But it doesn't matter if my argument is inconclusive. I take it that the burden of proof runs the other way: if the opponent of the possibility of time travel wishes to mount a *reductio* based on the objectionable nature of causal loops, then it is up to him to

show that, on balance, Lewis's conjecture is probably true. Moving on to the second step in the argument, there is an important very general objection to causal loops that I shall not address directly. Hugh Mellor (1981, 1995) has argued in an ingenious variety of ways that causation properly understood – that when one event causes another it boosts its probability – does not permit causal loops, on the ground that the assumption that loops obtain entails inconsistent frequencies. I think Mellor's arguments have been effectively rebutted in Riggs (1997), Berkovich (2001), and Dowe (2001), and I have nothing to add. I will instead consider some different varieties of objection, directed at different varieties of causal loops.

4. Object Loops

In Robert Heinlein's 'By His Bootstraps', the time traveler Bob Wilson finds a notebook. It proves very useful as a translation manual between his native English, and the language of a future tribe he lives with. The book suffers wear-and-tear, and Wilson eventually copies out the contents into a fresh notebook. He later takes the new notebook back in time, where he leaves it to be found by his younger self. There is a causal loop here, and we can pick out some salient events in it: the finding of the notebook, the copying of the information in the notebook (to itself), the taking of it back in time, the leaving of it in the place it will be found.

The copying of the notebook to itself avoids what I shall call, following MacBeath (1982), an *object loop*. Other stories include such loops. P. Schuyler Miller's story 'As Never Was', tells of the finding of a strange knife in the future by the time-traveling archaeologist Toynbee, the return of Toynbee and the knife to the present, the removal in the present of a sliver of the blade for testing, followed by the placement of the knife in the Toynbee Museum, and the finding of it there, 300 years in the future, by . . . Toynbee. In the movie *Somewhere in Time*, a young man is given a

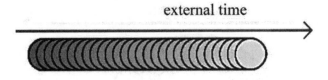

Figure 18.3

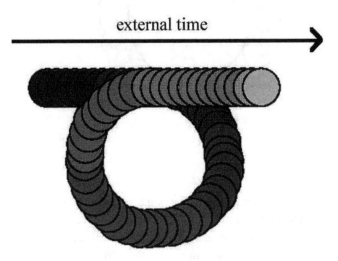

Figure 18.4

pocket watch by an old woman, which he takes back in time, to give to a young woman, who grows into the old woman. In both cases, what appears to be an artifact turns out never to have been *made* at all. Similarly, in Harry Harrison's *The Technicolor Time Machine*, Barney Hendrickson gives his younger self a piece of paper with a diagram on it, which he puts in his wallet, where it stays until he takes it out and gives it to his younger self. And in R. M. Farley's 'The Man Who Met Himself', there is 'One time machine, found in 1935 and brought back to 1925 – found in 1935 *because* brought back to 1925'.

To simplify matters, I shall assume perdurantism – the view that a persistent object is an aggregate of temporal parts.[14] I shall regard an object as an aggregate of causally ordered object-stages, stages in the 'life' of that object. A non-time traveling object then appears as in Figure 18.3.

Bob Wilson's notebook appears as in Figure 18.4.

In the other stories, the knife, the watch, the paper, and the time machine have 'lives' which are in themselves causal loops, and appear as in Figure 18.5.[15]

The oddity of an object represented in Figure 18.5 is not simply that it is never made or destroyed. One can assign no consistent age to such an object. It is clear that the object cannot simply age all the way around the loop. Hence, the only way to have a consistent object loop is for every change that the object undergoes at any point on the loop to be changed back at another point on the loop. Consider the sliver of the blade that is removed from the knife in Miller's story – somehow the sliver must be reattached to the knife at another time. But this point has, I think, been under-appreciated. In discussing a case like that of the watch in *Somewhere in Time*, Paul Nahin imagines the watch being tarnished, scratched and so on, and surmises that the problem can be fixed by polishing, repairing, and the like.[16] But something far more unlikely is required – for

external time

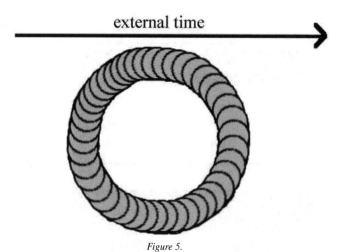

Figure 5.

Figure 18.5

instance, every molecule of the object that is lost along the way must be reattached, and in exactly the right position. Call two different stages of the object, S_1 and S_2. S_1 is both an earlier and a later stage than S_2. If there are (as there are bound to be) qualitative differences between the two stages, then whatever processes turn S_1 into S_2, must have their net effects strictly reversed to turn S_2 into S_1.[17] Call this the *restoration problem*.[18] Such loops are logically possible, it seems, but are they physically possible?[19] It seems we cannot intentionally produce or control such odd processes, but could they occur, in a world like ours?[20]

Here the earlier discussion of *temporal reversal* (Section 2) is relevant. Notice that (local) temporal reversal might provide a way for the restoration problem to be solved in particular cases. During part of its existence, an object like the watch might literally 'de-age', with local reversal of entropy, scratches disappearing as molecules reattach themselves, and so on. But it seems a mistake to think that temporal reversal is *required*. I was careful to claim above only that the *net effects* of the processes that turn S1 into S2 must be strictly reversed. If there is more than one causal pathway that can achieve this reversal (obviously temporal reversal could provide one

such pathway), then consistency demands only that one of them be instantiated. (Other causal pathways might even be simpler.)

A major difficulty with an object loop is that, given the connection between causal and counterfactual dependence, the causal relations between stages of the object must be counterfactual supporting. In the case of an ordinary object, as in Figure 18.3, or even in the odd case in Figure 18.4, the later stages depend counterfactually on the earlier ones, but not vice versa. In an object loop, there is counterfactual dependence both ways. While I do not think this physically impossible, there seems only one possible explanation for it: *coincidence*. Object loops require massive coincidence, if they are to obtain.

It may be thought that there is an entirely independent motivation for rejecting object loops. As I noted earlier, the knife, the watch, the paper, and the time machine are not really artifacts at all, since they are not made. (Grant me for the sake of the argument that there is no maker of the universe.) This in itself is not a problem – there are "found" objects that we can appropriate for purposes we normally would, or could, make something for (e.g., a river stone might make a good paperweight). But the further objection is that, unlike the river stone, which comes from somewhere, the knife, the watch, the paper, and the time machine *come from nowhere* – they are *ex nihilo*.

I confess I have never seen much force to this objection. It would be odd, yes. But impossible? No. Consider that one cosmological conjecture, taken very seriously, is that the entire universe is a causal loop (such a loop seems similar to a 'detached' one, in that there may be no external causal influences on it). Were this so, then the entire universe is *ex nihilo*. In cosmology, this doesn't particularly count against the conjecture, partly, I suppose, because all the alternatives have oddities of their own. Yet it would be specious reasoning to reject the very possibility of local loops on grounds that apply equally to the admitted possibility of a global one.[21] (Note that said cosmologists take the global thesis seriously as a candidate account of the *actual* nature of the world, which shows that they regard it as at least a physical possibility.)

There are other ways to object on scientific grounds, though. Niven (1971, 112) writes:

Travel to the past violates certain of what we regard as laws of nature. . . . A vehicle which travels from the thirtieth century AD to the twentieth, may be regarded as appearing from nowhere. Thus it violates the law of conservation of matter. . . . To say that an equivalent tonnage of matter disappears a thousand years later is no answer. For ten centuries there was an extra time machine around.

As an argument against time travel in general, this one has little merit, despite its popularity.[22] If it were successful, then we could equally show that it was physically impossible for my grandparents to have had any more children than they in fact did. (There would have been extra human organisms around!) It is obviously faulty counterfactual reasoning to change one thing and hold *everything* else fixed, since this immediately produces a contradiction. And the same goes for Niven's argument. He imagines holding the

amount of matter in the universe fixed and then adding a time machine to it. Of course, that would violate conservation laws.[23] Niven's argument might establish that some time travel processes are largely beyond prediction and control, since they require coincidences of various sorts if conservation laws are not to be violated. But this does not show they are *unphysical*, only that they are *unlikely*.

But what if we direct the argument at a more specific target – object loops? Here the conservation problem seems more acute, since we seem to have an object with its *matter* in a loop. We might then agree with MacBeath, who after noting the restoration problem, writes:

I propose, then, that we try to banish, if we can, objects whose paths in space-time are closed loops . . . (1982, 417)

But there is a way to resolve both problems – conservation and restoration – at once. If an object is composed of replaceable parts, such as in the case of the watch, then the object itself can have a 'path in space-time' that is a causal loop, and yet restoration is avoided, as long as its parts do not have looped paths. So, for instance, imagine a revision of the story of the watch in *Somewhere in Time*. All other details remain the same, but the watch undergoes a process of gradual, complete, new-for-old part replacement. Suppose that as each old part is removed, it is destroyed. Each part, then, has a history like that of Bob Wilson's notebook (cf. Figure 18.4), yet the watch itself has a history that is a causal loop (cf. Figure 18.5). This of course still involves a kind of coincidence: each 'new' part is in fact the ancestor of the 'old' part it replaces. But this seems a less formidable kind than that involved in the restoration problem. Call this the *replacement solution* to the restoration problem. How general this solution is depends of course upon one's metaphysics of objects, but artifacts at least look like good candidates for object loops of this sort.

One oddity remains about object loops like those of the knife and the watch. But this is an oddity in some other causal loops as well, to be addressed in Section 5.

5. Information Loops

Lewis does not discuss object loops directly. In discussing causal loops in general, he writes:

> Each event on the loop has a causal explanation, being caused by events elsewhere on the loop. That is not to say that the loop as a whole is caused or explicable. It may not be. Its inexplicability is especially remarkable if it is made up of the sort of causal processes that transmit information. (1986, 74)

Lewis does not claim that *all* causal loops are inexplicable, and just as well. Suppose that a time traveler visits a couple that is about to have a baby, but have not yet chosen a name. Since he is from the future, he knows that they will call the baby Ben. In a conversation about baby names, he says, "How about *Ben*?" The couple had not previously considered this name, and now that they do, they like it. The baby is born, and they name him Ben. If it is the case that the time traveler would not have suggested the name had he not already known it, and if it is the case that the couple would not have named the baby thus had it not been suggested by the time traveler, then we have a causal loop involving information. I, for one, see nothing inexplicable in or about this loop. Perhaps more interesting, in Mack Reynolds' story "Compounded Interest", a time traveler pays for his time machine by journeying to the past and depositing a small sum, which thanks to compound interest, grows into the fortune he needs, by the time he needs it. As long as no money is in an object loop, there is nothing inexplicable here, either.

Both cases may require coincidence. For instance, it may be completely unintentional that

a time traveler suggests the name he has 'recently' heard to a particular couple, or happens to open a bank account for himself in the past. But these are very *ordinary* coincidences. On the other hand, the actions of the time travelers may be intentional, in which case it is coincidental that they happen to know what they need to know, in order to do what they do. But again, the sorts of coincidence involved are completely ordinary.

Lewis himself proceeds to give the case, mentioned in Section 3, of the time traveler who relates the design of the time machine to his younger self. He continues:

> But where did the information come from in the first place? Why did the whole affair happen? There is simply no answer. The parts of the loop are explicable, the whole of it is not. Strange! But not impossible, and not too different from the inexplicabilities we are already inured to. (1986, 74)

As we shall see, I think Lewis's diagnosis of this case is incorrect. But he is correct that there is something strange about this loop. Levin (1980), though, regards the strangeness as merely apparent. Considering a similar story, in which the instructions for the time machine are written in a book, the question arises, 'Who wrote the book about building a time machine?'. Levin writes that this question is:

> . . . no different from questions about where *anything* originally came from. We can ask about the origin of the atoms that make up [a character in the story]; their time line is not neatly presented to us. The atoms either go back endlessly, or if the universe is finite, they just start. In either case the question of ultimate origin is as unanswerable as the question of the book's origin. What makes us think that when such questions are asked about the loop they are different and *ought* to be answerable is that the entire loop is open to

inspection. *Sub specie aeternitais* this difference disappears. (1980, 70)

First, notice that the restoration problem need not arise for information in a loop. Lewis could have the older man give a complete set of plans, on paper, to the younger man. The plans are retained without alteration, but the pages get worn. So, just before embarking on a journey into the past, the older man photocopies the plans, (on a copier that 'filters out' wrinkles and tears in the paper), and takes the new set with him, to give to his younger self. Similarly, Levin could have the instruction book copied out. The information does not change, so no restoration is required.

Lewis asks, 'Where did the information come from in the first place?' and the implied answer is, 'There is no answer'. This is correct, but not for the reason Lewis offers. The right reason is that the question is malformed. Since the information is in a loop, in which it is copied to itself, there is no 'first place'. The well-formed question 'Where did the information come from?' has a straightforward answer: from itself, by completely ordinary causal means (the mechanical operation of the photocopier).

Lewis's answer, and his appeal to 'companions in guilt' when it comes to inexplicability, parallels the response I made to the *ex nihilo* objection to object loops. So perhaps the charitable interpretation of Lewis's claim here is that the information is *ex nihilo*. But this claim doesn't fare any better. Distinguish first two senses of 'information': decoded and undecoded. It is something of a truism that 'everything encodes everything else', which is to say that with an appropriate decoder, one can extract information about my DNA from such an unlikely source as my astrological chart (or from yours, for that matter). But a decoder (however horribly complicated) is just more information, so that's encoded in everything, too. Hence, there's a sense in which all information exists, most of it undecoded.

Clearly, then, no objection can be mounted on the ground that the time machine information is *ex nihilo* in the undecoded sense. (And in this respect, Levin's argument seems to apply: all information, *sub specie aeternitatis*, is bound to appear undecoded.)

So if there's an objection here, it must be that the time machine information is *ex nihilo* in the decoded sense. However, this too is an ordinary phenomenon, hardly warranting the epithet 'inexplicable', so it should not count against the time machine information loop. Consider Einstein's hitting upon '$E = mc^2$'. Sometimes we get ideas like this in odd ways. Suppose that the raindrops on Einstein's window formed a pattern that looked like the formula when written in terms he was familiar with. Or suppose that he was only half paying attention to the conversation of another, and completely misheard what was said.[24] Perhaps it took an Einstein to extract the information from the misinformational context, together with what he knew, and if Einstein would not have thought of it unless presented with such a 'gift', then the information is *ex nihilo* in the required sense. But it is not an inexplicable occurrence at all.

There is a difference between this case and that of information in a loop. In the Einstein case, the information goes from being undecoded to being decoded. Since the time machine information is in a loop, it cannot go from being undecoded to being decoded unless it also goes from being decoded to being undecoded. This latter is highly implausible. Hence, we should regard the time machine information as either decoded all the way around the loop, or else as undecoded all the way around the loop. It seems obvious that it is decoded, since that is part of the explanation for its continued transmission. Decoded information is useful, and its utility explains why we bother to retain it.

Lewis also asks, 'Why did the whole affair happen?' and answers, 'There is no answer'. This, again, seems to me to be mistaken. It would be the correct answer if the loop was 'detached', but the loop in Lewis's story is not detached. The time machine causal loop is embedded in the causal fabric of the world, and the explanation of the whole affair will be the usual sort of causal explanation (modulo some of the chains being reversed). It's not true that the world would have been otherwise the same, had the loop not existed. Hence I do not think it true of causal loops (except for 'detached' loops), that, 'The parts of the loop are explicable, the whole of it is not'. Since the explanation of each event on the loop involves causes both internal and external to the loop, the explanation of all the parts of the loop is an explanation of the loop.[25]

But there is something puzzling about information in loops, Levin's argument notwithstanding. I hope to have shown that 'Where does the information come from?' does not begin to capture the puzzle. What question does? The clue is in the fact that the information is decoded all the way around the loop. The really puzzling question is, 'Why does the information work?' Even here, we must be careful. It's no mystery *how* the information works. Take the example of Bob Wilson's notebook. It works as a translation manual because all the graphemes (and phonemes?) that look (and sound) just like the future tribe's words for things, correspond in the manual to graphemes (and phonemes) that look (and sound) just like the English words for those things. The interesting question is *why* this is so. And the only possible answer is: *coincidence*.

Consider the usual sort of answer to such a question, concerning a more ordinary translation manual. We would explain that a lot of fieldwork was done, and so forth. In the ordinary case, when we give the causal genesis of the information concerned, the explanation of why it is useful comes for free. Because the information in a loop has an unusual causal genesis, the explanation does not come for free, except in the odd sense that it turns out to be just dumb luck that the information works. This is the point that Levin's argument misses.

Is the unusual genesis of utility always

puzzling? No. Consider a 'found' object such as the river stone. Sometimes we use things just because we recognize that they will be useful. The explanation of why the river stone is a good paperweight comes entirely from what it can do, not from how it came to be able to do it. The same goes in the Einstein case. In both cases, however, the 'decoding' involved is relatively simple. The object loops that are the knife and the watch are much more complicated, as is the case with Bob Wilson's notebook, and the time machine plans. So although in all such cases, the explanation is coincidence, some of the coincidences required are much more unlikely than others.

An unexpectedly philosophical objection to information in loops, and more generally to CTCs, comes from physicist David Deutsch. He writes:

> The real problem with closed timelike lines under classical [i.e., non-quantum] physics is that they could be used to generate knowledge in a way that conflicts with the principles of philosophy of science, specifically with the evolutionary principle. (1991, 3216)

Deutsch believes that no such problem arises with CTCs under quantum mechanical physics, but what of the above claim? The 'evolutionary principle' is the Popperian conjecture that 'knowledge comes into existence only by evolutionary, rational processes, and that solutions to problems do not spring fully-formed into the universe' (1991, 3198). Deutsch admits that 'knowledge' here is not what is normally meant by the term; nor is it equivalent to 'information'. But Deutsch speculates that the 'evolutionary principle' is satisfied if a (stronger) principle is invoked: 'that a system contain no independent information' (1991, 3204). I think it clear enough that this is just, once again, the objection that information not arise *ex nihilo*—as suggested by the apparent clarification of the principle, that 'solutions to problems do not spring fully-formed into the universe'—and can be disposed of as above. As for the "evolutionary principle" itself, we can take one of two approaches: either accept the principle, and so deny that information in a loop is 'knowledge'; or else regard the possibility of information in loops as a counterexample to the principle. My own inclination is toward the latter.

An information loop of independent interest is involved in the so-called *genetic paradox*. It is commonly claimed that a story like Heinlein's '_All You Zombies_' wherein a person is his own father and mother, is biologically impossible.[26] Jonathan Harrison tells the story of time-traveling Dum, who fathers himself by impregnating Jocasta with Dee, who turns out to grow up into Dum. William Godfrey-Smith responds:

> The biological problem is the following. Dee is the son of Dum and Jocasta. So Dee obtained half his genes from Dum and half from Jocasta. But Dum is diachronically identical with Dee, and is therefore genotypically identical with him (i.e., himself). That is, Dee is both genotypically identical with and distinct from Dum, which is absurd. (1980, 72)

Harrison replies by saying that this is a 'law of nature, not of logic'. Nahin, rehearsing the arguments, calls the story, 'biologically flawed, fatally so', and maintains:

> The biological objection raised by Godfrey-Smith to Harrison's story is, of course, equally valid for those of Harness, Heinlein, and Benford, too.[27]

This popular claim is false. It turns out that such stories require colossally unlikely coincidence, but are not (at least, not on this account), impossible.[28] The mistake in Godfrey-Smith's argument is the assumption that if Dee obtained half his genes from his mother Jocasta, then he cannot be genotypically identical with his father.[29]

The easiest way to see this error is to focus on Heinlein's story. Since mother, father and child in Heinlein's story are genetically identical, the coincidence required is that father and mother deliver the exact complement of each other's genetic input to the child. Heinlein's story avoids a second sort of coincidence: it is no mystery that father and mother in his story have so much of their genetic make-up in common.

Not so for other such stories, and MacBeath recognizes this. Concerning an imagined story in which the time-traveling Dr Arthur Who fathers himself, being both husband and son to Annabel, he writes:

> it would require either that Annabel contribute nothing to Arthur junior's genetic inheritance, or that Annabel and Arthur senior, by a coincidence of the utmost remoteness, have in common one copy of every last one of their genes. . . . (1982, 428)

MacBeath rightly rejects the first option, but he overestimates one coincidence here, and ignores the other: even if Arthur and Annabel are genetically identical, this would require the further coincidence noted above for Heinlein's story. Annabel must genetically endow Arthur junior with whatever Arthur senior doesn't, but this requires that Arthur and Annabel have 50% of their genetic material in common, not 100% as MacBeath would have it.

Interestingly, it is possible to construct cases of distinct individuals parenting a child, where MacBeath's requirement of genetic identity does hold. Suppose we revise MacBeath's story so that both Arthur (upper line) and Annabel (lower line) are time travelers, as in Figure 18.6.

Arthur is born at i, and at j travels back to h. At i, his son (himself) is born. At k, he and Annabel travel back to f, and at g their daughter is born. Annabel is of course their daughter, who is born at g, gives birth to Arthur at i, and at k, travels back with Arthur to f. This story requires *three* massive coincidences: that Arthur and Annabel

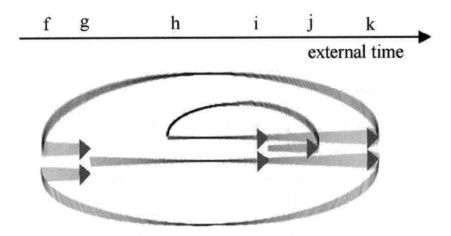

Figure 18.6

are genetically identical, and that each delivers the genetic complement of the other's contribution, *twice*—just before i, and just before g. (If you are worried about two genetically identical individuals being of different gender, we can adapt Heinlein's device: each is born with two sets of functional genitalia, Arthur keeping the male ones while Annabel keeps the female ones.)

In all three cases—Heinlein's MacBeath's, and the revised story just given—another coincidence lurks. In Heinlein's story, an entire person's genetic make-up is in an information loop. Once again, the oddity of this is that there is no explanation but coincidence for why the information in the loop is human, genetic information—the plans for a particular human being. In the revised version of MacBeath's story represented in Figure 18.6, we have information in a loop that is the plans for two distinct individuals (this seems a logically possible case of a pseudo-Möbius loop). In MacBeath's story, 50% of Arthur's genes are in a loop. In a story in which a time traveler is his own grandfather, and other things are equal, he shares 75% of his genes with his father-and-son, but only 25% is in a loop. And so on. In R. Dee's 'The Poundstone Paradox', a man becomes his own ancestor, 50 generations earlier, and this requires only that a tiny percentage of his genes be in a loop – about

2^{-50}. So, even for stories with genetic 'paradoxes', some loops seem much more coincidental than others.[30]

As a final example of an information loop, consider a startling proposal by the physicists Lossev and Novikov (1992), for using the possibility of CTCs to discover the location of wormholes. Assume that we know enough to build an automatic plant that is capable of following *any* sequence of suitable instructions, and provide it with enough suitable raw materials for spacecraft construction. The final step in any automated instruction sequence is to program the completed spaceship with three items of information:

(1) the instruction used for the construction of the spacecraft;
(2) the directions from Earth to the 'entry' mouth of a wormhole that leads back in time.
(3) the directions from the 'exit' mouth (in the past) to Earth.

We then simply withdraw from the scene, and here's what happens. A *very old* spacecraft appears. It contains the information (1)–(3), which the plant automatically extracts, and uses (1) to build a spacecraft and program it with (1)–(3). The very old one is put in a museum. The new one is launched. It travels to the 'entry' mouth (growing quite old), goes back in time, and comes out of the 'exit' mouth, then journeys back to Earth (growing *very* old), and lands at the construction site.[31]

Lossev and Novikov claim that, thanks to the existence of this causal loop, people now have acquired knowledge of (1)–(3). This is a little ingenuous, since the entire system is automated. People could obtain (1)–(3) if they downloaded the information from the spacecraft or the plant, but it isn't necessary that they do this, since in principle they could send an independent information gatherer on the journey with the spacecraft. And even if it were sufficient for their knowing (1)–(3) to download the information from the spacecraft or the plant, this by itself isn't a mysterious process. The only puzzling thing is, once again, the fact that the information in (1)–(3) *works*. And once again, the correct explanation is, *coincidence*, on a massive scale.[32]

6. Person Loops

The replacement solution to the restoration problem raises a further, intriguing, possibility. Towards the end of 'As Never Was', Shuyler Miller writes of the knife's history:

It was a simple pattern – as simple as ever was. Must we think only in terms of a beginning and an end? Cannot a thing – even a person – exist in a closed cycle without beginning or end?

Suppose first that a person is identical with his or her body. Given the normal recycling of cells, it may be that a person's body has entirely replaceable parts.[33] If so, then is Shuyler Miller's suggestion correct? Can a person exist *as* a causal loop?

Only two stories that I know of explore the possibility. In Harry Harrison's *The Stainless Steel Rat Saves the World*, a character called only 'He' apparently exists as a causal loop. But as I read the story, He (although certifiable) has a psychological history much like any of us. To put it loosely, His psychology 'ages' all the way around the loop, so the restoration problem seems fatal to the coherence of the story.[34] In Terry Pratchett's *Pyramids*, the High Priest Dios is a person in a loop, living 7,000 years only to be thrown back in time 7,000 years. Dios apparently changes hardly at all over time, so Pratchett may be aware of the restoration problem; but it is not resolved satisfactorily (apart from anything else, the story involves many magical occurrences, so it is far from clear what is true in it).

We can do better. The information in a person's psychology does not normally remain unchanged over time. This both raises, and offers a solution to, the restoration problem. To put a person in a loop, *as* a loop, there must be compensating gains and losses. But that there are gains and losses is not particularly miraculous, so the restoration problem is in one respect easier to solve in the case of a person. Indeed, a further intriguing possibility is a dualist one: the person just *is*, in some appropriate sense, information.[35] Suppose there is a 'time machine' that works as follows: the subject is scanned, and then killed. The scanned information is sent by tachyon transmission back in time. At the destination, the scanned information is used to 'assemble' a person from the information sent. (This may require that assembly machines have been built in the past.) The process is a 'lossy' one, involving much compression of data. Psychologically and physically, there may be considerably more difference between the scanned subject and the assembled one, than there is between the adjoining stages in a typical person's life, but no more than there is in some 'normal' cases. Given such a machine, and stipulating that no other transmissions of the same information occur, it seems possible (given enough coincidence, of course), to have a person as a causal loop. Suppose she lives relatively normally for 10 years from 'arrival' to 'departure'. During these 10 years, she will age, learn things, and forget things.

In the process from 'departure' to 'arrival' 10 years in the past, she has a qualitatively different body, literally 10 years younger, and the net profit and loss in her psychology exactly counterbalances that of her 10 years experience. This person has a life that is a causal loop. Her body is not in an object loop, but much of the information contained in her body, such as her entire "genetic" code, is in an information loop.

7. The Role of Coincidence

The common theme running through the discussion of the varieties of causal loops is that all require coincidences in order to obtain. This result tallies nicely with a thread of research in quantum mechanics, philosophy and computer science. We have already seen the Wheeler and Feynman 'logically pernicious self-inhibitor', in Section 2. Their correct solution to the paradox leaves one important question. Given that the 'attenuation' is not itself reached by the usual means (a process with duration), why does that attenuation obtain? (I.e., exactly the correct attenuation for the existence of the loop?) Only one answer is possible: it's a lucky coincidence. It's rather like tossing a coin and it coming up neither heads nor tails, but balancing on one edge.

In Section 3 I noted Mellor's probability arguments against causal loops. Berkovich and Dowe show in their respective replies to Mellor that there is indeed a consistent solution to assignment of frequencies in causal loops; but it requires assigning a unique value to the initial frequency. (To put it another way, the values of what would normally be independent choices of the *other* frequencies, in the case of a causal loop entail a particular initial frequency.) In order for the loop to be *actual*, then – for a loop to obtain with exactly the frequencies scribed – the initial frequency must be one exact value. But why would such a state of affairs obtain? *Coincidence.*

Consider also the work done by computer scientist Hans Moravec (1991), on hypothetical logic gate circuits, where the components have normal outputs of 0 or 1, but involving reverse causation. The components are either amplifiers, which have the same output as input, or NOT-gates, which output 1 if the input is 0, and vice versa. Moravec considers three cases. First is a simple feedback loop, where an amplifier's output is connected to its input, and there are no other inputs. Without reverse causation, the circuit "will lock up with its output permanently at either 0 or 1". If a 'negative time delay' is inserted into the circuit (i.e., with reverse causation involved), in such a way that it 'cancels' the forward delay, we have a consistent causal loop: 'when first switched on, it can permanently assume either 0 or 1 without contradiction'. The case I gave above of naming a baby 'Ben' is only slightly more complicated than this. Moravec does not address the question of why the circuit settles on one value rather than the other. There is only one answer: *coincidence,* and not such an unlikely one at that.

Second is a case of a simple NOT-gate feedback loop, with a single NOT-gate with its output connected to its input, and no other input. Without reverse causation, the circuit will:

oscillate rapidly between 0 and 1, at a rate that depends on its [forward] delay. It is possible to slow down this oscillation by inserting extra delay into the loop. Conversely, a negative delay element would speed up the oscillation.

If a negative time delay is inserted into the circuit in such a way that it cancels the forward delay, then we have, according to Moravec:

a simple case of the classical time travel grandfather paradox, a paradoxical causal loop. An input of 1 to the inverter gives an output of 0, which is brought back in time to contradict the input.

But not so fast. Moravec goes on to show that the

application of quantum mechanics to the problem – making the circuits *physical* – reveals consistent solutions. In one:

> somewhat like a ball balanced on a knife-edge
> that, against all odds, teeters indefinitely
> instead of falling to one side or the other. . . .
> The circuit finds itself perpetually in a dark
> fringe of an interference pattern.[36]

In another:

> the inverter's 1/2 state is extremely
> unlikely – a small deviation in the input
> would cause the output to saturate at one of
> the two extremes. Yet the circuit indefinitely
> maintains precisely that unlikely situation . . .
> by eliminating the standard possibilities,
> negative time delays make likely things that
> are otherwise nearly impossible.

This arrangement resembles a certain resolution
of a grandfatherish paradox, in which a time
traveler tries to shoot dead his earlier self, but
only wounds himself, because his ability to shoot
is impaired by the wound he received from the
shot.[37]

Third, Moravec presents a 'more complicated' arrangement:

> Make a computing box that accepts an input,
> which represents an approximate solution to
> some problem, and produces an output that is
> an improved approximation. Conventionally
> you would apply such a computation repeat-
> edly a finite number of times, and then settle
> for the better, but still approximate, result.
> Given an appropriate negative delay some-
> thing else is possible. . . .
> the result of each iteration of the function
> is brought back in time to serve as the "first"
> approximation. As soon as the machine is
> activated, a so-called "fixed-point" of [the
> function], an input which produces an iden-
> tical output, usually signaling a perfect
> answer, appears (by an extraordinary coinci-

dence!) immediately and steadily, just as
either 1 or 0 appears in the simple amplifier
loop. If the iteration does not converge, that
is, if [the function] has no fixed point, the
computer outputs and inputs will shut down
or hover in an unlikely intermediate state, like
the inverting loop.

The 'fixed point' possibility resembles the cases
of complicated information loops we have examined, such as undesigned time machines, Lossev
and Novikov's spaceship plans, and genetic
paradoxes. And it is obvious why there are no
instances of the 'no fixed point' possibility in
time travel stories: either a loop obtains in which
nothing of interest to us happens, or more likely
no loop obtains at all.[38] This last is of course what
would almost certainly happen if we followed
Lossev and Novikov's advice. If we build it, they
won't come.

8. Conclusion: Intentional Loops

To end where we began, time travel to the past
entails reverse causation. I hope to have shown
that, even if reverse causation entails causal
loops, such loops are not impossible, and some
are not even unlikely. All causal loops require
coincidence, but for some of the loops, the
coincidences required are really rather ordinary – the sort that we grant occur every day.
Some causal loops are extremely unlikely,
though. Should time travel to the past ever occur,
many of the weird situations envisaged in science
fiction stories probably will not obtain. But for
all we know, we will have to learn to live with the
others.

But perhaps we have been thinking about
causal loops in an unhelpful way. A common
objection to causal loops involving intentional
action is that they are incompatible with free
will. It is tempting to think that anyone
'trapped' in a causal loop will have their actions
inexorably, externally determined for them, and
lose the freedom to genuinely deliberate. This is

a topic worthy of at least an entire article, but suffice it to say here that the most this objection establishes is that, given causal loops, some agents in some circumstances do not act of their own free will. Since this last is true whether or not there are causal loops, I discern no real objection here. Indeed, it would in my view improve discussion of causal loops to place a moratorium on the discussion of free will, since in most circumstances the latter notion is no better understood than the former, and frequently it is not even as well understood.[39]

In general, then, physicists have tried to avoid free will problems by ignoring causal loops involving intentional agency, but I find this ironic. Consistent science fiction stories involving causal loops focus on agents, and divide into two sorts: either the time traveler is drunk or confused, and blunders into one situation or another (as in Michael Moorcock's *Behold The Man*, in which Jesus turns out to be a benighted time traveler, or in *Twelve Monkeys*, or its French inspiration, *La Jetée*); or else the time traveler makes a 'bilking' attempt which inevitably fails (as in Weisinger's 'Thompson's Time Traveling Theory', where the time traveler merely wounds rather than kills his younger self, or *The Terminator*). In both cases the past is apparently brought about willy-nilly, and this only reinforces the impression that time travel is an impediment to acting of one's own free will. It also encourages the postulation of a temporal censor, making causal loops seem rather unlikely.

But such fiction, not to mention much physics and philosophy, seems to take a dim view of human nature. A relatively unmined science fiction possibility (Heinlein providing obvious exceptions) is that informed time travellers will regard the fact that some past event occurred *as a reason to bring it about if necessary*. After all, *why would the informed person engage in futile 'bilking' attempts?* Whether or not such situations remove free will – and I am skeptical even of this claim –

is beside the point. Hence it may be that causal loops involving intentional action require less coincidence overall (and so are more likely), than causal loops not involving intentional action.

There is also a middle possibility. It seems a common temptation to suppose that time travelers will (unless they are drunk or inattentive) know what will happen in the past. Hence it might be thought that there is an asymmetry between our deliberative approaches to past events on the one hand, and to future events on the other. But any such difference seems at most one of degree. There is a lot we know about the future, and a lot we don't know about the past. So I'm inclined to think that the rational approach to acting in the past is to mostly behave just as you would in the present. Perhaps the best example of this behavior (outside of Heinlein's stories) is to be found in the movie *Bill and Ted's Excellent Adventure*. This fiction also contains a wonderful example of using time travel to one's own advantage. Early in the movie we learn that keys belonging to Ted's policeman father are missing. A few days later the boys, now in possession of a time machine, need to get into the Police Station. They decide to remember to go back in time, take the keys, and hide them behind a nearby sign. They simply look behind the sign, and sure enough, there are the keys!

This cute sequence involves a causal loop that depends for its existence on intentional action. And it can seem on first examination that it's a lucky coincidence that the keys are missing. (Otherwise, the specter of 'changing the past' looms large.) But of course, it's not a coincidence at all – the keys are missing precisely because the boys decided to take them. And they are quite properly resigned to take the future journey to the past to obtain the keys, precisely because *someone has to do it*. Ironically, in rendering them less improbable, the existence of agency may be the very thing that permits causal loops to obtain.

Notes

* Thanks to John Bigelow, Stephen Coleman, Michael Rea, and Aubrey Townsend, for valuable discussion; and to Tim Jones for the graphics.

1 I myself do not distinguish a further modality of metaphysical possibility, since I think it just is my notion of logical possibility. But I do not think that settling this issue matters to my purposes here.

2 Many of them, almost single-handedly, by Lewis (1986).

3 Special mention should be made here of an extraordinary article by 'hard' science fiction author Larry Niven (1971). Although not entirely lacking in merit, the article contains just about every fallacy of reasoning possible in connection with time travel. Indeed, I'm not entirely convinced of the sincerity of the piece, but I suspect it has many, many readers – far more than Lewis (1986), to judge from my anecdotal experience – who take it as both sincere and generally cogent.

4 MacBeath (1982, 410f) points out that it is a fallacy to suppose otherwise, and Smith (1997) even gives it a name, the *second-time-around* fallacy.

5 E.g., in Townsend (1997).

6 Special Relativity, in ruling out absolute simultaneity, does not thereby rule out the possibility of a closed causal chain in which there is no reverse causation. Any metaphysician who takes Special Relativity seriously must in any case distinguish *privileged* frames of reference (otherwise reverse causation obtains with or without time travel), and simultaneity in all such frames is simultaneity enough.

7 See, e.g., Hall (2000).

8 Riggs also points this out (1997, 59f).

9 This 'solution' has been presented to me at least a dozen times in personal communication, by non-philosophers. See also Niven (1971, 115f.). It doesn't really involve a Möbius loop, of course.

10 See, e.g., Niven's derivation of the immodestly named 'Niven's Law' (1971).

11 In Gregory Benford's *Timescape*, a theoretical physicist gives a very similar resolution in a similarly misleading way. Moravec (1991) describes such loops in both the right and the wrong way (refer-

ring approvingly to Niven's (1971) discussion of his 'Law'), apparently conflating the two.

12 D. Franson's story, 'Package Deal', uses the same idea.

13 In order, to avoid a particular causal loop in his story, MacBeath gives Arthur amnesia (1982, 418f). We could do the same for Max, post-journey, to remove any likelihood that, had he lived, he would have sought to influence events that are later in external time, but earlier in his personal time.

14 This is no mere assumption. I think that time travel all but requires that perdurantism is true, but I cannot argue for this claim here.

15 We can without harm think of the objects themselves (not just their "lives") as causal loops, by either extending the definition of a causal loop to include causation between temporal parts of objects, or else by redescribing objects as series of events. Lossev and Novikov (1992) call an object that is a loop a 'jinn'.

16 Nahin (1999, 315–316). Nahin says of the knife case that "I do not find this quite the puzzle Miller and Nerlich [1981] do. It is simply a variation of the grandfather paradox. If the knife is found flawless in the future, then it was not (will not) be nicked in the past". Nahin seems not to have grasped the point of the story here. His 'solution' is to change the story, but the issue is what has to be true for the original story to be consistent.

17 If it were possible for the watch to persist without any change in its intrinsic properties, that would provide one way out of the problem. I cannot discern any logical impossibility here, but I doubt that it is physically possible, given that the watch (even if useless as a timepiece) is causally interacting with the rest of the world.

18 As far as I am aware, Nerlich (1981) and MacBeath (1982) are the only previous explicit acknowledgements in the philosophical literature of the restoration problem affecting object loops. Nerlich writes (238, note 10), that David Lewis "is well aware of the problem". I see little evidence of recognition of the problem amongst physicists, however – they seem mostly concerned with problems of conservation of energy, e.g., Lossev and Novikov (1992).

19 Riggs (1997, 59f) gives an argument that might

be taken to show that such loops are not logically possible. In order to argue that what I have called a 'detached' loop is "plagued with serious conceptual incoherencies", Riggs uses the example of a time traveler whose life is a causal loop like that in Figure 18.5. He says, "There would be a point on the chain . . . where an adult time traveler would spontaneously metamorphosise into his newly born self! Such a state of affairs is clearly absurd". I cannot discern a conceptual incoherence where Riggs apparently does, but even if there is one, the source of it is more likely to be that the loop is 'detached', than that the time traveler's life is a loop (cf. Section 6). In any case, there is no need to suppose that normal aging of the time traveler must be undone instantaneously to return him to 'newly-born' state – for one thing, since the time traveler is clearly never born at all, there is no need to suppose he is ever that 'young'; and even if he was, there might be an equally gradual, 'de-aging', restoration process.

20 In Section 4, I described the physical notion of a closed timelike curve, or CTC, and I can now state why I find the notion metaphysically imprecise. If a CTC is to be understood concretely, then an object whose world line is a CTC would be in an 'object loop' of the sort represented in Figure 18.5 (hence the existence of CTCs entails the existence of causal loops); unless CTCs do not actually close, but merely come close enough to closing (cf. Figure 18.4). But it is common enough to claim that a CTC can be traversed repeatedly, which suggests that it is to be understood abstractly. It may be that physicists have no consistent notion, regarding timelike world lines concretely except in the case of CTCs. Understood in the abstract sense, CTCs clearly entail reverse causation, but I am not certain whether or not they entail the existence of causal loops (it is clear enough that abstract CTCs permit causal loops).

21 In Harry Harrison's story, the inventor of the time machine gives the following unhelpful response to the *ex nihilo* objection. After explaining how a two-sided piece of paper can be converted into a one-sided Möbius strip, he replies to the "where did the paper in the wallet come from?" question: "If you must have a source, you may say that it came from the same place that the missing side of the Möbius strip has gone to".

22 Nahin (1999, 159–160), reports that the argument goes back at least to 1937. He also notes (388, note 34), that global conservation laws are somewhat in doubt at present; and Deutsch (1991) argues that global conservation laws are respected in time travel cases without requiring unlikely expedients, if the 'many-worlds' interpretation of quantum mechanics is true. Lossev and Novikov (1992) address the issue of conservation of energy in a causal loop, since it might be expected that entropy increases all the way around the loop, leading to a contradiction. They conclude that this apparent problem disappears for any loop that has causal interaction with things external to the loop (i.e., if it is not 'detached'). The 'increasing entropy' problem resembles one of the 'increasing probability boosting' objections made by Mellor (1981, 1995), as mentioned in Section 3.

23 A banal expedient, by no means necessary, is to have an equally massive time machine making a well-timed complementary journey, from the twentieth century AD to the thirtieth.

24 Smith (1997) uses the example of mishearing, to make an analogous point.

25 Levin (1980) asks of a loop in a story, "How did it get started?" If this means, "Why did it obtain?" then the answer is the one I just gave.

26 See MacBeath (1982), Godfrey-Smith (1980), Harrison (1980), and Nahin (1999, 319–323).

27 The Benford story is another in which a man fathers himself; in the Harness story, a woman is her own mother and daughter.

28 David Gerrold's 'The Man Who Folded Himself', is yet another story in which a man is his own father, but this story is impossible for quite independent reasons.

29 Godfrey-Smith (now known as William Grey) has since recanted (2000).

30 MacBeath (1982), apparently on the basis of the fact that the Arthur story involves an information loop, concludes his article with, "there are contingent facts about the way in which men father offspring which preclude a man from fathering himself", and, "Respect for the scientific facts compels us to conclude that the Who who was Dr

Who's father was not Dr Who – that is, not the Dr Who whose father he was". I hope my discussion of information loops is an effective antidote to this reasoning, for science does not preclude coincidences. (Moreover, the scientific facts in question may include time traveling!)

31   I have simplified Lossev and Novikov's example somewhat, in that they have the spacecraft traversing the wormhole as many times as is necessary to get far enough back in time. I have merely assumed that only one wormhole trip is necessary, which may be physically less realistic (!); this removes a feature of Lossev and Novikov's example which can, if one doesn't go into the physics of it, seem paradoxical in itself.

32   Lossev and Novikov's answer, to the question of where the information came from, is that it came from the energy gained by interaction with the rest of the universe on the spacecraft's journey (see note 22) This seems to answer only a worry about conservation of energy, though, and doesn't touch the real puzzle.

33   Even non-replaceable parts, as neurons are supposed to be, may themselves consist entirely of replaceable, and replaced, smaller components.

34   For instance, this odd situation is supposed to explain why He already knows the hero of the story, even at their 'first' meeting.

35   Both Parfit (1984), and Lewis (1976), endorse the view that unbranching psychological continuity is a sufficient condition of personal identity. This is compatible with the thesis that a person is information.

36   Moravec's use of the terms 'permanently' (in the case of the amplifier loop) and 'perpetually' (in the case of the NOT-gate loop) should be ignored as a carry-over from thinking about feedback loops more generally. They have no helpful application to causal loops.

37   Clarke (1977), and following him, Riggs (1997), discuss this case, and correctly judge it analogous to the Wheeler and Feynman 'logically pernicious self-inhibitor', which is of course not logically pernicious.

38   Once again, take terms like 'shut down' and 'hover' with the appropriate grain of salt. The circuit will neither activate and then shut down, nor activate, and then hover – it simply will not activate, or else activate in an intermediate, colossally unlikely, state.

39   It does not help, either, that there is a tendency to conflate *eternalism* – the four-dimensional "block universe" view – with causal determinism.

References

Berkovich, J.: 2001, 'On Chance in Causal Loops', *Mind* **437**, 1–23.

Clarke, C. J. S.: 1977. 'Time in General Relativity', in J. Earman, C. Glymour, and J. Stachel (eds.), *Minnesota Studies in the Philosophy of Science, Volume VIII: Foundations of Space-Time Theories*, University of Minnesota Press, Minneapolis, pp. 94–108.

Deutsch, D.: 1991, 'Quantum Mechanics near Closed Timelike Lines', *Physical Review D* **44**, 3197–3217.

Dowe, P.: 2001, 'Causal Loops and the Independence of Causal Facts', *Philosophy of Science* **68**, 89–97.

Faye, J.: 2001 'Backward Causation', in E. N. Zalta (ed.), *The Stanford Encyclopedia of Philosophy* (Winter 2001 Edition). URL = <http://plato.stanford.edu/arch-ives/win2001/entries/causation-backwards/>.

Godfrey-Smith, W.: 1980, 'Traveling in Time', *Analysis* **40**, 72–73.

Grey [formerly Godfrey-Smith], W.: 1999, 'Troubles with Time Travel', *Philosophy* 55–70.

Hall, N.: 2000, 'Causation and the Price of Transitivity', *Journal of Philosophy* **97**, 198–222.

Harrison, J.: 1980, 'Report on *Analysis* Problem No. 18', *Analysis* **40**, 65–69.

Levin, M.: 1980, 'Swords' Points', *Analysis* **40**, 69–70.

Lewis, D.: 1986, in D. Lewis, *Philosophical Papers*, Vol. II, Oxford University Press, Oxford, pp. 67–80. (Reprint of Lewis, D.: 1976, "The Paradoxes of Time Travel", *American Philosophical Quarterly* **13**, 145–152.)

Lewis, D.: 1976, 'Survival and Identity', in A. Rorty (ed.), *The Identities of Persons*. University of California Press, Berkeley, pp. 17–40.

Lossev, A. and I. Novikov: 1992. 'The Jinn of the Time Machine: Nontrivial Self-Consistent Solutions', *Classical and Quantum Gravity* **9**, 2309–2321.

Mellor, H.: 1981, *Real Time*, Cambridge University Press, New York.

Mellor, H.: 1995, *The Facts of Causation*, Routledge, London.

MacBeath, M.: 1982, 'Who was Dr Who's Father?', *Synthese* **51**, 397–430.

Moravec, H.: 1991, 'Time Travel and Computing'. URL:

http://www.frc.ri.cmu.edu/hpm/project.archive/general/articles/1991/TempComp.html

Nahin, P.: 1999, *Time Machines: Time Travel in Physics, Metaphysics, and Science Fiction*, 2nd edn, Springer-Verlag, New York.

Nerlich, G.: 1981, 'Can Time Be Finite?', *Pacific Philosophical Quarterly* **62**, 227–239.

Niven, L.: 1971, 'The Theory and Practice of Time Travel', in *All the Myriad Ways*, Del Rey, New York, pp. 110–123.

Parfit, D.: 1984, *Reasons and Persons*, Clarendon Press, Oxford.

Price, H.: 1996, *Time's Arrow and Archimedes' Point*, Oxford University Press, New York.

Riggs, P.: 1997, 'The Principal Paradox of Time Travel', *Ratio* **10**, 48–64.

Riggs, P.: 1991, 'A Critique of Mellor's Argument against 'Backwards' Causation', *British Journal for the Philosophy of Science* **42**, 75–86.

Smith, N. J. J.: 1997, 'Bananas Enough for Time Travel?', *British Journal for the Philosophy of Science* **48**, 363–389.

Townsend, Aubrey, 'Time Travel, Freedom and Deliberation', in A. Townsend (ed.), *Time, Self and Freedom*, Monash University, Melbourne.

Wheeler, J. and R. Feynman: 1949, 'Classical Electro-Dynamics in Terms of Direct Interparticle Action', *Reviews of Modern Physics* **21**, 425–433.

PART 3

Change and Identity

INTRODUCTION TO PART 3

CENTRAL TO OUR COMMONSENSE WORLDVIEW is the idea that the world is made up of things that are able to persist through a wide variety of changes. Almost since the dawn of the discipline, however, philosophers have seen the phenomenon of change as fraught with virtually intractable difficulties. The pre-Socratic Greek philosopher Parmenides and his followers marshaled challenging arguments against the possibility of change, and these arguments exerted a great deal of influence on subsequent philosophy. Many in the wake of Parmenides, including Plato, were captivated by the idea that *fundamental reality*—whatever it is that underlies or explains appearances in the world—is unchanging, and they developed sophisticated and interesting ontological views in order to accommodate this notion. It is widely believed that ancient Greek worries about change also influenced the theistic tradition, particularly in providing the most important philosophical motivation for the controversial but traditional view that God is absolutely simple and unchanging.

This part of our text opens with a brief selection from the work of Parmenides, and with one of the most widely discussed contemporary puzzles about change, the so-called problem of temporary intrinsics.

For Parmenides, the problem with change is that it involves non-existence, and non-existence is unintelligible. If Socrates is generated, then there must have been a time when Socrates did not exist; if he is destroyed, then there will be such a time; and if Socrates changes (say, from being short to being tall) then there must be some time when his shortness does not exist and some time when his tallness does not exist. But, on Parmenides' view, non-existence claims can never be true. Thus, change is impossible.

As we have already seen in Part 1, non-existence is a topic for contemporary philosophical discussion as well; but in the recent literature on change, it is not Parmenides' arguments that have taken center stage, but the problem of temporary intrinsics. One way of stating the problem (different from Lewis's statement) is as follows: Let F be some intrinsic property, and let L be some location. It is quite natural to think that we can, in general, infer from "x is F at L" the conclusion that "x is F". After all, if Fred is human-shaped in Australia, then Fred is human-shaped, right? But change occurs only when one and the same thing has a property at one time that it lacks at another. Thus, if x changes from being F to being not-F, then there are times t1 and t2 such that:

(1) x is F at t1 and x is not-F at t2

By our principle about properties and locations, however, we can infer from (1) the contradictory claim that

(2)   *x* is F and *x* is not-F.

So, then, change is impossible because it entails a contradiction. To solve this problem—to show that change does not involve contradiction after all—one must do one of the following two things: (a) provide some reason for rejecting the principle about properties and locations that allows us to drop the temporal indices in (1) in order to derive (2), or (b) show that, contrary to what we initially thought, change does not imply anything resembling (1).

We also take up a third puzzle about change in this section: the so-called Ship of Theseus puzzle. Plutarch (*Life of Theseus* 23) tells us that, according to the Athenians anyway, Theseus's original ship was preserved for many, many years in working order by the continuous, gradual replacement of worn-out planks. According to Plutarch, the ship then became a topic for philosophical discussion, because philosophers wondered whether the *same* ship could retain its identity through such extensive— eventually, no doubt, complete—part replacement. Much later, Thomas Hobbes added a twist to the problems raised by Theseus's ship by inviting us to consider what we would say if all of the original parts were preserved as they were replaced and then eventually rebuilt into their original form. Which would be *the* Ship of Theseus—the one that has been continuously repaired and sailing for so many years, or the one that has been reconstructed from the original planks? This question is, in essence, the Ship of Theseus puzzle as it is discussed today.

This puzzle is one instance of a more general problem about material constitution. Material constitution occurs when an object *a* and an object *b* share all of the same material parts in common. The *problem of material constitution* arises whenever objects *a* and *b* share all of the same material parts but seem to have different properties. In the case of Theseus' ship, the relevant *a* and *b* might be thought to be the continuously repaired ship and the sum of all of the original planks. But we can illustrate the problem with different examples as well. Consider, for example, a table and the collection of parts that now constitutes it. Is the table something "over and above" the collection? It certainly seems so. After all, the table could have been composed of some different parts (different screws but the same pieces of wood, for example); but, obviously, the collection of parts couldn't itself have been composed of different parts (different parts would make for a different collection). So the table and the collection seem to have different essential properties: the collection, but not the table, has essentially the property of being composed of these parts. But now it looks as if the table and the collection must be *distinct objects* that are located in the same place at the same time. And isn't that puzzling? Moreover, it seems that there are still other objects located where the table is. Assembling the table, for example, is one way of piling the parts. So don't we have, in addition to the collection and the table a *pile*? It is tempting to say no; but bear in mind that when the parts were scattered on the floor, there was a collection but no table or pile; and if the parts had simply been piled, the pile and the collection would have existed, but not the table. So it looks as if pile, collection, and table have to be distinct. We can try to dodge the problem by denying the existence of the pile or the collection or the table (or all three); but if we do this, we will want principled grounds for doing so, and whatever principle we employ will likely have unwanted consequences in addition to the consequences we desire. Likewise in the Ship of Theseus puzzle: We can insist that the original ship was identical to what is now the "continuously repaired ship" and deny that there ever was any such thing as "the collection of original planks." (What is now composed of those planks is a brand new ship.) Or we can deny that what we now call the continuously repaired ship existed at the beginning of the story: replacing planks with new ones simply began the process of disassembling the original ship and replacing it with a brand new one that is now sailing the route. There are other ways of avoiding the problem; but those ways also have their costs.

The first four essays in this section focus on the three problems just identified. The remaining essays and stories focus on problems and puzzles concerning the survival of persons. Much of our interest in puzzles about change in material objects arises out of our deeper concerns about personal identity and survival. Not only do we think that we are able to survive radical, non-fatal changes in our bodies and minds; but many of us also think that we can ultimately survive even the death of our bodies. But, of course, if puzzles about change are to be solved (as many think they are) by denying, in one way or another, the existence of things that survive change, these beliefs of ours are in serious trouble.

Many of the questions that might be asked about personal identity over time are no different from the sorts of questions we want to ask about the persistence of non-persons. Some, however, are different. In particular, many philosophers have wondered whether and to what extent psychological continuity suffices for personal survival. Relatedly, many have wondered whether survival and identity might come apart. Thus, for example, some think that psychological continuity is what is most important in survival, but that it could, in principle, turn out that two different people, A and B, stand in the right sorts of psychological continuity relations to a previously existing person C. In such cases, some want to say, it makes sense to say that C has *survived as* both A and B even though C cannot possibly be identical to both A and B. If this is right, then survival and identity come apart. Others, however, think that survival and identity cannot possibly come apart; and so they face questions about what to do with the sorts of thought-experiments that motivate the idea that one person can somehow "survive as" two. Some of these issues are vividly raised in the stories by Greg Egan and Daryl Gregory. The essay by Derek Parfit defends a well-known version of the psychological theory, and the essay by Olson defends an alternative, organic theory of personal identity.

Chapter 19

Parmenides and David Lewis

PROBLEMS ABOUT CHANGE
Selections from the Writings of Parmenides and David Lewis

Excerpt from *The Ways of Truth & Opinion*

Parmenides

[1] The mares that carry me as far as my heart ever aspires sped me on, when they had brought and set me on the far-famed road of the god, which bears the man who knows over all cities. On that road was I borne, for that way the wise horses bore me, straining at the chariot, and maidens led the way. And the axle in the naves gave out the whistle of a pipe, blazing, for it was pressed hard on either side by the two well-turned wheels as the daughters of the Sun made haste to escort me, having left the halls of Night for the light, and having thrust the veils from their heads with their hands.

There are the gates of the paths of Night and Day, and a lintel and a stone threshold enclose them. They themselves, high in the air, are blocked with great doors, and avenging Justice holds the alternate bolts. Her the maidens beguiled with gentle words and cunningly persuaded to push back swiftly from the gates the bolted bar. And the gates created a yawning gap in the door frame when they flew open, swinging in turn in their sockets the bronze-bound pivots made fast with dowels and rivets. Straight through them, on the broad way, did the maidens keep the horses and the chariot.

And the goddess greeted me kindly, and took my right hand in hers, and addressed me with these words: "Young man, you who come to my house in the company of immortal charioteers with the mares which bear you, greetings. No ill fate has sent you to travel this road—far indeed does it lie from the steps of men but right and justice. It is proper that you should learn all things, both the unshaken heart of well-rounded truth, and the opinions of mortals, in which there is no true reliance. But nonetheless you shall learn these things too, how what is believed would have to be assuredly, pervading all things throughout."

[2] Come now, and I will tell you (and you must carry my account away with you when you have heard it) the only ways of enquiry that are to be thought of. The one, that [it] is and that it is impossible for [it] not to be, is the path of Persuasion (for she attends upon Truth); the other, that [it] is not and that it is needful that [it] not be, that I declare to you is an altogether indiscernible track: for you could not know what is not—that cannot be done—nor indicate it.

[3] For the same thing is there both to be thought of and to be.

[4] But look at things which, though far off, are securely present to the mind; for you will not cut off for yourself what is from holding to what is, neither scattering everywhere in every way in order [i.e., cosmic order] nor drawing together.

[5] It is a common point from which I start; for there again and again I shall return.

[6] What is there to be said and thought

needs must be; for it is there for being, but nothing is not. I bid you ponder that, for this is the first way of enquiry from which I hold you back, but then from that on which mortals wander knowing nothing, two-headed; for helplessness guides the wandering thought in their breasts, and they are carried along, deaf and blind at once, dazed, undiscriminating hordes, who believe that to be and not to be are the same and not the same, and the path taken by them is backward-turning.

[7] For never shall this be forcibly maintained, that things that are not are, but you must hold back your thought from this way of enquiry, nor let habit, born of much experience, force you down this way, by making you use an aimless eye or an ear and a tongue full of meaningless sound: judge by reason the strife-encompassed refutation spoken by me.

[8] Only one way remains; that it is. To this way there are very many sign-posts: that being has no coming-into-being and no destruction, for it is whole of limb, without motion, and without end. And it never was, nor will be, because it is now, a whole all together, one, continuous; for what creation of it will you look? How, whence sprung? Nor shall I allow you to speak or think of it as springing from not-being; for it is neither expressible nor thinkable that what-is-not is. Also, what necessity impelled it, if it did spring from nothing, to be produced later or earlier? Thus it must be absolutely, or not at all. Nor will the force of credibility ever admit that anything should come into being, beside being itself, out of not-being. So far as that is concerned, justice has never released (*being*) from its fetters and set it free either to come into being or to perish, but holds it fast. The decision on these matters depends on the following: it is, or it is not. It is therefore decided, as is inevitable: ignore the one way as unthinkable and inexpressible (for it is no true way) and take the other as the way of being and reality. How could being perish? How could it come into being? If it came into being, it is not, and so too if it is

about-to-be at some future time. Thus coming-into-being is quenched, and destruction also into the unseen.

Nor is being divisible, since it is all alike. Nor is there anything there which could prevent it from holding together, nor any lesser thing, but all is full of being. Therefore it is altogether continuous; for being is close to being.

But it is motionless in the limits of mighty bonds, without beginning, without cease, since becoming and destruction have been driven very far away, and true conviction has rejected them. And remaining the same in the same place, it rests by itself and thus remains there fixed; for powerful necessity holds it in the bonds of a limit, which constrains it round about, because it is decreed by divine law that being shall not be without boundary. For it is not lacking; but if it were (*spatially infinite*), it would be lacking everything.

To think is the same as the thought that it is; for you will not find thinking without being to which it refers. For nothing else either is or shall be except being, since fate has tied it down to be a whole and motionless; therefore all things that mortals have established, believing in their truth, are just a name: becoming and perishing, being and not-being, and change of position, and alteration of bright color.

But since there is a (*spatial*) limit, it is complete on every side, like the mass of a well-rounded sphere, equally balanced from its center in every direction; for it is not bound to be at all either greater or less in this direction or that; nor is there not-being which could check it from reaching to the same point, nor is it possible for being to be more in this direction, less in that, than being, because it is an inviolate whole. For, in all directions equal to itself, it reaches its limits uniformly.

At this point I cease my reliable theory ⟨*Logos*⟩ and thought, concerning Truth; from here onwards you must learn the opinions of mortals, listening to the deceptive order of my words.

They have established (*the custom of*) naming two forms, one of which ought not to be (*mentioned*): that is where they have gone astray. They have distinguished them as opposite in form, and have marked them off from another by giving them different signs: on one side the flaming fire in the heavens, mild, very light (*in weight*), the same as itself in every direction, and not the same as the other. This (*other*) also is by itself and opposite: dark night, a dense and heavy body. This world-order I describe to you throughout as it appears with all its phenomena, in order that no intellect of mortal men may outstrip you.

[9] But since all things are named light and night, and names have been given to each class of things according to the power of one or the other, everything is full equally of light and invisible night, as both are equal, because to neither of them belongs any share (of the other).

[10] You shall know the nature of the heavens, and all the signs in the heavens, and the destructive works of the pure bright torch of the sun, and whence they came into being. And you shall learn of the wandering works of the round-faced moon, and its nature; and you shall know also the surrounding heaven, whence it sprang and how necessity brought and constrained it to hold the limits of the stars.

[11] (*I will describe*) how earth and sun and moon, and the aether common to all, and the milky way in the heavens, and outermost Olympus, and the hot power of the stars, hastened to come into being.

[12] For the narrower rings were filled with unmixed fire, and those next to them with night, but between (these) rushes the portion of flame. And in the center of these is the goddess who guides everything; for throughout she rules over cruel birth and mating, sending the female to mate with the male, and conversely again the male with the female.

[13] First of all the gods she devised Love.

[14] (*The moon*): Shining by night with a light not her own, wandering round the earth.

Excerpt from On the Plurality of Worlds

David Lewis

Let us say that something persists iff, somehow or other, it exists at various times; this is the neutral word.[1] Something perdures iff it persists by having different temporal parts, or stages, at different times, though no one part of it is wholly present at more than one time; whereas it endures iff it persists by being wholly present at more than one time. Perdurance corresponds to the way a road persists through space; part of it is here and part of it is there, and no part is wholly present at two different places. Endurance corresponds to the way a universal, if there are such things, would be wholly present wherever and whenever it is instantiated. Endurance involves overlap: the content of two different times has the enduring thing as a common part. Perdurance does not.

(There might be mixed cases: entities that persist by having an enduring part and a perduring part. An example might be a person who consisted of an enduring entelechy ruling a perduring body; or an electron that had a universal of unit negative charge as a permanent part, but did not consist entirely of universals. But here I ignore the mixed cases. And when I speak of ordinary things as perduring, I shall ignore their enduring universals, if such there be.)

Discussions of endurance versus perdurance tend to be endarkened by people who say such things as this: 'Of course you are wholly present at every moment of your life, except in case of amputation. For at every moment all your parts are there: your legs, your lips, your liver....' These endarkeners may think themselves partisans of endurance, but they are not. They are perforce neutral because they lack the conceptual resources to understand what is at issue. Their speech betrays – and they may acknowledge it willingly – that they have no concept of a temporal part. (Or at any rate none that applies to a person, say, as opposed to a process or a stretch of time.) Therefore they are on neither side of a dispute about whether or not persisting things are divisible into temporal parts. They understand neither the affirmation nor the denial. They are like the people – fictional, I hope – who say that the whole of the long road is in their little village, for not one single lane of it is missing. Meaning less than others do by 'part', since they omit parts cut crosswise, they also mean less than others do by 'whole'. They say the 'whole' road is in the village; by which they mean that every 'part' is; but by that, they only mean that every part cut lengthwise is. Divide the road into its least lengthwise parts; they cannot even raise the question whether those are in the village wholly or only partly. For that is a question about crosswise parts, and the concept of a crosswise part is what they lack. Perhaps 'crosswise part' really does sound to them like a blatant contradiction. Or perhaps it seems to them that they understand it, but the village philosophers have persuaded them that really they couldn't, so their impression to the contrary must be an illusion. At any rate, I have the concept of a temporal part; and for some while I shall be addressing only those of you who share it.[2]

. . . The principal and decisive objection against endurance, as an account of the persistence of ordinary things such as people or puddles, is the problem of temporary intrinsics. Persisting things change their intrinsic properties. For instance shape: when I sit, I have a bent shape; when I stand, I have a straightened shape. Both shapes are temporary intrinsic properties; I have them only some of the time. How is such change possible? I know of only three solutions.

(It is not a solution just to say how very commonplace and indubitable it is that we have different shapes at different times. To say that is only to insist – rightly – that it must be possible somehow. Still less is it a solution to say it in jargon – as it might be, that bent-on-Monday and straight-on-Tuesday are compatible because they are 'time-indexed properties' – if that just means that, somehow, you can be bent on Monday and straight on Tuesday.)

First solution: contrary to what we might think, shapes are not genuine intrinsic properties. They are disguised relations, which an enduring thing may bear to times. One and the same enduring thing may bear the bent-shape relation to some times, and the straight-shape relation to others. In itself, considered apart from its relations to other things, it has no shape at all. And likewise for all other seeming temporary intrinsics; all of them must be reinterpreted as relations that something with an absolutely unchanging intrinsic nature bears to different times. The solution to the problem of temporary intrinsics is that there aren't any temporary intrinsics. This is simply incredible, if we are speaking of the persistence of ordinary things. (It might do for the endurance of entelechies or universals.) If we know what shape is, we know that it is a property, not a relation.

Second solution: the only intrinsic properties of a thing are those it has at the present moment. Other times are like false stories; they are abstract representations, composed out of the materials of the present, which represent or misrepresent the way things are. When something has different intrinsic properties according to one of these ersatz other times, that does not mean that it, or any part of it, or anything else, just has them – no more so than when a man is crooked according to the Times, or honest according to the News. This is a solution that rejects endurance; because it rejects persistence altogether. And it is even less credible than the first solution. In saying that there are no other times, as opposed to false representations thereof, it goes against what we all believe. No man, unless it be at the moment of his execution, believes that he has no future; still less does anyone believe that he has no past.

Third solution: the different shapes, and the different temporary intrinsics generally, belong to different things. Endurance is to be rejected in favour of perdurance. We perdure; we are made up of temporal parts, and our temporary intrinsics are properties of these parts, wherein they differ one from another. There is no problem at all about how different things can differ in their intrinsic properties.

Notes

1 My discussion of this problem is much indebted to David M. Armstrong, 'Identity Through Time', in *Time and Cause: Essays Presented to Richard Taylor*, ed. by Peter van Inwagen (Dordrecht: D. Reidel, 1980); and to Mark Johnston. I follow Johnston in terminology.

2 I attempt to explain it to others in *Philosophical Papers*, vol. 1 (Oxford: Oxford University Press, 1983), pp. 76–7; reprinted in this volume as 'In Defense of Stages: Postscript B to "Survival and Identity"'. But I have no great hopes, since any competent philosopher who does not understand something will take care not to understand anything else whereby it might be explained.

Chapter 20

Brian Smart

HOW TO REIDENTIFY THE SHIP OF THESEUS

A ship, X, is composed of a thousand old, but perfectly seaworthy, planks. It is brought into dock A where at hour 1 one of X's planks is removed to dock B and is replaced by a new plank. At hour 2 the same process is repeated so that by hour 1000 we have a ship Y in dock A composed of a thousand new planks and (since X's old planks have been reassembled as a ship) a ship Z in dock B composed of a thousand old planks. The problem is: with which ship—Y or Z—, if either, is X identical?

Let us give this problem a fictitious, but practical, setting.

Two shipowners, Morion and Bombos, are involved in a legal dispute. Morion had ordered a new ship from the Proteus brothers, shipbuilders and shiprepairers. Bombos had sent his ship, X, along to the same firm for a complete renewal of all its parts. (It should be explained that such a renewal would involve only half the labour costs of building a new ship from scratch.) Now the scheming Proteus brothers had persuaded Morion that what he wanted was a ship with well-seasoned timber and told him that his "new" ship was under construction in dock B. They saw their way to an enormous profit. For, while they would require a thousand new planks for renovating the ship that belonged to the shrewder and potentially more troublesome Bombos, they would clearly not need a second batch of new planks for building Morion's ship: they would use Bombos's old ones.

However the brothers' plans misfired all too literally. Just after Morion and Bombos had paid their bills, but before they had taken possession of Y and Z, there was a fire in dock B and Z was reduced to ashes. Under the law of Oudamou, where all these events occurred, the brothers were responsible for Z until Morion had taken possession. Unfortunately, they had not had Z insured. The insurance would have had to be for a "new" ship but under Oudamou law the newness of a ship was decided by the newness of its component parts.

Seeing their vast profits about to disappear the Proteus brothers, in heavy disguise, left Oudamou abandoning Y in dock A.

Morion was quickly persuaded by his lawyer to claim ownership of Y as he had paid for a new ship and Y was new under Oudamou law. Bombos's lawyer naturally put in a claim on his client's behalf for possession of Y on the ground that Y was identical with X.

When the case was heard the judges were presented with the following four lines of argument:

(1) $X = Y; X \neq Z$ (In favour of Bombos).
(2) $X = Z; X \neq Y$ (In favour of Morion).
(3) $X \neq Y; X \neq Z; X \neq Y + Z$ (In favour of Morion).
(4) $X \neq Y; X \neq Z; X = Y + Z$ (In favour of Bombos).

Bombos's lawyer argued for (1) as follows. Over a period of time objects like the human body can undergo a change of identity in all their parts. All that is required is that the overall form of the object is retained and that it occupies a continuous space-time path. The ship in dock A satisfies this condition, and so X, his client's ship, is identical with Y. X is not identical with Z precisely because the form of Z cannot be linked to the form of X by a continuous space-time path.

Morion's lawyer attacked this argument with (2). He urged that the spatio-temporal continuity of form was neither a necessary nor a sufficient condition of identity. It was not a necessary condition since a watch could be dismantled and the same parts reassembled to form the same watch. X had in fact been gradually dismantled in dock A and reassembled in dock B. The necessary and sufficient condition to be met was the identity of the parts of X with the parts of Z. This condition had been met by Z. Hence it was Bombos's ship that had been destroyed and his client's ship which remained.

Morion's lawyer now added a second line to his attack. He brought in (3) in case (2) proved defective. He asked the judges to consider the possibility that there were two independent, but defeasible, sufficient conditions of identity: identity of parts and spatio-temporal continuity of form. All, that was sufficient to defeat either claim was the applicability of the other. Hence in this case neither Y nor Z could be identical with X. Because of the transitivity of identity it could not be the case that X was identical with each. What required no argument was that X was not identical with both Y and Z, that is identical with the pair. It followed that Bombos could have no possible claim upon Y.

Here Bombos's lawyer spotted a weakness in Morion's case. For, while it had to be conceded that X was not identical with each of Y and Z, it was not obvious that X could not be identical with the pair. His argument for (4) attached great weight to the fact that a continuous space-time path linked X with both Y and Z. It was true that this path divided, but was not this precisely what was involved in X becoming both Y and Z? If this were true then Y would be a part or member of the pair, a pair that was identical with his client's ship X.

The judges then retired to consider their verdict.

(4) was rejected because the question was not one simply of identity but of substance-identity. Now a substance like a ship cannot be identical with a pair of substances for no substance-concept could cover the pair of ships. This would emerge if we asked 'X and the pair Y and Z are the same what?' They could not be the same ship; equally they could not be the same pair of ships. 'A pair' is not a substance-concept at all but rather a compositum-concept. So if the answer to the identity question were to lie within the existing rules for identity (4) would have to be dismissed.

At this point Morion had two arguments in his favour to Bombos's one. But now (3) was considered. (4), it was contended, had quite rightly been rejected on the ground that there was no covering substance-concept. But this might be misinterpreted as the claim that Y and Z were the products of X's fission and that (4) provided an incorrect analysis of such fission. Admittedly if fission had occurred then (3) supplied the correct identity judgements. However fission had not occurred and two arguments would show this.

Firstly, if there had been fission, did it have to be X's fission into Y and Z? Why not describe it as the fission of X's matter into the matter of Y and Z? In the statement 'X becomes Y and Z' 'becomes' is the 'becomes' of composition, not identity. If so, then the truth of such a statement was entirely irrelevant to the question before them: what does X 'become' in the sense of identity?

Secondly, if the fission of X, rather than of its matter, occurred, when precisely did it occur? A change in the identity of only one of its parts could not be called fission, so fission must have taken place after the first hour. It could hardly have taken place at the 999th hour since Y would differ from the ship in dock A at that hour by only one part, just as Z would differ from the ship in dock B at the 999th hour by only one part. Perhaps the 500th hour was the answer, for then the original 1000 parts of X would be evenly divided between two ships. If so, then X would be identical with the ship in dock A at the 499th hour and thus would differ from the ship in dock A at the 500th hour by only one plank; but then X would not be identical with that ship, and this was unacceptable.

However it will be remembered that (3) had not been defended as a case of fission. Rather it had been claimed that two defeasible sufficient conditions for identity had been defeated. The judges now introduced a refutation of both (3) and (2).

The judges agreed that objects could be dismantled and reassembled elsewhere, still retaining their identity, and that identity of parts was a defeasible sufficient condition of identity. Both (2) and (3) presupposed that this condition applied, though while (3) claimed that the condition was defeated (2) claimed that it was not. The judges attacked the presupposition. They contended that the requirement was that the object's *parts* had been reassembled: only then was it appropriate to enquire whether the condition was defeated or not defeated. They claimed that Z did not contain X's parts at all. If the case had been one in which only the original planks were involved there would be no difficulty over identifying Z's parts with X's parts. But the case was not as simple as that.

Their reasoning was this. When a plank had been removed from X and replaced by a new plank, it was the new plank that was now a part of X. The old plank *had been* a part of X but was no longer. Rather it was a part of Z which gradually

came into being from hour 1 onwards. When completed Z was not composed of any of X's parts but rather of what had been X's parts. 'Being a part of X' was merely a temporary rôle in the career of the old planks which were now parts of Z. Using this line of argument it was clear that X had simply changed the identity of its parts and that now its parts were identical with the parts of Y. Hence X was identical with Y. X was not identical with Z for they had no parts in common.

Thus they found in favour of Bombos.

Bombos's feeling of exultation was short-lived since it was illegal to launch such a poorly constructed ship. So he was faced with the costs of having it dismantled and constructed anew in the proper manner.

Morion lodged an appeal. This consisted of the claim that judgements of identity in cases like this were to be decided by an arbitrary decision: once the decision was made future judges would have to be guided by it, but so far that decision had not been made and ordinary language had not been designed to supply it.

Unfortunately for Morion the appeal was dismissed. He had thought that if his submission had been accepted he would have had at least a fifty-fifty chance of success. However the judges considered that his appeal was to be rejected for at least two reasons.

(i) If the problem case required an arbitrary decision, had it not already been made? For if Morion's submission was correct the judges' verdict had not been supported by their arguments and was not supportable by any other argument: it had amounted to an arbitrary decision.

(ii) In fact the existing rules of identity had proved perfectly adequate for this unusual case and had yielded a non-arbitrary and clear-cut decision—a testimony to their extraordinary versatility.

Chapter 21

Roderick Chisholm

IDENTITY AND TEMPORAL PARTS

The identity of a person is a perfect identity; wherever it is real, it admits of no degrees; and it is impossible that a person should be in part the same, and in part different . . . For this cause, I have first considered personal identity, as that which is perfect in its kind, and the natural measure of that which is imperfect.

Thomas Reid[1]

1 The Ship of Theseus

To understand the philosophical problems involved in persistence, in the fact that one and the same thing may endure through a period of time, we will begin with what Reid would have called the 'imperfect' cases and remind ourselves of some ancient philosophical puzzles. One such puzzle is suggested by the familiar dictum of Heraclitus: 'You could not step twice in the same river; for other and yet other waters are ever flowing on.'[2] Another is the problem of the Ship of Theseus.[3]

Updating the latter problem somewhat, let us imagine a ship – the Ship of Theseus – that was made entirely of wood when it came into being. One day a wooden plank is cast off and replaced by an aluminum one. Since the change is only slight, there is no question as to the survival of the Ship of Theseus. We still have the ship we had before; that is to say, the ship that we have now is identical with the ship we had before. On another day, another wooden plank is cast off and also replaced by an aluminum one. Still the

same ship, since, as before, the change is only slight. The changes continue, in a similar way, and finally the Ship of Theseus is made entirely of aluminum. The aluminum ship, one may well argue, is the wooden ship we started with, for the ship we started with survived each particular change, and identity, after all, is transitive.

But what happened to the discarded wooden planks? Consider this possibility, suggested by Thomas Hobbes: 'If some man had kept the old planks as they were taken out, and by putting them afterwards together in the same order, had again made a ship of them, this, without doubt, had also been the same numerical ship with that which was at the beginning; and so there would have been two ships numerically the same, which is absurd.'[4] Assuming, as perhaps one has no right to do, that each of the wooden planks survived intact throughout these changes, one might well argue that the reassembled wooden ship is the ship we started with. 'After all, it is made up of the very same parts, standing in the very same relations, whereas that ugly aluminum object doesn't have a single part in common with our original ship.'

To compound the problem still further, let us suppose that the captain of the original ship had solemnly taken the vow that, if his ship were ever to go down, he would go down with it. What, now, if the two ships collide at sea and he sees them start to sink together? Where does his duty lie – with the aluminum ship or with the reassembled wooden ship?

'The carriage' is another ancient version of the problem. Socrates and Plato change the parts of their carriages piece by piece until, finally, Socrates's original carriage is made up of all the parts of Plato's carriage and Plato's carriage is made up of all the parts of Socrates's original carriage. Have they exchanged their carriages or not, and if so, at what point?

Perhaps the essence of the problem is suggested by an even simpler situation. Consider a child playing with his blocks. He builds a house with ten blocks, uses it as a garrison for his toy soldiers, disassembles it, builds many other things, then builds a house again, with each of the ten blocks occupying the position it had occupied before, and he uses it again as a garrison for his soldiers. Was the house that was destroyed the same as the one that subsequently came into being?

These puzzles about the persistence of objects through periods of time have their analogues for the extension of objects through places in space. Consider the river that is known in New Orleans as 'the Mississippi'. Most of us would say that the source of the river is in northern Minnesota. But what if one were to argue instead that the source is in Montana, where it is known as 'the Missouri'? Or that its source is in Pittsburgh, where it is known as 'the Ohio', or that its source is farther back where it is called 'the Allegheny', or in still another place where it is called 'the Monongahela'?[5]

The accompanying diagram provides us with a schematic illustration.

```
(a)     (b)     (c)
 x       x       x
      x   x   x
       xxx
        x
        x
        x
       (d)
```

Of the river that has its central point at (d), one might wonder whether it flows south-easterly from (a), or due south from (b), or south-westerly from (c). (For simplicity, we ignore the Allegheny and the Monongahela.) If we are puzzled about the beginning of the Mississippi, we should be equally puzzled about the end of the Rhine. Reading our diagram from bottom to top (and again oversimplifying), we could say that if the Rhine begins at (d), then it ends either with the Maas at (a), or with the Waal at (b), or with the Lek at (c).[6]

Perhaps we can imagine three philosophers looking down at the river(s) that end(s) at (d). One insists that the river flows between (a) and (d), another that it flows between (b) and (d) and the third that it flows between (c) and (d); and each insists that, since the arms (or tributaries) to which the other two philosophers refer are distinct not only from each other but from the river itself, neither of the other two can be right. Their dispute, clearly, would be analogous in significant respects to the problem of the Ship of Theseus.

What are we to say of such puzzles? We might follow the extreme course that Carneades took and simply deny the principle of the transitivity of identity.[7] In other words we might say that things identical with the same thing need not be identical with each other. But if we thus abandon reason and logic at the very outset, we will have no way of deciding at the end what is the most reasonable thing to say about ourselves and our persistence through time.

We might be tempted to deny the possibility of alteration. Thus one could say: 'Strictly speaking, nothing alters – nothing is such that at one time it has one set of properties and at another time it has another set of properties. What happens is, rather, that at one time there is a thing having the one set of properties and at the other time there is another thing having the other set of properties.' But this supposition, if we apply it to ourselves, is inconsistent with the data with which we have begun. Each of us knows with respect to himself that he now has properties he didn't have in the past and that formerly he had properties he doesn't have now. ('But a thing x isn't identical with a thing y unless they have all their properties in common. And if the present you has one set of properties and the past you another, how can they be the same thing?') The answer is, of course, that there aren't two you's, a present one having one set of properties, and a past one having another. It is rather that you *are* now such that you have these properties and lack those, whereas formerly you *were* such that you had those properties and lacked these. The 'former you' *has* the same properties that the 'present you' now has, and the 'present you' *had* the same properties that the 'former you' then had.[8]

Bishop Butler suggested that it is only in 'a loose and popular sense' that we may speak of the persistence of such familiar things as ships, plants and houses. And he contrasted this 'loose and popular sense' with 'the strict and philosophical sense' in which we may speak of the persistence of *persons*.[9] Let us consider these suggestions.

2 Playing Loose with the "Is" of Identity

We will not pause to ask what Butler meant in fact. Let us ask what he could have meant. He suggested that there is a kind of looseness involved when we say that such things as the Ship of Theseus persist through time. What kind of looseness is this?

It could hardly be that the Ship of Theseus, in contrast with other things, is only loosely identical with itself. Surely one cannot say that, while some things are only loosely identical with themselves, other things are tightly identical with themselves.[10] The statement 'This thing is more loosely identical with itself than that thing', if it says anything at all, tells us only that the first thing is more susceptible than the second to loss of identity, and this means only that the first is more readily perishable than the second.

We should construe Butler's remark as saying, not that there is a loose kind of identity, but rather that there is a loose sense of 'identity' – a loose (and popular) use of the 'is' of identity.

What would be a *loose* sense of 'A is B', or 'A is identical with B' – a sense of 'A is B' which is consistent with a denial of the *strict* sense of 'A is B'? I suggest this: we use the locution 'A is B', or 'A is identical with B', in a *loose* sense, if we use it in such a way that it is consistent with saying 'A has a certain property that B does not have' or 'Some things are true of A that aren't true of B'.

Do we ever use the locution 'A is B' in this loose way? It would seem, unfortunately, that we do.

I will single out five different types of such misuse.

(1) One may say: 'Route 6 is Point Street in Providence and is Fall River Avenue in Seekonk.' Here we would seem to have the 'is' of identity, since it is followed in each occurrence by a term ('Point Street' and 'Fall River Avenue') and not by a predicate expression. But since Point Street and Fall River Avenue have different properties (one is in Providence and not in Seekonk and the other is in Seekonk and not in Providence), the statement may be said to play loose with 'is'.

As our brief discussion of the rivers may make clear, this use of 'is' is readily avoided. We have only to replace 'is' by 'is part of' and then switch around the terms, as in: 'Point Street in Providence is part of Route 6 and Fall River Avenue in Seekonk is part of Route 6.' Or we could also say, of course: 'Point Street is part of Route 6 in Providence and Fall River Avenue is part of Route 6 in Seekonk.'[11]

(2) One may say 'This train will be two trains after Minneapolis', or, travelling in the other direction, 'Those two trains will be one train after Minneapolis'. In the first case ('fission'), we are not saying that there is one thing which will subsequently be identical with two things. We are saying, rather, that there is one thing which will be divided into two things, neither of them being identical with the original

thing, but each of them being a part of the original thing. And in the second case ('fusion'), we are not saying that there are two things which are subsequently to become identical with each other, or with a third thing. We are saying rather that there are two things which will both become parts of a third thing. (Why not cite an amoeba as an instance of 'fission'? There is the off-chance that amoebas are persons, or at least may be thought to be persons, and in such a case, as we shall see, our treatment would have to be somewhat different.)

(3) One may say: 'The President of the United States was Eisenhower in 1955, Johnson in 1965 and Ford in 1975.'[12] Here one may seem to be saying that there is, or was, something – namely, the President of the United States – which was identical with Eisenhower in 1955, with Johnson in 1965 and with Ford in 1975. And so, given that Eisenhower, Johnson and Ford were three different people, one may seem to be saying that there is one thing which has been identical with three different things. But this talk, too, is readily avoided. We have only to reformulate the original sentence in such a way that the temporal expression ('in 1955', 'in 1965' and 'in 1975') may be seen to modify, not the verb 'was', but the term 'the President of the United States'. Thus we could say: 'The President of the United States in 1955 (the person who officially presided over the United States in 1955) was Eisenhower; the President of the United States in 1965 was Johnson; and the President of the United States in 1975 was Ford.'[13]

(4) Pointing to a musical instrument, one man may say to another: 'What you have there is the same instrument that I play, but the one that I play isn't as old as that one.' The first 'is' might be taken to be the 'is' of identity, for it would seem to be followed by a term ('the same instrument that I play'), but the man is saying, of the thing designated by the first term ('what you have there'), that it is older than the thing designated by the second. But of course he didn't need to talk that way. He could have said: 'What

you have there is an instrument of the same sort as the one that I play.'

We note a second example of this way of playing loose with 'is' – not because the example introduces any new considerations (for it doesn't), but because it has attracted the attention of philosophers.

Consider the following list:

Socrates is mortal.
Socrates is mortal.

How many sentences have been listed? We could say either 'exactly one' or 'exactly two'. That these incompatible answers are both possible indicates that the question is ambiguous. And so it has been suggested that, to avoid the ambiguity, we introduce the terms 'sentence-token' and 'sentence-type' and then say 'There are two sentence-tokens on the list and one sentence-type'. But if we say this, then we can say: 'The first item on the list is the same sentence-type as the second (for they are syntactically just alike and say the same thing), but the two are different sentence-tokens (for they are two, one being in one place and the other in another).' Here, once again, we are playing loose with 'is'.[14] We *needn't* speak this way in order to deal with the ambiguity of 'How many sentences are there?' We could say there *are* two sentence-tokens and they are tokens of the same (sentence-) type. The example does not differ in principle, then, from 'The instrument Jones plays is the same as the one Smith plays but is somewhat older'.

It is sometimes said that we should distinguish the two locutions 'A is identical with B and A is a so-and-so' and 'A is the same so-and-so as B'. It has even been suggested that, for purposes of philosophy, the first of these two locutions should be abandoned in favour of the second.[15] According to this suggestion, we should never say, simply and absolutely, 'A is identical with B'; we should 'relativise the ascription of identity to a sortal' and say something of the form 'A is the same so-and-so as

B', where the expression replacing 'so-and-so' is a count-term, or sortal, such as 'man', 'dog', 'horse'. But this suggestion has point only if we can find instances of the following:

A is the same so-and-so as B, and A is a such-and-such but is not the same such-and-such as B.

Are there really any such AS and BS?

What would be an instance of the above formula? In other words, what would be an instance of an A which is 'the same so-and-so' as something B, but which is not 'the same such-and-such' as B? The only instances which have ever been cited, in defending this doctrine of 'relativised identity', would seem to be instances of one or the other of the four ways of playing loose with 'is' that we have just distinguished. For example: 'Different official personages may be one and the same man' or 'This is the same word as that'. What the suggestion comes to, then, is that we abandon the strict use of 'is' and replace it by one or more of the loose uses just discussed. There may be advantages to this type of permissiveness, but it will not help us with our philosophical problems.[16]

Do these ways of playing loose with 'is' suggest a true interpretation of the thesis we have attributed to Bishop Butler – the thesis according to which it is only in 'a loose and popular sense' that we may speak of the persistence through time of such familiar physical things as ships, plants and houses? Is it only by playing loose with 'is' that we may say, of the Ship of Theseus, that it is one and the same thing from one period of time to another?

We can, of course, play loose with 'is' in one or another of these ways when we talk about the Ship of Theseus. Knowing that it is going to be broken up into two ships, we might say: 'It's going to be two ships.' Or knowing that it was made by joining two other ships, we might say: 'Once it had been two ships.' Or knowing that it makes the same ferry run as does the Ship of

Callicles, we might say: 'The Ship of Theseus and the Ship of Callicles are the same ferry.' But the Ship of Theseus doesn't have to be talked about in these loose and popular ways any more than anything else does.

(5) It may be that the Ship of Theseus and the carriage and other familiar things involve still another way of playing loose with 'is'. Thus Hume said that it is convenient to 'feign identity' when we speak about things which, though they 'are supposed to continue the same, are such only as consist of succession of parts, connected together by resemblance, contiguity, or causation'.[17] What Hume here has in mind by 'feigning' may have been put more clearly by Thomas Reid. (Though Reid and Hume were far apart with respect to most of the matters that concern us here, they seem to be together with respect to this one.) Reid wrote:

All bodies, as they consist of innumerable parts that may be disjoined from them by a great variety of causes, are subject to continual changes of their substance, increasing, diminishing, changing insensibly. When such alterations are gradual, because language could not afford a different name for every different state of such a changeable being, it retains the same name, and is considered as the same thing. Thus we say of an old regiment that it did such a thing a century ago, though there now is not a man alive who then belonged to it. We say a tree is the same in the seed-bed and in the forest. A ship of war, which has successively changed her anchors, her tackle, her sails, her masts, her planks, and her timbers, while she keeps the same name is the same.[18]

I believe that Reid is here saying two things. The first is that, whenever there is a change of parts, however insignificant the parts may be, then some old thing ceases to be and some new thing comes into being. This presupposes that, strictly speaking, the parts of a thing are essential to it, and therefore when, as we commonly say, something loses a part, then that thing strictly and philosophically ceases to be.[19]

The second thing I take Reid to be saying is this. If, from the point of view of our practical concerns, the new thing that comes into being upon the addition of parts is sufficiently similar to the old one, then it is much more convenient for us to treat them as if they were one than it is for us to take account of the fact that they are diverse. This point could also be put by saying that such things as the Ship of Theseus and indeed most familiar physical things are really 'fictions', or as we would say today, 'logical constructions'. They are logical constructions upon things which *cannot* survive the loss of their parts.

If Reid is right, then, 'The Ship of Theseus was in Athens last week and will be in Kerkyra Melaina next week' need not be construed as telling us that there *is* in fact a certain ship that was in Athens last week and will be in Kerkyra Melaina next week. It does not imply that any ship that was in the one place is identical with any ship that will be in the other place. And so if this is true, and if all the same we say 'A ship that was in Athens last week is identical with a ship that will be in Kerkyra Melaina next week', then, once again, we are playing loose with the 'is' of identity.

3 An Interpretation of Bishop Butler's Theses

We have found a way, then, of interpreting Bishop Butler's two theses.

According to the first, familiar physical things such as trees, ships, bodies and houses persist 'only in a loose and popular sense'. This thesis may be construed as presupposing that these things are 'fictions', logical constructions or *entia per alio*. And it tells us that, from the fact that any such physical thing may be said to exist at a certain place P at a certain time t and also at a certain place Q at a certain other time t', we may *not* infer that what exists at P at t is identical with what exists at Q at t'.

According to the second thesis, persons persist 'in a strict and philosophical sense'. This may be construed as telling us that persons are not thus 'fictions', logical constructions or *entia per alio*. And so it implies that, if a person may be said to exist at a certain place P at a certain time t and also at a certain place Q at a certain other time t', then we *may* infer that something existing at P at t is identical with something existing at Q at t'.

We now consider the two theses in turn.

4 Feigning Identity

Could we think of familiar physical things, such as ships and trees and houses, as being logical constructions? Let us consider just one type of physical thing, for what we say about it may be applied, *mutatis mutandis*, to the others.

Mon	AB
Tue	BC
Wed	CD

Consider the history of a very simple table. On Monday it came into being when a certain thing A was joined with a certain other thing B. On Tuesday A was detached from B and C was joined to B, these things occurring in such a way that a table was to be found during every moment of the process. And on Wednesday B was detached from C and D was joined with C, these things, too, occurring in such a way that a table was to be found during every moment of the process. Let us suppose that no other separating or joining occurred.

I suggest that in this situation there are the following three wholes among others: AB, that is, the thing made up of A and B; BC, the thing made up of B and C; and CD, the thing made up of C and D. I will say that AB 'constituted' our table on Monday, that BC 'constituted' our table on Tuesday and that CD 'constituted' our table on Wednesday. Although AB, BC and CD are three different things, they all constitute the same table. We thus have an illustration of what Hume called 'a succession of objects'.[20]

One might also say, of each of the three wholes, AB, BC and CD, that it 'stands in for' or 'does duty for' our table on one of the three successive days. Thus if we consider the spatial location of the three wholes, we see that the place of the table was occupied by AB on Monday, by BC on Tuesday, and by CD on Wednesday. Again, the table was red on Monday if and only if AB was red on Monday, and it weighed 10 pounds on Monday if and only if AB weighed 10 pounds on Monday. And analogously for BC on Tuesday and for CD on Wednesday.

The situation may seem to involve two somewhat different types of individual thing. On the one hand, there is what might be called the *ens successivum* – the 'successive table' that is made up of different things at different times.[21] And on the other hand, there are the things that do duty on the different days for the successive table: namely, AB, BC and CD. But any *ens successivum* may be viewed as a logical construction upon the various things that may be said to do duty for it.

Considering, then, just the simple situation I have described, can we express the information we have about the *ens successivum* in statements that refer only to the particular things that stand in or do duty for it? It should be clear that we can, but let us consider the situation in some detail.

Looking back to our diagram, we can see that Monday's table evolved into Tuesday's table and that Tuesday's table evolved into Wednesday's table. We began with AB; then A was separated from B and replaced by C, but in such a way that there was a table to be found at every moment during the process; then, in a similar way, B was separated from C and replaced by D. We could say, then, that BC was a 'direct table successor' of AB, and that CD was a 'direct table successor' of AB.

Making use of the undefined concept of *part*, or *proper part*, we may define the concept of 'table successor' in the following way:

D.III.1   x is at t a direct table successor of y at $t' =_{Df}$ (i) t does not begin before t'; (ii) x is a table at t and y is a table at t'; and (iii) there is a z, such that z is a part of x at t and a part of y at t', and at every moment between t' and t, inclusive, z is itself a table.

Thus z is a table which is a proper part of a table. (If we cut off a small part of a table, we may still have a table left. But if the thing that is left is a table, then, since it was there before, it was then a table that was a proper part of a table.) The concept *part*, as it is understood here, will be discussed in detail in Appendix B ('Mereological Essentialism').

We may also say, more generally, that the CD of Wednesday is a 'table successor' of the AB of Monday, even though CD is not a *direct* table successor of AB. The more general concept is this:

D.III.2   x is at t a table successor of y at $t' =_{Df}$ (i) t does not begin before t'; (ii) x is a table at t and y is a table at t'; and (iii) x has at t every property P such that (a) y has P at t' and (b) all direct table successors of anything having P have P.

The definition assures us that a direct table successor of a direct table successor is a table successor; so, too, for a direct table successor of a direct table successor ... of a direct table successor.[22]

We may now say that things that are thus related by table succession 'constitute the same successive table'.

D.III.3   x constitutes at t the same successive table that y constitutes at $t' =_{Df}$ Either (a) x and only x is at t a table successor of y at t', or (b) y and only y is at t' a table successor of x at t.

Each such thing may be said to 'constitute a successive table'.

D.III.4   x constitutes at t a successive table = _{Df} There are a y and a t′ such that y is other than x and x constitutes at t the same table that y constitutes at t′.

We are on the way, then, to reducing our successive table to those things that are said to constitute it.

Certain propositions, ostensibly about the successive table, may be reduced in a straightforward way to propositions about the things that are said to constitute it. For example:

D.III.5   There is exactly one successive table at place P at time t = _{Df} There is exactly one thing at place P at time t that constitutes a successive table at t.

Our definition of 'constituting the same successive table' (D.III.3) assures us that nothing will constitute more than one successive table at any given time.

Some of the properties that the table has at any given time are thus such that the table borrows them from the thing that constitutes it at that time; but others are not. An example of a property of the first sort may be that of *being red*; an example of a property of the second sort may be that of *having once been blue*. How are we to mark off the former set of properties?

Some properties may be said to be 'rooted outside the times at which they are had'. Examples are the property of *being a widow* and the property of *being a future President*. If we know of anything that it has the former property at any given time, then we can deduce that the thing existed prior to that time. And if we know of anything that it has the latter property at any given time, then we can deduce that the thing continues to exist after that time. Let us say:

D.III.6   G is rooted outside times at which it is had = _{Df} Necessarily, for any x and for any period of time t, x has the property

G throughout t only if x exists at some time before or after t.

Some properties may – but need not – be rooted outside the times at which they are had. An example is the property of *being such that it is or was red*. Our successive table may derive this from its present constituent – if its present constituent is red. But it may derive it from a former constituent – if its present constituent is not red. The definition of this type of property is straightforward:

D.III.7   G may be rooted outside times at which it is had = _{Df} G is equivalent to a disjunction of two properties one of which is, and the other of which is not, rooted outside times at which it is had.

Some properties, finally, are *not* such that they may be rooted outside the times at which they are had.[23] An example is *being red*.

Of the properties that our successive table has at any given time, which are the ones that it borrows from the thing that happens to constitute it at that time? The answer is: those of its properties which are *not* essential to it, and those of its properties which are *not* such that they may be rooted outside the times at which they are had. But the essential properties of the successive table – e.g. that it is a successive table – and those of its properties which may be rooted outside the times at which they are had – e.g. that it was blue or that it was or will be blue – are not such that, for any time, they are borrowed from the thing that constitutes the successive table at that time.

We may say, more generally, of the *ens successivum* and the thing that constitutes it at any given time, that they are exactly alike at that time with respect to all those properties which are such that they are not essential to either and they may not be rooted outside the times at which they are had.

Consider now the following definitional schema:

D.III.8 The successive table that is at place P at time *t* is F at *t* = $_{\text{Df}}$ There is exactly one thing at place P at *t* that constitutes a successive table at *t* and that thing is F at *t*.

This definition is applicable only if the predicates that replace the schematic letter 'F' are properly restricted. For the properties designated by such predicates should be those which are not essential to either and are not such that they may be rooted outside the times at which they are had. Hence acceptable replacements for 'F' would be: 'red', '10 feet square', and 'such that it weights 10 pounds'.

But not all the properties of the successive table are derivable in this straightforward way from the properties of things that constitute it. For example, if AB ceased to be after Monday, we could say of the successive table on Monday, but not of AB, that it was going to persist through Wednesday. Or if CD came into being on Wednesday, we could say of the successive table on Wednesday, but not of CD, that it is at least two days old. Moreover, on Monday, the successive table, but not AB, was such that it would be constituted by CD on Wednesday; while on Wednesday, the successive table, but not CD, was such that it was constituted by AB on Monday.

Nevertheless all such truths about the successive table may be reduced to truths about AB, BC and CD. That this is so should be apparent from these definitions.

D.III.9 The successive table that is at place P at time *t* has existed for at least 3 days = $_{\text{Df}}$ There is exactly one *x* such that *x* is at place P at time *t* and *x* constitutes a successive table at *t*; there are a *y* and a time *t'* such that *x* is at *t* a table-successor of *y* at *t'*; and *t* and *t'* are separated by a period of three days.

This definition tells us, then, what it is for a successive table to persist through time. And the following definition suggests the way in which, at any time, the successive table may borrow its properties from things that constitute it at *other* times:

D.III.10 The successive table that is at place P at time *t* is constituted by *x* at *t'* = $_{\text{Df}}$ There is a *y* such that *y* is at place P at time *t*; *y* constitutes a successive table at *t*; and either *x* is identical with *y* and *t* is identical with *t'*, or *y* constitutes at *t* the same successive table that *x* constitutes at *t'*.

It should now be obvious how to say such things as 'the successive table is red on Monday and green on Wednesday'.

One may object, 'You are committed to saying that AB, BC, CD, and our table are four different things. It may well be, however, that each of the three things AB, BC, CD satisfies the conditions of any acceptable definition of the term 'table'. Indeed your definitions pre-suppose that each of them *is* a table. Hence you are committed to saying that, in the situation described, there are *four* tables. But this is absurd; for actually you have described only *one* table.'

We will find a reply to this objection, if we distinguish the strict and philosophical sense of such expressions as 'There are four tables' from their ordinary, or loose and popular, sense. To say that there are four tables, in the strict and philosophical sense, is to say that there are four different things, each of them a table. But from the fact that there are four tables, in this strict and philosophical sense, it will not follow that there are four tables in the ordinary, or loose and popular, sense. If there are to be four tables in the ordinary, or loose and popular, sense, it must be the case that there are four things, not only such that each constitutes a table, but also such that no two of them constitute the same table. In other words, there must be four *entia successiva*, each of them a table.

We may, therefore, explicate the ordinary, or

loose and popular, sense of 'There are n so-and-so's at t' (or 'The number of so-and-so's at t is n') in the following way:

D.III.11   There are, in the loose and popular sense, n so-and-so's at t = $_{\text{Df}}$ There are n things each of which constitutes a so-and-so at t, and no two of which constitute the same so-and-so at t.

The term 'so-and-so' in this schematic definition may be replaced by any more specific count-term, e.g. 'table' or 'ship'. And the definiendum could be replaced by 'The number of successive so-and-so's at t is n'.

Hence the answer to the above objection is this: in saying that there are exactly three tables in the situation described one is speaking in the strict and philosophical sense and not in the loose and popular sense. In saying that there is exactly one table one is speaking in the loose and popular sense and not in the strict and philosophical sense. But the statement that there are four tables – AB, BC, CD and the successive table – is simply the result of confusion. One is trying to speak both ways at once.[24] The sense in which we may say that there is the successive table is not the sense in which we may say that there is the individual thing AB, or BC, or CD.[25]

The foregoing sketch, then, makes clear one way in which we may feign identity when what we are dealing with is in fact only a 'succession of related objects'. The ways in which we do thus feign identity are considerably more subtle and complex. Playing loose with 'is' and 'same', we may even speak of the sameness of a table when we are dealing with successions of objects which are related, not by what I have called table succession, but in much more tenuous ways. Nevertheless it should be clear that if we are saying something we really know, when we thus speak of the sameness of a table, what we are saying could be re-expressed in such a way that we refer only to the related objects and not to the ostensible entities we think of them as making up. And so, too, for other familiar things – ships and trees and houses – that involve successions of related objects that stand in or do duty for them at different times.

We could say, then, that such things are entia per alio. They are ontological parasites that derive all their properties from other things – from the various things that do duty for them. An ens per alio never is or has anything on its own. It is what it is in virtue of the nature of something other than itself. At every moment of its history an ens per alio has something other than itself as its stand-in.

But if there are entia per alio, then there are also entia per se.

5 The Persistence of Persons through Time

Am I an ens per alio or an ens per se?

Consider the simplest of Cartesian facts – say, that I now hope for rain. Hoping for rain is one of those properties that are rooted only in the times at which they are had. And so if I am an ens per alio, an ens successivum, like our simple table or the Ship of Theseus, then I may be said to hope for rain only in virtue of the fact that my present stand-in hopes for rain. I borrow the property, so to speak, from the thing that constitutes me now.

But surely that hypothesis is not to be taken seriously. There is no reason whatever for supposing that I hope for rain only in virtue of the fact that some other thing hopes for rain – some stand-in that, strictly and philosophically, is not identical with me but happens to be doing duty for me at this particular moment.

If there are thus two things that now hope for rain, the one doing it on its own and the other such that its hoping is done for it by the thing that now happens to constitute it, then I am the former thing and not the latter thing. But this is to say that I am not an ens successivum.[26]

But might I not be a constituent of an ens successivum? If I am a constituent of an ens successivum, then

there have been other things that once constituted the same person that I do now and presumably there will be still others in the future.
But if this is so, then the things I think I know
about my past history may all be false (even
though they may be true of the person I happen
now to constitute) and I may have no grounds
for making any prediction at all about my future.
Is this the sort of thing I am?

Let us recall the data with which we began,
the list of things we have a right to believe
about ourselves. Among those things, we said, is
the fact that we do undergo change and persist
through time. Each of us is justified in believing
a great variety of things about his past. We are
justified in believing these things until we have
found some reason to doubt them. It is reasonable to treat these beliefs as being innocent, epistemically, until we have found some positive
reason for thinking them guilty.

What would such a positive reason be?

It is important to remind ourselves that we
do *not* find any such positive reason in the writings of those philosophers who have professed
to be sceptical about the persistence of persons
through time.

Consider, for example, Kant's discussion of
what he calls 'the third paralogism of transcendental psychology'. For all I can know, Kant there
says, the thing that calls itself 'I' at one time may
be other than the thing that calls itself 'I' at
another time. There might be a series of different
subjects which make up my biography, each of
them passing its thoughts and memories on to its
successor – each subject would 'retain the
thought of the preceding subject and so hand it
over to the subsequent subject'.[27] The relation
between the successive subjects, he says, could be
like that of a set of elastic balls, one of which
impinges on another in a straight line and 'communicates to the latter its whole motion, and
therefore its whole state (that is, if we take account
only of the positions in space)'. Kant goes on to
say: 'If, then, in analogy with such bodies, we
postulate substances such that the one communi-

cates to the other representations together with
the consciousness of them, we can conceive a
whole series of substances of which the first
transmits its state together with its consciousness
to the second, the second its own state with that of
the preceding substance to the third, and this in
turn the states of all the preceding substances
together with its own consciousness and with
their consciousness to another. The last substance
would then be conscious of all the states of the
previously changed substances, as being its own
states, because they would have been transferred
to it together with the consciousness of them.
And yet it would not have been one and the same
person in all these states.'[28]

Does *this* give us a reason for wondering
whether we have in fact persisted through time?
Surely not. What Kant has pointed out to us, in
these speculations, is simply that the following
is logically possible: instead of there being just
one person who makes up my biography, there
was a succession of different persons, all but
the first of them being deluded with respect to
its past. It is also logically possible, as Russell
pointed out, that the universe came into being
three seconds ago with all its ostensible traces
and relics of the past. And it is logically possible
that a malicious demon is deceiving each of us
with respect to what we think are the external
physical things around us. But the fact that these
are logically possible is itself no reason for thinking that they actually occur.

'Given the transitory nature of the ultimate
particles that make up the physical universe,
isn't it reasonable to suppose that, if I do persist
through time, then my consciousness may be
transferred, as John Locke seemed to suggest,
from one substance or individual thing to
another? And if my consciousness is thus transferred, wouldn't I, too, be transferred from one
substance to another?'

The supposition, I am certain, is not only
untenable but also incoherent. Philosophers have
taken it seriously, however, and so we should
consider it briefly.

Is it possible to transfer my consciousness from one substance to another with the result that, whereas the former substance but not the latter was I, the latter substance but not the former is now I? In such a case, I could truly say: 'This is other than that, but once I was that and now I'm this.'

Locke said that, 'it being the same consciousness that makes a man be himself to himself, personal identity depends on that only, whether it be annexed solely to one individual substance, or can be continued in a succession of several substances'.[29] The same consciousness, he said, *could* be thus continued in a succession of several substances, if it were 'transferred from one thinking substance to another', and if this does happen then the different 'thinking substances may make but one person'[30] And these different thinking substances will all be 'the same self'.[31] (In fairness to Locke, we should note that he does not quite bring himself to say that I might now be identical with this but not with that and then later identical with that but not with this. Although he suggests that it is possible to transfer my consciousness from one substance to another, he does not explicitly say that, whereas the former substance *was* I, the latter substance is *now* I. It may very well be that he, too, was playing loose with 'is'.)

A *part* of a thing or an *appendage* to a thing may be transferred to another thing, as an organ may be transplanted from one body to another. The *contents* of a thing may be transferred to another thing, as apples may be moved from one bag to another.

Speaking somewhat more metaphorically, we might also say that the *properties* of one thing may be transferred to another thing. If you are infected by my contagious disease and if I then recover, one *could* say that my sickness *including my aches and and pains* has been transferred from me to you. But the disease or sickness will not be transferred in the literal sense in which, say, its carriers might be transferred.

My personality traits could be said to be transferred to you if you acquire the kind of complexes and dispositions that are characteristic of me. My beliefs could be said to be transferred to you, if you begin to believe the same things I do. And my memories could even be said to be transferred from me to you, if you remember, or think you remember, the same things I do. (But if I remember or think I remember my doing the deed, the content of that memory could not be transferred to you.)[32] By thus acquiring my properties – or, more accurately, by thus instantiating some of the properties that I do – you may become so much like me that others will have difficulty in telling us apart – in that they are unable to decide, with respect to certain things that have happened, whether they belong to your biography or to mine. Perhaps the courts will have to make a decree. Perhaps it will even be reasonable for them to decide, with respect to some of the things that only I did in the past, that you and not I are responsible for them, and then they might decide, with respect to the name I formerly had, that you should be the one who bears it.

But none of these possibilities, perplexing as they may be, justifies us in saying that there could be two different substances which are such that I am transferred from one to the other.[33]

There is still another type of transfer which is quite naturally described in the way in which Locke described 'transfer of self'. This is illustrated in the transfer of a shadow ('the shadow of his hand moved from the wall to the table and became larger but more faint in the process'). But a shadow is an *ens per alio*; it borrows its properties from other things (most notably from shadowed objects). The kind of transfer that is involved in the passage of a shadow from one object to another, to the extent that it differs from the types of transfer we distinguished above, is typical of *entia per alio*. But persons, we have seen, are *entia per se*.

What could it mean, after all, to say that I might be 'annexed to' or 'placed in' a thinking thing or individual substance?

Whatever it might mean, either I am identical with the thinking substance in which I am thus placed or I am not identical with it.

If I am identical with the thinking substance in which I am thus placed, then I cannot be transferred from that substance to another thinking substance.

But if I am placed in a certain thinking substance and am not identical with that thinking substance, then there are two different things – the thinking substance and I. But if there are two things, which of us does the thinking? There are exactly four possibilities.

(1) Neither of us does the thinking – that is to say, neither of us thinks. But this we know is false.

(2) I think but the thinking substance does not think. Why call the latter a "thinking" substance, then? (It would be like calling an elevator a thinking substance because it contains someone who thinks.) And what relation do I bear to this thinking substance? I'm not a *property* of it, since properties do not think. Am I a proper *part*, then, of the thinking substance? But proper parts of substances are themselves substances. And so if I am myself a thinking substance, what is the point of saying there is *another* thinking substance in which I am 'placed' or to which I am 'annexed'?

(3) The thinking substance thinks but I do not. But isn't this absurd? 'It's not really I who think; it is some *other* thing that thinks in me – some other thing that does what I mistakenly take to be my thinking.' (Or should the latter clause have been: 'some other thing that does what it mistakenly takes to be my thinking'?)

(4) Both the thinking substance and I think. Isn't this multiplying thinkers beyond necessity? If I want my dinner, does it follow that two of us want my dinner? Or does the thinking substance want its dinner and not mine?

I think we may reasonably conclude that there is no significant sense in which we may speak of the transfer of a self from one substance or individual thing to another.

6 'Will I Be He?': Truth-Conditions and Criteria

Suppose that there is a person x who happens to know, with respect to a certain set of properties, that there is or will be a certain person y who will have those properties at some future time, and x asks himself: 'Will I be he?' Either x is identical with y, or x is diverse from y.

We cannot find the *answer* to the question, 'Is x identical with y?', merely by deciding what would be practically convenient. To be sure, if we lack sufficient evidence for making a decision, it may yet be necessary for the courts to *rule* that x is the same person as y, or that he is not. Perhaps the ruling will have to be based upon practical considerations and conceivably such considerations may lead the court later to 'defeat' its ruling. But one may always ask of any such ruling 'But is it *correct*, or *true*?' For a ruling to the effect that x is the same person as y will be correct, or true, only if x is identical with y.

We should remind ourselves, however, that the expression 'x is the same person as y' also has a use which is not this strict and philosophical one. Thus there are circumstances in which one might say: 'Mr Jones is not at all the same person he used to be. You will be disappointed. He is not the person that you remember.' We would not say this sort of thing if Mr Jones had changed only slightly. We would say it only if he had undergone changes that were quite basic and thorough-going – the kind of changes that might be produced by psychoanalysis, or by a lobotomy, or by a series of personal tragedies. But just *how* basic and thorough-going must these changes be if we are to say of Mr Jones that he is a different person? The proper answer would seem to be: 'As basic and thorough-going as you would like. It's just a matter of convention. It all depends upon how widely it is convenient for you to construe the expression "He's the same person he used to be". In so far as the rules of language are in your own hands, you may have it any way you would like.'[34] (Compare 'Jones is not himself today' or 'Jones was not himself when he said that'.)

This, however, is only playing loose with 'same' – or, more accurately, it is playing loose with 'not the same'. When we say, in the above sense, 'Jones is no longer the person he used to be', we do not mean that there is, or was, a certain entity such that Jones was formerly identical with that entity and is no longer so. What we are saying does not imply that there are (or have been) certain entities, x and y, such that at one time x is, or was, identical with y, and at another time x is not identical with y. For this is incoherent, but 'Jones is no longer the person he used to be' is not.

Nor do we mean, when we say 'Jones is no longer the person he used to be', that there *was* a certain entity, the old Jones, which no longer exists, and that there is a certain *different* entity, the new Jones, which somehow has taken his place. We are not describing the kind of change that takes place when one President succeeds another. In the latter case, there is a clear answer to the question 'What happened to the old one?' But when we decide to call Jones a new person, we are not confronted with such questions as: 'What happened, then, to the old Jones? Did he die, or was he annihilated, or disassembled, or did he retire to some other place?'

The old Jones did not die; he was not annihilated or disassembled; and he did not retire to any other place. He *became* the new Jones. And to say that he 'became' the new Jones is *not* to say that he 'became identical' with something he hadn't been identical with before. For it is only when a thing comes into being that it may be said to become identical with something it hadn't been identical with before. To say that our man 'became the new Jones' is to say that he, Jones, *altered* in a significant way, taking on certain interesting properties he had not had before. (Hence we should contrast the 'became' of 'Jones then became a married man', said when Jones ceased to be a bachelor, with that of 'The President then became a Republican', said when

President Johnson retired.) When we say of a thing that it has properties that it did not have before, we are saying that there is an x such that x formerly had such-and-such properties and x presently has such-and-such other properties.

It will be instructive, I think, to consider two somewhat different examples.

The first is suggested by C. S. Peirce.[35] Elaborating upon his suggestion, let us assume that you are about to undergo an operation and that you still have a decision to make. The utilities involved are, first, financial – you wish to avoid any needless expense – and, secondly, the avoidance of pain, the avoidance, however, just of *your* pain, for pain that is other than yours, let us assume, if of no concern whatever to you. The doctor proposes two operating procedures – one a very expensive procedure in which you will be subjected to total anaesthesia and no pain will be felt at all, and the other of a rather different sort. The second operation will be very inexpensive indeed; there will be no anaesthesia at all and therefore there will be excruciating pain. But the doctor will give you two drugs: first, a drug just before the operation which will induce complete amnesia, so that while you are on the table you will have no memory whatever of your present life; and, secondly, just after the agony is over, a drug that will make you completely forget everything that happened on the table. The question is: given the utilities involved, namely, the avoidance of needless expense and the avoidance of pain that *you* will feel, other pains not mattering, is it reasonable for you to opt for the less expensive operation?

My own conviction is that it would *not* be reasonable, even if you could be completely certain that both amnesia injections would be successful. *You* are the one who would undergo that pain, even though you, Jones, would not know at the time that it is Jones who is undergoing it, and even though you would never remember it. Consider after all, the hypothesis that it would *not* be you. What would be your status, in such a case, during the time of the operation? Would you have passed away? That is to say, would you have *ceased to be*, but with the guarantee that you – you, yourself – would come into being once again when the agony was over?[36] And what about the person who *would* be feeling the pain? Who would he be?

It may well be that these things would not be obvious to you if in fact you had to make such a decision. But there is one point, I think, that ought to be obvious.

Suppose that others come to you – friends, relatives, judges, clergymen – and they offer the following advice and assurance. 'Have no fear', they will say. 'Take the cheaper operation and we will take care of everything. We will lay down the convention that the man on the table is not you, Jones, but is Smith.' What *ought* to be obvious to you, it seems to me, is that the laying down of this convention should have no effect at all upon your decision. For you may still ask, 'But won't that person be I?' and, it seems to me, the question has an answer.

I now turn to the second example. Suppose you know that your body, like that of an amoeba, would one day undergo fission and that you would go off, so to speak, in two different directions. Suppose you also know, somehow, that the one who went off to the left would experience the most wretched of lives and that the one who went off to the right would experience a life of great happiness and value. If I am right in saying that one's question 'Will that person be I?' or 'Will I be he?' always has a definite answer, then, I think, we may draw these conclusions. There is no possibility whatever that *you* would be *both* the the person on the right and the person on the left. Moreover, there *is* a possibility that you would be *one or the other* of those two persons. And, finally, *you* could be one of those persons and yet have no memory at all of your present existence. In this case, there may well be no criterion by means of which you or anyone else could decide which of the two halves was in fact yourself. Yet it would be reasonable of you, if you were concerned with *your* future pleasures

and pains, to hope that you would be the one on the right and not the one on the left. It would also be reasonable of you, given such self-concern, to have this hope even if you knew that the one on the right would have no memory of your present existence. Indeed it would be reasonable of you to have it even if you know that the one on the *left* thought he remembered the facts of your present existence. And it seems to me to be absolutely certain that no fears that you might have, about being the half on the left, could reasonably be allayed by the adoption of a convention, even if our procedure were endorsed by the highest authorities.[37]

In trying to *decide* which one of the two persons, if either, you will be, you will, of course, make use of such *criteria* that you have and are able to apply. As we all know, there are intriguing philosophical questions about the criteria of the identity of persons through time. ('How are we to make sure, or make a reasonable guess, that that person at that time is the same as that person at the other time?')[38] What are we to do, for example, when bodily criteria and psychological criteria conflict? Suppose we know that the person on the left will have certain *bodily* characteristics that we have always taken to be typical only of you – and that the person on the right will have certain *psychological* characteristics that we have always taken to be typical only of you. In such a case there may be no sufficient reason at all for deciding that you are or that you are not one or the other of the two different persons. But from this it does not follow that you *will* not in fact be one or the other of the two persons.

We should remind ourselves of a very simple and obvious point. When you ask yourself, 'Will I be the person on the right?' your question is *not* 'Will the person on the right satisfy such criteria as I have, or such criteria as someone or other has, for deciding whether or not a given person is I?' To be sure, the best you can do, by way of answering the first question, is to try to answer the second. But the answers to the two questions are logically independent of each other.

What is a *criterion* of personal identity? It is a statement telling what constitutes evidence of personal identity – what constitutes a good reason for saying of a person x that he is, or that he is not, identical with a person y. Now there is, after all, a fundamental distinction between the *truth-conditions* of a proposition and the *evidence* we can have for deciding whether or not the proposition is true. The *truth-conditions* for the proposition that Caesar crossed the Rubicon consist of the fact, if it is a fact, that Caesar did cross the Rubicon. The only *evidence* you and I can have of this fact will consist of certain *other* propositions – propositions about records, memories and traces. It is only in the case of what is self-presenting (that I hope for rain or that I seem to me to have a headache) that the evidence for a proposition coincides with its truth-conditions. In all other cases, the two are logically independent; the one could be true while the other is false.[39]

The question 'Was it Caesar?' is not the same as the question: 'Do we have good evidence for thinking it was Caesar?' (or 'Have the criteria for saying that it was Caesar been fulfilled?'). This is true despite the fact that the most reasonable way of trying to find the answer to the first question is to try to answer the second.

And analogously for 'Will I be he?'

What I have said may recall this observation made by Leibniz: 'Suppose that some individual could suddenly become King of China on condition, however, of forgetting what he had been, as though being born again, would it not amount to the same practically, or as far as the effects could be perceived, as if the individual were annihilated, and a King of China were at the same instant created in his place? The individual would have no reason to desire this.'[40]

If I am being asked to consider the possibility that there is an *ens successivum* of which I happen to be the present constituent and which will subsequently be constituted by someone who will then be a King of China, then the fate of the later

constituent may well be no special concern of mine. But what if Leibniz were not thus playing loose with 'is'?

In such a case, the proper reply to his question is suggested by the following observation in Bayle's *Dictionary*: 'The same atoms which compose water are in ice, in vapours, in clouds, in hail and snow; those which compose wheat are in the meal, in the bread, the blood, the flesh, the bones etc. Were they unhappy under the figure or form of water, and under that of ice, it would be the same numerical substance that would be unhappy in these two conditions; and consequently all the calamities which are to be dreaded, under the form of meal, concern the atoms which form corn; and nothing ought to concern itself so much about the state or lot of the meal, as the atoms which form the wheat, though they are not to suffer these calamities, under the form of wheat.' Bayle concludes that 'there are but two methods a man can employ to calm, in a rational manner, the fears of another life. One is, to promise himself the felicities of Paradise; the other, to be firmly persuaded that he shall be deprived of sensations of every kind.'[41] [. . .]

THE DOCTRINE OF
TEMPORAL PARTS

1 Temporal Parts

The doctrine of temporal parts is accepted by a number of distinguished theologians, logicians and philosophers of science. Since it may appear to conflict with what I have said in Chapter III about identity through time, I will consider it briefly.

Jonathan Edwards set forth the doctrine in his *Doctrine of Original Sin Defended* (1758). He was there concerned with the question whether it is just to impute to you and me the sins that were committed by Adam. And he appealed to temporal parts to show that it is *as* just to attribute Adam's sins to you and me now as it is to attribute any other past sins to you and me now.

He based his view upon a general theological thesis: God not only created the world *ex nihilo*, he also constantly preserves or upholds the things he creates, for without God's continued preservation of the world, all created things would fall into nothingness. 'God's upholding created substance, or causing its existence in each successive moment, is altogether equivalent to an immediate *production out of nothing*, at each moment.'[42] In preserving the table in its being, God cannot make use of what existed at any prior moment. The table is not there waiting to be upheld or preserved, for if it were, then God would not *need* to uphold or preserve it.

Edwards compares the persistence of created substances with that of a reflection or image on the surface of a mirror. 'The image that exists this moment, is not at all *derived* from the image which existed the last preceding moment . . . If the succession of new *rays* be intercepted, by something interposed between the object and the glass, the image immediately ceases; the *past existence* of the image has no influence to uphold it, so much as for one moment. Which shows that the image is altogether completely remade every moment; and strictly speaking, is in no part numerically the same with that which existed in the moment preceding. And truly so the matter must be with the *bodies* themselves, as well as their images. They also cannot be the same with an absolute identity, but must be wholly renewed every moment . . .' Edwards summarises his doctrine of preservation this way: 'If the existence of created *substance*, in each successive moment, be wholly the effect of God's immediate power, in *that* moment, without any dependence on prior existence, as much as the first creation out of *nothing*, then what exists at this moment, by this power, is a *new effect*, and simply and absolutely considered, not the same with any past existence . . .'

This conception of persisting physical things, though not its theological basis, is also defended by a number of contemporary philosophers. It may be found, for example, in the axiom system concerning things and their parts that is developed in Carnap's *Introduction to Symbolic Logic*.[43] Carnap's system is derived from the systems developed by J. H. Woodger and Alfred Tarski, in Woodger's *The Axiomatic Method in Biology*.[44] These authors say that, for every moment at which a thing exists there is a set of momentary parts of the thing; none of these parts exists at any other moment; and the thing itself is the sum of its momentary parts.[45]

The thing that constitutes you now, according to this view, is diverse from the things that have constituted you at any other moment, just as you are diverse from every other person who exists now. But God, according to Jonathan Edwards, can contemplate a collection of objects existing at different times and 'treat them as one'. He can take a collection of various individuals existing at different times and think of them as all constituting a single individual. Edwards thus appeals to a doctrine of truth by divine convention; he says that God 'makes truth in affairs of this nature'. God could regard temporally scattered individuals – you this year, me last year, and the Vice-President the year before that – as comprising a single individual. And then he could justly punish you this year and me last year for the sins that the Vice-President committed the year before that. And so, Edwards concludes, 'no solid reason can be given, why God . . . may not establish a constitution whereby the natural posterity of Adam . . . should be treated as *one* with him, for the derivation, either of righteousness, and communion in rewards, or of the loss of righteousness, and consequent corruption and guilt'.[46]

Suppose that today I hope for rain and tomorrow I hope for snow instead. If Edwards's doctrine is correct, the situation would seem to involve at least *three* different individual things: today's temporal part of me, tomorrow's temporal part of me and the thing of which these two things *are* temporal parts.[47] Today's temporal part of me will be other than yesterday's and each will be other than any thing of which they are proper parts. Which is the thing that hopes for rain – today's temporal part of me, or the thing of which it is a part, or both? Can we say of the temporal parts – of the temporally dimensionless slices – that they are *entia per se*? If we can, can we say of the whole of which they are slices that it is *also an ens per se*?

If there were good reasons to accept the doctrine of temporal parts, we would have to deal with these difficult questions. But why should we accept it? I will consider two different reasons that have been offered on behalf of the doctrine. I believe we will find that, even when considered together, they do not seem to lend any significant presumption to the doctrine. And then I will ask whether the doctrine might throw light on our problems involving identity through time.[48]

2 The Argument from Spatial Analogy

The first of two arguments for the doctrine of temporal parts appeals to an analogy between space and time. One version of it might be put as follows. '(i) Whatever may be said about spatial continuity and identity may also be said, *mutatis mutandis*, about temporal continuity and identity. But (ii) every object extending undivided or unscattered through any portion of space during any given time has, for each subportion of that space, a set of *spatial parts* which exist during that time only in that subportion of space, and the only parts that the object then has are within that portion of space. (More exactly: every object extending undivided or unscattered through any portion of space during any given time has, for each subportion of that space, a set s of spatial parts which is such that all the members of s are in that subportion of space at that time and any part of the object in that space at that time is a member of s.) Therefore (iii) every object persisting uninterruptedly through any

period of time within a given place has, for each subperiod of that time, a set of *temporal* parts which exist within that place and only during that period of time.'

Is the first premise in this argument true? I would say that it is not. For there is a fundamental *disanalogy* between space and time.

The disanalogy may be suggested by saying simply: 'One and the same thing cannot be in two different places at one and the same time. But one and the same thing can be at two different times in one and the same place.' Let us put the point of disanalogy, however, somewhat more precisely.

When we say 'a thing cannot be in two different places at one and the same time', we mean that it is not possible for *all* the parts of the thing to be in one of the places at that one time and *also* to be in the other of the places at that same time. It *is* possible, of course, for *some* part of the thing to be in one place at a certain time and *another* part of the thing to be in another place at that time. And to remove a possible ambiguity in the expression 'all the parts of a thing', let us spell it out as 'all the parts that the thing ever will have had'.

Instead of saying simply 'a thing cannot be in two different places at one and the same time' let us say this: 'It is *not* possible for there to be a thing which is such that all the parts it ever will have had are in one place at one time and also in another place at that same time.' And instead of saying 'a thing can be at two different times in one and the same place', let us say this: 'It *is* possible for there to be a thing which is such that all the parts it ever will have had are in one place at one time and also in that same place at another time.'

It seems to me to be clear that each of these two theses is true and therefore that there is a fundamental disanalogy between space and time. And so I would reject the first premise of the argument above. (One may, of course, use the doctrine of temporal parts in order to *defend* the view that there is no such disanalogy. One may use it, in particular, to criticise the second of the two theses I set forth above – the thesis according to which it is possible for there to be a thing which is such that all the parts it ever will have had are in one place at one time and also in that same place at another time. But if we were to defend (i) in the argument above by appeal to (iii), then our reasoning would be circular.)

3 Phillip Drunk and Phillip Sober

A second argument for the doctrine of temporal parts is suggested by the following quotation from C. S. Peirce: 'Phillip is drunk and Phillip is sober would be absurd, did not time make the Phillip of this morning another Phillip than the Phillip of last night.'[49]

Thus one might construct a philosophical puzzle: '(i) For any *x* and *y*, if *x* is identical with *y*, then whatever can be truly said of *x* can also be truly said of *y*. But (ii) the Phillip of this morning is identical with the Phillip of last night. Now (iii) the Phillip of this morning was sober. And therefore (iv) the Phillip of this morning was not drunk. But (v) the Phillip of last night was drunk. And therefore (vi) something can truly be said of the Phillip of last night that cannot be truly said of the Phillip of this morning. How can this be?' The doctrine of temporal parts might now be invoked as a way of solving the puzzle: 'The second premise is false. The Phillip of this morning and the Phillip of last night are *different* temporal parts of one and the same thing and therefore the thing that was drunk is not identical with the thing that was sober.'

But there is another way of dealing with the puzzle. If 'The Phillip of this morning was sober' is something we know to be true, then it tells us no more, and no less, than that Phillip was sober this morning. And if 'The Phillip of last night was drunk' is something we know to be true, then it tells us no more, and no less, than that Phillip was drunk last night. Consider now step (iv) of our puzzle: 'The Phillip of this morning was not drunk.' This statement may be

taken either as saying 'Phillip was not drunk last night' or as saying 'Phillip was not drunk this morning'. If it is taken the first way, as saying 'Phillip was not drunk last night', then it does not follow from the premises that precede it. But if it is taken the second way, as saying 'Phillip was not drunk this morning', then we cannot derive the conclusion of the puzzle. That is to say, we cannot conclude, as we do in (vi), that something can truly be said of 'the Phillip of last night', i.e. Phillip, that cannot also be truly said of 'the Phillip of this morning'.

We spoke earlier of 'playing loose with the "is" of identity'. We could speak here of 'playing loose with the "isn't" of diversity'. This is exemplified in: 'Since Phillip differed last night from what he was this morning, the Phillip of last night is other than the Phillip of this morning.' Or, if we need an example that is not concerned with the point at issue: 'Since Phillip is considerate toward his friends and inconsiderate toward his employees, Phillip the friend is other than Phillip the employer.'

4 Does the Doctrine Help Us?

One consideration that seems to have led many philosophers to accept the doctrine of temporal parts is this: the doctrine enables us to deal satisfactorily with the problem of the Ship of Theseus and with other such puzzles about identity through time.

This point of view has been defended, in many different writings, by W. V. Quine.[50] He illustrates the doctrine in application to Heraclitus's puzzlement about whether or not one can bathe in the same river twice. Let us consider this application and ask whether in fact it *does* throw light upon Heraclitus's problem. What may be said about the river may also be said, of course, about the Ship of Theseus and the other objects of our initial puzzlement.

Quine suggests that the temporal parts of individual things are like the temporal parts of the careers, histories or biographies of those things: they are *events* or *processes*.[51] He does not hesitate to say, therefore, that the temporal parts of a thing are 'stages' of the thing. He writes: 'a physical thing – whether a river or a human body or a stone – is at any one moment a sum of simultaneous momentary states of spatially scattered atoms or other small physical constituents. Now just as the thing at a moment is a sum of these spatially small parts, so we may think of the thing over a period as a sum of the temporally small parts which are its successive states.'[52] A river is thus a *process* through time, a sum of momentary 'river stages'. Quine now says that this way of looking at the matter provides the solution to Heraclitus's problem. 'The truth is that you *can* bathe in the same river twice, but not in the same river stage.'[53]

We should note, however, that this way of looking at the matter, if it is thus to yield a solution to Heraclitus's problem, would seem to *presuppose* the concept of the persistence of an individual thing through time – the concept of one and the same individual existing at different times. Even if it is true that all rivers are sums of river stages, it is not true that all sums of river stages are rivers. Indeed a sum of river stages occupying a continuous period of time need not be a river. Thus the Merrimack, from 9 to 10 a.m., Eastern Standard Time, the Housatonic from 10 to 11, and the Blackstone from 11 to 12, would be such a sum of river stages, occupying a three-hour period. But this particular sum, if there is such an entity, does not constitute a river.

What more is required for a sum of river stages to yield a river? Five possible answers suggest themselves. (i) We could say, of course, that river stages *a*, *b* and *c*, occurring or existing at different times, are stages of the same river if and only if there is an *x* such that *x* is a river and such that *a*, *b* and *c* are all stages of *x*. This answer obviously presupposes the concept of *a river* persisting through the time in question. (ii) We could say that *a*, *b* and *c* are all to be found in the same river bed, or between the same river

banks.[54] But this would be to presuppose that the *river bed*, or the pair of *river banks*, persists through the time in question.

To be sure, we do not need to presuppose the concept of a persisting *physical thing* in order to say what sums of river stages make up rivers and what sums of river stages do not. Thus (iii) we might be able to define a persisting river in terms of its stages and their accessibility to the observation of some person or persons. But this would be to presuppose the concept of a person persisting through time. Or (iv), given the concept of a *place* persisting through time, we could say that a sum of river stages makes up a river provided its elements all occupy the same place. But this would presuppose an absolute theory of space, for we could not then expect to define the persistence of a place through time in terms of the persistence of the various physical things that might be said to occupy it.

Or, finally, (v) we could introduce a technical term – 'cofluvial' for example – and say that *a*, *b* and *c* are stages of the same river if and only if they are *cofluvial* with each other.[55]

Whatever there is to recommend this doctrine, it can hardly be that it throws light upon Heraclitus's problem: 'How do I step into the same river twice?' For the answer would be: 'By stepping at different times into things that are cofluvial.' And if we then ask what it is for things to be cofluvial, the answer, if there is one, could only be: 'Things are cofluvial provided they are parts of the same river.'[56]

Notes

1 *On the Intellectual Powers of Man*, Essay III, Chapter 14 in Sir William Hamilton, ed., *The Works of Thomas Reid, D.D.* (Edinburgh: Maclachlan & Stewart, 1854), p. 345.

2 Fragment 41–2, as translated in Milton C. Nahm, *Selections from Early Greek Philosophy* (New York: F. S. Crofts, 1934), p. 91.

3 See Plato, *Phaedo*, 58A and Xenophon, *Memorabilia*, 4, 8, 2. Leibniz speaks of the Ship of Theseus in the

New Essays Concerning Human Understanding, Book II, Chapter 27, Section 4, noting that any ordinary physical body may be said to be 'like a river which always changes its water, or like the ship of Theseus which the Athenians were always repairing' (Open Court edition), p. 240.

4 Thomas Hobbes, *Concerning Body*, Chapter XI ("Of Identity and Difference"), Section 7.

5 Cf. W. V. Quine: 'Thus take the question of the biggest fresh lake. Is Michigan-Huron admissible, or is it a pair of lakes? . . . Then take the question of the longest river. Is the Mississippi-Missouri admissible, or is it a river and a half?' *Word and Object* (New York: John Wiley, 1960), p. 128.

6 Using terms not commonly applied to rivers, we may note for future reference that when our diagram is read from top to bottom it illustrates *fusion* and when it is read from bottom to top it illustrates *fission*.

7 See Note C of the article 'Carneades' in Pierre Bayle's *A General Dictionary: Historical and Critical*, trans. Rev. J. P. Bernard, Rev. Thomas Birch, John Lockeman *et al.* (10 vols; London: James Bettenham, 1734–41): 'He found uncertainty in the most evident notions. All logicians know that the foundation of the syllogism, and consequently the faculty of reasoning, is built on this maxim: Those things which are identical with a third are the same with each other (*Quae sunt idem uno tertio sunt idem inter se*). It is certain that Carneades opposed it strongly and displayed all his subtleties against it.'

8 Further aspects of this kind of problem are discussed in Appendix A ('The Doctrine of Temporal Parts').

9 Dissertation I, in *The Whole Works of Joseph Butler, LL.D.* (London: Thomas Tegg, 1839), pp. 263–70. But compare Locke's third letter to the Bishop of Worcester: 'For it being his body both before and after the resurrection, everyone ordinarily speaks of his body as the same, though, in a strict and philosophical sense, as your lordship speaks, it be not the very same.'

10 I have heard it suggested, however, that (a) whereas the evening star is strictly identical with the evening star, nevertheless (b) the evening star is identical but not strictly identical with the morning star. The facts of the matter would seem to be only these: the evening star (i.e. the morning star) is necessarily self-identical; it is not necessarily such that it is visible in the evening or in the morning; it would be contradictory to say that the evening star exists and is not identical with the evening star, or that the morning star exists and is not identical with the morning star; but it would not be contradictory to say that the morning star exists and the evening star exists and the morning star is not identical with the evening star; and whatever is identical with the evening star (i.e. with the morning star) has all the properties that it does

11 This example of the roads, like that of the rivers above ('the Mississippi-Missouri'), may suggest that the key to our puzzles about identity through time may be found in the doctrine of "temporal parts". According to this doctrine, every individual thing *x* is such that, for every period of time through which *x* exists, there is a set of parts which are such that *x* is made up of them at that time and they do not exist at any other time. (Compare: every individual thing *x* is such that, for every portion of space that *x* occupies at any time, there is at that time a set of parts of *x* which then occupy that place and no other place.) I consider this doctrine in detail in Appendix A. I there conclude that it will not help us with our problems about identity through time and that there is no sufficient reason for accepting it.

12 Contrast P. T. Geach, *Reference and Generality* (Ithaca: The Cornell University Press, 1962), p. 157: '. . . different official personages may be one and the same man'. Possibly an illustration would be: 'The fire-chief isn't the same personage as the Sunday-school superintendent (for one is charged with putting out fires and the other with religious instruction); yet Jones is both.' But here one seems to be playing loose with 'isn't', for what one has in mind, presumably, is something of this sort: 'Being the fire-chief commits one to different things than does being the Sunday-school superintendent, and Jones is both.'

13 There may be temptations in thus playing loose with 'is'. Suppose there were a monarchy wherein the subjects found it distasteful ever to affirm that the monarch vacated his throne. Instead of saying that there have been so many dozen kings and queens in the history of their country, they will say that the monarch has now existed for many

hundreds of years and has had so many dozen different names. At certain times it has been appropriate that these names be masculine, like 'George' and 'Henry', and at other times it has been appropriate that they be feminine, like 'Victoria' and 'Elizabeth'. What, then, if we knew about these people and were to hear such talk as this: 'There has existed for many hundreds of years an x such that x is our monarch; x is now feminine, though fifty years ago x was masculine, and fifty years before that x was feminine'? We should not conclude that there was in that land a monarch who is vastly different from any of the people in ours. We should conclude rather that the speakers were either deluded or pretending.

14 Other examples are suggested by: 'He has a copy of *The Republic* on his desk and another on the table and he doesn't have any other books. How many books does he have?' 'He played the *Appassionata* once in the afternoon and once again in the evening, but nothing further. How many sonatas did he play?'

15 Compare P. T. Geach in *Logic Matters* (Berkeley and Los Angeles: The University of California Press, 1972), pp. 238–49; and *Reference and Generality* (Ithaca: Cornell University Press, 1962), pp. 149ff. The suggestion is criticised in detail by David Wiggins, in *Identity and Spatio-Temporal Continuity* (Oxford: Basil Blackwell, 1967), pp. 1–26. Compare W. V. Quine in a review of *Reference and Generality* in *Philosophical Review*, lxxiii (1964), 100–4, and Fred Feldman, 'Geach and Relativised Identity', *Review of Metaphysics*, xxii (1968), 547–55.

16 Compare P. T. Geach: 'Even if the man Peter Geach is the same person as the man Julius Caesar, they are certainly different men; they were for example born at different times to a different pair of parents.' P. T. Geach, *God and the Soul* (London: Routledge & Kegan Paul, 1969), p. 6. John Locke says very similar things; see the Fraser edition of the *Essay Concerning Human Understanding*, pp. 445, 450ff.

17 *A Treatise of Human Nature*, Book I, Part IV, Section VI; L. A. Selby-Bigge edition, p. 255.

18 Thomas Reid, *Essays on the Intellectual Powers of Man*, Essay III, Chapter IV. In *The Works of Thomas Reid, D.D.*, ed. Sir William Hamilton (Edinburgh: Maclachlan & Stewart, 1854), p. 346.

19 This thesis is discussed and defended in Appendix B ('Mereological Essentialism').

20 See *A Treatise of Human Nature*, Book I, Part iv, Section 6 (Selby-Bigge edition, p. 255): 'all objects, to which we ascribe identity, without observing their invariableness and uninterruptedness, are such as consist of a succession of related objects'. In this same section. Hume affirms a version of the principle of mereological essentialism.

21 We could define an *ens successivum* by saying, with St Augustine, that it is 'a single thing . . . composed of many, all of which exist not together'; see *Confessions*, Book IV, Chapter XI. St Thomas says in effect that a *successivum* is a thing such that some of its parts do not coexist with others of its parts ('una pars non est cum alia parte'); see the *Commentary on the Sentences*, Book 1, Dist. VIII, Q. II, Art. I, ad 4. The term '*ens successivum*' has traditionally been applied to such things as periods of time (e.g. days, weeks, months) and events; compare Aristotle's *Physics*, Book III, Chapter VI, 206a.

22 Definition D.III.2 thus makes use of the general device by means of which Frege defined the ancestral relation; see G. Frege, *The Foundations of Arithmetic* (Oxford: Basil Blackwell, 1950), section 79. A more intuitive reading of clause (iii) might be: '(iii) x belongs at t to every class c which is such that (a) y belongs to c at t' and (b) all direct table successors of anything belonging to c belong to c'.

23 The distinction among these several types of property will be used in the following chapter to mark off those states of affairs that are *events*. (We had noted in the previous chapter that, although 'John is walking' refers to an event, 'John will walk' and 'John is such that either he is walking or he will walk' do not refer to events.)

24 Compare Hume: 'Tho' we commonly be able to distinguish pretty exactly betwixt numerical and specific identity, yet it sometimes happens that we confound them, and in our thinking and reasoning employ the one for the other.' *A Treatise of Human Nature*, Book I, Part IV, Section vi ('Of Personal Identity'), Selby-Bigge edition, pp. 257–8.

25 It may be noted that we have defined the loose and popular sense of the expression, 'There are n so-and-so's at t' and not the more general 'The number of so-and-so's that there ever will have been is n'. For the loose and popular sense of this

latter expression is not sufficiently fixed to be explicated in any strict and philosophical sense. The following example may make this clear. In the infantry of the United States Army during World War II each private carried materials for half a tent – something like one piece of canvas, a pole and ropes. Two privates could then assemble their materials and create a tent which would be disassembled in the morning. On another night the two privates might find different tent companions. Occasionally when the company was in camp the various tent parts were collected, stored away, and then re-issued but with no attempt to assign particular parts to their former holders. Supposing, to simplify the matter considerably, that all the tents that there ever will have been were those that were created by the members of a certain infantry company, how, making use of our ordinary criteria, would we go about answering the question 'Just how many tents *have* there been?' Would an accounting of the history of the joinings of the various tent parts be sufficient to give us the answer?

26   And so if we say that men are mere *entia per alio* and that God is the only *ens per se*, it will follow that I am God and not a man. Compare Bayle's refutation of Spinoza's doctrine according to which men are modifications of God: '. . . when we say that a man denies, affirms, gets angry, caresses, praises, and the like, we ascribe all these attributes to the substance of his soul itself, and not to his thoughts as they are either accidents or modifications. If it were true then, as Spinoza claims, that men are modalities of God, one would speak falsely when one said, "Peter denies this, he wants that, he affirms such and such a thing"; for actually, according to this theory, it is God who denies, wants, affirm; and consequently all the denominations that result from the thoughts of all men are properly and physically to be ascribed to God. From which it follows that God hates and loves, denies and affirms the same things at the same time . . .' From note N of the article 'Spinoza'; the passage may be found in R. H. Popkin, ed., Pierre Bayle, *Historical and Critical Dictionary: Selections* (Indianapolis: Bobbs-Merrill, 1965) 309–10.

27   *Critique of Pure Reason*, Kemp Smith edition, p. 342. The passage is from page 363 of the first edition of the *Kritik*.

28   Page 342 of the Kemp Smith edition; pp. 363–4 of the first edition.

29   *Essay Concerning Human Understanding*, Book II, Chapter xxiii ('Our Complex Ideas of Substance'); A. C. Fraser edition, p. 451.

30   *Op. cit.*, Fraser edition, p. 454.

31   *Op. cit.*, Fraser edition, p. 458.

32   The defence of this observation may be found in Section 4 of Chapter 1.

33   Kant at least was clear about this point. When he states that the 'consciousness' of one substance may be transferred to another, as the motion of one ball may be transferred to another, and notes that the last of a series of such substances might be conscious of all the states of the previous substances, he adds that 'it would not have been one and the same person in all these states'; *Critique of Pure Reason*, Kemp Smith edition, p. 342 (first edition of *Kritik*, p. 364).

34   Compare Bernard Williams, *Problems of the Self* (Cambridge: The University Press, 1973), pp. 2ff.

35   ' "If the power to remember dies with the material body, has the question of any single person's future life after death any particular interest for him?" As you put the question, it is not whether the matter ought rationally to have an interest but whether as a fact it has; and perhaps this is the proper question, trusting as it seems to do, rather to instinct than to reason. Now if we had a drug which would abolish memory for a while, and you were going to be cut for the stone, suppose the surgeon were to say, "You will suffer damnably, but I will administer this drug so that you will during that suffering lose all memory of your previous life. Now you have, of course, no particular interest in your suffering as long as you will not remember your present and past life, you know, have you?" ' *Collected Papers*, Vol. V (Cambridge, Mass.: Harvard University Press, 1935), p. 355.

36   See Locke's *Essay*, Book II, Chapter xxvii, Section i: 'One thing cannot have two beginnings of existence.' Compare Thomas Reid, *Essays on the Intellectual Powers of Man*, Essay III, Chapter 4.

37   Some philosophers who have considered this type of situation have not presupposed, as I have, that persons are *entia per se*. Thus Derek Parfit has suggested it is a mistake to believe that in such cases the question 'Will I be he?' has a true answer. He

writes: 'If we give up this belief, as I think we should, these problems disappear. We shall then regard the case as like many others in which, for quite unpuzzling reasons, there is no answer to a question about identity. (Consider "Was England the same nation after 1066?")' Derek Parfit, 'Personal Identity', *Philosophical Review*, LXXX (1971), 3–27; the quotation is on page 8. P. F. Strawson has expressed a similar scepticism: 'Perhaps I should say, not that I do not understand Professor Chisholm's notion of strict personal identity, but rather that I understand it well enough to think there can be no such thing.' P. F. Strawson, 'Chisholm on Identity through Time', in H. E. Kiefer and M. K. Munitz, eds, *Language, Belief, and Metaphysics* (Albany: State University of New York Press, 1970), pp. 183–6; the quotation is on page 186. I think that the conception of persons set forth in Strawson's *Individuals* coheres more readily with the view that persons are *entia per se* than with the view that they are ontological parasites or *entia per alio*.

38   Compare Godfrey Vesey, *Personal Identity* (London: Macmillan, 1974), pp. 8ff., 80ff.; Bernard Williams, *Problems of the Self* (Cambridge: The University Press, 1973), pp. 8ff., 15ff; and Anthony Quinton, 'The Soul', *Journal of Philosophy*, LIX (1962), 393–409, and *The Nature of Things* (London and Boston: Routledge & Kegan Paul, 1973); and Richard Taylor, *With Heart and Mind* (New York: St Martin's Press, 1973), pp. 122–33.

39   I have attempted to throw light upon these distinctions in Chapter IV ('The Problem of the Criterion') of *Theory of Knowledge* (Englewood Cliffs, N.J.: Prentice-Hall, 1966). Compare the discussion of criteria of self-identity in Sydney Shoemaker, *Self-Knowledge and Self-Identity* (Ithaca: Cornell University Press, 1963), pp. 35–8, 211–12, 255–60.

40   G. W. Leibniz, *Discourse on Metaphysics*, Section XXXIV (Open Court edition, p. 58). Sydney Shoemaker cited this passage in criticising an earlier formulation of my views. This earlier formulation, Shoemaker's criticism, and my rejoinder may be found in Norman S. Care and Robert H. Grimm, eds, *Perception and Personal Identity* (Cleveland: Case Western Reserve Press, 1969), pp. 82–139.

41   Pierre Bayle, article 'Lucretius', Note Q, *A General Dictionary, Historical and Critical*, trans. Rev. J. P. Bernard,

Rev. Thomas Birch, John Lockeman *et al.* (10 volumes: London, James Bettenham, 1734–41.)

42   The quotations are from Edward's *Doctrine of Original Sin Defended* (1758), Part IV, Chapter II. This work is reprinted in C. H. Faust and T. H. Johnson, eds, *Jonathan Edwards* (New York: American Book Co., 1935).

43   Rudolf Carnap, *Introduction to Symbolic Logic* (New York: Dover Publications, 1958), pp. 213ff.

44   J. H. Woodger, *The Axiomatic Method in Biology* (Cambridge: Cambridge University Press, 1937); see especially pp. 55–63, and Appendix E by Alfred Tarski (pp. 161–72).

45   A thing a is said to be the *sum* of a class F, provided only every member of the class F is a part of a, and every part of a has a part in common with some member of the class. If, as these authors postulate, every non-empty class has a sum, there would be, for example, an *individual* thing which is the sum of the class of dogs. Every dog would be a part of this collective dog and every part of this collective dog would share a part with some individual dog. The same would hold for the class the only members of which are this man and that horse. An opposing view is that of Boethius: a man and a horse are not one thing. See D. P. Henry, *The Logic of Saint Anselm* (Oxford: The Clarendon Press, 1967), p. 56. In the following Appendix ('Mereological Essentialism') [Appendix B, *Person and Object*], a mereology or theory of part and whole is developed which does not presuppose that there are such sums.

46   Edwards is impressed by what he takes to be the analogy between space and time. To persuade his reader that God could reasonably regard Adam's posterity as being one with Adam, he asserts that there would be no problem at all if Adam's posterity *coexisted* with Adam. If Adam's posterity had 'somehow *grown out of him*, and yet remained contiguous and literally *united to him*, as the branches to a tree, or the members of the body to the head; and had all, before the fall, existed together at the *same time*, though in *different places*, as the head and members are in different places', surely then, Edwards says, God could treat the whole collection as 'one moral whole' with each of us as its parts. And if a collection of persons existing in different places can be thought of as a single moral whole, why not also a collection of persons existing at different times?

47 The doctrine implies, of course, that there are an infinite number of temporal parts of me – that there will have been an infinite number today and an infinite number tomorrow, if I can be said in any sense to persist into tomorrow. Hence it is misleading to speak, as we do above, of 'today's temporal part of me' and 'tomorrow's temporal part of me'. What we have to say could be put more precisely by speaking of 'any given one of my temporal parts of today' and 'any given one of my temporal parts of tomorrow'.

48 Jonathan Edwards's own argument for the doctrine might be put this way. '(i) At every moment of time God preserves or upholds all individual things that exist in time. But (ii) such preservation or upholding is equivalent to creation *ex nihilo*. And therefore (iii), for any moment at which an individual thing may exist, the thing is made up at that moment of things that exist only at that moment.'

49 C. S. Peirce, *Collected Papers*, Vol. I (Cambridge, Mass.: Harvard University Press, 1931), 1.494. But compare 1.493.

50 Quine's published discussions of these questions begin with his *o Sentido da Nova Logica* (Sao Paulo: Livraria Martins Editora, 1944), pp. 135–8, and continue in the works cited below, as well as in *Word and Object* (New York: John Wiley, 1960), pp. 114–18, 171–3.

51 This assumption, of course, is not essential to the doctrine of temporal parts. But given what we said in the Introduction about persons and processes, the assumption would bear directly on the question whether the temporal parts of persons are themselves persons and therefore capable of such things as hoping for rain.

52 *Methods of Logic* (New York: Holt Dryden, 1959), p. 210.

53 *From a Logical Point of View* (New York: Harper & Row, 1963), p. 65.

54 This view is suggested by St Thomas: 'The Seine river is not "this particular river" because of "this flowing water," but because of "this source" and "this bed," and hence is always called the same river, although there may be other water flowing down it; likewise a people is the same, not because of sameness of soul or of man, but because of the same dwelling place, or rather because of the same laws and the same manner of living, as Aristotle says in III *Politica*.' From *De Spiritualibus Creaturis*, Article IX, ad 16; *On Spiritual Creatures*, trans. M. C. Fitzpatrick and J. J. Wellmuth (Milwaukee: Marquette University Press, 1949), p. 109.

55 This is the procedure that Quine follows, but instead of 'cofluvial' he uses 'river kinship'. He writes: 'We begin, let us imagine, with momentary things and their interrelations. One of these momentary things, called *a*, is a momentary stage of the river Cayster, in Lydia, around 400 B.C. Another, called *b*, is a momentary stage of the Cayster two days later. A third, *c*, is a momentary stage, at this same latter date, of the same multiplicity of water molecules which were in the river at the time of *a*. Half of *c* is in the lower Cayster valley, and the other half is to be found at diffuse points in the Aegean Sea. Thus, *a*, *b*, and *c* are three objects, variously related. We may say that *a* and *b* stand in the relation of river kinship, and that *a* and *c* stand in the relation of water kinship. Now the introduction of rivers as single entities, namely, processes or time-consuming objects, consists substantially in reading identity in place of river kinship.' (*From a Logical Point of View*, p. 66).

56 A subtle defence of the doctrine of temporal parts may be found in Richard Cartwright's 'Scattered Objects', in Keith Lehrer, ed., *Analysis and Metaphysics* (Dordrecht: D. Reidel, 1975), pp. 153–71. Cartwright's defence presuppose (1) that for any two material things there is a material thing of which each is a part and (2) it is possible for a whole to survive the loss of some of its part. These two presuppositions are rejected in Appendix B [of *Person and Object*] ('Mereological Essentialism') that immediately follows.

Chapter 22

Mark Heller

TEMPORAL PARTS OF FOUR DIMENSIONAL OBJECTS*

Probably the best objection to there being so-called temporal parts is that no one has adequately made sense of what a temporal part is supposed to be. Such phrases as "temporal part", "temporal phase", and "temporal slice" have been used in ways that suggest such varied purported objects as processes, events, ways things are, sets, and portions of careers or histories. The account which comes closest to making sense of temporal parts is Judith Jarvis Thomson's in 'Parthood and identity across time'.[1] Consider an object O which exists from time t_0 to t_3. On Thomson's account, a temporal part of O, call it P, is an object that comes into existence at some time $t_1 \geq t_0$ and goes out of existence at some time $t_2 \leq t_3$ and takes up some portion of the space that O takes up for all the time that P exists.[2] Her account has the strength of being reasonably explicit about what she means by "temporal part". Furthermore, as she explains them, temporal parts do, at least on the face of it, seem to be parts. Her account, however, has the weakness of, as Thomson claims,[3] making the existence of temporal parts fairly implausible. I shall offer an account which is at once explicit and supportive.

The basic problem with Thomson's account is that it is developed against the background of an unhelpful presupposition about the nature of physical objects. She thinks of physical objects as being three dimensional and enduring through time. I admit from the outset that this is our normal philosophical way of thinking of physical

objects. But it is this way of thinking that makes temporal parts seem implausible. I see nothing in favor of it other than the fact that it is our standard view, and I put very little weight on this advantage. Furthermore, this view leads to having to choose between what I take to be unpleasant alternatives. The alternatives are:

(a)   there is no such physical object as my body,

(b)   there is no physical object in the space that we would typically say is now exactly occupied by all of me other than my left hand.

(c)   no physical object can undergo a loss of parts (in the ordinary sense of "parts"),

(d)   there can be distinct physical objects exactly occupying the same space at the same time,

(e)   identity is not transitive.

To deny each of these alternatives and to accept three dimensional enduring objects would lead to a contradiction. To show this I present an abbreviated, slightly altered version of an argument of Peter van Inwagen's.[4] If we deny alternative *a*, then there is such an object as my body. Call it Body. If we deny alternative *b*, then there is an object that is all of me other than my left hand. Call that object Body-minus. Now consider some time t at which my left hand is cut off. This does not affect Body-minus, so:

(1)   the thing that, before *t*, is Body-minus =
       the thing that, after *t*, is Body-minus.

If we also deny alternative *c*, then my losing my
hand does not end my body's existence, so:

(2)   the thing that, after *t*, is Body = the thing
       that, before *t*, is Body.

Further, if we deny *d*, it *seems* to follow that:

(3)   the thing that, after *t*, is Body-minus = the
       thing that, after *t*, is Body.

If we then deny *e*, by transitivity of identity it
follows that:

(4)   the thing that, before *t*, is Body-minus =
       the thing that, before *t*, is Body.

But since Body was bigger before t than Body-
minus was before t:

(5)   the thing that, before *t*, is Body-minus ≠
       the thing that, before *t*, is Body,

and (5) contradicts (4).

In the end, Thomson's preferred way of
avoiding this contradiction is to accept *d*.[5] In contrast, van Inwagen avoids the contradiction by
accepting *b*.[6] Roderick Chisholm instead accepts
c.[7] And Peter Geach seems to accept *e*.[8] My way of
avoiding the contradiction is to claim that (3)
does not follow from the denial of *d* unless we
accept the additional thesis that physical objects
are three dimensional and endure through time.
I will deny this additional thesis. Doing so will
allow me to claim that Body and Body-minus are
distinct objects that, even after *t*, do not occupy
the same space at the same time. It is incumbent
upon me, then, to offer a reasonable alternative to the three dimensional view of physical
objects.

I propose that a physical object is not an
enduring spatial hunk of matter, but is, rather, a
spatiotemporal hunk of matter. Instead of thinking of matter as filling up regions of space, we
should think of matter as filling up regions of
spacetime. A physical object is the material content of a region of spacetime. Just as such an
object has spatial extent, it also has temporal
extent—it extends along four dimensions, not
just three. To see the contrast clearly, consider an
object that is created at noon and destroyed at
one. If we think of the object as three dimensional and enduring though time, it would be
appropriate to say that the object exists at different times; the same object exists at noon and at
one. Such an object has boundaries along only
three dimensions. The whole object is that hunk
of matter which entirely fills up those boundaries. The whole object, therefore, exists at noon
and still exists at one. A four dimensional object,
on the other hand, has boundaries along an additional dimension. The whole object must fill up
all its boundaries and, therefore, does not exist at
a single moment. If we accept that physical
objects are four dimensional, the appropriate
thing to say about the object under consideration
is that it takes up more than an instantaneous
region of time. It does not exist *at* noon *and* one;
rather, it exists *from* noon *until* one. Instead of
thinking of an object as existing at various times,
we should think of it as existing within regions
of time.

In so far as time is just one more dimension,
roughly alike in kind to the three spatial dimensions, we should expect that our claims about an
object's spatial characteristics have analogues
with respect to its temporal characteristics. For
instance, just as we might talk about the distance
between two points along a line in space, we can
also talk about the distance between two points
in time. This allows us to understand the notion
of temporal boundaries as analogous to that of
spatial boundaries. Furthermore, there is an analogy with respect to the part-whole relationship.
Just as a spatial part fills up a sub-region of the
space occupied by the whole, a temporal part
fills up a subregion of the time occupied by the

whole. Another important analogy is that, for both spatial and temporal parts, we can, loosely speaking, point at or perceive or name a whole by pointing at, perceiving, or indicating a part. It should be noted that an object's temporal characteristics are not completely analogous to its spatial characteristics. This is because time is not completely alike in kind to the three spatial dimensions. Time, for instance, seems to have a direction. Also, our perception along the temporal dimension is only one directional (memory) and is discontinuous (I can remember what happened on my third birthday without remembering anything that happened between my third and fourth birthdays). Furthermore, temporal units of measurement are not of the same kind as spatial units of measurement. These disanalogies will not affect our present discussion.

One question that arises is whether it is possible to have zero extent along the temporal dimension. I do not have a strong opinion on this issue, although I tend towards the view that zero extent is impossible. What should be noted is that this is no more an issue with respect to the temporal dimension than with any of the spatial dimensions. Could there be any such thing as the surface of a cube? I do not know the answer. Thinking according to our standard three dimensional picture such an object would have zero extent along one of the spatial dimensions and could, therefore, be called a two dimensional object. According to our new four dimensional picture such an object would still have zero extent along one of the spatial dimensions. It could, therefore, be called a three dimensional object, one of the three being the temporal dimension. I shall, for convenience's sake, simply assume that zero extent along the temporal dimension, and along each of the other dimensions, is possible.

Now that we have some understanding of the notion of a four dimensional object, let us turn our attention to the parts of such objects. A four dimensional object is the material content of a filled region of spacetime. A spatiotemporal part of such an object is the material content of a sub-region of the spacetime occupied by the whole. For instance, consider a particular object O and the region R of spacetime that O fills. A spatiotemporal part of O is the material content of a sub-region of R. A spatiotemporal part, as long as it has greater than zero extent along every dimension, is itself a four dimensional physical object.[9] A spatiotemporal part is not a set or a process or a way something is at a place and time. It, like the object it is part of, is a hunk of matter. If Heller is a physical object, then so is Heller's-left-hand-from-(1:00 p.m., January 3, 1980)-to-(1:01 p.m., January 3, 1980). This spatiotemporal part of me could have, between 1:00 p.m. and 1:01 p.m. on January 3, 1980, been felt, seen, heard, smelled, and, if need be, tasted. It had weight and volume. Thinking of spatiotemporal parts as physical objects corresponds to the way we ordinarily think of parts on our old three dimensional picture. When not being swayed by philosophical considerations we have no doubt that my hand is a physical object. Accepting the account of four dimensional objects presented in this paper, we may continue to hold the general principle that a part of a physical object is itself a physical object.

It should be noted that the fact that any part of O is the material content of a sub-region of R does not entail that every filled sub-region of R contains a part of O. I happen to believe that this is true, but it is not a feature of the concept of a spatiotemporal part. One could consistently accept all three of the following:

(i)   there are four dimensional objects and spatiotemporal parts of such objects,
(ii)   not every filled region of spacetime contains a physical object,
(iii) even for a region of spacetime that does contain a physical object, not every sub-region contains a spatiotemporal part of that object.

I take it that typically someone who accepts all

three of these would be accepting (iii) because he accepts (ii). Someone might accept (ii) if he thought that there is good reason to reject scattered objects. Or (ii) might be accepted if independent grounds could be found for some claim like "every object must contain its principle of unity within itself" (whatever that might mean). My goal here is not to supply a means of answering every question of the form "is there a spatiotemporal part here?", but rather to make clear the concept of spatiotemporal parthood.

It is now easy to understand the notion of a temporal part. Any proper part of a four dimensional object is smaller than the whole object along at least one dimension. A proper temporal part is smaller along just one dimension, the temporal dimension. A temporal part of O is a spatiotemporal part that is the same spatial size as O for as long as that part exists, though it may be a smaller temporal size. Let us suppose that object O exactly fills the temporal region from t_0 to t_3. That is, the region of spacetime filled by O, namely region R, has the temporal boundaries t_0 and t_3. Now consider a certain sub-region of R has the temporal boundaries of which are $t_1 \geq t_0$ and $t_2 \leq t_3$ and the spatial boundaries of which are just the spatial boundaries of R from t_1 to t_2. Call this sub-region S. If the material content of S is an object, then it is a temporal part of O. In general, using the single letters as variables rather than names, a temporal part of O is the material content of a temporal sub-region of R. "Temporal sub-region of R" means spatiotemporal sub-region that shares all of R's spatial boundaries within that sub-region's temporal boundaries. A temporal part of me which exists from my fifth birthday to my sixth is the same spatial size I am from age five to age six.

One matter of detail that is particularly important for temporal parts specifically and four dimensional objects in general is how to understand such phrases as "____ exists in region ____" or "____ exists at time ____". Physical objects are four dimensional hunks of matter. They, therefore, have precise spatiotemporal

boundaries. Consider a particular physical object, this piece of paper.[10] Call it Whitey. Whitey has certain spatiotemporal boundaries—there is a region which it exactly occupies. But we also think that it is true to say that Whitey now exists. This way of talking may be misleading. If Whitey exists now and existed a minute ago, then it is the same object which exists at both times. But this suggests the old three dimensional picture that we have been denying.

This confusion is easily avoided. When we say that Whitey exists now this should be taken as a loose way of saying that part of Whitey exists now. If we meant strictly that Whitey exists now we would be saying something false. "Whitey" names the whole piece of paper,[11] and that object does not exist now. Strictly speaking, Whitey is temporally too large to exist now. Only a part of Whitey exists now. This, then, is the major difference between the three dimensional and four dimensional pictures. On the three dimensional picture if we said that Whitey exists now and really meant Whitey, the whole piece of paper, we would be saying something true. It is Whitey which exist at different times. On the other hand, on the four dimensional picture Whitey does not, strictly speaking, exist at different times. Whitey's parts exist at different times (different parts at different times), and, in virtue of this fact, we say that Whitey exists at those times.

This can be made clearer by considering a spatial analogy. Put Whitey mostly in a drawer, but leave a small corner sticking out. Now if asked where Whitey is you will answer that it is in the drawer. Strictly speaking, however, your answer would be false. Even on the three dimensional picture, part of Whitey is not in the drawer. But "Whitey" names the whole piece of paper, so if it is not the whole piece in the drawer, then it is not Whitey in the drawer. We say that Whitey is in the drawer because a part of Whitey is in there. Notice also that with some rewording it can be seen that how large a portion of the paper is in the drawer is not crucial. If only a corner of the paper were inside we would be less likely to say that Whitey is in the drawer when asked where Whitey is. But if asked "Does Whitey exist inside that drawer?", I think we would all say "yes". For another case consider Alice's mother screaming at her "Now, Alice, you stay out of that cookie jar!".

Recognizing that we have this loose way of speaking even when using our three dimensional picture, it is not surprising that we also have this loose way of speaking when using our four dimensional picture. Recognizing that such a phrase as "Whitey exists now" is just loose speaking, we see that, strictly speaking, Whitey only exists within the spatiotemporal region which it exactly fills and regions of which that one is a sub-region. To loosely say that Whitey exists now is to strictly say that the present time is within Whitey's temporal boundaries, and thus is equivalent to saying that Whitey has a temporal part that exists now (assuming that there are instantaneous temporal parts).

One nice ramification of these considerations is that an object and a proper part of that object do not, strictly speaking, exist in the same space at the same time. An object is not coincident with any of its proper parts. Intuitively, the problem with coincident entities is that of overcrowding. There is just not enough room for them. But an object and a part of that object do not compete for room. There is a certain spatiotemporal region exactly occupied by the part; the whole object is not in that region. There is only as much of the object there as will fit—namely, the part. This intuitive understanding of the relationship between part and whole is what I intended to capture with my discussion of our loose way of talking. When we say that Whitey is in the drawer, that is just a loose way of saying that part of Whitey is there. When we say Whitey exists now we are only saying that a part of Whitey exists now. Keeping this in mind allows us to avoid being committed to coincident entities.

Let us consider a spatial case. Even adopting a three dimensional picture, we are not tempted to

say that Heller and Heller's left hand are coincident entities. These are not two distinct entities in one place at one time. Strictly speaking, there is only one entity in that hand shaped region of space—my hand. Whatever truth there is in saying that I am in that region can be wholly captured by saying that a part of me is there. The relation between my hand and me is not that of coincidence, but, rather, that of part to whole. Similar points are relevant to cases of spatial overlap. My living room and dining room share a common wall. But this does not entail that there is a wall shaped region of space occupied by both my living room and my dining room. That region is occupied by the wall, and that wall happens to be part of both rooms.

If we adopt the four dimensional view of physical objects, then similar points can be made about the relation between an object and its temporal parts. Heller is not coincident with Heller-during-1983. The only truth there is in saying that I occupy the year long region of time is that I have a part that occupies that region. Strictly speaking, there is only one entity in the relevant spatiotemporal region—my 1983 part. Also, analogous to the case of spatial overlap, there may be cases of temporal overlap. If I were to undergo fission next year, that should not tempt us to say that prior to 1984 there were two objects in the same space at the same time.[12] Rather, we should say that two four dimensional objects overlapped prior to 1984—they shared a common temporal part. Perhaps a less controversial case would be a hunk of gold that is shaped into a ring. The ring then undergoes a gradual replacement of matter until it is entirely composed of silver. Many would be tempted to say that the ring and the hunk of gold were, for a period of time, coincident entities. However adopting the four dimensional view, we can say that the gold and the ring temporally overlap. The gold has a ring shaped temporal part, the ring has a golden temporal part, and the gold's part is identical to the ring's part. The relationship of the part of the one and the part of the other is identity, not coincidence. The relationship between the gold and the ring is that they share a common part, they overlap.[13]

In contrast, trying to make sense of temporal parts without shifting to a four dimensional picture would require a commitment to coincident entities. On Thomson's account, Heller and Heller-now are, in the strictest sense, two distinct entities occupying the same space at the same time.[14] Heller is, at any given time between his birth and his death, complete. Right now I exactly fill all of my three dimensional boundaries. But that supposed temporal part of me called Heller-now also exactly fills those same boundaries. Yet the two entities are distinct because I have a much longer career than Heller-now. Thomson cannot claim that strictly speaking I am temporally too big to be coincident with my instantaneous temporal part, because she avails herself of only three dimensions along which to measure. Along those dimensions I am now exactly the same size as Heller-now.

In fact Thomson's problem of coincident entities is a symptom of a much deeper problem with trying to explain temporal parts without rejecting the old three dimensional picture. Let us return to Whitey, the piece of paper. On the old picture it is, strictly speaking, true that Whitey exists now. It is the same three dimensional object which exists at different times. "Whitey" names the whole piece of paper. So it is true that the whole piece of paper does exist now. So even though Whitey will continue to exist for the next several hours, "Whitey-from-(now + one hour)-to-(now + two hours)" does not pick out a part of Whitey unless that part exists now. But if there were such a temporal part it would not yet have come into existence. So Whitey has no temporal parts other than the one which exists now. Indeed, it does not even have that temporal part, since Whitey (all of it) existed an hour ago, and the temporal part which supposedly exists now did not exist then. If one holds the three dimensional view of physical objects it is perfectly reasonable to think of

an ontology including temporal parts as a "crazy metaphysic".[15]

Of course, this is not Thomson's reason for calling it a crazy metaphysic. She does not draw attention to the three dimensional/four dimensional distinction at all. Thomson writes:

> I said this seems to me a crazy metaphysic. It seems to me that its full craziness only comes out when we take the spatial analogy seriously. The metaphysic yields that if I have had exactly one bit of chalk in my hand for the last hour, then there is something in my hand which is white, roughly cylindrical in shape, and dusty, something which also has a weight, something which is chalk, which was not in my hand three minutes ago, and indeed, such that no part of it was in my hand three minutes ago. As I hold the bit of chalk in my hand, new stuff, new chalk keeps constantly coming into existence *ex nihilo*. That strikes me as obviously false.[16]

I suggest that this attack on temporal parts depends on accepting the thesis that physical objects are three dimensional.

Why does Thomson think that temporal parts would come into existence *ex nihilo*? It is obviously not because nothing exists before the temporal part. It is not even because everything that exists before the temporal part continues to exist, for there are prior temporal parts that go out of existence at just the moment that the part in question comes into existence. I suggest that Thomson's claim is founded on the belief that there is no significant material change occurring at the time that the temporal part is supposed to be coming into existence. The piece of chalk does not undergo any alteration. No molecules need be altering their internal structure or their relationships to other molecules. No matter from outside the chalk is added, nor is any matter that was part of the chalk released into the surrounding atmosphere. In short, nothing has occurred that would be enough to bring an object into existence. The temporal part just seems to pop into existence without any sufficient cause.

But this argument ignores one significant change that takes place—the passage of time. It is this change which is responsible for the temporal part's coming into existence. Of course, this passage of time does not provide the whole causal explanation for why the temporal part exists. To give the full explanation we would have to account for why there is matter at that place at that time. It is this passage of time, however, that explains why that matter's being there at that time constitutes a new object's coming into existence. At t_0 the temporal part in question did not exist. At t_1 it did exist. The change which brought this object into existence was just the change in time from t_0 to t_1. Some philosophers—Thomson, for instance—will undoubtably feel that this kind of change is too superficial to bring an object into existence. But this feeling is based on an unwarranted prejudice in favor of the spatial over the temporal. This prejudice, in turn, is founded upon the thesis that physical objects are three dimensional and enduring. Once we surrender this thesis, adopting instead the four dimensional view, I can find no defense for the claim that temporal parts would have to come into existence *ex nihilo*.

To support temporal parts and the four dimensional view of physical objects, recall that earlier in this paper I argued that thinking of objects as three dimensional and enduring would commit us to one of the following five unpleasant alternatives:

(a)   there is no such physical object as my body,
(b)   there is no physical object in the space that we would typically say is now exactly occupied by all of me other than my left hand,
(c)   no physical object can undergo a loss of parts (in the ordinary sense of "parts"),
(d)   there can be distinct physical objects exactly occupying the same space at the same time,

(e)   identity is not transitive.

We are now in a position to see how viewing objects as four dimensional allows us to avoid all of these alternatives. Once we adopt the four dimensional picture, we can deny all five alternatives without having to be committed to:

(3)   the thing that, after t, is Body-minus = the thing that, after t, is Body.

The objects claimed to be identical in (3) are distinct and do not occupy, except in a loose sense, the same space at the same time.

Body and Body-minus are distinct four dimensional objects, since they have different spatial shapes before t. But then, it might be objected, they seem to be distinct but coincident entities—co-occupying a single spatiotemporal region R which begins at t. The response is that *strictly speaking* neither of them is in R. They are both temporally too big. They each take up a spatiotemporal region that is temporally larger than R, since their regions begin before t. Of course, each has a temporal part that is in R, but that does not entail that either Body or Body-minus is in that region. They overlap in R, but neither one exactly fills R.

Perhaps there may be another way of generating the difficulty. Instead of comparing Body with Body-minus, let us compare that part of Body which does exactly fill R with that part of Body-minus which also exactly fills R. It might be claimed that here we have an example of two distinct objects in the same space at the same time. But this again would be a mistake, for these temporal parts are not two distinct objects but, rather, one object under two descriptions. Body and Body-minus have a common temporal part, just as my living room and my dining room have a common spatial part.

I have tried to expound a metaphysic for temporal parts that is at least plausible. I have also tried to give one reason why it might be desirable to adopt such a metaphysic. Still, there is much work left to be done. We will have to develop an understanding of change as a relationship between temporal parts of a four dimensional whole. This will have effects on our understanding of causation and, in particular, of an agent's bringing about change. For instance, Paul Bunyan's cutting down a tree should be seen as a relationship between certain of Bunyan's spatiotemporal parts and certain of the tree's spatiotemporal parts. There is also other important work to be done with respect to the question of whether four dimensional objects have their spatiotemporal parts essentially. Still one more relevant task would be to see how issues concerning the relationship between the mental and physical might affect our considerations of four dimensional objects. These are just some of the chores left undone. At least now that we have a better understanding of what four dimensional objects and temporal parts are, we have a solid basis for carrying out these and other future projects.

Notes

* My thanks to Jonathan Bennett, Mark Brown, Jan Cover, Paul Hrycaj, Carl Matheson, Judith Jarvis Thomson, and Peter van Inwagen.

1 Judith Jarvis Thomson, 'Parthood and identity across time', *Journal of Philosophy* 80 (1983), pp. 201–220.

2 Thomson would have been better off calling this a spatiotemporal part of O, since it may be spatially

part of O at some of the times at which it exists. She also defines "cross-sectional temporal part", and this could appropriately be called a temporal part.

3 She calls it "a crazy metaphysic" on pp. 34 and 36.

4 Peter van Inwagen, 'The doctrine of arbitrary undetached parts' (Chapter 10 of this volume).

5 Thomson *op. cit.*

6 van Inwagen, *op. cit.*

7 Roderick Chisholm: 'Parts as essential to their wholes', *Review of Metaphysics* 26 (1973), pp. 581–603.

8 Peter Geach: 'Identity', *Review of Metaphysics* 21 (1967–1968), pp. 3–12.

9 I am using "object" to pick out the broadest ontological category. To be is to be an object. To be physical is to be a physical object.

10 Assuming that this piece of paper does have precise boundaries.

11 Notice that my claims here are not presupposing a description theory of names. On a causal theory of names "Whitey" refers to the whole piece of paper if and only if it was the whole piece which was originally baptised when the reference of "Whitey" was fixed.

12 Compare this to David Lewis's discussion in 'Survival and Identity', *The Identity of Persons*, ed. Amelie Oksenberg Rorty (Berkeley: University of California Press, 1976), pp. 17–40.

13 Compare this to John Perry's discussion in 'The same F', *The Philosophical Review* 79 (April 1970), pp. 181–200, esp. pp. 198–199.

14 See Thomson, p. 34.

15 See Note 3.

16 Thomson, p. 36.

Chapter 23

Greg Egan

DUST

I open my eyes, blinking at the room's unexpected brightness, then lazily reach out to place one hand in a patch of sunlight spilling onto the bed from a gap between the curtains. Dust motes drift across the shaft of light, appearing for all the world to be conjured into, and out of, existence—evoking a childhood memory of the last time I found this illusion so compelling, so hypnotic. I feel utterly refreshed—and utterly disinclined to give up my present state of comfort. I don't know why I've slept so late, and I don't care. I spread my fingers on the sun-warmed sheet, and think about drifting back to sleep.

Something's troubling me, though. A dream? I pause and try to dredge up some trace of it, without much hope; unless I'm catapulted awake by a nightmare, my dreams tend to be evanescent. And yet—

I leap out of bed, crouch down on the carpet, fists to my eyes, face against my knees, lips moving soundlessly. The shock of realization is a palpable thing: a red lesion behind my eyes, pulsing with blood. Like ... the aftermath of a hammer blow to the thumb—and tinged with the very same mixture of surprise, anger, humiliation, and idiot bewilderment. Another childhood memory: *I held a nail to the wood, yes—but only to camouflage my true intention. I was curious about everything, including pain. I'd seen my father injure himself this way—but I knew that I needed firsthand experience to understand what he'd been through. And I was*

sure that it would be worth it, right up to the very last moment—

I rock back and forth, on the verge of laughter, trying to keep my mind blank, waiting for the panic to subside. And eventually, it does—laced by one simple, perfectly coherent thought: *I don't want to be here.*

For a moment, this conclusion seems unassailable, but then a countervailing voice rises up in me: *I'm not going to quit. Not again. I swore to myself that I wouldn't ... and there are a hundred good reasons not to—*

Such as?

For a start, I can't afford it—

No? *Who* can't afford it?

I whisper, "I know *exactly* how much this cost, you bastard. And I honestly don't give a shit. I'm *not going through with it.*"

There's no reply. I clench my teeth, uncover my eyes, look around the room. Away from the few dazzling patches of direct sunshine, everything glows softly in the diffuse light: the matte-white brick walls, the imitation (imitation) mahogany desk; even the Dalf and Giger posters look harmless, domesticated. The simulation is perfect—or rather, finer-grained than my "visual" acuity, and hence indistinguishable from reality—as no doubt it was the other four times. Certainly, none of the other Copies complained about a lack of verisimilitude in their environments. In fact, they never said anything very coherent; they just ranted abuse, whined about their plight, and then terminated themselves—all within fifteen (subjective) minutes of gaining consciousness.

And me? What ever made me—him—think that I won't do the same? How am I different from Copy number four? Three years older. More stubborn? More determined? More desperate for success? *I was,* for sure . . . back when I was still thinking of myself as the one who'd stay real, the one who'd sit outside and watch the whole experiment from a safe distance.

Suddenly I wonder: What makes me so sure that I'm *not* outside? I laugh weakly. I don't remember anything after the scan, which is a bad sign, but I was overwrought, and I'd spent so long psyching myself up for "this" . . .

Get it over with.

I mutter the password, "Bremsstrahlung"—and my last faint hope vanishes, as a black-on-white square about a meter wide, covered in icons, appears in midair in front of me.

I give the interface window an angry thump; it resists me as if it were solid, and firmly anchored. *As if I were solid, too.* I don't really need any more convincing, but I grip the top edge and lift myself right off the floor. I regret this; the realistic cluster of effects of exertion—down to the plausible twinge in my right elbow—pin me to this "body," anchor me to this "place," in exactly the way I should be doing everything I can to avoid.

Okay. Swallow it: *I'm a Copy.* My memories may be those of a human being, but I will never inhabit a real body "again." Never inhabit *the real world* again . . . unless my cheapskate original scrapes up the money for a telepresence robot—in which case I could blunder around like the slowest, clumsiest, most neurologically impaired cripple. *My model-of-a-brain runs seventeen times slower than the real thing.* Yeah, sure, technology will catch up one day—and seventeen times faster for me than for him. In the meantime? I rot in this prison, jumping through hoops, carrying out his precious research—while he lives in my

apartment, spends my money, sleeps with Elizabeth. . . .

I close my eyes, dizzy and confused; I lean against the cool surface of the interface.

"His" research? I'm just as curious as him, aren't I? I wanted this; I did this to myself. Nobody forced me. I knew exactly what the drawbacks would be, but I thought I'd have the strength of will (this time, at last) to transcend them, to devote myself, monklike, to the purpose for which I'd been brought into being—content in the knowledge that my other self was as unconstrained as ever.

Past tense. Yes, I made the decision—but I never really faced up to the consequences. *Arrogant, self-deluding shit.* It was only the knowledge that "I" would continue, free, on the outside, that gave me the "courage" to go ahead—but that's no longer true, for me.

Ninety-eight percent of Copies made are of the very old, and the terminally ill. People for whom it's the last resort—most of whom have spent millions beforehand, exhausting all the traditional medical options. And despite the fact that they have no other choice, 15 percent decide upon awakening—usually in a matter of hours—that they just can't hack it.

And of those who are young and healthy, those who are merely curious, those who know they have a perfectly viable, living, breathing body outside?

The bail-out rate has been, so far, one hundred percent.

I stand in the middle of the room, swearing softly for several minutes, trying to prepare myself—although I know that the longer I leave it, the harder it will become. I stare at the floating interface; its dreamlike, hallucinatory quality helps, slightly. I rarely remember my dreams, and I won't remember this one—but there's no tragedy in that, is there?

I don't want to be here.

I don't want to be *this.*

And to think I used to find it so often disappointing, waking up yet again as the *real* Paul Durham: self-centered dilettante, spoiled by a medium-sized inheritance, too wealthy to gain any sense of purpose from the ordinary human struggle to survive—but insufficiently brain-dead to devote his life to the accumulation of ever more money and power. No status-symbol luxuries for Durham: no yachts, no mansions, no bioenhancements. He indulged other urges; threw his money in another direction entirely.

And I don't know, anymore, what he thinks it's done for *him*—but I know what it's done to *me*.

I suddenly realize that I'm still stark naked. Habit—if no conceivable propriety—suggests that I should put on some clothes, but I resist the urge. One or two perfectly innocent, perfectly ordinary actions like that, and I'll find I'm taking myself seriously, thinking of myself as real.

I pace the bedroom, grasp the cool metal of the doorknob a couple of times, but manage to keep myself from turning it. *There's no point even starting to explore this world.*

I can't resist peeking out the window, though. The view of the city is flawless—every building, every cyclist, every tree, is utterly convincing—and so it should be: it's a recording, not a simulation. Essentially photographic—give or take a little computerized touching up and filling in—and totally predetermined. What's more, only a tiny part of it is "physically" accessible to me; I can see the harbor in the distance, but if I tried to go for a stroll down to the water's edge . . .

Enough. Just get it over with.

I prod a menu icon labeled UTILITIES; it spawns another window in front of the first. The function I'm seeking is buried several menus deep—but for all that I thought I'd convinced myself that I wouldn't want to use it, I brushed up on the details just a week ago, and I know exactly where to look. For all my self-deception, for all that I tried to relate only to *the one who'd stay outside,* deep down, I must have understood full well that I had two separate futures to worry about.

I finally reach the EMERGENCIES menu, which includes a cheerful icon of a cartoon fig-ure suspended from a parachute. *Bailing out is*

what they call it—but I don't find that too cloy-ingly euphemistic; after all, I can't commit "sui-cide" when I'm not legally human. In fact, the law requires that a bail-out option be available, without reference to anything so troublesome as the "rights" of the Copy; this stipulation arises solely from the ratification of certain purely technical, international software standards.

I prod the icon; it comes to life, and recites a warning spiel. I scarcely pay attention. Then it says, "Are you absolutely sure that you wish to shut down this Copy of Paul Durham?"

Nothing to it. Program A asks Program B to confirm its request for orderly termination. Packets of data are exchanged.

"Yes, I'm sure."

A metal box, painted red, appears at my feet. I open it, take out the parachute, strap it on.

Then I close my eyes and say, "Listen, you selfish, conceited, arrogant turd: How many times do you need to be told? I'll skip the per-sonal angst; you've heard it all before—and ignored it all before. But when are you going to stop wasting your time, your money, your energy . . . when are you going to stop wasting your life . . . on something which you just don't have the strength to carry through? After all the evidence to the contrary, do you honestly still believe that you're brave enough, or crazy enough, to be your own guinea pig? Well, I've got news for you: *You're not.*"

With my eyes still closed, I grip the release lever.

I'm nothing: a dream, a soon-to-be-forgotten dream.

My fingernails need cutting; they dig pain-fully into the skin of my palm.

Have I never, in a dream, feared the extinction of waking? Maybe I have—but a dream is not a life. If the only way I can reclaim my body, reclaim my world, is to wake and forget—

I pull the lever.

After a few seconds, I emit a constricted sob—a sound more of confusion than any kind of emotion—and open my eyes.

The lever has come away in my hand.

I stare dumbly at this metaphor for . . . what?

A bug in the termination software? Some kind of hardware glitch?

Feeling—at last—truly dreamlike, I unstrap the parachute, and unfasten the neatly packaged bundle.

Inside, there is no illusion of silk, or Kevlar, or whatever else there might plausibly have been. Just a sheet of paper. A note.

Dear Paul,

The night after the scan was completed, I looked back over the whole preparatory stage of the project, and did a great deal of soul searching. And I came to the conclusion that—right up to the very last moment—my attitude was poisoned with ambivalence.

With hindsight, I very quickly came to realize just how foolish my qualms were—but that was too late for you. I couldn't afford to ditch you, and have myself scanned yet again. So, what could I do?

This: I put your awakening on hold for a while, and tracked down someone who could make a few alterations to the virtual environment utilities. I know, that wasn't strictly legal . . . but you know how important it is to me that you—that we—succeed this time.

I trust you'll understand, and I'm confident that you'll accept the situation with dignity and equanimity.

Best wishes,
Paul

I sink to my knees, still holding the note, staring at it in disbelief. *He can't have done this. He can't have been so callous.*

No? Who am I kidding? Too weak to be so cruel to anyone else—perhaps. Too weak to go through with this in person—certainly. But as for making a Copy, and then—once its future was no longer his future, no longer anything for him to fear—taking away its power to escape . . .

It rings so true that I hang my head in shame.

Then I drop the note, raise my head, and bellow with all the strength in my non-existent lungs:

"DURHAM! YOU PRICK!"

* * *

I think about smashing furniture. Instead, I take a long, hot shower. In part, to calm myself; in part, as an act of petty vengeance: I may not be adding to the cheapskate's water bill, but he can damn well pay for twenty virtual minutes of gratuitous hydrodynamic calculations. I scrutinize the droplets and rivulets of water on my skin, searching for some small but visible anomaly at the boundary between my body—computed down to subcellular resolution—and the rest of the simulation, which is modeled much more crudely. If there are any discrepancies, though, they're too subtle for me to detect.

I dress—I'm just not comfortable naked—and eat a late breakfast. The muesli tastes exactly like muesli, the toast exactly like toast, but I know there's a certain amount of cheating going on with both taste and aroma. The detailed effects of chewing, and the actions of saliva, are being faked from empirical rules, not generated from first principles; there are no individual molecules being dissolved from the food and torn apart by enzymes—just a rough set of evolving nutrient concentration values, associated with each microscopic "parcel" of saliva. Eventually, these will lead to plausible increases in the concentrations of amino acids, various carbohydrates, and other substances all the way down to humble sodium and chloride ions, in similar "parcels" of gastric juices . . . which in turn will act as input data to the models of my intestinal villus cells. From there, into the bloodstream.

The coffee makes me feel alert, but also slightly detached—as always. Neurons, of course, are modeled with the greatest care of all, and whatever receptors to caffeine and its metabolites were present on each individual neuron in my original's brain at the time of the scan, my model-of-a-brain should incorporate every one of them—in a simplified, but functionally equivalent, form.

I close my eyes and try to imagine the physical reality behind all this: a cubic meter of silent, motionless optical crystal, configured as a cluster of over a billion individual processors, one of a few hundred identical units in a basement vault . . . somewhere on the planet. I don't even know what city I'm in; the scan was made in Sydney, but the model's implementation would have been contracted out by the local node to the lowest bidder at the time.

I take a sharp vegetable knife from the kitchen drawer, and drive the point a short way into my forearm. I flick a few drops of blood onto the table—and wonder exactly which software is now responsible for the stuff. Will the blood cells "die off" slowly—or have they already been surrendered to the extrasomatic general-physics model, far too unsophisticated to represent them, let alone keep them "alive"?

If I tried to slit my wrists, when exactly would he intervene? I gaze at my distorted reflection in the blade. Maybe he'd let me die, and then run the whole model again from scratch, simply leaving out the knife. After all, I re-ran all the earlier Copies hundreds of times, tampering with various aspects of their surroundings, trying in vain to find some cheap trick that would keep them from wanting to bail out. It must be a measure of sheer stubbornness that it took me—him—so long to admit defeat and rewrite the rules.

I put down the knife. I don't want to perform that experiment. Not yet.

I go exploring, although I don't know what I'm hoping to find. Outside my own apartment, everything is slightly less than convincing; the architecture of the building is reproduced faithfully enough, down to the ugly plastic potplants, but every corridor is deserted, and every door to every other apartment is sealed shut—concealing, literally, nothing. I kick one door, as hard as I can; the wood seems to give slightly, but when I examine the surface, the paint isn't even marked. The model will admit to no damage here, and the laws of physics can screw themselves.

There are people and cyclists on the street—all purely recorded. They're solid rather than ghostly, but it's an eerie kind of solidity; unstop-

pable, unswayable, they're like infinitely strong, infinitely disinterested robots. I hitch a ride on one frail old woman's back for a while; she carries me down the street, heedlessly. Her clothes, her skin, even her hair, all feel the same to me: hard as steel. Not cold, though. Neutral.

This street isn't meant to serve as anything but three-dimensional wallpaper; when Copies interact with each other, they often use cheap, recorded environments full of purely decorative crowds. Plazas, parks, open-air cafés; all very reassuring, no doubt, when you're fighting off a sense of isolation and claustrophobia. There are only about three thousand Copies in existence—a small population, split into even smaller, mutually antagonistic, cliques—and they can only receive realistic external visitors if they have friends or relatives willing to slow down their mental processes by a factor of seventeen. Most dutiful next-of-kin, I gather, prefer to exchange video recordings. Who wants to spend an afternoon with great-grandfather, when it burns up half a week of your life? Durham, of course, has removed all of my communications facilities; he can't have me blowing the whistle on him and ruining everything.

When I reach the corner of the block, the visual illusion of the city continues, far into the distance, but when I try to step forward onto the road, the concrete pavement under my feet starts acting like a treadmill, sliding backward at precisely the rate needed to keep me motionless, whatever pace I adopt. I back off and try leaping over this region, but my horizontal velocity dissipates—without the slightest pretense of any "physical" justification—and I land squarely in the middle of the treadmill.

The people of the recording, of course, cross the border with ease. One man walks straight at me; I stand my ground, and find myself pushed into a zone of increasing viscosity, the air around me becoming painfully unyielding before I slip free to one side. The software impeding me is, clearly, a set of clumsy patches which aims to cover every contingency—but which might not in fact be complete. The sense that discovering a way to breach this barrier would somehow "liberate" me is compelling—but completely irrational. Even if I did find a flaw in the program which enabled me to break through, I doubt I'd gain anything but decreasingly realistic surroundings. The recording can only contain complete information for points of view within a certain, finite zone; all there is to "escape to" is a range of coordinates where my view of the city would be full of distortions and omissions, and would eventually fade to black.

I step back from the corner, half dispirited, half amused. What did I expect to find? A big door at the edge of the model, marked EXIT, through which I could walk out into reality? Stairs leading metaphorically down to some boiler room representation of the underpinnings of this world, where I could throw a few switches and blow it all apart? Hardly. I have no right to be dissatisfied with my surroundings; they're precisely what I ordered.

It's early afternoon on a perfect spring day; I close my eyes and lift my face to the sun. Whatever I believe intellectually, there's no denying that I'm beginning to feel a purely physical sense of integrity, of identity. My skin soaks up the warmth of the sunlight. I stretch the muscles in my arms, my shoulders, my back; the sensation is perfectly ordinary, perfectly familiar—and yet I feel that I'm reaching out from the self "in my skull" to the rest of me, binding it all together, staking some kind of claim. I feel the stirrings of an erection. *Existence is beginning to seduce me.* This body doesn't want to evaporate. This body doesn't want to bail out. It doesn't much care that there's another—"more real"—version of itself elsewhere. It wants to retain its wholeness. It wants to *endure.*

And this may be a travesty of life, now—but there's always the chance of improvement. Maybe I can persuade Durham to restore my communications facilities; that would be a start. And when I get bored with holovision libraries; news systems; databases; and, if any of them

deign to meet me, the ghosts of the senile rich? I could have myself suspended until processor speeds catch up with reality—when people will be able to visit without slow-down, and telepresence robots might actually be worth inhabiting.

I open my eyes, and shiver. I don't know what I want anymore—the chance to bail out, to declare this bad dream *over* . . . or the chance of virtual immortality—but I have to accept that there's only one way that I'm going to be given a choice.

I say quietly, "I won't be your guinea pig. A collaborator, yes. An equal partner. If you want cooperation, if you want meaningful data, then you're going to have to treat me like a *colleague,* not a piece of fucking apparatus. Understood?"

A window opens up in front of me. I'm shaken by the sight, not of his ugly face, but of the room behind him. It's only my study—and I wandered through the virtual equivalent, disinterested, just minutes ago—but this is still my first glimpse of the real world, in real time. I move closer to the window, in the hope of seeing if there's anyone else in the room with him—*Elizabeth?*—but the image is two-dimensional, the perspective doesn't change.

He emits a brief, high-pitched squeak, then waits with visible impatience while a second, smaller window gives me a slowed-down replay.

"Of course it's understood. That was always my intention. I'm just glad you've finally come to your senses and decided to stop sulking. We can begin whenever you're ready."

I try to look at things objectively.

Every Copy is already an experiment—in perception, cognition, the nature of consciousness. A sub-cellular mathematical model of a specific human body is a spectacular feat of medical imaging and computing technology—but it's certainly not itself a human being. A lump of gallium arsenic phosphide awash with laser light is not a member of *Homo sapiens*—so a Copy manifestly isn't "human" in the current sense of the word.

The real question is: What does a Copy have in *common* with human beings? Information-theoretically? Psychologically? Metaphysically?

And from these similarities and differences, what can be revealed?

The Strong AI Hypothesis declares that consciousness is a property of certain algorithms, independent of their implementation. A computer which manipulates data in essentially the same way as an organic brain must possess essentially the same mental states.

Opponents point out that when you model a hurricane, nobody gets wet. When you model a fusion power plant, no energy is produced. When you model digestion and metabolism, no nutrients are consumed—no *real digestion* takes place. So when you model the human brain, why should you expect *real thought* to occur?

It depends, of course, on what you mean by "real thought." How do you characterize and compare the hypothetical mental states of two systems which are, physically, radically dissimilar? Pick the right parameters, and you can get whatever answer you like. If consciousness is defined purely in terms of physiological events—actual neurotransmitter molecules crossing synapses between real neurons—then those who oppose the Strong AI Hypothesis win, effortlessly. A hurricane requires real wind and actual drops of rain. If consciousness is defined, instead, in information-processing terms—*this* set of input data evokes *that* set of output data (and, perhaps, a certain kind of internal representation)—then the Strong AI Hypothesis is almost a tautology.

Personally, I'm no longer in a position to quibble. *Cogito ergo sum.* But if I can't doubt my own consciousness, I can't expect my testimony—the output of a mere computer program—to persuade the confirmed skeptics. Even if I passionately insisted that my inherited memories of experiencing biological consciousness were qualitatively indistinguishable from my present condition, the listener would be free to treat this outburst as nothing but a computer's

(eminently reasonable) prediction of what my original *would have said*, had he experienced exactly the same sensory input as my model-of-a-brain has received (and thus been tricked into believing that he was nothing but a Copy). The skeptics would say that comprehensive modeling of *mental states that might have been* does not require any "real thought" to have taken place.

Unless you *are* a Copy, the debate is unresolvable. For *me*, though—and for anyone willing to grant me the same presumption of consciousness that they grant their fellow humans—the debate is almost irrelevant. The real point is that there are questions about the nature of this condition which a Copy is infinitely better placed to explore than any human being.

I sit in my study, in my favorite armchair (although I'm not at all convinced that the texture of the surface has been accurately reproduced). Durham appears on my terminal—which is otherwise still dysfunctional. It's odd, but I'm already beginning to think of him as a bossy little djinn trapped inside the screen, rather than a vast, omnipotent deity striding the halls of Reality, pulling all the strings. Perhaps the pitch of his voice has something to do with it.

Squeak. Slow-motion replay: "Experiment one, trial zero. Baseline data. Time resolution one millisecond—system standard. Just count to ten, at one-second intervals, as near as you can judge it. Okay?"

I nod, irritated. I planned all this myself, I don't need step-by-step instructions. His image vanishes; during the experiments, there can't be any cues from real time.

I count. Already, I'm proving something: my subjective time, I'm sure, will differ from his by a factor very close to the ratio of model time to real time. Of course, that's been known ever since the first Copies were made—and even then, it was precisely what everyone had been expecting—but from my current perspective, I can no longer think of it as a "trivial" result.

The djinn returns. Staring at his face makes it harder, not easier, to believe that we have so much in common. My image of myself—to the extent that such a thing existed—was never much like my true appearance—and now, in defense of sanity, is moving even further away.

Squeak. "Okay. Experiment one, trial number one. Time resolution five milliseconds. Are you ready?"

"Yes."

He vanishes. I count: "One. Two. Three. Four. Five. Six. Seven. Eight. Nine. Ten."

Squeak. "Anything to report?"

I shrug. "No. I mean, I can't help feeling slightly apprehensive, just knowing that you're screwing around with my . . . infrastructure. But apart from that, nothing."

His eyes no longer glaze over while he's waiting for the speeded-up version of my reply; either he's gained a degree of self-discipline—or, more likely, he's interposed some smart editing software to conceal his boredom.

Squeak. "Don't worry about apprehension. We're running a control, remember?"

I'd rather not. Durham has cloned me, and he's feeding exactly the same sensorium to my clone, but he's only making changes in the model's time resolution for one of us. A perfectly reasonable thing to do—indeed, an essential part of the experiment—but it's still something I'd prefer not to dwell on.

Squeak. "Trial number two. Time resolution ten milliseconds."

I count to ten. The easiest thing in the world—when you're made of flesh, when you're made of matter, when the quarks and the electrons just do what comes naturally. I'm not built of quarks and electrons, though. I'm not even built of photons—I'm comprised of the data *represented by* the presence or absence of pulses of light, not the light itself.

A human being is embodied in a system of continuously interacting matter—ultimately, fields of fundamental particles, which seem to me incapable of being anything other than themselves. I am embodied in a vast set of finite, digital representations of numbers. Representa-

tions which are purely conventions. Numbers which certainly *can be* interpreted as describing aspects of a model of a human body sitting in a room . . . but it's hard to see that meaning as intrinsic, as *necessary*. Numbers whose values are recomputed—according to reasonable, but only approximately "physical," equations—for equally spaced successive values of the model's notional time.

Squeak. "Trial number three. Time resolution twenty milliseconds."

"One. Two. Three."

So, when do I experience existence? During the computation of these variables—or in the brief interludes when they sit in memory, unchanging, doing nothing but *representing* an instant of my life? When both stages are taking place a thousand times a subjective second, it hardly seems to matter, but very soon—

Squeak. "Trial number four. Time resolution fifty milliseconds."

Am I the data? The process that generates it? The relationships between the numbers? *All of the above?*

"One hundred milliseconds."

I listen to my voice as I count—as if half expecting to begin to notice the encroachment of silence, to start perceiving the gaps in myself.

"Two hundred milliseconds."

A fifth of a second. "One. Two." Am I strobing in and out of existence now, at five subjective hertz? "Three. Four. Sorry, I just—" An intense wave of nausea passes through me, but I fight it down. "Five. Six. Seven. Eight. Nine. Ten."

The *djinn* emits a brief, solicitous squeak. "Do you want a break?"

"No. I'm fine. Go ahead." I glance around the sun-dappled room, and laugh. *What will he do if the control and the subject just gave two different replies?* I try to recall my plans for such a contingency, but I can't remember them—and I don't much care. It's *his* problem now, not mine.

Squeak. "Trial number seven. Time resolution five hundred milliseconds."

I count—and the truth is, I feel no different. A

little uneasy, yes—but factoring out any meta-physical squeamishness, everything about my experience remains the same. And "of course" it does—because nothing is being omitted, in the long run. My model-of-a-brain is only being fully described at half-second (model time) intervals—but each description still includes the effects of everything that "would have happened" in between. Perhaps not quite as accurately as if the complete cycle of calculations was being carried out on a finer time scale—but that's irrelevant. Even at millisecond resolution, my models-of-neurons behave only roughly like their originals—just as any one person's neurons behave only roughly like anyone else's. Neurons aren't precision components, and they don't need to be; brains are the most fault-tolerant machines in the world.

"One thousand milliseconds."

What's more, the equations controlling the model are far too complex to solve in a single step, so in the process of calculating the solutions, vast arrays of partial results are being generated and discarded along the way. These partial results *imply*—even if they don't directly *represent*—events taking place within the gaps between successive complete descriptions. So in a sense, the intermediate states are still being described—albeit in a drastically recoded form.

"Two thousand milliseconds."

"One. Two. Three. Four."

If I seem to speak (and hear myself speak) every number, it's because the effects of having said "three" (and having heard myself say it) are implicit in the details of calculating how my brain evolves from the time when I've just said "two" to the time when I've just said "four."

"Five thousand milliseconds."

"One. Two. Three. Four. Five."

In any case, is it so much stranger to hear words that I've never "really" spoken, than it has been to hear *anything at all* since I woke? Millisecond sampling is far too coarse to resolve the full range of audible tones. Sound isn't represented in this world by fluctuations in air pressure values—which couldn't change fast enough—but in terms of audio power spectra: profiles of intensity versus frequency. Twenty kilohertz is just a number here, a label; nothing can actually *oscillate* at that rate. Real ears analyze pressure waves into components of various pitch; mine are fed the pre-existing power spectrum values directly, plucked out of the non-existent air by a crude patch in the model.

"Ten thousand milliseconds."

"One. Two. Three."

My sense of continuity remains as compelling as ever. Is this experience arising in retrospect from the final, complete description of my brain . . . or is it emerging from the partial calculations as they're being performed? What would happen if someone shut down the whole computer, right now?

I don't know what that *means*, though. In any terms but my own, I don't know when "right now" is.

"Eight. Nine. Ten."

Squeak. "How are you feeling?"

Slightly giddy—but I shrug and say, "The same as always." And basically, it's true. Aside from the unsettling effects of contemplating what might or might not have been happening to me, I can't claim to have experienced anything out of the ordinary. No altered states of consciousness, no hallucinations, no memory loss, no diminution of self-awareness, no real disorientation. "Tell me—was I the control, or the subject?"

Squeak. He grins. "I can't answer that, Paul—I'm still speaking to both of you. I'll tell you one thing, though: the two of you are still identical. There were some very small, transitory discrepancies, but they've died away completely now—and whenever the two of you were in comparable representations, all firing patterns of more than a couple of neurons were the same."

I'm curiously disappointed by this—and *my clone must be, too*—although I have no good reason to be surprised.

I say, "What did you expect? Solve the same

set of equations two different ways, and of course you get the same results—give or take some minor differences in round-off errors along the way. You *must*. It's a mathematical certainty."

Squeak. "Oh, I agree. However much we change the details of the way the model is computed, the state of the subject's brain—whenever he has one—and everything he says and does— in whatever convoluted representation—*must* match the control. Any other result would be unthinkable." He writes with his finger on the window:

$$(1 + 2) + 3 = 1 + (2 + 3)$$

I nod. "So why bother with this stage at all? I *know*—I wanted to be rigorous, I wanted to establish solid foundations. All that naive *Principia* stuff. But the truth is, it's a waste of resources. Why not skip the bleeding obvious, and get on with the kind of experiment where the answer isn't a foregone conclusion?"

Squeak. He frowns. "I didn't realize you'd grown so cynical, so quickly. AI isn't a branch of pure mathematics; it's an empirical science. Assumptions have to be tested. Confirming the so-called 'obvious' isn't such a dishonorable thing, is it? Anyway, if it's all so straightforward, what do you have to fear?"

I shake my head. "I'm not afraid; I just want to get it over with. Go ahead. Prove whatever you think you have to prove, and then we can move on."

Squeak. "That's the plan. But I think we should both get some rest now. I'll enable your communications—for incoming data only." He turns away, reaches off-screen, hits a few keys on a second terminal.

Then he turns back to me, smiling—and I know exactly what he's going to say.

Squeak. "By the way, I just deleted one of you. Couldn't afford to keep you both running, when all you're going to do is laze around."

I smile back at him, although something

inside me is screaming. "Which one did you terminate?"

Squeak. "What difference does it make? I told you, they were identical. And you're still here, aren't you? Whoever you are. Whichever you *were*."

* * *

Three weeks have passed outside since the day of the scan, but it doesn't take me long to catch up with the state of the world; most of the fine details have been rendered irrelevant by subsequent events, and much of the ebb and flow has simply canceled itself out. Israel and Palestine came close to war again, over alleged water treaty violations on both sides—but a joint peace rally brought more than a million people onto the glassy plain that used to be Jerusalem, and the governments were forced to back down. Former US President Martin Sandover is still fighting extradition to Palau, to face charges arising from his role in the bloody *coup d'état* of thirty-five; the Supreme Court finally reversed a long-standing ruling which had granted him immunity from all foreign laws, and for a day or two things looked promising—but then his legal team apparently discovered a whole new set of delaying tactics. In Canberra, another leadership challenge has come and gone, with the Prime Minister undeposed. One journalist described this as *high drama*; I guess you had to be there. Inflation has fallen half a percent; unemployment has risen by the same amount.

I scan through the old news reports rapidly, skimming over articles and fast-forwarding scenes that I probably would have studied scrupulously, had they been "fresh." I feel a curious sense of resentment, at having "missed" so much—it's all here in front of me, *now*, but that's not the same at all.

And yet, shouldn't I be relieved that I didn't waste my time on so much ephemeral detail? The very fact that I'm now disinterested only goes to show how little of it really mattered, in the long run.

Then again, what does? People don't inhabit geological time. People inhabit hours and days; they have to care about things on that time scale.

People inhabit hours and days. I don't.

I plug into real time holovision, and watch a sitcom flash by in less than two minutes, the soundtrack an incomprehensible squeal. A game show. A war movie. The evening news. It's as if I'm in deep space, rushing back toward the Earth through a sea of Doppler-shifted broadcasts— and this image is strangely comforting: my situation isn't so bizarre, after all, if *real people* could find themselves in much the same relationship with the world as I am. Nobody would claim that Doppler shift or time dilation could render someone less than human.

Dusk falls over the recorded city. I eat a microwaved soya protein stew—wondering if there's any good reason now, moral or otherwise, to continue to be a vegetarian.

I listen to music until well after midnight. Tsang Chao, Michael Nyman, Philip Glass. It makes no difference that each note "really" lasts seventeen times as long as it should, or that the audio ROM sitting in the player "really" possesses no microstructure, or that the "sound" itself is being fed into my model-of-a-brain by a computerized sleight-of-hand that bears no resemblance to the ordinary process of hearing. The climax of Glass's *Mishima* still seizes me like a grappling hook through the heart.

If the computations behind *all this* were performed over millennia, by people flicking abacus beads, would I still feel exactly the same? It's outrageous to admit it—but the answer has to be *yes*.

What does that say about real time, and real space?

I lie in bed, wondering: *Do I still want to wake from this dream?* The question remains academic, though; I still don't have any choice.

"I'd like to talk to Elizabeth."

Squeak. "That's not possible."

"Not possible? Why don't you just ask her?"

Squeak. "I can't do that, Paul. She doesn't even know you exist."

I stare at the screen. "But . . . I was going to tell her! As soon as I had a Copy who survived, I was going to tell her everything, explain everything—"

Squeak. The *djinn* says drily, "Or so we thought."

"I don't believe it! Your life's great ambition is finally being fulfilled—and you can't even share it with the one woman . . ."

Squeak. His face turns to stone. "I really don't wish to discuss this. Can we get on with the experiment, please?"

"Oh, sure. Don't let me hold things up. I almost forgot: you turned forty-five while I slept, didn't you? Many happy returns—but I'd better not waste too much time on congratulations. I don't want you dying of old age in the middle of the conversation."

Squeak. "Ah, but you're wrong. I took some short cuts while you slept—shut down ninety percent of the model, cheated on most of the rest. You got six hours' sleep in ten hours' real time. Not a bad job, I thought."

"You had no right to do that!"

Squeak. "Be practical. Ask yourself what you'd have done in my place."

"It's not a *joke!*" I can sense the streak of paranoia in my anger; I struggle to find a rational excuse. "The experiment is worthless if you're going to intervene at random. Precise, controlled changes—that's the whole point. You have to promise me you won't do it again."

Squeak. "You're the one who was complaining about waste. Someone has to think about conserving our dwindling resources."

"Promise me!"

Squeak. He shrugs. "All right. You have my word: no more ad hoc intervention."

Conserving our dwindling resources? What will he do, when he can no longer afford to keep me running? Store me until he can raise the money to start me up again, of course. In the long term, set up a trust fund; it would only have to earn enough to run me part time, at first: keep me in touch with the world, stave off excessive culture shock. Eventually, computing technology is sure to transcend the current hurdles, and once again enter a phase of plummeting costs and increasing speed.

Of course, all these reassuring plans were made by a man with two futures. *Will he really want to keep an old Copy running, when he could save his money for a death-bed scan, and "his own" immortality?* I don't know. And I may not be sure if I *want* to survive—but I wish the choice could be *mine.*

We start the second experiment. I do my best to concentrate, although I'm angry and distracted—and very nearly convinced that my dutiful introspection is pointless. Until the model itself is changed—not just the detailed way it's computed—it remains a mathematical certainty that the subject and the control will end up with identical brains. If the subject claims to have experienced anything out of the ordinary, then *so will the control*—proving that the effect was spurious.

And yet, I still can't shrug off any of this as "trivial." Durham was right about one thing: there's no dishonor in confirming the obvious—and when it's as bizarre, as counterintuitive as this, the only way to believe it is to experience it firsthand.

This time, the model will be described at the standard resolution of one millisecond, throughout—but the order in which the states are computed will be varied.

Squeak. "Experiment two, trial number one. Reverse order."

I count, "One. Two. Three." After an initial leap into the future, I'm now traveling backward through real time. I wish I could view an external event on the terminal—some entropic cliché like a vase being smashed—and dwell on the fact that it was *me*, not the image, that was being rewound . . . but that would betray the difference between subject and control. Unless the control was shown an artificially reversed version of the

same thing? Reversed how, though, if the vase was destroyed in real time? The control would have to be run separately, after the event. Ah, but even the *subject* would have to see a delayed version, because computing his real-time-first but model-time-final state would require information on all his model-time-earlier perceptions of the broken vase.

"Eight. Nine. Ten." Another imperceptible leap into the future, and the djinn reappears.

Squeak. "Trial number two. Odd numbered states, then even."

In external terms, I will count to ten . . . then forget having done so, and count again.

And from my point of view? As I count, once only, the external world—even if I can't see it—is flickering back and forth between two separate regions of time, which have been chopped up into seventeen-millisecond portions, and interleaved.

So which of us is right? Relativity may insist upon equal status for all reference frames . . . but the coordinate transformations it describes are smooth—possibly extreme, but always continuous. One observer's spacetime can be stretched and deformed in the eyes of another—but it can't be sliced like a loaf of bread, and then shuffled like a deck of cards.

"Every tenth state, in ten sets."

If I insisted on being parochial, I'd have to claim that the outside world was now rapidly cycling through fragments of time drawn from ten distinct periods. The trouble is, this allegedly shuddering universe is home to all the processes that implement me, and they *must*—in some objective, absolute sense—be running smoothly, bound together in unbroken causal flow, or I wouldn't even exist. My perspective is artificial, a contrivance relying on an underlying, continuous reality.

"Every twentieth state, in twenty sets."

Nineteen episodes of amnesia, nineteen new beginnings. How can I swallow such a convoluted explanation for ten perfectly ordinary seconds of my life?

"Every hundredth state, in one hundred sets."

I've lost any real feeling for what's happening to me. I just count.

"Pseudo-random ordering of states."

"One. Two. Three."

Now I am dust. Uncorrelated moments scattered throughout real time. Yet the pattern of my awareness remains perfectly intact: it finds itself, assembles itself from these scrambled fragments. I've been taken apart like a jigsaw puzzle—but my dissection and shuffling are transparent to me. On their own terms, the pieces remain connected.

How? Through the fact that every state reflects its entire model-time past? Is the jigsaw analogy wrong—am I more like the fragments of a hologram? But in each millisecond snapshot, do I recall and review all that's gone before? Of course not! In each snapshot, I *do* nothing. In the computations between them, then? Computations that drag me into the past and the future at random—wildly adding and subtracting experience, until it all cancels out in the end—or rather, all adds up to the very same effect as ten subjective seconds of continuity.

"Eight. Nine. Ten."

Squeak. "You're sweating."

"Both of me?"

Squeak. He laughs. "What do you think?"

"Do me a favor. The experiment is over. Shut down one of me—control or subject, I don't care."

Squeak. "Done."

"Now there's no need to conceal anything, is there? So run the pseudorandom effect on me again—and stay on-line. This time, *you* count to ten."

Squeak. He shakes his head. "Can't do it, Paul. Think about it: You can't be computed non-sequentially when past perceptions aren't known."

Of course; the broken vase problem all over again. I say, "Record yourself, then, and use that."

He seems to find the request amusing, but he indulges me; he even slows down the recording,

so it lasts ten of my own seconds. I watch his blurred lips and jaws, listen to the drone of white noise.

Squeak. "Happy now?"

"You did scramble *me*, and not the recording?"

Squeak. "Of course. Your wish is my command."

"Yeah? Then do it again."

He grimaces, but obliges.

"Now, scramble *the recording*."

It looks just the same. Of course.

"Again."

Squeak. "What's the point of all this?"

"Just do it."

I'm convinced that I'm on the verge of a profound insight—arising, not from any revelatory aberration in my mental processes, but from the "obvious," "inevitable" fact that the wildest permutations of the relationship between model time and real time leave me perfectly intact. I've accepted the near certainty of this, tacitly, for twenty years—but the experience is provocative in a way that the abstract understanding never could be.

It needs to be pushed further, though. The truth has to be shaken out of me.

"When do we move on to the next stage?"

Squeak. "Why so keen all of a sudden?"

"Nothing's changed. I just want to get it over and done with."

Squeak. "Well, lining up all the other machines is taking some delicate negotiations. The network allocation software isn't designed to accommodate whims about geography. It's a bit like going to a bank and asking to deposit some money . . . at a certain location in a particular computer's memory. Basically, people think I'm crazy."

I feel a momentary pang of empathy, recalling my own anticipation of these difficulties. *Empathy verging on identification.* I smother it, though; we're two utterly different people now, with different problems and different goals, and the stupidest thing I could do would be to forget that.

Squeak. "I could suspend you while I finalize the arrangements, save you the boredom, if that's what you want."

I have a lot to think about, and not just the implications of the last experiment. If he gets into the habit of shutting me down at every opportunity, I'll "soon" find myself faced with decisions that I'm not prepared to make.

"Thanks. But I'd rather wait."

I walk around the block a few times, to stretch my legs and switch off my mind. I can't dwell on the knowledge of what I am, every waking moment; if I did, I'd soon go mad. There's no doubt that the familiar streetscape helps me forget my bizarre nature, lets me take myself for granted and run on autopilot for a while.

It's hard to separate fact from rumor, but apparently even the gigarich tend to live in relatively mundane surroundings, favoring realism over power fantasies. A few models-of-psychotics have reportedly set themselves up as dictators in opulent palaces, waited on hand and foot, but most Copies have aimed for an illusion of continuity. If you desperately want to convince yourself that you *are* the same person as your memories suggest, the worst thing to do would be to swan around a virtual antiquity (with mod cons), pretending to be Cleopatra or Ramses II.

I certainly don't believe that I "am" my original, but . . . why do I believe that I exist *at all*? What gives me my sense of identity? Continuity. Consistency. Once I would have dragged in *cause and effect*, but I'm not sure that I still can. The cause and effect that underlies me bears no resemblance whatsoever to the pattern of my experience—not now, and least of all when the software was dragging me back and forth through time. I can't deny that the computer which runs me is obeying the real-time physical laws—and I'm sure that, to a real-time observer, those laws would provide a completely satisfactory explanation for every pulse of laser light that constitutes my world, my flesh, my being. And

yet . . . if it makes *no perceptible difference to me* whether I'm a biological creature, embodied in real cells built of real proteins built of real atoms built of real electrons and quarks . . . or a randomly time-scrambled set of descriptions of a crude model-of-a-brain . . . then surely *the pattern* is all, and cause and effect are irrelevant. The whole experience might just as well have arisen by chance.

Is that conceivable? Suppose an intentionally haywire computer sat for a thousand years or more, twitching from state to state in the sway of nothing but electrical noise. *Might it embody consciousness?*

In real time, the answer is: *Probably not*—the chance of any kind of coherence arising at random being so small. Real time, though, is only one possible reference frame; what about all the others? If the states the machine passed through can be re-ordered in time arbitrarily (with some states omitted—perhaps *most* omitted, if need be) then who knows what kind of elaborate order might emerge from the chaos?

Is that fatuous? As absurd, as empty, as claiming that every large-enough quantity of rock—contiguous or not—contains Michelangelo's *David*, and every warehouse full of paint and canvas contains the complete works of Rembrandt and Picasso—not in any mere latent form, awaiting some skilful forger to physically rearrange them, but *solely by virtue of the potential redefinition of the coordinates of space-time?*

For a statue or a painting, yes, it's a hollow claim—where is the observer who perceives the paint to be in contact with the canvas, the stone figure to be suitably delineated by air?

If the pattern in question is *not* an isolated object, though, but *a self-contained world*, complete with at least one observer to join up the dots . . .

There's no doubt that it's possible. *I've done* it. I've assembled myself and my world—effortlessly—from the dust of randomly scattered states, from apparent noise in real time. Specially contrived noise, admittedly—but given enough of the real thing, there's no reason to believe that some subset of it wouldn't include patterns, embody relationships, as complex and coherent as the ones which underly me.

I return to the apartment, fighting off a sense of giddiness and unreality. *Do I still want to bail out?* No. No! I still wish that he'd never created me— but how can I declare that I'd happily wake and forget myself—wake and "reclaim" my life— when already I've come to an insight that he never would have reached himself?

The *djinn* looks tired and frayed; all the begging and bribery he must have been through to set this up seems to have taken its toll.

Squeak. "Experiment three, trial zero. Baseline data. All computations performed by processor cluster number four six two, Hitachi Super-computer Facility, Tokyo."

"One. Two. Three." *Nice to know where I am, at last. Never visited Japan before.* "Four. Five. Six." *And in my own terms, I still haven't. The view out the window is Sydney, not Tokyo. Why should I defer to external descriptions?* "Seven. Eight. Nine. Ten."

Squeak. "Trial number one. Model partitioned into five hundred sections, run on five hundred processor clusters, distributed globally."

I count. *Five hundred clusters.* Five only for the crudely modeled external world; all the rest are allocated to my body—and most to the brain, of course. I lift my hand to my eyes—and the information flow that grants me motor control and sight now traverses tens of thousands of kilometers of optical cable. This introduces no perceptible delays; each part of me simply hibernates when necessary, waiting for the requisite feedback from around the world. Moderately distributed processing is one thing, but this is pure lunacy, computationally and economically. I must be costing at least a hundred times as much as usual—not quite five hundred, since each cluster's capacity is only being partly used—and my model-time to real-time factor must be more like fifty than seventeen.

Squeak. "Trial number two. One thousand sections, one thousand clusters."

Brain the size of a planet—and here I am, counting to ten. I recall the perennial—naïve and paranoid—fear that all the networked computers of the world might one day spontaneously give birth to a global hypermind—but I am, almost certainly, the first planet-sized intelligence on Earth. I don't feel much like a digital Gaia, though. I feel like an ordinary human being sitting in an ordinary armchair.

Squeak. "Trial number three. Model partitioned into fifty sections and twenty time sets, implemented on one thousand clusters."

"One. Two. Three." I try to imagine the outside world in my terms, but it's almost impossible. Not only am I scattered across the globe, but widely separated machines are simultaneously computing different moments of model-time. Is the distance from Tokyo to New York now the length of my *corpus callosum*? Has the planet been shrunk to the size of my skull—and banished from time altogether, except for the fifty points that contribute to my notion of the present?

Such a pathological transformation seems nonsensical—but in some hypothetical space traveler's eyes, the whole planet is virtually frozen in time and flat as a pancake. Relativity declares that this point of view is perfectly valid—but mine is not. Relativity permits continuous deformation, but no cutting and pasting. *Why?* Because it must allow for *cause and effect*. Influences must be localized, traveling from point to point at a finite velocity; chop up space-time and rearrange it, and the causal structure would fall apart.

What if you're an observer, though, who has no *causal structure?* A self-aware pattern appearing by chance in the random twitches of a noise machine, your time coordinate dancing back and forth through causally respectable "real time"? Why should you be declared a second-class being, with no right to see the universe your way? What fundamental difference is there between so-called cause and effect, and any other internally consistent pattern of perceptions?

Squeak. "Trial number four. Model partitioned into fifty sections; sections and states pseudo-randomly allocated to one thousand clusters."

"One. Two. Three."

I stop counting, stretch my arms wide, stand. I wheel around once, to examine the room, checking that it's still intact, complete. Then I whisper, "This is dust. *All dust.* This room, this moment, is scattered across the planet, scattered across five hundred seconds or more—*and yet it remains whole.* Don't you see what that means?"

The djinn reappears, frowning, but I don't give him a chance to chastise me.

"Listen! If I can assemble myself, this room— if I can construct my own coherent space-time out of nothing but scattered fragments—*then what makes you think that you're not doing the very same thing?*

"Imagine . . . a universe completely without structure, without topology. No space, no time; just a set of random events. I'd call them 'isolated,' but that's not the right word; there's simply *no such thing as distance.* Perhaps I shouldn't even say 'random,' since that makes it sound like there's some kind of natural order in which to consider them, one by one, and find them random—but there isn't.

"What *are* these events? We'd describe them as points in space-time, and assign them coordinates—times and places—but if that's not permitted, what's left? Values of all the fundamental particle fields? Maybe even that's assuming too much. Let's just say that each event is a collection of numbers.

"Now, if the pattern that is *me* could pick itself out from the background noise of all the other events taking place on this planet . . . then why shouldn't the pattern we think of as 'the universe' assemble itself, find itself, in exactly the same way?"

The djinn's expression hovers between alarm and irritation.

Squeak. "Paul . . . I don't see the point of any of this. Space-time is a construct; the *real* universe is nothing but a sea of disconnected events . . . it's all just metaphysical waffle. An unfalsifiable hypothesis. What explanatory value does it have? What difference would it make?"

"*What difference?* We perceive—*we inhabit*—one arrangement of the set of events. But why should that arrangement be *unique?* There's no reason to believe that the pattern we've found is the only coherent way of ordering the dust. There must be billions of other universes coexisting with us, made of the very same stuff—just differently arranged. If I can perceive events thousands of kilometers and hundreds of seconds apart to be side-by-side and simultaneous, there could be worlds, and creatures, built up from what we'd think of as points in space-time scattered all over the galaxy, all over the universe. We're one possible solution to a giant cosmic anagram . . . but it would be ludicrous to think that we're the only one."

Squeak. "So where are all the left-over letters? If this primordial alphabet soup really is random, don't you think it's highly unlikely that we could structure the whole thing?"

That throws me, but only for a moment. "We *haven't* structured the whole thing. The universe is random, at the quantum level. Macroscopically, the pattern seems to be perfect; microscopically, it decays into uncertainty. We've swept the residue of randomness down to the lowest level. The anagram analogy's flawed; the building blocks are more like random pixels than random letters. Given a sufficient number of random pixels, you could construct virtually any image you liked— but under close inspection, the randomness would be revealed."

Squeak. "None of this is testable. How would we ever observe a planet whose constituent parts were scattered across the universe? Let alone communicate with its hypothetical inhabitants? I don't doubt that what you're saying has a certain—purely mathematical—validity: grind the universe down to a fine enough level, and I'm sure the dust could be rearranged in other ways that make as much sense as the original. If these rearranged worlds are inaccessible, though, it's all angels on the heads of pins."

"How can you say that? I've *been* rearranged! I've *visited* another world!"

Squeak. "If you did, it was an artificial world; created, not discovered."

"Found a pattern, created a pattern . . . there's no real difference."

Squeak. "Paul, you know that everything you experienced was due to the way your model was programmed; there's no need to invoke *other worlds.* The state of your brain at every moment can be explained completely in terms of *this* arrangement of time and space."

"Of course! Your pattern hasn't been violated; the computers did exactly what was expected of them. That doesn't make my perspective any less valid, though. Stop thinking of explanations, causes and effects; there are only *patterns.* The scattered events that formed my experience had an internal consistency every bit as real as the consistency in the actions of the computers. And perhaps the computers didn't provide all of it."

Squeak. "What do you mean?"

"The gaps, in experiment one. What filled them in? What was I made of, when the processors weren't describing me? Well . . . it's a big universe. Plenty of dust to *be me,* in between descriptions. Plenty of events—nothing to do with your computers, maybe nothing to do with your planet or your epoch—out of which to construct ten seconds of experience, consistent with everything that had gone before—and everything yet to come."

Squeak. The *djinn* looks seriously worried now. "Paul, listen: you're a Copy in a virtual environment under computer control. Nothing more, nothing less. These experiments prove that your internal sense of space and time is invariant—as expected. But your states are *computed,* your memories *have to be* what they would have been without manipulation. You haven't visited any other worlds, you haven't built yourself out of fragments of distant galaxies."

I laugh. "Your stupidity is . . . surreal. What the fuck did you *create me* for, if you're not even going to *listen* to me? We've stumbled onto some-

thing of cosmic importance! Forget about farting around with the details of neural models; we have to devote all our resources to exploring this further. We've had a glimpse of the truth behind . . . *everything*: space, time, the laws of physics. You can't shrug that off by saying that my states were *inevitable.*"

Squeak. "Control and subject are still identical."

I scream with exasperation. "Of *course* they are, you moron! That's the whole point! Like acceleration and gravity in General Relativity, it's the equivalent experience of two different observers that blows the old paradigm apart."

Squeak. The *djinn* mutters, dismayed, "Elizabeth said this would happen. She said it was only a matter of time before you'd lose touch."

I stare at him. "*Elizabeth?* You said you hadn't even told her!"

Squeak. "Well, I have. I didn't let you know, because I didn't think you'd want to hear her reaction."

"Which was?"

Squeak. "She wanted to shut you down. She said I was . . . seriously disturbed, to even think about doing this. She said she'd find help for me."

"Yeah? Well, what would *she* know? Ignore her!"

Squeak. He frowns apologetically, an expression I recognize from the inside, and my guts turn to ice. "Paul, maybe I should pause you, while I think things over. Elizabeth *does* care about me, more than I realized. I should talk it through with her again."

"No. Oh, shit, no." *He won't restart me from this point. Even if he doesn't abandon the project, he'll go back to the scan, and try something different, to keep me in line. Maybe he won't perform the first experiments at all—the ones which gave me this insight. The ones which made me who I am.*

Squeak. "Only temporarily. I promise. Trust me."

"Paul. Please."

He reaches off-screen.

"No!"

There's a hand gripping my forearm. I try to shake it off, but my arm barely moves, and a terrible aching starts up in my shoulder. I open my eyes, close them again in pain. I try again. On the fifth or sixth attempt, I manage to see a face through washed-out brightness and tears.

Elizabeth.

She holds a cup to my lips. I take a sip, splutter and choke, but then force some of the thin sweet liquid down.

She says, "You'll be okay soon. Just don't try to move too quickly."

"Why are you here?" I cough, shake my head, wish I hadn't. I'm touched, but confused. Why did my original lie, and claim that she wanted to shut me down, when in fact she was sympathetic enough to go through the arduous process of visiting me?

I'm lying on something like a dentist's couch, in an unfamiliar room. I'm in a hospital gown; there's a drip in my right arm, and a catheter in my urethra. I glance up to see an interface helmet, a bulky hemisphere of magnetic axon current inducers, suspended from a gantry, not far above my head. Fair enough, I suppose, to construct a simulated meeting place that looks like the room that her real body must be in; putting me in the couch, though, and giving me all the symptoms of a waking visitor, seems a little extreme.

I tap the couch with my left hand. "What's the point of all this? You want me to know exactly what you're going through? Okay. I'm grateful. And it's good to see you." I shudder with relief, and delayed shock. "Fantastic, to tell the truth." I laugh weakly. "I honestly thought he was going to wipe me out. The man's a complete lunatic. Believe me, you're talking to his better half."

She's perched on a stool beside me. "Paul. Try to listen carefully to what I'm going to say. You'll start to reintegrate the suppressed memories gradually, on your own, but it'll help if I talk you through it all first. To start with, you're not a Copy. You're flesh and blood."

I stare at her. "What kind of sadistic joke is that? Do you know how hard it was, how long it took me, to come to terms with the truth?"

She shakes her head. "It's not a joke. I know you don't remember yet, but after you made the scan that was going to run as Copy number five, you finally told me what you were doing. And I persuaded you not to run it—until you'd tried another experiment: putting yourself in its place. Finding out, first hand, what it would be forced to go through.

"And you agreed. You entered the virtual environment which the Copy would have inhabited—with your memories since the day of the scan suppressed, so you had no way of knowing that you were only a visitor."

Her face betrays no hint of deception—but software can smooth that out. "I don't believe you. How can I be the original? I *spoke to* the original. What am I supposed to believe? *He* was the Copy?"

She sighs, but says patiently, "Of course not. That would hardly spare the Copy any trauma, would it? The scan was never run. I controlled the puppet that played your 'original'—software provided the vocabulary signature and body language, but I pulled the strings."

I shake my head, and whisper, "Bremsstrahlung." No interface window appears. I grip the couch and close my eyes, then laugh. "You say I agreed to this? What kind of masochist would do that? I'm going out of my mind! *I don't know what I am!*"

She takes hold of my arm again. "Of course you're still disoriented—but trust me, it won't last long. And you *know* why you agreed. You were sick of Copies bailing out on you. One way or another, you have to come to terms with their experience. Spending a few days believing you were a Copy would make or break the project: you'd either end up truly prepared, at last, to give rise to a Copy who'd be able to cope with its fate—or you'd gain enough sympathy for their plight to stop creating them."

A technician comes into the room and

removes my drip and catheter. I prop myself up and look out through the windows of the room's swing doors; I can see half a dozen people in the corridor. I bellow wordlessly at the top of my lungs; they all turn to stare in my direction. The technician says, mildly, "Your penis might sting for an hour or two."

I slump back onto the couch and turn to Elizabeth. "You wouldn't pay for reactive crowds. I wouldn't pay for reactive crowds. Looks like you're telling the truth."

People, glorious *people*: thousands of strangers, meeting my eyes with suspicion or puzzlement, stepping out of my way on the street—or, more often, clearly, consciously refusing to. I'll never feel alone in a crowd again; I remember what *true* invisibility is like.

The freedom of the city is so sweet. I walked the streets of Sydney for a full day, exploring every ugly shopping arcade, every piss-stinking litter-strewn park and alley, until, with aching feet, I squeezed my way home through the evening rush-hour, to watch the real-time news.

There is no room for doubt: I am not in a virtual environment. Nobody in the world could have reason to spend so much money, simply to deceive me.

When Elizabeth asks if my memories are back, I nod and say, of course. She doesn't grill me on the details. In fact, having gone over her story so many times in my head, I can almost imagine the stages: my qualms after the fifth scan, repeatedly putting off running the model, confessing to Elizabeth about the project, accepting her challenge to experience for myself just what my Copies were suffering.

And if the suppressed memories haven't actually integrated, well, I've checked the literature, and there's a 2.5 percent risk of that happening.

I have an account from the database service which shows that I consulted the very same articles before.

I reread and replayed the news reports that I accessed from inside; I found no discrepancies.

In fact, I've been reading a great deal of history, geography, and astronomy, and although I'm surprised now and then by details that I'd never learnt before, I can't say that I've come across anything that definitely contradicts my prior understanding.

Everything is consistent. Everything is explicable.

I still can't stop wondering, though, what might happen to a Copy who's shut down, and never run again. A normal human death is one thing—woven into a much vaster tapestry, it's a process that makes perfect sense. From the internal point of view of a Copy whose model is simply *halted*, though, there is no explanation whatsoever for this "death"—just an edge where the pattern abruptly ends.

If a Copy could assemble itself from dust scattered across the world, and bridge the gaps in its existence with dust from across the universe, why should it ever come to an *inconsistent* end? Why shouldn't the pattern keep on finding itself? Or find, perhaps, a *larger* pattern into which it could merge?

Perhaps it's pointless to aspire to know the truth. If I *was* a Copy, and "found" this world, this arrangement of dust, then the seam will be, *must* be, flawless. For the patterns to merge, both "explanations" must be equally true. If I was a Copy, then it's also true that I was the flesh-and-blood Paul Durham, believing he was a Copy.

Once I had two futures. Now I have two pasts.

Elizabeth asked me yesterday what decision I'd reached: to abandon my life's obsession, or to forge ahead, now that I know firsthand what's involved. My answer disappointed her, and I'm not sure if I'll ever see her again.

In this world.

Today, I'm going to be scanned for the sixth time. I can't give up now. I can't discover the truth—but that doesn't mean that nobody *else* can. If I make a Copy, run him for a few virtual days, then terminate him abruptly . . . then *he*, at least, will know if his pattern of experience continues. Again, there will be an "explanation"; again, the "new" flesh-and-blood Paul Durham will have an extra past. Inheriting my memories, perhaps he will repeat the whole process again.

And again. And *again*. Although the seams will always be perfect, the "explanations" will necessarily grow ever more "contrived," less convincing, and the dust hypothesis will become ever more compelling.

I lie in bed in the predawn light, waiting for sunrise, staring into the future down this corridor of mirrors.

One thing nags at me. I could swear I had a dream—an elaborate fable, conveying some kind of insight—but my dreams are evanescent, and I don't expect to remember what it was.

Chapter 24

Daryl Gregory

SECOND PERSON, PRESENT TENSE

If you think, "I breathe," the "I" is extra. There is no you to say "I." What we call "I" is just a swinging door which moves when we inhale or when we exhale.
—Shun Ryu Suzuki

I used to think the brain was the most important organ in the body, until I realized who was telling me that.
—Emo Phillips

When I enter the office, Dr. S is leaning against the desk, talking earnestly to the dead girl's parents. He isn't happy, but when he looks up he puts on a smile for me. "And here she is," he says, like a game show host revealing the grand prize. The people in the chairs turn, and Dr. Subramaniam gives me a private, encouraging wink.

The father stands first, a blotchy, square-faced man with a tight belly he carries like a basketball. As in our previous visits, he is almost frowning, struggling to match his face to his emotions. The mother, though, has already been crying, and her face is wide open: joy, fear, hope, relief. It's way over the top.

"Oh, Therese," she says. "Are you ready to come home?"

Their daughter was named Therese. She died of an overdose almost two years ago, and since then Mitch and Alice Klass have visited this hospital dozens of times, looking for her. They desperately want me to be their daughter, and so in their heads I already am.

My hand is still on the door handle. "Do I have a choice?" On paper I'm only seventeen years old. I have no money, no credit cards, no job, no car. I own only a handful of clothes. And Robierto, the burliest orderly on the ward, is in the hallway behind me, blocking my escape.

Therese's mother seems to stop breathing for a moment. She's a slim, narrow-boned woman who seems tall until she stands next to anyone. Mitch raises a hand to her shoulder, then drops it.

As usual, whenever Alice and Mitch come to visit, I feel like I've walked into the middle of a soap opera and no one's given me my lines. I look directly at Dr. S, and his face is frozen into that professional smile. Several times over the past year he's convinced them to let me stay longer, but they're not listening anymore. They're my legal guardians, and they have Other Plans. Dr. S looks away from me, rubs the side of his nose.

"That's what I thought," I say.

The father scowls. The mother bursts into fresh tears, and she cries all the way out of the building. Dr. Subramaniam watches from the entrance as we drive away, his hands in his pockets. I've never been so angry with him in my life—all two years of it.

The name of the drug is Zen, or Zombie, or just Z. Thanks to Dr. S I have a pretty good idea of how it killed Therese.

"Flick your eyes to the left," he told me one

afternoon. "Now glance to the right. Did you see the room blur as your eyes moved?" He waited until I did it again. "No blur. No one sees it."

This is the kind of thing that gets brain doctors hot and bothered. Not only could no one see the blur, their brains edited it out completely. Skipped over it—left view, then right view, with nothing between—then fiddled with the person's time sense so that it didn't even *seem* missing.

The scientists figured out that the brain was editing out shit all the time. They wired up patients and told them to lift one of their fingers, move it any time they wanted. Each time, the brain started the signal traveling toward the finger up to 120 milliseconds *before* the patient consciously decided to move it. Dr. S said you could see the brain warming up right before the patient consciously thought, *now*.

This is weird, but it gets weirder the longer you think about it. And I've been thinking about this a lot.

The conscious mind—the "I" that's thinking, hey, I'm thirsty, I'll reach for that cold cup of water—hasn't really decided anything. The signal to start moving your hand has already traveled halfway down your arm by the time *you* even realize *you* are thirsty. *Thought* is an afterthought. By the way, the brain says, we've decided to move your arm, so please have the thought to move it.

The gap is normally 120 milliseconds, max. Zen extends this minutes. Hours.

If you run into somebody who's on Zen, you won't notice much. The person's brain is still making decisions, and the body still follows orders. You can talk to the them, and they can talk to you. You can tell each other jokes, go out for hamburgers, do homework, have sex.

But the person isn't conscious. There is no "I" there. You might as well be talking to a computer. And *two* people on Zen—"you" and "I"—are just puppets talking to puppets.

It's a little girl's room strewn with teenager.

Stuffed animals crowd the shelves and window sills, shoulder to shoulder with stacks of Christian rock CDs and hair brushes and bottles of nail polish. Pin-ups from *Teen People* are taped to the wall, next to a bulletin board dripping with soccer ribbons and rec league gymnastics medals going back to second grade. Above the desk, a plaque titled "I Promise . . ." exhorting Christian youth to abstain from premarital sex. And everywhere taped and pinned to the walls, the photos: Therese at Bible camp, Therese on the balance beam, Therese with her arms around her youth group friends. Every morning she could open her eyes to a thousand reminders of who she was, who she'd been, who she was supposed to become.

I pick up the big stuffed panda that occupies the place of pride on the bed. It looks older than me, and the fur on the face is worn down to the batting. The button eyes hang by white thread—they've been re-sewn, maybe more than once.

Therese's father sets down the pitifully small bag that contains everything I've taken from the hospital: toiletries, a couple of changes of clothes, and five of Dr. S's books. "I guess old Boo Bear was waiting for you," he says.

"Boo W. Bear."

"Yes, Boo W!" It pleases him that I know this. As if it proves anything. "You know, your mother dusted this room every week. She never doubted that you'd come back."

I have never been here, and *she* is not coming back, but already I'm tired of correcting pronouns. "Well, that was nice," I say.

"She's had a tough time of it. She knew people were talking, probably holding her responsible—both of us, really. And she was worried about them saying things about you. She couldn't stand them thinking that you were a wild girl."

"Them?"

He blinks. "The Church."

Ah. *The Church.* The term carried so many feelings and connotations for Therese that months ago I stopped trying to sort them out. The

Church was the red-brick building of the Davenport Church of Christ, shafts of dusty light through rows of tall, glazed windows shaped like gravestones. The Church was God and the Holy Ghost (but not Jesus—he was personal, separate somehow). Mostly, though, it was the congregation, dozens and dozens of people who'd known her since before she was born. They loved her, they watched out for her, and they evaluated her every step. It was like having a hundred overprotective parents.

I almost laugh. "The Church thinks Therese was wild?"

He scowls, but whether because I've insulted the Church or because I keep referring to his daughter by name, I'm not sure. "Of course not. It's just that you caused a lot of worry." His voice has assumed a sober tone that's probably never failed to unnerve his daughter. "You know, the Church prayed for you every week."

"They did?" I do know Therese well enough to be sure this would have mortified her. She was a pray-er, not a pray-ee.

Therese's father watches my face for the bloom of shame, maybe a few tears. From contrition it should have been one small step to confession. It's hard for me to take any of this seriously.

I sit down on the bed and sink deep into the mattress. This is not going to work. The double bed takes up most of the room, with only a few feet of open space around it. Where am I going to meditate?

"Well," Therese's father says. His voice has softened. Maybe he thinks he's won. "You probably want to get changed," he says.

He goes to the door but doesn't leave. I stand by the window, but I can feel him there, waiting. Finally the oddness of this makes me turn around.

He's staring at the floor, a hand behind his neck. Therese might have been able to intuit his mood, but it's beyond me.

"We want to help you, Therese. But there's so many things we just don't understand. Who gave you the drugs, why you went off with that boy,

why you would—" His hand moves, a stifled gesture that could be anger, or just frustration. "It's just . . . hard."

"I know," I say. "Me too."

He shuts the door when he leaves, and I push the panda to the floor and flop onto my back in relief. Poor Mr. Klass. He just wants to know if his daughter fell from grace, or was pushed.

When I want to freak myself out, "I" think about "me" thinking about having an "I." The only thing stupider than puppets talking to puppets is a puppet talking to itself.

Dr. S says that nobody knows what the mind is, or how the brain generates it, and nobody *really* knows about consciousness. We talked almost every day while I was in the hospital, and after he saw that I was interested in this stuff— how could I *not* be?—he gave me books and we'd talk about brains and how they cook up thoughts and make decisions.

"How do I explain this?" he always starts. And then he tries out the metaphors he's working on for his book. My favorite is the Parliament, the Page, and the Queen.

"The brain isn't one thing, of course," he told me. "It's millions of firing cells, and those resolve into hundreds of active sites, and so it is with the mind. There are dozens of nodes in the mind, each one trying to out-shout the others. For any decision, the mind erupts with noise, and that triggers . . . how do I explain this . . . Have you ever seen the British Parliament on C-SPAN?" Of course I had: in a hospital, TV is a constant companion. "These members of the mind's parliament, they're all shouting in chemicals and electrical charges, until enough of the voices are shouting in unison. Ding! That's a 'thought,' a 'decision.' The Parliament immediately sends a signal to the body to act on the decision, and at the same time it tells the Page to take the news—"

"Wait, who's the Page?"

He waves his hand. "That's not important right now." (Weeks later, in a different discussion, Dr. S will explain that the Page isn't one thing, but a cascade of neural events in the temporal area of the limbic system that meshes the neural map of the new thought with the existing neural map—but by then I know that "neural map" is just another metaphor for another deeply complex thing or process, and that I'll never get to the bottom of this. Dr. S said not to worry about it, that nobody gets to the bottom of it.) "The Page takes the news of the decision to the Queen."

"All right then, who's the Queen? Consciousness?"

"Exactly right! The self itself."

He beamed at me, his attentive student. Talking about this stuff gets Dr. S going like nothing else, but he's oblivious to the way I let the neck of my scrubs fall open when I stretch out on the couch. If only I could have tucked the two hemispheres of my brain into a lace bra.

"The Page," he said, "delivers its message to Her Majesty, telling her what the Parliament has decided. The Queen doesn't need to know about all the other arguments that went on, all the other possibilities that were thrown out. She simply needs to know what to announce to her subjects. The Queen tells the parts of the body to act on the decision."

"Wait, I thought the Parliament had already sent out the signal. You said before that you can see the brain warming up before the self even knows about it."

"That's the joke. The Queen announces the decision, and she thinks that her subjects are obeying her commands, but in reality, they have already been told what to do. They're already reaching for their glasses of water."

I pad down to the kitchen in bare feet, wearing Therese's sweatpants and a T-shirt. The shirt is a little tight; Therese, champion dieter and Olympic-level purger, was a bit smaller than me.

Alice is at the table, already dressed, a book open in front of her. "Well, you slept in this morning," she says brightly. Her face is made up, her hair sprayed into place. The coffee cup next to the book is empty. She's been waiting for hours.

I look around for a clock, and find one over the door. It's only nine. At the hospital I slept in later than that all the time. "I'm starved," I say. There's a refrigerator, a stove, and dozens of cabinets.

I've never made my own breakfast. Or any lunch or dinner, for that matter. For my entire life, my meals have been served on cafeteria trays. "Do you have scrambled eggs?"

She blinks. "Eggs? You don't—" She abruptly stands. "Sure. Sit down, Therese, and I'll make you some."

"Just call me 'Terry,' okay?"

Alice stops, thinks about saying something—I can almost hear the clank of cogs and ratchets—until she abruptly strides to the cabinet, crouches, and pulls out a non-stick pan.

I take a guess on which cabinet holds the coffee mugs, guess right, and take the last inch of coffee from the pot. "Don't you have to go to work?" I say. Alice does something at a restaurant supply company; Therese has always been hazy on the details.

"I've taken a leave," she says. She cracks an egg against the edge of the pan, does something subtle with the shells as the yolk squeezes out and plops into the pan, and folds the shell halves into each other. All with one hand.

"Why?"

She smiles tightly. "We couldn't just abandon you after getting you home. I thought we might need some time together. During this adjustment period."

"So when do I have to see this therapist? Whatsisname." My executioner.

"Her. Dr. Mehldau's in Baltimore, so we'll drive there tomorrow." This is their big plan. Dr. Subramaniam couldn't bring back Therese, so they're running to anyone who says they can. "You know, she's had a lot of success with people in your situation. That's her book." She nods at the table.

"So? Dr. Subramaniam is writing one too." I pick up the book. *The Road Home: Finding the Lost Children of Zen.* "What if I don't go along with this?"

She says nothing, chopping at the eggs. I'll be eighteen in four months. Dr. S said that it will become a lot harder for them to hold me then. This ticking clock sounds constantly in my head, and I'm sure it's loud enough for Alice and Mitch to hear it too.

"Let's just try Dr. Mehldau first."

"First? What then?" She doesn't answer. I flash on an image of me tied down to the bed, a priest making a cross over my twisting body. It's a fantasy, not a Therese memory—I can tell the difference. Besides, if this had already happened to Therese, it wouldn't have been a priest.

"Okay then," I say. "What if I just run away?"

"If you turn into a fish," she says lightly, "then I will turn into a fisherman and fish for you."

"What?" I'm laughing. I haven't heard Alice speak in anything but straightforward, earnest sentences.

Alice's smile is sad. "You don't remember?"

"Oh, yeah." The memory clicks. "*Runaway Bunny.* Did she like that?"

Dr. S's book is about me. Well, Zen O.D.-ers in general, but there are only a couple thousand of us. Z's not a hugely popular drug, in the U.S. or anywhere else. It's not a hallucinogen. It's not a euphoric or a depressant. You don't speed, mellow out, or even get high in the normal sense. It's hard to see what the attraction is. Frankly, I have trouble seeing it.

Dr. S says that most drugs aren't about making you feel better, they're about not feeling anything at all. They're about numbness, escape. And Zen is a kind of arty, designer escape hatch. Zen disables the Page, locks him in his room, so that he can't make his deliveries to the Queen. There's no update to the neural map, and the Queen stops hearing what Parliament is up to. With no orders to bark, she goes

silent. It's that silence that people like Therese craved.

But the real attraction—again, for people like Therese—is the overdose. Swallow way too much Zen and the Page can't get out for weeks. When he finally gets out, he can't remember the way back to the Queen's castle. The whole process of updating the self that's been going on for years is suddenly derailed. The silent Queen can't be found.

The Page, poor guy, does the only thing he can. He goes out and delivers the proclamations to the first girl he sees.

The Queen is dead. Long live the Queen.

"Hi, Terry. I'm Dr. Mehldau." She's a stubby woman with a pleasant round face, and short dark hair shot with gray. She offers me her hand. Her fingers are cool and thin.

"You called me Terry."

"I was told that you prefer to go by that. Do you want me to call you something else?"

"No . . . I just expected you to make me say my name is 'Therese' over and over."

She laughs and sits down in a red leather chair that looks soft but sturdy. "I don't think that would be very helpful, do you? I can't make you do anything you don't want to do, Terry."

"So I'm free to go."

"Can't stop you. But I do have to report back to your parents on how we're doing."

My parents.

She shrugs. "It's my job. Why don't you have a seat and we can talk about why you're here."

The chair opposite her is cloth, not leather, but it's still nicer than anything in Dr. Subramaniam's office. The entire office is nicer than Dr. S's office. Daffodil walls in white trim, big windows glowing behind white cloth shades, tropically colored paintings.

I don't sit down.

"Your job is to turn me into Mitch and Alice's daughter. I'm not going to do that. So any time we spend talking is just bullshit."

"Terry, no one can turn you into something you're not."

"Well then we're done here." I walk across the room—though "stroll" is what I'm shooting for—and pick up an African-looking wooden doll from the bookshelf. The shelves are decorated with enough books to look serious, but there are long open spaces for arty arrangements of candle-sticks and Japanese fans and plaques that advertise awards and appreciations. Dr. S's bookshelves are for holding books, and books stacked on books. Dr. Mehldau's book-shelves are for selling the idea of Dr. Mehldau.

"So what are you, a psychiatrist or a psychologist or what?" I've met all kinds in the hospital. The psychiatrists are MDs like Dr. S and can give you drugs. I haven't figured out what the psychologists are good for.

"Neither," she says. "I'm a counselor."

"So what's the 'doctor' for?"

"Education." Her voice didn't change, but I get the impression that the question's annoyed her. This makes me strangely happy.

"Okay, Dr. Counselor, what are you supposed to counsel me about? I'm not crazy. I know who Therese was, I know what she did, I know that she used to walk around in my body." I put the doll back in its spot next to a glass cube that could be a paperweight. "But I'm not her. This is my body, and I'm not going to kill myself just so Alice and Mitch can have their baby girl back."

"Terry, no one's asking you to kill yourself. Nobody can even make you into who you were before."

"Yeah? Then what are they paying you for, then?"

"Let me try to explain. Please, sit down. Please."

I look around for a clock and finally spot one on a high shelf. I mentally set the timer to five minutes and sit opposite her, hands on my knees. "Shoot."

"Your parents asked me to talk to you because I've helped other people in your situation, people who've overdosed on Z."

"Help them what? Pretend to be something they're not?"

"I help them take back what they are. Your experience of the world tells you that Therese was some other person. No one's denying that. But you're in a situation where biologically and legally, you're Therese Klass. Do you have plans for dealing with that?"

As a matter of fact I do, and it involves getting the hell out as soon as possible. "I'll deal with it," I say.

"What about Alice and Mitch?"

I shrug. "What about them?"

"They're still your parents, and you're still their child. The overdose convinced you that you're a new person, but that hasn't changed who they are. They're still responsible for you, and they still care for you."

"Not much I can do about that."

"You're right. It's a fact of your life. You have two people who love you, and you're going to be with each other for the rest of your lives. You're going to have to figure out how to relate to each other. Zen may have burned the bridge between you and your past life, but you can build that bridge again."

"Doc, I don't want to build that bridge. Look, Alice and Mitch seem like nice people, but if I was looking for parents, I'd pick someone else."

Dr. Mehldau smiles. "None of us get to choose our parents, Terry."

I'm not in the mood to laugh. I nod toward the clock. "This is a waste of time."

She leans forward. I think she's going to try to touch me, but she doesn't. "Terry, you're not going to disappear if we talk about what happened to you. You'll still be here. The only difference is that you'll reclaim those memories as your own. You can get your old life back *and* choose your new life."

Sure, it's that easy. I get to sell my soul and keep it too.

I can't remember my first weeks in the hospital, though Dr. S says I was awake. At some point I realized that time was passing, or rather, that there was a me who was passing through time. I had lasagna for dinner yesterday, I am having meat loaf today. I am this girl in a bed. I think I realized this and forgot it several times before I could hold onto it.

Every day was mentally exhausting, because everything was so relentlessly *new*. I stared at the TV remote for a half hour, the name for it on the tip of my tongue, and it wasn't until the nurse picked it up and turned on the TV for me that I thought: *Remote*. And then sometimes, this was followed by a raft of other ideas: *TV. Channel. Gameshow.*

People were worse. They called me by a strange name, and they expected things of me. But to me, every visitor, from the night shift nurse to the janitor to Alice and Mitch Klass, seemed equally important—which is to say, not important at all.

Except for Dr. S. He was there from the beginning, and so he was familiar before I met him. He belonged to me like my own body.

But everything else about the world—the names, the details, the *facts*—had to be hauled into the sunlight, one by one. My brain was like an attic, chock full of old and interesting things jumbled together in no order at all.

I only gradually understood that somebody must have owned this house before me. And then I realized the house was haunted.

After the Sunday service, I'm caught in a stream of people. They lean across the pews to hug Alice and Mitch, then me. They pat my back, squeeze my arms, kiss my cheeks. I know from brief dips into Therese's memories that many of these people are as emotionally close as aunts or uncles. And any of them, if Therese were ever in trouble, would take her in, feed her, and give her a bed to sleep in.

This is all very nice, but the constant petting has me ready to scream.

All I want to do is get back home and take off this dress. I had no choice but to wear one of Therese's girly-girl extravaganzas. Her closet was full of them, and I finally found one that fit, if not comfortably. She loved these dresses, though. They were her floral print flak jackets. Who could doubt the purity of a girl in a high-necked Laura Ashley?

We gradually make our way to the vestibule, then to the sidewalk and the parking lot, under assault the entire way. I stop trying to match their faces to anything in Therese's memories.

At our car, a group of teenagers take turns on me, the girls hugging me tight, the boys leaning into me with half hugs: shoulders together, pelvises apart. One of the girls, freckled, with soft red curls falling past her shoulders, hangs back for awhile, then abruptly clutches me and whispers into my ear, "I'm so glad you're okay, Miss T." Her tone is intense, like she's passing a secret message.

A man moves through the crowd, arms open, smiling broadly. He's in his late twenties or early thirties, his hair cut in a choppy gelled style that's ten years too young for him. He's wearing pressed khakis, a blue Oxford rolled up at the forearms, a checked tie loosened at the throat.

He smothers me in a hug, his cologne like another set of arms. He's easy to find in Therese's memories: This is Jared, the Youth Pastor. He was the most spiritually vibrant person Therese knew, and the object of her crush.

"It's so good to have you back, Therese," he says. His cheek is pressed to mine. "We've missed you."

A few months before her overdose, the youth group was coming back from a weekend-long retreat in the church's converted school bus. Late into the trip, near midnight, Jared sat next to her, and she fell asleep leaning against him, inhaling that same cologne.

"I bet you have," I say. "Watch the hands, *Jared*."

His smile doesn't waver, his hands are still on my shoulders. "I'm sorry?"

"Oh please, you heard me."

He drops his hands, and looks questioningly

at my father. He can do sincerity pretty well. "I don't understand, Therese, but if—"

I give him a look that makes him back up a step. At some point later in the trip Therese awoke with Jared still next to her, slumped in the seat, eyes closed and mouth open. His arm was resting between her thighs, a thumb against her knee. She was wearing shorts, and his flesh on hers was hot. His forearm was inches from her warm crotch.

Therese believed that he was asleep.

She believed, too, that it was the rumbling of the school bus that shifted Jared's arm into contact with the crease of her shorts. Therese froze, flushed with arousal and embarrassment.

"Try to work it out, Jared." I get in the car.

The big question I can help answer, Dr. S said, is why there is consciousness. Or, going back to my favorite metaphor, if the Parliament is making all the decisions, why have a Queen at all?

He's got theories, of course. He thinks the Queen is all about storytelling. The brain needs a story that gives all these decisions a sense of purpose, a sense of continuity, so it can remember them and use them in future decisions. The brain can't keep track of the trillions of possible *other* decisions it could have made every moment; it needs one decision, and it needs a who, and a why. The brain lays down the memories, and the consciousness stamps them with identity: I did this, I did that. Those memories become the official record, the precedents that the Parliament uses to help make future decisions.

"The Queen, you see, is a figurehead," Dr. S said. "She represents the kingdom, but she isn't the kingdom itself, or even in control of it."

"I don't feel like a figurehead," I said.

Dr. S laughed. "Me neither. Nobody does."

Dr. Mehldau's therapy involves occasional joint sessions with Alice and Mitch, reading aloud from Therese's old diaries, and home movies. Today's video features a pre-teen Therese dressed in sheets, surrounded by kids in bathrobes, staring fixedly at a doll in a manager.

Dr. Mehldau asks me what Therese was thinking then. Was she enjoying playing Mary? Did she like being on stage?

"How would I know?"

"Then imagine it. What do you think Therese is thinking here?"

She tells me to do that a lot. Imagine what she's thinking. Just pretend. Put yourself in her shoes. In her book she calls this "reclaiming." She makes up a lot of her own terms, then defines them however she wants, without research to back her up. Compared to the neurology texts Dr. S lent me, Dr. Mehldau's little book is an Archie comic with footnotes.

"You know what, Therese was a good Christian girl, so she probably loved it."

"Are you sure?"

The wise men come on stage, three younger boys. They plop down their gifts and their lines, and the look on Therese's face is wary. Her line is coming up.

Therese was petrified of screwing up. Everybody would be staring at her. I can almost see the congregation in the dark behind the lights. Alice and Mitch are out there, and they're waiting for every line. My chest tightens, and I realize I'm holding my breath.

Dr. Mehldau's eyes on mine are studiously neutral.

"You know what?" I have no idea what I'm going to say next. I'm stalling for time. I shift my weight in the big beige chair and move a leg underneath me. "The thing I like about Buddhism is Buddhists understand that they've been screwed by a whole string of previous selves. I had nothing to do with the decisions Therese made, the good or bad karma she'd acquired."

This is a riff I've been thinking about in Therese's big girly bedroom. "See, Therese was a Christian, so she probably thought by overdosing that she'd be born again, all her sins forgiven. It's the perfect drug for her: suicide without the corpse."

"Was she thinking about suicide that night?"

"I *don't know*. I could spend a couple weeks mining through Therese's memories, but frankly, I'm not interested. Whatever she was thinking, she wasn't born again. I'm here, and I'm still saddled with her baggage. I am Therese's donkey. I'm a karma donkey."

Dr. Mehldau nods. "Dr. Subramaniam is Buddhist, isn't he?"

"Yeah, but what's . . .?" It clicks. I roll my eyes. Dr. S and I talked about transference, and I know that my crush on him was par for the course. And it's true that I spend a lot of time—still—thinking about fucking the man. But that doesn't mean I'm wrong. "This is not about that," I say. "I've been thinking about this on my own."

She doesn't fight me on that. "Wouldn't a Buddhist say that you and Therese share the same soul? Self's an illusion. So there's no rider in charge, no donkey. There's just *you*."

"Just forget it," I say.

"Let's follow this, Terry. Don't you feel you have a responsibility to your old self? Your old self's parents, your old friends? Maybe there's karma you *owe*."

"And who are you responsible to, Doctor? Who's your patient? Therese, or me?"

She says nothing for a moment, then: "I'm responsible to you."

You.

You swallow, surprised that the pills taste like cinnamon. The effect of the drug is intermittent at first. You realize that you're in the back seat of a car, the cell phone in your hand, your friends laughing around you. You're talking to your mother. If you concentrate, you can remember answering the phone, and telling her which friend's house you're staying at tonight. Before you can say goodbye, you're stepping out of the car. The car is parked, your phone is away—and you remember saying goodnight to your mother and riding for a half hour before finding this parking garage. Joelly tosses her red curls and tugs you toward the stairwell: *Come on, Miss T!*

Then you look up and realize that you're on the sidewalk outside an all-ages club, and you're holding a ten dollar bill, ready to hand it to the bouncer. The music thunders every time the door swings open. You turn to Joelly and—

You're in someone else's car. On the Interstate. The driver is a boy you met hours ago, his name is Rush but you haven't asked if that's his first name or his last. In the club you leaned into each other and talked loud over the music about parents and food and the difference between the taste of a fresh cigarette in your mouth and the smell of stale smoke. But then you realize that there's a cigarette in your mouth, you took it from Rush's pack yourself, and you don't like cigarettes. Do you like it now? You don't know. Should you take it out, or keep smoking? You scour your memories, but can discover no reason why you decided to light the cigarette, no reason why you got into the car with this boy. You start to tell yourself a story: he must be a trustworthy person, or you wouldn't have gotten into the car. You took that one cigarette because the boy's feelings would have been hurt.

You're not feeling like yourself tonight. And you like it. You take another drag off the cigarette. You think back over the past few hours, and marvel at everything you've done, all without that constant weight of self-reflection: worry, anticipation, instant regret. Without the inner voice constantly critiquing you.

Now the boy is wearing nothing but boxer shorts, and he's reaching up to a shelf to get a box of cereal, and his back is beautiful. There is hazy light outside the small kitchen window. He pours Froot Loops into a bowl for you, and he laughs, though quietly because his mother is asleep in the next room. He looks at your face and frowns. He asks you what's the matter. You look down, and you're fully dressed. You think back, and realize that you've been in this boy's apartment for hours. You made out in his bedroom, and the boy took off his clothes, and you kissed his chest and ran your hands along his legs. You let him put his hand under your shirt and cup your breasts, but you didn't go any further. Why didn't you have sex? Did he not interest you? No—you were wet. You were excited. Did you feel guilty? Did you feel ashamed?

What were you thinking?

When you get home there will be hell to pay. Your parents will be furious, and worse, they will pray for you. The entire church will pray for you. Everyone will know. And no one will ever look at you the same again.

Now there's a cinnamon taste in your mouth, and you're sitting in the boy's car again, outside a convenience store. It's afternoon. Your cell phone is ringing. You turn off the cell phone and put it back in your purse. You swallow, and your throat is dry. That boy—Rush—is buying you another bottle of water. What was it you swallowed? Oh, yes. You think back, and remember putting all those little pills in your mouth. Why did you take so many? Why did you take another one at all? Oh, yes.

Voices drift up from the kitchen. It's before 6 AM, and I just want to pee and get back to sleep, but then I realize they're talking about me.

"She doesn't even *walk* the same. The way she holds herself, the way she talks . . ."

"It's all those books Dr. Subramaniam gave her. She's up past one every night. Therese never read like that, not *science*."

"No, it's not just the words, it's how she *sounds*. That low voice . . ." She sobs. "Oh hon, I didn't know it would be this way. It's like she's right, it's like it isn't her at all."

He doesn't say anything. Alice's crying grows louder, subsides. The clink of dishes in the sink. I step back, and Mitch speaks again.

"Maybe we should try the camp," he says.

"No, no, no! Not yet. Dr. Mehldau says she's making progress. We've got to—"

"Of course she's going to say that."

"You said you'd try this, you said you'd give this a chance." The anger cuts through the

weeping, and Mitch mumbles something apologetic. I creep back to my bedroom, but I still have to pee, so I make a lot of noise going back out. Alice comes to the bottom of the stairs. "Are you all right, honey?"

I keep my face sleepy and walk into the bathroom. I shut the door and sit down on the toilet in the dark.

What fucking camp?

"Let's try again," Dr. Mehldau said. "Something pleasant and vivid."

I'm having trouble concentrating. The brochure is like a bomb in my pocket. It wasn't hard to find, once I decided to look for it. I want to ask Dr. Mehldau about the camp, but I know that once I bring it into the open, I'll trigger a showdown between the doctor and the Klasses, with me in the middle.

"Keep your eyes closed," she says. "Think about Therese's tenth birthday. In her diary, she wrote that was the best birthday she'd ever had. Do you remember Sea World?"

"Vaguely." I could see dolphins jumping—two at a time, three at a time. It had been sunny and hot. With every session it was getting easier for me to pop into Therese's memories. Her life was on DVD, and I had the remote.

"Do you remember getting wet at the Namu and Shamu show?"

I laughed. "I think so." I could see the metal benches, the glass wall just in front of me, the huge shapes in the blue-green water. "They had the whales flip their big tail fins. We got drenched."

"Can you picture who was there with you? Where are your parents?"

There was a girl, my age, I can't remember her name. The sheets of water were coming down on us and we were screaming and laughing. Afterward my parents toweled us off. They must have been sitting up high, out of the splash zone. Alice looked much younger: happier, and a little heavier. She was wider at the hips. This was before she started dieting and exercising, when she was Mom-sized.

My eyes pop open. "Oh God."

"Are you okay?"

"I'm fine—it was just . . . like you said. Vivid." That image of a younger Alice still burns. For the first time I realize how *sad* she is now.

"I'd like a joint session next time," I say.

"Really? All right. I'll talk to Alice and Mitch. Is there anything in particular you want to talk about?"

"Yeah. We need to talk about Therese."

Dr. S says everybody wants to know if the original neural map, the old Queen, can come back. Once the map to the map is lost, can you find it again? And if you do, then what happens to the new neural map, the new Queen?

"Now, a good Buddhist would tell you that this question is unimportant. After all, the cycle of existence is not just between lives. *Samsara* is every moment. The self continuously dies and recreates itself."

"Are you a good Buddhist?" I asked him.

He smiled. "Only on Sunday mornings."

"You go to church?"

"I golf."

There's a knock and I open my eyes. Alice steps into my room, a stack of folded laundry in her arms. "Oh!"

I've rearranged the room, pushing the bed into the corner to give me a few square feet of free space on the floor.

Her face goes through a few changes. "I don't suppose you're praying."

"No."

She sighs, but it's a mock-sigh. "I didn't think so." She moves around me and sets the laundry on the bed. She picks up the book there, *Entering the Stream.* "Dr. Subramaniam gave you this?"

She's looking at the passage I've highlighted. But loving kindness—maitri—toward ourselves doesn't mean getting rid of anything. The point is not to try to change ourselves. Meditation practice isn't about trying to throw ourselves away and become something better. It's about befriending who we already are.

"Well." She sets the book down, careful to leave it open to the same page. "That sounds a bit like Dr. Mehldau."

I laugh. "Yeah, it does. Did she tell you I wanted you and Mitch to be at the next session?"

"We'll be there." She works around the room, picking up T-shirts and underwear. I stand up to get out of the way. Somehow she manages to straighten up as she moves—righting books that had fallen over, setting Boo W. Bear back to his place on the bed, sweeping an empty chip bag into the garbage can—so that as she collects my dirty laundry she's cleaning the entire room, like the Cat in the Hat's cleaner-upper machine.

"Alice, in the last session I remembered being at Sea World, but there was a girl next to me. Next to Therese."

"Sea World? Oh, that was the Hammel girl, Marcy. They took you to Ohio with them on their vacation that year."

"Who did?"

"The Hammels. You were gone all week. All you wanted for your birthday was spending money for the trip."

"You weren't there?"

She picks up the jeans I left at the foot of the bed. "We always meant to go to Sea World, but your father and I never got out there."

"This is our last session," I say.

Alice, Mitch, Dr. Mehldau: I have their complete attention.

The doctor, of course, is the first to recover. "It sounds like you've got something you want to tell us."

"Oh yeah."

Alice seems frozen, holding herself in check. Mitch rubs the back of his neck, suddenly intent on the carpet.

"I'm not going along with this anymore." I make a vague gesture. "Everything: the memory exercises, all this imagining of what Therese felt. I finally figured it out. It doesn't matter to you if I'm Therese or not. You just want me to think

I'm her. I'm not going along with the manipulation anymore."

Mitch shakes his head. "Honey, you took a *drug*." He glances at me, looks back at his feet. "If you took LSD and saw God, that doesn't mean you really saw God. Nobody's trying to manipulate you, we're trying to *undo* the manipulation."

"That's bullshit, Mitch. You all keep acting like I'm schizophrenic, that I don't know what's real or not. Well, part of the problem is that the longer I talk to Dr. Mehldau here, the more fucked up I am."

Alice gasps.

Dr. Mehldau puts out a hand to soothe her, but her eyes are on me. "Terry, what your father's trying to say is that even though you feel like a new person, there's a *you* that existed before the drug. That exists now."

"Yeah? You know all those O.D.-ers in your book who say they've 'reclaimed' themselves? Maybe they only *feel* like their old selves."

"It's *possible*," she says. "But I don't think they're fooling themselves. They've come to accept the parts of themselves they've lost, the family members they've left behind. They're people like you." She regards me with that standard-issue look of concern that doctors pick up with their diplomas. "Do you really want to feel like an orphan the rest of your life?"

"What?" From out of nowhere, tears well in my eyes. I cough to clear my throat, and the tears keep coming, until I smear them off on my arm. I feel like I've been sucker punched. "Hey, look Alice, just like you," I say.

"It's normal," Dr. Mehldau says. "When you woke up in the hospital, you felt completely alone. You felt like a brand new person, no family, no friends. And you're still just starting down this road. In a lot of ways you're not even two years old."

"*Damn* you're good," I say. "I didn't even see that one coming."

"Please, don't leave. Let's—"

"Don't worry, I'm not leaving yet." I'm at the door, pulling my backpack from the peg by the door. I dig into the pocket, and pull out the brochure. "You know about this?"

Alice speaks for the first time. "Oh honey, no . . ."

Dr. Mehldau takes it from me, frowning. On the front is a nicely posed picture of a smiling teenage boy hugging relieved parents. She looks at Alice and Mitch. "Are you considering this?"

"It's their big stick, Dr. Mehldau. If you can't come through for them, or I bail out, *boom*. You know what goes on there?"

She opens the pages, looking at pictures of the cabins, the obstacle course, the big lodge where kids just like me engage in "intense group sessions with trained counselors" where they can "recover their true identities." She shakes her head. "Their approach is different than mine . . ."

"I don't know, doc. Their *approach* sounds an awful lot like 'reclaiming.' I got to hand it to you, you had me going for awhile. Those visualization exercises? I was getting so good that I could even visualize stuff that never happened. I bet you could visualize me right into Therese's head."

I turn to Alice and Mitch. "You've got a decision to make. Dr. Mehldau's program is a bust. So are you sending me off to brainwashing camp or not?"

Mitch has his arm around his wife. Alice, amazingly, is dry-eyed. Her eyes are wide, and she's staring at me like a stranger.

It rains the entire trip back from Baltimore, and it's still raining when we pull up to the house. Alice and I run to the porch step, illuminated by the glare of headlights. Mitch waits until Alice unlocks the door and we move inside, and then pulls away.

"Does he do that a lot?" I ask.

"He likes to drive when he's upset."

"Oh." Alice goes through the house, turning on lights. I follow her into the kitchen.

"Don't worry, he'll be all right." She opens the refrigerator door and crouches down. "He just doesn't know what to do with you."

"He wants to put me in the camp, then."

"Oh, not that. He just never had a daughter who talked back to him before." She carries a Tupperware cake holder to the table. "I made carrot cake. Can you get down the plates?"

She's such a small woman. Face to face, she comes up only to my chin. The hair on the top of her head is thin, made thinner by the rain, and her scalp is pink.

"I'm not Therese. I never will be Therese."

"Oh, I know," she says, half sighing. And she does know it; I can see it in her face. "It's just that you look so much like her."

I laugh. "I can dye my hair. Maybe get a nose job."

"It wouldn't work, I'd still recognize you." She pops the lid and sets it aside. The cake is a wheel with icing that looks half an inch thick. Miniature candy carrots line the edge.

"Wow, you made that before we left? Why?"

Alice shrugs, and cuts into it. She turns the knife on its side and uses the blade to lever a huge triangular wedge onto my plate. "I thought we might need it, one way or another."

She places the plate in front of me, and touches me lightly on the arm. "I know you want to move out. I know you may never want to come back."

"It's not that I—"

"We're not going to stop you. But wherever you go, you'll still be my daughter, whether you like it or not. You don't get to decide who loves you."

"Alice . . ."

"Shhh. Eat your cake."

Chapter 25

Derek Parfit

PERSONAL IDENTITY[1]

We can, I think, describe cases in which, though we know the answer to every other question, we have no idea how to answer a question about personal identity. These cases are not covered by the criteria of personal identity that we actually use.

Do they present a problem?

It might be thought that they do not, because they could never occur. I suspect that some of them could. (Some, for instance, might become scientifically possible.) But I shall claim that even if they did they would present no problem.

My targets are two beliefs: one about the nature of personal identity, the other about its importance.

The first is that in these cases the question about identity must have an answer.

No one thinks this about, say, nations or machines. Our criteria for the identity of these do not cover certain cases. No one thinks that in these cases the questions "Is it the same nation?" or "Is it the same machine?" must have answers.

Some people believe that in this respect they are different. They agree that our criteria of personal identity do not cover certain cases, but they believe that the nature of their own identity through time is, somehow, such as to guarantee that in these cases questions about their identity must have answers. This belief might be expressed as follows: "Whatever happens between now and any future time, either I shall still exist, or I shall not. Any future experience will either be my experience, or it will not."

This first belief—in the special nature of personal identity—has, I think, certain effects. It makes people assume that the principle of self-interest is more rationally compelling than any moral principle. And it makes them more depressed by the thought of aging and of death.

I cannot see how to disprove this first belief. I shall describe a problem case. But this can only make it seem implausible.

Another approach might be this. We might suggest that one cause of the belief is the projection of our emotions. When we imagine ourselves in a problem case, we do feel that the question "Would it be me?" must have an answer. But what we take to be a bafflement about a further fact may be only the bafflement of our concern.

I shall not pursue this suggestion here. But one cause of our concern is the belief which is my second target. This is that unless the question about identity has an answer, we cannot answer certain important questions (questions about such matters as survival, memory, and responsibility).

Against this second belief my claim will be this. Certain important questions do presuppose a question about personal identity. But they can be freed of this presupposition. And when they are, the question about identity has no importance.

I

We can start by considering the much-discussed case of the man who, like an amoeba, divides.[2]

Wiggins has recently dramatized this case.[3] He first referred to the operation imagined by Shoemaker.[4] We suppose that my brain is transplanted into someone else's (brainless) body, and that the resulting person has my character and apparent memories of my life. Most of us would agree, after thought, that the resulting person is me. I shall here assume such agreement.[5]

Wiggins then imagined his own operation. My brain is divided, and each half is housed in a new body. Both resulting people have my character and apparent memories of my life.

What happens to me? There seem only three possibilities: (1) I do not survive; (2) I survive as one of the two people; (3) I survive as both.

The trouble with (1) is this. We agreed that I could survive if my brain were successfully transplanted. And people have in fact survived with half their brains destroyed. It seems to follow that I could survive if half my brain were successfully transplanted and the other half were destroyed. But if this is so, how could I *not* survive if the other half were also successfully transplanted? How could a double success be a failure?

We can move to the second description. Perhaps one success is the maximum score. Perhaps I shall be one of the resulting people.

The trouble here is that in Wiggins' case each half of my brain is exactly similar, and so, to start with, is each resulting person. So how can I survive as only one of the two people? What can make me one of them rather than the other?

It seems clear that both of these descriptions —that I do not survive, and that I survive as one of the people—are highly implausible. Those who have accepted them must have assumed that they were the only possible descriptions.

What about our third description: that I survive as both people?

It might be said, "If 'survive' implies identity, this description makes no sense—you cannot be two people. If it does not, the description is irrelevant to a problem about identity."

I shall later deny the second of these remarks. But there are ways of denying the first. We might say, "What we have called 'the two resulting people' are not two people. They are one person. I do survive Wiggins' operation. Its effect is to give me two bodies and a divided mind."

It would shorten my argument if this were absurd. But I do not think it is. It is worth showing why.

We can, I suggest, imagine a divided mind. We can imagine a man having two simultaneous experiences, in having each of which he is unaware of having the other.

We may not even need to imagine this. Certain actual cases, to which Wiggins referred, seem to be best described in these terms. These involve the cutting of the bridge between the hemispheres of the brain. The aim was to cure epilepsy. But the result appears to be, in the surgeon's words, the creation of "two separate spheres of consciousness,"[6] each of which controls one half of the patient's body. What is experienced in each is, presumably, experienced by the patient.

There are certain complications in these actual cases. So let us imagine a simpler case.

Suppose that the bridge between my hemispheres is brought under my voluntary control. This would enable me to disconnect my hemispheres as easily as if I were blinking. By doing this I would divide my mind. And we can suppose that when my mind is divided I can, in each half, bring about reunion.

This ability would have obvious uses. To give an example: I am near the end of a maths exam, and see two ways of tackling the last problem. I decide to divide my mind, to work, with each half, at one of two calculations, and then to reunite my mind and write a fair copy of the best result.

What shall I experience?

When I disconnect my hemispheres, my consciousness divides into two streams. But this division is not something that I experience. Each of my two streams of consciousness seems to have been straightforwardly continuous with my one stream of consciousness up to the moment of division. The only changes in each stream are the disappearance of half my visual field and the loss of sensation, in, and control over, half my body.

Consider my experiences in what we can call my "right-handed" stream. I remember that I assigned my right hand to the longer calculation. This I now begin. In working at this calculation I can see, from the movements of my left hand, that I am also working at the other. But I am not aware of working at the other. So I might, in my right-handed stream, wonder how, in my left-handed stream, I am getting on.

My work is now over. I am about to reunite my mind. What should I, in each stream, expect? Simply that I shall suddenly seem to remember just having thought out two calculations, in thinking out each of which I was not aware of thinking out the other. This, I submit, we can imagine. And if my mind was divided, these memories are correct.

In describing this episode, I assumed that there were two series of thoughts, and that they were both mine. If my two hands visibly wrote out two calculations, and if I claimed to remember two corresponding series of thoughts, this is surely what we should want to say.

If it is, then a person's mental history need not be like a canal, with only one channel. It could be like a river, with islands, and with separate streams.

To apply this to Wiggins' operation: we mentioned the view that it gives me two bodies and a divided mind. We cannot now call this absurd. But it is, I think, unsatisfactory.

There were two features of the case of the exam that made us want to say that only one person was involved. The mind was soon reunited, and there was only one body. If a mind was permanently divided and its halves

developed in different ways, the point of speaking of one person would start to disappear. Wiggins' case, where there are also two bodies, seems to be over the borderline. After I have had his operation, the two "products" each have all the attributes of a person. They could live at opposite ends of the earth. (If they later met, they might even fail to recognize each other.) It would become intolerable to deny that they were different people.

Suppose we admit that they are different people. Could we still claim that I survived as both, using "survive" to imply identity?

We could. For we might suggest that two people could compose a third. We might say, "I do survive Wiggins' operation as two people. They can be different people, and yet be me, in just the way in which the Pope's three crowns are one crown."[7]

This is a possible way of giving sense to the claim that I survive as two different people, using "survive" to imply identity. But it keeps the language of identity only by changing the concept of a person. And there are obvious objections to this change.[8]

The alternative, for which I shall argue, is to give up the language of identity. We can suggest that I survive as two different people without implying that I am these people.

When I first mentioned this alternative, I mentioned this objection: "If you new way of talking does not imply identity, it cannot solve our problem. For that is about identity. The problem is that all the possible answers to the question about identity are highly implausible."

We can now answer this objection.

We can start by reminding ourselves that this is an objection only if we have one or both of the beliefs which I mentioned at the start of this paper.

The first was the belief that to any question about personal identity, in any describable case, there must be a true answer. For those with this belief, Wiggins' case is doubly perplexing. If all the possible answers are implausible, it is hard to decide which of them is true, and hard even to keep the belief that one of them must be true. If we give up this belief, as I think we should, these problems disappear. We shall then regard the case as like many others in which, for quite unpuzzling reasons, there is no answer to a question about identity. (Consider "Was England the same nation after 1066?")

Wiggins' case makes the first belief implausible. It also makes it trivial. For it undermines the second belief. This was the belief that important questions turn upon the question about identity. (It is worth pointing out that those who have only his second belief do not think that there must *be* an answer to this question, but rather that we must decide upon an answer.)

Against this second belief my claim is this. Certain questions do presuppose a question about personal identity. And because these questions *are* important, Wiggins' case does present a problem. But we cannot solve this problem by answering the question about identity. We can solve this problem only by taking these important questions and prizing them apart from the question about identity. After we have done this, the question about identity (though we might for the sake of neatness decide it) has no further interest.

Because there are several questions which presuppose identity, this claim will take some time to fill out.

We can first return to the question of survival. This is a special case, for survival does not so much presuppose the retaining of identity as seem equivalent to it. It is thus the general relation which we need to prize apart from identity. We can then consider particular relations, such as those involved in memory and intention.

"Will I survive?" seems, I said, equivalent to "Will there be some person alive who is the same person as me?"

If we treat these questions as equivalent, then the least unsatisfactory description of Wiggins' case is, I think, that I survive with two bodies and a divided mind.

Several writers have chosen to say that I am neither of the resulting people. Given our equivalence, this implies that I do not survive, and hence, presumably, that even if Wiggins' operation is not literally death, I ought, since I will not survive it, to regard it *as* death. But this seemed absurd.

It is worth repeating why. An emotion or attitude can be criticized for resting on a false belief, or for being inconsistent. A man who regarded Wiggins' operation as death must, I suggest, be open to one of these criticisms.

He might believe that his relation to each of the resulting people fails to contain some element which is contained in survival. But how can this be true? We agreed that he *would* survive if he stood in this very same relation to only *one* of the resulting people. So it cannot be the nature of this relation which makes it fail, in Wiggins' case, to be survival. It can only be its duplication.

Suppose that our man accepts this, but still regards division as death. His reaction would now seem wildly inconsistent. He would be like a man who, when told of a drug that could double his years of life, regarded the taking of this drug as death. The only difference in the case of division is that the extra years are to run concurrently. This is an interesting difference. But it cannot mean that there are *no* years to run.

I have argued this for those who think that there must, in Wiggins' case, be a true answer to the question about identity. For them, we might add, "Perhaps the original person does lose his identity. But there may be other ways to do this than to die. One other way might be to multiply. To regard these as the same is to confuse nought with two."

For those who think that the question of identity is up for decision, it would be clearly absurd to regard Wiggins' operation as death. These people would have to think, "We could have chosen to say that I should be one of the resulting people. If we had, I should not have regarded it as death. But since we have chosen to say that I am neither person, I *do*." This is hard even to understand.[9]

My first conclusion, then, is this. The relation of the original person to each of the resulting people contains all that interests us—all that matters—in any ordinary case of survival. This is why we need a sense in which one person can survive as two.[10]

One of my aims in the rest of this paper will be to suggest such a sense. But we can first make some general remarks.

II

Identity is a one-one relation. Wiggins' case serves to show that what matters in survival need not be one-one.

Wiggins' case is of course unlikely to occur. The relations which matter are, in fact, one-one. It is because they are that we can imply the holding of these relations by using the language of identity.

This use of language is convenient. But it can lead us astray. We may assume that what matters *is* identity and, hence, has the properties of identity.

In the case of the property of being one-one, this mistake is not serious. For what matters is in fact one-one. But in the case of another property, the mistake *is* serious. Identity is all-or-nothing. Most of the relations which matter in survival are, in fact, relations of degree. If we ignore this, we shall be led into quite ill-grounded attitudes and beliefs.

The claim that I have just made—that most of what matters are relations of degree—I have yet to support. Wiggins' case shows only that these relations need not be one-one. The merit of the case is not that it shows this in particular, but that it makes the first break between what matters and identity. The belief that identity is what matters is hard to overcome. This is shown in most discussions of the problem cases which actually occur: cases, say, of amnesia or of brain damage.

Once Wiggins' case has made one breach in this belief, the rest should be easier to remove.[11]

To turn to a recent debate: most of the relations which matter can be provisionally referred to under the heading "psychological continuity" (which includes causal continuity). My claim is thus that we use the language of personal identity in order to imply such continuity. This is close to the view that psychological continuity provides a criterion of identity.

Williams has attacked this view with the following argument. Identity is a one-one relation. So any criterion of identity must appeal to a relation which is logically one-one. Psychological continuity is not logically one-one. So it cannot provide a criterion.[12]

Some writers have replied that it is enough if the relation appealed to is always in fact one-one.[13]

I suggest a slightly different reply. Psychological continuity is a ground for speaking of identity when it is one-one.

If psychological continutity took a one-many or branching form, we should need, I have argued, to abandon the language of identity. So this possibility would not count against this view.

We can make a stronger claim. This possibility would count in its favor.

The view might be defended as follows. Judgments of personal identity have great importance. What gives them their importance is the fact that they imply psychological continuity. This is why, whenever there is such continuity, we ought, if we can, to imply it by making a judgment of identity.

If psychological continuity took a branching form, no coherent set of judgments of identity could correspond to, and thus be used to imply, the branching form of this relation. But what we ought to do, in such a case, is take the importance which would attach to a judgment of identity and attach this importance directly to each limb of the branching relation. So this case helps to show that judgments of personal identity do derive their importance from the fact that they imply psychological continuity. It helps to show that when we can, usefully, speak of identity, this relation is our ground.

This argument appeals to a principle which Williams put forward.[14] The principle is that an important judgment should be asserted and denied only on importantly different grounds.

Williams applied this principle to a case in which one man is psychologically continuous with the dead Guy Fawkes, and a case in which two men are. His argument was this. If we treat psychological continuity as a sufficient ground for speaking of identity, we shall say that the one man is Guy Fawkes. But we could not say that the two men are, although we should have the same ground. This disobeys the principle. The remedy is to deny that the one man is Guy Fawkes, to insist that sameness of the body is necessary for identity.

Williams' principle can yield a different answer. Suppose we regard psychological continuity as more important than sameness of the body.[15] And suppose that the one man really is psychologically (and causally) continuous with Guy Fawkes. If he is, it would disobey the principle to deny that he is Guy Fawkes, for we have the same important ground as in a normal case of identity. In the case of the two men, we again have the same important ground. So we ought to take the importance from the judgment of identity and attach it directly to this ground. We ought to say, as in Wiggins' case, that each limb of the branching relation is as good as survival. This obeys the principle.

To sum up these remarks: even if psychological continuity is neither logically, nor always in fact, one-one, it can provide a criterion of identity. For this can appeal to the relation of *non-branching* psychological continuity, which is logically one-one.[16]

The criterion might be sketched as follows. "X and Y are the same person if they are psychologically continuous and there is no person who is contemporary with either and psychologically continuous with the other." We should need to explain what we mean by "psychologically continuous" and say how much continuity the criterion requires. We should then, I think, have described a sufficient condition for speaking of identity.[17]

We need to say something more. If we admit that psychological continuity might not be one-one, we need to say what we ought to do if it were not one-one. Otherwise our account would be open to the objections that it is incomplete and arbitrary.[18]

I have suggested that if psychological continuity took a branching form, we ought to speak in a new way, regarding what we describe as having the same significance as identity. This answers these objections.[19]

We can now return to our discussion. We have three remaining aims. One is to suggest a sense of "survive" which does not imply identity. Another is to show that most of what matters in survival are relations of degree. A third is to show that none of these relations needs to be described in a way that presupposes identity.

We can take these aims in the reverse order.

III

The most important particular relation is that involved in memory. This is because it is so easy to believe that its description must refer to identity.[20] This belief about memory is an important cause of the view that personal identity has a special nature. But it has been well discussed by Shoemaker[21] and by Wiggins[22] So we can be brief.

It may be a logical truth that we can only remember our own experiences. But we can frame a new concept for which this is not a logical truth. Let us call this "q-memory."

To sketch a definition[23] I am q-remembering an experience if (1) I have a belief about a past experience which seems in itself like a memory belief, (2) someone did have such an experience, and (3) my belief is dependent upon this experience in the same way (whatever that is) in which a memory of an experience is dependent upon it.

According to (1) q-memories seem like memories. So I q-remember *having* experiences.

This may seem to make q-memory presuppose identity. One might say, "My apparent memory of *having* an experience is an apparent memory of *my* having an experience. So how could I q-remember my having other people's experiences?"

This objection rests on a mistake. When I seem to remember an experience, I do indeed seem to remember *having* it.[24] But it cannot be a part of what I seem to remember about this experience that I, the person who now seems to remember it, am the person who had this experience.[25] That I am is something that I automatically assume. (My apparent memories sometimes come to me simply as the belief that I had a certain experience.) But it is something that I am justified in assuming only because I do not in fact have q-memories of other people's experiences.

Suppose that I did start to have such q-memories. If I did, I should cease to assume that my apparent memories must be about my own experiences. I should come to assess an apparent memory by asking two questions: (1) Does it tell me about a past experience? (2) If so, whose?

Moreover (and this is a crucial point) my apparent memories would now come to me *as* q-memories. Consider those of my apparent memories which do come to me simply as beliefs about my past: for example, "I did that." If I knew that I could q-remember other people's experiences, these beliefs would come to me in a more guarded form: for example, "Someone—probably I—did that." I might have to work out who it was.

I have suggested that the concept of q-memory is coherent. Wiggins' case provides an illustration. The resulting people, in his case, both have apparent memories of living the life of the original person. If they agree that they are not

this person, they will have to regard these as only q-memories. And when they are asked a question like "Have you heard this music before?" they might have to answer "I am sure that I q-remember hearing it. But I am not sure whether I remember hearing it. I am not sure whether it was I who heard it, or the original person."

We can next point out that on our definition every memory is also a q-memory. Memories are, simply, q-memories of one's own experiences. Since this is so, we could afford now to drop the concept of memory and use in its place the wider concept q-memory. If we did, we should describe the relation between an experience and what we now call a "memory" of this experience in a way which does not presuppose that they are had by the same person.[26]

This way of describing this relation has certain merits. It vindicates the "memory criterion" of personal identity against the charge of circularity.[27] And it might, I think, help with the problem of other minds.

But we must move on. We can next take the relation between an intention and a later action. It may be a logical truth that we can intend to perform only our own actions. But intentions can be redescribed as q-intentions. And one person could q-intend to perform another person's actions.

Wiggins' case again provides the illustration. We are supposing that neither of the resulting people is the original person. If so, we shall have to agree that the original person can, before the operation, q-intend to perform their actions. He might, for example, q-intend, as one of them, to continue his present career, and, as the other, to try something new.[28] (I say "q-intend *as* one of them" because the phrase "q-intend *that* one of them" would not convey the directness of the relation which is involved. If I intend that someone else should do something, I cannot get him to do it simply by forming this intention. But if I am the original person, and he is one of the resulting people, I can.)

The phrase "q-intend *as* one of them" reminds

us that we need a sense in which one person can survive as two. But we can first point out that the concepts of q-memory and q-intention give us our model for the others that we need: thus, a man who can q-remember could q-recognize, and be a q-witness of, what he has never seen; and a man who can q-intend could have q-ambitions, make q-promises, and be q-responsible for.

To put this claim in general terms: many different relations are included within, or are a consequence of, psychological continuity. We describe these relations in ways which presuppose the continued existence of one person. But we could describe them in new ways which do not.

This suggests a bolder claim. It might be possible to think of experiences in a wholly "impersonal" way. I shall not develop this claim here. What I shall try to describe is a way of thinking of our own identity through time which is more flexible, and less misleading, than the way in which we now think.

This way of thinking will allow for a sense in which one person can survive as two. A more important feature is that it treats survival as a matter of degree.

IV

We must first show the need for this second feature. I shall use two imaginary examples.

The first is the converse of Wiggins' case: fusion. Just as division serves to show that what matters in survival need not be one-one, so fusion serves to show that it can be a question of degree.

Physically, fusion is easy to describe. Two people come together. While they are unconscious, their two bodies grow into one. One person then wakes up.

The psychology of fusion is more complex. One detail we have already dealt with in the case of the exam. When my mind was reunited, I remembered just having thought out two

calculations. The one person who results from a fusion can, similarly, q-remember living the lives of the two original people. None of their q-memories need be lost.

But some things must be lost. For any two people who fuse together will have different characteristics, different desires, and different intentions. How can these be combined?

We might suggest the following. Some of these will be compatible. These can coexist in the one resulting person. Some will be incompatible. These, if of equal strength, can cancel out, and if of different strengths, the stronger can be made weaker. And all these effects might be predictable.

To give examples—first, of compatibility: I like Palladio and intend to visit Venice. I am about to fuse with a person who likes Giotto and intends to visit Padua. I can know that the one person we shall become will have both tastes and both intentions. Second, of incompatibility: I hate red hair, and always vote Labour. The other person loves red hair, and always votes Conservative. I can know that the one person we shall become will be indifferent to red hair, and a floating voter.

If we were about to undergo a fusion of this kind, would we regard it as death?

Some of us might. This is less absurd than regarding division as death. For after my division the two resulting people will be in every way like me, while after my fusion the one resulting person will not be wholly similar. This makes it easier to say, when faced with fusion, "I shall not survive," thus continuing to regard survival as a matter of all-or-nothing.

This reaction is less absurd. But here are two analogies which tell against it.

First, fusion would involve the changing of some of our characteristics and some of our desires. But only the very self-satisfied would think of this as death. Many people welcome treatments with these effects.

Second, someone who is about to fuse can have, beforehand, just as much "intentional control" over the actions of the resulting individual as someone who is about to marry can have, beforehand, over the actions of the resulting couple. And the choice of a partner for fusion can be just as well considered as the choice of a marriage partner. The two original people can make sure (perhaps by "trial fusion") that they do have compatible characters, desires, and intentions.

I have suggested that fusion, while not clearly survival, is not clearly failure to survive, and hence that what matters in survival can have degrees.

To reinforce this claim we can now turn to a second example. This is provided by certain imaginary beings. These beings are just like ourselves except that they reproduce by a process of natural division.

We can illustrate the histories of these imagined beings with the aid of a diagram (below). The lines on the diagram represent the spatiotemporal paths which would be traced out by the bodies of these beings. We can call each single line (like the double line) a "branch"; and we can call the whole structure a "tree." And let us suppose that each "branch" corresponds to what is thought of as the life of one individual. These individuals are referred to as "A," "B+1," and so forth.

Now, each single division is an instance of Wiggins' case. So A's relation to both B+1 and B+2 is just as good as survival. But what of A's relation to B+30?

I said earlier that what matters in survival could be provisionally referred to as "psychological continuity." I must now distinguish this relation from another, which I shall call "psychological connectedness."

Let us say that the relation between a q-memory and the experience q-remembered is a "direct" relation. Another "direct" relation is that which holds between a q-intention and the q-intended action. A third is that which holds between different expressions of some lasting q-characteristic.

"Psychological connectedness," as I define it, requires the holding of these direct psychological relations. "Connectedness" is not transitive, since these relations are not transitive. Thus, if X q-remembers most of Y's life, and Y q-remembers most of Z's life, it does not follow that X q-remembers most of Z's life. And if X carries out the q-intentions of Y, and Y carries out the q-intentions of Z, it does not follow that X carries out the q-intentions of Z.

"Psychological continuity," in contrast, only requires overlapping chains of direct psychological relations. So "continuity" *is* transitive.

To return to our diagram. A is psychologically continuous with B+30. There are between the two continuous chains of overlapping relations. Thus, A has q-intentional control over B+2, B+2 has q-intentional control over B+6, and so on up to B+30. Or B+30 can q-remember the life of B+14, B+14 can q-remember the life of B+6, and so on back to A.[29]

A, however, need not be psychologically

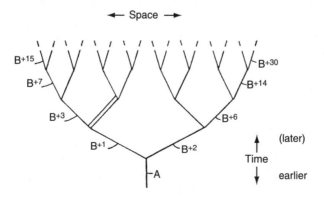

connected to B+30. Connectedness requires direct relations. And if these beings are like us, A cannot stand in such relations to every individual in his indefinitely long "tree." Q-memories will weaken with the passage of time, and then fade away. Q-ambitions, once fulfilled, will be replaced by others. Q-characteristics will gradually change. In general, A stands in fewer and fewer direct psychological relations to an individual in his "tree" the more remote that individual is. And if the individual is (like B+30) sufficiently remote, there may be between the two *no* direct psychological relations.

Now that we have distinguished the general relations of psychological continuity and psychological connectedness, I suggest that connectedness is a more important element in survival. As a claim about our own survival, this would need more arguments than I have space to give. But it seems clearly true for my imagined beings. A is as close psychologically to B+1 as I today am to myself tomorrow. A is as distant from B+30 as I am from my great-great-grandson.

Even if connectedness is not more important than continuity, the fact that one of these is a relation of degree is enough to show that what matters in survival can have degrees. And in any case the two relations are quite different. So our imagined beings would need a way of thinking in which this difference is recognized.

V

What I propose is this.

First, A can think of any individual, anywhere in his "tree," as "a descendant self." This phrase implies psychological continuity. Similarly, any later individual can think of any earlier individual on the single path[30] which connects him to A as "an ancestral self."

Since psychological continuity is transitive, "being an ancestral self of" and "being a descendant self of" are also transitive.

To imply psychological connectedness I suggest the phrases "one of my future selves" and "one of my past selves."

These are the phrases with which we can describe Wiggins' case. For having past and future selves is, what we needed, a way of continuing to exist which does not imply identity through time. The original person does, in this sense, survive Wiggins' operation: the two resulting people are his later selves. And they can each refer to him as "my past self." (They can share a past self without being the same self as each other.)

Since psychological connectedness is not transitive, and is a matter of degree, the relations "being a past self of" and "being a future self of" should themselves be treated as relations of degree. We allow for this series of descriptions: "my most recent self," "one of my earlier selves," "one of my distant selves," "hardly one of my past selves (I can only q-remember a few of his experiences)," and, finally, "not in any way one of my past selves—just an ancestral self."

This way of thinking would clearly suit our first imagined beings. But let us now turn to a second kind of being. These reproduce by fusion as well as by division.[31] And let us suppose that they fuse every autumn and divide every spring. This yields the following diagram:

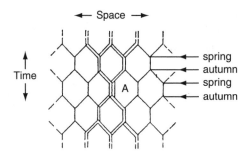

If A is the individual whose life is represented by the three-lined "branch," the two-lined "tree" represents those lives which are psychologically continuous with A's life. (It can be seen that each individual has his own "tree," which overlaps with many others.)

For the imagined beings in this second world, the phrases "an ancestral self" and "a descendant self" would cover too much to be of much use. (There may well be pairs of dates such that every individual who ever lived before the first date was an ancestral self of every individual who ever will live after the second date.) Conversely, since the lives of each individual last for only half a year, the word "I" would cover too little to do all of the work which it does for us. So part of this work would have to be done, for these second beings, by talk about past and future selves.

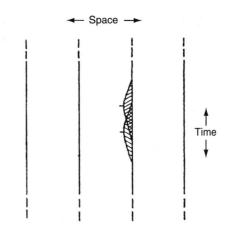

We can now point out a theoretical flaw in our proposed way of thinking. The phrase "a past self of" implies psychological connectedness. Being a past self of is treated as a relation of degree, so that this phrase can be used to imply the varying degrees of psychological connectedness. But this phrase can imply only the degrees of connectedness between different lives. It cannot be used within a single life. And our way of delimiting successive lives does not refer to the degrees of psychological connectedness. Hence there is no guarantee that this phrase, "a past self of," could be used whenever it was needed. There is no guarantee that psychological connectedness will not vary in degree within a single life.

This flaw would not concern our imagined beings. For they divide and unite so frequently, and their lives are in consequence so short, that within a single life psychological connectedness would always stand at a maximum.

But let us look, finally, at a third kind of being.

In this world there is neither division nor union. There are a number of everlasting bodies, which gradually change in appearance. And direct psychological relations, as before, hold only over limited periods of time. This can be illustrated with a third diagram (above). In this diagram the two shadings represent the degrees of psychological connectedness to their two central points.

These beings could not use the way of think-ing that we have proposed. Since there is no branching of psychological continuity, they would have to regard themselves as immortal. It might be said that this is what they are. But there is, I suggest, a better description.

Our beings would have one reason for thinking of themselves as immortal. The parts of each "line" are all psychologically continuous. But the parts of each "line" are not all psychologically connected. Direct psychological relations hold only between those parts which are close to each other in time. This gives our beings a reason for *not* thinking of each "line" as corresponding to one single life. For if they did, they would have no way of implying these direct relations. When a speaker says, for example, "I spent a period doing such and such," his hearers would not be entitled to assume that the speaker has any memories of this period, that his character then and now are in any way similar, that he is now carrying out any of the plans or intentions which he then had, and so forth. Because the word "I" would carry none of these implications, it would not have for these "immortal" beings the useful-ness which it has for us.[32]

To gain a better way of thinking, we must revise the way of thinking that we proposed above. The revision is this. The distinction between successive selves can be made by refer-ence, not to the branching of psychological continuity, but to the degrees of psychological connectedness. Since this connectedness is a matter of degree, the drawing of these distinctions can be left to the choice of the speaker and be allowed to vary from context to context.

On this way of thinking, the word "I" can be used to imply the greatest degree of psychological connectedness. When the connections are reduced, when there has been any marked change of character or style of life, or any marked loss of memory, our imagined beings would say, "It was not I who did that, but an earlier self." They could then describe in what ways, and to what degree, they are related to this earlier self.

This revised way of thinking would suit not only our "immortal" beings. It is also the way in which we ourselves could think about our lives. And it is, I suggest, surprisingly natural.

One of its features, the distinction between successive selves, has already been used by several writers. To give an example, from Proust: "we are incapable, while we are in love, of acting as fit predecessors of the next persons who, when we are in love no longer, we shall presently have become. . . ."[33]

Although Proust distinguished between successive selves, he still thought of one person as being these different selves. This we would not do on the way of thinking that I propose. If I say, "It will not be me, but one of my future selves," I do not imply that I will be that future self. He is one of my later selves, and I am one of his earlier selves. There is no underlying person who we both are.

To point out another feature of this way of thinking. When I say, "There is no person who we both are," I am only giving my decision. Another person could say, "It will be you," thus deciding differently. There is no question of either of these decisions being a mistake. Whether to say "I," or "one of my future selves," or "a descendant self" is entirely a matter of choice. The matter of fact, which must be agreed, is only whether the disjunction applies. (The question "Are X and Y the same person?" thus becomes "Is X at least an ancestral [or descendant] self of Y?")

VI

I have tried to show that what matters in the continued existence of a person are, for the most part, relations of degree. And I have proposed a way of thinking in which this would be recognized.

I shall end by suggesting two consequences and asking one question.

It is sometimes thought to be especially rational to act in our own best interests. But I suggest that the principle of self-interest has no force. There are only two genuine competitors in this particular field. One is the principle of biased rationality: do what will best achieve what you actually want. The other is the principle of impartiality: do what is in the best interests of everyone concerned.

The apparent force of the principle of self-interest derives, I think, from these two other principles.

The principle of self-interest is normally supported by the principle of biased rationality. This is because most people care about their own future interests.

Suppose that this prop is lacking. Suppose that a man does not care what happens to him in, say, the more distant future. To such a man, the principle of self-interest can only be propped up by an appeal to the principle of impartiality. We must say, "Even if you don't care, you ought to take what happens to you then equally into account." But for this, as a special claim, there seem to me no good arguments. It can only be supported as part of the general claim, "You ought to take what happens to everyone equally into account."[34]

The special claim tells a man to grant an *equal* weight to all the parts of his future. The argument for this can only be that all the parts of his future are *equally* parts of *his* future. This is true. But it is a truth too superficial to bear the weight of the argument. (To give an analogy: The unity of a nation is, in its nature, a matter of degree. It is therefore only a superficial truth that all of a man's compatriots are *equally* his compatriots. This truth cannot support a good argument for nationalism.)[35]

I have suggested that the principle of self-interest has no strength of its own. If this is so, there is no special problem in the fact that what we ought to do can be against our interests. There is only the general problem that it may not be what we want to do.

The second consequence which I shall mention is implied in the first. Egoism, the fear not of near but of distant death, the regret that so much of one's *only* life should have gone by—these are not, I think, wholly natural or instinctive. They are all strengthened by the beliefs about personal identity which I have been attacking. If we give up these beliefs, they should be weakened.

My final question is this. These emotions are bad, and if we weaken them we gain. But can we achieve this gain without, say, also weakening loyalty to, or love of, other particular selves? As Hume warned, the "refined reflections which philosophy suggests . . . cannot diminish . . . our vicious passions . . . without diminishing . . . such as are virtuous. They are . . . applicable to all our affections. In vain do we hope to direct their influence only to one side."[36]

That hope *is* vain. But Hume had another: that more of what is bad depends upon false belief. This is also my hope.

Notes

1 I have been helped in writing this by D. Wiggins, D. F. Pears, P. F. Strawson, A. J. Ayer, M. Woods, N. Newman, and (through his publications) S. Shoemaker.

2 Implicit in John Locke, *Essay Concerning Human Understanding*, ed. by John W. Yolton (London, 1961), Vol. II, Ch. XXVII, sec. 18, and discussed by (among others) A. N. Prior in "Opposite Number," *Review of Metaphysics*, 11 (1957–1958), and "Time, Existence and Identity," *Proceedings of the Aristotelian Society*, LVII (1965–1966); J. Bennett in "The Simplicity of the Soul," *Journal of Philosophy*, LXIV (1967); and R. Chisholm and S. Shoemaker in

"The Loose and Popular and the Strict and the Philosophical Senses of Identity," in *Perception and Personal Identity: Proceedings of the 1967 Oberlin Colloquium in Philosophy*, ed. by Norman Care and Robert H. Grimm (Cleveland, 1967).

3 In *Identity and Spatio-Temporal Continuity* (Oxford, 1967), p. 50.

4 In *Self-Knowledge and Self-Identity* (Ithaca, N.Y., 1963), p. 22.

5 Those who would disagree are not making a mistake. For them my argument would need a different case. There must be some multiple transplant, faced with which these people would both find it hard to believe that there must be an answer to the question about personal identity, and be able to be shown that nothing of importance turns upon this question.

6 R. W. Sperry, in *Brain and Conscious Experience*, ed. by J. C. Eccles (New York, 1966), p. 299.

7 Cf. David Wiggins, *op. cit*, p. 40.

8 Suppose the resulting people fight a duel. Are there three people fighting, one on each side, and one on both? And suppose one of the bullets kills. Are there two acts, one murder and one suicide? How many people are left alive? One? Two? (We could hardly say, "One and a half.") We could talk in this way. But instead of saying that the resulting people *are* the original person—so that the pair is a trio—it would be far simpler to treat them as a pair, and describe their relation to the original person in some new way. (I owe this suggested way of talking, and the objections to it, to Michael Woods.)

9 Cf. Sydney Shoemaker, in *Perception and Personal Identity: Proceedings of the 1967 Oberlin Colloquim in Philosophy*, loc. cit.

10 Cf. David Wiggins, *op. cit.*, p. 54.

11 Bernard Williams' "The Self and the Future," *Philosophical Review*, LXXIX (1970), 161–180, is relevant here. He asks the question "Shall I survive?" in a range of problem cases, and he shows how natural it is to believe (1) that this question must have an answer, (2) that the answer must be all-or-nothing, and (3) that there is a "risk" of our reaching the *wrong* answer. Because these beliefs are so natural, we should need in undermining them to discuss their causes. These, I think, can be found in the ways in which we misinterpret what it is to

remember (cf. Sec. III below) and to anticipate (cf. Williams' "Imagination and the Self," *Proceedings of the British Academy*, LII [1966], 105–124); and also in the way in which certain features of our egoistic concern—e.g., that it is simple, and applies to all imaginable cases—are "projected" onto its object. (For another relevant discussion, see Terence Penelhum's *Survival and Disembodied Existence* [London, 1970], final chapters.)

12 "Personal Identity and Individuation," *Proceedings of the Aristotelian Society*, LVII (1956–1957), 229–253; also *Analysis*, 21 (1960–1961), 43–48.

13 J. M. Shorter, "More about Bodily Continuity and Personal Identity," *Analysis*, 22 (1961–1962), 79–85; and Mrs J. M. R. Jack (unpublished), who requires that this truth be embedded in a causal theory.

14 *Analysis*, 21 (1960–1961), 44.

15 For the reasons given by A. M. Quinton in "The Soul," *Journal of Philosophy*, LIX (1962), 393–409.

16 Cf. S. Shoemaker, "Persons and Their Pasts," to appear in the *American Philosophical Quarterly*, and "Wiggins on Identity," *Philosophical Review*, LXXIX (1970), 542.

17 But not a necessary condition, for in the absence of psychological continuity bodily identity might be sufficient.

18 Cf. Bernard Williams, "Personal Identity and Individuation," *Proceedings of the Aristotelian Society*, LVII (1956–1957), 240–241, and *Analysis*, 21 (1960–1961), 44; and also Wiggins, *op. cit.*, p. 38: "if coincidence under [the concept] f is to be *genuinely* sufficient we must not withhold identity . . . simply because transitivity is threatened."

19 Williams produced another objection to the "psychological criterion," that it makes it hard to explain the difference between the concepts of identity and exact similarity (*Analysis*, 21 [1960–1961], 48). But if we include the requirement of causal continuity we avoid this objection (and one of those produced by Wiggins in his note 47).

20 Those philosophers who have held this belief, from Butler onward, are too numerous to cite.

21 *Op. cit.*

22 In a paper on Butler's objection to Locke (not yet published).

23 I here follow Shoemaker's "quasi-memory." Cf. also Penelhum's "retro-cognition," in his article on "Personal Identity," in the *Encyclopedia of Philosophy*, ed. by Paul Edwards.

24 As Shoemaker put it, I seem to remember the experience "from the inside" (*op. cit.*).

25 This is what so many writers have overlooked. Cf. Thomas Reid: "My memory testifies not only that this was done, but that it was done by me who now remember it" ("Of Identity," in *Essays on the Intellectual Powers of Man*, ed. by A. D. Woozley [London, 1941], p. 203). This mistake is discussed by A. B. Palma in "Memory and Personal Identity," *Australasian Journal of Philosophy*, 42 (1964), 57.

26 It is not logically necessary that we only q-remember our own experiences. But it might be necessary on other grounds. This possibility is intriguingly explored by Shoemaker in his "Persons and Their Pasts" (*op. cit.*). He shows that q-memories can provide a knowledge of the world only if the observations which are q-remembered trace out fairly continuous spatiotemporal paths. If the observations which are q-remembered traced out a network of frequently interlocking paths, they could not, I think, be usefully ascribed to persisting observers, but would have to be referred to in some more complex way. But in fact the observations which are q-remembered trace out single and separate paths; so we can ascribe them to ourselves. In other words, it is epistemologically necessary that the observations which are q-remembered should satisfy a certain general condition, one particular form of which allows them to be usefully self-ascribed.

27 Cf. Wiggins' paper on Butler's objection to Locke.

28 There are complications here. He could form *divergent* q-intentions only if he could distinguish, in advance, between the resulting people (e.g., as "the left-hander" and "the right-hander"). And he could be confident that such divergent q-intentions would be carried out only if he had reason to believe that neither of the resulting people would change their (inherited) mind. Suppose he was torn between duty and desire. He could not solve this dilemma by q-intending, as one of the resulting people, to do his duty, and, as the other, to do what he desires. For the one he q-intended to do his duty would face the same dilemma.

29 The chain of continuity must run in one direction

of time. B + 2 is not, in the sense I intend, psychologically continuous with B + 1.

30 Cf. David Wiggins, *op.cit.*

31 Cf. Sydney Shoemaker in "Persons and Their
Pasts," *op.cit.*

32 Cf. Austin Duncan Jones, "Man's Mortality," *Analy-sis*, 28 (1967–1968), 65–70.

33 *Within a Budding Grove* (London, 1949), 1, 226 (my
own translation).

34 Cf. Thomas Nagel's *The Possibility of Altruism* (Oxford,
1970), in which the special claim is in effect
defended as part of the general claim.

35 The unity of a nation we seldom take for more than

what it is. This is partly because we often think of
nations, not as units, but in a more complex way. If
we thought of ourselves in the way that I proposed,
we might be less likely to take our own identity
for more than what it is. We are, for example,
sometimes told, "It is irrational to act against your
own interests. After all, it will be you who will
regret it." To this we could reply, "No, not me. Not
even one of my future selves. Just a descendant
self."

36 "The Sceptic," in "Essays Moral, Political and Liter-ary," *Hume's Moral and Political Philosophy* (New York,
1959), p. 349.

Chapter 26

Eric T. Olson

AN ARGUMENT FOR ANIMALISM

It is a truism that you and I are human beings. It is also a truism that a human being is a kind of animal: roughly a member of the primate species *Homo sapiens*. It would seem to follow that we are animals. Yet that claim is deeply controversial. Plato, Augustine, Descartes, Spinoza, Leibniz, Locke, Berkeley, Hume, Kant, and Hegel all denied it. With the notable exception of Aristotle and his followers, it is hard to find a major figure in the history of Western philosophy who thought that we are animals. The view is no more popular in non-Western traditions. And probably nine out of ten philosophers writing about personal identity today either deny outright that we are animals or say things that are clearly incompatible with it.

This is surprising. Isn't it obvious that we are animals? I will try to show that it isn't obvious, and that Plato and the others have their reasons for thinking otherwise. Before doing that I will explain how I understand the claim that we are animals. My main purpose, though, is to make a case for this unpopular view. I won't rely on the brief argument I began with. My strategy is to ask what it would mean if we weren't animals. Denying that we are animals is harder than you might think.

1. What Animalism Says

When I say that we are animals, I mean that each of us is numerically identical with an animal.

There is a certain human organism, and that organism is you. You and it are one and the same. This view has been called animalism (not a very nice name, but I haven't got a better one). Simple though it may appear, this is easily misunderstood. Many claims that sound like animalism are in fact different.

First, some say that we are animals and yet reject animalism.[1] How is that possible? How can you be an animal, and yet not be one? The idea is that there is a sense of the verb to be in which something can "be" an animal without being identical with any animal. Each of us "is" an animal in the sense of being "constituted" by one. That means roughly that you are in the same place and made of the same matter as an animal. But you and that animal could come apart (more on this later). And since a thing can't come apart from itself, you and the animal are not identical.

I wish people wouldn't say things like this. If you are not identical with a certain animal, that animal is something other than you. And I doubt whether there is any interesting sense in which you can be something other than yourself. Even if there is, expressing a view on which no one is identical with an animal by saying that we *are* animals is badly misleading. It discourages us from asking important questions: what we *are* identical with if not animals, for instance. Put plainly and honestly, these philosophers are saying that each of us is a non-animal that relates in some intimate way to an animal. They put it by saying that we *are* animals because that sounds more plausible. This is salesman's hype, and we shouldn't be fooled. In any case, the "constitutionalists" do not say that we are animals in the straightforward sense in which I mean it. They are not animalists.

The existence of the constitution view shows that animalism is not the same as *materialism*. Materialism is the view that we are material things; and we might be material things but not animals. Animalism implies materialism (animals are material things), but not vice versa. It may seem perverse for a materialist to reject animalism. If we are material things of any sort, surely we are animals? Perverse or not, though, the view that we are material non-organisms is widely held.

Animalism says that *we* are animals. That is compatible with the existence of non-animal people (or persons, if you prefer). It is often said that to be a person is to have certain mental qualities: to be rational, intelligent, and self-conscious, say. Perhaps a person must also be morally responsible, and have free will. If something like that is right, then gods or angels might be people but not animals.

Nor does our being animals imply that all animals, or even all human animals, are people. Human beings in a persistent vegetative state are biologically alive, but their mental capacities are permanently destroyed. They are certainly human animals. But we might not want to call them people. The same goes for human embryos.

So the view that we are animals does not imply that to be a person is nothing other than to be an animal of a certain sort—that being an animal is part of what it is to be a person. Inconveniently enough, this view has also been called animalism. It isn't the animalism that I want to defend. In fact it looks rather implausible. I don't know whether there could be inorganic people, as for instance traditional theism asserts. But mere reflection on what it is to be a person doesn't seem to rule it out. Of course, if people are animals by definition, it

follows that we are animals, since we are obviously people. But the reverse entailment doesn't hold: we might be animals even if something could be a person without being an animal.

If I don't say that all people are animals, which people do I mean? Is animalism the mere tautology that all animal people are animals? No. I say that you and I and the other people who walk the earth are animals. If you like, all *human* people are animals, where a human person is roughly someone who relates to a human animal in the way that you and I do, whatever way that is. (Even idealists can agree that we are in some sense human, and not, say, feline or angelic.) Many philosophers deny that *any* people are animals. So there is nothing trivial about this claim.

"Animalism" is sometimes stated as the view that we are *essentially or most fundamentally* animals. We are essentially animals if we couldn't possibly exist without being animals. It is less clear what it is for us to be most fundamentally animals, but this is usually taken to imply at least that our identity conditions derive from our being animals, rather than from our being, say, people or philosophers or material objects—even though we *are* people and philosophers and material objects.

Whether our being animals implies that we are essentially or most fundamentally animals depends on whether human animals are essentially or most fundamentally animals. If the animal that you are is essentially an animal, then so are you. If it is only contingently an animal, then you are only contingently an animal. Likewise, you are most fundamentally an animal if and only if the animal that you are is most fundamentally an animal. The claim that each of us is identical with an animal is neutral on these questions. Most philosophers think that every animal is essentially and most fundamentally an animal, and I am inclined to agree. But you could be an animalist in my sense without accepting this.

Is animalism the view that we are identical with our bodies? That depends on what it is for something to be someone's body. If a person's body is by definition a sort of animal, then I suppose being an animal amounts to being one's body. It is often said, though, that someone could have a partly or wholly inorganic body. One's body might include plastic or metal limbs. Someone might even have an entirely robotic body. I take it that no animal could be partly or wholly inorganic. If you cut off an animal's limb and replace it with an inorganic prosthesis, the animal just gets smaller and has something inorganic attached to it. So perhaps after having some or all of your parts replaced by inorganic gadgets of the right sort you would be identical with your body, but would not be an animal. Animalism may imply that you are your body, but you could be your body without being an animal. Some philosophers even say that being an animal rules out being identical with one's body. If you replaced enough of an animal's parts with new ones, they say, it would end up with a different body from the one it began with.

Whether these claims about bodies are true depends on what it is for something to be someone's body. What does it *mean* to say that your body is an animal, or that someone might have a robotic body? I have never seen a good answer to this question (see van Inwagen 1980 and Olson 2006). So I will talk about people and animals, and leave bodies out of it.

Finally, does animalism say that we are *merely* animals? That we are nothing more than biological organisms? This is a delicate point. The issue is whether being "more than just" or "not merely" an animal is compatible with being an animal—that is, with being identical with an animal.

If someone complains that the committee is more than just the chairman, she means that it is not the chairman: it has other members too. If we are more than just animals in something like this sense, then we are not animals. We have parts that are not parts of any animal: immaterial souls, perhaps.

On the other hand, we say that Descartes was more than just a philosopher: he was also a mathematician, a Frenchman, a Roman Catholic, and many other things. That is of course compatible with his being a philosopher. We can certainly be more than "mere" animals in this sense, and yet still be animals. An animal can have properties other than being an animal, and which don't follow from its being an animal. Our being animals does not rule out our being mathematicians, Frenchmen, or Roman Catholics—or our being people, socialists, mountaineers, and many other things. At least there is no evident reason why it should. Animalism does not imply that we have a fixed, "animal" nature, or that we have only biological or naturalistic properties, or that we are no different, in any important way, from other animals. There may be a vast psychological and moral gulf between human animals and organisms of other species. We may be very special animals. But for all that we may be animals.

2. Alternatives

One reason why it may seem obvious that we are animals is that it is unclear what else we could be. If we're not animals, what are we? What are the alternatives to animalism? This is a question that philosophers ought to ask more often. Many views about personal identity clearly rule out our being animals, but leave it a mystery what sort of things we might be instead. Locke's account is a notorious example. His detailed account of personal identity doesn't even tell us whether we are material or immaterial.

Well, there is the traditional idea that we are simple immaterial substances, or, alternatively, compound things made up of an immaterial substance and a biological organism.

There is the view, mentioned earlier, that we are material objects "constituted by" human animals. You and a certain animal are physically indistinguishable. Nonetheless you and it are two different things.

Some say that we are temporal parts of

animals. Animals and other persisting objects exist at different times by having different temporal parts or "stages" located at those times. You are made up of those stages of a human animal (or, in science fiction, of several animals) that are "psychologically interconnected" (Lewis 1976). Since your animal's embryonic stages have no mental properties at all, they aren't psychologically connected with anything, and so they aren't parts of you. Hence, you began later than the animal did.

Hume famously proposed that each of us is "a bundle or collection of different perceptions, which succeed each other with an inconceivable rapidity, and are in a perpetual flux and movement" (1888: 252). Strictly speaking you are not made of bones and sinews, or of atoms, or of matter. You are literally composed of thoughts. Whether Hume actually believed this is uncertain; but some do (e.g. Quinton 1962).

Every teacher of philosophy has heard it said that we are something like computer programs. You are a certain complex of information "realized" in your brain. (How else could you survive Star-Trek teletransportation?) That would mean that you are not a concrete object at all. You are a universal. There could literally be more than one of you, just as there is more than one concrete instance of the web browser *Netscape* 6.2.

There is even the paradoxical view that we don't really exist at all. There are many thoughts and experiences, but no beings that *have* those thoughts or experiences. The existence of human people is an illusion—though of course no one is deluded about it. Philosophers who have denied or at least doubted their own existence include Parmenides, Spinoza, Hume, Hegel (as I read them, anyway), Russell (1985: 50), and Unger (1979). We also find the view in Indian Buddhism.

There are other views about what we might be, but I take these to be animalism's main rivals. One of these claims, or another one that I haven't mentioned, must be true. There must be *some* sort of thing that we are. If there is anything sitting in your chair and reading these words, it must have some basic properties or other.

For those who enjoy metaphysics, these are all fascinating proposals. Whatever their merits, though, they certainly are strange. No one but a philosopher could have thought of them. And it would take quite a bit of philosophy to get anyone to believe one of them. Compared with these claims, the idea that we are animals looks downright sensible. That makes its enduring unpopularity all the more surprising.

3. Why Animalism is Unpopular

Why is animalism so unpopular? Historically, the main reason (though by no means the only one) is hostility to materialism. Philosophers have always found it hard to believe that a material object, no matter how physically complex, could produce thought or experience. And an animal is a material object (I assume that vitalism is false). Since it is plain enough that *we* can think, it is easy to conclude that we couldn't be animals.

But why do modern-day materialists reject animalism, or at least say things that rule it out? The main reason, I believe, is that when they think about personal identity they don't ask what sort of things we are. They don't ask whether we are animals, or what we might be if we aren't animals, or how we relate to the human animals that are so intimately connected with us. Or at least they don't ask that first. No one who *began* by asking what we are would hit on the idea that we must be computer programs or bundles of thoughts or non-animals made of the same matter as animals.

The traditional problem of personal identity is not what we are, but what it takes for us to persist. It asks what is necessary, and what is sufficient, for a person existing at one time to be identical with something present at another time: what sorts of adventures we could survive, and what would inevitably bring our existence to an end. Many philosophers seem to think that an answer to this question would tell us all there is to know about the metaphysics of personal identity. This is not so. Claims about what it takes for us to persist do not by themselves tell us what other fundamental properties we have: whether we are material or immaterial, simple or composite, abstract or concrete, and so on. At any rate, the single-minded focus on our identity over time has tended to put other metaphysical questions about ourselves out of philosophers' minds.

What is more, the most popular solution to this traditional problem rules out our being animals. It is that we persist by virtue of some sort of psychological continuity. You are, necessarily, that future being that in some sense inherits its mental features—personality, beliefs, memories, values, and so on—from you. And you are that past being whose mental features you have inherited. Philosophers disagree about what sort of inheritance this has to be: whether those mental features must be continuously physically realized, for instance. But most accept the general idea. The persistence of a human animal, on the other hand, does not consist in mental continuity.

The fact that each human animal starts out as an unthinking embryo and may end up as an unthinking vegetable shows that no sort of mental continuity is necessary for a human animal to persist. No human animal is mentally continuous with an embryo or vegetable.

To see that no sort of mental continuity is sufficient for a human animal to persist, imagine that your cerebrum is put into another head. The being who gets that organ, and he alone, will be mentally continuous with you on any account of what mental continuity is. So if mental continuity of any sort suffices for you to persist, you would go along with your transplanted cerebrum. You wouldn't stay behind with an empty head.

What would happen to the human animal associated with you? Would it go along with its cerebrum? Would the surgeons pare that animal down to a small chunk of yellowish-pink tissue, move it across the room, and then supply it with a new head, trunk, and other parts? Surely not. A detached cerebrum is no more an organism than a detached liver is an organism. The empty-headed thing left behind, by contrast, is an animal. It may even remain alive, if the surgeons are careful to leave the lower brain intact. The empty-headed being into which your cerebrum is implanted is also an animal. It looks for all the world like there are two human animals in the story. One of them loses its cerebrum and gets an empty head. The other has its empty head filled with that organ. No animal moves from one head to another. The surgeons merely move an organ from one animal to another. If this is right, then no sort of psychological continuity suffices for the identity of a human animal over time. One human animal could be mentally continuous with another one (supposing that they can have mental properties at all).

If we tell the right kind of story, it is easy enough to get most people, or at any rate most Western-educated philosophy students, to say that you would go along with your transplanted cerebrum. After all, the one who got that organ would act like you and think she was you. Why deny that she would be who she thinks she is? But "your" animal—the one you would be if you were any animal—would stay behind. That means that you and that animal could go your separate ways. And a thing and itself can never go their separate ways.

It follows that you are not that animal, or indeed any other animal. Not only are you not essentially an animal. You are not an animal at all, even contingently. Nothing that is even contingently an animal would move to a different head if its cerebrum were transplanted. The human animals in the story stay where they are and merely lose or gain organs.[2]

So the thought that leads many contemporary philosophers to reject animalism—or that would lead them to reject it if they accepted the consequences of what they believe—is something like this: You would go along with your transplanted cerebrum; but no human animal would go along with its transplanted cerebrum. More generally, some sort of mental continuity suffices for us to persist, yet no sort of mental continuity suffices for an animal to persist. It follows that we are not animals. If we were animals, we should have the identity conditions of animals. Those conditions would have nothing to do with psychological facts. Psychology would be irrelevant to our identity over time. That goes against 300 years of thinking about personal identity.

This also shows that animalism is a substantive metaphysical thesis with important consequences. There is nothing harmless about it.

4. The Thinking-Animal Argument

I turn now to my case for animalism.

It seems evident that there is a human animal intimately related to you. It is the one located where you are, the one we point to when we point to you, the one sitting in your chair. It seems equally evident that human animals can think. They can act. They can be aware of themselves and the world. Those with mature nervous systems in good working order can, anyway. So there is a thinking, acting human animal sitting where you are now. But you think and act. You are the thinking being sitting in your chair.

It follows from these apparently trite observations that you are an animal. In a nutshell, the argument is this: (1) There is a human animal sitting in your chair. (2) The human animal sitting in your chair is thinking. (If you like, every human animal sitting there is thinking.) (3) You are the thinking being sitting in your chair. The one and only thinking being sitting in your chair is none other than you. Hence, you are that animal. That animal is you. And there is nothing special about you: we are all animals. If anyone suspects a trick, here is the argument's logical form:

1. $(\exists x)(x$ is a human animal & x is sitting in your chair$)$
2. $(x)((x$ is a human animal & x is sitting in your chair$) \rightarrow x$ is thinking$)$
3. $(x)((x$ is thinking & x is sitting in your chair$) \rightarrow x =$ you$)$
4. $(\exists x)(x$ is a human animal & $x =$ you$)$

The reader can verify that it is formally valid. (Compare: A man entered the bank vault. The man who entered the vault—any man who did—stole the money. Snodgrass, and no one else, entered the vault and stole the money. Doesn't it follow that Snodgrass is a man?)

Let us be clear about what the thinking-animal argument purports to show. Its conclusion is that we are human animals. That is, one of the things true of you is that you are (identical with) an animal. That of course leaves many metaphysical questions about ourselves unanswered. It doesn't by itself tell us whether we are essentially or most fundamentally animals, for instance, or what our identity conditions are. That depends on the metaphysical nature of human animals: on whether human animals are essentially animals, and what their identity conditions are. These are further questions. I argued in the previous section that no sort of mental continuity is either necessary or sufficient for a human animal to persist. If that is right, then our being animals has important and highly contentious metaphysical implications. But it might be disputed, even by those who agree that we are animals. The claim that we are animals is not the end of the story about personal identity. It is only the beginning. Still, it is important to begin in the right place.

The thinking-animal argument is deceptively simple. I suspect that its very simplicity has prevented many philosophers from seeing its point. But there is nothing sophistical about it. It has no obvious and devastating flaw that we teach our students. It deserves to be better known.[3]

In any case, the argument has three premises, and so there are three ways of resisting it. One could deny that there is any human animal sitting in your chair. One could deny that any such animal thinks. Or one could deny that you are the thinking being sitting there. Anyone who denies that we are animals is committed to accepting one of these claims. They are not very plausible. But let us consider them.

5. Alternative One: There Are No Human Animals

Why suppose that there is no human animal sitting in your chair? Presumably because there are no human animals anywhere. If there are any human animals at all, there is one sitting there. (I assume that you aren't a Martian foundling.) And if there are no human animals, it is hard to see how there could be any organisms of other sorts. So denying the argument's first premise amounts to denying that there are, strictly speaking, any organisms. There appear to be, of course. But that is at best a well-founded illusion.

There are venerable philosophical views that rule out the existence of organisms. Idealism, for instance, denies that there are any material objects at all (so I should describe it, anyway). And there is the view that nothing can have different parts at different times (Chisholm 1976: 145–158). Whenever something appears to lose or gain a part, the truth of the matter is that one object, made of the first set of parts, ceases to exist (or becomes scattered) and is instantly replaced by a numerically different object made of the second set of parts. Organisms, if there were such things, would constantly assimilate new particles and expel others. If nothing can survive a change of any of its parts, organisms are metaphysically impossible. What we think of as an organism is in reality only a succession of different "masses of matter" that each take on organic form for a brief moment—until a single particle is gained or lost—and then pass that form on to a numerically different mass.

But few opponents of animalism deny the

existence of animals. They have good reason not to, quite apart from the fact that this is more or less incredible. Anything that would rule out the existence of animals would also rule out most of the things we might be if we are not animals. If there are no animals, there are no beings constituted by animals, and no temporal parts of animals. And whatever rules out animals may tell against Humean bundles of perceptions as well. If there are no animals, it is not easy to see what we could be.

6. Alternative Two: Human Animals Can't Think

The second alternative is that there is an animal sitting in your chair, but it isn't thinking. (Let any occurrence of a propositional attitude, such as the belief that it's raining or the hope that it won't, count as "thinking".) You think, but the animal doesn't. The reason for this can only be that the animal can't think. If it were able to think, it would be thinking now. And if that animal can't think—despite its healthy, mature human brain, lengthy education, surrounding community of thinkers, and appropriate evolutionary historythen no human animal can. And if no human animal can think, no animal of any sort could. (We can't very well say that dogs can think but human animals can't.) Finally, if no animal could ever think—not even a normal adult human animal—it is hard to see how any organism could have any mental property whatever. So if your animal isn't thinking, that is apparently because it is impossible for any organism to have mental properties.

The claim, then, is that animals, including human animals, are no more intelligent or sentient than trees. We could of course say that they are "intelligent" in the sense of being the bodies of intelligent people who are not themselves animals. And we could call organisms like dogs "sentient" in the sense of being the bodies of sentient non-animals that stand to those animals as you and I stand to human animals. But that is loose talk. The strict and sober truth would be that only non-organisms could ever think.

This is rather hard to believe. Anyone who denies that animals can think (or that they can think in the way that we think) needs to explain why they can't. What stops a typical human animal from using its brain to think? Isn't that what that organ is for?

Traditionally, those who deny that animals can think deny that any material object could do so. That seems natural enough: if *any* material thing could think, it would be an animal. Thinking things must be immaterial, and so must we. Of course, simply denying that any material thing could think does nothing to explain why it couldn't. But again, few contemporary opponents of animalism believe that we are immaterial.

Someone might argue like this: "The human animal sitting in your chair is just your body. It is absurd to suppose that your body reads or thinks about philosophy. The thinking thing there—you—must therefore be something other than the animal. But that doesn't mean that you are immaterial. You might be a material thing other than your body."

It may be false to say that your body is reading. There is certainly *something* wrong with that statement. What is less clear is whether it is wrong because the phrase "your body" denotes something that you in some sense have—a certain human organism—that is unable to read. Compare the word "body" with a closely related one: mind. It is just as absurd to say that Alice's mind weighs 120 pounds, or indeed any other amount, as it is to say that Alice's body is reading. (If that seems less than obvious, consider the claim that Alice's mind is sunburned.) Must we conclude that Alice has something—a clever thing, for Alice has a clever mind—that weighs nothing? Does this show that thinking beings have no mass? Surely not. I think we should be equally wary of drawing metaphysical conclusions from the fact that the phrase "Alice's body" cannot always be substituted for the name

"Alice". In any case, the "body" argument does nothing to explain why a human animal should be unable to think.

Anyone who claims that some material objects can think but animals cannot has his work cut out for him. Shoemaker (1984: 92–97, 1999) has argued that animals cannot think because they have the wrong identity conditions. Mental properties have characteristic causal roles, and these, he argues, imply that psychological continuity must suffice for the bearers of those properties to persist. Since this is not true of any organism, no organism could have mental properties. But material things with the right identity conditions *can* think, and organisms can "constitute" such things. I have discussed this argument in another place (Olson 2002b). It is a long story, though, and I won't try to repeat it here.

7. Alternative Three: You Are Not Alone

Suppose, then, that there is a human animal sitting in your chair. And suppose that it thinks. Is there any way to resist the conclusion that you are that thinking animal? We can hardly say that the animal thinks but you don't. (If anything thinks, you do.) Nor can we deny that you exist, when there is a rational animal thinking your thoughts. How, then, could you fail to be that thinking animal? Only if you are not the only thinker there. If you are not the thinking thing sitting there, you must be one of at least two such thinkers. You exist. You think. There is also a thinking human animal there. Presumably it has the same psychological qualities as you have. But it isn't you. There are two thinking beings wherever we thought there was just one. There are two philosophers, you and an animal, sitting there and reading this. You are never truly alone: wherever you go, a watchful human animal goes with you.

This is not an attractive picture. Its adherents may try to comfort us by proposing linguistic hypotheses. Whenever two beings are as intimately related as you and your animal are, they will say, we "count them as one" for ordinary purposes (Lewis 1976). When I write on the copyright form that I am the sole author of this essay, I don't mean that every author of this essay is numerically identical with me. I mean only that every author of this essay bears some relation to me that does not imply identity: that every such author is co-located with me, perhaps. My wife is not a bigamist, even though she is, I suppose, married both to me and to the animal. At any rate it would be seriously misleading to describe our relationship as a *ménage à quatre*.

This is supposed to show that the current proposal needn't contradict anything that we say or believe when engaged in the ordinary business of life. Unless we are doing metaphysics, we don't distinguish strict numerical identity from the intimate relation that each of us bears to a certain human animal. Ordinary people have no opinion about how many numerically different thinking beings there are. Why should they? What matters in real life is not how many thinkers there are strictly speaking, but how many *non-overlapping* thinkers.

Perhaps so. Still, it hardly makes the current proposal easy to believe. Is it not strange to suppose that there are two numerically different thinkers wherever we thought there was just one?

In any event, the troubles go beyond mere overcrowding. If there really are two beings, a person and an animal, now thinking your thoughts and performing your actions, you ought to wonder which one you are. You may think you're the person (the one that isn't an animal). But doesn't the animal think that it is a person too? It has all the same reasons for thinking so as you have. Yet it is mistaken. If you *were* the animal and not the person, you'd still think you were the person. So for all you know, you're the one making the mistake. Even if you are a person and not an animal, you could never have any reason to believe that you are.[4]

For that matter, if your animal can think, that ought to make it a person. It has the same mental features as you have. (Otherwise we should expect an explanation for the difference, just as we should if the animal can't think at all.) It is, in Locke's words, "a thinking intelligent being, that has reason and reflection, and can consider itself as itself, the same thinking thing, in different times and places" (1975: 335). It satisfies every ordinary definition of "person". But it would be mad to suppose that the animal sitting in your chair is a *person* numerically different from you—that each human person shares her location and her thoughts with *another* person. If nothing else, this would contradict the claim that people—all people—have psychological identity conditions, thus sweeping away the main reason for denying that we are animals in the first place.

On the other hand, if ordinary human animals are not people, familiar accounts of what it is to be a person are all far too permissive. Having the psychological and moral features that you and I have would not be enough to make something a person. There could be rational, intelligent, self-conscious *non*-people. In fact there would be at least one such rational non-person for every genuine person. That would deprive personhood of any psychological or moral significance.

8. Hard Choices

That concludes my argument for animalism. We could put the same point in another way. There are about six billion human animals walking the earth. Those animals are just like ourselves. They sit in our chairs and sleep in our beds. They work, and talk, and take holidays. Some of them do philosophy. They have just the mental and physical attributes that we take ourselves to have. So it seems, anyway. This makes it hard to deny that *we* are those animals. The apparent existence of rational human animals is an inconvenient fact for the opponents of animalism. We might call it the *problem of the thinking animal*.

But what of the case against animalism? It seems that you would go along with your cerebrum if that organ were transplanted. More generally, some sort of mental continuity appears to suffice for us to persist.[5] And that is not true of any animal. Generations of philosophers have found this argument compelling. How can they have gone so badly wrong?

One reason, as I have said, is that they haven't asked the right questions. They have thought about what it takes for us to persist through time, but not about what we are.

Here is another. If someone is mentally just like you, that is strong evidence for his being you. Even stronger if there is continuously physically realized mental continuity between him and you. In fact it is conclusive evidence, given that brain transplants belong to science fiction. Moreover, most of us find mental continuity more interesting and important than brute physical continuity. When we hear a story, we don't much care which person at the end of the tale is the same animal as a given person at the beginning. We care far more who is psychologically continuous with that person. If mental and animal continuity often came apart, we might think differently. But they don't.

These facts can easily lead us to suppose that the one who remembers your life in the transplant story is you. Easier still if we don't know how problematic that claim is—if we don't realize that it would rule out our being animals. To those who haven't reflected on the problem of the thinking animal—and that includes most philosophers—it can seem dead obvious that we persist by virtue of mental continuity. But if we are animals, this is a mistake, though an understandable one.

Of course, opponents of animalism can play this game too. They can attempt to explain why it is natural to suppose that there are human animals, or that human animals can think, or that you are the thinking thing sitting in your chair, in a way that does not imply that those claims are true. (That is the point of the linguistic hypotheses I mentioned earlier.) What to do? Well, I invite you to compare the thinking-

animal argument with the transplant argument. Which is more likely: That there are no animals? That no animal could ever think? That you are one of at least two intelligent beings sitting in your chair? Or that you would not, after all, go along with your transplanted cerebrum?

9. What It Would Mean If We Were Animals

What would it mean if we were animals? The literature on personal identity gives the impression that this is a highly counterintuitive, "tough-minded" idea, radically at odds with our deepest convictions. It is certainly at odds with most of that literature. But I doubt whether it conflicts with anything that we all firmly believe.

If animalism conflicts with any popular beliefs, they will have to do with the conditions of our identity over time. As we have seen, the way we react (or imagine ourselves reacting) to certain fantastic stories suggests that we take ourselves to persist by virtue of mental continuity. Our beliefs about *actual* cases, though, suggest no such thing. In every actual case, the number of people we think there are is just the number of human animals. Every actual case in which we take someone to survive or perish is a case where a human animal survives or perishes.

If anything, the way we regard actual cases suggests a conviction that our identity does not consist in mental continuity, or at any rate that mental continuity is unnecessary for us to persist. When someone lapses into a persistent vegetative state, his friends and relatives may conclude that his life no longer has any value. They may even conclude that he has ceased to exist *as a person*. But they don't ordinarily suppose that their loved one no longer exists at all, and that the living organism on the hospital bed is something numerically different from him—even when they come to believe that there is no mental continuity between the vegetable and the person. *That* would be a tough-minded view.

And most of us believe that we were once foetuses. When we see an ultrasound picture of a 12-week-old foetus, it is easy to believe we are seeing something that will, if all goes well, be born, learn to talk, go to school, and eventually become an adult human person. Yet none of us is in any way mentally continuous with a 12-week-old foetus.

Animalism may conflict with religious beliefs: with the belief in reincarnation or resurrection, for instance (though whether there is any real conflict is less obvious than it may seem: see van Inwagen 1978). But few accounts of personal identity are any more compatible with those beliefs. If resurrection and reincarnation rule out our being animals, they probably rule out our being anything except immaterial substances, or perhaps computer programs. On this score animalism is no worse off than its main rivals.

And don't we have a strong conviction that we are animals? We all think that we are human beings. And until the philosophers got hold of us, we took human beings to be animals. Of course that doesn't show that we *are* animals. But it shows that we seem to be. It is the opponents of animalism who insist that this appearance is deceptive: that the animal you see in the mirror is not really you. That we are animals ought to be the default position. If anything is hard to believe, it's the alternatives.[6]

Notes

1 E.g. Shoemaker 1984: 113f. For what it's worth, my opinion of "constitutionalism" can be found in Olson 2001.

2 For more on this crucial point see Olson 1997: 114–119.

3 The argument is not entirely new. As I see it, it only makes explicit what is implicit in Carter 1989, Ayers 1990: 283f., Snowdon 1990, and Olson 1997: 100–109.

4 Some say that revisionary linguistics can solve this problem too (Noonan 1998). The idea is roughly

this. First, not just any rational, self-conscious being is a person, but only those that have psychological identity conditions. Human animals, despite their mental properties, are not people because they lack psychological identity conditions. Second, the word "I" and other personal pronouns refer only to people. Thus, when the animal associated with you says "I", it doesn't refer to itself. Rather, it refers to you, the person associated with it. When it says, "I am a person," it does not say falsely that it is a person, but truly that *you* are. So the animal is not mistaken about which thing it is, and neither are you. You can infer that you are a person from the linguistic facts that you are whatever you refer to when you say "I", and that "I" refers only to people. I discuss this ingenious proposal in Olson 2002c.

5 In fact this is not so. Let the surgeons transplant each of your cerebral hemispheres into a different head. Both offshoots will be mentally continuous with you. But they can't both *be* you, for the simple reason that one thing (you) cannot be identical with two things. We cannot say in general that anyone who is mentally continuous with you must be you. Exceptions are possible. So it ought to come as no great surprise if the original cerebrum transplant is another exception.

6 I thank Trenton Merricks and Gonzalo Rodriguez-Pereyra for comments on an earlier version.

References

Ayers, M. 1990. *Locke*, vol. 2. London: Routledge.

Carter, W. R. 1989. How to change your mind. *Canadian Journal of Philosophy* 19: 1–14.

Chisholm, R. 1976. *Person and Object*. La Salle, IL: Open Court.

Hume, D. 1888. *Treatise of Human Nature*, ed. by L. A. Selby-Bigge. Oxford: Clarendon Press. (Original work 1739. Partly reprinted in Perry 1975.)

Lewis, D. 1976. Survival and identity. In A. Rorty, ed., *The Identities of Persons*. Berkeley: California. (Repr. in his *Philosophical Papers* vol. I. New York: Oxford University Press. 1983.)

Locke, J. 1975. *An Essay Concerning Human Understanding*, ed. P. Nidditch. Oxford: Clarendon Press. (Original work, 2nd ed., originally published 1694. Partly reprinted in Perry 1975.)

Noonan, Harold. 1998. Animalism versus Lockeanism: a current controversy. *Philosophical Quarterly* 48: 302–318.

Olson, E. 1997. *The Human Animal: Personal Identity Without Psychology*. New York: Oxford University Press.

——. 2001. Material coincidence and the indiscernibility problem. *Philosophical Quarterly* 51: 337–355.

——. 2002b. What does functionalism tell us about personal identity? *Noûs* 36.

——. 2002c. Thinking animals and the reference of "I". *Philosophical Topics* 30.

——. 2006. There is no bodily criterion of personal identity. In F. MacBride, ed. *Identity and Modality*, Oxford: Clarendon Press.

Perry, J., ed. 1975. *Personal Identity*. Berkeley: University of California Press.

Quinton, A. 1962. The soul. *Journal of Philosophy* 59: 393–403. (Reprinted in Perry 1975.)

Russell, B. 1985. *The Philosophy of Logical Atomism*. La Salle, IL: Open Court. Original work 1918.

Shoemaker, S. 1984. Personal identity: a materialist's account. In S. Shoemaker and R. Swinburne, *Personal Identity*. Oxford: Blackwell.

——. 1999. Self, body, and coincidence. *Proceedings of the Aristotelian Society, Supplementary Volume* 73: 287–306.

Snowdon, Paul. 1990. Persons, animals, and ourselves. In C. Gill, ed., *The Person and the Human Mind*. Oxford: Clarendon Press.

Unger, P. 1979. I do not exist. In G. F. MacDonald, ed., *Perception and Identity*. London: Macmillan. (Reprinted in M. Rea, ed., *Material Constitution*. Lanham, MD: Rowman and Littlefield. 1997.)

van Inwagen, P. 1978. The possibility of resurrection. *International Journal for the Philosophy of Religion* 9: 114–121. (Reprinted in his *"This Possibility of Resurrection" and Other Essays in Christian Apologetics*. Boulder: Westview. 1997.)

——. 1980. Philosophers and the words "human body". In van Inwagen, ed., *Time and Cause*. Dordrecht: Reidel.

PART 4

Freedom

INTRODUCTION TO PART 4

OUR SECTION ON FREEDOM opens with a story about a biologically engineered Satyr who is rational, and thus capable of moral reasoning, but also (in his own view, anyway) genetically determined to engage in various kinds of morally reprehensible behavior. The second story, "What's Expected of Us," describes a device that infallibly signals to whomever is holding it that the person will press a button on the device exactly one second after the signal is given. People who play with the device try all manner of ways of foiling its predictions, but find that they cannot. Concluding that the device demonstrates that they are unfree, many of them fall into a catatonic state. Our third story presents the case of a person who is told by God that he will die in a crash. As in the case of Oedipus, the prediction is ultimately fulfilled by the efforts to prevent it. Together these stories raise two of the central problems associated with free will: What we might call the *compatibility problem* and the *fatalism problem*.

The compatibility problem is just the question whether the determination of our actions by deterministic laws of nature, genetics, or other factors is compatible with our freedom or (if this can be separated from freedom) with our own moral responsibility. If factors outside of my control—the laws of nature and some past state of the universe, for example, or my own brain chemistry, or a divine decree—make it absolutely inevitable that I will perform a certain action, how could I possibly be said to perform that action freely? How could I possibly be thought to be responsible for the action?

The fatalism problem arises out of the apparent fact that, if it is infallibly believed (or simply true) in advance of my doing A that I *will* do A, then I cannot do anything other than A. A central feature of classical logic is the supposition that every proposition has a truth value. So suppose you are now contemplating whether to marry a certain person. The fact that every proposition has a truth value means that either it has been true from the beginning of time that you will marry the person, or it has been false from the beginning of time that you will do so. Suppose it's the first option: it has been true from the beginning of time that you will marry the person. This fact *logically entails* that the two of you will marry. Moreover, you weren't around at the beginning of time, so it is hard to see how you could possibly have had any control over whether it was true or false way back at that time that you would eventually marry this person. How, then, can you possibly be free with respect to marrying this person?

The first four essays after the stories address these two problems directly. (On fatalism, see also Chapter 13 by Horwich, and the "June 22, 1905" entry in Chapter 10 by Lightman.) The remaining essays take up two related questions. In Chapter 34, Peter van Inwagen argues that not only is there a problem reconciling freedom with determinism, but there also is a problem reconciling freedom with *indeterminism*. If this is right, then it looks as if freedom is impossible. But, van Inwagen argues, we *know* that we are free. Thus, what we ought to conclude is that freedom is mysterious. Finally, in Chapter 35, Harry Frankfurt poses a challenge to the idea, central to many people's concept of freedom, that freedom requires *alternative possibilities*—i.e., we perform an act A freely only if we could have done something other than A.

Chapter 27

Stephen Robinett

THE SATYR

No women! No booze! What do they take me for, some kind of animal? They keep me caged like an animal. What did I ever do to them? What did I ever do to anyone, even Hench?

I should have seen it coming. For that, I blame Hench. The whole thing is his fault, his responsibility. A starship to the middle of nowhere and a life in the mines—how could he do it? and to *me*, of all creatures!

I should have seen most of it coming the day Hench said we were going to see the Merton woman's father. Hench seldom took me out. He called our trips out disasters.

I remember Hench putting me in a new tunic, parting my hair in the middle, combing it over my ears and stepping back to admire his work.

"You'll do."

I eyed him, suspicious. "For what?"

Hench flicked a piece of lint off my shoulder. "What's it to you?"

"I like to keep track of what's going on in your head, Hench." I tugged at the front of my tunic. "New clothes, shined shoes, going out—something's fishy. You're not planning anything foolish like marrying that Merton woman, are you?"

"Not yet." He told me about the appointment with her father.

I frowned. I knew Merton's reputation. He exploited worlds, most of them hostile. "What's the appointment about?"

Hench ignored the question and started for the door. "Let's go."

We took the mono downtown to Merton Planetary Development. Even public transportation put a strain on Hench's small budget. In spite of his hybrid genius, crossing biogenetic engineer and artist, things had gone poorly for Hench. As a businessman, he left something to be desired, namely, money. He mortgaged everything—laboratory, equipment, car—to create me. He could balance that incredibly complex process of genetic transplantation, followed by biochemical gestation, followed by education through artificial engram implantation, but not his checkbook. They repossessed the car first. Eventually, everything would go, except me, of course. I had no intention of going anywhere.

Hench's money problems stemmed from one source. No one wanted his product. Better cows and horses through genetic manipulation, yes, better dogs and cats—people could accept improvements on what they already knew—but new creatures, unique creatures, they found repulsive.

They even found *me* repulsive. No one objected to a chest-high, two-toed helper with bristly hair, a broad nose and leaf-shaped ears. They had seen pictures of satyrs. No one even objected to my strength and intelligence. What they claimed to object to was my pleasant disposition. They considered me unreliable. I take a drop now and then. I like the ladies. Does that make me unreliable? Still, no one wanted me. No one, except, perhaps, Merton.

Hench and I took the elevator up to Merton's offices.

"Hench, I thought you'd given up on this hare-brained scheme."

"What hare-brained scheme?"

"Selling me."

Hench avoided looking at me. I knew the reaction. I had guessed right. Every time Hench told me about a potential customer, he avoided looking at me. Every time he reported failure, he looked relieved. At first, I took this as a sign Hench liked me. Finally, I realized the true basis of his attitude. He felt responsible for me. I was his creation. A peculiar notion, responsibility, but useful.

The elevator arrived at Merton's offices. I could see the entire floor from the reception area, a central bay with row after row of gnome-like computer technicians at their consoles, all monitoring Merton's empire. Lights appeared and faded in front of them. Information filled screens and vanished. The empire was safe under their bloodshot eyes.

Of more immediate interest was the receptionist, a bird-legged girl with acne. She did have one point in her favor. She was female. Any port in a storm.

Hench talked to the receptionist a few seconds, then glanced at me. "Wait here."

I gave the receptionist an appreciative once-over. "Anything you say, Hench."

I waited on the couch opposite the bird-legged receptionist. When Hench disappeared into Merton's office, I grinned at her. Hench had told me not to grin in public. He said people found scraggly teeth repulsive. What did he know? I made out better with the ladies than he did. All he had was the Merton woman.

The receptionist noticed me grinning at her and shifted uneasily on her chair. Her eyes returned to the paperwork on her desk. She knew I was watching, inspecting, appreciating. She tried to concentrate in spite of me.

She failed. "Is there something I can do for you, sir?"

My grin widened. "Indeed, there is."

"What?"

"Is there someplace we can be alone and . . . talk?"

She looked around. For help? Possibly. "What did you want to talk about, Mr.—?" Her almost nonexistent eyebrows remained elevated, waiting for my answer.

"Silenus. Where can we chat?"

"I think right here will be satisfactory."

"I don't mind, but . . ." I glanced toward the gnomes at their computers. ". . . you may find it a little too public. Is there, perhaps, a bar in the building with romantically subdued lighting?"

"Yes, on the top floor, but—"

"Good." I stood up and extended my elbow. "Shall we go?"

I could see the struggle going on behind her eyes. She found me repulsive—bristly hair, scraggly teeth, faintly jaundiced complexion—yet, interesting. Both are common reactions.

I decided to nudge her interest. "I come equipped with a sizeable advantage."

Wrong nudge. Persnickety type. All interest faded from her eyes. She looked slightly sick. I knew I would have to resort to stronger measures to give her the kind of memories she would secretly cherish for a lifetime.

I started toward her. "You're absolutely right, my dear. Actions do speak louder than words."

Before I reached her, she bolted, scooping up an armload of papers and heading across the computer bay on her bird legs. I considered chasing her—I love a good chase—but decided against it. She would probably scream and bring Hench.

"Miss," I called after her. "I shall return. If Mr. Hench comes out of his meeting, tell him I'm in the bar."

I took the elevator up to the top floor. The doors opened on a sign reading Olympus Club. The name put me in a good mood. Part of my basic education includes large doses of Greek mythology. Hench wanted my personality to reflect my appearance. Hench makes all sorts of mistakes.

I went unnoticed in the subdued light. Along with the new suit, Hench had given me a few coins to squander. I climbed up on a barstool and ordered a half-dozen screwdrivers in a large brandy glass. I go through phases, wine, beer, bourbon, Scotch—at the time, it was vodka.

I paid and downed half the snifter. The bartender, shining a glass, watched me. Shortly, I felt good enough to sing.

I sang.

The bartender, evidently no music lover, stopped shining the glass, frowning. Several people at the bar turned to listen. The bartender asked me to stop.

"Stop? Are you kidding? This is one of my favorite songs."

He said there were ladies in the room.

"Ladies? Ladies?" I looked around. Here and there, I could see several lovely faces watching me. "Why so there are!"

I climbed up on the barstool, stepped onto the bar and began singing for the ladies, doing a soft-shoe down the shiny surface and playing to them with open arms. Several of the women looked shocked at the lyrics. Most of the men smiled.

I sang on.

The bartender, still frowning, tried to catch me.

I evaded him, tapping out a two-step before I hopped away from each swipe of his thick arms. My polished shoes sounded on the bar and glittered in the light. I sang my heart out, pathos, bathos—you name it. Then I made a mistake. I stopped long enough to pluck up my drink from the bar. The bartender, aided by two other tone-deaf men in white aprons from the kitchen, grabbed me, ejected me and told me to leave the building before they called a security guard.

I ignored this insensitive criticism of my performance and touched the button for Merton's floor. I reentered Merton's offices feeling pleasantly amorous, the full effect of the screwdrivers beginning to take hold. I wondered whether I could coax, chase, or threaten the bird-legged receptionist into the elevator long enough to have her.

She saw me coming but stood her ground, or rather sat it, remaining at her desk. I walked up, went around the desk and faced her. With her seated, we were the same height.

"Madame," I began, an ingratiating smile on my face.

"You've been drinking."

"Don't scold. A bit of the grape, or, in this case the potato."

"What do you want?"

In sexual matters, I believe in being frank. I put my hand on her thigh.

Her eyes enlarged noticeably, making them close to normal size. "Please take your hand off me."

I stroked.

She slapped my hand.

I stepped closer, inhaling her perfume—a scent that reminded me, subtly, of Hench's laboratory—and put my arms around her waist. Delicately, I kissed her throat.

She thrashed, arms flailing.

I ignored this mild protest. Resistance adds something special to their inevitable submission. I persisted.

She kicked.

I avoided.

Her chair teetered. I dragged her to the floor. A wastebasket overturned near our heads, thunk, spilling balls of paper around us.

I murmured. "My sweet rose, it will not be long now. My jewel, my buttercup, my plum, I burn with desire for you."

She responded to this eloquence by continuing to thrash and squirm.

"Submit, my treasure. You need not tell your husband. You will only hurt his feelings."

She screamed.

I felt hands grabbing at my tunic. I clutched my treasure to me and rolled away from them, ignoring the gathering crowd, continuing to murmur.

"Ahh, my wondrous blossom, my—"

Abruptly, a sharp pain went through my ribs. I was jerked away from my wondrous, bird-legged blossom.

Hench, glaring into my face, shook me. My head bobbed with each shake. "Why (shake, bob), why do you do these things?"

"What things?"

"Can't you control yourself, dammit, even in public?"

"I tried to get her to go someplace private, Hench. She wouldn't listen."

"Why can't you at least control yourself for five minutes?"

"Is it my fault?"

"It's your responsibility."

"Don't be silly, Hench. Only human beings are responsible. I am what I am."

A murmur went through the crowd. Not human? An animal? Someone, probably Merton, explained.

A biosynthetic? They looked at me with renewed interest, their mood changed. Able to classify me as something other than human, they no longer considered me a rapist, only an animal, poorly trained or perhaps not yet housebroken.

They backed off slightly. Even the receptionist, now on her feet, looked sympathetic, or semisympathetic.

Hench grabbed me by the shoulder and pushed me through the crowd toward Merton's office.

I glanced up at him. "What are you going to do?"

He pushed again, harder.

I looked over my shoulder and shouted to the crowd. "*If you hear screams, he's beating me. Call the police or the humane society or someone.*"

"Shut up," growled Hench, "or I'll crack your skull."

He gave me a shove into Merton's office.

I had to stand in the middle of the room. Hench and Merton inspected me as though I

were a new piece of office equipment. Hench, the salesman, demonstrating my finer points, Merton, nodding and willing to listen but unwilling to be sold a useless product.

Hench listed my virtues: the strength of ten (Hench exaggerates), the endurance of a machine, capable of independent action—

"Speaking of independent action, John," interrupted Merton, "can you explain that incident with our receptionist?"

Hench looked embarrassed. He scowled in my direction and tried to explain. "He has the ability to reproduce, another advantage from your point of view."

Though to me the advantage seemed obvious—as well as sizeable—Merton looked dubious.

Hench persevered. "A creature like this would only have to be seeded on a planet. After that, nature would provide you with as many workers as needed."

"An army," I added, imagining my only mission in life to populate an entire planet. But Hench had forgotten one important point. "Hench."

"What?" snapped Hench, annoyed.

"It takes two to tango—at *least* two—but the more the merrier I always say."

"The creature's right, John. Can you produce females of his species?"

"The brides of Frankenstein," I suggested.

"Yes, that's possible," answered Hench.

I shook my head, exasperated with Hench. "All these years, Hench, you've been holding out on me."

"Did you hear me tell you to shut up?"

"Do I care what you tell me?"

"You'd better care or you won't eat tonight."

I shut up. I did want to eat. Hench was forever holding that over my head. He had worked up a penalty scale, tying it to my food. The more I disobeyed, the less I ate. I found myself on an involuntary diet most of the time.

Hench continued his explanation. "The entire process takes about two years. The female version—I have had a few problems making one up to now—the female version would be ready to reproduce five years after that."

"Hench, you don't have to go to all that trouble just for me. There are plenty of women around."

"I told you to shut up."

"Yep, Hench, you did do that."

We glared at each other, deadlocked.

Merton intervened. "He doesn't seem to follow orders very well."

"You have to kick him occasionally, or take away his food."

"Go ahead, Hench, beat me—but I'll scream. You'll have the humane society on your neck."

Hench snorted. He threatened to beat me frequently. He seldom did. He usually snorted and wandered away, muttering about the allowances people had to make for creatures like me.

"And the life span, how long do they live?"

"Frankly, I don't know. He's a prototype."

I gave a prototypical grin, teeth clenched, lips folded back.

Merton automatically started to respond to the grin, then caught himself, his expression degenerating to a sort of sick look. He addressed me directly for the first time. "You do seem like an intelligent creature."

"So do you."

"Perhaps too intelligent."

"Actually," interrupted Hench, probably envisioning the entire deal going down the drain, "it's only a superficial intelligence. His real level of understanding is rudimentary." Hench turned to me, his face taking on the expression adults use with children. He pronounced his words distinctly. "Go and sit down. Do you understand me? Go and sit down."

I considered standing on my head to defy Hench. It would only have made his point, dumb animal. I walked to the nearest chair and sat down.

Merton looked like he bought exactly zero of Hench's "superficial intelligence" argument. Still, I suspected it gave him a rationalization to pass along to the board of directors. They would

not be consigning a quasi-human to this hostile world they wanted populated, but only a "superficially intelligent biosynthetic construct," i.e., me.

Merton stood up, indicating an end to the interview. He shook hands with Hench and said he would give his answer within a week. Hench led the way out the door.

In the elevator, after a prolonged parting wink at the receptionist, I asked Hench about the odds on Merton accepting the deal. Hench told me about Merton. Overextended in six directions from earth, Merton had sunk most of the company's remaining assets into colonizing and exploiting some world in the middle of nowhere. Merton had one problem. No one wanted to colonize it. That part bothered me. It reminded me too much of "hostile worlds." If no one wanted to go, they had reasons. Merton needed manpower or his empire would collapse. Hench, on the other hand, needed money.

The Merton woman had convinced her father to consider solving both problems with a single blow. Instead of manpower, she suggested satyr-power. She even went so far as to suggest I ought to work for my keep, a truly vicious idea.

I asked Hench if he intended to sell me into slavery.

He avoided looking at me and told me to shut up.

"Selling your only begotten—or, rather, synthesized—son into slavery! Hench, you're an immoral man, no better than us beasts."

"What do you know about morality?"

"I know human beings talk about it a lot. What else do I need . . ."

"I told you to shut up. I'm thinking."

"Do I care if you're thinking? Sell me off like a sack of potatoes. Hench, you're of dubious value as a father figure."

The elevator reached the ground floor, slowed and stopped. Hench snapped his finger. "Got it!"

"You've got it all right. I don't know what it is, but you've got it. The more I think about it, the more I think you got it from that Merton woman."

"If I change the thyroid hormone balance, along with the aldosterone level, inactivating the glutamic dehydrogenase so there's less glutamic acid and consequently less ammonia and alpha-keloglutaric acid . . ."

Hench kept babbling in this manner all the way back to the laboratory, his eyes becoming progressively more glazed the deeper he go into the problem. I had to lead him the last few blocks by the hand. When we got to the laboratory, he wrote down his brainstorm, covering large sheets of paper with cryptic chemical symbols and mathematics. He stayed at it for hours, oblivious to distraction.

An hour past my dinner time, he sat back, head lolling, writing arm dangling, drained. "Finished."

"Finished what?"

"Your mate, a Maenad, a nymph or whatever you call them."

"Fine, let's see the wench."

I moved up to the desk, expecting at least a drawing. Hench showed me formulas, page after page of them. Added to the computerful of formulas he had prepared to create me, they would produce my mate. I hope she looked better than Hench's chicken scratchings.

I looked up at Hench. "Only one?"

"As many as you like."

"I like a lot, but won't mass production spoil quality?" I looked at the bland formulas. "Frankly, Hench, I'd rather see a production model, or a reproduction model."

Hench gave me an exasperated glance. "You dwell on sex, do you know that?"

"Only as does a starving man of food. Speaking of food—"

"Why do you do that?"

"What?"

"Dwell on sex."

"You're the one who gave me the extra Y-chromosome. You're the one who wanted to make sure I could reproduce. You tell me."

Hench grunted. "Talk about something else."

"Okay, let's talk about this slave sale you're conducting. Why are you selling me?"

The question annoyed him. "Look, I'm in business. I make creatures, then I sell them. Business is business."

"Materialist."

Hench grunted again and avoided looking at me.

"What do they do on this godforsaken planet, anyway?"

"Mining."

"Mining! You're sending me off to the salt mines! You're inhuman, Hench."

"Business is business. Do you know what you cost? Plus—"

"Prototypes are always expensive."

"Plus, you aren't good for anything more complicated than physical labor. You can't concentate on anything but sex for more than two minutes."

"That's not true. I just don't want to concentrate on most of the things human beings do."

"It amounts to the same thing on the job market."

"The job market! Money again! Is that all you can think about, Hench? You dwell on money, do you know that? Since you met that Merton woman, that's all you can think about—money, money, money. She's got you by the bank book, Hench."

"I don't have a bank book."

"You will, as soon as old man Merton ships me off to the salt mines, you and that Merton woman will be rolling in dough, not to mention the hay. I'd like to get that woman in the hay for five minutes and show her what life's all about. It isn't money."

Abruptly, Hench slapped me.

I just about grabbed him and threw him across the room. My sense of enlightened self-interest asserted itself. I controlled the urge. If I threw him across the room, I would never be able to work on his conscience.

I let my face sting and glared at him. "You're

responsible for me, Hench! I'm your creation! If you sell me, you'll be selling your self-respect!"

That night, Hench locked me in my room to prevent escape. The next day, he let me out long enough to clean the laboratory and myself, then locked me up again, a broom returned to its closet. It sounds cruel, night after night locked away from life, liquor and the ladies. Except for my profound ability with locks, it would have been cruel. Every night, when Hench left for his rendezvous with the Merton woman, I unlocked the door and crept out.

Without money, spirits are hard to come by. I rifled coin return slots on public phones, occasionally turning up enough loose change for a short snort. I looked for women but found none alone. When I got cold or tired or hungry, I went back to the laboratory. I decided to give Hench until the last possible minute to change his mind. Why leave a warm bed and good food before necessary?

During my daily outings to scrub and sweep, I noticed Hench's anxiety. He suffered from conscience. I let him suffer. The more it ate at him—his desire for the Merton woman, money and possibly fame warring with his sense of responsibility for me—the better chance I had. I watched the moral battles played out on his face. The closer we got to the date of Merton senior's decision, the more intense the battles became, attack and counterattack causing Hench to pace the laboratory, scowling and mumbling, or pause long minutes in an abstracted trance.

Toward the end of the week, I was off in one corner of the main workroom, filling the autoclave with glassware, when the Merton woman came in. She failed to notice me. Hench, engaged in hand-to-hand combat with his conscience, had forgotten me.

She walked across the workroom to Hench, hugged him and gave him a perfunctory kiss on the cheek, announcing *good news*.

The only good news I could see her bringing were those flanks, sleek, solid—no bird legs there. I ached to have her on the spot.

Hench gazed at her with a lovestruck smile on his face, his moral dilemma temporarily forgotten as his hormones took over. "What good news?"

"Father has decided to use your creature."

Bad news, definitely bad news.

Her delighted enthusiasm continued. "It's just marvelous, darling. I'm sure father will give us enough in advance to pay off those horrible debts and have a long honeymoon." She noticed a change in Hench's expression and frowned slightly. "Is something wrong?"

"I'm not sure I should do it."

She gave an exasperated sigh and shook her head. "We've been all through this a million times, dear. It's only an animal. You've sold animals before."

"Not like him."

"Darling, you're too close to the situation. You created it. You've begun to see more in it than is there. I appreciate your feelings. It must be like selling a very smart pet. It's regrettable but necessary. It's not just me you have to worry about. It's your work. Without money, your work will stop completely. You are a great man, John. Don't let that *thing* keep you from being all you can be."

That *thing* continued to listen to this line of bullshit until its teeth ground. Hench's conscience needed help. I cupped my hands around my mouth and shouted across the workroom. *"She's only after your money, Hench!"*

Both of them became aware of me. The Merton woman turned a look of acid contempt in my direction. "John, please get that filthy animal out of here."

"Filthy or not, I'm right. Old man Merton's done for without me. Hench, she's just trying to soft soap you into becoming a millionaire slave trader. Don't listen to her."

The Merton woman kept looking at me, disgust evident on her face. "And just what is wrong with becoming a millionaire?"

I ignored her. "Slave trader, Hench. It's cost you your dignity and your soul and your self-respect. You're responsible for me. You made me. Sending me to the mines is evil and wrong."

Words like "evil" and "wrong," "responsibility" and "self-respect" usually struck a responsive chord in Hench. In spite of that, he told me to go to my room or he would crack my skull.

Reluctantly, I went, winking at the Merton woman (what flanks!) on the way out.

I could hear them arguing from my room. Even on their way to dinner, I heard Hench stressing words like "responsibility" and "doing the right things," while the Merton woman stressed eternal, nuptial bliss "and the money, darling. Don't forget the money."

That night, I resolved to leave. If I waited too long, the Merton woman would seduce Hench in more senses than one. Hench, guilty as he felt, would deport me. I put on my suit, unlocked the door and started out.

I followed the corridor past the laboratory workrooms and downstairs. Hench's office door was open, a sharp rectangle of light falling across the darkened hall. I would have to sprint past the office to get to the double doors at the end of the corridor.

I readied myself for the dash, getting down into a half-crouch, fingers arched against the polished floor.

I hesitated, hearing voices—Hench and the Merton woman arguing in his office. I tiptoed to the doorway, pressing myself against the wall and listening. The Merton woman was pleading with Hench.

"Darling, you *have* to do it. As much as you hate it, you don't have any choice."

"I do have a choice. Until I sign that contract with your father, I have a choice. I created him. I'm responsible for him."

I hesitated a moment longer. Hench's conscience seemed to be holding its own.

"It's not like it was human, darling. In the most basic sense, it's simply a product."

"That's exactly the point, he's not human. In some ways, he's completely inhuman. If he were human, at some point he would begin to take care of himself and be responsible for what he does. But he's not human at all. He's my creation and my responsibility."

"You'll lose the laboratory. You owe—"

Something slammed down on Hench's desk, cutting her off. "I know what I owe, *dammit!* Money, money, money—is that all anyone thinks about?"

"It's a vicious animal, dear. It belongs someplace away from people. You know the kinds of things it's done. It's utterly amoral."

Hench's voice took on a note of despair. "That's my fault, too. He's what I made him, whether I intended it or not. I'm responsible for everything he is, including that."

The Merton woman gave one last, unreasoned appeal. "Darling, please get rid of it—for me."

A long pause followed. I heard Hench get up and pace the office. A shadow, Hench's, filled the rectangle of light on the floor in front of me. I pressed myself closer to the wall.

At last, Hench spoke. "I can't."

My heart sang! Saved by Hench's conscience!

I tiptoed away from the door and back upstairs. Going to my room, I whistled and sang and cavorted, doing several forward flips (my favorites). I relocked the door, took off my clothes and went to bed. I drifted off to a pleasant sleep composing a song to Hench's conscience. Fortunately, before inflicting too many verses on myself, I fell asleep.

Something scraped. My eyes blinked open. A key turned in the lock. I glanced at the window. No daylight. A midnight visit from Hench? Unlikely. The light came on. The door opened.

The Merton woman, still dressed for her evening out with Hench—a sleek tube dress, black, glittering, low cut, a single strand of pearls around her throat—stepped into the cell and stood by the door, looking at me.

I looked past her at the partially open door. "Where's Hench?"

"He's gone home. I came back."

I sat up on the bed. "Does he know you're here?"

She looked at me, her revulsion (and something else—what? A spark of fascination?) clear on her face. "Please cover yourself."

I grinned.

She picked my tunic off the chair and tossed it across my lap.

I continued grinning. "Satisfied?"

"You are a disgusting creature."

"I know." I watched her flanks, the muscles clearly visible through the shiny cloth. "What do you want?"

"John has decided to keep you."

"Good news."

"Bad news. It will bankrupt him."

"So? What's the tragedy?"

"Don't you care?"

"He'll find work to support us." I hesitated. "The three of us."

Her back went rigid. "I'm not going to let it happen."

"I don't see how you can stop it. Hench is a man of conscience."

Her hand came around from behind her. She held one of the dart guns Hench uses to tranquilize, occasionally kill, us beasts. I could tell the setting by the color coding on the chamber. She had it set on kill.

Her hand shook slightly. "You will go tomorrow."

"Why do you hate me?"

Her expression, stern, wavered. The question caught her offguard. "This is for John."

I laughed. "Human beings only do things for themselves. Don't you know that yet?"

"It's for John. I won't have our lives ruined by a freak."

"I'm only a freak because I'm too much like you. Hench is different, but you and I are two of a kind. We do what we have to do to get what we want."

"If you don't agree to go tomorrow, I'll kill you now."

"I agree."

She had expected an argument, resistance. Her surprise showed on her face.

I shrugged. "I'm a coward."

I am also a liar, but it seemed best to avoid mentioning that.

Her determination softened. Some thought or speculation flitted behind her eyes. Enough of it showed to let me recognize it. I glanced at the dart gun. Distracted by her speculation, she had let her thumb wander from the trigger button.

I looked at her flanks a moment, then up at her eyes, catching her attention. Once I had it, I lunged. I knocked aside the gun. It flew out of her hand, hit the wall and discharged ineffectually against the floor, the propellant exploding with a loud *poomp* in the small room.

I grabbed her and pulled her down on the bed, beginning to whisper softly. "We are alone, my blossom. No one will interrupt. We may do as we wish, as you have always wished. There's no one here but us satyrs."

I slept soundly until mid-morning. I expected Hench to wake me early. He usually arrived at the laboratory before seven and let me out to make coffee. When I finally heard him rummaging around outside my door, sunlight already streamed through the window.

I was about to get up and go out when the door—still unlocked from the Merton woman's visit—came open. Hench entered, his hands thrust into his jacket pockets, dark circles under his red eyes, looking shaken. The expression on his face was new to me.

"Hi, Hench, What's up? You look terrible. You look like a ton of bricks fell on you. What happened?"

Hench looked directly at me. "Why did you do it?"

"Do what? What are you talking about?"

"Don't lie. I talked to Audrey."

"Oh, that." I shrugged. "How do I know why I do things? It seemed like a good idea at the time. I am what I am, Hench." I grinned and folded back my upper lip.

Hench's expression hardened. I could see I was in trouble. I fell back on my usual argument.

"Listen, Hench, you're the one who made me like this. I'm not responsible for the way I am."

"You're responsible for what you *do*."

"Ha! I am what I am, Hench. You know that as well as I do."

The struggle on Hench's face looked nothing like his earlier dilemma. Something else was going on in his head. He looked like a sickly twin brother to the Hench I knew—to the Hench I understood.

He repeated his question. "Why did you do it?"

"What do you want from me, Hench? An accounting?"

"Yes."

"You certainly don't want the truth. That's clear enough from your face. By the way, your face could use a shave. Someone's liable to mistake you for me. We can't have that, can we? After all, you're a man and I'm just a—"

"Answer me."

I made calming gestures with my hands and stalled for time. What did I see in Hench's face? More importantly, what did he see when he looked at me? A rival? a defiler? A—what?

"Stay calm, Hench. I'm not some mere human being you can shove up against a wall and—"

"I want the truth."

He didn't. That was part of what I saw in his face. He wanted answers, yes, but not the truth, either about me or about the Merton woman. He wanted something from me to take away the pain he felt, the guilt and the responsibility. He wanted his accounting, not the truth.

But what do I know about such things? I am what I am, not what someone else sees in me. What could I have said to avoid a starship to some godforsaken hell hole and a life in the mines? Hench saw what he wanted to see. If I had lied, he would have heard only what he wanted to hear.

I leaned back on the bed, smiled and gave him what he said he wanted. "Pickings have been slim lately, Hench. I just took what she offered. She only struggled at first. After that, she liked it. It's what she wanted all along anyway, so what's the big deal? No harm done." I changed my smile to sincere. "And she really wasn't that bad, Hench, not that bad at all, especially after she let herself go."

Hench's hand came out of his jacket pocket. The last thing I remember was the *poomp* of the dart gun and the expression on Hench's face. In that instant before the dart hit, I realized what he saw when he looked at me, what he had seen since he came into my room. A rival? Yes. A defiler? Yes. And more. A man.

Chapter 28

Ted Chiang

WHAT'S EXPECTED OF US

This is a warning. Please read carefully.

By now you've probably seen a Predictor; millions of them have been sold by the time you're reading this. For those who haven't seen one, it's a small device, like a remote for opening your car door. Its only features are a button and a big green LED. The light flashes if you press the button. Specifically, the light flashes one second *before* you press the button.

Most people say that when they first try it, it feels like they're playing a strange game, one where the goal is to press the button after seeing the flash, and it's easy to play. But when you try to break the rules, you find that you can't. If you try to press the button without having seen a flash, the flash immediately appears, and no matter how fast you move, you never push the button until a second has elapsed. If you wait for the flash, intending to keep from pressing the button afterward, the flash never appears. No matter what you do, the light always precedes the button press. There's no way to fool a Predictor.

The heart of each Predictor is a circuit with a negative time delay—it sends a signal back in time. The full implications of the technology will become apparent later, when negative delays of greater than a second are achieved, but that's not what this warning is about. The immediate problem is that Predictors demonstrate that there's no such thing as free will.

There have always been arguments showing that free will is an illusion, some based on hard

physics, others based on pure logic. Most people agree these arguments are irrefutable, but no one ever really accepts the conclusion. The experience of having free will is too powerful for an argument to overrule. What it takes is a demonstration, and that's what a Predictor provides.

Typically, a person plays with a Predictor compulsively for several days, showing it to friends, trying various schemes to outwit the device. The person may appear to lose interest in it, but no one can forget what it means—over the following weeks, the implications of an immutable future sink in. Some people, realizing that their choices don't matter, refuse to make any choices at all. Like a legion of Bartleby the Scriveners, they no longer engage in spontaneous action. Eventually, a third of those who play with a Predictor must be hospitalized because they won't feed themselves. The end state is akinetic mutism, a kind of waking coma. They'll track motion with their eyes, and change position occasionally, but nothing more. The ability to move remains, but the motivation is gone.

Before people started playing with Predictors, akinetic mutism was very rare, a result of damage to the anterior cingulate region of the brain. Now it spreads like a cognitive plague. People used to speculate about a thought that destroys the thinker, some unspeakable lovecraftian horror, or a Gödel sentence that crashes the human logical system. It turns out that the disabling thought is one that we've all encountered: the idea that free will doesn't exist. It just wasn't harmful until you believed it.

Doctors try arguing with the patients while they still respond to conversation. We had all been living happy, active lives before, they reason, and we hadn't had free will then either. Why should anything change? "No action you took last month was any more freely chosen than one you take today," a doctor might say. "You can still behave that way now." The patients invariably respond, "But now I know." And some of them never say anything again.

Some will argue that the fact the Predictor causes this change in behavior means that we *do* have free will. An automaton cannot become discouraged, only a free-thinking entity can. The fact that some individuals descend into akinetic mutism whereas others do not just highlights the importance of making a choice.

Unfortunately, such reasoning is faulty: every form of behavior is compatible with determinism. One dynamic system might fall into a basin of attraction and wind up at a fixed point, whereas another exhibits chaotic behavior

indefinitely, but both are completely deterministic.

I'm transmitting this warning to you from just over a year in your future: it's the first lengthy message received when circuits with negative delays in the mega-second range are used to build communication devices. Other messages will follow, addressing other issues. My message to you is this: pretend that you have free will. It's essential that you behave as if your decisions matter, even though you know that they don't. The reality isn't important: what's important is your belief, and believing the lie is the only way to avoid a waking coma. Civilization now depends on self-deception. Perhaps it always has.

And yet I know that, because free will is an illusion, it's all predetermined who will descend into akinetic mutism and who won't. There's nothing anyone can do about it—you can't choose the effect the Predictor has on you. Some of you will succumb and some of you won't, and my sending this warning won't alter those proportions. So why did I do it?

Because I had no choice.

Chapter 29

Richard Taylor

THE STORY OF OSMO

Now, then, let us make one further supposition, which will get us squarely into the philosophical issue these ideas are intended to introduce. Let us suppose that God has revealed a particular set of facts to a chosen scribe who, believing (correctly) that they came from God, wrote them all down. The facts in question then turned out to be all the more or less significant episodes in the life of some perfectly ordinary man named Osmo. Osmo was entirely unknown to the scribe, and in fact to just about everyone, but there was no doubt concerning whom all these facts were about, for the very first thing received by the scribe from God, was: "He of whom I speak is called Osmo." When the revelations reached a fairly voluminous bulk and appeared to be completed, the scribe arranged them in chronological order and assembled them into a book. He at first gave it the title *The Life of Osmo, as Given by God*, but thinking that people would take this to be some sort of joke, he dropped the reference to God.

The book was published but attracted no attention whatsoever, because it appeared to be nothing more than a record of the dull life of a very plain man named Osmo. The scribe wondered, in fact, why God had chosen to convey such a mass of seemingly pointless trivia.

The book eventually found its way into various libraries, where it gathered dust until one day a high school teacher in Indiana, who rejoiced under the name of Osmo, saw a copy on the shelf.

The title caught his eye. Curiously picking it up and blowing the dust off, he was thunderstruck by the opening sentence: "Osmo is born in Mercy Hospital in Auburn, Indiana, on June 6, 1965, of Finnish parentage, and after nearly losing his life from an attack of pneumonia at the age of five, he is enrolled in the St. James school there." Osmo turned pale. The book nearly fell from his hands. He thumbed back in excitement to discover who had written it. Nothing was given of its authorship nor, for that matter, of its publisher. His questions of the librarian produced no further information, he being as ignorant as Osmo of how the book came to be there.

So Osmo, with the book pressed tightly under his arm, dashed across the street for some coffee, thinking to compose himself and then examine this book with care. Meanwhile he glanced at a few more of its opening remarks, at the things said there about his difficulties with his younger sister, how he was slow in learning to read, of the summer on Mackinac Island, and so on. His emotions now somewhat quieted, Osmo began a close reading. He noticed that everything was expressed in the present tense, the way newspaper headlines are written. For example, the text read, "Osmo is born in Mercy Hospital," instead of saying he *was* born there, and it recorded that he quarrels with his sister, is a slow student, is fitted with dental braces at age eight, and so on, all in the journalistic present tense.

But the text itself made quite clear approximately when all these various things happened, for everything was in chronological order, and in any case each year of its subject's life constituted a separate chapter and was so titled – "Osmo's Seventh Year," "Osmo's Eighth Year," and so on through the book.

Osmo became absolutely engrossed, to the extent that he forgot his original astonishment, bordering on panic, and for a while even lost his curiosity concerning authorship. He sat drinking coffee and reliving his childhood, much of which he had all but forgotten until the memories were revived by the book now before him. He had almost forgotten about the kitten, for example, and had entirely forgotten its name, until he read, in the chapter called "Osmo's Seventh Year," this observation: "Sobbing, Osmo takes Fluffy, now quite dead, to the garden, and buries her next to the rose bush." Ah yes! And then there was Louise, who sat next to him in the eighth grade – it was all right there. And how he got caught smoking one day. And how he felt when his father died. On and on. Osmo became so absorbed that he quite forgot the business of the day, until it occurred to him to turn to Chapter 26, to see what might be said there, he having just recently turned twenty-six. He had no sooner done so than his panic returned, for lo! what the book said was true! That it rains on his birthday for example, that his wife fails to give him the binoculars he had hinted he would like, that he receives a raise in salary shortly thereafter, and so on. Now how in God's name, Osmo pondered, could anyone know that apparently before it had happened? For these were quite recent events, and the book had dust on it. Quickly moving on, Osmo came to this: "Sitting and reading in the coffee shop across from the library, Osmo, perspiring copiously, entirely forgets, until it is too late, that he was supposed to collect his wife at the hairdresser's at four." Oh my god! He had forgotten all about that. Yanking out his watch, Osmo discovered that it was nearly five o'clock –too late. She would be on her way home by now, and in a very sour mood.

Osmo's anguish at this discovery was nothing, though, compared with what the rest of the day held for him. He poured more coffee, and it now occurred to him to check the number of chapters in this amazing book: only twenty-nine! But surely, he thought, that doesn't mean anything. How anyone could have gotten all this stuff down so far was puzzling enough, to be sure, but no one on God's earth could possibly know in advance how long this or that person is going to live. (Only God could know that sort of thing; Osmo reflected.) So he read along; though not without considerable uneasiness and even depression, for the remaining three chapters were on the whole discouraging. He thought he had gotten that ulcer under control, for example. And he didn't see any reason to suppose his job was going to turn out that badly, or that he was really going to break a leg skiing; after all, he could just give up skiing. But then the book ended on a terribly dismal note. It said: "And Osmo, having taken Northwest flight 569 from O'Hare, perishes when the aircraft crashes on the runway at Fort Wayne, with considerable loss of life, a tragedy rendered the more calamitous by the fact that Osmo had neglected to renew his life insurance before the expiration of the grace period." And that was all. That was the end of the book.

So *that's* why it had only twenty-nine chapters. Some idiot thought he was going to get killed in a plane crash. But, Osmo thought, he just wouldn't get on that plane. And this would also remind him to keep his insurance in force.

(About three years later our hero, having boarded a flight for St. Paul, went berserk when the pilot announced they were going to land at Fort Wayne instead. According to one of the flight attendants, he tried to hijack the aircraft and divert it to another airfield. The Civil Aeronautics Board cited the resulting disruptions as contributing to the crash that followed as the plane tried to land.)

Chapter 30

Peter van Inwagen

FATALISM

1. Fatalism, as I shall use the term, is the thesis that it is a logical or conceptual truth that no one is able to act otherwise than he in fact does; that the very idea of an agent to whom alternative courses of action are open is self-contradictory.[1] The word 'fatalism' is used in philosophy in at least two other senses: it is used (i) for the thesis that what is going to happen is *inevitable*, and (ii) for the thesis that no one is able to act otherwise than he in fact does. (This latter thesis is entailed by but does not entail what I am calling fatalism.) So long as it is understood that neither of these theses is what I mean by 'fatalism', no confusion will result from this plurality of senses. But the idea of the inevitability of what is going to happen is so commonly associated with the word 'fatalism' that I feel I should say something about it.

2. Suppose a witch predicts that I shall drown within the next twenty-four hours. She also predicts that I shall attempt to evade this fate, and that my efforts will be in vain. Here are two stories about how her prediction might come true.

(a)   I determine to spend the next twenty-four hours at the top of a high hill. But as I leave the witch's hovel, I am overpowered by three assailants in the employ of an enemy of mine, who, despite my struggles, carry me to a nearby pond and hold me under water till I am dead.

(b)   I determine to spend the next twenty-four hours at the top of a high hill. While climbing the hill, I fall into a hidden well and drown. Moreover, if I had simply gone about my business and done nothing in particular to avoid drowning, I should not have drowned.

In each of these stories, the witch's prediction, that my efforts to avoid drowning would be in vain, came true. But there is an important difference between them. In story (a), I should have drowned no matter what I had done, and this is not a feature of story (b). And yet story (b) produces—in me at any rate—the sort of feeling one might express by saying, "Yes, that's what inescapable fate means". How is this feeling produced? Let us examine a more artful story of the same kind.

SHEPPY: I wish now I'd gone down to the Isle of Sheppey when the doctor advised it. You wouldn't 'ave thought of looking for me there.

DEATH: There was a merchant in Bagdad who sent his servant to market to buy provisions and in a little while the servant came back, white and trembling, and said, Master, just now when I was in the market-place I was jostled by a woman in the crowd and when I turned I saw it was death that jostled me. She looked at me and made a threatening gesture;

now, lend me your horse, and I will ride away from this city and avoid my fate. I will go to Samarra and there death will not find me. The merchant lent him his horse, and the servant mounted it, and he dug his spurs in its flanks and as fast as the horse could gallop he went. Then the merchant went down to the market-place and he saw me standing in the crowd and he came to me and said, Why did you make a threatening gesture to my servant when you saw him this morning? That was not a threatening gesture, I said, it was only a start of surprise. I was astonished to see him in Bagdad, for I had an appointment with him to-night in Samarra.

SHEPPY: [With a shudder.] D'you mean there's no escaping you?

DEATH: No.[2]

Death seems to imply that she and the merchant's servant would have met that very night, no matter what he had done. But this is false. They would not have met that night if he had remained in Bagdad. (Otherwise, the point of the story is lost.) But then why does Death's story have the effect on us of making her seem inescapable? Well, because her story leads us to believe that whatever one attempts to do to avoid her will be just the wrong thing. In this sense, she is inescapable. But notice that the fact that there's no escaping her depends on our inevitable ignorance of what she has got written down in her little (presumably black) book. Such stories as story (b) above and Death's story and the story of Oedipus depend for their effect on the ignorance of their protagonist about the way in which a prediction will come true. Story (a) does not depend on the ignorance of its protagonist. Even if the witch in story (a) had told me exactly how I should be drowned, this would not have enabled me to escape drowning.

Let us introduce some philosophical jargon. Let us say of a certain future event (an event that is in fact going to happen) that it is *strongly inevitable for me* if it would happen no matter what I

did.[3] Similarly, a future *state of affairs* is strongly inevitable for me if it would *obtain* no matter what I did. Let us say that a future event, or state of affairs, is *weakly inevitable for me* if both of the following conditions hold: (i) it is not strongly inevitable, and (ii) if I tried to take measures to prevent it, then I should choose the wrong measures out of ignorance, and it is strongly inevitable for me that I should be ignorant of the right measures.

In story (a), my death by drowning at a certain moment was strongly inevitable for me at the time of the witch's prediction. In story (b), my death by drowning at a certain moment was weakly inevitable for me at the time of the witch's prediction, at least assuming that nothing I might have done thereafter would have been sufficient for getting a more detailed prediction from the witch. In Death's story, it was weakly inevitable for the servant that he should meet her in Samarra that night, at least assuming that nothing he might have done before arriving in Samarra would have been sufficient for discovering that it was 'Samarra' and not 'Bagdad' that was written beside his name in her appointment book. (The "effect" of these stories, their "atmosphere" of inescapable fate, is not due solely to the fact that they are stories about men whose death at a certain moment is weakly inevitable. These literary qualities also owe a great deal to the fact that their protagonists' incomplete foreknowledge has magical or supernatural sources, to the fact that their protagonists in fact attempt to escape death, and to the fact that the very measures their protagonists take to escape death contribute to their deaths.)

It is obviously possible, magical or supernatural prediction aside, that *some* events be strongly inevitable, and possible that *some* events be weakly inevitable. It is, for example, strongly inevitable for me and for anyone else that the sun rise tomorrow. As to weak inevitability, suppose I am in a burning building—I do not yet realize it is burning, but shall in a moment—from which there are exactly two possible exits. And suppose that all the following propositions are true:

(i)   if I do not try to leave the building, I shall be burned to death;
(ii)   if I try to leave by the nearer exit, I shall be burned to death;
(iii)   if I try to leave by the more remote exit, I shall succeed and save my life;
(iv)   I have no reason to think that either exit is more likely to lead to safety than the other, and have no way of finding out if either exit is preferable;
(v)   if I believed I were in danger and saw two routes of possible escape, I should always choose the nearer unless I had some good reason to regard the more distant as preferable.

If (i)–(v) are true, then my death by burning is now weakly inevitable for me.

But if it is possible that some events be inevitable, in either sense, for someone, could it be that all events are inevitable, in either sense, for anyone or everyone? Let us first consider weak inevitability. Taken literally, this question must be answered "No": it is certainly not weakly inevitable for me that I shall continue writing for at least the next five minutes, though, unless I am very much mistaken, I shall in fact do this. A more interesting question is whether some important subclass of the class of future events is weakly inevitable for everyone. For example, everyone will die at some particular moment; could it be that, for every living person, there is some future moment such that it is weakly inevitable for him that he shall die at that moment?

Let us look carefully at this question. Consider the class of people who will die at noon tomorrow. Many of these people, unfortunately, are in excellent health, and no one could now predict any of the fires, bathing accidents, acts of political terrorism, and so on, that will cause their deaths. But this is not sufficient for the weak inevitability of any of their deaths. It seems enormously likely

that at least one of these people is such that if now, contrary to fact, he were to come to think that there was good reason to believe he should die tomorrow at noon, then he would not die tomorrow at noon. Consider, for example, Mergendus, who will die in a boating accident at noon tomorrow. Suppose, contrary to fact, that you or I were to predict in Mergendus's hearing that he should die at noon tomorrow, and that Mergendus—he is a superstitious man—took our prediction seriously enough to believe that his life was in danger, and that he had better take care. What would happen? What I should expect would happen is that Mergendus would refuse to leave his house tomorrow (much less, go boating) and that, owing to this precaution, he would not die at noon tomorrow. But, of course, there is no intrinsic absurdity in supposing that what would happen is that Mergendus would refuse to leave his house tomorrow and would be killed in his own bed by a meteorite at just the moment at which he would have drowned if he had gone boating. In fact, someone or other has probably been in just this doubly unfortunate position: even if he had taken steps sufficient to avoid whatever it was that in fact caused his death at a certain moment, he would, none the less, have died at just that same moment because, to speak theromorphically, another death was lying in wait for him.

There seems to be no conceptual absurdity in supposing that this is always the case: it is conceptually possible that, for every person, there is a moment such that he will die at that moment and such that his death at that moment is weakly inevitable for him if it is not strongly inevitable. But we cannot take seriously any suggestion that this conceptual possibility is in fact realized. If it were realized, this would either be simply an enormous, meaningless multiple accident, an accident of more than astronomical improbability, or else the result of the manipulations of some cosmic "puppet-master" like Death or Death's employers in Maugham's play. And surely a belief in a personified Death or Fate, or whatever one might want to call a cosmic puppet-master, is a belief for which 'superstition' is, if anything, too flattering a word.[4]

Let us turn now to strong inevitability. Is there any reason to think that all future events, or some important and interesting class of future events, are strongly inevitable for us? To believe this is to believe that the future would be the way it is in fact going to be, even if we should choose to behave differently and no matter *how* we should choose to behave. To affirm this thesis is simply to deny the reality of cause and effect. Thus baldly stated, the thesis that all future events (or all those of some important kind) are strongly inevitable has nothing whatever to recommend it. It is therefore not surprising that there exist philosophical arguments for it. I offer the reader two. One is a chestnut, and one is, as the White Knight would say, my own invention. It may be regarded as a generalization of the first.

It's no good summoning a physician if you are ill, for a physician can't help you. For either you're going to recover or you aren't. If you aren't going to recover, the physician can't help you. If you are going to recover, the physician can't help you, since you don't need help.[5]

Let E be any event that might happen. Consider the theorem of logic '$(q \supset p) \lor (r \supset \sim p)$'. In virtue of this theorem, one or the other of the following two propositions must be true:

If I try, by any means whatever, to prevent E, E will happen;

If I try, by any means whatever, to bring about E, E will not happen.

Therefore, either E or the non-occurrence of E is strongly inevitable for me.

Each of these arguments is sheerest sophistry. (I leave them to the reader to expose.) And, so far as I know, there is no reason for thinking that all

events, or all events of some important kind, are strongly inevitable always and for everyone, other than the reasons, such as they are, that are supplied by sophistical arguments like these.

We may summarize our conclusions about the "inevitability of what is going to happen" as follows. If one's belief that what is going to happen is inevitable is a belief in the *weak* inevitability of all, or all of some important class of, future events, then one's belief is a belief in an accidental, meaningless, and staggeringly improbable aggregation of circumstances, or else mere superstition. If one's belief is a belief in the *strong* inevitability of all, or all of some important class of, future events, then one's belief, if it is founded upon anything at all, is founded upon sophistry.

3. Let us now turn to fatalism proper. The fatalist is not an "inevitabilist", strong or weak. The strong inevitabilist affirms the counter-factual conditional

If Caesar had taken ship for Spain on 14 March, Caesar would have been murdered on 15 March

but neither the fatalist nor the weak inevitabilist affirms this proposition. (Perhaps they don't *deny* it either; after all, for all anyone knows, if Caesar had suddenly decided to leave for Spain on 14 March, a storm would have forced his ship back to port, and the assassination would have gone through as planned. But the fatalist and the weak inevitabilist see no particular *reason* to affirm this proposition.) The weak inevitabilist affirms the counter-factual conditional

If Caesar had taken seriously the soothsayer's warning, Caesar would have been murdered on 15 March

and the fatalist does not affirm this proposition, though perhaps he doesn't *deny* it; he simply sees no particular reason to think it's true. What the fatalist does believe is that, since Caesar didn't take ship for Spain on 14 March, he couldn't have done this. And since Caesar didn't in fact take the soothsayer's warning seriously, he couldn't have. And, of course, he believes this not because he thinks he knows some special facts about Caesar, but as an instance of a general thesis: it is a logical or conceptual truth that if an agent in fact does some particular thing, then that thing is the only thing the agent is able to do. And, as regards the future, the fatalist believes that if an agent is in fact going to do some particular thing, then that thing is the only thing he can do, the only thing it is open to him to do.

Now if there is any good reason to think that fatalism is true, it is a very important thesis. It seems to be a feature of our concept of moral responsibility that we hold a person morally responsible for the way he has acted only if we believe he could have acted otherwise. And it seems to be a feature of our concept of deliberation that we can deliberate about which of various mutually exclusive courses of action to pursue only if we believe that each of these courses of action is open to us. Therefore, anyone who accepts fatalism must regard all ascriptions of moral responsibility as incorrect, and must, on pain of self-contradiction, refrain from deliberating about future courses of action.[6] But deliberation and the ascription of moral responsibility are extremely important; in fact it is hard to imagine what human life would be like without them. But these very facts that show that fatalism is extremely important if there is any reason to think it true, also seem to show that there could not be any reason to think it true. If fatalism is true, then the ideas expressed by sentences like 'he alone is to blame for the accident' and 'I am trying to decide whether to have my father declared mentally incompetent' are conceptually defective. The former is, if fatalism is true, a straightforward conceptual falsehood, like 'he alone has trisected the angle'. The second, while it could be used to express a truth even if fatalism were true, would be like 'I am

trying to devise a method for trisecting the angle': these sentences could be used to express a truth only by one who *believed* a conceptual falsehood.

I think it is incoherent to suppose that any thesis could be true that has the consequence of rendering conceptually defective sentences so utterly *basic* to human life as the sentences about blame and deliberation mentioned above. But I shall not argue for this thesis. It could not, I think, be adequately argued for in print: philosophers who disagree about such deep matters as these can hope to resolve their disagreement, if at all, only in conversation. In any case, this is not a book of metaphilosophy but of metaphysics. In such a book as this, the wisest course is to look at various arguments for fatalism and see what can be made of them. It will probably not surprise the reader to discover that I think that the arguments we shall examine are houses built upon sand. But I shall not claim to show that fatalism is false, since, for all I shall show, there may be arguments for fatalism that are not open to the objections I shall raise. Unless I am mistaken, however, most arguments for fatalism depend upon premises that are among or are variants on the premises of the two arguments I shall discuss.[7] Therefore, what I shall say will be directly relevant to, if it does not actually refute, just about any argument for fatalism.

I shall not examine directly the classical sources of fatalism. The meaning of Aristotle's famous passage (*De Interpretatione*, IX) is in dispute; the very structure of the Master Argument of Diodorus is a matter of scholarly conjecture. I, who am no historian, do not propose to undertake an investigation of what these philosophers may have meant. If any of the blunders I shall doubtless make in the sequel could have been avoided by more careful attention to Aristotle, Cicero, Epictetus, or their modern commentators, I expect someone will be good enough to point this out.

4. Fatalistic arguments typically depend on the

notions of truth and falsity. But what are truth and falsity? Truth and falsity are properties. But properties of what? They are properties of propositions. I do not mean anything mysterious by 'proposition'. I use this word as a general term for the things people *assent to, reject, find doubtful, accept for the sake of argument, attempt to verify, deduce things from,* and so on.[8] (Some of the phrases in this list take more than one sort of object. One may, for example, reject not only propositions but bribes. I hope no one is going to be difficult about this.) We have plenty of "specialized" words for propositions in the language of everyday life, just as we have plenty of specialized words for human beings. On various occasions we call propositions 'doctrines', 'theses', 'theories', 'premisses', 'conclusions', 'theorems', 'views', 'positions', 'conjectures', 'statements', 'hypotheses', 'dogmas', 'beliefs', and 'heresies', just as, on various occasions we call human beings 'women', 'babies', 'thieves', 'Trotskyites', 'Australians', and 'Catholics'.

It is thus uncontroversial that there are propositions. The only question that could arise is: "What *are* propositions?" Many philosophers apparently think propositions are sentences, since they think sentences are what are true or false. But I can make no sense of the suggestion that propositions are sentences, and I shall not discuss it further. It is true that I am willing on occasion to speak of sentences being true or false, but this is only shorthand. When I say that a given sentence is *true*, I mean that the proposition—a non-sentence—that that sentence expresses is true. (To say that an English sentence *expresses* a given proposition is to say, roughly, that the result of concatenating 'the proposition that' and that sentence *denotes* that proposition.) Similarly, when I say that a name is *honourable*, I mean that the individual or family that bears that name is honourable. I can no more understand the suggestion that a sentence might be true otherwise than in virtue of its expressing a true proposition than I can understand the suggestion that a name might be honourable otherwise than in virtue of its being borne by an honourable individual or family.

There are philosophers who will demand at this point that I state a "principle of identity" for propositions. I will not do this. When one attempts to give a general way of determining whether two predicates applying to propositions are coextensive, a number of vexed questions arise. What I want to say about fatalism can be said without answering most of them. But there is one sort of question about propositional identity that we must be able to answer. We might call questions of this sort, 'questions about propositions expressed by sentences containing indexical expressions'. Suppose a madman says, "I am Napoleon", and that a second madman, perhaps at another time and in another place, speaks these same words. Do these madmen assert or express the same thing?—what we might call 'the proposition that one is Napoleon'. Or, again, suppose that at a certain moment I believe I am about to die and that at another moment, years later, I believe I am about to die. Do I believe the same thing to be true on these two occasions ("the proposition that one is about to die"), or two different things?

It seems to me that only one answer is possible: the madmen say, and I believe, different things.[9] Take the former case. Suppose, to simplify the argument, that one of the madmen *was* Napoleon. Then what one said was true and what the other said was false, and, therefore, by the non-identity of discernibles, what one said was not what the other said. (If we had supposed neither of the madmen to be Napoleon, then what each said would have been false; but this would not have changed matters essentially, since they would none the less have been in *disagreement* about the identity of Napoleon, and therefore saying distinct things.) More or less the same argument can be given in respect of the two occasions on which I believe I am about to die: there are possible circumstances in which what I believe on the earlier occasion is false and what I believe on the later occasion is true. But there are no possible circumstances in which some one thing is both true and false. Of course someone might say that what I believed on the earlier occasion was *then* false but later *became* true. But if that were right, I could say on the later occasion, "When I thought I was about to die twenty years ago I was *then* wrong. But what I then believed has now become true. When I look at my diary of twenty years ago and see the words 'I am about to die', I am comforted in my present affliction by the thought that what I wrote has become true and that, in consequence, nothing said in my diary is *now* false." And this would be an absurd thing to say.

So the two madmen said, and I believed, two different things. That is, in each of our two cases, two numerically distinct propositions are involved. To take a more extreme example, if someone asks me how I feel and I say, "I am tired", and, five seconds later I am again asked how I feel and again say, "I am tired", then I assert or express two distinct propositions: at a certain moment, I express the proposition that I am then tired; five seconds later, I express a distinct proposition, the proposition that I am then tired.[10]

This is a very sketchy account of "propositions", but perhaps it will do for our purposes. Truth and falsity are, as we said earlier, properties of propositions. There are, of course, many other properties whose extensions comprise propositions. Propositions, in addition to being true or false, may be empirically verifiable, hard to understand, inexpressible in the tongue of a certain tribe, and so on. But I take it that each of us knows *what* properties truth and falsity are. Anyone sufficiently pervicacious to claim *not* to know, may perhaps be helped by two famous passages from Aristotle's *Metaphysics* (Ross's translation):[11]

To say of what is that it is not, or of what is not that it is, is false, while to say of what is that it is, and of what is not that it is not, is true . . . (r, 1011^b.)

It is not because we think truly that you are white, but because you *are* white, but because you are white that we who say this have the truth. (Θ, 1051^b.)

Let us now turn to an argument for fatalism.

5. The argument we shall now consider turns on the notion of an agent's "ability to render a proposition false". This notion will be defined in Section 3.4 [of *An Essay on Free Will*, not reproduced here]. For the present, however, let us suppose that we have a sufficient intuitive grasp of the schema '*s* can render *p* false' to go on with.

Let us consider some proposition about the future—say the proposition that I shall shave tomorrow morning. This proposition—call it 'S', for short—is true if and only if I shall shave during the morning of 4 June 1976. Since I shall shave during this period (I *might* be wrong about this; but then I *might* be wrong about almost anything), S is true. That is, S is true now. But it would seem that if a proposition is true at some particular moment then it must be true at every moment. If this were not the case, then the following would be part of a conceivable "history" of S: S was false all through April 1902, but early in May it became true and remained true till Good Friday 1936, after which it was false until V-E day. . . . But this sort of history is not conceivable, and, hence, if S is true, S is unchangeably true. We might put the matter this way: there are possible worlds in which S is always true and possible worlds in which S is always false; but there are no possible worlds in which S is at one time true and at another false. But if S is unchangeably true, then I cannot render S false, for the same reason that, if a certain king is unchangeably powerful, then I cannot render him helpless. But if I cannot render S false, then I cannot refrain from shaving tomorrow morning; for if I could refrain from shaving tomorrow morning, then I could render S false.

Now this argument is sound only if a certain factual claim I have made—that I shall shave tomorrow morning—is true.[12] But even if I am mistaken in thinking I shall shave tomorrow morning, then, though the argument we have been considering is not sound, an essentially identical argument for the conclusion that I cannot shave tomorrow morning *is* sound. Thus, either I cannot refrain from shaving tomorrow morning or else I cannot shave tomorrow morning: my belief that, of two incompatible courses of action, shaving and not shaving, both are open to me, is shown to be false.

This reasoning can, of course, be generalized. If it is correct, then for every true proposition about the future there is a similar argument, also sound, for the conclusion that I cannot (nor can anyone else) render that proposition false. That is to say, if anyone is in fact going to act in a certain way then just *that* way is the only way he *can* act. Or, to put our conclusion another way, fatalism is true.

Various philosophers have found this way of arguing compelling. Such philosophers do not usually, at least in modern times, become fatalists. But they do think that this way of arguing forces us to choose between fatalism and some almost equally unattractive alternative, such as the recognition of some third truth-value in addition to truth and falsity. I cannot myself say whether this is the case, for the above paragraphs contain phrases I do not understand.[13] Among them are: 'true at some particular moment', 'true at every moment', 'became true', 'remained true', 'is unchangeably true', and so on. That is—and we must be very careful about this—I do not see what these phrases mean if they are used as they are used in the above argument for fatalism. If I were to say, "Municipal bonds are a good investment", and someone replied, "That used to be true but it isn't true any more", his words would be a model of lucidity. But if someone were to speak to me as follows:

> Consider the proposition that municipal bonds are a good investment. *This very proposition* used to be true but is no longer true

then I should have grave problems in understanding what he meant. Let us pretend that 'T' denotes in our dialect, yours and mine, the moment at which my imagined respondent spoke. When he spoke the words 'the proposition that municipal bonds are a good investment' he referred to a proposition that is true if and only if municipal bonds were a good investment at T. (I do not say the proposition he referred to *is* the proposition that municipal bonds were a good investment at T; whether this is the case is one of the questions about identifying propositions that I don't have to answer.) If he had spoken these same words one day earlier, he would have referred to a proposition that is true if and only if municipal bonds were a good investment one day earlier than T. What could he mean by saying of such a proposition that it "was once" true but "is no longer" true? My understanding of the ordinary use of 'was once true' and 'is no longer true' is of no help to me. Normally, if I utter a certain sentence and am told, "That was once true",[14] my respondent means *something* like: 'If you had used those same words on a certain *earlier* occasion, then you *would have* said something true' or 'The words you have spoken *used* to express a true proposition'.

If anyone thinks this an *ad hoc* description of what 'was once true' means, let him consider the following case, which raises exactly analogous difficulties. Suppose I say, "The number of committee members is odd, so the vote won't be a tie", and you, who know of a change in the structure of the committee reply, "It used to be odd, but it isn't any more". You are *not* saying that there is a certain number—twelve, say—that used to be odd but isn't nowadays; rather, you are saying *something* like this: the phrase 'the number of committee members' *used* to denote an odd number, but now it denotes a different number, one that isn't odd. I think that most philosophers will agree that we are on the right track in the "used to be odd" case; I think we are also on the right track in the "used to be true" case.

In any event, the analogy between the two cases is instructive. Suppose someone were to say, "There is a number that used to be odd", and I replied, as indeed I should, that I didn't understand what he meant. My failure to understand him might or might not be justified, but, however, this might be, clearly I should not be helped towards understanding him by an explanation like this one: 'Look, you understand what I mean if I say that the number of committee members used to be odd. But the number of committee members is a number; therefore you understand what it means to say there is a number that used to be odd'. Similarly, my difficulties about sentences like 'There is a proposition that used to be true' are not going to be cleared up by explanations like: 'The proposition that municipal bonds are a good investment used to be true. So it is clear what it means to say that there is a proposition that used to be true'.

I have argued that, when, in ordinary speech, we appear to say of a certain proposition that it used to be true, we are in fact saying of a certain propositional name that it used to denote, or of a certain sentence that it used to express, a proposition that is true, just as when we appear to say of a certain number that it used to be odd, we are in fact saying of a certain descriptive phrase that it used to denote a number that is odd. If I am right, then our ordinary use of 'used to be true' and similar phrases (of which a parallel account could be given) will not enable us to understand the use made of such phrases in the argument for fatalism that we are considering.

What I have done so far is to argue that temporal qualification of a copula connecting 'true' or 'false' and a name of a proposition cannot be explained in a certain way, namely, by reference to *apparent* instances of it in ordinary speech. But it may very well be that there is some other way to make sense of such qualification. To make sense of this idea, it would be sufficient to make sense of the open sentence:

(The proposition) x is true at (the moment) t,

since all the other locutions involving temporal qualification of the possession of truth by a proposition that are required by the fatalistic argument we are examining can be defined in terms of this sentence.

I know of only one explanatory paraphrase of this open sentence that is worthy of serious consideration.[15] It is this:

If someone were to assert x and nothing else at t, then what he asserted at t would be true.

Thus, for example, according to the proponents of this explanation, the sentence

The proposition that Queen Victoria died in 1901 was true in 1878

expresses a truth, since, if anyone had said in 1878, "Queen Victoria will die in 1901"—which are words that were suitable in 1878 for asserting the proposition we *now* call 'the proposition that Queen Victoria died in 1901'—he would have been right. (This sort of device can be applied in all manner of cases. For example, someone could say, "The number twelve is even in Tibet", and explain these strange words as just another way of saying, "If someone were to refer to the number twelve in Tibet, he would be referring to something even".) Now I do not think that what we have been offered is a good *explanation* of the meaning of 'x is true at t' since I don't think this sentence means anything—just as I don't think 'The number twelve is even in Tibet' means anything—and thus I don't think that *anything* is or could be an explanation, good or bad, of its meaning. But perhaps this is not terribly important, since we can always regard what we have been offered as a stipulative definition: it is, after all, a sentence containing the proper variables free, and that is the only formal requirement on the *definiens* of a stipulative definition. That is to say, we may regard 'x is true at t' as simply a convenient abbreviation, without antecedent meaning, for what has mistakenly been offered as an analysis or explanation of 'x is true at t'.[16] We now have a way of interpreting (apparent) temporal qualifications of the ascription of truth-values to propositions. Let us return to our argument for fatalism and see whether its premises appear plausible when the temporal qualifications they contain are interpreted in this way.

The crucial premiss in this argument seems to be the proposition that S is unchangeably true. The sentence 'S is unchangeably true' can, I think, be paraphrased in terms of our "basic" locution 'x is true at t' in this way (by analogy to, e.g., 'God is unchangeably powerful'):

$(\exists x)$ (S is true at x) & ~ $\diamond$ $(\exists x)$ $(\exists y)$ (S is true at x & ~ S is true at y)

where '$\diamond$' abbreviates 'it is possible that'. Expanding the second conjunct of this sentence in terms of our stipulative definition of 'x is true at t', we obtain:

(a) ~$\diamond$ $(\exists x)$ $(\exists y)$ (If someone were to assert S at x, then what he asserted at x would be true & ~ If someone were to assert S at y, then what he asserted at y would be true).

Now this sentence seems to express a truth: consider the conjunctive open sentence got by dropping '~$\diamond$ $(\exists x)$ $(\exists y)$' from it; there is no possible world in which there exists a pair of moments of time that satisifies this open sentence. Have we then proved fatalism? Not unless we can deduce 'I cannot render S false' from 'S is unchangeably true'. Why should anyone accept this consequence? Earlier I wrote:

But if S is unchangeably true, then I cannot render S false, for the same reason that, if a certain king is unchangeably powerful, then I cannot render him helpless (p. 34),

and this appears to be a conclusive argument. But does the analogy really hold? When we say,

"Edward III was powerful in 1346", our use of the adverbial phrase 'in 1346' is transparent; it does not need to be given a meaning. But when we say, "S was true in 1346", the phrase 'in 1346' is not transparent; it needs to be given a meaning. Well, we gave it a meaning in the only way in which anything can be given a meaning: by stipulation. Having done this, we proceeded to define 'S is unchangeably true' in such a way that this phrase would have the same logical properties as 'Edward is unchangeably powerful', provided 'S is true at t' had the same logical properties as 'Edward is powerful at t'. Do they have the same logical properties? The answer to this question is not obvious. After all, the logical properties of, for example, 'Edward III was powerful in 1346' are determined by the rules, embedded in our linguistic practice, for the use of the words it contains, and this is not the case with 'S was true in 1346': its logical properties are determined by the rules for the use of the words contained in its stipulated definiens. Perhaps the wisest course we could take would be to refrain from framing our questions in terms of the stipulatively defined sentence 'S is unchangeably true' and, instead, frame them in terms of the definiens we have provided for this sentence. That is, instead of asking whether 'I cannot render S false' follows from 'S is unchangeably true', let us ask whether it follows from the conjunction of

$(\exists x)$ (if someone were to assert S at x, then what he asserted at x would be true)

with proposition (a). Informally, suppose S has these two features: (i) there is a time such that if anyone were to assert S at that time, his assertion would be true, and (ii) there could not be a pair of times such that, if someone were to assert S at one of these times, he would say something true, and if someone were to assert S at the other of these times, he would say something false. Does it follow from this supposition that I cannot render S false? Well, perhaps it does; but I don't see any reason to think so. Suppose someone said yesterday (Thursday) that I should shave on Saturday morning, and that what he said on Thursday is true. It is, of course, quite impossible for this to be the case *and* for it to be the case that he should say tonight, "You are going to shave tomorrow morning", and be wrong. Moreover, it is simply not possible that he should have said on Thursday "You are going to shave on Saturday" *and* have been right *and* it be the ease that I shall not shave on Saturday. But, I think, nothing of interest about my free will with respect to shaving on Saturday follows; the argument-form

$$p$$
$$\sim\Diamond\,(p\ \&\ q)$$
hence, $\sim\Diamond q$

is notoriously fallacious. But perhaps clever fatalists do not rely on this fallacious form of reasoning. The clever fatalist may claim to reason as follows:

Look, you admit that S was true yesterday. But it's not *now* up to you what was the case yesterday: it is not within your power to change the fact that S was true yesterday. And it is a logical consequence of S's having been true yesterday that you will shave tomorrow. Therefore, it is not within your power to change the fact that you will shave tomorrow. If I am making use of any "modal" argument-form, it is this:

$\sim$ P p
the fact that q is a logical consequence of the fact that p hence, $\sim$P q,

where "P" abbreviates 'it is within one's power to change the fact that'.[17]

I am not convinced by this argument. Its proponent says, "But it's not now up to you what was the case yesterday", and this has the ring of an extremely plausible assertion. If the adverb 'yesterday' that occurs in 'It's not now up to you what was the case yesterday' has its usual sense, then it can hardly be denied that this sentence expresses a truth. But if the argument we are considering is to avoid the fallacy of equivocation, then 'yesterday' must be used in the same sense in the argument's first and second sentences. And if its first sentence is to make sense, then 'yesterday' must have in that sentence a sense of the sort we have stipulated for temporal adverbs that qualify copulae flanked by 'true' or 'false' and propositional names, or some other purely stipulative sense. I shall ignore this second possibility, since I do not know what other sense might be given to these adverbs. Therefore, in evaluating this argument we must interpret

It's not *now* up to you what was the case yesterday

in accordance with our stipulation. And I see no reason to think that this sentence, so interpreted, expresses a truth. In particular, I see no reason to assent to

If S was true yesterday, then it's not now up to me whether S was true yesterday,

though I see every reason to assent to, for example,

If S was believed yesterday, then it's not now up to me whether S was believed yesterday.

In the second of these sentences, 'yesterday' has the sense it has in everyday usage; in the first it has a peculiar sense stipulated by the fatalist, just as 'in Tibet' has a special sense in 'The number twelve is even in Tibet' if this peculiar sentence is interpreted as was suggested earlier.

If we expand the first of these sentences in accordance with our stipulation, we obtain:

If (if someone had asserted S yesterday, then he would have asserted something true), then it's not now up to me whether it is the case that (if someone had asserted S yesterday, then he would have asserted something true).

Now I think the antecedent of this conditional is true. But I see no reason to think that its consequent isn't false. That is, I see no reason to think that the truth-value of

If someone had asserted S yesterday, then he would have asserted something true

isn't now up to me, for it is up to me just in the case that I can shave tomorrow and can refrain from shaving tomorrow. And I see no reason to doubt that both these things are within my power. Moreover, even if I am wrong about this and I am either unable to shave or unable to refrain from shaving, I do not see that the fatalist has ever suggested any *logical* or *conceptual* reason why this might be so. Someone might, I suppose, offer the following argument: 'If S was true yesterday and if you have it within your power to render S false, then you have the power to make it the case that S was at one time true and at another time false, which is impossible'. But such a consequence doesn't follow. What follows is that it is within my power to make it the case that S was always false. When I say this, I am talking the fatalist's language. If it sounds strange to say that I now have it within my power to make it the case that a certain true proposition was always false, that is the fatalist's fault. It is he, after all, who has invented a strange sense for the word 'always', a sense such that, using the word in that sense, I can truly describe my ability to refrain from shaving tomorrow morning as an ability to make it the case that the true proposition S "was always" false.

I realize that neither the fatalist nor the philosopher who feels drawn to fatalism is likely to be convinced by these arguments. Richard Taylor has responded to them in conversation along these lines: 'You say you have the ability to

render false the proposition that you will shave tomorrow—that is, to make it the case that this proposition has always been false—even though this proposition is in fact true. And you say there are ever so many true propositions about the future that you have this sort of power over. Very well then, let us see you exercise this power that you claim: pick any true proposition about the future, and then so act that this proposition has always been false'. But this is an illegitimate demand. I claim to have a certain power and the description I give of this power depends for its application on this power's not being exercised. (The description is 'the power to render certain always true propositions always false'.) What Taylor demands is that I show that I have such a power by exercising it. If this sort of demand were legitimate, fatalism could be established very easily. Fatalism may be looked upon as the doctrine that the only powers one has are—of logical necessity—powers that one in fact exercises. Suppose I say that fatalism is false since I have powers I never in fact exercise, and the fatalist replies, "Very well then, if you have such powers, *let's see you exercise one*". This is not perhaps a very convincing argument. In fact, it depends on the same fallacy as an infamous sophistical demand sometimes made by not very able Berkeleians: 'You say that objects continue to exist while they're not being observed; very well then, *let's see one*'.

To recapitulate: Either the use that the fatalist makes of "temporal" qualifications of the possession of truth and falsity by a proposition is meaningless, or else this use must be explained by a stipulation like the one I have suggested. If it is explained by such a stipulation, then sentences like 'Every proposition is, if true, unchangeably true' express, in his usage, truths. (And there is no other usage in which they express anything.) But the proposition expressed by this sentence is quite consistent with its being the case that there are many true propositions about, for example, what will happen tomorrow that I have it within my power to render false. Or, at least, I have never seen any compelling argument for the conclusion that this is not the case.

6. Richard Taylor has offered a puzzling and ingenious argument for fatalism.[18] His argument may be put as follows:

Suppose I am a naval commander who is deliberating about whether to issue order O or to refrain from issuing order O. Suppose that, under the conditions that in fact prevail, my issuing O would result in there being a naval battle tomorrow, while my refraining from issuing O would result in there being *no* naval battle tomorrow.

We shall show that either it is not within my power to issue O, or else it is not within my power to refrain from issuing O.

(i) Suppose no naval battle will occur tomorrow. Then a condition necessary for my issuing O is absent: namely, a naval battle tomorrow. For, since my issuing O is a condition *sufficient* for there being a naval battle tomorrow, then a naval battle tomorrow is a condition *necessary* for my issuing O. If someone feels it is odd to talk of my *now* doing something "in the absence of", for example, a naval battle *tomorrow*, we may agree with him. Let us say that our use of 'in the absence of' is an *extension* of normal English usage. We may in our present usage say I am now writing *in the absence* of an earthquake in London tomorrow, provided there will be no earthquake in London tomorrow. As regards the past, we may say I am now writing *in the absence* of a German invasion of the British Isles in 1940. While there is an element of artificiality in this way of speaking, the truth-conditions for assertions that involve it are none the less intelligible enough. The first of our illustrative sentences expresses just the same proposition as, or a proposition necessarily equivalent to, that expressed by

I am now writing and there will be no earthquake in London tomorrow.

The second illustrative sentence expresses the same proposition as, or a proposition necessarily equivalent to, that expressed by

I am now writing and the Germans did not invade the British Isles in 1940.

Now consider the following principle:

(A) No agent is able to perform an act in the absence of a condition necessary for its accomplishment.

Taylor says of this principle, 'This is no law of logic, and in fact cannot be expressed even in the contemporary modal logics, but it is nonetheless manifestly true' (p. 58). It follows from (A) and from what we have already established—that a condition necessary for my issuing O is absent—that I cannot issue O.

(ii) Suppose a naval battle will occur tomorrow. Then a condition necessary for my refraining from issuing O is absent: namely, the non-occurrence of a naval battle tomorrow. But then, by principle (A), I cannot refrain from issuing O.

Therefore, either I cannot issue O or else I cannot refrain from issuing O. That is to say, it is not up to me whether I issue O. This argument, of course, can be generalized. If it is sound, then, for any case of an agent who is deliberating about which of various courses of action to pursue, we can show by a similar argument that at most *one* of these courses of action is open to him; that at most one is such that he can pursue it; that it is not up to him which if any of these courses he shall pursue.

The crucial premiss in Taylor's argument is Principle (A). If we accept this principle, then we can derive fatalism by a much simpler argument than Taylor's. For it is obvious that whenever I am *not* performing a certain act, then there is absent a condition necessary for my performing it: namely, my performing it.[19] And, of course, whenever I am performing a certain act, there is absent a certain condition necessary for my *not* performing it: my not performing it.[20] Thus, Principle (A) leads *directly* to the collapse of the distinction between what one does and what one can do: one who accepts Principle (A) has already got fatalism in his pocket and need not shop for it in Taylor's elaborate naval bazaar, diverting though the wares offered there may be.

Is Principle (A) true? The question is complex, for Principle (A) is ambiguous. We shall see that there are two ways it might be interpreted. Interpreted in one of these ways, it is obviously true but does not yield Taylor's conclusion; interpreted in the other way, it indeed yields Taylor's conclusion, though there is no reason to think it is true.

Let us call an *ability-sentence* a complete, grammatical, declarative sentence that consists of a subject term that denotes or purports to denote a person ('I'; 'Richard Taylor'), followed by an "ability-copula" such as 'can', 'am able to', or 'has it within his power to', followed by any string of words.

Ability-sentences containing adverbs or adverbial phrases are often ambiguous. Consider:

I can refrain from talking at any time.

Does the adverbial phrase 'at any time' modify the verb-phrase 'refrain from talking' or does it modify 'can'? In the former case, the sentence means something like 'It is within my power to keep a vow of perpetual silence'; in the latter case, something like 'At any given moment, I can at that moment refrain from talking'.

In normal English usage, this ambiguity is usually not very important. It is resolved by such factors as intonation or one of the syntactically possible interpretations being wildly inappropriate. If there were some real possibility of confusion, the speaker might reposition the adverbial phrase:

I can, at any time, refrain from talking.

It will be convenient for us to introduce a more explicit device than these for the disambiguation of ability-sentences. Let us use round brackets in this fashion:

I can (refrain from talking) at any time;

I can (refrain from talking at any time).

The import of the round brackets is this: in the first of these sentences, 'at any time' must modify 'can', since both 'can' and 'at any time' are outside the brackets; in the second sentence, 'at any time' must modify 'refrain from talking', since both these phrases are inside the brackets. Roughly speaking, the presence of a pair of disambiguating brackets in an ability-sentence "forces" an adverb or adverbial phrase to modify a verb or verb-phrase that is on the "same side" of the pair of brackets.

Or, if the reader is willing to include in his ontology abstract entities called "acts" and is willing to recognize 'refraining from talking' and 'refraining from talking at any time' as phrases naming acts, then he may regard the round brackets as marking the boundaries of names of acts. Thus, on this way of looking at matters, the above pair of sentences may be read:

I can perform the act *refraining from talking* at any time;

I can perform the act *refraining from talking at any time.*

Perhaps even the reader whose ontology is not so copious as to include such acts will regard this explanation as intuitively useful if ontologically dubious, like an explanation of the derivative as a quotient of infinitesimal quantities.

A third way of looking at this pair of sentences is to regard them as marking the same distinction as:

I can obey the command 'Refrain from talking' at any time;

I can obey the command 'Refrain from talking at any time'.

But this is not quite satisfactory, since the propositions expressed by these sentences seem to have unwanted entailments, as, for example, that I can understand English. Let us, therefore, regard our first explanation of our use of brackets as official, and the second and third explanations as being offered for the sake of such intuitive value as they may have.

Let us now return to principle (A). Let us look at some instances of this principle. First a "trivial" instance:

(a)   I cannot move my finger when my finger is not moving.

This sentence may be disambiguated as follows:

(b)   I cannot (move my finger) when my finger is not moving;
(c)   I cannot (move my finger when my finger is not moving).

If an English speaker were to utter sentence (a), he would most naturally be taken to mean (c). But (b) is a *possible* reading of (a), though what is expressed by (b) would normally be expressed by 'Whenever my finger is not moving, I lack the ability to move my finger'. Obviously, if someone uttered sentence (c), or uttered (a) *meaning* (c), he would be right. But what about (b)? Could a person utter this sentence and say something true? Well, consider the following case. My finger is paralysed, but it is important to me that it move, so I am continuously straining to move it. During intermittent and unpredictable intervals I become able to move my finger and then, of course, it begins to move; then it again becomes paralysed and ceases to move. In that case, if I were to utter (b), I should say

something true. There is therefore a semantic difference between (b) and (c); sentence (a) is not merely syntactically ambiguous. But if (a) is an instance of (A), then it would seem to follow that (A) is ambiguous. Is it (b) or (c) that is an instance of (A)?

A similar point can be made about

(d)   I cannot issue O in the absence of a naval battle tomorrow.

Does Taylor intend this sentence to mean (e) or (f)?

(e)   I cannot (issue O) in the absence of a naval battle tomorrow.
(f)   I cannot (issue O in the absence of a naval battle tomorrow).

Which of these sentences is an instance of (A)? Obviously this question has no answer. For (A) itself is ambiguous. We must distinguish between:

(A)1   No agent is able to (perform an act) in the absence of a condition necessary for its accomplishment,

and

(A)2   No agent is able to (perform an act in the absence of a condition necessary for its accomplishment).

In which of these ways shall we read (A)? Let us try it both ways. Suppose (A) means A(2). From A(2) we may deduce (f), though there seems to be no reason to think we can deduce (e). Does it follow from (f) together with the proposition that there will be no naval battle tomorrow that I cannot issue O? I see no reason to think it follows. Certainly not just any inference of this form can convincingly claim to be valid. For example, the inference

I cannot (move my finger in the absence of my finger's moving);

My finger is not moving;

hence, I cannot move my finger

does not *seem* to be valid. In fact, it seems to be invalid. For its premises are true, but its conclusion certainly seems to be false. As one philosopher (an unlooked-for ally) has put the matter:

> The statement "I can move my finger," as well as the statement "I can hold my finger still," are both true (though their joint truth obviously does not entail that I can do both at once). This I take to be quite certain . . . if there is any philosophical theory implying that one or the other of these statements must be false, then that theory is doubtful.[21]

Is there then some special reason, some reason having to do with naval battles and orders, to suppose that the proposition that I cannot issue O follows from (f)? This would be hard to maintain. Proposition (f) is the same proposition as, or, at least, is entailed by, the proposition that I cannot issue O without a naval battle tomorrow resulting. And the following inference hardly seems valid:

> I cannot issue O without a naval battle tomorrow resulting;
>
> There will be no naval battle tomorrow;
>
> hence, I cannot issue O.

Of course, if fatalism is true, then this inference is valid, as is the inference about the movement of my finger we looked at earlier. But I am not arguing that fatalism is false; rather that a certain argument does not show that it is true.

It seems, therefore, that, while A(2) is true, there is no reason to think that it can be used to prove fatalism. What about A(1)? A(1) does indeed entail (e), and hence fatalism. But is there any reason to think that A(1) is true? I see none. The only argument Taylor offers in support of (A) does not produce—in me, at any rate—any tendency to accept A(1). His argument consists simply in exhibiting instances of situations in which he is unable to perform some act and in which a condition necessary for his performing that act is absent and in which his inability to perform that act is a result of the absence of that condition:

> I cannot, for example, live without oxygen, or swim five miles without ever having been in water, or read a given page of print without having learned Russian, or win a certain election without having been nominated, and so on. (p. 58.)

But this argument is invalid. Since my being able to perform a certain act is a necessary condition for my performing it, any condition necessary for my being able to perform that act is a condition necessary for my performing it. Therefore, since there are indeed conditions necessary for my being able to perform various acts, there are conditions that are necessary for my performing various acts that are also necessary for my being *able* to perform those acts. What Taylor has done is simply to list certain conditions necessary for his being able to perform certain acts, conditions that are *a fortiori* necessary for his performing those acts. But such a list lends no support to A(1). One might as well try to show that one cannot live in America if some condition necessary for one's living in California is absent by arguing:

> I cannot, for example, live in America, if I do not live in the Western Hemisphere, live upon dry land, live north of the Equator . . .

I conclude that Taylor's attempt to establish fatalism is a failure. Principle A is ambiguous. On one interpretation, A(2), it is true but there is no reason to think it entails fatalism; on the other, A(1), it entails fatalism but there is no reason to think it true.

7. Discussions of the "Law of the Excluded Middle" bulk large in most treatments of fatalism. But I have not discussed this "law" at all, and it does not appear as a premiss in either of the fatalistic arguments we have examined. It would be possible to maintain, however, that these two arguments do make covert use of the Law of the Excluded Middle. My formulation of Taylor's argument, for example, depends for its validity on the validity of the inference-form

$p \supset q$
$\sim p. \supset q$
hence, q

which certainly seems to depend, in some sense, on the Law of the Excluded Middle. And perhaps it is arguable that the argument discussed in 2.5 depends, again "in some sense", on the Law of the Excluded Middle.

But what is the Law of the Excluded Middle (hereinafter 'LEM')? Here are three candidates:

(i) If p is any English sentence, then the sentence that results from writing p and then writing 'or it is not the case that' and then once more writing p, expresses (as an English sentence) a true proposition;[22]
(ii) Every proposition is either true or false;
(iii) For every proposition, either that proposition is true or its denial is true.

Candidate (i) must be provided with some informal qualification if it is even to be plausible. Obviously 'sentence' must be understood to mean 'declarative sentence', where, one hopes, the class of 'declarative' sentences of English is one that can be specified by purely syntactical means. But even if this can be done, a more serious problem remains: (i) seems to be a report of a fact about English that is at best contingently

true. And this would be the case even if 'true' in (i) were replaced with 'necessarily true'. After all, 'or' and 'not' might have meant something other than what they in fact mean. Of course, (i) might be elaborated to meet this difficulty, but the objection might be elaborated, too. On the whole, I think it would be more profitable for us to turn our attention to (ii) and (iii), than to play modification-and-counter-example with (i).

There are two main differences between (ii) and (iii): (ii) contains 'false' and (iii) does not, and (iii) contains 'denial' and (ii) does not. But what does 'false' mean if not 'not true'; what is falsehood but the complement of truth in the domain of propositions? And what is the "denial" of a proposition if not the proposition that it is not true? Some philosophers, I know, think that 'true' and 'false' are like 'transparent' and 'opaque': just as there are visible objects that are neither transparent nor opaque, so there are propositions that are neither true nor false. It has been argued, for example, that the proposition that the present king of France is bald is neither true nor false. These well-known arguments, however, establish at best that it is not clear whether 'the proposition that the present king of France is bald' denotes anything, given the political conditions that actually prevail in France. But if this description does denote something—presumably it denotes the proposition that someone is now the only king of France and is bald, if it denotes anything—what it denotes is, I should think, either true or false; if it denotes nothing, then no counter-example to the thesis that falsehood is, in the domain of propositions, the complement of truth, has been produced. (The thesis that propositions "about the future" are neither true nor false we shall consider presently.)

If, as I have argued, 'false' means 'not true', and the denial of a proposition is the proposition that it is not true, then (ii) and (iii) come to much the same thing. I shall treat them as equivalent and equally good expressions of LEM.

Is LEM true? Various reasons for saying it is

not have been offered. One class of interesting reasons for rejecting LEM arises in physical science, from considerations involving the physical interpretation of the formal mathematical theory of quantum mechanics; another class of reasons arises in pure mathematics from considerations involving non-constructive descriptions of infinite sets. I have nothing interesting to say about these reasons, which are, in any case, of no direct relevance to those questions about LEM that arise in discussions of fatalism. (They may, of course, be of indirect relevance; if they are persuasive, they may lead the erstwhile champion of LEM to mistrust his intuitions concerning the application of this principle even in cases involving only macroscopic objects and constructive predicates.)

What is of direct relevance to the problem of fatalism is the question whether LEM "applies" to propositions "about the future". Does this principle give us licence to say that, for example, the proposition that I shall one day kill myself (K) is either true or false? Let us say that it does, and then ask whether the principle, so interpreted, is true. It will, I think, be sufficient to ask whether K is either true or false. If K is neither true nor false, then LEM is false; if K is either true or false then—I should think—just any proposition "about the future" is either true or false, at least assuming it involves only assertions about macroscopic objects and properties expressible by means of constructive predicates.

The question whether K is either true of false is just the question whether it is the case that either I shall kill myself or I shall not. For consider the argument:

(1)   The proposition that I shall kill myself is true if and only if I shall kill myself
(2)   The proposition that I shall kill myself is false if and only if I shall not kill myself
(3)   Either I shall kill myself or I shall not

hence,

(4)   Either the proposition that I shall kill myself is true or it is false.

By way of commentary on this argument: (a) it is formally valid, being an instance of the form '$p \equiv q; r \equiv s; q \lor s;$ hence $p \lor r$';[23] (b) the sentence displayed to the right of '(1)' is formed by filling the blank in 'The proposition that . . . is true if and only if . . .'. Such a sentence expresses—as a sentence of English and relative to a given context of utterance (I shall from now on leave it to the reader to supply such qualification as this)— a true proposition provided the sentence that fills the blank expresses any proposition. (I shall presently discuss the contention that 'I shall kill myself' does not express any proposition.) If anyone denies this, I do not understand what he means by 'true'. The same remarks apply mutatis mutandis to the sentence to the right of '(2)'. (c) Therefore—leaving aside the question whether 'I shall kill myself' and its negation express propositions—(4) is true if (3) is true.

Is (3) true? It is certainly the case that if I were to utter the sentence displayed to the right of '(3)' above, I should say something true. (Or at least this is the case if we suppose I utter this sentence in a context in which my uttering it constitutes my asserting that I either shall or shall not kill myself, and not a mere phonetic exercise. But such a context is easily imagined: suppose you and I are discussing the advisability of my buying a certain type of life insurance, and I utter this sentence as a preface to an argument by cases.) But if that is the case, then how could (3) be anything but true? Could it be the case that there is a certain sentence s such that (i) if I were to utter s I should in uttering s say something true, and (ii) the proposition expressed by s is not true? To answer "Yes" to this question is surely to contradict oneself.

Therefore, (4) is true unless 'I shall kill myself' fails to express a proposition, unless there is no such proposition as the proposition that I shall kill myself, just as there is no such proposition as the proposition about kangaroos I just now asserted. How could there be no such proposition? Surely someone may believe or assert or even know that I shall one day kill myself. But if a sentence can be meaningfully concatenated with 'he believes that . . .' or 'he knows that . . .' or can be used as the vehicle of an assertion, then that sentence expresses a proposition. That is what it is for a sentence to express a proposition.

Perhaps the opponent of LEM will want to protest: "I grant you that it is possible for someone to utter, say, 'he will someday kill himself' and make an assertion. What I am saying is that the assertion he makes, or the proposition he expresses, is neither true nor false". But to say this is simply to grant the premiss of my argument—that it is possible to make assertions about the future—and to deny the conclusion: that any such assertion is either true or false. And that would be to deny that my argument is valid without attempting to find a flaw in it.

There is a good deal more that could be said about LEM, but I shall not say it. I have attempted in 2.7 to show that LEM is true because I think it is true and because certain writers on fatalism have denied it, thinking that such a denial constitutes the only escape from fatalism. But since there are no known compelling arguments for fatalism, this is not the case. Such writers are like atheists who become Parmenideans in order to deny the premiss of St. Thomas's First Way. To enter into an extended debate about LEM would be as profitless an undertaking as writing a treatise proving that some things are in motion.

Notes

1 C. D. Broad was a fatalist by the terms of this definition. The argument of his inaugural lecture, "Determinism, Indeterminism and Libertarianism" (in Ethics and the History of Philosophy, New York: 1952), might be summarized as follows: free will is incompatible with both determinism and indeterminism and is therefore impossible (though this bald summary does not do justice to Broad's beautifully finished lecture). In the present chapter we shall be concerned with fatalistic arguments in a narrow sense (I resist the tempta-

tion to pun): those arguments that depend on the notions of time and truth. The question of the compatibility of free will with determinism and indeterminism will be considered in Chapters III and IV.

2 The Collected Plays of W. Somerset Maugham, (London: 1931), 298–9. The quotation is from "Sheppy", Act III.

3 There is a problem about defining no matter what I do (he does, etc.). Suppose you were to say "She would have died no matter what he had done", and a carping critic replied "That's not true! She wouldn't have died if he'd prevented her death, made an effective medicine out of the materials at hand, transported a doctor to her bedside by magic, or if he'd done any of a great variety of things." The obvious way of dealing with this critic is to stipulate that 'no matter what one does' means 'no matter which of the things one can do one does'. But if we accept this stipulation, then it will follow from fatalism that the man who delayed seeing a doctor about his cough till it was too late would have died of the disease the cough signalled no matter what he had done (since, according to fatalism, what he could have done and what he did coincide). And, in general, if we accepted this stipulation, it would be a consequence of fatalism that all events are strongly inevitable for everyone. That this is a consequence of fatalism is a thesis that one of the most prominent contemporary authorities on fatalism has been at pains to deny. (See Steven Cahn, Fate, Logic, and Time, New Haven and London: 1967, ch. 2, passim.) It would hardly do, therefore, to make this thesis true by definition. Perhaps the solution to this problem is to stipulate that no matter what one does means no matter what choices or decisions one makes.

4 To believe that God plays the role of a cosmic puppet-master would be to have a superstitious belief about God.

5 This is the infamous "idle argument" of antiquity, considered, according to Cicero, by Chrysippus.

6 For a detailed treatment of these issues, see Chapter V.

7 The one exception I know of is "Time, Truth, and Modalities" by "Diodorus Cronus" (Steven Cahn and Richard Taylor), Analysis (1965).

8 This is true in the same sense as that in which it is

true that I use 'cardinal number' as a general term for the things people count with. But, of course, most numbers are too large for us to count with, and—in my view—most propositions are too complex for us to entertain. It would be more accurate, therefore, to say that I use *proposition* as a term for a certain class of objects, some of the simpler members of which are the things people *assent to*, etc. If anyone finds the "further" or "unentertainable" propositions mysterious, I ask him to lay aside his objections for the moment. Unentertainable propositions will play no role in the argument of the present chapter, though they will figure in our attempts to define determinism in Chapter III.

9 For the sake of convenience, I shall frequently use 'believe' and 'say' transitively when talking about the relations people bear to propositions, despite the fact that sentences of the form 'S says p' and 'S believes p' are usually too odd-sounding for me to feel at all comfortable about them, except for the case in which 'p' is replaced by certain 'wh'-nominalizations. For example, we certainly can't say 'John said Newton's First Law of Motion' and *my* ear doesn't much care for 'John believes Newton's First Law of Motion'—but 'John believes what Newton postulated about motion' is perfectly all right.

10 Thus, sentences containing indexical terms can, strictly speaking, be said to express propositions only in or relative to a situation or a "context of utterance", just as denoting phases containing indexicals can be said to denote objects only in or relative to a situation or context of utterance. We may therefore say that a sentence containing indexical terms expresses a given proposition in a given context of utterance, provided that the result of concatenating 'the proposition that' and that sentence denotes that proposition in that context of utterance.

11 We shall return to the topic of truth and falsity in sec. 2.7.

12 I use 'sound' and 'valid' in what have become their usual technical senses: a valid argument is an argument whose conclusion follows from its premises; a sound argument is a valid argument with true premises.

13 The remainder of this section owes a great deal to A. J. Ayer's essay "Fatalism", in *The Concept of a Person* (London: 1963).

14 I take it that when someone speaks these words, he uses the demonstrative pronoun to refer to the proposition expressed by the sentence the person he is speaking with has uttered, and not to the sentence uttered. To deny this would be like saying that in the following fragment of conversation,

> "How many have you invited to the wedding?"
> "Four hundred."
> "That's too many.",

the demonstrative pronoun refers not to the number four hundred but to the *words* 'four hundred'.

15 This paraphrase, I believe, captures Aristotle's view of truth-at-a-time. At any rate it is suggested by the language he uses in *De Interpretatione*, IX, particularly at 18b. A typical and especially suggestive passage is ". . . if a thing is white now, it was true before to say that it would be white, so that of anything that has taken place it was always true to say 'it is' or 'it will be'." (W. D. Ross (ed.), *The Works of Aristotle Translated into English*, vol. I (Oxford: 1928), tr. E. M. Edghill.) About twenty lines later, in discussing the alleged necessity of the events referred to in a correct prediction, he says, ". . . a man may predict an event . . . and another predict the reverse; that which was truly predicted at the moment in the past will of necessity take place in the fullness of time. Further, it makes no difference whether people have or have not actually made the contradictory statements . . .". Steven Cahn employs essentially this Aristotelian conception of truth-at-a-time. See his *Fate, Logic, and Time* (cited in note 3), 33 note 15.

16 This definition faces a great many purely technical difficulties. Suppose, for example, that no propositions were asserted in 10,000,000 BC or earlier. Then, it would seem, it was true in 10,000,000 BC that no propositions had yet been asserted; or, at least, this would seem to be the right thing to say if the temporal qualification of the possession of truth makes sense. But, of course, if anyone had asserted this proposition in 10,000,000 BC he would have said something false.

17 This argument-form is essentially the principle that will be called 'Rule (β)' in the parts of this book [*An Essay on Free Will*] that deal with free will

and determinism. I have no wish to dispute the validity of this argument-form, for the validity of (β) comes very close to being the single premiss upon which the argument of this book is based. [. . .]

18 *Metaphysics* (Englewood Cliffs, NJ: 1963), ch. 5.

19 Note that this point does not depend on our artificially extended sense of *in the absence of*. It therefore seems unlikely that Taylor's argument is defective owing to some incoherency in the notion of one's performing an act "in the absence of" conditions that, if they obtained, would obtain at times different from the time at which one performs the act.

20 Taylor has told me that he intended Principle (A) to apply only in the case of conditions causally but not logically necessary for one's acts. But what is the point of this restriction? Surely if it's plausible to suppose that I can't do a thing in the absence of a condition causally necessary for my doing it, then it's even more plausible to suppose that I can't do a thing in the absence of a condition logically necessary for my doing it. That is to say, if there were any good reason to reject the principle

> No agent is able to perform an act in the absence of a condition logically necessary for its accomplishment.

that reason would be an even better reason for rejecting the principle

> No agent is able to perform an act in the absence of a condition causally but not logically necessary for its accomplishment.

21 Richard Taylor, "I Can", *The Philosophical Review* (1960), 81.

22 This is as close as I can come to making sense of the syntactical *lusus naturae* (or *artis*) "(p) (p v ~p)". One might try 'Everything is such that either it or it is not the case that it'.

23 This argument-form certainly does not in any clear sense "pre-suppose" LEM.

Chapter 31

WILLIAM L. ROWE

TWO CONCEPTS OF FREEDOM

In his life of Samuel Johnson, Boswell reports Johnson as saying: "All theory is against freedom of the will; all experience for it." The first part of this remark would be agreeable to many eighteenth century philosophers: those believing that certain theoretical principles concerning explanation or causality support the doctrine of necessity. But the second part, that experience is on the side of free will, would be somewhat puzzling to those eighteenth century philosophers who hold that free will is a power and that a power, as opposed to an activity, is not something we can directly experience or be conscious of.[1] In his journal, however, which presumably was written shortly after the actual conversation with Johnson, Boswell reports Johnson's remark differently. There he has Johnson saying: "All theory against freedom of will, all practice for it."[2] Here the second part makes better philosophical sense, for that our practice of moral praise and blame is on the side of free will was a standard theme among eighteenth century advocates of free will, and it is perfectly understandable, therefore, that Johnson would have cited practice as on the side of freedom. But what is the *concept* of freedom that lies behind this remark by Johnson? And more generally, what *conceptual issues* were at the center of the controversy over freedom and necessity that occupied the last half of the seventeenth and most of the eighteenth century, a controversy bringing forward as its champions, on one side or another, such

formidable figures as Hobbes, Locke, Samuel Clarke, Leibniz, Hume, and Thomas Reid? I want to answer these questions, not simply in order to deepen our understanding of this historical episode in the controversy over freedom and necessity, as important as that may be, but because I believe a clear understanding of this episode in the controversy can help us in our current thinking about the problem of freedom and necessity.

My belief is that when all is said and done there are two fundamentally different conceptions of freedom that occupy center stage in the controversy that we may arbitrarily date as beginning with Thomas Hobbes and Bishop Bramhall (in the second half of the seventeenth century) and ending with Thomas Reid and Joseph Priestley (in the late eighteenth century). Vestiges of these two conceptions are very much alive in the twentieth century. I intend, however, to examine these two conceptions in their earlier setting, analyzing and evaluating them in the light of criticisms advanced against them, both then and now. The first of these conceptions, of which John Locke is a major advocate, I will call *Lockean freedom*. The other conception, of which Thomas Reid is the leading advocate, I will call *Reidian freedom*. The history of the controversy in the period we are considering is fundamentally a dispute over which of these two concepts of freedom is more adequate to our commonsense beliefs about freedom and our general metaphysical and scientific principles.

Before we begin with Locke's conception of freedom, it is best to note that all participants in the controversy embraced what has come to be known as the volitional theory of action. Since this theory is common to the controversy we are examining, it plays no significant role in the controversy itself. Nevertheless, some brief description of it will help us understand certain points that emerge in the controversy. According to this theory, actions are of two sorts: those that involve thoughts and those that involve motions of the body. What makes the occurrence of a certain thought or bodily motion an *action* is its being preceded by a certain act of will (a volition) which brings about the thought or motion. Volitions, then, are "action starters." On the other hand, they are also themselves referred to as "actions." Of course, if we do classify volitions as actions, we cannot say that *every* action must be preceded by a volition. For then no action could occur unless it were preceded by an absolutely infinite number of volitions. But we still can say that thoughts and bodily motions are actions only if *they* are preceded by volitions that cause them. It is not clear whether volitions that start actions are viewed as distinct from the actions started, or as a part of the actions. It is also unclear just what the agent wills when his volition starts (or is part of) a certain action. These uncertainties, however, will have little bearing on our examination of the two conceptions of freedom that dominated eighteenth century thought.

I. Lockean Freedom

Locke distinguished between a free action and a voluntary action. For your action to be voluntary all that is required is that you will to do that action and perform it, presumably as a result of your willing to do it. Suppose you are sitting in your chair and someone invites you to go for a walk. You reject the idea, choosing instead to remain just where you are. Your so remaining, Locke would say, is a voluntary act. But was it a free act? This is a further question for Locke, and it depends on whether you could have done otherwise had you so willed. If I had injected you with a powerful drug, so that at the time—perhaps without your being aware of it—your legs were paralyzed, then your act of remaining in the chair was voluntary but not free, for you could not have got up and walked had you willed to do so. A free act, says Locke, is not just a voluntary act.[3] An act is free if it is voluntary *and* it is true that had you willed to do otherwise you would have been able to do otherwise. For Locke, then, we can say that you are free with respect to a certain action provided it is in your power to do it if you will to do it *and* in your power to refrain from doing it if you should will to refrain. Locke tells us that a man who is chained in prison does not stay in prison freely—even if that is what he wants to do—because it is not in his power to leave if he should will to leave. But if the prison doors are thrown open, and his chains are removed, he is free to leave and free to stay—for he can do either, depending on his will.

So far, of course, little or nothing has been said about the question of whether the will is free. And this was what Locke preferred, thinking on the whole that the question of freedom is the question of whether you are free *to do* what you will; much confusion, he thought, results from asking whether you are free *to will* what you will. But the chief merit of Locke's conception of freedom, or so it seemed to many, is that it fits nicely with the belief that our acts of will are causally necessitated by prior events and circumstances. Anthony Collins, Locke's friend and follower, took up this topic in his book, *A Philosophical Inquiry Concerning Human Liberty*, published in London in 1717. Collins argued that all our actions are subject to causal necessity; he argued, that is, that our actions are so determined by the causes preceding them that, given the causes and circumstances, no other actions were possible. What are the causes of our actions? Well, the immediate cause of the action is you decision or act of will to perform that action. What is the cause of your making that decision? According to Locke and Collins, the cause of that act of will is your desires, judgments, and the circumstances that prevailed just prior to that decision. Given your desires and judgments at the time, and given the circumstances that prevailed, it was impossible for you not to will as you did. And given the desires, judgments, circumstances, and the act of will, it was impossible for you not to act as you did. Now this impossibility of willing and acting otherwise does not conflict with Lockean freedom. For Lockean freedom does not require that *given the causes*, we somehow could have acted differently. All it requires is that if we had decided or willed differently *then* we could have acted differently. Indeed, Locke is careful to note that the absolute determination of the will or preference of the mind does not preclude freedom so far as the action flowing from the will or preference of the mind is concerned. He remarks:

> But though the preference of the Mind be always determined . . .; yet the Person who has the power, in which alone consists liberty to act, or not to act, according to such preference, is nevertheless free; such determination abridges not that Power. He that has his Chains knocked off, and the Prison doors set open to him, is perfectly at liberty, because he may either go or stay as he best likes; though his preference be determined to stay by the darkness of the Night, or illness of the Weather, or want of other Lodging. He ceases not to be free; though that which at that time appears to him the greater Good absolutely determines his preference, and *makes* him stay in his Prison.[4]

Let us call those who believe both that we have Lockean freedom and that our actions and acts of will are subject to causal necessity, 'necessitarians.' It is likely that Locke was a necessitarian; Hobbes and Collins most certainly were. Those who, like Clarke and Reid, hold that

necessity and freedom are really inconsistent with one another do not disagree with the necessitarians concerning the consistency of *Lockean freedom* with the causal necessity of our actions and acts of will. What they reject is the whole notion of Lockean freedom. Before we state their conception of freedom, however, we had best consider what their objections are to the Lockean idea of freedom.[5]

Lockean freedom, as we saw, exists solely at the level of *action*: you are free with respect to some action provided that you have the power to do the act if you will to do it, and have the power not to do it if you will not to do it. But what about the *will*? What if you don't have the power to will the action, or don't have the power not to will it? To see the difficulty here, let's return to our example where you are sitting down, someone asks you get up and walk over to the window to see what is happening outside, but you are quite satisfied where you are and choose to remain sitting. We earlier supposed that I had injected you with a powerful drug so that you can't move your legs. Here Locke would say that you don't sit freely, since it was not in your power to do otherwise if you had willed otherwise—say, to get up and walk to the window. But let's now suppose that instead of paralyzing your legs I had hooked up a machine to your brain so that I can and do cause you to will to sit, thus depriving you of the *capacity* to will to do otherwise. It's still true that you have the power to get up and walk if you should will to do so—I haven't taken away your physical capacity to walk, as I did when I paralyzed your legs. Here the problem is that you can't *will* to do anything other than sit. In this case, it seems clear that you sit of necessity, not freely. You can't do otherwise than sit, not because you lack the power to get up and walk if you should manage to choose to do that, but because you lack the power to *choose* to get up and walk. On Locke's account of freedom, however, it remains true that you sit freely and not of necessity. And this being so, we must conclude that Locke's account of freedom is simply inadequate. It is not sufficient that you have the power to do otherwise if you so will; it must also be true that you have the power to will to do otherwise. Freedom that is worth the name, therefore, must include power *to will*, not simply power *to do if we will*.

There is a second objection to Lockean freedom, an objection based on the fact that Lockean freedom is consistent with the causal necessity of our actions and decisions. According to the necessitarians, you are totally determined to will and act as you do by your motives and circumstances. Indeed, Leibniz quotes with favor Bayle's comparison of the influence of motives on an agent to the influence of weights on a balance. Referring to Bayle, Leibniz remarks: "According to him, one can explain what passes in our resolutions by the hypothesis that the will of man is like a balance which is at rest when the weights of its two pans are equal, and which always inclines either to one side or the other according to which of the pans is the more heavily laden."[6] Bayle's idea is that just as the heavier weight determines the movement of the balance, so does the stronger motive determines the movement of your will. If your motive to get up and walk to the window is stronger than whatever motive you have to remain sitting, then it determines you to will to get up and walk to the window. Given the respective strength of these motives, it is no more possible for you to will to remain sitting than it is possible for a balance to stay even when a heavier weight is placed in one of its pans than in the other. Motives, on this view, are determining causes of the decisions of our will in precisely the way in which weights are the determining causes of the movements of the balance. But if all this is so, claim the opponents of the necessitarians, then no one acts freely, no one has power over his will. For it was generally agreed that our motives are determined by factors largely beyond our control, and if these motives determine our acts of will as weights determine the movement of a balance, then we can no more control our will than the

balance can control its movements. Just as a balance has no freedom of movement, so the person would have no freedom of will. Freedom would be an illusion if our will is subjected to causal necessity by motives and circumstances. Since Lockean freedom is consistent with such causal necessity, Lockean freedom is really not freedom at all.[7]

We've looked at two major objections to Lockean freedom. According to Locke, freedom to do a certain thing is (roughly) the power to do that thing if we will to do it. Our first objection is that we might have the power to do something if we willed to do it and yet lack the power to will to do it. Surely, freedom must include the power to will, and not just the power to do if we will. Our second objection is against the necessitarian view that our acts of will are causally necessitated by prior events and circumstances. If that is so then we *now* have no more control over what we will to do than a balance has over how it moves once the weights are placed in its pans. Causal necessitation of our acts of will denies to us any real power over the determinations of our will. And without such power we do not act freely. To be told, as Locke would tell us, that we could have done something else if we had so willed, is of course interesting, and perhaps not unimportant. But if we are totally determined to will as we do and cannot will otherwise, then it is absurd to say we act freely simply because had we willed otherwise—which we could not do—we could have acted otherwise.

I believe these objections to Lockean freedom are in the end totally convincing. Indeed, it puzzles me that the notion of Lockean freedom continues to survive in the face of such utterly devastating objections. But before passing on to the second concept of freedom, *Reidian freedom*, we should note an attempt or two to defend or amend Lockean freedom so that it will appear less implausible.

At the level of action we are free, for Locke, provided we could have done otherwise if we had chosen or willed to do otherwise. Basically, our objections to Lockean freedom point out the need to supplement freedom at the level of action with freedom at the level of the will. The problem for the necessitarian is how to do this without abandoning the causal necessitation of the will by our motives and circumstances. Now one might be tempted to suggest that at the level of the will we are free provided we could have willed to do otherwise if we had been in different circumstances or had different motives—a thesis that in no way conflicts with the act of will being causally necessitated by our actual motives and circumstances. Such a suggestion of what it means to have free will fully merits, I believe, the contempt and ridicule that Kant meant when he spoke of a "wretched subterfuge" and William James meant when he spoke of "a quagmire of evasion."[8] If Lockean freedom is to be saved, we need a better account of free will than this suggestion provides.

In his discussion of Locke's account of freedom, Leibniz generally endorses Locke's view but points out its failure to provide any account of free will. He suggests two accounts of free will, one in contrast to the bondage of the passions, an account drawn from the Stoics; a second in contrast to necessity, an account that is Leibniz's own.[9] Although neither account removes the causal necessitation of the will, the first account does appear to soften the blow. Leibniz remarks: "the Stoics said that only the wise man is free; and one's mind is indeed not free when it is possessed by a great passion, for then one cannot will as one should, i.e., with proper deliberation. It is in that way that God alone is perfectly free, and that created minds are free only in proportion as they are above passion; . . ."[10] Here we have a nice amendment to Lockean freedom. For an action to be free it must not only be willed and such that we could have done otherwise if we had willed otherwise, but also the act of will must have been free in the sense of resulting at least partially from the proper exercise of reason. If the passions totally determine the act of will and the consequent

action, we need not say that the person acts freely. However, if the judgments of reason and our circumstances totally determine our will so that given those judgments and circumstances no other act of will was possible, we can still say that we act freely, provided we could have done otherwise had we chosen or willed to do otherwise, for as rational beings we are willing as we should. This amendment, I believe, softens the necessitarian view; but it fails to solve the basic problem. For to will as we should is one thing, and to will freely is another. The problem with Lockean freedom is not that it fails to rule out necessitation of the will *by the passions*; the problem is that it fails to rule out the necessitation of the will *period*. It is time to turn to our second concept of freedom.

II. Reidian Freedom

The clearest statement of our second concept of freedom is by the Scottish philosopher, Thomas Reid. Here is what Reid says.

> By the liberty of a moral agent, I understand, a power over the determinations of his own will.
>
> If, in any action, he had power to will what he did, or not to will it, in that action he is free. But if, in every voluntary action, the determination of his will be the necessary consequence of something involuntary in the state of his mind, or of something in his external circumstances, he is not free; he has not what I call the liberty of a moral agent, but is subject to necessity.[11]

It is helpful, I believe, to divide Reid's view of freedom into two themes: a negative thesis and a positive thesis. The negative thesis is this: if some action of ours is free then our decision or act of will to do that action cannot have been causally necessitated by any prior events, whether they be internal or external. If I have a machine hooked up to your brain in such a manner that my flip of a switch causally necessitates your decision to get up and walk across the room, it follows that you are not free in your action of getting up and walking across the room. In this case your decision to do that action is causally necessitated by some prior *external* event, the flipping of the switch. On the other hand, if your decision to do the act was causally necessitated by your motives and circumstances, then the causally necessitating event is *internal*, and the action again is not free. You are free in some action only if your decision to do that act is not causally necessitated by any involuntary event, whether internal or external. This is the negative thesis.

All too often, it is assumed that this second concept of freedom, which I have called *Reidian freedom*, consists in nothing more than this negative thesis. And the major objection of the necessitarians to Reidian freedom is based on this assumption. According to Reid, our free acts of will are not caused by any prior events, whether external or internal. And the difficulty with this, so the objection goes, is that it conflicts with the view that every event has a cause, a view that most eighteenth century philosophers, including Reid, accepted. What this objection reveals, however, is that the necessitarians hold to only one sort of causation, causation by prior events. Thus once it was denied that our free acts of will are caused by any prior events, the necessitarians concluded that the advocates of Reidian freedom were committed to the view that our free acts of will are totally uncaused events. But Reid, following Samuel Clarke, Edmund Law, and others, believed in another sort of causation, causation by persons or agents. And what they affirmed in their positive thesis is that free acts of will are caused by the agent whose acts they are. Reid, then, no less than the necessitarians affirmed that all events, including our free acts of will, are caused. As he remarks: "I grant, then, that an effect uncaused is a contradiction, and that an event uncaused is an absurdity. The question that remains is whether a volition, undetermined by motives, is an event uncaused. This I deny.

The cause of the volition is the man that willed it."[12]

What we've just seen is that the advocates of Reidian freedom agree with the necessitarians in holding that every event has a cause. What they deny is that every event has an event-cause. In the case of our free acts of will the cause is not some prior event but the agent whose acts they are. To understand Reidian freedom, therefore, we need to look at the foundation on which it rests, the idea of agent causation.

Reid believed that the original notion of 'cause' is that of an agent who brings about changes in the world by *acting*. To be such a cause, Reid held that a thing or substance must satisfy three conditions: first, it must have the power to bring about the change in the world; second, it must exert its power to bring about that change. It will help us understand and appreciate his view if we contrast two examples. Suppose a piece of zinc is dropped into some acid, and the acid dissolves the zinc. In this example, we might say that the acid has the power to bring about a certain change in the zinc. We might also be willing to say that in this instance the acid *exerted* its power to bring about this change, it *exerted* its power to dissolve the zinc. But can we reasonably say that the acid had the power not to bring about this change? Clearly we cannot. The acid has no power to refrain from dissolving the zinc. When the conditions are right, the acid must dissolve the zinc. So Reid's third condition is not satisfied. The acid, therefore, is not an agent-cause of the zinc's dissolving. Turning to our second example, suppose I invite you to write down the word "cause." Let's suppose that you have the power to do so and that you exert that power with the result that a change in the world occurs, and the world "cause" is written on a piece of paper. Here, when we look at Reid's third condition, we believe that it does obtain. We believe that you had the power to refrain from initiating your action of writing down the word "cause." The acid had no power to refrain from dissolving the zinc, but you had the power not to bring about your action of writing down the word "cause." If these things are so, then in this instance you are a true agent-cause of a certain change in the world, for you had the power to bring about that change, you exerted that power by acting, and finally, you had the power not to bring about that change.

There is one very important point to note concerning Reid's idea of agent causation. We sometimes speak of causing someone to cause something else. But if we fully understand Reid's notion of agent causation we can see, I think, that no event or agent can cause someone to agent-cause some change. And this, again, is because of Reid's third condition of agent causation, the condition that requires that you have the power to refrain from bringing about the change. Suppose an event occurs that causes you to cause something to happen—some boiling water spills on your hand, say, causing you to drop the pot of boiling water. Now if the spilling of the boiling water on your hand really does cause you to bring about your dropping the pot, if it causally necessitates you to cause your dropping of the pot, then given the spilling of the boiling water on your hand it wasn't in your power not to bring about your dropping the pot. But you are the agent-cause of some change only if it was in your power at the time not to cause that change. This being so, it is quite impossible that anything should ever cause you to agent-cause some change. Since having the power not to cause a change is required for you to be the agent-cause of some change, and since being caused to cause some change implies that you cannot refrain from causing that change, it follows that no one can be caused to agent-cause a change. If you are the agent-cause of some change, it follows that you were not caused to agent-cause that change.

Having taken a brief look at Reid's notion of agent causation, we can return to what I have been calling Reidian freedom. According to Reidian freedom, any action we perform as a result of our act of will to do that action is a free action, provided that we were the agent-cause of

the act of will to perform that action. And since to agent-cause an act of will includes the power not to cause it, we can say that every act of will resulting in a *free* action is an act of will we had power to produce and power not to produce. As Reid says: "If, in any action, he had power to will what he did, or not to will it, in that action he is free."

Suppose someone wills to perform a certain action, say revealing a secret of great importance that he has been entrusted with. Since his act of will must have a cause, either it is caused by the agent himself—in which case he is the agent-cause of that act of will and his action is free—or something else causes his act of will and his action, although voluntary, is not free. In some cases, it will not be difficult to decide the matter. Suppose our person has been offered a small bribe and, as a result, reveals the important secret. Here, we would judge that the person does act freely, believing that the desire for the bribe is not sufficient of itself to cause the agent to will as he did. On the other hand, if our agent is placed on the rack and made to suffer intensely over a period of time and finally, after much pain, divulges the secret, we would all judge that the intense pain was such as to cause directly the volition to reveal the important secret. The volition was not agent-caused and the action of revealing the secret was not *free*. But these are the easy cases. Clearly, between these two extremes there is a continuum of cases in which we would find the judgment between agent-cause and other cause extraordinarily difficult to make with any assurance. To help us here, we need to note another important element in Reid's theory of human freedom.

Reid believes that freedom is a *power*, a power over the determinations of our will. Now power is something that can come in degrees—you may have more or less of it. Presumably, under torture on the rack, your power over your will may be reduced to zero and your freedom thereby destroyed. On the other hand, your desire for a small bribe is unlikely to diminish significantly your power not to will to reveal the secret. Between these two extremes the mounting strength of your desires and passions will make it increasingly difficult for you to refrain from willing to reveal the secret. But so long as their strength is not irresistible, if you do will to reveal it, you will be at least a *partial agent-cause* of your act of will, and, therefore, will act with a certain degree of freedom and a corresponding degree of responsibility. Of course, people may differ considerably in terms of the power they possess over their wills. So a desire of a given strength may overwhelm one person while only slightly diminishing another person's power over his will. Therefore, in order to determine whether a person acted freely and with what degree of freedom, we need to judge two things: we need to judge the degree of power over the will that the person possesses *apart* from the influence of his desires and passions; and we need to judge the strength of his desires and passions. Clearly these are matters about which at best only reasonable or probable judgments can be made.

Leibniz once remarked concerning a version of the free will doctrine: "What is asserted is impossible, but if it came to pass it would be harmful."[13] This remark nicely captures most of the objections to the view of Reid and other free will advocates. For these objections divide into those that argue that the view is impossible because it is internally inconsistent or inconsistent with some well-established principle of causality or explanation, and those that argue that the possession of free will would be harmful because the agent's actions would then be capricious, uninfluenced by motives, rewards or punishment. I want here to look at two different objections that fall into the first category. The first of these, and by far the most popular, is, I believe, a spurious objection. Since it is spurious, I will bury it in a footnote.[14] The second, however, is a very serious objection, revealing, I believe, a real difficulty in Reid's agent-cause account of freedom.

The second objection (the serious one), like the first, arrives at the absurd conclusion that any action requires an infinite series of antecedent events, each produced by the agent who produces the action. This absurd conclusion, I believe, does follow from Reid's view of agent-causation in conjunction with the principle that every event has a cause. I propose here to explain how this absurdity is embedded in Reid's theory and what can be done to remove it.

On Reid's theory, when an agent wills some action, the act of will is itself an event and, as such, requires a cause. If the act of will is free, its cause is not some event, it is the agent whose act of will it is. Being the casue of the act of will, the agent must satisfy Reid's three conditions of agent-causation. Thus the agent must have had the power to bring about the act of will as well as the power to refrain from bringing about the act of will, and she must have *exerted* her power to bring about the act of will. It is the last of these conditions that generates an infinite regress of events that an agent must cause if she is to cause her act of will. For what it tells us is that to produce the act of will the agent must *exert* her power to bring about the act of will. Now an exertion of power is itself an event. As such, it too must have a cause. On Reid's view the cause must again be the agent herself. But to have caused this exertion the agent must have had the power to bring it about and must have *exerted* that power. Each exertion of power is itself an event which the agent can cause only by having the power to cause it and by *exerting* that power. As Reid reminds us, "In order to the production of any effect, there must be in the cause, not only power, but the exertion of that power: for power that is not exerted produces no effect."[15] The result of this principle, however, is that in order to produce any act of will whatever, the agent must cause an infinite number of exertions. Reid's theory of agent-causation, when conjoined with the principle that every event has a cause, leads to the absurdity of an infinite regress of agent-produced exertions for every act of will the agent produces.

It is remarkable that Reid appears never to have seen this difficulty in his theory. Occasionally he joins the causal principle and his view of agent-causation into a single remark, with the result that the difficulty fairly leaps up from the page. For example, in discussing Leibniz's view that every action has a sufficient reason, Reid remarks: "If the meaning of the question be, was there a cause of the action? Undoubtedly there was: of every event there must be a cause, that had power sufficient to produce it, and that exerted that power for the purpose."[16] If exertions of power are events—and what else could they be?—the infinite regress of exertions produced by the agent who performs any action is abundantly apparent in this remark. Perhaps Reid didn't see the problem because he always had in mind the basic distinction between the *effects* agents produce by their actions and the *actions* of the agents by which they produce those effects. With this distinction in mind, it is natural to suppose that *everything* an agent causes (the effects) she causes not simply by virtue of having a certain power but by acting, by exerting that power. Put this way, Reid's notion that an agent can cause something only by acting, by *exerting* her power, is intuitively attractive—so attractive, perhaps, that one may be blind to the difficulty that appears when actions themselves are held to be among the things that an agent causes.

One solution to the difficulty requires that we view some acts of the agent as caused by the agent, but not caused by some *exertion* of the agent's power to produce them. Perhaps we should think of the act of will as in some way a special sort of action, a *basic act*. A basic act of an agent is one that she causes but not by any exertion of power or any other act. Short of some such view, it seems that we must either accept the absurdity of the infinite regress, view some act of the agent as itself uncaused (thus abandoning the causal principle), or take the view that an act of will is not itself an event and, therefore, does not fall under the causal principle. This last move, however, would leave the act of will as

absurd in Reid's theory and plainly conflicts with his stated position that acts of will are effects. "I consider the determination of the will as an effect."[17]

The solution I've proposed requires a significant change in Reid's view of agent-causation. Not every act of the agent can be produced by the agent only by the agent's *exerting* her power to produce it. Acts of will that are produced by the agent whose acts they are, we shall say, are such that the agent causes them but not by any other act or any exertion of the power she has to produce the acts of will. We thus can halt the regress of acts of exertions that is implied by the conjunction of the causal principle and Reid's analysis of what it is to be a cause "in the strict and proper sense." The price, of course, is a significant modification of Reid's account of agent-causation.

Can we afford this price? Many philosophers would agree with Jonathan Edwards in holding that it is simply impossible that the agent should *cause* his act of will without an *exertion* of his power to produce that act of will, an exertion that is *distinct* from the act of will that is produced.[18]

The answer to Edwards is that although some actions (moving one's arm, e.g.) can be caused by the agent only by the agent exerting his power to produce his action of moving his arm, other actions such as acts of will are produced directly by the agent and not by means of exertions that are distinct from the acts of will produced. To deny the possibility of the latter is simply to claim that ultimately only events can be causes of events—thus if there is no exertion of power by the agent (and no other event causes the volition), no act of will can be produced. But the whole idea of agent-causation is that agents are causes of events, that in addition to event-causes there are causes of a wholly different kind—agents. If we take the view that persons really are active, rather than passive, in the production of their acts, then the modification I've suggested is precisely what one might expect the theory of agency embraced by Reid ultimately to imply.

For, on the one hand, it is Reid's view that events and circumstances and other agents do not cause the person to agent-cause his acts of will. If other agents or prior events cause the person to do something, then the person lacks power to refrain and, therefore, is not the agent-cause of those doings: he is in fact passive with respect to his actions. And, on the other hand, if the person is the agent-cause of some act of his then on pain of infinite regress there must be some exertion or act he brings about without engaging in some other exertion or act in order to bring it about. In short, once we fully grasp the idea of agent-causation we can see, I believe, that it implies that when an agent causes his action there is some event (an act of will, perhaps) that the agent causes without bringing about any other event as a means to producing it.[19]

III. Reidian Freedom and Responsibility

We started with Johnson's remark that although all theory is against free will, all experience or practice is for it. Among the several arguments Reid advanced in favor of free will, his argument from our *practice* of holding persons morally responsible for their actions and decisions is undoubtedly the strongest. I believe that Reid's argument from the fact of moral responsibility to the existence of Reidian freedom merits careful examination. But I have no time here to do that. Instead, I want to sharpen our grasp of Reidian freedom by considering just what it implies with respect to the vexing question of whether the agent could have done or willed otherwise. For there are, I believe, good reasons to doubt the traditional claim that an agent is morally responsible for doing A only if she could have avoided doing A. And there appear to be good reasons to doubt the claim that an agent is morally responsible for doing A only if she could have refrained from willing to do A. Now if this should be so, then if Reidian freedom implies either of these claims, it will not be true that an

agent is morally responsible only if she possesses Reidian freedom—Reid's strongest argument for Reidian freedom will stand refuted.

According to Locke, the agent freely does A only if she could have refrained from doing A had she so willed. Reid says that freedom must include power over the determinations of our will. Perhaps then, Reidian freedom is simply Lockean freedom with the addition of the power to will to do A and the power to will to refrain from doing A.[20] If so, I'm afraid that moral responsibility does not entail Reidian freedom. For moral responsibility does not entail Lockean freedom. One of Locke's examples is of a man who wills to stay in a room, not knowing that he is locked in. We may hold such a person responsible even though he would not have been able to avoid staying in the room had he willed not to stay in the room. For the agent who willingly does what he does, believing it to be in his power to do otherwise, must be distinguished from the person who stays in the room unwillingly because he is unable to leave. And if such a person is morally accountable for what he does, moral responsibility does not entail Reidian freedom if Reidian freedom is correctly understood as Lockean freedom with the addition of power over the will. But a careful look at Reid's account of a free action shows that it is a mistake so to understand Reidian freedom. What he says is this: "If, in any action, he had power to will what he did, or not to will it, in that action he is free." There is nothing in Reid's account to suggest that the agent must have had the power to do otherwise had he so willed. What Reid says is that if a person wills to perform some action and does so, then he performs that action freely provided he had the power not to will to do that action.

An interesting challenge to the idea that we are morally responsible for our action only if we could have refrained from willing it has been advanced by Frankfurt and Nozick.[21] To see the challenge, consider the following example. Suppose a mad scientist has gained access to your volitional capacity and not only can tell what act of will you are about to bring about but, worse yet, can send electrical currents into your brain that will cause a particular act of will to occur even though it is not the act of will that you would have brought about if left to your own devices. We will suppose that you are deliberating on a matter of great concern: killing Jones. Our mad scientist happens to be interested in Jones's going on to his reward, but he wants Jones to die by your hand. His complicated machinery tells him that you are about to conclude your deliberations by willing *not* to kill Jones. Quickly, he pushes the buttons sending certain currents into your brain with the result that the volition to kill Jones occurs in you and results, let us say, in your actually killing Jones. Clearly you are not here morally accountable for your act of will and subsequent action of killing Jones. Were matters left to you, you would have willed not to kill Jones and would not have killed him. Although on Reid's account of this case it would be true that you willed to kill Jones, it is also true that you were not the agent-cause of your act of will and are therefore not morally accountable for your willing and your action.

Our second case is similar to, but also crucially different from, the first case. The mad scientist is intent on seeing to it that Jones is killed by your hand. But rather than activate the machine to cause your act of will to kill Jones, he would prefer that you bring about that act of will and the subsequent action of killing Jones. This time, however, your deliberations result in your act of will to kill Jones. The mad scientist could and would have caused that act of will in you had you been going to will not to kill Jones. But no such action on his part was necessary. There is a process in place (the machine, etc.) that assures that you shall will to kill Jones. But the process is activated *only if* you are not going to initiate your act of will to kill Jones. Given the machine, it was not in your power to avoid willing to kill Jones. But this fact *played no role* in what actually led to your willing to kill Jones and the actual killing

that resulted. In this case, we do wish to hold you morally responsible for your act of will and the resulting action. And this is so even though it was not in your power to prevent your willing to kill Jones and not in your power to refrain from killing Jones.

Frankfurt argues that the fact that there are circumstances that make it impossible for an agent to avoid performing a certain action diminishes or extinguishes moral accountability for the action only if those circumstances in some way *bring it about* that the agent performs the action in question. This is true in our first case, where the mad scientist pushes the buttons that send the current causing your volition to kill Jones. Here the circumstances that prevent you from *not* willing to kill Jones *bring about* your volition to kill Jones. But in the second case, the circumstances that make it impossible for you not to will to kill Jones *play no role* in bringing it about that you willed to kill Jones. As Frankfurt remarks: "For those circumstances, by hypothesis, actually had nothing to do with his having done what he did. He would have done precisely the same thing, . . ., even if they had not prevailed."[22] It is because these circumstances play no role in what the agent willed and did that the agent bears moral responsibility for his volition and act even though it was not in his power to refrain from doing what he did. I believe Frankfurt is right about this matter. What remains to be seen, however, is whether Reid's basic intuition of a necessary connection between moral accountability and power over the will is unable to accommodate the case in which the agent is morally accountable but cannot prevent willing to kill Jones.

The second mad scientist example shows that an agent may be morally accountable for an act of will to do A even though it is not in the agent's power not to will that action. This certainly *appears* to conflict with Reid's theory. But we need to recall here that what is *crucial* for Reid's view of moral accountability is that the person be the *agent-cause* of her volition to do A. His view is that the agent is morally accountable for her voluntary action only if she is the agent-cause of her volition to do A. Now we already have seen that she may be the agent-cause of her volition to do A and not have it in her power not to will that action. This is what we learned, in part, from our second mad scientist case. But here, I believe, we need to distinguish between

1. It was in the agent's power not to will doing A.

and

2. It was in the agent's power *not* to cause her volition to do A.

In our second mad scientist case, (1) is false. But (2) is not false. The agent does have the power not to cause her volition to do A. The mad scientist has so arranged matters that the machine automatically causes the volition to do A in our agent if, but only if, the agent is about not to will to do A. This being so, (1) is clearly false. The agent cannot prevent her willing to do A; for if she does not cause her willing to do A the machine will cause her act of will to do A. But it still may be up to the agent whether *she* shall be the cause of her volition to do A. This power, Reid would argue, depends on a number of factors: the will of God, the continued existence of the agent, the absence of prior internal events and circumstances determining the occurrence of the volition to do A, etc. It also depends on the mad scientist's decision to activate the machine *only* if the agent is about not to will to do A. The scientist can cause our agent to will to do A. He does this by causing that act of will in the agent.[23] But if he does so then the agent does not agent-cause her volition to do A. The real agent-cause is the scientist. So if the agent has the power to cause her volition to do A she also has the power *not to cause* that volition. If she does not cause the volition and the machine activates, she, nevertheless, wills to do A—but *she* is not the

cause of that act of will. I propose, therefore, the following as representing Reid's basic intuition concerning the connection between moral accountability and power:

(P) A person is morally accountable for his action A only if he causes the volition to do A and it was in his power not to cause his volition to do A.[24]

(I believe this principle expresses Reid's view of our moral accountability for volitions as well. Simply replace "action A" with "volition to do A.")

Principle P accords with our intuitions concerning both of the mad scientist's cases. In the first case, when the machinery causes the volition to kill Jones, we do not wish to hold the agent morally accountable for the volition and its causal products. After all, if left to himself he would have willed to refrain from killing Jones. In the second case, where the machinery is not activated, we do hold the agent responsible for the volition and the action of killing Jones. And this is just what principle P will support. For the agent caused his volition to kill Jones and had it in his power not to cause that volition. I suggest, therefore, that the Frankfurt–Nozick examples do not refute the thesis that moral responsibility for a voluntary action implies Reidian freedom with respect to that action.[25]

Conclusion

Some philosophical questions eventually yield to fairly definitive answers, answers which succeeding generations of philosophers accept, thereby contributing to our sense of progress in the discipline. Other philosophical questions seem to defy progress in the sense of definitive answers that are commonly accepted. Progress regarding them consists largely in deeper understanding and clarity concerning the questions and their possible answers. These are the deep philosophical questions. My conviction is that the question of human freedom is of the latter sort. I know that by setting forth the two concepts of freedom that were at the center of the eighteenth century controversy over freedom and necessity, and by criticizing the one, Lockean freedom, and recommending the other, Reidian freedom, I have not contributed to philosophical progress in the first sense. I haven't given any definitive answer. And in these compatibilist days, I certainly haven't given any answer that would be commonly accepted in my own department, let alone the discipline. My hope is that I have made some of these issues clearer and more understandable and have thereby contributed to philosophical progress in the second sense, helping us to grasp more clearly the philosophical question of human freedom and its relation both to causality and to moral responsibility.

Notes

1 Thus Thomas Reid remarks: "Power is not an object of any of our external senses, nor even an object of consciousness" (*Essays on the Active Powers of Man*, IV, ch. I, p. 512; references are to the 1983 printing by Georg Olms Verlag of *The Works of Thomas Reid DD*, 8th ed., edited by Sir William Hamilton [James Thin, 1895]).

2 I am grateful to the distinguished Johnson scholar, Donald Green, for pointing this out to me.

3 Don Locke in "Three Concepts of Free Action" *Proceedings of the Aristotelian Society* (suppl., 1975), p. 96, fails to see that John Locke distinguishes between a voluntary and a free act. Thus he wrongly interprets Locke as holding "that to act freely is to act as you want to: the man who wants to get out of a locked room does not remain there freely but, Locke insists, a man who wants to stay there, to speak to a friend, does stay freely, even if the door is locked."

4 *An Essay Concerning Human Understanding*, Peter H. Nidditch, ed. (Oxford: Clarendon Press, 1975), bk. II, section 33.

5 There is an objection by J. L. Austin that also should be considered, since it attacks a point that is assumed by the other objections. Locke and Collins, as we just saw, took the view that given the causes of your action A, you could not have done anything other than A. Yet this does not preclude it being true that you could have done something else if you had willed to do something else. For with a difference in the causes, we might expect a difference in our powers. Now this nice harmony of causal necessity and freedom of action presupposes that the "if" in statements of the form 'S could have done X if S had chosen or willed to do X' is an "if" of causal condition. And Austin had an apparently devastating argument to show that the "if" in 'S could have done X if S had chosen or willed to do X' is not the "if" of causal condition. (See "Ifs and Cans," *Proceedings of the British Academy* 42 (1956), pp. 107–32.) The argument is this: if we consider an "if" of causal condition, as in the statement "This zinc will dissolve if placed in that acid," we can note two points. First, it will follow that if this zinc does not dissolve then it has not been placed in that acid. Second, it will not follow simpliciter that this zinc will dissolve. Just the opposite holds, however, of statements of the form 'S could have done X if S had chosen or willed to do X.' First, it will not follow that if S could not have done X, then S has not chosen or willed to do X. And second, it will follow simpliciter that S could have done X. From these premises Austin concludes that the "if" in 'S could have done X if S had chosen or willed to do X' is not the "if" of causal condition. But all that really follows from these premises is that the "if" in 'S could have done X if S had chosen or willed to do X' does not present a condition of the *main clause*, 'S could have done X.' It may still be, for all Austin has shown, an "if" of causal condition of something else. What else? Clearly, as Kurt Baier has argued, it would have to be of S's doing X ("Could and Would," *Analysis* 13 [suppl., 1963], pp. 20–29). The "if" in 'S could have done X if S had chosen or willed to do X' is an "if" of causal condition of the doing of X by S. What statements of this form tell us is that a set of conditions necessary for S's doing X obtained at the time in question, and had S chosen or willed to do X there would then have been a set of conditions sufficient for S's doing X. On this account, 'S could have done X if S had chosen or willed to do X' implies the genuinely conditional statement form, 'S would have done X if S had

chosen or willed to do X.' So Austin's argument fails to establish that Locke and Collins were wrong to suppose that the "if" in 'S could have done X if S had chosen or willed to do X' is an "if" of condition.

6 *Theodicy*, Austin Farrer, ed., and E. M. Huggard, trans. (LaSalle, IL: Open Court, 1985), para. 324.

7 These two objections, and others, are expressed by Reid, Clarke, and Edmund Law. Perhaps their most forceful presentation is contained in Clarke's stinging attack on Collin's work. See *Remarks upon a Book, entitled, A Philosophical Enquiry Concerning Human Liberty* (1717), in Samuel Clarke, *The Works* (1738), vol. 4. The 1738 edition has been reprinted by Garland Publishing, 1978.

8 See Kant's *Critique of Practical Reason*, Lewis W. Beck, trans. (Indianapolis: Bobbs-Merrill Co., 1956), p. 99. Also see W. James's "The Dilemma of Determinism," in *The Writings of William James*, John J. McDermott, ed. (Chicago: The University of Chicago Press, 1977), p. 590.

9 In his second account of free will, Leibniz insists that the act of will must be free in the sense of not being necessitated by the motives and circumstances that give rise to it. His often repeated dictum on this matter is that motives "incline without necessitating." This remark has the appearance of giving the free will advocate just what he wants, the power to have willed otherwise even though the motives and circumstances be unchanged. But Leibniz meant no such thing. The motive that inclines most determines the will and the action, just as the weight that is heaviest determines the movement of the balance. Motives and circumstances necessitate the act of will in the sense that it is logically or causally impossible that those motives and circumstances should obtain and the act of will not obtain. Leibniz's claim that they don't necessitate the act of will means only that the act of will itself is not thereby rendered an absolute or logical necessity. Since Spinoza, Hobbes, and Collins held that the act of will is itself absolutely necessary, Leibniz's point is well taken. But, as we noted, it does nothing to remove the causal necessity of the act of will.

10 *New Essays on Human Understanding*, P. Remnant and J. Bennett, trans. and ed. (Cambridge: Cambridge University Press, 1982), bk. II, ch. xxi, sect 8.

11 *Active Powers*, IV, ch. I, p. 599.

12 Letter to Dr. James Gregory, 1793, in Hamilton, *Works*, p. 87.

13 "Observations on the book concerning 'The Origin of Evil,' " in *Theodicy*, p. 406.

14 The spurious objection is that the doctrine of the freedom of the will implies that each act of will that is free is itself the result of a prior act of will, ad infinitum. According to the free will position, an action is free provided it is willed and the agent freely determined or brought about that act of will. But, so the spurious objection goes, to determine freely an act of will is to will freely that act of will. So an act of will is freely determined only if it is freely chosen. But an agent freely chooses an act of will only if his choice of that act of will is itself freely determined by the agent, in which case the choice of the act of will is itself the result of a prior free choice by the agent. And so we are off to the races, each determination of the will by the agent being preceded by an infinite series of determinations of the will by the agent. This objection fails, however, because it supposes that what it is for the agent to determine his will (that is, bring it about that he wills X, rather than something else) is for the agent to *Will* that his will be determined in a certain manner. (See, for example, Jonathan Edwards, *Freedom of the Will*, Paul Ramsey, ed. [New Haven, CT: Yale University Press, 1957], p. 172). But it is very doubtful that any free will advocate held this view. Many free will advocates attributed to the agent a power of self-determination, a self-moving principle. But by this they meant only that when the volitional act is produced by the self-moving principle, it is produced by the agent himself and not by any other thing or agent. (See "Unpublished Letters of Thomas Reid to Lord Kames, 1762–1782," collected by Ian Simpson Ross, *Texan Studies in Literature and Language* 7 [1965], p. 51.) They did not mean that in causing his volition the agent first chose or willed to produce that volition. To attribute such a view to them is to misunderstand what they claimed. According to the free will advocates, the soul or mind determines the will but does not do so by choosing or willing that the mind will X, rather than some other act. This objection, therefore, fails.

15 *Active Powers*, IV, ch. II, p. 603.

16 Ibid., ch. IX, p. 625.

17 Ibid., ch. I, p. 602.

18 See Edwards, *Freedom of the Will*, pp. 175–76.

19 The solution I present in the text requires a major modification of Reid's theory of agent causation: dropping the requirement that the agent must *exercise* his power to bring about an act of will if the agent is to *cause* that act of will. There is, however, a way of solving the problem of the infinite regress that leaves Reid's theory intact. The whole problem vanishes if we take the view that the *exercise* of the agent's power (in order to produce his volition) is not itself an *event*. Not being an event, we require no cause of it, thus preventing the regress from starting. Is there any basis for such a view? Perhaps so. First, we must note that on Reid's view an event is a *change* in a substance. (Actually, Reid also includes the coming into existence of a substance as an event.) The occurrence of a volition in the agent is an event. The agent causes that event by exercising his power to cause it. What then of the agent's *exercise of power?* Here we may turn to Aristotle and his view of a *self-mover*. A self-mover is distinguished from a moved-mover. The latter (for example, a stick moving a stone) has a capacity to bring about movement in something else (the stone), but the exercise of that capacity is itself a movement. The *exercise* of the moved-mover's capacity to bring about motion in another is, therefore, an event. But the agent who causes the stick to move must be an unmoved mover—the exercise of its capacity to cause movement in another is *not itself a movement*. Not being a movement, it is not a change in a substance and is, therefore, not an event. Thus Aristotle holds that a *self-mover* has a part that is moved (undergoes a change) and a part that moves but is not itself in motion (does not undergo a change). The part that moves but is not itself in motion must, of course, *exercise* its capacity to produce motion in the part that is moved. But this *exercise* of the unmoved part's capacity to produce motion is not itself a change in the part that is not itself in motion (not itself a change in the part that is an unmoved mover; see Aristotle's *Physics*, bk. viii, sections 4 and 5). Following Aristotle, we might take Reid to hold that the exercise of the agent's power to produce the volition to do A is *not itself* a change in the agent, it is not a change the agent undergoes. Now the causal principle, as Reid interprets it, holds that every event (every change in a substance) has a cause. The exertion of power to produce a *basic* change (e.g., an act of will), however, is not itself a change the substance undergoes. Therefore, it is not an event, and, therefore, does not require a cause. It would be an interesting and important addition to historical scholarship to see if Reid's theory can bear this interpretation.

20 For such an account of Reid, see Timothy Duggan's essay, "Active Power and the Liberty of Moral Agents," in Stephen F. Barker and Tom L. Beauchamp, eds. *Thomas Reid: Critical Interpretations* (Philadelphia: Philosophical Monographs, 1976), p. 106.

21 See Harry G. Frankfurt's "Alternate Possibilities and Moral Responsibility," *Journal of Philosophy* 66 (1969), pp. 829–39.

22 Frankfurt, "Responsibility," p. 837.

23 I take Reid to hold (rightly) that causing a volition to do A in an agent is to cause *the agent's willing to do A*. Thus, when an agent wills to do A we can raise the question of whether the cause of his so willing is the agent himself or something else.

24 Of course, we hold persons accountable for actions that they do not will. If I will to open my car door and do so, with the result that I knock you off your bicycle, I may be accountable for what I did through culpable ignorance—knocking you off your bicycle—even though I did not will to do it. But we may take Reid's account of freedom as what is entailed by those *voluntary* actions for which we are morally responsible.

25 Could not a supersophisticated scientist so arrange his machine that if the agent were about not to cause his volition to do A the machine would activate, causing him to *cause* his volition to do A? If so, and if our agent does cause his volition, with the result that the machine is not activated, isn't our agent responsible even though it is not in his power *not to cause* his volition? The Reidian reply to this is that it is *conceptually impossible* to cause an *agent* to cause (in Reid's sense) his volition. For an agent has active power to cause only if he has power not to cause. This last is a conceptual truth for Reid. "Power to produce any effect, implies power not to produce it" (*Active Powers*, IV, ch. I, p. 523).

Chapter 32

Susan Wolf

FREEDOM WITHIN REASON

Perhaps no problem in philosophy is easier to motivate than the problem of free will, for it is not just philosophers occupied with academic puzzles but thoughtful people of all sorts who can be struck and upset by the thought that the direction of their lives might be determined by things wholly beyond their control. In earlier times, this thought was perhaps chiefly connected with the contemplation of the idea of divine predestination. Today, the worry that there is no such thing as free will might as easily arise from other sources. Free will seems to be threatened not only by what may be called divine determinism, but also by psychological determinism – that is, by the view of human psychology that holds that one's interests and beliefs and values, and consequently one's decisions for action, are wholly a product of one's heredity and environment. Moreover, the very reality of our status as valuing, deliberating agents whose thoughts, desires, and wills are effective in guiding our behavior can be called into question by the scientific perspective that views human beings as wholly physical creatures whose behavior, like the behavior of all other natural objects, can be completely explained in terms of the interaction of atomic or subatomic particles.

I have said that we are "upset" by the thought that we may not have free will. But, to quote *Mad Magazine*, "Why worry?" What difference does it make if we lack free will? Because people differ in the aspects of the free-will problem that concern them and because philosophical discussions of this issue vary accordingly, it is best to be explicit about the specific worries one cares to address. Some people, I think, are shaken up primarily because in ordinary day-to-day life we assume that we do have free will, and the recognition that we might be wrong about this would imply that we are living an illusion. That is, in day-to-day life we see ourselves – at least in good circumstances of psychic health and political liberty – as "calling the shots" about our own lives, as making our own decisions about where, and how, and with whom to live, as choosing whether to eat a peach, go to Italy, rob a bank, become a hairdresser. If we lack free will, it means we are not calling the shots – our lives are in the hands, rather, of God or physics or the past, and reflection on this makes us feel like fools, duped by superficial appearances. Others are less concerned about being duped than about the lack of freedom itself. They fear the absence of power and of ultimate control. If their lives or their individual acts are not theirs to create in whatever image they choose, this seems to rob their lives of significance, their acts of any meaning. My own concern, somewhat more specific than this, has to do with issues of responsibility. Among the things that we feel to be licensed by the ordinary assumption that we are in control of our lives and our acts is the appropriateness of holding ourselves and each other responsible for how we live and what we do. We blame, resent, feel indignant toward those who act in ways they ought not to; we praise, admire, feel grateful to those who act well . . . or better than the rest of us. We form these attitudes, at least so it appears, only on the assumption that those who acted badly could have acted better, that those who acted especially well did not have to do what they did. Our attitudes and affections rest on the assumption that what people do expresses and reveals qualities that are especially and deeply attributable to them. If free will is an illusion and we are not calling the shots, then these attitudes appear to be inappropriate and unjustifiable, and so do the practices of reward and punishment, of credit- and discredit-giving that reflect and express these attitudes. To imagine a world without these attitudes and the practices related to them is to imagine an extraordinarily different world, a world much colder, much bleaker, much less human. Were we thoroughly and consistently to eradicate from our lives all traces of the assumption that we are responsible beings, we would have to see ourselves as well as other people not as persons but as objects. Such a feat might well be impossible to achieve. At any rate, most of us would not want to achieve it. So we have reason to hope that the world is not such as to make that perspective the only rational option. We have reason to hope, that is, that the metaphysical truth about the world and our relation to it is not such as to imply that we are not responsible beings.

What *does* the world imply about our status as responsible beings? This is the fifty million dollar question – not only because there may be relevant facts about the world that are beyond our grasp, but because our understanding of the concept of responsibility is so murky as to leave it unclear what facts about the world would be relevant. It is the latter aspect of the question to which philosophers may hope to provide illumination and with which I will be concerned here.

Though we begin with a murky and possibly confused understanding of the concept of responsibility, we tend to have plenty of intuitions about who is and isn't responsible in individual cases. Indeed, reflection on individual cases and the implications that follow from them is one of the most common paths to the philosophical worries about freedom and responsibility that I have been discussing. Although we go through life with the background assumption that, barring special circumstances, we – that is, adult human beings of normal intelligence and emotional stability – are responsible for what we do, reflection on the incidents and circumstances in which we withdraw our attributions of responsibility leads to puzzlement about whether and, if so, how any of us can ever be responsible for anything at all.

Imagine, for example, that while you are standing in a hallway, minding your own business, someone walking by jostles you or steps on your foot, without even stopping to apologize. Other things being equal, you are apt to blame and resent him for his behavior – you hold him responsible for his behavior, and his behavior was bad. But you are apt to withdraw your blame and your attribution of responsibility if you subsequently discover that the man was pushed into you or unwittingly hypnotized by someone else. Similarly, you will withdraw your resentment if you should learn that the man had been in the midst of an epileptic seizure or a hallucinatory episode in which you appeared to him as someone or something else.[1]

Why do we hold people responsible in ordinary circumstances but not in the special sorts of cases just described? A first attempt to articulate the difference might suggest that, in ordinary circumstances, we assume that a person's actions or behavior *originates* in the person himself; he *initiates* the chain of events; the action is *up to him*. But when a person is pushed or hypnotized, he is not the initiator but rather a link in a chain. To be sure, he is the one who bumps into you, but there is something else, behind him, as it were, causing him or compelling him to do so. Importantly, it is irrelevant to the issue of his responsibility whether the force behind him takes the form of another human or otherwise conscious agent. A wind, a seizure, or a psychotic delusion can as easily take the control of his movements out of his hands or his mind.

So it seems that we hold an agent responsible for an action when, and only when, his actions originate from within himself, when nothing beyond or behind his self is forcing him to act as he does. I shall use the word "autonomy" to refer to this condition. That is, I shall say that a person is autonomous when, and only when, his actions are governed by his self, and there is nothing behind or beyond his self, making it govern actions the way he does.[2] The Autonomy View of responsibility, then, is the view that beings are responsible just insofar as they are autonomous. If their actions are governed by things external to their selves or if their selves are themselves governed by things external to them, then they are not responsible for the actions that ensue.

The Autonomy View seems to me the most natural and intuitive view of what responsibility requires. As I have suggested, it seems to follow directly from a first attempt to articulate what lies behind our individual intuitive judgments about responsibility. But the Autonomy View is problematic for at least two reasons.

The first is that if responsibility does require autonomy, it is questionable whether any of us is ever responsible for anything. For autonomy requires that our actions be governed by our selves and that our selves not be governed by anything beyond our control. Now, it is undeniable that many of our actions are governed by our selves — that is, they result from our own decisions and choices. Moreover, it is fairly rare that these decisions and choices are overtly caused or determined by such obviously external forces as a gunman or a hypnotist or the wind or a seizure. But neither do our choices or decisions or selves arise spontaneously out of nothing. Though the factors that shape who we are and what we value, and consequently that shape how we respond to the circumstances that confront

us, are rarely so easy to point to as they are in the examples of what I called "special circumstances," it is plausible that such factors are always operative nonetheless, calling into doubt the assumption that even the strongest candidates for autonomous action really are as autonomous as they appear.

The second problem with the autonomy view is perhaps more purely philosophical. It is that even if autonomous action is possible, even if we are, most or all of the time, autonomous agents, it remains disturbingly opaque why or how this should make us responsible agents. That is, it seems easy enough to grasp why nonautonomous agents might not be responsible for what they do. If their actions are governed by their selves, but their selves are governed by something outside their control, then it is not really they who are calling the shots; they are not in ultimate control. But if being autonomous means that instead of one's self being a product of external forces, one's self is a spontaneous, undetermined entity, it is hard to see why one should be any more responsible for the decisions, choices, and actions that flow out of that. One is in no more control of a self that has arisen out of nothing than one is if one's self has arisen out of something. An undetermined self seems no more responsible than a determined self.

In light of the serious difficulties faced by the Autonomy View, some philosophers have taken a different approach. Noting that autonomy appears at once impossible and of uncertain value in the vindication of our sense of ourselves as responsible agents, they have tried to develop an account of responsibility for which autonomy is not required. These philosophers argue that the intuitions and the reasoning that lead us to think that determinism of any sort is incompatible with free will is confused and mistaken. Rather, they say, the conditions that need to be satisfied in order for us to be generally responsible are ones that we have good reason to think are commonly met.

We may organize our sense of the problem of free will (understood in terms of its connection to responsibility) around what I shall call "the dilemma of autonomy." That is, beginning with the strong appearance that free will and responsibility require autonomy, we may try to attack or resolve the problem along one of two paths. On the one hand, we may hold fast to the appearance and overcome the problems with the Autonomy View to which I have already referred. Alternatively, we may tackle the appearance, trying at once to break the tendency to see freedom as involving independence from all external causes and to provide a positive account of what freedom does involve, given that it doesn't involve that. Because supporters of the Autonomy View typically regard their position as committed to the incompatibility of free will with any sort of determinism, they are often labeled "incompatibilists" in academic philosophy; supporters of the alternate approach typically believe free will to be compatible with at least some forms of determinism, and so they are called compatibilists.

My own view, which I shall be sketching below, falls strictly in the second category – it holds that autonomy is not necessary for the kind of freedom required by responsibility. However, the positive account of freedom and responsibility I endorse is so different from what most people in this category take to be sufficient that few philosophers who have identified themselves with the compatibilist tradition show much sympathy for my view. (Regrettably, philosophers in the incompatibilist tradition show little sympathy for my view as well. My only hope is that, if the criticisms from both directions balance equally, this will count as a point in favor of my view to those who are so far uncommitted to one tradition or the other.)

I have already described the problem confronted by the Autonomy View. The difficulties encountered by nonautonomous views will present themselves in due course. Specifically, I shall present what seems to me the most compelling version of a nonautonomous account of free will (my own account excluded) in a way that I hope will bring out both the insights and the problems that I believe are endemic to such accounts.

I have mentioned that one of the tasks confronting a proponent of a nonautonomous view is that of showing that the reasoning that leads us to think responsibility requires autonomy is mistaken. To see how this is done, let us return to our example of the various ways in which special circumstances lead us to exempt people from responsibility and blame. Earlier, reflecting on the case of the person who had been pushed or hypnotized or seized by epilepsy or delusions, I offered the suggestion that such a person was not responsible because, although he was the one who bumped into you, his behavior was ultimately determined by someone or something that was ultimately beyond his control. The problem we immediately confronted, however, was that this more general description could arguably be applied to all human agents, not just to those who are unusually beset by domineering people or oppressive circumstances.

Taking a more fine-grained approach to these examples, however, we may find a somewhat less general description that locates the source of their unfreedom in something that distinguishes their situations from ours: Specifically, a difference between a person who is pushed and someone who bumps into another person intentionally is that in the latter case but not in the former the person's behavior is determined by his will. Hypnotism is not quite like being pushed, for the hypnotist typically works on the will rather than circumvents it. But of the person acting under hypnosis, we can say that, though he moves according to his will, his will is not determined by his own desires.

These reflections suggest an account of freedom much more moderate in its requirements than the autonomy view: namely, one according to which a person is free and responsible for his behavior when, and only when, his behavior can be governed by his will and his will can be governed by his desires. Note that this account of freedom would exclude the victims of physical force and hypnosis (and also the victims of some sorts of mental and physical disorders), without excluding us. For most of us, most of the time, can and do act as we choose—we decide to walk or stand, to eat or refrain from eating, to attend a lecture or go to the movies. Moreover, we decide what to do on the basis of our desires—our desires and not the desires of a hypnotist or gunman.

As an account of freedom and responsibility, the idea that freedom consists in the ability to do what one wants goes back at least as far as the eighteenth-century philosopher David Hume. But in the form so far presented, it suffers from being both too broad and too vague. It is too broad because it can apply to lower animals and young children as easily as it can apply to adults. An unharnessed horse in an unfenced field may be able to do what it wants to do, and so perhaps can a one-year-old with a lenient, perhaps too lenient, caretaker. Though there is indeed a sense in which it is natural and appropriate to call such individuals free, this is not the kind of freedom that licenses us to hold the agents in question responsible for their actions.

The account is too vague because it does not differentiate between relevantly different desires. There are many desires that we would prefer to be without – a desire for nicotine or even chocolate, a desire to sleep with one's best friend's spouse, or, to borrow an example from Gary Watson, to smash one's opponent's face with a squash racquet after suffering an ignominious defeat.[3] Sometimes such desires are a result of circumstances beyond the agent's control, and sometimes they are so irresistibly powerful as to give the agent no choice but to try to satisfy them. (Consider, for example, the heroin addict or the compulsive handwasher.) Taken literally, such cases are ones in which the agent acts on the basis of desires he has. But in another sense, the agent does not want to act on those desires –

he does not even want to have those desires and would resist them if he could. According to the nonautonomous account of freedom and responsibility I've offered, a person is free whenever he acts on the basis of his desires. But these examples suggest that there are cases in which a person can be overwhelmed by his desires. The mere fact that one acts according to one's will and one wills according to one's desires, then, does not seem sufficient to guarantee the freedom necessary for responsibility.

In recent years, a number of philosophers have developed more sophisticated versions of the account just described in ways that rid that account of the difficulties just mentioned. Specifically, they have called attention to the complexity of the motivational systems of mature human beings, noting particularly that not all of our desires, interests, and dispositions are on the same level.[4] Some of our desires, as we have seen, are desires we would just as soon be without. We find them in us – whether as a result of biology or conditioning – but we do not value them or identify with them. Other desires, or, more generally, other features of our character, we cherish – we claim them for our own, whether we have cultivated them by design or approved them after we had come to see them as parts of us, and we would go to considerable length, not just to satisfy these desires, but to preserve them. These latter desires may be referred to as comprising our systems of *value*. These are what we think of as constituting our deepest selves.

In light of the distinction between values and other "mere" desires, or between one's whole, partly superficial, partly alienated self and one's deeper or real self, we can improve on the earlier proposal to understand freedom in terms of the ability to do what one wants. The kind of freedom necessary for responsibility, it might be suggested, is the freedom to do what one *really* wants – that is, the freedom to do what one's core, deep, or real self wants, which may be different from what one's strongest desires would urge upon one. To put it another way, the freedom necessary for responsibility on this account consists in the ability not just to behave in accordance with one's will and to will in accord with one's desires, but more specifically in the ability to govern one's will (and so one's actions) in accordance with the specific set of desires that constitute one's system of values.

In my book, I referred to this view as the Real Self View.[5] It has much to commend it – among other things, that it explains in a satisfying way not just why people are exempted from responsibility in the special circumstances that were on our initial list, but also why lower animals and young children are not suitable candidates for responsibility. For lower animals and young children do not yet have real selves – unlike mature human beings, their desires are all on one level, and they seem fairly pictured as tossed around by whatever desires have been given to them.

Despite the appeal of the Real Self View, however, it has a serious flaw. What makes the Real Self View a distinctively nonautonomous account of free will is its insistence that one's status as a free and responsible being lies not in whether but in how one's actions are determined. Specifically, freedom and responsibility are held to depend solely on whether one's behavior can be governed by the dictates of one's real self – never mind where one's real self came from or why it came to dictate the behavior that it does. But it is not at all clear that we should never mind where one's real self comes from in evaluating one's status as a free and responsible agent.

An example will bring the problem more sharply into focus. Consider someone who was raised in an unusually sheltered environment, by authoritarian albeit loving parents, in a community in which open debate and reflection are discouraged. As an adult, the man has as complex a psychology as most, with a system of values as well as other mere desires. But because the community and the family in which he was raised are deeply racist, he also grows up to be a racist, and his racism is reflected in his values. We may assume that he is aware of his racist values and approves of them. They are among his values, and, insofar as his actions exhibit racism or even directly promote it, he happily claims responsibility for them. He regards them as expressions of his real self.

In fact, the man's racist values *are* part of his real self. For one's real self just is one's collection of values, of features with which one identifies and approves – that is how the notion of a real self was defined. Despite this, however, it seems to me highly questionable that the man is responsible – and thus blameworthy – for his racist activities. For although these activities are governed by his values, his life – at least so I am imagining – had no room in it for questioning, for coming to see the reasons why racism is wrong. He didn't have a chance to not be a racist, and so it seems unfair to blame him for acting out and expressing a racism he had no choice but to have. Indeed, it seems to me that this case is not significantly relevantly different from the case of the child or even the compulsive hand-washer. For, although the man himself sees his racism in a different light from the way the child sees his urges or the handwasher his compulsion – the racist I am imagining is proud of his racism and wishes to claim responsibility for it – the fact is that he is just as "tossed around" with respect to his racism as the others are by their desires. He, like these others, is helplessly moved to act in accordance with a desire that he did not choose to acquire.

Obviously, my characterization of the racist is structurally similar to stories we might tell of others who, due to the values of their communities, could not but be Nazis or sexists or snobs. Only slightly less obvious is its similarity to stories of victims of different sorts of deprived childhoods, people who, due to abuse or neglect or exposure to nothing but violent, uncaring people, inevitably develop real selves that care little for human life and love and much for physical power or wealth.

In general terms, the case of the racist exemplifies those cases in which an agent's behavior is determined by the agent's values (or real self), but the agent's values (real self) are themselves inescapably determined by forces external to the agent's control. The flaw in the Real Self View is that it takes such cases to be unproblematic cases of responsible behavior. Many people share my view that these may not be cases of responsible behavior at all. Even if they are cases of responsible behavior, we must be given some explanation of why they are – of why an agent is more responsible for actions that are governable by his values than he is for actions that are governed by his nonvalued desires, if his values are no more within his control and are no more products of his choice than are the mere desires for which he is recognized not to be responsible.

Thus, I conclude that the Real Self View is unsatisfactory. What is particularly troublesome, however, is that the objection that led to this conclusion seems to force us straight back to the Autonomy View, a view that we have seen is riddled with problems of its own. If the racist, the Nazi, the victim of the deprived childhood are not responsible for their behavior because their behavior is governed by values that are shaped by forces beyond their control, aren't we all deprived responsibility on the same grounds? After all, we are as much a product of our cultures as these individuals are of theirs. Is there any way to solve the problem of the Real Self View without returning to the problems of the Autonomy View? I think that there is – that there is a way between the Scylla and Charybdis of the traditional responses to the problem of free will and responsibility.

To see the way out, it is useful to notice a feature common to the cases that pose a problem for the Real Self View. The cases of the racist, the Nazi, and the victim of the deprived childhood are all cases of people whose behavior and whose values are faulty, deficient, bad. They are cases of people, who, were they responsible for their actions, would thereby be blameworthy.

Reflecting on the supposition that they could not help but have those values, then, inclines us to exempt them not just of responsibility, but of blame.

If we turn our attention to cases of good action and admirable behavior, however, we find somewhat different intuitions applying to these cases. Consider for a moment, not the racist or the Nazi, but an abolitionist or a member of the French Resistance or the woman in my former home city who single-handedly set up soup kitchens and shelters for Baltimore's homeless. When we reflect on the sources of these people's values or of their courage and commitment and integrity, we are not so concerned or upset by the thought that they are products of their environments. Perhaps one of our heroes was especially moved by a parent, another by a teacher or a neighbor or a priest. Perhaps the trauma of losing a sibling at an early age, witnessing a lynch mob, or battling cancer and surviving was instrumental in the development of their dedication to relieve suffering or to make the world a better place. Of course, these people didn't choose to have wise and inspiring role models. They couldn't help but experience or witness the tragedies that molded their characters. But it seems crazy that this should be a reason to withhold the praise or credit that we initially judge them to deserve.

When we focus on these positive cases, it seems bizarre to regard it as a condition of responsibility that the values on which one acts be formed independently of one's environment – what better way can there be to form one's values than to listen to and observe and reflect on the views of the people one encounters and on the experiences one has?

Focusing on cases of good-acting agents suggests that it is no obstacle to responsibility that one acts on values that themselves have been formed by forces external to the agent's control. Reflecting on bad-acting agents, however, seemed to lead us to the opposite conclusion. Are these intuitions simply contradictory, or is there a relevant distinction between these sets of cases that can make sense of our different attitudes?

Let me describe one proposal that I believe to be mistaken before offering the one that I endorse.

It might be noted that when we look at cases of bad-acting agents, our tendency to exempt them from responsibility (and thus from blame) rests heavily on our imagining cases in which it is posited that the agent could not but have become vicious or disturbed. Their environments (or, as it may be, their physiologies) leave them no choice whatsoever; their characters and consequent behaviors are inevitable, irresistible, determined absolutely by forces beyond their control. When we understand similar cases somewhat differently – noting perhaps that not all Germans in the 1930s approved of the Nazis or that not all ghetto children become criminals, we are less likely to exempt the individuals in question from blame.

When we reflect upon the good-acting agents we do not similarly focus on the narrowness of their options. Even when one traces a person's courage or altruism to a specific influence or source, we are not apt to think of it as an overpowering influence, one that could not have been resisted. One might suspect, then, that we are not comparing truly analogous pairs of cases: We exempt the bad-acting agent from responsibility, one might suppose, because we think he was shaped absolutely and irresistibly by forces beyond his control. We do not exempt the good-acting agent because we covertly, perhaps even unconsciously, imagine the agent as one who was encouraged by good influences, but who was not compelled to become good. Rather, we assume that the decision to accept these influences was more truly up to him.

This suggestion would effectively bring us back to the Autonomy View. For it contains the idea that however much an agent is shaped by physical or cultural influences, responsibility requires that the agent must ultimately decide

whether to submit to these influences and that this decision must be in the hands of a self even deeper than the real self of the Real Self View, a self independent of all external influences.

I believe this suggestion is mistaken. There is no such ultrareal or superdeep self, independent of all external influences, arising from nothing; and even if there were, it is hard to see why a being with such a self would be any more responsible than a being without it. But the attractions of this view can be analyzed as a misplaced attempt to put one's finger on a different view.

This other view I call the Reason View. The title of this chapter (and my book) comes from it. According to this view, the relevant difference between the good-acting agents, shaped, say, by inspiring role models, whom we view as responsible and praiseworthy, and the bad-acting agents, shaped, say, by horrible role models or by the absence of role models or by brutal and impoverished upbringing, whom we exempt from responsibility and blame, is that the former have been led through reason, perception, good sense, and good data to adopt their values and live by them, while the latter have been shaped in ways that have kept reason and truth out.

In other words, I think that there is something to the image of the good and praiseworthy person as one who is not merely passively molded by good influences but who actively chooses and affirms them. But I believe that this image is misidentified when it is thought to involve an autonomous metaphysically independent chooser. What matters rather is that the agent's embrace of these good values be an expression of her understanding that they are good, of her appreciation, that is, of the reasons that make these values preferable to others. It is by being rationally persuaded that these values are good ones that the agent makes them her own in a way for which she is responsible. But there is no analogous story to be told of the agent who acquires bad values from his culture. We cannot say that the racist is responsible for his racism if it results from his understanding of what is good about racism – for there is nothing good about racism for him to understand. Nor can we say that the racist is responsible for his racism if it results from his understanding about what is bad about racism – for no sane person chooses values because he understands them to be bad.

Insofar as a person is shaped by his culture to adopt bad values, then, it is in the nature of the case that he is shaped by forces of unreason. Our tendency to excuse those whom we think could not help but develop bad values or perverse ideals, then, is due to our seeing them as having been pushed blindly along a path that, through no fault of their own, they could not recognize as undesirable or wrong. Their vision was inescapably distorted, their power to question or simply to see was helplessly limited or blocked. Those whom we think are responsible for developing good values may be no less strongly influenced by their backgrounds than the people with bad values whom we exempt from blame, but the development of their values invoked and made use of, rather than interfered with, these agents' powers of reason and perception. If their values are formed, or revised or affirmed, in accordance with their reason and perception, then they have exercised all the powers of self-determination it is sensible to want, or at least all the powers of self-determination that our status as responsible agents requires.

We are attracted by the view that responsibility requires autonomy – that it requires, in other words, the ability to resist all external forces, the power to choose either one's own character or one's acts independently of anything outside one's control because we think of "external forces" as inimical to our powers as agents. "External forces" suggests violence, or at least something brute and blind; things or circumstances "beyond one's control" suggest accidents or hardships one would have preferred to avoid. But in fact, of course, education is as external a force as indoctrination, and exposure to intelligent discussion of new ideas is as little within one's control as exposure to bullets. In other words, the sources of our freedom are as external as are the forces that inhibit and interfere with it. Realizing this should lead us to see that what is required for freedom and responsibility is not independence from external forces. It is not, in other words, the metaphysical property of autonomy. Rather, we require independence from specifically bad forces in the world – forces that either interfere with or deprive us of the ability to act on our values or disrupt and prevent us from forming our values in the light of reason and truth. Moreover, we are in other respects positively dependent on the world for our freedom and responsibility – for we are dependent on the world, both on our biology and on our environment, for giving us both the abilities and the opportunities to transcend the status of lower animals and young children and become responsible agents.

According to the Reason View, then, the freedom necessary for responsibility is a freedom within reason. This is more freedom than is required by the Real Self View – for it requires that the responsible agent not only be free to govern her actions in accordance with her values, but that she be free to form or revise her values (or, if you like, to revise her Real Self) in accordance with what reason and truth would suggest. It is less freedom than is required by the Autonomy View – for it neither requires nor values an agent's freedom from those aspects of the world that provide us with the faculties of thought and perception and the data on which these faculties can operate to yield an appreciation of what the world is and can be like.

Before closing, let me make a few remarks that may prevent some misunderstandings.

The development of my view about responsibility laid stress on a disanalogy between good-acting and bad-acting agents. As we have seen, my view accepts the intuition that if a bad-acting agent "never had a chance" to do or to want to do something better than what he does, then he is not fairly held responsible and blameworthy for his acting badly. At the same time, I have argued that a good-acting agent, whose decision to align herself with good values is as strongly a product of her background as the former agent's choices are a consequence of his, may nonetheless deserve credit for her behavior. In audiences to whom I have presented my view in other forms before, this asymmetry has been the source of both misinterpretation and criticism.

Specifically, some people have understood my view to be too free to give praise – to imply, in particular, that anyone who acts well and does so on the basis of values she has gained from her culture or her upbringing can fairly be held responsible and praiseworthy for it. Still more have been concerned with the thought that my view automatically excuses virtually all criminals and exempts from blame anyone whose wrongful behavior can be traced to bad influences in his culture or upbringing. But these inferences rest on a misunderstanding.

Although I believe that there is an important disanalogy between good-acting agents and bad-acting agents, the disanalogy is quite specific: It is that a good-acting agent may have been irresistibly drawn to accept good values as a result of the exercise of good reason, whereas this can never be said of the agent who acts in a blameworthy way. It may be precisely because a person holds the values of her society up to reflection and questioning that she has no choice but ultimately to affirm (or reject) them. But if a man is irresistibly led to affirm bad values, this can only be because he was deprived of the ability to appreciate the reasons why those values are bad. This stress on the ability to appreciate reasons – reasons why one set of values deserves affirmation, while another set ought to be reconsidered and revised – is all-important. It is the possession or lack of this ability, and not the desirable or undesirable nature of the acts or the values themselves, that, on my account, makes the difference between responsible and non-responsible agency.

Thus, according to the Reason View, a person who does the right thing for the wrong reasons deserves no more praise than a person who doesn't do the right thing at all. Moreover, a person who does the right thing on the basis of values she doesn't understand (a person whose acceptance of good values, in other words, is as blind and unreasoned as the acceptance of the racist's values in our earlier example) is as little responsible for what she does as those whose paths lead to more objectionable behavior.

Moreover, a person who does the wrong thing, though it must be for bad reasons, is not necessarily exempt from responsibility and blame. It is crucial to establish whether the person in question had reasons to act better available to him. In the cases I dwelt on, we imagined people who could not but have acquired bad values or false beliefs and so could not but have made bad decisions on the basis of them. But it is a real and difficult question how often such cases occur. If a person acts badly despite his ability to appreciate the reasons for acting better, then he is fully responsible and blameworthy for his choice. If, therefore, as some people believe, almost anyone is able to tell good values from bad (whatever her cultural or subcultural background), then almost anyone will be blameworthy should she choose a bad path.

Understanding the Reason View in more detail and seeing how it is to be applied in practice may quell some of the doubts that a cruder understanding of the view may call to mind. But it will not quell all of them. Even if one doesn't overestimate the practical significance of the Reason View's acknowledged disanalogy between good and bad, one may find the associated asymmetry between the conditions of praise and blame conceptually disconcerting. The Reason View admits that two people who are equally products of their respective heredities and environments may nonetheless not be equally responsible agents. And this may seem at once unfair and rationally arbitrary. There is something powerfully compelling about the thought that insofar as we are all products of our environments or of our physiologies or our genes, then we should all be in the same boat with respect to our status as responsible agents. Indeed, this thought, though rejected by the Reason View, is affirmed by both of its otherwise contrasting opponents. The Autonomy View insists that no responsible agent can be purely a product of external forces, while the Real Self View regards such external determinism as nowhere posing a threat.

That the Reason View takes issue with both its traditional alternatives with respect to this question marks what may be its most distinctive and controversial feature. Specifically, it marks the fact that according to the Reason View, the problem of free will and responsibility is not as purely nor as fundamentally a metaphysical problem as it has traditionally seemed to be. Proponents of the Autonomy View have felt that responsible agents need to be metaphysically distinctive from the rest of the world − they have felt that responsibility requires contracausal powers, the ability to stand back from the physical and psychological forces in the world, to be removed from the world at the same time as being able to act upon it. Proponents of the Real Self View have argued that no such special powers are necessary, that, to the contrary, the powers possessed by normal mature human agents, such as the power to form values and to deliberate and act in accordance with them, are sufficient for responsibility. Both views have taken the question at least to be "How much metaphysical power is necessary?" How free from external forces does a responsible agent have to be?

According to the Reason View, however, the difference between responsible and nonresponsible agents is not fundamentally metaphysical − it is normative. What we need in order to be responsible is not the power to form and revise our values independently of the world, but rather the power to form and revise our values well rather than badly, in light of an understanding of the world and of what is important

and worthwhile in it. The freedom needed for responsibility involves the freedom to see things aright − the freedom, if you will, to appreciate the True and the Good.

There is no privileged perspective from which one can pronounce whether or to what extent we have this freedom. There can be no guarantee that one does, or that one can, see things aright, that one has, as it were, mentally grasped the True and the Good. And so, if the Reason View is right, there can be no guarantee that we are fully and in every respect free and responsible agents. At the same time, I see no reason to doubt that these powers are at least partly open to us. The ability to understand and appreciate the world poses no obvious conflict with our status as metaphysically ordinary parts of the physical universe, as products both of physics and the past.

The Reason View, then, may be thought to be more pessimistic than some views that take our status as free and responsible agents as more or less guaranteed. But it is less pessimistic than others, according to which the conditions of responsibility are so strong as to be wildly unlikely, or impossible, or even incoherent. Moreover, the Reason View offers the hope that insofar as we are not free, we can do something about it. For, on this view, Reason, broadly construed to include powers of imagination and perception as well as logical thought, opens the path to freedom. The more we are able to understand and correctly and sensitively evaluate our world, the more responsible we are able to be in acting within and upon it. Insofar as we want to promote freedom and responsibility, then, both across the population and within ourselves, we can do so by promoting as well as by exercising faculties of reason, perception, and reflection, by encouraging as well as by cultivating open and active minds and attitudes of alertness and sensitivity to the world. These are what we need if we are to have the freedom and the ability to see things aright. If we have this freedom and the associated freedom to form our values accordingly, and if in addition we have the freedom to govern our actions in accordance with the values we form, then we have all the freedom that responsibility requires.

Notes

1 A similar example is found in P.F. Strawson, "Freedom and Resentment," *Proceedings of the British Academy* 48 (1962): 1–25. This chapter is much indebted to that article.

2 This metaphysical use of the term "autonomy" derives from Immanuel Kant. It is an important question, which I shall not pursue here, how this relates to the use of the term in political theory.

3 Gary Watson, "Free Agency," *Journal of Philosophy* 72 (1975): 205–220.

4 See, e.g., Harry Frankfurt, "Freedom of the Will and the Concept of a Person," *Journal of Philosophy* 68 (1971): 5–20; and Watson, "Free Agency."

5 Susan Wolf, *Freedom within Reason* (New York: Oxford University Press, 1990).

Chapter 33

Derk Pereboom

DETERMINISM *AL DENTE*

Al dente means "firm to the bite," and that is how Italians eat pasta. Soft pasta is no more fit to eat than a limp and soggy slice of bread. As soon as pasta begins to lose its stiffness and becomes just tender enough so that you can bite through without snapping it, it is done. Once you have learned to cook and eat pasta *al dente*, you'll accept it no other way.

(Marcella Hazan, *The Classic Italian Cookbook*, pp. 90–1)

The demographic profile of the free will debate reveals a majority of soft determinists, who claim that we possess the freedom required for moral responsibility, that determinism is true, and that these views are compatible. Libertarians, incompatibilist champions of the freedom required for moral responsibility, constitute a minority. Not only is this the distribution in the contemporary philosophical population, but in Western philosophy it has always been the pattern. Seldom has hard determinism —the incompatibilist endorsement of determinism and rejection of the freedom required for moral responsibility—been defended.[1] One would expect hard determinism to have few proponents, given its apparent renunciation of morality. I believe, however, that the argument for hard determinism is powerful, and furthermore, that the reasons against it are not as compelling as they might at first seem.

The categorization of the determinist position by 'hard' and 'soft' masks some important distinctions, and thus one might devise a more fine-grained scheme. Actually, within the conceptual space of both hard and soft determinism there is a range of alternative views. The softest version of soft determinism maintains that we possess the freedom required for moral responsibility, that having this sort of freedom is compatible with determinism, that this freedom includes the ability to do otherwise than what one actually will do, and that even though determinism is true, one is yet deserving of blame upon having performed a wrongful act. The hardest version of hard determinism claims that since determinism is true, we lack the freedom required for moral responsibility, and hence, not only do we never deserve blame, but, moreover, no moral principles or values apply to us. But both hard and soft determinism encompass a number of less extreme positions. The view I wish to defend is somewhat softer than the hardest of the hard determinisms, and in this respect it is similar to some aspects of the position recently developed by Ted Honderich.[2] In the view we will explore, since determinism is true, we lack the freedom required for moral responsibility. But although we therefore never deserve blame for having performed a wrongful act, most moral principles and values are not thereby undermined.

I

Let us, for the sake of counterargument, devise a soft-determinist position that incorporates the essential features of three widespread compatibilist notions of freedom. First, perhaps the most prominent compatibilist conception is found in the Humean tradition—a notion of freedom of action. In this view, an action is free in the sense required for moral responsibility when it is one the agent really wanted to perform. More precisely, an action is free in the right sense just in case desires that genuinely belong to the agent make up the immediate causal history of the action. An action is unfree, by contrast, when, for example, it is performed as a result of brainwashing or some types of mental illness. In such cases, desires that genuinely belong to the agent do not play the causal role necessary for the action to be genuinely free.[3]

Second, in Harry Frankfurt's view, to be morally responsible, one's effective desires to perform actions must conform to one's second-order desires.[4] Frankfurt has us suppose "that a person has done what he wanted to do, that he did it because he wanted to do it, and that the will by which he was moved when he did it was his will because it was the will he wanted."[5] Such a person, in his view, acted freely in the sense required for moral responsibility.

Third, Bernard Gert and Timothy Duggan have argued that the type of freedom required for moral responsibility is *the ability to will*, or, in John Fischer's development of this view, *responsiveness to reasons*.[6] For an action to be free in the right sense, it must result from the agent's rational consideration of reasons relevant to the situation, such that, in at least some alternative circumstances in which there are sufficient reasons for her to do otherwise than she actually does, she would be receptive to these reasons and would have done otherwise by the efficacy of the same deliberative mechanism that actually results in the action. Hence, I am free in the right sense when I decide to harvest the wheat next

week rather than this week, if, in circumstances in which I knew it would rain next week, I would, by the deliberative mechanism that actually results in my deciding to harvest next week, appreciate the different reasons and harvest this week instead. If my practical reasoning would not differ in varying circumstances, I am neither free nor morally responsible.[7]

Let us consider a situation involving an action that is free in all of the three senses we have just discussed. Mr. Green kills Ms. Peacock for the sake of some personal advantage. His act of murder is caused by desires that are genuinely his, and his desire to kill Ms. Peacock conforms to his second-order desires. Mr. Green's desires are modified, and some of them arise, by his rational consideration of the relevant reasons, and his process of deliberation is reasons-responsive. For instance, if he knew that the bad consequences for him resulting from his crime would be much more severe than they are actually likely to be, he would not have murdered Ms. Peacock. Given that determinism is true, is it plausible that Mr. Green is responsible for his action?

In the deterministic view, the first and second-order desires and the reasons-responsive process that result in Mr. Green's crime are inevitable given their causes, and those causes are inevitable given their causes. In assessing moral responsibility for his act of murder, we wind our way back along the deterministic chain of causes that results in his reasoning and desires, and we eventually reach causal factors that are beyond his control—causal factors that he could not have produced, altered, or prevented. The incompatibilist intuition is that if an action results from a deterministic causal process that traces back to factors beyond the control of the agent, he is not morally responsible for the action.

A compatibilist rejoinder to this intuition is that moral responsibility does not leave Mr. Green behind as the deterministic causal process traces backwards in time. Even though the chain of sufficient causes for his crime reaches far beyond him, to a time before he ever existed, he retains moral responsibility. Mr. Green is morally responsible for the act of murder because his first-order desires caused the action, and these first-order desires conform to his second-order desires, and all of these desires are generated in a context of his rational evaluation of reasons. Since the causal history of his action has the right pattern, he is free and morally responsible.

Let us consider a series of different ways in which the above type of situation might come about, in order to undermine soft determinism and to support the contrary claim that moral responsibility precludes being determined in virtue of a causal process that traces back to factors beyond the agent's control.[8]

> Case 1: Mr. Green is like an ordinary human being, except that he was created by neuroscientists, who can manipulate him directly through the use of radio-like technology. Suppose these neuroscientists directly manipulate Mr. Green to undertake the process of reasoning by which his desires are modified and produced, and his effective first-order desire to kill Ms. Peacock conforms to his second-order desires. The neuroscientists manipulate him by, among other things, pushing a series of buttons just before he begins to reason about his situation, thereby causing his reasoning process to be rationally egoistic. His reasoning process is reasons-responsive, because it would have resulted in different choices in some situations in which the egoistic reasons were otherwise. Mr. Green does not think and act contrary to character, since the neuroscientists typically manipulate him to be rationally egoistic.

Mr. Green's action would seem to meet the criteria of the various compatibilist theories of freedom we have examined. But intuitively, he is not morally responsible because he is determined by the neuroscientists' actions, which are beyond his control.

The intuitions generated by this case challenge the suppositions of many soft determinists. Fischer argues that in "case of direct manipulation of the brain, it is likely that the process issuing in the action is not reasons-responsive, whereas the fact that a process is causally deterministic does not in itself bear on whether it is reasons-responsive."[9] He claims that although Frankfurt's sort of freedom can be induced neurophysiologically, a process that is reasons-responsive cannot.[10] But Fischer's claim is mistaken. As long as a process requires only abilities that are physically realized, it can be induced by sufficiently equipped scientists.

One might argue that although in Case 1 the process resulting in the action is reasons-responsive, it is induced by direct manipulation near the time of the action, and this makes the case very much like one of brainwashing. Or one might contend that Mr. Green's reasons-responsiveness is too superficial, because the neuroscientists could make him lack reasons-responsiveness just by controlling him differently. It is not clear how deeply these objections cut, but in reply, let us consider a further case:

> Case 2: Mr. Green is like an ordinary human being, except that he was created by neuroscientists, who, although they cannot control him directly, have programmed him to be a rational egoist, so that, in any circumstances like those in which he now finds himself, he is causally determined to undertake the reasons-responsive process and to possess the set of first and second-order desires that results in his killing Ms. Peacock.

Case 2 is more similar than Case 1 to the ordinary human situation, since the agent is not directly manipulated near the time of the action. But again, although the agent is free in each of our compatibilist senses, intuitively he is not morally responsible because he is determined in virtue of the neuroscientists' actions, which are beyond his control. Furthermore, it would seem unprincipled to claim that whether Mr. Green is morally responsible depends on the length of the temporal interval between the programming and the action. Whether the programming takes place two seconds or thirty years before the action is irrelevant.

> Case 3: Mr. Green is an ordinary human being, except that he was determined by the rigorous training practices of his home and community to be a rational egoist. His training took place at too early an age for him to have had the ability to prevent or alter the practices that determined his character. Mr. Green is thereby caused to undertake the reasons-responsive process and to possess the organization of first and second-order desires that result in his killing Ms. Peacock.

If the compatibilist wishes to argue that Mr. Green is morally responsible under these circumstances, he must point out a morally relevant feature present in Case 3 but not in the first two cases, and such a difference is difficult to detect. In each of these cases Mr. Green is free in all of the compatibilist senses. Causal determination by agents whose determining activity is beyond Mr. Green's control most plausibly explains his lack of moral responsibility in the first two cases, and accordingly, we would seem forced to concede that he is not morally responsible in the third case as well.

> Case 4: Physicalist determinism is true. Mr. Green is a rationally egoistic but (otherwise) ordinary human being, raised in normal circumstances. Mr. Green's killing of Ms. Peacock comes about as a result of his undertaking the reasons-responsive process of deliberation, and he has the specified organization of first and second-order desires.

Just as in Cases 1–3, Mr. Green's action in Case 4 results from a deterministic causal process that traces back to factors beyond his control. Given that we are constrained to deny moral responsibility to Mr. Green in the first three cases, what principled reason do we have for holding him morally responsible in this more ordinary case? One distinguishing feature of Case 4 is that the causal determination of Mr. Green's crime is not, in the last analysis, brought about by other agents.[11] But if we were to revise the first three cases so that the determination is brought about by a spontaneously generated, mindless machine, the intuition that Mr. Green is not morally responsible would persist. Hence, the best explanation for this intuition in these first three cases is just that Mr. Green's action results from a deterministic causal process that traces back to factors beyond his control. Consequently, because Mr. Green is also causally determined in this way in Case 4, we must, despite our initial predilections, conclude that here too Mr. Green is not morally responsible. And more generally, if every action results from a deterministic causal process that traces back to factors beyond the agent's control, then no agents are ever morally responsible for their actions.

The soft determinist might point out that according to ordinary intuitions, in Case 4 Mr. Green is morally responsible, and that these intuitions should be given more weight than we have given them. But in the incompatibilist view, one consequence of determinism is that ordinary intuitions about moral responsibility in specific cases are based on a mistake. In making moral judgments in everyday life, we do not assume that agents' choices and actions result from deterministic causal processes that trace back to factors beyond their control. Our ordinary intuitions do not presuppose that determinism is true, and they may even presuppose that it is false. Indeed, in Case 4 it is specified that determinism is true, but ordinary intuitions are likely to persist regardless of this stipulation, especially if the implications of determinism are not thoroughly internalized. If we did assume determinism and internalize its implications, our intuitions might well be different. Consequently, a reply to incompatibilism requires something more powerful than an analysis of freedom and moral responsibility designed to capture ordinary intuitions about moral responsibility in specific cases. What is needed is an argument against the fundamental incompatibilist claim, that if one's action results from a deterministic causal process that traces back to factors beyond one's control, to factors that one could not have produced, altered, or prevented, then one is not free in the sense required for moral responsibility.[12]

II

It has often been assumed that there is an alternative and equivalent statement of the fundamental incompatibilist claim. According to this variant formulation, moral responsibility requires that, given all of the factors that precede one's choice, one could have done otherwise than what one actually did.[13] Furthermore, some have argued that because this variant formulation can be defeated, the incompatibilist view is mistaken. But the variant formulation is not equivalent to the original, and since the original is more forceful, it would be best to reject the view that a successful challenge to the "responsibility only if she could have done otherwise" intuition also undermines the "responsibility only if her action does not result from a deterministic causal process that traces back to factors beyond her control" intuition.

As Peter Van Inwagen points out, if physicalist determinism is true, there is a clear sense in which no agent could have done otherwise than what he in fact did.[14] By Van Inwagen's characterization, physicalist determinism is true just in case a proposition that expresses the entire state of the universe at some instant in time, in conjunction with the physical laws, entails any proposition that expresses the state of the universe at any other instant.[15] So if physicalist

determinism is true, given the entire state of the universe at some instant in time, every subsequent state of the universe is thereby rendered inevitable. Suppose Ms. White murdered Mr. Green last Tuesday. Given physicalist determinism, Ms. White's crime is inevitable given the state of the universe 100 years before she was born and the natural laws. So if Ms. White was able to do otherwise last Tuesday, then she must at that time have been able to alter the state of the universe 100 years before she was born, or to change the natural laws. Since she was able to do neither, last Tuesday she could not have done otherwise than to murder Mr. Green.

But soft determinists have argued that one can be morally responsible for one's actions even if one could not have done otherwise. Frankfurt has devised a case similar to this one:

> Ms. Scarlet is seriously considering whether to kill Colonel Mustard. Meanwhile Professor Plum, a neuroscientist, very much wants the Colonel dead, and is worried that Ms. Scarlet will not choose to kill him. So Professor Plum has implanted a device in Ms. Scarlet's brain, which, just in case Ms. Scarlet were to be swayed by a reason not to kill Colonel Mustard, would cause her to choose to kill him. But Ms. Scarlet chooses to kill, and carries out the deed, without even beginning to be swayed by a reason for making the alternative choice.[16]

Our intuition is that Ms. Scarlet is responsible for killing Colonel Mustard, although she could not have done otherwise, and thus, the conclusion of Frankfurt's argument is that the variant intuition is mistaken. This argument is powerful and resilient. For example, it succeeds not only against the intuition that moral responsibility requires the ability to *do* otherwise, but also against the intuition that it requires the ability to *choose* otherwise. For Ms. Scarlet could not even have chosen otherwise, because the device would have arrested the deliberative process before it resulted in any alternative choice.

Frankfurt's argument strongly suggests that the incompatibilist (and everyone else) must relinquish the "responsibility only if she could have done otherwise" intuition. As Fischer has shown, however, this type of argument does not establish that the incompatibilist must also abandon the claim that moral responsibility requires that one's action not be causally determined, or, in my formulation, that moral responsibility requires that one's action not result from a deterministic causal process that traces back to factors beyond one's control.[17] (One might note that Frankfurt does not state that his argument has this result). In the Frankfurt-style example it is not specified that Ms. Scarlet is causally determined to choose or act as she did. Our intuition that she is responsible might well depend on the assumption that although the device prevents her from being able to choose to do otherwise, her choice does not result from a deterministic causal process that traces back to factors beyond her control. And indeed, if it were specified that her choice is caused in this way, incompatibilists, among others, would no longer agree that Ms. Scarlet is morally responsible.

That one's choice and action result from a deterministic causal process that traces back to factors beyond one's control entails that one cannot choose to do otherwise (in at least one sense), but not vice versa. For as Fischer points out, it is possible that one's choice not come about as a result of a deterministic process at all, and yet there be mechanisms that prevent one's choosing to do otherwise.[18] Ms. Scarlet might have been the undetermined agent-cause of the murder of Colonel Mustard even if Professor Plum's device renders her incapable of choosing to do otherwise. The incompatibilist's most fundamental claim is that moral responsibility requires that one's choice and action not result from a deterministic causal process that traces back to factors beyond one's control. An argument of the sort that Frankfurt advances cannot dislodge

this claim. This incompatibilist premise does not entail the proposition that moral responsibility requires that one be able to choose to do otherwise, and this proposition, for the reasons Frankfurt has advanced, is best rejected.[19]

III

Let us now consider the libertarians, who claim that we have a capacity for indeterministically free action, and that we are thereby morally responsible. According to one libertarian view, what makes actions free is just their being constituted (partially) of indeterministic natural events. Lucretius, for example, maintains that actions are free just in virtue of being made up partially of random swerves in the downward paths of atoms.[20] These swerves, and the actions they underlie, are random (at least) in the sense that they are not determined by any prior state of the universe. If quantum theory is true, the position and momentum of microparticles exhibit randomness in this same sense, and natural indeterminacy of this sort might also be conceived as the metaphysical foundation of indeterministically free action. But natural indeterminacies of these types cannot, by themselves, account for freedom of the sort required for moral responsibility. As has often been pointed out, such random physical events are no more within our control than are causally determined physical events, and thus, we can no more be morally responsible for them than, in the indeterminist opinion, we can be for events that are causally determined.[21]

Alternatively, many libertarians advocate the theory of agent causation, the view that freedom of action is accounted for not (simply) by randomly occurring events of the sort we have described, but by agents capable of causing their actions deliberately. In this view, an agent's causation of her action is not itself produced by processes beyond her control.[22] Positing such agent-causes, in my view, involves no internal incoherence. There is no internal incoherence in the idea of an agent having a non-Humean causal power to cause her actions deliberately in such a way that her causation of her actions is not itself produced by processes beyond her control. It is unclear, however, whether we have any reason to believe that such entities exist.[23]

Furthermore, we have not encountered any divergences from the predictions of our physical theories. The libertarian could, of course, advocate a theory that embraces such divergences, but this, by itself, would provide a powerful reason to reject such a view. So let us focus on those theories that attempt to reconcile agent-causation with the predictions of our physical theories.

Suppose first that the physical world is a deterministic system. If this is so, then the physical component of any action—constituent events describable, for example, by neurophysiology, physiology, chemistry, physics—will be causally determined. As Kant argues, it is *possible* that undetermined, non-physical agents always make free choices for just those potential actions whose physical components are causally determined.[24] In Kant's view, this possibility is all we need for rational faith in indeterministic freedom. But is it credible that this possibility is actually realized? There would certainly be nothing incredible about an undetermined agent-cause making a free choice *on some particular occasion* for a possible action whose physical component was causally determined. However, it would be incredible if for any substantial period of human history all free choices made by agent-causes should be for just those possible actions whose physical components are causally determined to occur, and none of these choices should be for the alternatives. Independent of an idealistic theory according to which agents construct the physical world, the coincidences this view implies are too wild to believe.[25]

To try to solve this problem of wild coincidences, the libertarian might invoke indeterminacy in nature. Nevertheless, in ordinary cases, quantum indeterminacy only allows for an extremely small probability of counterfactual

events at the scale of human actions.[26] Suppose, by analogy, that the soda can on the table remains where it is for the next minute. Given quantum indeterminacy, there is some probability that instead it would spontaneously move one inch to the left sometime during this minute. But for this event to occur, each of many quantum indeterminacies would have to be resolved in a specific alternative way, the probability of which is extremely small. The prospects for counterfactual human actions are similarly bad. Even if quantum indeterminacy results in the indeterminacy of certain neural events, like the firing of individual neurons, so that at certain times both the probability that the neural event will occur and that it will not are significant, the likelihood of physical components of counterfactual actions occurring is insignificant. The reason is that the making of a decision is an event of a much larger scale than is an event like the firing of a neuron. When a decision is made, a very large number of individual quantum and neural events are involved, and quantum indeterminacy would not undergird a significant probability for counterfactual events of this magnitude.

Let us assume that what determines an indeterministically free agent's choices is how she finally weighs the reasons. The weighing of each reason will be (partially) realized in a very large complex of neural and quantum events. But this complex will be too large for quantum indeterminacy to substantiate a significant probability of counterfactual actions. Suppose an agent actually makes a decision to perform action A rather than action B, and that the physical realization of her weighing of reasons is large-scale neural pattern of type X. Given quantum indeterminacy, there is some antecedent probability—the probability, let us say, just as the agent begins to weigh the reasons for action—that her brain should realize a very different neural pattern upon weighing the reasons, one of type Y, which is correlated with performing action B. But for a pattern of type B to come about, each of many indeterminacies would have to be resolved in a specific alternative way, the antecedent probability of which is extremely small. More generally, the antecedent probability of the occurrence of the physical component of any counterfactual action is extremely small. And it would be too wildly coincidental to believe that for any substantial interval of human history all or even almost all indeterministically free choices made by agent-causes should be for just those possible actions the occurrence of whose physical components has the extremely high antecedent physical probability, and not for any of the alternatives. Thus the fact that quantum theory allows counterfactual actions to have non-zero antecedent probability fails to remedy the problem of wild coincidences posed by the attempt to reconcile libertarianism with strict determinism.

Now it might be objected that the problem of wild coincidences arises only if it turns out that, at the neurophysiological level, counterfactual events do not have significant antecedent probability. Yet there are examples, such as the moving of the needle on a Geiger counter, of microphysical indeterminacies that are magnified to significantly indeterminate events at the macrolevel. Perhaps similar magnifications occur in the brain.[27] Randolph Clarke suggests that a libertarian might take advantage of macrolevel natural indeterminacy of this sort by positing agent causes who have the power to make the difference as to which of a series of naturally possible actions is performed.[28] Might this picture not offer the libertarian a way out of the wild coincidences problem? No. Suppose that physical components of counterfactual actions do have a significant antecedent probability of occurring. Consider a class of possible actions each of which has a physical component whose antecedent probability of occurring is approximately 0.32. If indeterminist free action is to be compatible with what our physical theories predict to be overwhelmingly likely, then over a long enough period of time these possible

actions would have to be freely chosen almost exactly 32% of the time. Yet their actually being freely chosen almost exactly 32% of the time would constitute a coincidence no less wild than the coincidence of possible actions whose physical components have an antecedent probability of about 0.99 being freely chosen about 99% of the time. The problem of wild coincidences, therefore, is independent of the physical components of actions having any particular degree of antecedent probability.[29]

This point reveals the fundamental difficulty for libertarian agent causation. Whether the physical laws are deterministic or quantum indeterministic, the antecedent probabilities of the physical components of human actions are fixed. With deterministic laws, the antecedent probability of any such component is either 1 or 0. According to quantum theory, such probabilities will be different. But regardless of which view is true, it would be wildly coincidental, and hence too bizarre a scenario to believe, if for any substantial span of human history frequencies of indeterministically free choices should happen to dovetail with determinate physical probabilities.

Thus, barring revolutionary discoveries in neurophysiology or physics, it seems unlikely that libertarianism is true. Accordingly, let us focus our attention on the hard determinist version of incompatibilism. But first, our discussion of libertarianism reveals the need to revise our characterization of the wider issues: assuming the truth of our best scientific theories, determinism turns out to be false. However, the kinds of indeterminacies these theories posit provide us with no more control over our actions than we would have if determinism were true. Our actions may not result from deterministic causal processes that trace back to factors over which we have no control, but yet there are processes, either deterministic or indeterministic, over which we have no control, that produce our actions, and this is enough to rule out freedom of the sort required for moral responsibility.

Hence the fundamental incompatibilist intuition turns out to be "responsibility only if her action is not produced by processes, either deterministic or indeterministic, beyond her control." For the sake of simplicity and meshing with the traditional discussion, however, I shall continue to describe the position I am defending as "hard determinism," with the understanding that this term is strictly speaking inaccurate, but not in a way that makes a difference to the issues we shall now explore.

IV

The alternative to soft determinism and libertarianism is hard determinism, the view that because determinism is true, we lack the freedom required for moral responsibility. Let us examine this option to ascertain whether it must be as unacceptable as it may initially seem.

One instinctive reaction to hard determinism is that if it were true, we would have no reason to attempt to accomplish anything—to try to improve our lives or the prospects of society—because our deliberations and choices could make no difference. This challenge has also been directed towards soft determinists, and they have responded persuasively. Ayer and Dennett, among others, have pointed out that the determination of our deliberations, choices, actions, and their consequences does not undermine their causal efficacy.[30] The hard determinist can legitimately appropriate this position. It is true that according to hard determinism we are not free in the sense required for moral responsibility, and therefore, what happens cannot be affected by choices that are free in this sense. But what happens may nevertheless be caused by the deliberations we engage in and the choices we make.

It is undeniable that we feel we have the ability to choose or do otherwise; for example, that you feel that it is now possible for you either to continue or to stop reading this article. In the hard determinist's judgment, this feeling of freedom is an illusion (and soft determinists of some types agree). This judgment would be challenged by those who believe that our introspective sense provides us with infallible beliefs about our own abilities. But it is a familiar fact that such an assessment of introspection is implausible. Kant, however, provide us with a different reason not to discount the feeling of freedom. He suggests that engaging in a process of deliberation requires that one suppose that more than one choice for action is causally possible.[31] This view seems compelling: could one deliberate about which roads to take if one believed that one was causally capable of choosing only one of them? But according to hard determinism, one cannot choose otherwise than the way one actually does. Thus, as Van Inwagen argues, whenever one engages in a process of deliberation, one would be making a false supposition, and hence if one were a self-professed hard determinist, one would often have inconsistent beliefs; "anyone who denies the existence of free will must, inevitably, contradict himself with monotonous regularity."[32]

There are two replies available to the hard determinist. The first grants that when we deliberate, at the moment of choice we must indeed make the false and unjustified assumption that more than one course of action is open to us. But it is legitimate to assume this cognitive posture, because the practical gains of engaging in deliberation are significant enough to outweigh the losses of having false and unjustified beliefs. In this view, deliberation requires us to choose between theoretical and practical irrationality. One is irrational in the theoretical sense when, for example, one has a belief that has no justification, or a belief one knows to be false, and one is irrational in the practical sense if, for instance, one does something one knows will frustrate what one wants, all things considered. Hard determinism would seem to leave us with the following choice: either deliberate and have a belief that you know to be false whenever you do, or cease to deliberate. Practical rationality would appear to have the upper hand.

It is nevertheless disturbing to maintain that one must be theoretically irrational whenever one deliberates. There is, however, a more attractive alternative which does not require that one override the canons of theoretical rationality. The hard determinist might deny that at the moment of choice, one must assume that more than one option is causally possible. One might instead believe that one's actions are determined by way of one's choices, that one's choices are determined by means of one's deliberation, and that one does not know in advance of deliberation which action one will choose. As long as one's actions are determined by deliberation and choice, and one does not know beforehand what the result of one's deliberation will be, there will be no interference with the deliberative process. Indeed, the deliberative process might be jeopardized if one had previous knowledge of the choice that would result. Perhaps it is even incoherent to suppose that one might know in advance of deliberation which of two roads one will choose, for in such a situation genuine deliberation would be undermined. But given that one cannot know the results of one's deliberation in advance, the process can go on unimpeded.

V

A very prominent feature of our ordinary conception of morality that would be undermined if hard determinism were true is our belief that people deserve credit and praise when they deliberately perform morally exemplary actions, and that they deserve blame when they deliberately perform wrongful actions. To deserve blame is to be morally liable to blame by deliberately choosing to do the wrong thing. Hard determinism rules out one's ever deserving blame for deliberately choosing to act wrongly, for such choices are always produced by processes that are beyond one's control.

Someone might argue that even if no one ever deserves blame, it would nevertheless be best for us to think and act as if people sometimes do,

because thinking and acting this way is a superb method for promoting moral reform and education. More generally, even if no one is ever really morally responsible, it would still be best sometimes to hold people morally responsible. Such a view might be justified on practical grounds, were we confident, for example, that thinking and acting as if people sometimes deserve blame is often necessary for effectively promoting moral reform and education. But this option would have the hard determinist thinking that someone deserves blame when she also believes him not to, which is an instance of theoretical irrationality, and would have her blaming someone when he does not deserve to be blamed, which would seem to be morally wrong.

There is, however, an alternative practice for promoting moral reform and education which would suffer neither from irrationality nor apparent immorality. Instead of blaming people, the determinist might appeal to the practice of moral admonishment and encouragement. One might, for example, explain to an offender that what he did was wrong, and then encourage him to refrain from performing similar actions in the future. One need not, in addition, blame him for what he has done. The hard determinist can maintain that by admonishing and encouraging a wrongdoer one might communicate a sense of what is right, and a respect for persons, and that these attitudes can lead to salutary change.[33] Hence, one need not hold the wrongdoer morally responsible for what he has done, but rather consider him responsive to moral admonishment and encouragement. Likewise, although one could not justifiably think of one's own wrongful actions as deserving of blame, one could legitimately regard them as wrongful, and thereby admonish oneself, and resolve to refrain from similar actions in the future. But like blame of others, blame of self, and more generally, holding oneself morally responsible, would be best avoided.

But what of the character who regularly and deliberately does wrong, and refuses to make a commitment to doing what is right? Doesn't the hard determinist have little to say to such a person? While the hard determinist can only admonish, the advocate of moral responsibility can also blame. But having recourse to blame in such circumstances is not clearly a significant practical advantage. One might argue that hard determinism is a threat to moral practice because the character we have described might offer determinism as an excuse for his behavior. Certainly, the hard determinist would have to accept his excuse, whereas the proponent of moral responsibility would not. But the practical advantages from this point on do not favor either side. Both face the task of moral education and imparting a respect for persons, and it is not obvious that the hard determinist has fewer resources for this project than those available to her opposition.

The hard determinist position implies that the appalling actions of persons are much more similar to earthquakes and epidemics than they are according to views that hold persons morally responsible. The justification we assume for regarding especially wrongful actions of persons as deeply different from natural disasters is that persons are typically responsible for their actions. But according to hard determinism, because a person's actions are the result of processes over which he has no control, we cannot consider him responsible for them, just as we cannot hold earthquakes or epidemics responsible for their effects. One still might legitimately have a feeling of moral concern about what persons do, or about what persons who are reasons-responsive do, which would differ from one's attitudes to earthquakes and epidemics. This feeling would be legitimate supposing it has no cognitive component that conflicts with hard determinism. But as I shall soon argue in further detail, the various attitudes that presuppose the cognitive component that persons are morally responsible would be unjustified.

Honderich contends rightly, I believe, that in the face of determinism we must eschew retribution, but he also argues that

we can persist in certain responses to the desires and intentions of others, and hence to them. There is no obstacle to my abhorrence of the desires and intentions of the treacherous husband foreseeing his divorce, or, more important, to my abhorrence of him, a man whose personality and character are consistent with these desires and intentions, and support them.[34]

But the determinist must be more abstemious here. Abhorrence of a person because of the actions he has performed at least typically involves blaming him for those actions, which, in turn, presupposes that his actions and character did not result from processes beyond his control. If one were to discover that an especially wrongful "action" was caused by some non-psychological, physiological reaction in the person, one's abhorrence would tend to vanish, and this would suggest that one's abhorrence was founded in blame. It is legitimate to feel moral concern in response to a wrongful action, and to be deeply saddened that there are persons with immoral characters, but at least most often one's response of abhorrence, because it involves blaming someone, is unjustified.[35]

Perhaps one can learn to abhor people because of the wrongful actions they perform without blaming them, just as one might abhor soggy Corn Flakes because of their sogginess without blaming them. But it is doubtful that developing such an attitude towards people could be justified on moral grounds if determinism is true. One might be able to abhor people for their wrongful actions without being theoretically irrational, but it seems unlikely that one would advance the good by fostering this attitude, by contrast, for example, with attitudes such as moral concern or sadness.

Susan Wolf has argued that whereas deserved blame cannot be justified if determinism is true, deserved praise does not collapse along with it.[36] As she puts it, she is "committed to the curious claim that being psychologically determined to perform good actions is compatible with deserving praise for them, but that being psychologically determined to perform bad actions is not compatible with deserving blame."[37] Wolf, in effect, endorses the hard determinist's view about deserved blame, but not about deserved praise. She cites the following example in support of her view:

> Two persons, of equal swimming ability, stand on equally uncrowded beaches. Each sees an unknown child struggling in the water in the distance. Each thinks "The child needs my help" and directly swims out to save him. In each case, we assume that the agent reasons correctly—the child *does* need her help—and that, in swimming out to save him, the agent does the right thing. We further assume that in one of these cases, the agent has the ability to do otherwise, and in the other case not.[38]

Wolf says that whereas according to the libertarian only the first of these agents is responsible, "there seems to be nothing of value that the first agent has but the second agent lacks." Perhaps the second agent does not have the ability to do otherwise because "her understanding of the situation is so good and her moral commitment so strong." Wolf concludes that the fact that the second agent is determined to do the right thing for the right reasons does not make her any less deserving of praise than the first agent.

First of all, Wolf's argument is susceptible to an objection inspired by the point Fischer raises in connection with Frankfurt's case. Given the way Wolf presents her lifesaver case, the reader might yet presuppose that the swimmer who cannot do otherwise is not causally determined to deliberate and act as she does. If it were specified that her action results from a deterministic causal process that traces back to factors she could not have produced, altered, or prevented—perhaps by adding that she is controlled by neuroscientists—the intuition that she

deserves praise might well vanish. Wolf's case may indicate that an agent might deserve praise even if she could not have done otherwise, but it fails to show that an agent deserves praise even if her action results from a deterministic causal process that traces back to factors beyond her control.

But suppose that the intuition that the second swimmer deserves praise persists even if it is specified that she is causally determined. The hard determinist can now argue that while according to ordinary intuitions both swimmers deserve praise, the second swimmer really does not. Ordinarily, we consider persons praiseworthy for their great intelligence, good looks, or native athletic ability, even though these qualities are not due to any agency of theirs, and hence, even though they in no sense really deserve praise for these qualities. Thus it comes as no surprise that we would ordinarily consider the second swimmer, who is determined to do the right thing for the right reasons, praiseworthy. She may be considered praiseworthy because she is a good person, and has acted in pursuit of the good, but as in the case of the person of great intelligence, we need not conclude that she is genuinely deserving of praise.

Sometimes it may well be a good thing to praise someone despite her not deserving it, perhaps because praise can at times simply be an expression of approbation or delight about the actions or accomplishments of another. By contrast, blaming someone who does not deserve it would seem always to be (at least *prima facie*) wrong. The reason for this (as Wolf notes) might be that because blaming typically causes pain, it must be wrong unless it is deserved, whereas since praise is far from painful, it can be appropriate beyond cases in which it is deserved. Whatever may be the case here, the intuition that the determined swimmer is praiseworthy fails to undermine the hard determinist view, that not only deserved blame but also deserved praise is incompatible with determinism.

VI

Another feature of our ordinary conception of morality that would be threatened if we accepted hard determinism is the belief that statements of the following form are sometimes true: 'Although you did not choose x, you ought, morally, to have chosen x.' There are different senses of the moral 'ought,' but the central senses might well be undermined in a hard determinist picture. It would seem that in all cases in which one could never have performed an action, it is never true that one ought to have performed the action.[39] Consequently, if because one is causally determined one can never choose otherwise than the way one actually does, then it is false that one ever morally ought to choose otherwise. And further, if it is never true that one ought to have chosen otherwise than the way one does, then what would be the point of a system of moral 'ought's? Hard determinism imperils this system, because it would seem that if 'A ought to choose x' is true at all, it must be true not only when A comes to choose x, but also when A does not come to choose x.

But even if moral 'ought' statements are never true, moral judgments, such as 'it is morally right for A to do x,' or 'it is a morally good thing for A to do x,' still can be. Thus, even if one is causally determined to refrain from giving to charity, and even if it is therefore false that one ought to give to charity, it still might be the right thing or a good thing to do.[40] Cheating on one's taxes might be a wrong or a bad thing to do, even if one's act is causally determined, and hence, even if it is false that one ought not to do so. These alternative moral judgments would indeed lack the deontic implications they are typically assumed to have, but nevertheless, they can be retained when moral 'ought' statements are undermined. In addition, the various benefits of the system of moral 'ought's can be recouped. For instance, when one is encouraging moral action, one can replace occurrences of 'you ought to do x' with 'it would be right for you to

do x,' or with 'it would be a good thing for you to do x.' Discouragement of wrongful action could be revised analogously.

One might argue that if moral 'ought' statements were never true, we could have no reason to do what is right. But this view is mistaken. Although it is false that one ought to eat boiled rather than poached eggs, one might still have reason to choose one over the other, perhaps in virtue of one's preference for boiled eggs, or even because one thinks that one type is objectively better than the other, and one has resolved to aspire to excellence. Similarly, one might treat others with respect because one prefers to do so, or because one has resolved to do what is right, even if it is not the case that one ought to do so. If one has resolved to do what is right, by whatever motivation, one thereby has reason to act in accordance with this resolution.

It may seem that relinquishing the moral 'ought' together with deserved praise and blame restricts hard determinism to a consequentialist position in ethics. One might be tempted by the claim that although rejection of the moral 'ought' is consistent with the goodness of certain consequences and, derivatively, with the goodness of actions that bring about such consequences, abandoning the moral 'ought' does rule out principles of right that are based on non-consequentialist considerations. But this claim seems mistaken for the reason that insofar as they have been developed, the metaphysical bases for non-consequentialist positions do not clearly involve an essential appeal to a notion of freedom unavailable to the hard determinist. One might argue that the hard determinist is restricted to consequentialism because her rejection of deserved praise and blame confines her to forward-looking ethical views, and such forward-looking views are consequentialist. But although the hard determinist may not look to the past to assess praise and blame, she can legitimately make judgments about the rightness and wrongness of past actions. Furthermore, not all forward-looking ethical views are consequentialist. The Kantian principle, "Act only on that maxim which you can also will to be a universal law" is no less forward-looking than the utilitarian principle, "Act so as to maximize happiness." The hard determinist seems free to accept non-consequentialist ethical views.

VII

If hard determinism is true, how would it be best to regard our reactive attitudes, for example, our resentment and anger upon being betrayed, or our gratitude upon receiving help in trouble? In the face of a deterministic universe, the Stoics urge self-discipline aimed at eradicating at least the negative reactive attitudes. David Hume and P. F. Strawson, on the other hand, advance the psychological thesis that our reactive attitudes cannot be affected by a general belief in determinism, or by any such abstract metaphysical view, and that therefore the project of altering or eliminating our reactive attitudes by a determinist conviction would be ineffectual.[41]

Let us address two issues: first, whether the reactive attitudes really are immune from alteration by a belief in determinism, and second, whether it would be good for them to be altered by such a belief (if they could be). On the first issue, Gary Watson provides a compelling example, the case of Robert Harris, who brutally murdered two teenage boys in California in 1978.[42] When we read an account of these murders "we respond to his heartlessness and viciousness with loathing."[43] But an account of the atrocious abuse he suffered as a child "gives pause to the reactive attitudes."[44] Upon absorbing such information, not everyone relinquishes his attitude of blame completely, but this attitude is at least typically tempered. It is not only that we are persuaded to feel pity for the criminal. In addition, our attitude of blame is mitigated by our coming to believe that the criminal was at least partially determined to behave as he did. One might claim that although belief in determinism about a particular situation can affect

reactive attitudes, the general belief in determinism never can. But I can think of no reason to accept this view. Because particular cases of determinism can be vividly described, they can much more readily affect one's attitudes, but there is no reason to believe that the general conviction cannot have a similar effect.

It would be implausible to maintain that in every case the presence or the intensity of one's reactive attitudes can be affected by a belief in determinism. Sometimes a wrong committed might be too horrible for such a belief to have any effect on one's subsequent reaction. The Stoics maintained that we can always prevent or eradicate attitudes like grief and anger, regardless of their intensity, with the aid of a determinist conviction. But they might well have overestimated the extent of the control we have over our emotional lives. If someone were brutally to murder your family, it might well be psychologically impossible for you ever to eradicate feelings of intense anger toward the killer. This fails to show, however, that a determinist conviction cannot affect reactive attitudes, even in typical cases.

Let us suppose, therefore, that a determinist conviction can affect our reactive attitudes. Would it be a good thing if they were affected by this means? According to Strawson, human beings would stand to lose much if reactive attitudes were dislodged by a belief in determinism, for we would then be left with a certain "objectivity of attitude." A stance of this sort, Strawson believes, conflicts with the types of attitudes required for good interpersonal relationships:

> To adopt the objective attitude to another human being is to see him, perhaps, as an object of social policy; as a subject for what, in a wide range of sense, might be called treatment; as something certainly to be taken account, perhaps precautionary account, of; to be managed or handled or cured or trained; perhaps simply to be avoided. . . .

The objective attitude may be emotionally toned in many ways: it may include repulsion or fear, it may include pity or love, though not all kinds of love. But it cannot include the range of reactive feelings and attitudes which belong to involvement or participation with others in interpersonal human relationships; it cannot include resentment, gratitude, forgiveness, anger, or the sort of love which two adults can sometimes be said to feel reciprocally, for each other.[45]

Strawson is right to believe that objectivity of attitude would destroy interpersonal relationships. But he is mistaken to think that objectivity of attitude would result or be appropriate if determinism were to undermine the reactive attitudes. As Honderich argues, a reasonable determinist attitude towards the moral life "recommends no such bloodlessly managerial an attitude toward others."[46]

In his analysis, Honderich points out that one's reactive attitudes presuppose certain beliefs about the persons to whom they are directed, and that these beliefs can sometimes be undermined by determinist convictions.[47] I agree, and I would develop the claim in this way. One's reactive attitudes presuppose beliefs of this sort, and when these presuppositions lack adequate justification, or when one believes them to be false, or when they have little or no justification and conflict with justified beliefs one holds, then maintaining attitudes that have such presuppositions is irrational in the theoretical sense. Suppose, for example, that you are angry with the guests because they are very late for dinner. Your anger presupposes the belief that they reasonably could have been on time. But you come to know that they are late because an airplane crashed on the freeway, and the resulting traffic jam trapped them for an hour. Given that your presupposition no longer has justification, and since it conflicts with a justified belief you hold, it is theoretically irrational for you to maintain your anger, and you would

therefore have to give up your anger to escape irrationality.

Now suppose that you have a justified belief that hard determinism is true, and that you are angry with a friend because he has betrayed a confidence. Your anger presupposes the belief that he deserves blame and that his betrayal was not produced by processes beyond his control. You have no justification for this presupposition, let us suppose, and it conflicts with your justified belief that his action was produced by processes beyond his control. Consequently, your anger is irrational in the theoretical sense, and in order to escape this irrationality, you must give up your anger.

Someone might point out, however, that such anger may not be practically irrational, and since practical and theoretical rationality may conflict, an issue may arise about which sort it would then be best to secure. If one's anger is practically rational in virtue of playing a part in a system of attitudes required for interpersonal relationships, but it is nevertheless theoretically irrational because of its presuppositions, how would it be best to act? For Hume and Strawson, the issue would happily be resolved by facts about human psychology, since we would be psychologically incapable of theoretical rationality in such situations. But since their psychological claim is implausible, the issue again becomes live.

If the hard determinist were to acknowledge that a determinist conviction could affect the reactive attitudes, but that adopting an objectivity of attitude would be practically irrational in virtue of being destructive to human relationships, she might well override theoretical rationality by retaining her normal reactive attitudes. If she acted in this way, however, she would be reduced to the uncomfortable position of maintaining attitudes that are theoretically irrational. But the hard determinist is not clearly forced into such a difficult situation. For first, although many ordinary reactive attitudes might be irrational, these reactive attitudes are not obviously required for good interpersonal relationships. Some reactive attitudes, like certain kinds of anger and resentment, may well not be good for relationships at all. And secondly, the reactive attitudes one would want to retain have analogues that do not have false presuppositions. Such analogues by no means amount to Strawson's objectivity of attitude, and they are sufficient to sustain good interpersonal relationships.

In Strawson's view, some of the attitudes most important for interpersonal relationships are resentment, anger, forgiveness, gratitude, and mature love. As I have suggested, a certain measure of resentment and anger is likely to be beyond our power to affect, and thus even supposing that one is committed to doing what is right and rational, one would still not be able to eradicate all of one's resentment and anger. As hard determinists, we might expect these attitudes to occur in certain situations, and we might regard them as inevitable and exempt from blame when they do. But we sometimes have the ability to prevent, alter, or eliminate resentment and anger, and given a belief in hard determinism, we might well do so for the sake of morality and rationality. Modification of anger and resentment, aided by a determinist conviction, could well be a good thing for relationships (supposing that no unhealthy repression is induced). At very least, the claim that it would be harmful requires further argument.

The attitude of forgiveness seems to presuppose that the person being forgiven deserves blame, and therefore, forgiveness is indeed imperiled by hard determinism. But there are certain features of forgiveness that are not threatened by hard determinism, and these features can adequately take the place this attitude usually has in relationships. Suppose your companion has wronged you in similar fashion a number of times, and you find yourself unhappy, angry, and resolved to loosen the ties of your relationship. Subsequently, however, he apologizes to you, which, consistent with hard determinism, signifies his recognition of the wrongness of his behavior, his wish that he had not wronged you, and his genuine commitment to improvement. As a result, you change your mind and decide to continue the relationship. In this case, the feature of forgiveness that is consistent with hard determinism is the willingness to cease to regard past wrongful behavior as a reason to weaken or dissolve one's relationship. In another type of case, you might, independently of the offender's repentance, simply choose to disregard the wrong as a reason to alter the character of your relationship. This attitude is in no sense undermined by hard determinism. The sole aspect of forgiveness that is jeopardized by a hard determinist conviction is the willingness to overlook deserved blame or punishment. But if one has given up belief in deserved blame and punishment, then the willingness to overlook them is no longer needed for relationships.

Gratitude would seem to require the supposition that the person to whom one is grateful is morally responsible for an other-regarding act, and therefore hard determinism might well undermine gratitude.[48] But certain aspects of this attitude would be left untouched, aspects that can play the role gratitude commonly has in interpersonal relationships. No feature of the hard determinist position conflicts with one's being joyful and expressing joy when people are especially considerate, generous, or courageous in one's behalf. Such expression of joy can produce the sense of mutual well-being and respect frequently brought about by gratitude. Moreover, just as in the case of gratitude, when one expresses joy for what another person has done, one can do so with the intention of developing a human relationship.

Finally, the thesis that love between mature persons would be subverted if hard determinism were true requires much more thorough argument than has been provided. One might note, first of all, that parents love their children rarely, if ever, because these children possess the freedom required for moral responsibility, or because they freely (in this sense) choose the good, or because they deserve to be loved. But moreover, when adults love each other, it is also seldom, if at all, for these kinds of reasons. Explanations for love are complex. Besides moral character and action, factors such as appearance, manner, intelligence, and affinities with persons or events in one's history all have a part. But suppose we agree that moral character and action are of paramount importance in producing and maintaining love. Even then, it is unlikely that one's love would be undermined if one were to believe that moral character and action do not come about through free and morally responsible choice. Love of another involves, most fundamentally, wishing well for the other, taking on many of the aims and desires of the other as one's own, and a desire to be together with the other. Hard determinism threatens none of this.

While certain reactive attitudes might well be irrational because of the presuppositions these attitudes have, turning to analogues of the sort we have described is in no sense irrational, and it is far from assuming the objectivity of attitude so destructive to interpersonal relationships. Furthermore, nothing about hard determinism recommends assuming an objectivity of attitude. The specter of this outlook arises from the sense that the hard determinist is constrained to view other persons as mere mechanical devices, to be used and not respected. The hard determinist, however, is not forced to view persons in this way. She is not compelled to deny that human beings are rational and responsive to reasons, and no feature of her view threatens the appropriateness of respecting persons for their rational capacities.

Accordingly, someone's thinking and acting in harmony with her hard determinist conviction would not endanger her interpersonal relationships. She would resist anger, blame, and resentment, but she would not be exempt from pain and unhappiness upon being wronged. She might, if wronged, admonish, disregard the wrongdoing, or terminate the relationship.

Although she would avoid gratitude, she could enjoy and express joy about other persons' efforts in her behalf. No obstacle would be posed to her loving others. Only if, in addition, she had an unappealing tendency to control another, would she see him "as an object of social policy; as a subject for what, in a wide range of sense, might be called treatment; as something certainly to be taken account, perhaps precautionary account, of; to be managed or handled or cured or trained; perhaps simply to be avoided ...".[49] But taking on such an objectivity of attitude would not be justified by her hard determinist conviction.

VIII

Given that free will of some sort is required for moral responsibility, then libertarianism, soft determinism, and hard determinism, as typically conceived, are jointly exhaustive positions (if we allow the "deterministic" positions the view that events may result from indeterministic processes of the sort described by quantum mechanics). Yet each has a consequence that is difficult to accept. If libertarianism were true, then we would expect events to occur that are incompatible with what our physical theories predict to be overwhelmingly likely. If soft determinism were true, then agents would deserve blame for their wrongdoing even though their actions were produced by processes beyond their control. If hard determinism were true, agents would not be morally responsible—agents would never deserve blame for even the most cold-blooded and calmly executed evil actions. I have argued that hard determinism could be the easiest view to accept. Hard determinism need not be of the hardest sort. It need not subvert the commitment to doing what is right, and although it does undermine some of our reactive attitudes, secure analogues of these attitudes are all one requires for good interpersonal relationships. Consequently, of the three positions, hard determinism might well be the most attractive, and it is surely worthy of more serious consideration than it has been accorded.[50]

Notes

1 The terms 'soft determinism' and 'hard determinism' originate in William James' essay "The Dilemma of Determinism," in *The Will to Believe and Other Essays*, New York: Longman, 1909). The most prominent attempts to develop a hard determinist theory are in Baruch de Spinoza, *Ethics* (especially Part II, Proposition 48, and Part III, Scholium to Proposition 2), in Baron d'Holbach, *System of Nature* (1770), and in John Hospers, "Meaning and Free Will," *Philosophy and Phenomenological Research* X (1950), pp. 313–330, and *Human Conduct* (New York: Harcourt, Brace, and World, 1961), pp. 493–524. For Charles Stevenson, morality accords with determinism only because the backward-looking elements that many have thought to be essential to morality are not genuinely so; see "Ethical Judgments and Avoidability," *Mind* 47, (1938), and *Facts and Values* (New Haven and London: Yale University Press, 1963) pp. 138–152. The view I develop is similar to Stevenson's in that I argue that there is a conception of ethics, different from the common sense version, which is compatible with determinism, but I contend, while Stevenson does not, that any conception which is compatible with determinism must relinquish moral responsibility. Elizabeth Beardsley argues that the hard deterministic perspective must be taken seriously, but only as one among several perspectives, each of which has its proper role in the moral life, "Determinism and Moral Perspectives," *Philosophy and Phenomenological Research* XXI (1960), pp. 1–20.

2 My attention was drawn to Honderich's position in *A Theory of Determinism* (Oxford: Oxford University Press, 1988) by a referee for *Noûs*. I do not endorse Honderich's strategies for arguing against soft determinism and libertarianism, and my approach for undermining these views differs from his. Neither do I sympathize with his contention that determinism is true despite the evidence of quantum mechanics. But despite Honderich's claim to reject both compatibilism and incompatibilism, I agree with several important aspects of his conception of *affirmation* (pp. 488–540), as will become evident as this discussion progresses. Honderich believes that he can reject both compatibilism and incompatibilism because, contrary to tradition, he does not construe these notions as jointly exhaustive of the determinist positions on freedom and morality. Compatibilism, in his schema, is the claim that determinism is compatible with all of our practices of moral evaluation, that it "leaves moral approval and disapproval untouched," whereas incompatibilism is the claim that determinism is compatible with none of these practices, that it "destroys [moral approval and disapproval]" (p. 539, cf. pp. 451–487). In my conception, compatibilism is the view that determinism is compatible with whatever sort of freedom is sufficient for moral responsibility, while incompatibilism is the view that determinism is not compatible with this type of freedom.

3 David Hume, *A Treatise of Human Nature*, L. A. Selby-Bigge, ed., (Oxford: Oxford University Press, 1962), pp. 399–412; *An Enquiry Concerning Human Understanding*, Eric Steinberg, ed., (Indianapolis: Hackett Publishing Co., 1981), §8; A. J Ayer, "Freedom and Necessity," in *Free Will*, Gary Watson, ed., (Oxford: Oxford University Press, 1982), pp. 15–23.

4 Harry Frankfurt, "Freedom of the Will and the Concept of a Person," in Gary Watson, ed., *Free Will*, (Oxford: Oxford University Press, 1982), pp. 81–95.

5 Frankfurt, p. 94.

6 Bernard Gert and Timothy J. Duggan, "Free Will as the Ability to Will," *Noûs* XIII (May 1979), pp. 197–217, reprinted in *Moral Responsibility*, John Martin Fischer ed., (Ithaca: Cornell University Press, 1986) pp. 205–224); John Martin Fischer, "Responsiveness and Moral Responsibility," in *Responsibility, Character, and the Emotions*, Ferdinand Schoeman, ed., (Cambridge: Cambridge University Press, 1987), pp. 81–106, at pp. 88–9.

7 In Honderich's view, compatibilists ignore a widespread attitude about our actions, that moral responsibility presupposes *origination*, or agent causation. He claims, accordingly, that compatibilists are *intransigent* in maintaining their notions of moral responsibility in the face of determinism, and that this counts against them (pp. 482–487).

While I agree that moral responsibility presupposes origination, I also believe that pointing out that compatibilists ignore this conception has little force against their position. What is needed is an argument against the view that the types of freedom that soft determinisms have advocated are sufficient for moral responsibility, and I develop such an argument here.

8 Richard Taylor discusses cases of these sorts in *Metaphysics*, (Englewood Cliffs: Prentice Hall, 1983), pp. 43–4.

9 Fischer, p. 102.

10 Fischer, pp. 104–5.

11 For example, in the course of developing his soft determinist view, William G. Lycan argues that in the kinds of cases Richard Taylor discusses (in *Metaphysics*, pp. 43–4) the agent lacks responsibility just because he "is a puppet of another person" and not simply because he is causally determined (*Consciousness*, Cambridge, MA: MIT Press, 1987, pp. 117–18).

12 Some compatibilists might argue that one should construe the slide to slope the other way. One should begin with one's strong intuition that in Case 4 Mr. Green is morally responsible, and since there are no good reasons to believe that there is a morally relevant distinction between Mr. Green in Case 4 and his counterpart in Cases 1–3, one should conclude that Mr. Green in the first three cases is also morally responsible. My own intuition that Mr. Green in Cases 1 and 2 is not morally responsible is much stronger than my intuition that Mr. Green in Case 4 is, but some compatibilists may differ. What follows may provide these compatibilists with a clearer picture of an alternative view.

13 Honderich, for example, seems to suppose that these intuitions, on some interpretation of 'could have done otherwise,' are equivalent, e.g. pp. 400–409.

14 Peter Van Inwagen, "The Incompatibility of Free Will and Determinism," in *Free Will*, Gary Watson, ed., (Oxford: Oxford University Press, 1982), pp. 96–110; *An Essay on Free Will*, (Oxford: Oxford University Press, 1983), pp. 55–78.

15 "The Incompatibility of Free Will and Determinism," p. 47.

16 Harry Frankfurt, "Alternate Possibilities and Moral Responsibility," *Journal of Philosophy* 1969, pp. 829–839; for a precursor to certain elements of my variation on Frankfurt's case see John Martin Fischer, "Responsibility and Control," *Moral Responsibility*, Fischer, ed., pp. 174–190.

17 Fischer, "Responsibility and Control," pp. 182–185.

18 Fischer, "Responsibility and Control," pp. 182–185.

19 Given this view, the incompatibilist would still be right to claim that one is morally responsible for an action only if one could not have done otherwise due the action's resulting from a deterministic causal process that traces back to factors beyond one's control.

20 Lucretius, *De Rerum Natura*, translated by W. H. D. Rouse, Loeb Classical Library, (Cambridge: Harvard University Press, 1982), 2.216–293; ". . . but what keeps the mind itself from having necessity within it in all actions . . . is the minute swerving of the first beginnings at no fixed place and at no fixed time" (2.289–293).

21 See, for example, A. J. Ayer, "Freedom and Necessity," p. 18; Honderich, pp. 184ff, 332–334.

22 cf. Randolph Clarke, "Toward a Credible Agent-Causal Account of Free Will," *Noûs* XXVII (June 1993), pp. 191–203, at p. 192. Theories of agent causation have been advanced by Roderick Chisholm, for example in "Human Freedom and the Self," in Gary Watson, ed. *Free Will*, pp. 24–35, and in *Person and Object*, (La Salle: Open Court, 1976), pp. 53–88, and by Richard Taylor, for instance in *Action and Purpose*, (Englewood Cliffs: Prentice-Hall, 1966), pp. 99–152, and in *Metaphysics*, pp. 33–50.

23 Clarke, in "Toward a Credible Agent-Causal Account of Free Will," provides an argument for agent causation and for libertarianism more generally at pp. 199–200; cf. Immanuel Kant, *Critique of Pure Reason*, Bxxix–xxxiii.

24 Immanuel Kant, *Critique of Pure Reason*, A538/B566–A558/B586. For a related view, focussed not on defending libertarianism but on interactionist concerns, see Tyler Burge, "Philosophy of Language and Mind: 1950–1990," *The Philosophical Review* CI (January 1992), pp. 3–51, at pp. 36–39.

25 One might attempt a nonreductive materialist defense of the compatibility of libertarian freedom with determinism at the physical level, by arguing that since psychological laws do not reduce to

physical laws, everything's being causally determined at the physical level does not entail that events at the psychological level are causally determined. But although the existence of deterministic physical laws does not entail the existence of deterministic psychological laws, this argument fails. According to the nonreductive materialist view, although psychological laws do not reduce to physical laws, the fact that every token event is completely physically realized places restrictions on the genesis of token psychological events such as actions. For if the physical realization of every token event is causally determined, and an action (and everything implicated in its individuation) is completely physically realized, it must be that the action is also causally determined. Hence, if nonreductive materialism is true, and determinism is true at the physical level, then actions are no less determined than their physical realizations. For a characterization of nonreductive materialism, see Hilary Putnam, "Philosophy and Our Mental Life" *Readings in the Philosophy of Psychology*, v. 1, Ned Block, ed., (Cambridge, Mass.: Harvard University Press, 1980), pp. 134–143.

26 For an extensive discussion of the relation between freedom and quantum theory, see Honderich, pp. 304–336. See also Daniel Dennett, *Elbow Room: Varieties of Free Will Worth Wanting*, (Cambridge: MIT Press, 1984), pp. 135–6.

27 Cranston Paull raised this issue in discussion of this article. See Peter Van Inwagen, *An Essay on Free Will*, (Oxford: Oxford University Press, 1983), pp. 191–201.

28 Randolph Clarke, "Toward a Credible Agent-Causal Account of Free Will," p. 193.

29 Thanks to David Christensen for helping to formulate the argument of this paragraph. Clarke says that on his theory "there is no observational evidence that could tell us whether our world is an indeterministic world with agent causation or an indeterministic world without it . . . even highly improbable behavior could occur in a world without agent causation" (p. 199). But as we can now see, there is observational evidence that bears on the question. Only in the absence of agent causation should we, in the long run, *expect* observed frequencies to match the frequencies that our physical theories predict.

30 A. J. Ayer, "Freedom and Necessity," p. 23; Daniel Dennett, *Elbow Room*, pp. 100–130.

31 Immanuel Kant, *Groundwork of the Metaphysics of Morals*, Part III, Ak IV, 448.

32 Peter Van Inwagen, *An Essay on Free Will*, pp. 153–161, the quote is on p. 160; see also Richard Taylor, *Metaphysics*, pp. 46–7.

33 I have, so far, avoided discussion of punishment. One current theory of punishment that would be undermined by hard determinism is the retribution theory, since it justifies punishment by way of desert. But hard determinism provides no special reason to reject any other current view about the justification of punishment, for example, the deterrence, self-defense, or moral education theories. For a thorough discussion of the relation between determinism and punishment practices see Honderich, pp. 541–613.

34 Honderich, p. 533.

35 Thanks to Rachel Wertheimer for convincing me to make this point.

36 Susan Wolf, *Freedom Within Reason*, (Oxford: Oxford University Press, 1990), pp. 79–85; see also her "Asymmetrical Freedom," *Journal of Philosophy* 77 (March 1980): pp. 151–66.

37 *Freedom Within Reason*, p. 79.

38 *Freedom Within Reason*, pp. 81–2.

39 For a discussion of issues of this sort, see Walter Sinnott-Armstrong, " 'Ought' Conversationally Implies 'Can'," *The Philosophical Review* XCIII (April 1984), pp. 249–261, and " 'Ought To Have' and 'Could Have'," *Analysis* 45 (1985), pp. 44–48.

40 Honderich argues (pp. 525–530) that although determinism is incompatible with retributive attitudes, since these attitudes presuppose that agents causally originate actions, it is not incompatible with judgements of right and wrong, goodness and badness. The picture I am developing here is close to his, although the way I prefer to articulate and argue for my view is somewhat different.

41 David Hume, *An Enquiry Concerning Human Understanding*, §8, part II; P. F. Strawson, "Freedom and Resentment," in *Free Will*, Gary Watson, ed., (Oxford: Oxford University Press, 1982), pp. 59–80. For an important discussion of the reactive attitudes, see Jonathan Bennett, "Accountability," in *Philosophical Topics, Essays in Honor of*

P. F. *Strawson*, Zak Van Straaten, ed., (Oxford: Oxford University Press, 1979), pp. 14–47.

42 Gary Watson, "Responsibility and the Limits of Evil," in *Responsibility, Character, and the Emotions*, Ferdinand Schoeman, ed., (Cambridge: Cambridge University Press, 1987), pp. 256–286.

43 Watson, pp. 268–271.

44 Watson, pp. 272–274.

45 P. F. Strawson, "Freedom and Resentment," p. 66.

46 Honderich, p. 532–3.

47 Honderich, pp. 400–409.

48 See Honderich's discussion of gratitude, pp. 518–519.

49 Strawson, p. 66.

50 This article benefitted greatly from suggestions for revision by Marilyn Adams, Robert Adams, Lynne Rudder Baker, Randolph Clarke, Keith De Rose, Emily Fleschner, Bernard Gert, Hilary Kornblith, Arthur Kuflik, Isaac Levi, Don Loeb, William Mann, Michael Otsuka, Cranston Paull, Seana Schiffren, George Sher, Walter Sinnott-Armstrong, Rachel Wertheimer and the referees for *Noûs*. The philosophers at Dartmouth College provided a stimulating and useful discussion of an earlier draft. I wish to thank David Christensen for especially thorough, careful and incisive commentary.

Chapter 34

Peter van Inwagen

THE MYSTERY OF METAPHYSICAL FREEDOM

There are many kinds of freedom – or, as I prefer to say, the word "freedom" has many senses. In one sense of the word, an agent is "free" to the extent that his actions are not subject to control by the state. It is, however, obvious that an agent may be free in this sense but unfree in other senses. However little the state may interfere with my actions, I may be unfree because I am paralyzed from the waist down or because I am subject to a neurotic fear of open spaces that makes it impossible for me to venture out of doors or because I am so poor that I am unable to afford the necessary means to what I want to do. These examples suggest that freedom is a merely negative concept – that freedom is freedom from constraint, that freedom consists in the mere absence of constraint. If freedom is in this sense a negative concept, this explains why there are many kinds of freedom: there are many kinds of freedom because there are many kinds of constraint. Because there are political constraints, there is political freedom, which exists in their absence; because there are internal psychological constraints (such as neurosis), there is psychological freedom, which exists in their absence; because there are economic constraints, there is economic freedom, which exists in their absence – and so on.

When we turn from politics and psychology and economics to metaphysics, however, we encounter discussions of freedom – discussions involving words like "freedom," "free," and "freely" – that it is hard to account for if freedom is no more than a negative concept. Consider, for example, the following words of Holbach:

> Man's life is a line that nature commands him to describe upon the surface of the earth, without his ever being able to swerve from it, even for an instant. . . . Nevertheless, in spite of the shackles by which he is bound, it is pretended he is a free agent. . . .

Or consider the ancient problem of future contingents, which would seem to depend on considerations different from those adduced by Holbach, for it has only to do with whether statements about future events must be either true or false, and has nothing to do with causation and physical law. Consider, again, the problem of divine knowledge of future human action. Consider, finally, the problem of evil and the attempts to solve that problem that appeal to the freedom of creatures and the alleged impossibility of a free creature that is certain to do no evil.

I think it is fairly evident that the concept of freedom that figures in the discussions raised by these metaphysical problems is the same concept. I think it is not easy to see how this concept could be understood as a merely negative concept, as a concept that applies to any agent just in the case that that agent's acts are not subject to some sort of constraint.

Consider, for example, the problem of free will and determinism, the problem that is raised by the above quotation from Holbach. Although my present actions may be determined by the laws of nature and the state of the world before my birth (indeed, millions of years ago), it does not follow that this state of affairs places me under any sort of constraint. A constraint on one's behavior is an impediment to the exercise of one's will. If the state places me in chains, then my will to be elsewhere, if I attempt to exercise it, will soon come into conflict with the length and solidity of my chain. If I am an extreme agoraphobe, then my will to go about the ordinary business of life will come into conflict with sensations of panic and dislocation the moment I step out of doors. If I am very poor, my will to own a warm overcoat will come into conflict with my lack of the price of the coat. It is things of these sorts that are meant by "constraint." And it is evident that determinism places me under no constraints. It is true that in a deterministic world, *what my will is on a given occasion* will be a consequence of the way the world was millions of years ago and the laws of nature. It is true that in a deterministic world, *whether my will happens to encounter an obstacle on a given occasion* will be a consequence of the way the world was millions of years ago and the laws of nature. But it is certainly not inevitable that my will encounter an obstacle on any given occasion in a deterministic world, and even in an indeterministic world, my will must encounter obstacles on many occasions. Indeed, there is no reason to suppose that my will will encounter obstacles more frequently in a deterministic world than in an indeterministic world. Anyone who believes that freedom is a negative concept will therefore conclude that the so-called problem of free will and determinism is founded on confusion. (So Hobbes, Hume, Mill, and many other philosophers have concluded.)

The situation is similar with the problem of divine knowledge of future human actions. We are often told that there really is no problem about this, since the fact that God knows that one is going to tell a lie (for example) in no way forces one to lie. Since God's knowledge does not interfere with the exercise of one's will, since the false words that issue from one's mouth are the words that it was one's will to speak, God's knowledge that one was going to lie is consistent with the lie's being a free act.

All this can sound very sensible. And yet one is left with the feeling that the freedom this leaves us with is, in Kant's words, a "wretched subterfuge." This feeling can be embodied in an argument. The argument is, to my mind, a rather powerful one. If the argument is correct, then freedom is not a merely negative concept. Or, at any rate, there is *a* concept of freedom that is not a merely negative concept, and this concept is a very important one. It is this concept, I believe, that figures in the metaphysical problems I have cited. I will call it metaphysical freedom. In calling it metaphysical freedom, however, I do not mean to imply that it is of interest only to the metaphysician. I believe that this concept is also of importance in everyday life, and that the concept that metaphysicians employ is just this everyday concept, or perhaps a refinement of it. (I should be willing to argue that all concepts that we employ in philosophy or science or any other area of inquiry are either everyday concepts or explicable in terms of everyday concepts.)

In ordinary English, the concept of metaphysical freedom finds its primary expression in simple, common words and phrases, and not in the grand, abstract terms of philosophical art that one is apt to associate with metaphysics. (The situation is similar in French, German, and Latin. I should be surprised to learn of a language in which the concept I am calling "metaphysical freedom" could not be expressed in simple, common words and phrases.) It is true that philosophical analysis is needed to distinguish those uses of these simple words and phrases on which they express this concept from other uses on which they express other concepts.

Nevertheless, in particular concrete contexts, these simple words express that very concept of freedom (not, as we shall see, a negative concept) that figures in metaphysical problems like the problem of freedom and determinism. But perhaps the meaning of these abstract remarks will not be clear without an example.

One of the simple words that expresses the concept of metaphysical freedom in English is "can." What are we asking when we ask whether I am free to tell the truth tomorrow if it has been determined by events in the remote past and the laws of nature that when, tomorrow, I confront a choice between lying and telling the truth, I shall lie? Only this: "I am free to tell the truth" means "I *can* tell the truth," and "I am not free to tell the truth" means "I *cannot* tell the truth." Metaphysical freedom, therefore, is simply what is expressed by "can." If we accept this thesis, however, we must take care to understand it properly. We must take care to avoid two possible sources of confusion: the ambiguity of the word "can" and false philosophical theories about what is expressed by certain sentences in which it occurs.

As to the first point, the word "can" is extremely versatile, and can be used to express many ideas other than the idea of metaphysical freedom (a fact illustrated by this sentence). One example must suffice. In negative constructions, "can" sometimes expresses an idea that might be called "moral impossibility." One might say to a hard-hearted son, "You can't refuse to take your own mother into your house" – even though one knows perfectly well that in the sense of "can" we have been discussing he certainly *can* refuse to take his own mother into his house because he has already done so. We must take care that if we propose to use the simple word "can" as our means to an understanding of metaphysical freedom, we do not allow our understanding of metaphysical freedom to be influenced by any of the many other concepts this simple word can be used to express. The best way to avoid such influence is not to rely on the word "can" alone in our attempt to understand metaphysical freedom, but to examine also as many as possible of the other simple, ordinary words and phrases that can be used to express the concept of metaphysical freedom (or unfreedom). To illustrate what I mean, here are three sentences in which idioms of ordinary speech that do not involve "can" are used to express the concepts of metaphysical freedom and unfreedom:

- He will *be able* to be there in time for the meeting.
- You must not blame her for missing the meeting; she *had no choice* about that.
- It was simply *not within my power* to attend the meeting.

(Oddly enough, the phrase "of his own free will" does not express the concept of metaphysical freedom, despite the fact that "free will," as a philosophical term of art, means just exactly what I mean by "metaphysical freedom". To say that someone attended a meeting of his own free will is simply to say that no one forced him to attend the meeting. The phrase "of his own free will" thus expresses a merely negative concept, the concept of the absence of coercion.)

False theories about the meanings of philosophically important words and phrases abound, and the philosophically important word "can" is no exception to this generalization. There are those who, recognizing the importance of idioms like "I can do X" for the metaphysical problems of freedom, have simply insisted that this word means something that supports their favorite philosophical theories. An example of such a theory would be: "I can do X" means "There exists no impediment, obstacle, or barrier to my doing X; nothing prevents my doing X." I will not argue specifically for the conclusion that this theory is false; the argument I will later present for the incompatibility of metaphysical freedom and determinism, however, will have the consequence that this theory about the meaning of "I can" is false — since, if the theory were true, metaphysical freedom would be compatible with determinism. At this point, I wish merely to call attention to the fact that there do exist tendentious theories about the meaning of "I can do X."

If we consider carefully the meaning of "I can do X" ("I am able to do X"; "It is within my power to do X") do we find that the idea expressed by this form of words is a merely negative one, the idea of the absence of some constraint or barrier or obstacle to action? It would seem not. It is true that the presence of an obstacle to the performance of an action can be sufficient for one's being unable to perform that action. But it does not follow that the absence of all obstacles to the performance of an action is sufficient for one's being *able* to perform that action. And the idea that ability could consist in the absence of obstacles does seem, on consideration, to be a very puzzling idea indeed. To see this, let us examine carefully the relation between the concept of ability and the concept of an obstacle. We should note that not just any obstacle to one's performance of an action is such that its presence renders one unable to perform that action — for some obstacles can be surmounted or eliminated or by-passed (in short: some obstacles can be overcome). Let us ask a simple question: *which* obstacles to the performance of an action are such that their presence renders one unable to perform that action? Why, just those obstacles that one is *unable* to overcome, of course. And it seems fairly obvious that the concept of an obstacle that one is unable to overcome cannot be analyzed or explained in terms of the concept of an obstacle *simpliciter*. (Is the concept of an obstacle that one cannot overcome the concept of an obstacle such that there is some "decisive" obstacle to one's overcoming it? — No, not unless a "decisive" obstacle is understood as an obstacle that one is unable to overcome. . . .) These reflections suggest very strongly that the concept expressed by the words "I can do X" or "I am able to do X"

cannot be a merely negative concept, the concept of the absence of some sort of obstacle or barrier or impediment to action. But let us turn now to the question of the compatibility of determinism and metaphysical freedom. I shall present an argument for the conclusion that determinism is incompatible with metaphysical freedom. Since, as we have seen, determinism and metaphysical freedom are compatible if metaphysical freedom (the concept expressed by "I can do X") is a merely negative concept, this argument will be in effect an argument for the conclusion that metaphysical freedom is not a merely negative concept.

As Carl Ginet has said, our freedom can only be the freedom to add to the actual past — for the past is unalterable; it is what we *find ourselves with* in any situation in which we are contemplating some course of action. (Or to put this point in the terms I have been recommending, all we *can* do, all we are *able to do*, is add to the actual past.) And, unless we are bona fide miracle workers, we can make only such additions to the actual past as conform to the laws of nature. But the only additions to the actual past that conform to a deterministic set of laws are the additions that are actually made, the additions that collectively make up the actual present and the actual future. This is simply a statement of what is meant by determinism, which is the thesis that the laws of nature and the past together determine a unique future. Therefore, if the laws of nature are deterministic, we are free to do only what we in fact do — that is, we are unable to act otherwise than we do and are ipso facto not free in the sense in which the term "free" is properly used in metaphysics.

This little argument has great persuasive power, and it is probably no more than an articulation of the reasons that lead, almost without exception, the undergraduates to whom I lecture to join Kant in regarding the merely negative freedom of Hobbes and Hume as a wretched subterfuge. If the argument is correct, as I have said, it refutes the idea that metaphysical freedom is a merely negative concept, for the past and the laws of nature are not impediments to the exercise of one's will. But, more generally, we may well ask what we are to say of this argument and its consequences, for these consequences go far beyond establishing that metaphysical freedom is not a negative concept. One possible reaction to the argument would be to say, with Holbach, that, because determinism is true, we therefore do not possess metaphysical freedom. (An epistemologically more modest reaction would be to say that, because we do not know whether determinism is true, we do not know whether we possess metaphysical freedom.) I shall return to the possibility that we lack freedom (or that we do not know whether we have freedom). For the moment, let us see where the argument leaves those of us who would like to say that we are free and that we know this. Many philosophers have regarded it as evident that we are free, and have accepted something like our argument for the incompatibility of determinism and metaphysical freedom. These philosophers, therefore, have denied that the world is deterministic, have denied that the laws of nature and the past together determine a unique future.

These philosophers (among whom I count myself) face a difficult problem. They assert or postulate that the laws of nature are indeterministic. One might ask how they know this, or what gives them the right to this postulate. These are good questions, but I will not consider them. I want to consider instead another question that these philosophers must answer: does postulating or asserting that the laws of nature are indeterministic provide any comfort to those who would like to believe in metaphysical freedom? If the laws are indeterministic, then more than one future is indeed consistent with those laws and the actual past and present – but how can anyone have any choice about which of these futures becomes actual? Isn't it just a matter of chance which becomes actual? If God were to "return" an indeterministic world to precisely its state at some time in the past, and then let the world go forward again, things might indeed happen differently the "second" time. But then, if the world is indeterministic, isn't it just a matter of chance how things *did* happen in the one, actual course of events? And if what we do is just a matter of chance – well, who would want to call that freedom?

It seems, therefore, that, in addition to our argument for the incompatibility of metaphysical freedom and determinism, we have an argument for the incompatibility of metaphysical freedom and indeterminism. But the world must be either deterministic or indeterministic. It follows that, unless one of the two arguments contains some logical error or proceeds from a false premise, metaphysical freedom must be a contradiction in terms, as much an impossibility as a round square or a liquid wine bottle. We may in fact *define* the problem of metaphysical freedom as the problem of discovering whether either of the two arguments is defective, and (if so) of locating the defect or defects.

The problem of metaphysical freedom, so conceived, is a very *abstract* problem. Although, for historical reasons, it is natural to think of the problem as essentially involving reference to the physical world and its supposedly intransigent laws ("man's life is a line that nature commands him to describe on the surface of the earth . . ."), it does not. For suppose that man's life is in fact *not* a line that nature commands him to describe on the surface of the earth. Suppose that nature presents us with two or seventeen or ten thousand lines inscribed on the surface of the earth, and says to us (in effect), "Choose whichever one of them you like." How could it be that we really had any choice about which "line" we followed, when any deliberations we might undertake would themselves have to be segments of the lines that nature has offered us? Imagine that two of the lines that nature offers me diverge at some point – that is, imagine that the lines present the aspect of a fork in a road or a river. The common part of the two lines, the segment that immediately precedes their divergence, represents the course of my deliberations; their divergence from a common origin represents diagrammatically the fact that *either* of two futures is a possible outcome of my deliberations. My deliberations, therefore, do not determine which future I shall choose. But then what *does* determine which future I shall choose? Only chance, it would seem, and if only chance determines which of two paths into the future I follow, then how can it be that I have a choice about which of them I follow?

The problem of metaphysical freedom is so abstract, so very nearly independent of the features of the world in which agents happen to find themselves, that it could – it would; it must – arise in essentially the same form in a world inhabited only by immaterial intelligences, a world whose only inhabitants were, let us say, angels.

Let us consider such a world. It is true that if there were only angels, there would be no physical laws – or at any rate there would be nothing for the laws to apply to, so we might as well say there would be none. But if we assume the angels make choices, we have to assume that time (somehow) exists in this non-physical world, and that the agents are in different "states" at different times. And what is responsible for the way an angel changes its states with the passage of time? One possibility is that it is something structurally analogous to the laws of physics – something that stands to angels as our laws of physics stand to electrons and quarks. (I'm assuming, by the way, that these angels are metaphysical simples, that they are not composed of smaller immaterial things. If they were, we could conduct the argument in terms of the smallest immaterial things, the "elementary particles" of this imaginary immaterial world.) This "something" takes the properties of the angels at any time (and the relations they bear to one another at that time: the analogue, whatever it may be, of spatial relations in a material world) as "input," and delivers as output a sheaf of

possible futures and histories of the world. In other words, given the "state of the world" at any time, it tells you what temporal sequences of states could have preceded the world's being in that state at that time, and it tells you what temporal sequences of states could follow the world's being in that state at that time. Maybe it couldn't be written as a set of differential equations (since nothing I have said implies that the properties of and relations among angels are quantifiable) as the laws of our physical world presumably can, but I don't think that affects the point. And the point is: either "the sheaf of possible futures" relative to each moment has only one member or it has more than one. If it has only one, the world of angels is deterministic. And then where is their free will? (Their freedom is the freedom to add to the actual past. And they can only add to the actual past in accordance with the laws that govern the way angels change their properties and their relations to one another with time.) If it has more than one, then the fact that one possible future rather than another, equally possible, future becomes actual seems to be simply a matter of chance. And then where is their free will?

I said above that this way of looking at a postulated "world of angels" was one possibility. But are there really any others? We have to think of the angels as being temporal and as changing their properties with the passage of time if we are to think of them as making choices. And we have to think of them as bearing various relations to one another if we are to think of them as belonging to the same world. And we have to think of them as having natures if we are to think of them as being real things. Every real thing that is in time must have a nature that puts some kinds of constraints on how it can change its states with the passage of time. Or so, at any rate, it seems to me. But if we grant this much, it seems that, insofar as we can imagine a world of non-physical things (angels or any others) we must imagine the inhabitants of this world as being subject to something analogous to the laws of physics. If this "something" is deterministic, then (it seems) we can't think of the inhabitants of our imaginary world as having free will. And if this "something" is indeterministic, then (it seems) we can't think of the inhabitants of our imaginary world as having free will. Thus, the "problem of metaphysical freedom" is a problem so abstract and general that it arises in any imaginable world in which there are beings who make choices. The problem, in fact, arises in exactly the same way in relation to God. God, the theologians tell us, although He did in fact create a world, was free not to. (That is, He was *able* not to create a world.) But God has His own nature, which even He cannot violate and cannot change. (He cannot, for example, make Himself less than omnipotent; He cannot break a promise He has made; He cannot command immoral behavior.) And either this nature determines that He shall create a world or it does not. If it does, He was not free not to create. If it does not, then, it would seem, the fact that He *did* create a world was merely a matter of chance. For what, other than chance, could be responsible for the fact that He created a world? His choice or His will? But what determined that he should make *that* choice when the choice not to make a world was also consistent with His nature? What determined that His will should be set on making a world, when a will set on *not* making a world was also consistent with His nature? We should not be surprised that our dilemma concerning metaphysical freedom applies even to God, for the dilemma does not depend on the nature of the agent to whom the concept of metaphysical freedom is applied. The dilemma arises from the concept of metaphysical freedom itself, and its conclusion is that metaphysical freedom is a contradictory concept. And a contradictory concept can no more apply to God than it can apply to anything else.

The concept of metaphysical freedom seems, then, to be contradictory. One way to react to the seeming contradiction in this concept would be to conclude that it was real: metaphysical freedom seems contradictory because it *is* contradictory. (This was the conclusion reached by C. D. Broad.)

But none of us really believes this. A philosopher may argue that consciousness does not exist or that knowledge is impossible or that there is no right or wrong. But no one really believes that he himself is not conscious or that no one knows whether there is such a city as Warsaw; and only interested parties believe that there is nothing morally objectionable about child brothels or slavery or the employment of poison gas against civilians. And everyone really believes in metaphysical freedom, whether or not he would call it by that name. Dr Johnson famously said, "Sir, we know our will's free, and there's an end on't." Perhaps he was wrong, but he was saying something we all believe. Whether or not we are all, as the existentialists said, condemned to freedom, we are certainly all condemned to *believe* in freedom – and, in fact, condemned to believe that we *know* that we are free. (I am not disputing the sincerity of those philosophers who, like Holbach, have denied in their writings the reality of metaphysical freedom. I am saying rather that their beliefs are contradictory. Perhaps, as they say, they believe that there is no freedom—but, being human beings, they also believe that there is. In my book on freedom, I compared them to the Japanese astronomer who was said to have believed, in the 1930s, that the sun was an astronomically distant ball of hot gas vastly larger than the earth, and also to have believed that the sun was the ancestress of the Japanese imperial dynasty.)

I would ask you to try a simple experiment. Consider some important choice that confronts you. You must, perhaps, decide whether to marry a certain person, or whether to undergo a dangerous but promising course of medical treatment, or whether to report to a superior a colleague you suspect of embezzling money. (Tailor the example to your own life.) Consider the two courses of action that confront you;

since I don't know what you have chosen, I'll call them simply A and B. Do you really not believe that you are *able* to do A and *able* to do B? If you do not, then how can it be that you are trying to decide which of them to do? It seems clear to me that when I am trying to decide which of two things to do, I commit myself, by the very act of attempting to decide between the two, to the thesis that I am able to do each of them. If I am trying to decide whether to report my colleague, then, by the very act of trying to reach a decision about this matter, I commit myself both to the thesis that I am able to report him and to the thesis that I am able to refrain from reporting him: although I obviously cannot do *both* these things, I can (I believe) do *either*. In sum: whether we are free or not, we believe that we are − and I think we believe, too, that we *know* this. We believe that we know this even if, like Holbach, we *also* believe that we are not free, and, therefore, that we do not know that we are free.

But if we know that we are free − indeed, if we are free and do not know it − there is some defect in one or both of our two arguments. Either there is something wrong with our argument for the conclusion that metaphysical freedom is incompatible with determinism or there is something wrong with our argument for the conclusion that metaphysical freedom is incompatible with indeterminism − or there is

something wrong with both arguments. But which argument is wrong, and why? (Or are they both wrong?) I do not know. I think no one knows. That is why my title is, "The *Mystery* of Metaphysical Freedom." I believe I know, as surely as I know anything, that at least one of the two arguments contains a mistake. And yet, having thought very hard about the two arguments for almost thirty years, I confess myself unable to identify even a possible candidate for such a mistake. My *opinion* is that the first argument (the argument for the incompatibility of freedom and determinism) is essentially sound, and that there is, therefore, something wrong with the second argument (the argument for the incompatibility of freedom and indeterminism). But if you ask me *what* it is, I have to say that I am, as current American slang has it, absolutely clueless. Indeed the problem seems to me to be so evidently impossible of solution that I find very attractive a suggestion that has been made by Noam Chomsky (and which was developed by Colin McGinn in his recent book *The Problems of Philosophy*) that there is something about our biology, something about the ways of thinking that are "hardwired" into our brains, that renders it impossible for us human beings to dispel the mystery of metaphysical freedom. However this may be, I am certain that I cannot dispel the mystery, and I am certain that no one else has in fact done so.

Chapter 35

Harry G. Frankfurt

ALTERNATE POSSIBILITIES AND MORAL RESPONSIBILITY

A dominant role in nearly all recent inquiries into the free-will problem has been played by a principle which I shall call "the principle of alternate possibilities." This principle states that a person is morally responsible for what he has done only if he could have done otherwise. Its exact meaning is a subject of controversy, particularly concerning whether someone who accepts it is thereby committed to believing that moral responsibility and determinism are incompatible. Practically no one, however, seems inclined to deny or even to question that the principle of alternate possibilities (construed in some way or other) is true. It has generally seemed so overwhelmingly plausible that some philosophers have even characterized it as an *a priori* truth. People whose accounts of free will or of moral responsibility are radically at odds evidently find in it a firm and convenient common ground upon which they can profitably take their opposing stands.

But the principle of alternate possibilities is false. A person may well be morally responsible for what he has done even though he could not have done otherwise. The principle's plausibility is an illusion, which can be made to vanish by bringing the relevant moral phenomena into sharper focus.

I

In seeking illustrations of the principle of alternate possibilities, it is most natural to think of situations in which the same circumstances both bring it about that a person does something and make it impossible for him to avoid doing it. These include, for example, situations in which a person is coerced into doing something, or in which he is impelled to act by a hypnotic suggestion, or in which some inner compulsion drives him to do what he does. In situations of these kinds there are circumstances that make it impossible for the person to do otherwise, and these very circumstances also serve to bring it about that he does whatever it is that he does.

However, there may be circumstances that constitute sufficient conditions for a certain action to be performed by someone and that therefore make it impossible for the person to do otherwise, but that do not actually impel the person to act or in any way produce his action. A person may do something in circumstances that leave him no alternative to doing it, without these circumstances actually moving him or leading him to do it—without them playing any role, indeed, in bringing it about that he does what he does.

An examination of situations characterized by circumstances of this sort casts doubt, I believe, on the relevance to questions of moral responsibility of the fact that a person who has done something could not have done otherwise. I propose to develop some examples of this kind in the context of a discussion of coercion and to suggest that our moral intuitions concerning these examples tend to disconfirm the principle of alternate possibilities. Then I will discuss the principle in more general terms, explain what I think is wrong with it, and describe briefly and without argument how it might appropriately be revised.

II

It is generally agreed that a person who has been coerced to do something did not do it freely and is not morally responsible for having done it. Now the doctrine that coercion and moral responsibility are mutually exclusive may appear to be no more than a somewhat particularized version of the principle of alternate possibilities. It is natural enough to say of a person who has been coerced to do something that he could not have done otherwise. And it may easily seem that being coerced deprives a person of freedom and of moral responsibility simply because it is a special case of being unable to do otherwise. The principle of alternate possibilities may in this way derive some credibility from its association with the very plausible proposition that moral responsibility is excluded by coercion.

It is not right, however, that it should do so. The fact that a person was coerced to act as he did may entail both that he could not have done otherwise and that he bears no moral responsibility for his action. But his lack of moral responsibility is not entailed by his having been unable to do otherwise. The doctrine that coercion excludes moral responsibility is not correctly understood, in other words, as a particularized version of the principle of alternate possibilities.

Let us suppose that someone is threatened convincingly with a penalty he finds unacceptable and that he then does what is required of him by the issuer of the threat. We can imagine details that would make it reasonable for us to

think that the person was coerced to perform the action in question, that he could not have done otherwise, and that he bears no moral responsibility for having done what he did. But just what is it about situations of this kind that warrants the judgment that the threatened person is not morally responsible for his act?

This question may be approached by considering situations of the following kind. Jones decides for reasons of his own to do something, then someone threatens him with a very harsh penalty (so harsh that any reasonable person would submit to the threat) unless he does precisely that, and Jones does it. Will we hold Jones morally responsible for what he has done? I think this will depend on the roles we think were played, in leading him to act, by his original decision and by the threat.

One possibility is that Jones$_1$ is not a reasonable man: he is, rather, a man who does what he has once decided to do no matter what happens next and no matter what the cost. In that case, the threat actually exerted no effective force upon him. He acted without any regard to it, very much as if he were not aware that it had been made. If this is indeed the way it was, the situation did not involve coercion at all. The threat did not lead Jones$_1$ to do what he did. Nor was it in fact sufficient to have prevented him from doing otherwise: if his earlier decision had been to do something else, the threat would not have deterred him in the slightest. It seems evident that in these circumstances the fact that Jones$_1$ was threatened in no way reduces the moral responsibility he would otherwise bear for his act. This example, however, is not a counterexample either to the doctrine that coercion excuses or to the principle of alternate possibilities. For we have supposed that Jones$_1$ is a man upon whom the threat had no coercive effect and, hence, that it did not actually deprive him of alternatives to doing what he did.

Another possibility is that Jones$_2$ was stampeded by the threat. Given that threat, he would have performed that action regardless of what decision he had already made. The threat upset him so profoundly, moreover, that he completely forgot his own earlier decision and did what was demanded of him entirely because he was terrified of the penalty with which he was threatened. In this case, it is not relevant to his having performed the action that he had already decided on his own to perform it. When the chips were down he thought of nothing but the threat, and fear alone led him to act. The fact that at an earlier time Jones$_2$ had decided for his own reasons to act in just that way may be relevant to an evaluation of his character; he may bear full moral responsibility for having made *that* decision. But he can hardly be said to be morally responsible for his action. For he performed the action simply as a result of the coercion to which he was subjected. His earlier decision played no role in bringing it about that he did what he did, and it would therefore be gratuitous to assign it a role in the moral evaluation of his action.

Now consider a third possibility. Jones$_3$ was neither stampeded by the threat nor indifferent to it. The threat impressed him, as it would impress any reasonable man, and he would have submitted to it wholeheartedly if he had not already made a decision that coincided with the one demanded of him. In fact, however, he performed the action in question on the basis of the decision he had made before the threat was issued. When he acted, he was not actually motivated by the threat but solely by the considerations that had originally commended the action to him. It was not the threat that led him to act, though it would have done so if he had not already provided himself with a sufficient motive for performing the action in question.

No doubt it will be very difficult for anyone to know, in a case like this one, exactly what happened. Did Jones$_3$ perform the action because of the threat, or were his reasons for acting simply those which had already persuaded him to do so? Or did he act on the basis of two motives, each of which was sufficient for his action? It is not impossible, however, that the situation

should be clearer than situations of this kind usually are. And suppose it is apparent to us that Jones$_3$ acted on the basis of his own decision and not because of the threat. Then I think we would be justified in regarding his moral responsibility for what he did as unaffected by the threat even though, since he would in any case have submitted to the threat, he could not have avoided doing what he did. It would be entirely reasonable for us to make the same judgment concerning his moral responsibility that we would have made if we had not known of the threat. For the threat did not in fact influence his performance of the action. He did what he did just as if the threat had not been made at all.

III

The case of Jones$_3$ may appear at first glance to combine coercion and moral responsibility, and thus to provide a counterexample to the doctrine that coercion excuses. It is not really so certain that it does so, however, because it is unclear whether the example constitutes a genuine instance of coercion. Can we say of Jones$_3$ that he was coerced to do something, when he had already decided on his own to do it and when he did it entirely on the basis of that decision? Or would it be more correct to say that Jones$_3$ was not coerced to do what he did, even though he himself recognized that there was an irresistible force at work in virtue of which he had to do it? My own linguistic intuitions lead me toward the second alternative, but they are somewhat equivocal. Perhaps we can say either of these things, or perhaps we must add a qualifying explanation to whichever of them we say.

This murkiness, however, does not interfere with our drawing an important moral from an examination of the example. Suppose we decide to say that Jones$_3$ was *not* coerced. Our basis for saying this will clearly be that it is incorrect to regard a man as being coerced to do something unless he does it *because* of the coercive force exerted against him. The fact that an irresistible threat is made will not, then, entail that the person who receives it is coerced to do what he does. It will also be necessary that the threat is what actually accounts for his doing it. On the other hand, suppose we decide to say that Jones₃ *was* coerced. Then we will be bound to admit that being coerced does not exclude being morally responsible. And we will also surely be led to the view that coercion affects the judgment of a person's moral responsibility only when the person acts as he does because he is coerced to do so—i.e., when the fact that he is coerced is what accounts for his action.

Whichever we decide to say, then, we will recognize that the doctrine that coercion excludes moral responsibility is not a particularized version of the principle of alternate possibilities. Situations in which a person who does something cannot do otherwise because he is subject to coercive power are either not instances of coercion at all, or they are situations in which the person may still be morally responsible for what he does if it is not because of the coercion that he does it. When we excuse a person who has been coerced, we do not excuse him because he was unable to do otherwise. Even though a person is subject to a coercive force that precludes his performing any action but one, he may nonetheless bear full moral responsibility for performing that action.

IV

To the extent that the principle of alternate possibilities derives its plausibility from association with the doctrine that coercion excludes moral responsibility, a clear understanding of the latter diminishes the appeal of the former. Indeed the case of Jones₃ may appear to do more than illuminate the relationship between the two doctrines. It may well seem to provide a decisive counterexample to the principle of alternate possibilities and thus to show that this principle is false. For the irresistibility of the threat to which Jones₃ is subjected might well be taken to mean

that he cannot but perform the action he performs. And yet the threat, since Jones₃ performs the action without regard to it, does not reduce his moral responsibility for what he does.

The following objection will doubtless be raised against the suggestion that the case of Jones₃ is a counterexample to the principle of alternate possibilities. There is perhaps a sense in which Jones₃ cannot do otherwise than perform the action he performs, since he is a reasonable man and the threat he encounters is sufficient to move any reasonable man. But it is not this sense that is germane to the principle of alternate possibilities. His knowledge that he stands to suffer an intolerably harsh penalty does not mean that Jones₃, strictly speaking, *cannot* perform any action but the one he does perform. After all it is still open to him, and this is crucial, to defy the threat if he wishes to do so and to accept the penalty his action would bring down upon him. In the sense in which the principle of alternate possibilities employs the concept of "could have done otherwise," Jones₃'s inability to resist the threat does not mean that he cannot do otherwise than perform the action he performs. Hence the case of Jones₃ does not constitute an instance contrary to the principle.

I do not propose to consider in what sense the concept of "could have done otherwise" figures in the principle of alternate possibilities, nor will I attempt to measure the force of the objection I have just described.[1] For I believe that whatever force this objection may be thought to have can be deflected by altering the example in the following way.[2] Suppose someone—Black, let us say—wants Jones₄ to perform a certain action. Black is prepared to go to considerable lengths to get his way, but he prefers to avoid showing his hand unnecessarily. So he waits until Jones₄ is about to make up his mind what to do, and he does nothing unless it is clear to him (Black is an excellent judge of such things) that Jones₄ is going to decide to do something *other* than what he wants him to do. If it does become clear that Jones₄ is going to decide to do something else,

Black takes effective steps to ensure that Jones$_4$ decides to do, and that he does do, what he wants him to do.[3] Whatever Jones$_4$'s initial preferences and inclinations, then, Black will have his way.

What steps will Black take, if he believes he must take steps, in order to ensure that Jones$_4$ decides and acts as he wishes? Anyone with a theory concerning what "could have done otherwise" means may answer this question for himself by describing whatever measures he would regard as sufficient to guarantee that, in the relevant sense, Jones$_4$ cannot do otherwise. Let Black pronounce a terrible threat, and in this way both force Jones$_4$ to perform the desired action and prevent him from performing a forbidden one. Let Black give Jones$_4$ a potion, or put him under hypnosis, and in some such way as these generate in Jones$_4$ an irresistible inner compulsion to perform the act Black wants performed and to avoid others. Or let Black manipulate the minute processes of Jones$_4$'s brain and nervous system in some more direct way, so that causal forces running in and out of his synapses and along the poor man's nerves determine that he chooses to act and that he does act in the one way and not in any other. Given any conditions under which it will be maintained that Jones$_4$ cannot do otherwise, in other words, let Black bring it about that those conditions prevail. The structure of the example is flexible enough, I think, to find a way around any charge of irrelevance by accommodating the doctrine on which the charge is based.[4]

Now suppose that Black never has to show his hand because Jones$_4$, for reasons of his own, decides to perform and does perform the very action Black wants him to perform. In that case, it seems clear, Jones$_4$ will bear precisely the same moral responsibility for what he does as he would have borne if Black had not been ready to take steps to ensure that he do it. It would be quite unreasonable to excuse Jones$_4$ for his action, or to withhold the praise to which it would normally entitle him, on the basis of the fact that he could not have done otherwise. This fact played no role at all in leading him to act as he did. He would have acted the same even if it had not been a fact. Indeed, everything happened just as it would have happened without Black's presence in the situation and without his readiness to intrude into it.

In this example there are sufficient conditions for Jones$_4$'s performing the action in question. What action he performs is not up to him. Of course it is in a way up to him whether he acts on his own or as a result of Black's intervention. That depends upon what action he himself is inclined to perform. But whether he finally acts on his own or as a result of Black's intervention, he performs the same action. He has no alternative but to do what Black wants him to do. If he does it on his own, however, his moral responsibility for doing it is not affected by the fact that Black was lurking in the background with sinister intent, since this intent never comes into play.

V

The fact that a person could not have avoided doing something is a sufficient condition of his having done it. But, as some of my examples show, this fact may play no role whatever in the explanation of why he did it. It may not figure at all among the circumstances that actually brought it about that he did what he did, so that his action is to be accounted for on another basis entirely. Even though the person was unable to do otherwise, that is to say, it may not be the case that he acted as he did *because* he could not have done otherwise. Now if someone had no alternative to performing a certain action but did not perform it because he was unable to do otherwise, then he would have performed exactly the same action even if the *could* have done otherwise. The circumstances that made it impossible for him to do otherwise could have been subtracted from the situation without affecting what happened or why it happened in any way. Whatever it was that actually led the person to do what he did, or that made him do it, would have led him to do it or made him do it even if it had been possible for him to do something else instead.

Thus it would have made no difference, so far as concerns his action or how he came to perform it, if the circumstances that made it impossible for him to avoid performing it had not prevailed. The fact that he could not have done otherwise clearly provides no basis for supposing that he might have done otherwise if he had been able to do so. When a fact is in this way irrelevant to the problem of accounting for a person's action it seems quite gratuitous to assign it any weight in the assessment of his moral responsibility. Why should the fact be considered in reaching a moral judgment concerning the person when it does not help in any way to understand either what made him act as he did or what, in other circumstances, he might have done?

This, then, is why the principle of alternate possibilities is mistaken. It asserts that a person bears no moral responsibility—that is, he is to be excused—for having performed an action if there were circumstances that made it impossible for him to avoid performing it. But there may be circumstances that make it impossible for a person to avoid performing some action without those circumstances in any way bringing it about that he performs that action. It would surely be no good for the person to refer to circumstances of this sort in an effort to absolve himself of moral responsibility for performing the action in question. For those circumstances, by hypothesis, actually had nothing to do with his having done what he did. He would have done precisely the same thing, and he would have been led or made in precisely the same way to do it, even if they had not prevailed.

We often do, to be sure, excuse people for what they have done when they tell us (and we believe them) that they could not have done otherwise. But this is because we assume that what they tell us serves to explain why they did what they did. We take it for granted that they are not being disingenuous, as a person would be who cited as an excuse the fact that he could not have avoided doing what he did but who knew full well that it was not at all because of this that he did it.

What I have said may suggest that the principle of alternate possibilities should be revised so as to assert that a person is not morally responsible for what he has done if he did it because he could not have done otherwise. It may be noted that this revision of the principle does not seriously affect the arguments of those who have relied on the original principle in their efforts to maintain that moral responsibility and determinism are incompatible. For if it was causally determined that a person perform a certain action, then it will be true that the person performed it because of those causal determinants. And if the fact that it was causally determined that a person perform a certain action means that the person could not have done otherwise, as philosophers who argue for the incompatibility thesis characteristically suppose, then the fact that it was causally determined that a person perform a certain action will mean that the person performed it because he could not have done otherwise. The revised principle of alternate possibilities will entail, on this assumption concerning the meaning of 'could have done otherwise', that a person is not morally responsible for what he has done if it was causally determined that he do it. I do not believe, however, that this revision of the principle is acceptable.

Suppose a person tells us that he did what he did because he was unable to do otherwise; or suppose he makes the similar statement that he did what he did because he had to do it. We do often accept statements like these (if we believe them) as valid excuses, and such statements may well seem at first glance to invoke the revised principle of alternate possibilities. But I think that when we accept such statements as valid excuses it is because we assume that we are being told more than the statements strictly and literally convey. We understand the person who offers the excuse to mean that he did what he did *only because* he was unable to do otherwise, or *only because* he had to do it. And we understand him to mean, more particularly, that when he did what he did it was not because that was what he really wanted to do. The principle of alternate possibilities should thus be replaced, in my opinion, by the following principle: a person is not morally responsible for what he has done if he did it only because he could not have done otherwise. This principle does not appear to conflict with the view that moral responsibility is compatible with determinism.

The following may all be true: there were circumstances that made it impossible for a person to avoid doing something; these circumstances actually played a role in bringing it about that he did it, so that it is correct to say that he did it because he could not have done otherwise; the person really wanted to do what he did; he did it because it was what he really wanted to do, so that it is not correct to say that he did what he did only because he could not have done otherwise. Under these conditions, the person may well be morally responsible for what he has done. On the other hand, he will not be morally responsible for what he has done if he did it only because he could not have done otherwise, even if what he did was something he really wanted to do.

Notes

1 The two main concepts employed in the principle of alternate possibilities are "morally responsible"

and "could have done otherwise." To discuss the principle without analyzing either of these concepts may well seem like an attempt at piracy. The reader should take notice that my Jolly Roger is now unfurled.

2 After thinking up the example that I am about to develop I learned that Robert Nozick, in lectures given several years ago, had formulated an example of the same general type and had proposed it as a counterexample to the principle of alternate possibilities.

3 The assumption that Black can predict what Jones$_4$ will decide to do does not beg the question of determinism. We can imagine that Jones$_4$ has often confronted the alternatives—*A* and *B*—that he now confronts, and that his face has invariably twitched when he was about to decide to do *A* and never when he was about to decide to do B. Knowing this, and observing the twitch, Black would have a basis for prediction. This does, to be sure, suppose that there is some sort of causal relation between Jones$_4$'s state at the time of the twitch and his subsequent states. But any plausible view of decision or of action will allow that reaching a decision and performing an action both involve earlier and later phases, with causal relations between them, and such that the earlier phases are not themselves part of the decision or of the action. The example does not require that these earlier phases be deterministically related to still earlier events.

4 The example is also flexible enough to allow for the elimination of Black altogether. Anyone who thinks that the effectiveness of the example is undermined by its reliance on a human manipulator, who imposes his will on Jones$_4$, can substitute for Black a machine programmed to do what Black does. If this is still not good enough, forget both Black and the machine and suppose that their role is played by natural forces involving no will or design at all.

PART 5

Worlds and Worldmaking

INTRODUCTION TO PART 5

IT IS ENTIRELY COMMONPLACE to talk about "the world" as if there is just *one* world—namely, the one four-dimensional universe in which, as it were, we live and move and have our being. But many philosophers and scientists believe that, in fact, there are many things that deserve to be called "worlds"—not just other planets, but parallel universes with different laws of nature, or abstract states of affairs that constitute complete alternative ways in which our one universe (or multiverse, as some have it) might have turned out.

There are various motivations for believing in other worlds. In this part of the book, we focus on two. The first three essays focus on other worlds that are posited for *scientific* reasons. In the article by Max Tegmark, we see that some "other worlds" are believed in because their existence is probable on the assumption that spacetime is infinite; others are posited to explain certain features of quantum mechanics; and still others are posited because, if we don't believe in them, then it appears that, certain features of the universe can only be explained by positing the existence of a designer. This last reason is explored in more detail in the article by John Leslie. Leslie notes that certain features of the universe appear to have been "fine-tuned" for the existence of life—fine-tuned in the sense that, had those features been different even in relatively small ways, life would have been impossible. Advocates of belief in a designing agent claim that such fine-tuning is evidence of design: it is precisely what we would expect if the universe had been created as a home for living beings, and it is not at all what we would expect (because it is vastly improbable) had the universe not been so created. Belief in many universes is supposed by some to undermine this sort of argument from apparent fine-tuning to the existence of a designer, in part because it allows us to explain our observation of fine-tuning as a "selection effect." The idea, roughly, is that we observe a fine-tuned universe because that is the only sort of universe in which we could live; but there's nothing objectively surprising or in need of explanation about the *existence* of a fine-tuned universe because the existence of such a thing is precisely what we would expect in light of the fact that a vast plenitude of universes exist. The third article, by Peter Forrest, takes up the interesting question of whether (as some think) belief in the many-worlds interpretation of quantum mechanics implies that death is an illusion.

The remaining articles focus on other worlds of various sorts that are posited for philosophical reasons. But first a bit of background is in order.

The idea that some things might have been different than they are whereas other things couldn't have been any different is central to our commonsense and scientific ways of thinking about the world. We blame people only for things that we think they *could have* refrained from doing. We don't leap off of tall buildings and flap our arms in an effort to fly because we think that (given the existing laws of nature) it is *impossible* that we fly simply by flapping our arms. Religious believers pray for God to heal their loved ones because they think that God *can* do so. But most acknowledge that some things even an omnipotent God cannot do. (God cannot make a two dimensional cube; God cannot bring it about that 2+2=22; and God cannot sin, for example.)

In metaphysics (and other areas of philosophy) we often make inferences involving the modalities of possibility and necessity; and there are various different logical systems—modal logics—that purport to tell us the rules that govern these inferences. For example, one contemporary version of the famous ontological argument for the existence of God reasons from the premise that it is *possible* that a *necessary* (and otherwise perfect) being exist to the conclusion that such a being actually exists. The inference is valid in some systems of modal logic, but not in others. Likewise, some views about properties imply (a) that all properties are necessary beings, but (b) some properties might have been contingent beings. Some modal logics will allow that views like this are coherent; other modal logics will not. So metaphysicians will naturally have an interest in modal logic; and they will naturally wonder how, if at all, to determine which of the various competing modal systems is correct.

But how would one do this? How, for example, would we determine whether we ought to endorse a modal logic that sanctions the following inference (where "□" and "◇" represent necessity and possibility, respectively):

(1) ◇□*p*
(2) Therefore: □*p*

It seems that what we need is an interpretation of the "modal operators" (here, "□" and "◇") that gives us a more intuitive grip on what premises like (1) *mean*. In 1963, Saul Kripke proposed what was to become the standard interpretation for the modal operators. According to Kripke's interpretation, sentences with modal operators in them are sentences about other *possible worlds*. Thus, "□*p*" is true if, and only if, *p* is true in *every* world that is possible relative to ours, and "◇*p*" is true if, and only if, *p* is true in *some* world that is possible relative to ours. This way of interpreting the symbols helped philosophers to get an intuitive grip on the differences among various rival systems of modal logic—it was seen that some of the differences, at any rate, boiled down to differences in suppositions about the way in which the "relative possibility" relation works.

Kripke's way of thinking about modal operators provided philosophers with a useful tool for thinking about and addressing a variety of metaphysical questions, but it also raised metaphysical questions in its own right. What *are* possible worlds? Are they abstract things or concrete things? These and related questions are taken up in the selections by Lewis and Plantinga.

The final chapter focuses on a different sort of world altogether. It is a rather mundane fact that different people sometimes conceive of the world in very different ways. They categorize things differently; they adopt different theories to explain roughly the same experiential data; and so on. According to some philosophers, however, there is a very real sense in which people who conceive of the world differently *live in different worlds*. The reason is that our ways of thinking about the world, on this view, *make the world into the sort of thing that it is*. In other words, on this view, the *character* and the *contents* of the world are at least partly constituted by our ways of thinking about the world.

How could someone think a thing like this? Perhaps an example will help to illustrate. Consider a (wet) clay statue (call it "Clay"). In the region occupied by Clay, we seem to have a statue; we also seem to have a lump of clay. But this is problematic. Statues cannot survive being squashed and reshaped; lumps of wet clay can. So it *looks* as if we have two objects in the same place at the same time; but we don't want to say that either. What then is the truth of the matter? Is Clay *really* a statue? Or is it *really* a lump? Or is there perhaps no such thing as Clay at all, but only particles arranged statuewise or something like that? (This, of course, is just an instance of the problem of material constitution, mentioned in the introduction to Part 3.) On our commonsense way of thinking about things—what philosophers might call a *realist* or *objectivist* way of thinking about things—these questions are meaningful and it makes sense to try to answer them.

On the other way of thinking that I am trying to describe here, however, the world lacks the sort of intrinsic structure that metaphysical realism presupposes. Thus, one might think that what it is for there to be a statue is just for there to be stuff arranged statuewise *and* for us to conceive of that stuff as constituting a statue. On this view, it is not the case that there is an objective, mind-independent fact about whether the stuff in question constitutes a statue or a mere lump. There are no genuinely *natural* kinds; objects do not come ready-made, pre-sorted into well-defined classes that determine what they are and what sorts of changes they can and cannot survive. Thus, what Clay is—indeed, whether there is any such thing as Clay at all—depends importantly upon how we think or talk or theorize about the stuff in the region allegedly occupied by Clay. Thus, as some would have it anyway, our ways of thinking and talking about the world can, in some very meaningful sense, be said to *bring into existence* the very stars and planets. Apart from us and our thoughts about them, there would have been no such things.

In describing these two ways of thinking I have glossed over a variety of important issues and I have run together a variety of distinct positions. But the descriptions at least provide a rough and ready contrast; and the important point for present purposes is that the dispute between the two positions is one about the role our concepts play in giving "structure" to the world. According to the realists, the world has an intrinsic structure: there are natural kinds, and kind-membership (perhaps together with the laws) plays a role in determining the possibilities for and the powers of a thing. According to the anti-realists, on the other hand, if there is structure at all to the world, it is in some hard-to-articulate sense partly or entirely in our heads. If the anti-realists are right, facts about what exists might vary across persons or across communities, depending on differences in conceptual schemes. In other words, there would be a kind of existential relativity. The essay by Goodman lays out this sort of view.

Chapter 36

Max Tegmark

PARALLEL UNIVERSES

Is there a copy of you reading this article? A person who is not you but who lives on a planet called Earth, with misty mountains, fertile fields and sprawling cities, in a solar system with eight other planets? The life of this person has been identical to yours in every respect. But perhaps he or she now decides to put down this article without finishing it, while you read on.

The idea of such an alter ego seems strange and implausible, but it looks as if we will just have to live with it, because it is supported by astronomical observations. The simplest and most popular cosmological model today predicts that you have a twin in a galaxy about 10 to the 10^{28} meters from here. This distance is so large that it is beyond astronomical, but that does not make your doppelgänger any less real. The estimate is derived from elementary probability and does not even assume speculative modern physics, merely that space is infinite (or at least sufficiently large) in size and almost uniformly filled with matter, as observations indicate. In infinite space, even the most unlikely events must take place somewhere. There are infinitely many other inhabited planets, including not just one but infinitely many that have people with the same appearance, name and memories as you, who play out every possible permutation of your life choices.

You will probably never see your other selves. The farthest you can observe is the distance that light has been able to travel during the 14 billion years since the big bang expansion began. The most distant visible objects are now about 4×10^{26} meters away—a distance that defines our observable universe, also called our Hubble volume, our horizon volume or simply our universe. Likewise, the universes of your other selves are spheres of the same size centered on their planets. They are the most straightforward example of parallel universes. Each universe is merely a small part of a larger "multiverse."

By this very definition of "universe," one might expect the notion of a multiverse to be forever in the domain of metaphysics. Yet the borderline between physics and metaphysics is defined by whether a theory is experimentally testable, not by whether it is weird or involves unobservable entities. The frontiers of physics have gradually expanded to incorporate ever more abstract (and once metaphysical) concepts such as a round Earth, invisible electromagnetic fields, time slowdown at high speeds, quantum superpositions, curved space, and black holes. Over the past several years the concept of a multiverse has joined this list. It is grounded in well-tested theories such as relativity and quantum mechanics, and it fulfills both of the basic criteria of an empirical science: it makes predictions, and it can be falsified. Scientists have discussed as many as four distinct types of parallel universes. The key question is not whether the multiverse exists but rather how many levels it has.

Level I: Beyond our Cosmic Horizon

The Parallel Universes of your alter egos constitute the Level I multiverse. It is the least controversial type. We all accept the existence of things that we cannot see but could see if we moved to a different vantage point or merely waited, like people watching for ships to come over the horizon. Objects beyond the cosmic horizon have a similar status. The observable universe grows by a light-year every year as light from farther away has time to reach us. An infinity lies out there, waiting to be seen. You will probably die long before your alter egos come into view, but in principle, and if cosmic expansion cooperates, your descendants could observe them through a sufficiently powerful telescope.

If anything, the Level I multiverse sounds trivially obvious. How could space not be infinite? Is there a sign somewhere saying "Space Ends Here—Mind the Gap"? If so, what lies beyond it? In fact, Einstein's theory of gravity calls this intuition into question. Space could be finite if it has a convex curvature or an unusual topology (that is, interconnectedness). A spherical, doughnut-shaped or pretzel-shaped universe would have a limited volume and no edges. The cosmic microwave background radiation allows sensitive tests of such scenarios [see "Is Space Finite?" by Jean-Pierre Luminet, Glenn D. Starkman and Jeffrey R. Weeks; SCIENTIFIC AMERICAN, April 1999]. So far, however, the evidence is against them. Infinite models fit the data, and strong limits have been placed on the alternatives.

Another possibility is that space is infinite but matter is confined to a finite region around us—the historically popular "island universe" model. In a variant on this model, matter thins out on large scales in a fractal pattern. In both cases, almost all universes in the Level I multiverse would be empty and dead. But recent observations of the three-dimensional galaxy distribution and the microwave background have shown that the arrangement of matter gives way to dull uniformity on large scales, with no coherent structures larger than about 10^{24} meters. Assuming that this pattern continues, space beyond our observable universe teems with galaxies, stars and planets.

Observers living in Level I parallel universes experience the same laws of physics as we do but with different initial conditions. According to current theories, processes early in the big bang spread matter around with a degree of randomness, generating all possible arrangements with nonzero probability. Cosmologists assume that our universe, with an almost uniform distribution of matter and initial density fluctuations of one part in 100,000, is a fairly typical one (at least among those that contain observers). That assumption underlies the estimate that your closest identical copy is 10 to the 10^{28} meters away. About 10 to the 10^{92} meters away, there should be a sphere of radius 100 light-years identical to the one centered here, so all perceptions that we have during the next century will be identical to those of our counterparts over there. About 10 to the 10^{113} meters away should be an entire Hubble volume identical to ours.

These are extremely conservative estimates, derived simply by counting all possible quantum states that a Hubble volume can have if it is no hotter than 10^3 kelvins. One way to do the calculation is to ask how many protons could be packed into a Hubble volume at that temperature. The answer is 10^{113} protons. Each of those particles may or may not, in fact, be present, which makes for 2 to the 10^{113} possible arrangements of protons. A box containing that many Hubble volumes exhausts all the possibilities. If you round off the numbers, such a box is about 10 to the 10^{113} meters across. Beyond that box, universes—including ours—must repeat. Roughly the same number could be derived by using thermodynamic or quantum-gravitational estimates of the total information content of the universe.

Your nearest doppelgänger is most likely to be much closer than these numbers suggest, given the processes of planet formation and biological evolution that tip the odds in your favor. Astronomers suspect that our Hubble volume has at least 10^{20} habitable planets; some might well look like Earth.

The Level I multiverse framework is used routinely to evaluate theories in modern cosmology, although this procedure is rarely spelled out explicitly. For instance, consider how cosmologists used the microwave background to rule out a finite spherical geometry. Hot and cold spots in microwave background maps have a characteristic size that depends on the curvature of space, and the observed spots appear too small to be consistent with a spherical shape. But it is important to be statistically rigorous. The average spot size varies randomly from one Hubble volume to another, so it is possible that our universe is fooling us—it could be spherical but happen to have abnormally small spots. When cosmologists say they have ruled out the spherical model with 99.9 percent confidence, they really mean that if this model were true, fewer than one in 1,000 Hubble volumes would show spots as small as those we observe.

The lesson is that the multiverse theory can be tested and falsified even though we cannot see the other universes. The key is to predict what the ensemble of parallel universes is and to specify a probability distribution, or what mathematicians call a "measure," over that ensemble. Our universe should emerge as one of the most probable. If not—if, according to the multiverse theory, we live in an improbable universe—then the theory is in trouble. As I will discuss later, this measure problem can become quite challenging.

Level II: Other Postinflation Bubbles

If the Level I multiverse was hard to stomach, try imagining an infinite set of distinct Level I multiverses, some perhaps with different spacetime dimensionality and different physical constants. Those other multiverses—which constitute a Level II multiverse—are predicted by the currently popular theory of chaotic eternal inflation.

Inflation is an extension of the big bang theory and ties up many of the loose ends of that theory, such as why the universe is so big, so uniform and so flat. A rapid stretching of space long ago can explain all these and other attributes in one fell swoop [see "The Inflationary Universe," by Alan H. Guth and Paul J. Steinhard; SCIENTIFIC AMERICAN, May 1984; and "The Self-Reproducing Inflationary Universe," by Andrei Linde, November 1994]. Such stretching is predicted by a wide class of theories of elementary particles, and all available evidence bears it out. The phrase "chaotic eternal" refers to what happens on the very largest scales. Space as a whole is stretching and will continue doing so forever, but some regions of space stop stretching and form distinct bubbles, like gas pockets in a loaf of rising bread. Infinitely many such bubbles emerge. Each is an embryonic Level I multiverse: infinite in size and filled with matter deposited by the energy field that drove inflation.

Those bubbles are more than infinitely far away from Earth, in the sense that you would never get there even if you traveled at the speed of light forever. The reason is that the space between our bubble and its neighbors is expanding faster than you could travel through it. Your descendants will never see their doppelgängers elsewhere in Level II. For the same reason, if cosmic expansion is accelerating, as observations now suggest, they might not see their alter egos even in Level I.

The Level II multiverse is far more diverse than the Level I multiverse. The bubbles vary not only in their initial conditions but also in seemingly immutable aspects of nature. The prevailing view in physics today is that the dimensionality of spacetime, the qualities of elementary particles and many of the so-called physical constants are not built into physical laws but are the outcome of processes known as symmetry breaking. For instance, theorists think that the space in our universe once had nine dimensions, all on an equal footing. Early in cosmic history, three of them partook in the cosmic expansion and became the three dimensions we now observe. The other six are now unobservable, either because they have stayed microscopic with a doughnutlike topology or because all matter is confined to a three-dimensional surface (a membrane, or simply "brane") in the nine-dimensional space.

Thus, the original symmetry among the dimensions broke. The quantum fluctuations that drive chaotic inflation could cause different symmetry breaking in different bubbles. Some might become four-dimensional, others could contain only two rather than three generations of quarks, and still others might have a stronger cosmological constant than our universe does.

Another way to produce a Level II multiverse might be through a cycle of birth and destruction of universes. In a scientific context, this idea was introduced by physicist Richard C. Tolman in the 1930s and recently elaborated on by Paul J. Steinhardt of Princeton University and Neil Turok of the University of Cambridge. The Steinhardt and Turok proposal and related models involve a second three-dimensional brane that is quite literally parallel to ours, merely offset in a higher dimension [see "Been There, Done That," by George Musser; News Scan, SCIENTIFIC AMERICAN, March 2002]. This parallel universe is not really a separate universe, because it interacts with ours. But the ensemble of universes—past, present and future—that these branes create would form a multiverse, arguably with a diversity similar to that produced by chaotic inflation. An idea proposed by physicist Lee Smolin of the Perimeter Institute in Waterloo, Ontario, involves yet another multiverse comparable in diversity to that of Level II but mutating and sprouting new universes through black holes rather than through brane physics.

Although we cannot interact with other Level II parallel universes, cosmologists can infer their presence indirectly, because their existence can account for unexplained coincidences in our universe. To give an analogy, suppose you check into a hotel, are assigned room 1967 and note that this is the year you were born. What a coincidence, you say. After a moment of reflection, however, you conclude that this is not so surprising after all. The hotel has hundreds of rooms, and you would not have been having these thoughts in the first place if you had been assigned one with a number that meant nothing to you. The lesson is that even if you knew nothing about hotels, you could infer the existence of other hotel rooms to explain the coincidence.

As a more pertinent example, consider the mass of the sun. The mass of a star determines its luminosity, and using basic physics, one can compute that life as we know it on Earth is possible only if the sun's mass falls into the narrow range between 1.6×10^{30} and 2.4×10^{30} kilograms. Otherwise Earth's climate would be colder than that of present-day Mars or hotter than that of present-day Venus. The measured solar mass is 2.0×10^{30} kilograms. At first glance, this apparent coincidence of the habitable and observed mass values appears to be a wild stroke of luck. Stellar masses run from 10^{29} to 10^{32} kilograms, so if the sun acquired its mass at random, it had only a small chance of falling into the habitable range. But just as in the hotel example, one can explain this apparent coincidence by postulating an ensemble (in this case, a number of planetary systems) and a selection effect (the fact that we must find ourselves living on a habitable planet). Such observer-related selection effects are referred to as "anthropic," and although the "A-word" is notorious for triggering controversy, physicists broadly agree that these selection effects cannot be neglected when testing fundamental theories.

What applies to hotel rooms and planetary systems applies to parallel universes. Most, if not all, of the attributes set by symmetry breaking appear to be fine-tuned. Changing their values by modest amounts would have resulted in a qualitatively different universe—one in which we probably would not exist. If protons were 0.2 percent heavier, they could decay into neutrons, destabilizing atoms. If the electromagnetic force were 4 percent weaker, there would be no hydrogen and no normal stars. If the weak interaction were much weaker, hydrogen would not exist; if it were much stronger, supernovae would fail to seed interstellar space with heavy elements. If the cosmological constant were much larger, the universe would have blown itself apart before galaxies could form.

Although the degree of fine-tuning is still debated, these examples suggest the existence of parallel universes with other values of the physical constants [see "Exploring Our Universe and Others," by Martin Rees; SCIENTIFIC AMERICAN, December 1999]. The Level II multiverse theory predicts that physicists will never be able to determine the values of these constants from first principles. They will merely compute probability distributions for what they should expect to find, taking selection effects into account. The result should be as generic as is consistent with our existence.

Level III: Quantum Many Worlds

The Level I and Level II multiverses involve parallel worlds that are far away, beyond the domain even of astronomers. But the next level of multiverse is right around you. It arises from the famous, and famously controversial, many-worlds interpretation of quantum mechanics—the idea that random quantum processes cause the universe to branch into multiple copies, one for each possible outcome.

In the early 20th century the theory of quantum mechanics revolutionized physics by explaining the atomic realm, which does not abide by the classical rules of Newtonian mechanics. Despite the obvious successes of the theory, a heated debate rages about what it really means. The theory specifies the state of the universe not in classical terms, such as the positions and velocities of all particles, but in terms of a mathematical object called a wave function. According to the Schrödinger equation, this state evolves over time in a fashion that mathematicians term "unitary," meaning that the wave function rotates in an abstract infinite-dimensional space called Hilbert space. Although quantum mechanics is often described as inherently random and uncertain, the wave function evolves in a deterministic way. There is nothing random or uncertain about it.

The sticky part is how to connect this wave function with what we observe. Many legitimate wave functions correspond to counterintuitive situations, such as a cat being dead and alive at the same time in a so-called superposition. In the 1920s physicists explained away this weirdness by postulating that the wave function "collapsed" into some definite classical outcome whenever someone made an observation. This add-on had the virtue of explaining observations, but it turned an elegant, unitary theory into a kludgy, nonunitary one. The intrinsic randomness commonly ascribed to quantum mechanics is the result of this postulate.

Over the years many physicists have abandoned this view in favor of one developed in 1957 by Princeton graduate student Hugh Everett III. He showed that the collapse postulate is unnecessary. Unadulterated quantum theory does not, in fact, pose any contradictions. Although it predicts that one classical reality gradually splits into superpositions of many such realities, observers subjectively experience this splitting merely as a slight randomness, with probabilities in exact agreement with those from the old collapse postulate. This superposition of classical worlds is the Level III multiverse.

Everett's many-worlds interpretation has been boggling minds inside and outside physics for more than four decades. But the theory becomes easier to grasp when one distinguishes between two ways of viewing a physical theory: the outside view of a physicist studying its mathematical equations, like a bird surveying a landscape from high above it, and the inside view of an observer living in the world described by the equations, like a frog living in the landscape surveyed by the bird.

From the bird perspective, the Level III multiverse is simple. There is only one wave function. It evolves smoothly and deterministically over time without any kind of splitting or parallelism. The abstract quantum world described by this evolving wave function contains within it a vast number of parallel classical story lines, continuously splitting and merging, as well as a number of quantum phenomena that lack a classical description. From their frog perspective, observers perceive only a tiny fraction of this full reality. They can view their own Level I universe, but a process called decoherence—which mimics wave function collapse while preserving unitarity—prevents them from seeing Level III parallel copies of themselves.

Whenever observers are asked a question, make a snap decision and give an answer, quantum effects in their brains lead to a superposition of outcomes, such as "Continue reading the article" and "Put down the article." From the bird perspective, the act of making a decision causes a person to split into multiple copies: one who keeps on reading and one who doesn't. From their frog perspective, however, each of these alter egos is unaware of the others and notices the branching merely as a slight randomness: a certain probability of continuing to read or not.

As strange as this may sound, the exact same situation occurs even in the Level I multiverse. You have evidently decided to keep on reading the article, but one of your alter egos in a distant galaxy put down the magazine after the first paragraph. The only difference between Level I and Level III is where your doppelgängers reside. In Level I they live elsewhere in good old three-dimensional space. In Level III they live on another quantum branch in infinite-dimensional Hilbert space.

The existence of Level III depends on one crucial assumption: that the time evolution of the wave function is unitary. So far experimenters have encountered no departures from unitarity. In the past few decades they have confirmed unitarity for ever larger systems, including carbon 60 buckyball molecules and kilometer-long optical fibers. On the theoretical side, the case for unitarity has been bolstered by the discovery of decoherence [see "100 Years of Quantum Mysteries," by Max Tegmark and John Archibald Wheeler; SCIENTIFIC AMERICAN, February 2001]. Some theorists who work on quantum gravity have questioned unitarity; one concern is that evaporating black holes might destroy information, which would be a nonunitary process. But a recent breakthrough in string theory known as AdS/CFT correspondence suggests that even quantum gravity is unitary. If so, black holes do not destroy information but merely transmit it elsewhere.

If physics is unitary, then the standard picture of how quantum fluctuations operated early in the big bang must change. These fluctuations did not generate initial conditions at random. Rather they generated a quantum superposition of all possible initial conditions, which coexisted simultaneously. Decoherence then caused these initial conditions to behave classically in separate quantum branches. Here is the crucial point: the distribution of outcomes on different quantum branches in a given Hubble volume (Level III) is identical to the distribution of outcomes in different Hubble volumes within a single quantum branch (Level I). This property of the quantum fluctuations is known in statistical mechanics as ergodicity.

The same reasoning applies to Level II. The process of symmetry breaking did not produce a unique outcome but rather a superposition of all outcomes, which rapidly went their separate ways. So if physical constants, spacetime dimensionality and so on can vary among parallel quantum branches at Level III, then they will also vary among parallel universes at Level II.

In other words, the Level III multiverse adds nothing new beyond Level I and Level II, just more indistinguishable copies of the same universes—the same old story lines playing out again and again in other quantum branches. The passionate debate about Everett's theory therefore seems to be ending in a grand anticlimax, with the discovery of less controversial multiverses (Levels I and II) that are equally large.

Needless to say, the implications are profound, and physicists are only beginning to explore them. For instance, consider the ramifications of the answer to a long-standing question: Does the number of universes exponentially increase over time? The surprising answer is no. From the bird perspective, there is of course only one quantum universe.From the frog perspective, what matters is the number of universes that are distinguishable at a given instant—that is, the number of noticeably different Hubble volumes. Imagine moving planets to random new locations, imagine having married someone else, and so on. At the quantum level, there are 10 to the 10^{118} universes with temperatures below 10^3 kelvins. That is a vast number, but a finite one.

From the frog perspective, the evolution of the wave function corresponds to a never-ending sliding from one of these 10 to the 10^{118} states to another. Now you are in universe A, the one in which you are reading this sentence. Now you are in universe B, the one in which you are reading this other sentence. Put differently, universe B has an observer identical to one in universe A, except with an extra instant of memories. All possible states exist at every instant, so the passage of time may be in the eye of the beholder—an idea explored in Greg Egan's 1994 sciencefiction novel *Permutation City* and developed by physicist David Deutsch of the University of Oxford, independent physicist Julian Barbour, and others. The multiverse framework may thus prove essential to understanding the nature of time.

Level IV: Other Mathematical Structures

The initial conditions and physical constants in the Level I, Level II and Level III multiverses can vary, but the fundamental laws that govern nature remain the same. Why stop there? Why not allow the laws themselves to vary? How about a universe that obeys the laws of classical physics, with no quantum effects? How about time that comes in discrete steps, as for computers, instead of being continuous? How about a universe that is simply an empty dodecahedron? In the Level IV multiverse, all these alternative realities actually exist.

A hint that such a multiverse might not be just some beerfueled speculation is the tight correspondence between the worlds of abstract reasoning and of observed reality. Equations and, more generally, mathematical structures such as numbers, vectors and geometric objects describe the world with remarkable verisimilitude. In a famous 1959 lecture, physicist Eugene P. Wigner argued that "the enormous usefulness of mathematics in the natural sciences is something bordering on the mysterious." Conversely, mathematical structures have an eerily real feel to them. They satisfy a cntral criterion of objective existence: they are the same no matter who studies them. A theorem is true regardless of whether it is proved by a human, a computer or an intelligent dolphin. Contemplative alien civilizations would find the same mathematical structures as we have. Accordingly, mathematicians commonly say that they discover mathematical structures rather than create them.

There are two tenable but diametrically opposed paradigms for understanding the correspondence between mathematics and physics, a dichotomy that arguably goes as far back as Plato and Aristotle. According to the Aristotelian paradigm, physical reality is fundamental and mathematical language is merely a useful approximation. According to the Platonic paradigm, the mathematical structure is the true reality and observers perceive it imperfectly. In other words, the two paradigms disagree on which is more basic, the frog perspective of the observer or the bird perspective of the physical laws. The Aristotelian paradigm prefers the frog perspective, whereas the Platonic paradigm prefers the bird perspective.

As children, long before we had even heard of mathematics, we were all indoctrinated with the Aristotelian paradigm. The Platonic view is an acquired taste. Modern theoretical physicists tend to be Platonists, suspecting that mathematics describes the universe so well because the universe is inherently mathematical. Then all of physics is ultimately a mathematics problem: a mathematician with unlimited intelligence and resources could in principle compute the frog perspective—that is, compute what self-aware observers the universe contains, what they perceive, and what languages they invent to describe their perceptions to one another.

A mathematical structure is an abstract, immutable entity existing outside of space and time. If history were a movie, the structure would correspond not to a single frame of it but to the entire videotape. Consider, for example, a world made up of pointlike particles moving around in three-dimensional space. In four-dimensional spacetime—the bird perspective—these particle trajectories resemble a tangle of spaghetti. If the frog sees a particle moving with constant velocity, the bird sees a straight strand of uncooked spaghetti. If the frog sees a pair of orbiting particles, the bird sees two spaghetti strands intertwined like a double helix. To the frog, the world is described by Newton's laws of motion and gravitation. To the bird, it is described by the geometry of the pasta—a mathematical structure. The frog itself is merely a thick bundle of pasta, whose highly complex intertwining corresponds to a cluster of particles that store and process information. Our universe is far more complicated than this example, and scientists do not yet know to what, if any, mathematical structure it corresponds.

The Platonic paradigm raises the question of why the universe is the way it is. To an Aristotelian, this is a meaningless question: the universe just is. But a Platonist cannot help but wonder why it could not have been different. If the universe is inherently mathematical, then why was only one of the many mathematical structures singled out to describe a universe? A fundamental asymmetry appears to be built into the very heart of reality.

As a way out of this conundrum, I have suggested that complete mathematical symmetry holds: that all mathematical structures exist physically as well. Every mathematical structure corresponds to a parallel universe. The elements of this multiverse do not reside in the same space but exist outside of space and time. Most of them are probably devoid of observers. This hypothesis can be viewed as a form of radical Platonism, asserting that the mathematical structures in Plato's realm of ideas or the "mindscape" of mathematician Rudy Rucker of San Jose State University exist in a physical sense. It is akin to what cosmologist John D. Barrow of the University of Cambridge refers to as "π in the sky," what the late Harvard University philosopher Robert Nozick called the principle of fecundity and what the late Princeton philosopher David K. Lewis called modal realism. Level IV brings closure to the hierarchy of multiverses, because any self-consistent fundamental physical theory can be phrased as some kind of mathematical structure.

The Level IV multiverse hypothesis makes testable predictions. As with Level II, it involves an ensemble (in this case, the full range of mathematical structures) and selection effects. As mathematicians continue to categorize mathematical structures, they should find that the structure describing our world is the most generic one consistent with our observations. Similarly, our future observations should be the most generic ones that are consistent with our past observations, and our past observations should be the most generic ones that are consistent with our existence.

Quantifying what "generic" means is a severe problem, and this investigation is only now beginning. But one striking and encouraging feature of mathematical structures is that the symmetry and invariance properties that are responsible for the simplicity and orderliness of our universe tend to be generic, more the rule than the exception. Mathematical structures tend to have them by default, and complicated additional axioms must be added to make them go away.

What Says Occam?

The scientific theories of parallel universes, therefore, form a four-level hierarchy, in which universes become progressively more different from ours. They might have different initial conditions (Level I); different physical constants and particles (Level II); or different physical laws (Level IV). It is ironic that Level III is the one that has drawn the most fire in the past decades, because it is the only one that adds no qualitatively new types of universes.

In the coming decade, dramatically improved cosmological measurements of the microwave background and the large-scale matter distribution will support or refute Level I by further pinning down the curvature and topology of space. These measurements will also probe Level II by testing the theory of chaotic eternal inflation. Progress in both astrophysics and high-energy physics should also clarify the extent to which physical constants are fine-tuned, thereby weakening or strengthening the case for Level II.

If current efforts to build quantum computers succeed, they will provide further evidence for Level III, as they would, in essence, be exploiting the parallelism of the Level III multiverse for parallel computation. Experimenters are also looking for evidence of unitarity violation, which would rule out Level III. Finally, success or failure in the grand challenge of modern physics—unifying general relativity and quantum field theory—will sway opinions on Level IV. Either we will find a mathematical structure that exactly matches our universe, or we will bump up against a limit to the unreasonable effectiveness of mathematics and have to abandon that level.

So should you believe in parallel universes? The principal arguments against them are that they are wasteful and that they are weird. The first argument is that multiverse theories are vulnerable to Occam's razor because they postulate the existence of other worlds that we can never observe. Why should nature be so wasteful and indulge in such opulence as an infinity of different worlds? Yet this argument can be turned around to argue for a multiverse. What precisely would nature be wasting? Certainly not space, mass or atoms—the uncontroversial Level I multiverse already contains an infinite amount of all three, so who cares if nature wastes some more? The real issue here is the apparent reduction in simplicity. A skeptic worries about all the information necessary to specify all those unseen worlds.

But an entire ensemble is often much simpler than one of its members. This principle can be stated more formally using the notion of algorithmic information content. The algorithmic information content in a number is, roughly speaking, the length of the shortest computer program that will produce that number as output. For example, consider the set of all integers. Which is simpler, the whole set or just one number? Naively, you might think that a single number is simpler, but the entire set can be generated by quite a trivial computer program, whereas a single number can be hugely long. Therefore, the whole set is actually simpler.

Similarly, the set of all solutions to Einstein's field equations is simpler than a specific solution. The former is described by a few equations, whereas the latter requires the specification of vast amounts of initial data on some hypersurface. The lesson is that complexity increases when we restrict our attention to one particular element in an ensemble, thereby losing the symmetry and simplicity that were inherent in the totality of all the elements taken together.

In this sense, the higher-level multiverses are simpler. Going from our universe to the Level I multiverse eliminates the need to specify initial conditions, upgrading to Level II eliminates the need to specify physical constants, and the Level IV multiverse eliminates the need to specify anything at all. The opulence of complexity is all in the subjective perceptions of observers—the frog perspective. From the bird perspective, the multiverse could hardly be any simpler.

The complaint about weirdness is aesthetic rather than scientific, and it really makes sense only in the Aristotelian world-view. Yet what did we expect? When we ask a profound question about the nature of reality, do we not expect an answer that sounds strange? Evolution provided us with intuition for the everyday physics that had survival value for our distant ancestors, so whenever we venture beyond the everyday world, we should expect it to seem bizarre.

A common feature of all four multiverse levels is that the simplest and arguably most elegant theory involves parallel universes by default. To deny the existence of those universes, one needs to complicate the theory by adding experimentally unsupported processes and ad hoc postulates: finite space, wave function collapse and ontological asymmetry. Our judgment therefore comes down to which we find more wasteful and inelegant: many worlds or many words. Perhaps we will gradually get used to the weird ways of our cosmos and find its strangeness to be part of its charm.

Chapter 37

John Leslie

WORLD ENSEMBLE, OR DESIGN

(i) Did God create a universe specially suited to life's evolution? (ii) Alternatively, Do there exist vastly many universes with very varied properties, ours being one of a rare kind in which life occurs? (iii) Or again, May there be nothing too surprising in our universe's life-containing character? (Perhaps more or less any universe would be life-containing, or perhaps there is some other ground for us to feel no surprise. Might we reason that if the cosmos weren't life-containing then nobody would be around to ask whether to be astonished, and that this shows there is nothing to be astonished at?) The chapter introduces some main arguments in reaction to these, the book's three main questions. 'God or Multiverse' is a phrase taken from Henry Adams.[1]

God or Multiverse

1. The Argument from Design is an argument for God's reality based on the fact that our universe looks much as if designed.

The Argument for Multiple Worlds starts from the same fact. But it concludes instead that there exist many small-u universes – Soviet cosmologists sometimes call them "metagalaxies" – inside the capital-U Universe which is The Whole of Reality.

These 'universes', 'mini-universes', 'Worlds' with a capital W to distinguish them from mere planets, can be of immense size. There may be immensely many of them. And their properties are thought of as very varied. Sooner or later, somewhere, one or more of them will have life-permitting properties. Our universe can indeed look as if designed. In reality, though, it may be merely the sort of thing to be expected sooner or later. Given sufficiently many years with a typewriter even a monkey would produce a sonnet.[2]

Suppose there existed ninety-seven trillion universes, all but three of them life-excluding. Obviously, only the three life-permitting universes could ever be observed by living beings. This suggests that an interesting kind of observational selection effect could underlie our seeing of a world whose conditions permit life to evolve. (Recognizing this is not the same as proposing paradoxically that the world is a causal consequence of human existence.)

2. While the Multiple Worlds (or World Ensemble) hypothesis is impressively strong, the God hypothesis is a viable alternative.

Rightly or wrongly, however, this book shows no interest in the kind of God who designs the structures of individual organisms, plague germs perhaps, or who interferes with Nature's day-to-day operations. If God exists then of the various ways in which he may act on the universe there are only two which will be considered in these pages.

First, he makes the universe obey a particular

set of laws (I prefer to think of them all as laws of physics), also 'sustaining' it in existence if this is necessary: recreating it, so to speak, from moment to moment, to prevent it from vanishing.

Second, he creates its initial state in such-and-such a fashion. He starts it off with this or that many particles in this or that arrangement; or at least he does this just so long as it has not been done already through his specifying what Nature's laws are to be. It might be that the laws themselves dictated the number and arrangement of the particles.

If the universe has existed for ever, replace 'creating its initial state' by something like 'deciding the number of its particles, and their arrangement at at least one time'.

3. Referring to God as 'he' or 'him' is just following convention. If God is real then his reality seems to me most likely to be as described by the Neoplatonist theological tradition. He is then not an almighty person but an abstract Creative Force which is 'personal' through being concerned with creating persons and acting as a benevolent person would.

To be more specific, Neoplatonism's God is *the world's creative ethical requiredness*. Or, which comes to the same thing, he is *the creatively effective ethical requirement that there be a good universe or universes*. Or again, he is the Principle that the ethical need for a universe or universes *is itself responsible for the actual existence of that universe or those universes*.[3]

However, it might instead be that God was a divine person creating everything else. Such a person might owe his existence and creative power to the fact that this was ethically required, a position suggested by the philosopher A. C. Ewing.

It is no insult to a divine person to suggest that he exists for that kind of reason. If anything, what would be uncomplimentary would be to call his existence utterly reasonless.

The Fine Tuning

4. This chapter introduces some of the book's chief arguments. One is that it looks as if our universe is spectacularly 'fine tuned for Life'.

By this I mean only that it looks as if small changes in this universe's basic features would have made life's evolution impossible. Thus talk of 'fine tuning' does not presuppose that a divine Fine Tuner, or Neoplatonism's more abstract God, must be responsible.

In the modern cosmological literature you find many claims like the following.

- Large regions coming out of a Big Bang could be expected to be uncoordinated since not even influences travelling at the speed of light would have had time to link them. When they made contact tremendous turbulence would occur, yielding a cosmos of black holes or of temperatures which stopped galaxies forming for billions of years, after which everything would be much too spread out for them to form. Placing a pin to choose our orderly world from among the physically possible ones, God could seem to have been called on to aim with immense accuracy. Cosmologists refer to this as the *Smoothness Problem*.

- The cosmos threatened to recollapse within a fraction of a second or else to expand so fast that galaxy formation would be impossible. To avoid these disasters its rate of expansion at early instants needed to be fine tuned to perhaps one part in 10^{55} (which is 10 followed by 54 zeros). That would make Space remarkably "flat", so this is often called the *Flatness Problem*.

- Smoothness and Flatness Problems might be avoided through what is known as 'Inflation': after initial deceleration, a short burst of *accelerating* expansion at very early times could have increased the universe's size by a factor of as much as $10^{1,000,000}$. This could mean that everything now visible to us had grown from a region whose parts were originally well co-ordinated, which would give the observed smoothness. Also, a greatly expanded space might be very flat like the surface of a much inflated balloon.

However, *Inflation could itself seem to have required fine tuning* for it to occur at all and for it to yield irregularities neither too small nor too great for galaxies to form. Thus, besides having to select a Grand Unified Theory (GUT) or Theory of Everything (TOE) very carefully, a deity wishing to bring about life-permitting conditions would seemingly need to have made two components of an expansion-driving 'cosmological constant' cancel each other with an accuracy better than of one part in 10^{50}. ('Bare lambda', the cosmological constant as originally pro-posed by Einstein, has to be in almost but not quite perfect balance with 'quantum lambda'. With a balance that was perfect, Inflation would probably not occur.) A change by one part in 10^{100} in the present strengths either of the nuclear weak force or of gravity might end this cancellation, disastrously.

- Had *the nuclear weak force* been appreciably stronger then the Big Bang would have burned all hydrogen to helium. There could then be neither water nor long-lived stable stars. Making it appreciably weaker would again have destroyed the hydrogen: the neutrons formed at early times would not have decayed into protons.

  Again, this force had to be chosen appropriately if neutrinos were to interact with stellar matter both weakly enough to escape from a supernova's collapsing core and strongly enough to blast its outer layers into space so as to provide material for making planets.

- For carbon to be created in quantity inside stars *the nuclear strong force* must be to within

perhaps as little as 1 per cent neither stronger nor weaker than it is. Increasing its strength by maybe 2 per cent would block the formation of protons – so that there could be no atoms – or else bind them into diprotons so that stars would burn some billion billion times faster than our sun. On the other hand *decreasing* it by roughly 5 per cent would unbind the deu-teron, making stellar burning impossible. (Increasing Planck's constant by over 15 per cent would be another way of prevent-ing the deuteron's existence. So would making the proton very slightly lighter or the neutron very slightly heavier, as it would then not be energetically advanta-geous for pairs of protons to become deuterons.)

- With *electromagnetism* very slightly stronger, stellar luminescence would fall sharply. Main sequence stars would then all of them be red stars: stars probably too cold to encourage Life's evolution and at any rate unable to explode as the supernovae one needs for creating elements heavier than iron. Were it very slightly *weaker* then all main sequence stars would be very hot and short-lived blue stars.

  Again, a slight strengthening could transform all quarks (essential for con-structing protons, and hence for all atoms) into leptons or else make protons repel one another strongly enough to prevent the existence of atoms even as light as those of helium.

  Again, strengthening by 1 per cent could have doubled the years needed for intelligent life to evolve, by making chem-ical changes more difficult. A doubled strength could have meant that 10^{62} years were needed – and in a much shorter time almost all protons would have decayed.

  Again, there is this. The electromagnetic fine structure constant gives the strength of the coupling between charged particles and electromagnetic fields. Increasing it to above 1/85 (from its present 1/137) could result in too many proton decays for there to be long-lived stars, let alone living beings who were not killed by their own radioactivity.

- The need for electromagnetism to be fine tuned if stars are not to be all of them red, or all of them blue, can be rephrased as a need for fine tuning of *gravity* because it is the ratio between the two forces which is crucial. Gravity also needs fine tuning for stars and planets to form, and for stars to burn stably over billions of years. It is roughly 10^{39} times weaker than electromagnetism. Had it been only 10^{33} times weaker, stars would be a billion times less massive and would burn a million times faster.

- Various *particle masses* had to take appropriate values for life of any plausible kind to stand a chance of evolving. (i) If the neutron–proton mass difference – about one part in a thousand – had not been almost exactly twice the electron's mass then all neutrons would have decayed into protons or else all protons would have changed irreversibly into neutrons. Either way, there would not be the couple of hundred stable types of atom on which chemistry and biology are based. (ii) Superheavy particles were active early in the Bang. Fairly modest changes in their masses could have led to disastrous alterations in the ratio of matter particles to photons, giving a universe of black holes or else of matter too dilute to form galaxies. Further, the superheavies had to be very massive to prevent rapid decay of the proton. (iii) The intricacy of chemistry and the existence of solids depend on the electron's being much less massive than the proton. (iv) The masses of a host of scalar particles could affect whether the cosmological constant would ever be the right size for Inflation to occur appropriately, and whether it would later be small enough to allow space to be very flat – failing which it would be expanding or contracting very violently. Today the constant is zero to one part in 10^{120}. (v) Forces can vary with range in seemingly very odd ways: the nuclear strong force, for instance, is repulsive at extremely short ranges while at slightly greater ones it is first attractive and then disappears entirely. The explanation for this lies in force 'screening' and 'antiscreening' and in how force-conveying 'messenger particles' can vanish before having had time to deliver their messages. These effects are crucially dependent on particle masses. The actual masses make forces enter into intricate checks and balances which underlie the comparatively stable behaviour of galaxies, stars, planets, and living organisms.

5. No doubt some of these claimed facts are mistakes – although many seem as well established as facts about the reality of quarks or black holes or neutron stars, or of the Big Bang itself. Others, again, may be dictated by physical principles so fundamental that they are not fine tunable. But clues heaped upon clues can constitute weighty evidence despite any doubts attaching to each element in the pile. Important, too, is that force strengths and particle masses are distributed across enormous ranges. The nuclear strong force is (roughly) a hundred times stronger than electromagnetism, which is in turn ten thousand times stronger than the nuclear weak force, which is itself some ten thousand billion billion billion times stronger than gravity. So we can well be impressed by any apparent need for a force to be 'just right' even to within a factor of ten, let alone to within one part in a hundred or in 10^{100} – especially when nobody is sure why the strongest force tugs any more powerfully than the weakest.

Ways of Getting a World Ensemble

6. As indicated earlier, one way of accounting for fine tuning of the world's properties to suit Life's needs would be suppose that there exists an ensemble of vastly many 'Worlds' or 'universes' with very varied properties. Ours would be one of the rare ones in which living beings could evolve. There is no need to say 'infinitely many universes' or 'all possible universes' instead of 'vastly many', although people often write as if this were essential. For a car number plate such as 'LOOK 1234 WOW' to be explained, *rendered unmysterious*, it can be enough that very numerous permutations of letters and numbers appear on cars. Again, a sufficiently mighty army of monkeys at type-writers could type a page of poetry unmysteri-ously without having to type infinitely many pages or all possible pages.

People have proposed a wide variety of mech-anisms for generating multiple universes. They include these:

(a) The cosmos oscillates: Big Bang, Big Squeeze, Big Bang, and so on. As was suggested by J. A. Wheeler, each oscillation could count as a new World or (small-u) universe because of having new properties, or because the oscilla-tions are separated by knotholes of intense com-pression in which information about previous cycles is lost – or in which Time breaks down entirely so that we cannot talk of other cycles as being 'previous'.

(b) Many-Worlds quantum theory, origin-ated by H. Everett III, is usually understood as giving us a capital-U Universe which branches into more and more Worlds that interact hardly at all. Each World represents one choice among the sets of events which quantum mechanics views as having been truly possible.

Some people treat such branching as an offence against Simplicity. They prefer to regard Worlds other than our own as useful fictions at best. But various experiments – for instance, the double slit experiment in which we see what looks like interference between two separate sets of waves – seem to show that these supposed fictions are *complexly active*. The paths which particles *might have taken* appear able to affect in complex ways the paths which they actually take, setting up what looks like a 'jostling' of all the possibilities. It is then doubtful whether Simplicity is served by denying that the Worlds are all of them fully real.

(c) Worlds, small-u universes, could occur as quantum fluctuations, as was suggested by E. P. Tryon in 1973. Maybe such fluctuations would occur from time to time in a Superspace, although some have denied the need for any such already existing background.

That an entire universe could occur as a fluc-tuation can seem absurd. In fact, however, it forms the basis of what is fast becoming the accepted account of how our universe began. Quantum fluctuations, in which particles spring into existence at unpredictable places and times, are happening constantly even in empty space. A fluctuation can be long-lasting if its energy is very small. And it is very ordinary physics to treat binding energies – for instance, the energy which binds an electron to a nucleus – as *negative energies*. Now, gravitational energy is binding energy, and our universe is richly supplied with it. It may be a universe having a total energy of zero or nearly zero when this is taken into account. Moreover even a small fluctuation could give birth to hugely much, because at very early times more and more new matter could spring into existence without 'costing' anything: its mass-energy could be exactly balanced by its gravitational energy.

(d) If Space is 'open' instead of being 'closed' like the surface of a sphere then on the most straightforward models it is infinitely large and contains infinitely much material. Gigantic regions situated far beyond our 'particle hori-zon' (the horizon set by how far light can have travelled to us since the Bang) could well be counted as 'other universes', particularly if their properties were very different.

(e) Even a 'closed' cosmos could be of any size, and the nowadays very popular Inflationary Cosmos is in fact gigantic. It is quite probably split into hugely many domains, markedly different in their properties. A. H. Guth and P. J. Steinhardt suggest that our own domain stretches 10^{25} times further than we can see,[4] so of course we can see none of the others.

7. Even granted ideal conditions, life might evolve only with great difficulty: its first beginnings could depend, for instance, on tremendously lucky molecular combinations in some primeval soup. If so, then multiple universes could help produce it by sheer force of numbers: toss fifty coins sufficiently often and some day the lot will land heads together. However, a multiplicity of universes could be all the more helpful if the universes varied widely, so making it more likely that conditions would somewhere be ideal. Now, modern Unified Theories do suggest that very wide variations could be expected.

Why? Well, at early times there may have been only a single force and a single general type of particle. As the Big Bang cooled this unity would have been destroyed by a process known as 'symmetry breaking'. It would have become energetically advantageous for a scalar field (or more probably *fields*) to take a non-zero value (or values). The choice of any such value in any particular region may have been a random affair. Alternatively, field values may have varied from region to region not randomly but deterministically. Now, interacting with a field can make particles take on mass—and particle masses, besides being of great direct importance to the possibility of Life, also underlie the differences between the strengths of Nature's four main forces. Hence *any theory giving us multiple universes might also fairly readily provide multiply different combinations of force strengths and masses.*

When many scalar fields were involved and when each affected different particles in different ways, the range of variations would be enormous.

This way of looking on things is favoured by, for example, A. D. Linde, who speaks of the multiple domains of an Inflationary Cosmos as forming 'a lunch at which all possible dishes are available'.[5] It could then be unsurprising that at least a few of the dishes were food for intelligent living beings.

Observing only a single domain inside that cosmos, a single small-u universe, any such being could be greatly puzzled by how that domain's properties were accurately tuned to Life's requirements. Unless suspecting the existence of the greatly many other domains whose properties were life-discouraging, the being could feel forced to believe in a divine Fine Tuner.

A Few Stories

8. Let us ask, however, whether a life-containing universe really does stand in special need of explanation, and if so, whether a multiplicity of Worlds or universes with varied properties could provide the best explanation.

An initial point to notice is that neither a Multiple Worlds explanation nor an explanation by reference to a Fine Tuner would supply a substitute for a long, scientifically very ordinary causal account of Life's evolution. What these explanations could instead provide would be insight into how it came to be inevitable, likely, or very possible that there would be, *somewhere*, a situation whose characteristics – force strengths, particle masses, etc. – made Life's evolution inevitable or likely or very possible.

Next, I find it helpful to tell a succession of stories.

9. First comes the Fishing Story. You know that a lake's impenetrably cloudy waters contained a fish 23.2576 inches long, for you have just caught the fish in question. Does this fact about the lake stand in specially strong need of explanation? Of course not, you tend to think. Every fish must have some length! Yet you next

discover that your fishing apparatus could accept only fish of this length, plus or minus one part in a million. Competing theories spring to mind: the first, that there are millions of differently lengthed fish in the lake, your apparatus having in the end found one fitting its requirements; and the second, that there is just the one fish, created by someone wishing to give you a fish supper. Either explanation will serve; and so for that matter will the explanation that the well-wisher created so many fish of different lengths that there would be sure to be one which you could catch. (God and Multiple Worlds are far from being flatly incompatible.) In contrast, *that the one and only fish in the lake just happened to be of exactly the right length* is a suggestion to be rejected at once. Similarly with the suggestion *that the lake contains many fish, all of a length which just happens to be the right one.*

10. The tale has countless variants: for example, the Poker Game Story. (This is a nice response to those who say that the 'improbability' of our universe is no more impressive than that of just any hand of cards, every possible hand being equally improbable.) You seem to see mere rubbish in your opponent's poker hand of an eight, six, five, four, and three. It is natural to assume that Chance gave it to him. But you then recall that poker has many versions; that you had agreed on one in which his Little Tiger ('eight high, three low, no pair') defeats your seemingly much stronger hand; that a million dollars are at stake; and that card players occasionally cheat. At once your suspicions are aroused.

Again, an old arch collapses exactly when you pass through. You congratulate yourself on a narrow escape from purely accidental death – until you notice your rival in love tiptoeing from the scene.

Again, consider a tale told by Ernest Bramah about an ingenious merchant. 'Mok Cho had been seen to keep his thumb over a small hole in a robe of embroidered silk'; now, 'although the tolerant-minded pointed out that in exhibiting a piece of cloth even a magician's thumbs must be somewhere . . .'.

11. The main moral must by now be plain. Our universe's elements do not carry labels announcing whether they are in special need of explanation. A chief (or the only?) reason for thinking that something stands in such need, i.e. for justifiable reluctance to dismiss it as how things just happen to be, is that one in fact glimpses some tidy way in which it might be explained.

In the case of catching the 23.2576 inch fish, a fish of the only length which can be caught and observed, the first of the tidy explanations which suggested themselves could be called a Fish Ensemble explanation. It runs parallel to the World Ensemble (or multiple universes) explanation of how it came to be at all likely that anyone would ever observe a cosmos.

12. There are subsidiary morals too. Thus, notice how you cannot account for catching your fish by considering many *merely possible* fish, remarking that only fish of just about exactly 23.2576 inches could be caught, and then declaring that this would sufficiently explain the affair even if yours had been the only fish in the lake. What you instead need is either a benevolent fish-creating person or else a lake with many *actual* fish of varied lengths. The fish, really existing fish, of lengths which cannot be caught, help to render unmysterious the catching of the fish which can be.

Is this wildly paradoxical? Surely not. Firing an arrow at random into a forest, you hit Mr Brown: persuasive evidence, surely, that the forest is full of people, despite how the other people gave Mr Brown no greater chance of being hit. You may need a well-populated forest to have much likelihood of there being somebody precisely where your arrow lands. You may need fish of many different lengths to have much likelihood that at least one of them will be of precisely the right length for your fishing apparatus.

When the fish is captured then the details of how it came to be captured and of how it came to be of the right length will form a long causal story perhaps entirely unaffected by the other fish in the lake. The complex details of how Mr Brown came to stand precisely where he stood may be uninfluenced by the others in the forest. But I have already (in section 8) drawn attention to this kind of point. I said, remember, that a Multiple Worlds explanation *would not be a substitute for* a long, scientifically very ordinary causal account of Life's evolution. Instead it would offer insight into why it was inevitable, likely, or very possible that Life would evolve *somewhere*.

13. But aren't there *infinitely many* infinitesimally different fish lengths which the fishing apparatus could accept? *Just as many*, in fact, as the lengths which it would reject?

Well, there being infinitely many points inside a bull's-eye is no ground for optimism that a dart will hit this tiny target.

One sometimes meets with the flat announcement that there could be nothing impressive in the supposed evidence of fine tuning unless among all possible sets of force strengths and particle masses *only one* could lead to Life's evolution. I see no excuse for such an announcement. Surely the fine tuning could be impressive if the Life-permitting possibilities constituted, say, only a thousandth of the range of possibilities under consideration. To deny this is almost as bad as announcing that the evidence could be impressive only if every single aspect of our universe were fine tuned, or only if the fine tuning made Life's evolution 100 per cent certain.

14. Would you protest that if fish appeared one after another with randomized lengths then there would be nothing particularly unlikely in the right length's being had by the very first fish of all?

You would be trading on an ambiguity. Yes,

the very first fish would be no more unlikely to be 'just right' than the second or the millionth. *In that sense* its just-rightness 'wouldn't be particularly unlikely'. But it could still be particularly unlikely where this meant that it was very, very unlikely. Assuming that no benevolent fish-creator is at work, no just-right fish is likely to exist unless there are many fish.

15. Yet, you exclaim, aren't we in fact virtually compelled to accept the God hypothesis? The alternative is to assume, so to speak, that the lake contains many fish and that we had been waiting until a catchable fish – a universe we could observe – came along. Yet surely we weren't *disembodied spirits lying in wait* until there came to be a universe containing bodies for us! Isn't *our being specifically us* tied to our being in this specific universe, a universe in which our minds are just parts or aspects of the bodies which we say they inhabit? So aren't we forced to believe in a divine hand which made our universe one in which life was likely to evolve?

Not so, I think. Let us agree that in God's absence our births could only be a matter of tremendous luck. Let it be supposed that if the breaking apart of Nature's four main forces had occurred slightly differently in our universe then living beings could never have evolved in it, and that exactly how it occurred was a random affair. So what? The hypothesis of many universes shows how it could be likely that *some* set of living beings should have the luck of being born. While they could be extremely lucky, their luck would not be unbelievably amazing.

Remember Mr Brown's sad case when the arrow hits him. Extremely unlucky? Yes. But his bad luck is unmysterious if there were many people in the forest. It is unmysterious despite how the others in the forest could in no way have increased the chance that he, Mr Brown in particular, would be hit.

Here we could tell a story of a lottery. When the hundred thousand lottery tickets were being printed one of them was given a number which made it worth a million dollars. Most of the tickets were actually sold. Anyone winning the million dollars—Mr Green, perhaps—should presumably feel no compulsion to seek some very special explanation for having won: some explanation of a kind inapplicable to just any other winner. Yes, the absence of such an explanation would mean that he personally had enjoyed immense good luck, but it was very likely that somebody would enjoy it. The greater the number of tickets sold after Mr Green purchased his, the less amazing his win, although the improbability of his winning would have been precisely as great no matter how many were sold.

True enough, Mr Green's immense good luck is firmly tied to the specific fact that he is Mr Green. If someone else had won the million dollars then Mr Green would be groaning. But the amazingness or otherwise of his win is not firmly tied to the luck involved. For if enough tickets were sold then it would be utterly unamazing that somebody or other – somebody who would be forced to be a specific somebody because nobody can avoid being somebody specific – should be the lucky winner.

16. This particular lottery story, however, fails to reflect an important extra element in the cosmological case: namely, that it is a case in which (so to speak) the winning of a lottery *is a prerequisite of observing anything*. Given this extra element, we cannot argue in the following style:

> While it would not be unbelievably amazing that somebody had won a million dollars by mere chance, it could still be very amazing *to me* that somebody should be *specifically me*. Not, perhaps, unbelievably amazing – because one presumably ought to be reluctant to say that *no matter who* wins a lottery by mere chance, that person ought to be flatly unwilling to believe that it was Chance that settled the affair – but still amazing enough to make me doubt

whether Chance, rather than, say, my girlfriend who works at lottery company headquarters, really did give me my victory. For *what I should expect to be observing* is a situation in which I hold a non-winning ticket.

One cannot argue in this style because in the cosmological case a queer kind of observational selection effect guarantees that a "non-winning ticket" – a lifeless universe – will never be seen by anyone.

To highlight this extra element we might tell a new version of the Fishing Story. A mad scientist allocates numbers to millions of human ova, fertilized and then frozen. She fishes for ten seconds with an apparatus able to catch only a 23.2576 inch fish. If unsuccessful she destroys ovum number one. She then fishes for another ten seconds on behalf of ovum number two; and so on. Any test-tube boy baby born because 'his' fishing period led to success can (after mastering mathematics) be extremely thankful to have survived this savage weeding. He has been extremely lucky. But not unbelievably lucky. He presumably need not feel compelled to reject the mad scientist's report on how he came to be born. For with respect to *believability* this report is much on a par with a report that the scientist fished repeatedly on behalf of the same ovum for successive ten-second periods until triumph crowned her efforts. It is just that the two cases differ markedly with respect to how *fortunate* he is to have been born. In the case of the many ova it would have been only through immense good fortune that *his* ovum gave rise to a conscious being.

If, in contrast, the mad scientist reported to him that she had set aside only a single ovum for the fishing experiment and fished for just one ten-second period, then he should refuse to believe this. It would not be enough for him to comment, 'If that ovum hadn't had such tremendous luck then I shouldn't be here to ask whether to be surprised, so there's nothing for me to be surprised at.'

17. The Firing Squad Story can help us to see the correctness of that last point. When the fifty sharpshooters all miss me, 'If they hadn't all missed then I shouldn't be considering the affair' is not an adequate response. What the situation demands is, 'I'm popular with the sharpshooters—unless, perhaps, immensely many firing squads are at work and I'm among the very rare survivors.'

18. The proposed observational selection effect which inspires these stories – namely, that the universe which we observe must be in the class of life-permitting universes since how otherwise could we living beings be observing it? – cannot operate unless there is *more than one actual universe*. (No Observational Selection Effect without Actual Things from Which to Select! Section 12 in effect made this the second moral to be drawn from the Fishing Story. The tale of the Firing Squad is just another way of making the point.) But equally, a multiplicity of actual universes cannot help us much *unless the observational selection effect is joined to it*. Given vastly many universes very varied in their properties, we could be less puzzled that some universe or other was life-containing; but mightn't we be tempted to feel almost as astonished as ever that our universe was a life-containing one? Well, the temptation could disappear when we reflected that any universe which wasn't life-containing could not be 'our universe' to anybody. As 16 pointed out, we must not say things parallel to, 'What I personally should expect to be observing is a non-winning ticket.'

19. Perhaps a Typing Monkey Story will make things clearer. Contemplating the World Ensemble hypothesis we are not like Mr Henry who is called into a room, shown a monkey and a typewritten sonnet, told that the monkey has typed the sonnet just by chance, and then invited to feel less astonished – or else much less deeply suspicious that he has been told a lie – when he is further informed that vastly many men have

been called into similar rooms at the same moment: sufficiently many men to have made it likely that at least one of them would be looking at a monkey-written sonnet.

Nor again are we like Mr Richard who is instead told that this was the one and only time that a monkey had been given a typewriter to play with, but that if no sonnet had been typed – faultlessly and without any prior errors – then he would have been unable to observe or think anything. 'You would have been shot as soon as the monkey made its first error, and therefore the sonnet is nothing for you to be astonished at.'

Rather, we are like Mr Thomas who is told both that there were vastly many monkeys typing away in different rooms and that each monkey was paired with a different Mr So-and-So, the arrangement being that no Mr So-and-So would remain unshot unless 'his' monkey generated a sonnet.

'There exist many universes, very varied in their properties', is of little use if in splendid isolation. The same applies to, 'Without life-permitting conditions we shouldn't be here to discuss a universe.' The two must work in harness.

How could the existence of other universes have affected the situation here? The answer is that it couldn't have affected it. The existence of countless other universes couldn't have made it any more likely that this universe, which in point of fact became 'ours' to living beings through (let us say) a breaking apart of Nature's four main forces which just chanced to take a fortunate turn, would have its forces break apart in that fashion so that life could evolve in it. But on the other hand the existence of countless universes may well have made it virtually sure that at least one universe would become 'ours' to living beings, thanks to the forms which its forces chanced to take when they broke apart. Those living beings, while having cause to thank their luck, could seem to have little ground for astonishment. Beings like them may have been practically bound to evolve somewhere – and wherever they evolved would be their 'our universe', 'this universe', 'here'. An observational selection effect would guarantee that the particular universe which they observed was life-containing; and the existence of the many universes could have meant that there had been more than just a faint possibility that such a selection effect would operate. If the universes really were sufficiently many then there would have been a virtual certainty that it would operate.

(Even if there were only a single universe, mightn't that universe be 'subject to an observational selection effect' in the following strained sense, that it was only through its being life-containing that it could be observed? Perhaps so. But as the Firing Squad Story shows, this strained sense could not enter into any satisfying explanation.)

20. Yet – you protest – we have no firm reason to think that universes really could have any of a wide range of features much as fishes can have many lengths. Mightn't only the one kind of universe be possible? Or mightn't only universes like ours be at all likely?

Let us not linger over the idea that only the one kind of universe is logically possible. Today, 'the logically possible' means what could be described without self-contradiction; and *that only the actual universe could be described non-self-contradictorily* looks a very odd claim.

How, though, should we react to the idea that there is something about Nature's actual force strengths, particle masses, and so forth which makes them alone '*really* possible or likely'?

While it looked to us as if God had very skilfully hit a bull's-eye, a tiny 'window' of light encouraging force strengths, particle masses, etc., mightn't having this window have been hard or impossible to avoid? When we represented the situation on graph paper, couldn't we be using the wrong kinds of scale? Mightn't a truly appropriate graph show the so-called window as filling most or all of the field of real possibilities?

21. My answer is that all this might conceivably be so but that it ought not to trouble us much.

A fanciful example could illustrate the point. Suppose that the words MADE BY GOD are found all over the world's granite. Their letters recur at regular intervals in this rock's crystal patterns. Two explanations suggest themselves. Perhaps God put the words there or perhaps very powerful visitors from Alpha Centauri are playing a practical joke. Both explanations might account for the facts fairly well, yet along comes a philosopher with the hypothesis that the only 'really possible' natural laws are ones which make granite carry such words. And in that case, says he, there is no need for anything to be 'fine tuned' in order for there to be such words. Nothing else is genuinely possible! Explanation fully provided! So-called bull's-eye, tiny window, in fact fills the entire field! Yes, there are countless logically possible natural laws, but the only *really possible* ones are the laws which yield electrons, pebbles, stars, and MADE BY GOD.

Surely this would be ingeniously idiotic. We must not turn our backs on tidy explanations, replacing them by a hand waved towards the obscure notion of 'limits to what is really possible'. Prior to our discovering that there are messages in granite or that any of a hundred small changes in force strengths, particle masses, and so forth would seemingly have prevented Life's evolution – *prior to* our discovering this, I agree, it might be attractive to theorize that only the one kind of granitic crystal pattern or the one set of strengths and masses 'is really possible'. But *afterwards*? Surely the attractiveness has vanished. Blind Necessity must be presumed not to run around scattering messages or making a hundred different factors each look exactly as if chosen in order to produce living beings.

22. It might still be that all force strengths, particle masses, etc. were dictated by the laws which applied to our cosmos, laws cohering elegantly

in some Totally Unified Theory or Theory of Everything. For these laws could be due not to Blind Necessity but to divine selection of a Totally Unified Theory which provided automatically the results which lead people to talk of fine tuning. (Rather similarly, a very carefully chosen Theory might perhaps yield granitic messages automatically. We might then say that 'the real fine tuning' was a matter of God's very careful choice.) Or again, it might just conceivably be that immensely many such Totally Unified Theories happened to be correct, each in a different universe. There would then be no Blind Necessity stating that all universes must be life-permitting – although it would of course be necessary that any universe in which living beings found themselves was in fact life-permitting.

23.   Concluding that it was no Blind Necessities that gave life-permitting forms to a hundred factors, we should be showing cheerful disregard of the possibility that it was 'a priori tremendously likely' that such Necessities had dictated those factors. (Or else that they had made them highly probable – so that, in the cases of absolutely all the factors, the seeming needs for fine tuning were mere artefacts of graphs wrongly scaled. Or else, perhaps, that they had set up a situation in which those factors, while apparently so multitudinously distinct, in truth formed a web such that every attempt to ruin Life's prospects by changing one factor would only produce compensatory changes in others.) Yet such a cheerful disregard can be reasonable even if we grant that some clear sense can here be attached to the words 'a priori tremendously likely'. The Story of the Granite is an attempt to show how very reasonable this sort of disregard could sometimes be.

Again, consider the following case. Feeling two balls in an urn but knowing nothing about their colours, you draw a ball, replace it, draw again, replace, and so on for a hundred draws. Every single time a red ball is drawn. A tidy explanation suggests itself: that both the balls are red. Would you resist this on the grounds that 'maybe it was tremendously likely' that one of them was blue?

24.   But, you object, wouldn't it be silly to suppose that we can, albeit only in thought or on computer screens, inspect absolutely all possible universes so as to be able to find that only a very tiny proportion would be life-permitting?

It would indeed be silly. However, the Story of the Fly on the Wall shows that we need inspect only the universes of 'the local area': the possible universes which are much like ours in their basic laws yet differ in their force strengths, particle masses, expansion speeds, degrees of turbulence, and so on. A wall bears a fly (or a tiny group of flies) surrounded by a largish empty area. The fly (or one of the group) is hit by a bullet. With appropriate background assumptions – e.g. our not knowing that short-sighted, frugal Uncle Harry was the one and only firer – we might fairly confidently say, 'Many bullets are hitting the wall and/or a marksman fired this particular bullet', without bothering about whether distant areas of the wall are thick with flies. All that is relevant is that there are no further flies locally.

The point of this story is not that the Many Bullets or Else Marksman theory is undeniably superior to the Uncle Harry Fired Just Once theory. Instead it is that the latter theory would get no support from any mere fact that the wall was crawling with flies, if there were only the one fly locally.

When telling the story I have sometimes suggested that the alternative to the marksman would be that many bullets *were hitting the wall near the fly*. This was a blunder. For suppose the wall carried many solitary flies each surrounded by a largish empty area. There could now be a good chance of a bullet's hitting some solitary fly provided only that many bullets *were hitting the wall*. So from the fact that there is only one fly locally (only one life-permitting kind of possible universe inside 'the local group' of possible universes, those much like ours in their basic laws) we have no firm right to conclude that in the absence of a marksman (God) there are probably many bullets locally (many actually existing universes much like ours in their basic laws). It need only be supposed that there are many bullets hitting the wall at varying places: many actually existing universes with differing characters. Although the basic laws of these other universes could plausibly be thought to be much like those of our universe, they might conceivably be very different.

25. It is often objected that only one universe is open to our inspection and that judgments of probability cannot be made on the basis of a single trial. The Telepathized Painting Story is a suitable reply. After doing his best to paint a countryside, Jones tries to transmit the horrid results to Smith by mere power of thought. Behold, Smith reproduces every messy tree and flower and cloud. Whereupon a philosopher reacts as follows: 'Can't conclude anything from *that*! Must have more than one trial!'

Faced by such a reaction we ought to protest that Smith's painting is complex. Although only a single painting it is many thousand blobs of paint. Much could be learned from it. And experiencing many thousand billion parts of our universe, mightn't we rather similarly gain some right to draw conclusions about the whole? After learning about ordinary messages we could be justifiably reluctant to dismiss as mere chance, or even as 'neither probable nor improbable because we haven't experienced other universes', any MADE BY GOD messages which we found in the rocks. *After a little acquaintance with physics and biology* we could fairly confidently perform thought-experiments showing how dim Life's prospects would have been, had various force strengths and particle masses been slightly different; now, couldn't this well encourage us to believe in God or in an ensemble of universes? (Yet philosophers have argued solemnly that a Creator would find it impossible to leave any signs of his creative action because, poor fellow, he would be limited to showing us just a single universe. Hence, one presumes, even writing MADE BY GOD all over it would have no tendency to prove anything. And if that were so then of course the mere fact of its containing living beings could give us no reason to believe in God – or in Multiple Worlds, for that matter.)

Hostile Stories: Little Puddle etc.

26. Let us now turn to a story apparently damaging to my case: the oft-told tale of the Great Rivers Flowing through the Principal Cities of Europe. What superb evidence of the Creator's action!

A variant points to the Mississippi. See how wonderfully it threads its way under every bridge!

Another concerns pond life. The rotifers of Little Puddle marvel at the deity who has provided filthy water and mud. Had their ancestors evolved in arsenic-filled waters then they would be marvelling at the Creator's benevolence in supplying arsenic. An atrocious case of thinking backwards! How blind to Darwin's point that just as cities and bridges conform to the positions of rivers, so organisms adapt themselves to their environments! What parochial concern with the prerequisites of rotiferhood!

My reply is that even those defending the unfortunately named Anthropic Principle often take pains to deny that their concern is only with *anthropos, homo sapiens*, mankind. As was made plain enough by B. Carter, who baptized the Principle and so has a right to be heard on the subject, what is involved is a possible observational selection effect stemming from the nature not of manhood but of *observerhood*. The Anthropic Principle reminds us that if there were many actually existing universes most of which had properties utterly hostile to the evolution of intelligent life then, obviously, we intelligent products of evolution could be observing only one of the rare universes in which intelligent life could indeed evolve. The fact that such a selection effect could be helpful in explaining any observations of fine tuning – could help them to become unmysterious since (section 8) such observations would have been likely to occur somewhere, and (16) no situations tuned in life-excluding ways could ever be observed – provides by far the strongest reason for believing in multiple universes. The mere truth that a slightly different universe could not be seen *by mankind* is much less interesting. It could be ludicrous to view that truth as any reason at all for accepting more than one universe. And similarly, those who believe in God rather than in multiple universes could be being absurd if their grounds for belief were that various natural conditions seemed crucial to human existence in particular. The key point is instead that *intelligent life of any plausible kind* seems crucially dependent on those natural conditions. People who tell sarcastic tales about rotifers could seem to have missed the point.

27. Alternatively, perhaps these people do not miss it but instead have minds dominated by the curious idea that intelligent life could evolve just about anywhere: for instance, in frozen hydrogen or near neutron star surfaces or in the interiors of ordinary stars like the sun or deep inside planet Earth, or in interstellar gas clouds.[6] But they then invite responses such as the following.

First, there are quite powerful reasons for thinking that frozen hydrogen, neutron stars, etc. would be inhospitable environments. There are for instance grounds for thinking that chemistry – impossible in neutron stars or inside the sun – is very special in the intricate structures which it makes possible. And our sort of life, at any rate, is chemical life. Are we to suppose that this, the only kind of life we know, is highly unusual, *other kinds* being nowhere near as suggestive of fine tuning? That could look too reminiscent of an argument which Bertrand Russell thought he heard voiced by various

eighteenth-century optimists: that since, so to speak, the oranges at the top of the barrel looked rotten, those underneath were probably delicious.

Second, if intelligent life were as easily achieved as such people fancy then Fermi's celebrated 'Where are they?' conundrum, the puzzle of why we have no evidence of extraterrestrial intelligent beings, could become very hard to solve. Maybe the solution would now be that it is a huge step from mere *life processes*, perhaps something pretty simple going on in frozen hydrogen, to *intelligent life*. But in this case a multiplicity of universes or a divine Fine Tuner could be needed to make intelligent life at all likely to evolve.

Third, there could never have been any frozen hydrogen, neutron stars, ordinary stars, interstellar gas clouds, or even individual atoms, if the Big Bang had been followed by recollapse within ten seconds or if any of a large number of other unfortunate happenings had happened – happenings seemingly avoidable only by tuning that is extremely accurate. (See parts of section 4.) So even if living beings of many very different kinds filled our universe, a universe very slightly differently tuned would still be utterly lifeless.

28. 'If rotifers could talk . . .' is sometimes replaced by 'If carbon could talk. . . .' The sceptic may say that the prerequisites of intelligent life are just whatever are the prerequisites of carbon, of water, of long-lived stable stars, and maybe of a handful of further things. Now, how would matters look to a Philosophical Club consisting of carbon atoms, water molecules, long-lived stable stars, and so forth? Instead of an Anthropic Principle, wouldn't there be a Carbonic Principle? Instead of worshipping a Creator benevolent towards humans, wouldn't club members pray to one who loved stellar stability?

In reply it can be helpful to insist that intelligent life seems to depend on a very lengthy list of things. When the Philosophical Club came to its grand conclusion that carbon, water, long-lived stars, and so forth are what are truly important here, or are at any rate just as important as the intelligent life which so obsesses humans, then surely the length of the list, plus the fact that all the items listed *were listed because of being prerequisites of intelligent life*, would show the wrongness of this.

29. Still, suppose for argument's sake that nothing but carbon was required for producing living intelligence. The prerequisites of carbon and of living intelligence thus being identical, might it not be arbitrary to concentrate on the latter?[7] Why not forget about the Difficulty of Generating Intelligence? Why not talk instead of How Hard It Is to Produce Carbon? Now, the existence of carbon might indeed act as a 'selection function' picking out our kind of universe from the field of all possible universes. Many scientific theories might fail through being incompatible with the observed fact of there being carbon. Yet — says the sceptic — this is all very ordinary science. Compare how the theory that rock becomes fluid at a pressure of two tons per square inch is refuted by the existence of Mount Everest whose lower regions would in that case have flowed away. There is nothing in this to justify talk of God, of a multiplicity of universes, or of the 'Mount Everestic Principle'!

This seems to me very wrong. It overlooks the point of the Fishing Story, the Poker Game Story, the Collapsing Arch Story, and the tale of the Silk Merchant's Thumb. It forgets that carbon particles do not talk, observe nothing, and could not plausibly be loved for their own sakes by a benevolent deity.

How are those tales relevant, and what is so special about observerhood or about being such as a benevolent deity could well love? It is all a question of tidiness of explanation. Every thumb must be somewhere, but the placement of the silk merchant's is 'special' because it suggests a plausible ground — a love of money — for its being where it is and not elsewhere. Likewise,

the reason why a 23.2576 inch fish is special is that nothing else can be observed with the help of your fishing apparatus and that this, when combined with belief in many fish of varied lengths swimming by the apparatus, very neatly explains why the fish is being observed. In place of a mere 'selection function' we have a possible observational selection effect: one which operates if there are many actual fish from which the apparatus can select.

30. True, the catching of the fish *also* gives grounds for believing in a benevolent fish-creator. But such double suggestiveness need not dismay us. Bob's empty treasure chest, on an island whose only inhabitants are Bob, Mike, and Jim, can fairly powerfully suggest that Mike is a thief despite also suggesting just as powerfully that theft has been committed by Jim. (In fact, the two of them may have committed it in partnership.)

Some Conclusions

31. Contemporary religious thinkers often approach the Argument from Design with a grim determination that their churches shall not again be made to look foolish. Recalling what happened when churchmen opposed first Galileo and then Darwin, they insist that religion must be based not on science but on faith. Philosophy, they announce, has demonstrated that Design Arguments lack all force.

I hope to have shown that philosophy has demonstrated no such thing. Our universe, which these religious thinkers believe to be created by God, does look, greatly though this may dismay them, very much as if created by God. Many of its basic features seem fine tuned to Life's requirements. Various parables ('Stories') suggest that this is indeed a ground for belief in God so long as we use reasoning such as serves us well in ordinary affairs. Let us trust it even here. The question of whether our universe is God-created is no ordinary question, but that cannot itself provide any strong excuse for abandoning ordinary ways of thinking. Theology is not a call to reject common sense.

Still, we must bear in mind two main points.

First: World Ensemble plus Observational Selection could provide a powerful means of accounting for any fine tuning which we felt tempted to ascribe to Divine Selection. Now, this does not say that belief in God could gain no support from fine tuning. (Remember the empty treasure chest of section 30.) Still, fine tuning could not point towards God in an unambiguous way. Of my various Stories, not one gives any support to the God hypothesis which it does not also give to the World Ensemble hypothesis.

Second: A cosmos too very obviously God-made might tend to be a cosmos not of freedom but of puppetry. This is one of several grounds for thinking that God's creative role would not be made entirely plain.

It would be quite another matter, though, for God to avoid every possible indication of his existence even when this meant selecting physical laws and force strengths and particle masses which were prima facie far less satisfactory than others he would otherwise have chosen. A God of that degree of deviousness looks uncomfortably close to the kind of deity who creates the universe in 4004 BC complete with fossils in the rocks.

32. A frequently heard protest is that no amount of finite evidence could support a belief in God, who is infinite.

A balance pan contains butter to the weight of one kilogram. The pan rises. What can we conclude about the weight in the balance's other pan? Answer: It is above one kilogram. We certainly cannot conclude that there is an infinite weight there.

My reply is that in science and elsewhere we should seek simplicity, and *infinity* can at times be simpler than, say, *five million and seventy*. Consider the theory that only five million and seventy universes will ever appear as quantum fluctuations (section 6[c]). It could seem sim-

pler to believe that infinitely many would appear in this way.

In the case of the divine infinity, what is crucial to a Neoplatonist like me is God's infinite power to create what is good. But why should I prefer to think that this power is only finite? Why suppose that a creatively effective ethical requirement (section 3) could be responsible for a world's existence but only if that world were a non-intricate world, or a world containing no more than sixty million and thirty-one cabbages? (Would intricacy tax the intelligence of Neoplatonism's God? No. Creatively effective ethical requirements *act as* if intelligent but are not themselves intelligent in any way that could encourage us to speak of an intelligence which could be taxed. Among Neoplatonists, Plotinus was specially clear on that sort of point.)

33. Later chapters will expand the arguments of this first one. Sometimes it will be at the cost of making things look more complicated than they actually are.

In reading them, please remember section 4's point about words like 'fine tuned for producing Life'. Such words must not be read as begging the question of whether there is anything like a divine Fine Tuner. Physicists often say such things as this: that a particular theory might account for various facts, but only if various numbers which the theory allows to have any of many values are 'fine tuned', i.e. *fall within certain narrow limits*.[8] Nothing about a Fine Tuner there! – and the business need have nothing to do with Life. True, the fine tuning talked of in this book will almost always have to do with it; yet context will sometimes show otherwise. Assuming, for example, that fish must have lengths falling within narrow limits if they are to be caught by your fishing apparatus, then any fish which it catches are 'fine-tuned fish' even if the reason why there are any such fish is just that the lake contains vastly many fish of randomized lengths. In this context, calling the fish 'fine tuned' clearly says only that ones slightly different in length would not have been caught. Again, the fact that many of my Stories have involved the suspicion that *conscious agents* have been fine tuning things – the position of a thumb, say, or the constitution of a hand of cards – is of no particular significance. Any explanations given for 'fine tuning' need not be *agent*-explanations. If all natural pearls have grit grains at their centres then the positions of those grains are fine tuned in ways suggesting the theory that pearls are secreted by oysters to envelop irritating grit. The positions count as 'fine tuned' for suggesting this theory just because very slightly different ones wouldn't suggest it –and not because oysters are conscious beings intent on minimizing their irritations. Oysters aren't.

34. Please bear in mind also that satisfying various of Life's prerequisites (its necessary conditions) may often be fairly far distant from guaranteeing Life's presence. While this should be plain enough, the line between the two affairs can be difficult to draw; it will usually be left to your good sense to draw it in a flexible way. In this region, making the philosopher's beloved distinction between necessary and sufficient conditions can often be both a hard and a pointless task. For on the one hand, virtually nothing is 100 per cent guaranteed in a world of quantum uncertainties let alone in the realm of great chemical complexities (where luck can be very important). And on the other hand, in a large enough Reality anything which is at all possible could be expected somewhere or other.

Notes

The chapter draws on Leslie, 1988d. As in the cases of later chapters which also draw on various of my papers, I thank all those whose criticisms led to changes.

1 See Adams's, *The Education of Henry Adams* (New York, 1931), esp. p. 429. 'If he were obliged to insist on a Universe, he seemed driven to the Church'—so he opted for a 'multiverse' of largely or entirely separate worlds with very different characteristics.

2 I consider the Argument for Multiple Worlds in many places. See esp. Leslie 1982, 1983a and b, 1985, 1986a and b, 1987, 1988a, b, c, d, and e, and 1989a and b. In early treatments of the Argument, 1978a and 1979 (ch. 7), I underestimated its power.

3 Neoplatonism is defended in my *Value and Existence* (Leslie, 1979) and in several articles, esp. Leslie, 1970, 1978b, and 1980. Also see Leslie, 1972, for the ethical theory underlying it, and 1986c for a reply to J. L. Mackie's chapter discussing *Value and Existence* in his *The Miracle of Theism* (Oxford, 1982).

4 Guth and Steinhardt, 1984.

5 Linde, 1983, p. 245. Compare Weinberg, 1983, p. 140: 'Did the universe freeze into domains? Do we live in one such domain, in which the symmetry between the weak and electromagnetic interactions has been broken in a particular way?'

6 For all this and also the Little Puddle tale, see G. Feinberg and R. Shapiro, *Life Beyond Earth* (New York, 1980).

7 Here and in section 1.28 I particularly have in mind Sylvan, 1986, pp. 160–8. (While J. Earman's paper in *American Philosophical Quarterly*, October 1987, pp. 307–17, could seem to revolve around similar reasoning, I believe that the key to this paper is instead Earman's doubts about whether such things as carbon really are essential.) Sylvan also challenges the point made in section 1.12: that those fish need to be *actual* fish.

8 Cf. p. 664 of S. Coleman, *Nuclear Physics* B310, 12 December 1988, pp. 643–68: 'When we describe a phenomenon as unnatural we may mean either that it requires fine tuning of short-distance physics or that it requires fine tuning of initial conditions. The original cosmological-constant problem was unnatural in the first sense; the slightest alteration in the parameters of microphysics would produce an enormous cosmological constant.'

References

Guth, A. H. and Steinhardt, P. J. (1984) 'The inflationary universe', *Scientific American*. May, pp. 116–28.

Leslie, J. (1970) 'The theory that the world exists because it should', *American Philosophical Quarterly*, October, pp. 286–98.

—— (1972) 'Ethically required existence', *American Philosophical Quarterly*, July, pp. 215–24.

—— (1978a) 'God and scientific verifiability', *Philosophy*, January, pp. 71–9.

—— (1978b) 'Efforts to explain all existence', *Mind*, April, pp. 181–94.

—— (1979) *Value and Existence*, Oxford: Blackwell.

—— (1982) 'Anthropic principle, world ensemble, design', *American Philosophical Quarterly*, April, pp. 141–51 (with some misprints corrected in the October number).

—— (1983a) 'Cosmology, probability and the need to explain life', in N. Rescher (ed.), *Scientific Explanation and Understanding*, Pittsburgh: Center for Philosophy of Science, and Lanham and London: University Press of America, pp. 53–82.

—— (1983b) 'Observership in cosmology: the anthropic principle', *Mind*, October, pp. 573–9.

—— (1985) 'Modern cosmology and the creation of life', in E. McMullin (ed.), *Evolution and Creation*, Notre Dame: University of Notre Dame Press, pp. 91–120.

—— (1986a) 'The scientific weight of anthropic and teleological principles', in N. Rescher (ed.), *Current Issues in Teleology*, Lanham and London: University Press of America, pp. 111–19.

—— (1986b) 'Anthropic explanations in cosmology', in *PSA 1986: Volume One* (Proceedings of the Philosophy of Science Association). Ann Arbor: Edwards Bros, pp. 87–95.

—— (1987) 'Probabilistic phase transitions and the anthropic principle', in J. Demaret (ed.), *Origin and Early History of the Universe*, Liège: Institut d'Astrophysique, University of Liège, and Presses of the University of Liège, pp. 439–44.

—— (1988a) 'No inverse gambler's fallacy in cosmology', *Mind*, April, pp. 269–72. (A reply to I. Hacking.)

—— (1988b). 'The Leibnizian richness of our universe', in N. Rescher (ed.), *Leibnizian Inquiries*, Lanham: University Press of America, pp. 139–48.

—— (1988c) 'The prerequisites of life in our universe', in G. V. Coyne, M. Heller, and J. Zycinski (eds), *Newton and the New Direction in Science*, Vatican City: Specola Vaticana, pp. 229–58. (Reprinted in *Truth*, Fall, 1990, an issue on the cosmological argument edited by W. L. Craig.)

—— (1988d) 'How to draw conclusions from a fine-tuned universe', in R. J. Russell, W. R. Stoeger, and G. V. Coyne (eds), *Physics, Philosophy and Theology*, Vatican City: Vatican Observatory, pp. 297–311. (Coming from a September 1987 papal workshop at Castel Gandolfo; distributed by University of Notre Dame Press.)

—— (1988e) 'Dialectics and metaphysics', *Explorations in Knowledge*, vol. 6, no. 1, pp. 1–12. (A debate with D. Goldstick.)

—— (1989a) *Physical Cosmology and Philosophy* (edited, with introduction and annotated bibliography). New York: Macmillan.

—— (1989b) "Multiple universes", to appear in R. F. Kitchener (ed.), *The Origin of the Universe*. (Coming from a September 1988 conference of Colorado State University.)

Linde, A. D. (1983) 'The new inflationary universe scenario', in G. W. Gibbons, S. W. Hawking, and S. T. C. Siklos (eds), *The Very Early Universe*, Cambridge: Cambridge University Press, pp. 205–49.

Sylvan, R. (1986) 'Toward an improved cosmo-logical synthesis', *Grazer Philosophische Studien*, vols 25 and 26, pp. 135–79.

Weinberg, S. (1983) *The First Three Minutes* (2nd edn with afterword), London: Fontana.

Chapter 38

Peter Forrest

THE TREE OF LIFE
Agency and Immortality in a Metaphysics Inspired by Quantum Theory

Recently several philosophers including Huw Price, Peter Lewis, and David Lewis have argued that on one interpretation of quantum theory (genus *Indeterminacy*, species *No Collapse*) death is an illusion.[1] Taking Schröedinger's unhappy cat as the standard example, this interpretation tells us that it is as if the whole universe splits into two copies in one of which the cat survives and in the other there is a corpse. Fission into a living organism on the one hand and a corpse on the other is, most of us agree, a way of surviving.[2] So we arrive at the first premise, namely that organisms survive situations like that of Schrödinger's cat. Moreover—and this is the second premise—the causes of death are, it is said, always relevantly similar to those in the Schrödinger's cat thought experiment. From these two premises it is inferred that death is an illusion.

That interpretation also implies *over-survival*, that is, the repeated fission of organisms so that each one of us survives more than once, in fact more times than we naively thought there were human beings on Earth. Moreover, we are ourselves survivors of past fission. Such repeated over-survival is counter-intuitive, and might well be taken as a *reductio ad absurdum* of the interpretation that leads to it.

This paper is not intended as a contribution to a debate over whether quantum theory implies that death is an illusion, although it is inspired by and, as I argue in the Appendix, coherent with contemporary physics. Apart from the Appendix it is an independent investigation of the metaphysical hypothesis that the Universe undergoes fission in such a way that we survive death. I hope it will not cause confusion, however, if the Twin Slit thought experiment is used to illustrate indeterminacy. This is not intended as an appeal to quantum theory; rather, it is just a familiar example.

After a note on coherence with Science, I shall first state the unmodified Tree of Life hypothesis for survival, showing that it has motivation quite independent of the belief in survival after death. Then I explain why it needs modifying, resulting in a rather more complicated Dividing Bundle hypothesis, based upon a *fibrous universe*.

1. Coherence with Science

I seek a metaphysics that *coheres* with the sciences. By that I do not mean mere consistency. What I mean by coherence is that the result of adjoining the metaphysics to contemporary scientific theories is an aggregate theory that has the standard theoretical virtue of overall simplicity. If we measure complexity in such a way that the complexity of a consistent conjunction never exceeds, but sometimes equals, the sum of the complexities of the conjuncts, two theories may be said to cohere well if the complexity of the conjunction is significantly less than the sum of the complexities.

My reason for seeking such coherence is a basic commitment to the principle that simpler theories are *significantly* more probable than more complicated ones. That simpler theories are *somewhat* more probable can be argued for on the assumption that we have countably many pairwise inconsistent theories compatible with the data. They can be arranged in order of increasing complexity with only finitely many simpler than any given theory. The sum of their probabilities cannot exceed 100 percent. So, unless they all have 0 percent (or infinitesimal) probability as Karl Popper taught, their probability must on the whole decrease with complexity. The details of this argument are hardly worth developing, for it does not show that there is *significant* decrease with increasing complexity. I assume, however, that there is a significant decrease and that this applies to philosophy and theology as much as to the sciences.

When it comes to metaphysical hypotheses concerning survival after death, coherence with the sciences is not that easy to achieve. An example of a speculation about survival that is not even intended to cohere with the sciences in this way is Peter van Inwagen's suggestion that God removes the dying, replacing them by corpses.[3] If we postulate an extra spatial dimension, then such removal would merely be a matter of moving sideways. This idea has the advantage of making sense of the accounts of the risen Jesus, who seemed to appear and disappear and yet was solid. I mention this as setting a standard to which other accounts of survival should aspire. In particular, van Inwagen avoids any temporal gaps in persons, avoids fission of one person into many persons, and avoids any appeal to ghostly bodies made of subtle matter. These might all be considered implausible, although subtle matter does have popularity on its side.

2. The Unmodified Tree of Life Hypothesis

There is a straightforward metaphysical hypothesis that permits survival. It is inspired by Storrs McCall's branching universe.[4] For convenience. I shall throughout this paper take Time to be represented as an extra spatial dimension. Hence the branching universe can be thought of as like a tree. The idea of the Tree of Life is that the universe continually branches but that agents have the power to prune the resulting tree, so that most branches survive for only for a very short time—a jiffy, as Paul Davies would call it: too short a time to support consciousness. (See Fig. 38.1, but be warned: in all the diagrams a few branches represent many.)

Either as a result of divine providence or the human will to survive only once, we undergo no fission ourselves.[5] So on this proposal the universe itself undergoes fission into two or more parts that last for more than a jiffy only if the set of all human beings is correspondingly divided into two or more disjoint subsets. That is,

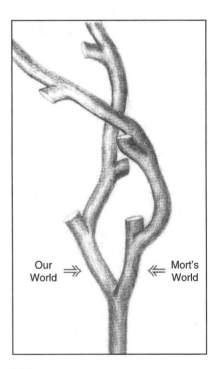

Figure 38.1

each subset has for its members precisely those who survive in the corresponding branch. Peter Geach suggested something like this as a model for the separation of the blessed from the damned on Judgment Day.[6] But we may use it to provide an account of survival after death. In this context "death" amounts to separation from the rest of us, rather than death strictly speaking. The "dead" person, whom I shall call Mort, lives on in a side branch, presumably alone. I say "presumably" because each death is a distinct event and hence is associated with a distinct branching. Perhaps if you die at the same time as one you love you could go off on in tandem, or perhaps you could ensure your otherwise lonely branches fuse together. But it is highly speculative what happens in Mort's branch. So my advice to suicidal young lovers is not to count on union immediately after death.

To the obvious objection that the Mort was in a bad way and would die in the side branch, I reply that the branches that begin to form do so in numbers proportionate to the probability of the events occurring in them. Current physical theories allow a very small probability of our surviving just about anything—perhaps even falling into a black hole. So we may suppose that of the very many branches that begin to form a small proportion are ones in which Mort survives if that branch continues for more than a jiffy; and divine providence or a will to survive ensures that Mort continues to exist in one of those branches.

This account, along with the Dividing Bundle hypothesis provided below, has motivation independent of any belief in survival. This motivation is based upon the idea that agency is not the sort of thing for which there is an adequate scientific account. That generates the problem of giving an overall theory that includes agency on the one hand and, without undue alteration, the scientific account of the natural order on the other. The Tree of Life is such a theory. For we replace the usual scientific account of the natural order by a variant, to the effect that so long as a branch

exists then the laws of nature hold in it without exception. We then adjoin to it first an account of universe-fission and then an agency account of pruning. I appeal to readers to judge that this coheres with the sciences somewhat better than van Inwagen's suggestion, and much better than, say, the outrageous suggestion that on apparent death we shrink and come to dwell on the surface of a subatomic particle which looks surprisingly like planet Earth.

The acts of different agents are coordinated in the following way. If X brings it about that a situation of type T occurs, then X prunes all the branches in which X exists but a T does not occur. There are very many branches not thus pruned. If this is the only act occurring at the time then which of these T-occurring branches survives is random. But if there is another agent Y bringing it about that a situation of type U occurs, then Y prunes all the branches in which Y exists but no U occurs. So their combined action results in many branches in which both X and Y exist and situations of types T and U occur. Again if there are no other agents acting apart from X and Y it is random which of these T&U-occurring branches survives.

In what state will Mort be after separation from the rest of us? Divine providence might ensure any possible state for Mort; but if survival is due solely to a will to survive without fission, then the resulting state depends quite critically on whether the pruning occurs before or after further branching. Suppose it occurs after several "generations" of branching, and after enough time has lapsed for very badly damaged organisms to die, but still before it could constitute fission of a person. Then there would be a selection effect, in which the fitter organisms undergo more fission. Hence by the time the pruning occurs it is likely that the random survivor will be fairly fit. If, as I suspect, there is no time for such a selection effect then we may predict that poor Mort only just survives, with whatever degree of consciousness is required for survival. It would be like a brain in a vat, except there is no vat, and only part of a brain. In that case we should expect Mort to "rest in peace", asleep until . . . Until what? The Tree of Life hypothesis does not have much to say about the Resurrection of the Dead, but its successor, the Dividing Bundle hypothesis will.

3. How Lovely is the Tree of Life?

The Tree of Life hypothesis is open to the objection that a permanent sleep does not correspond to the hoped for—or feared—survival. To the extent that such hopes are adequately grounded our metaphysics should accommodate them. How could this be done? One suggestion is that there is a further project of providing an eschatology coherent with science, and that Muslims and Jews could think of the dead resting, in peace or otherwise, until Judgment Day. But I fail to see how Christians could fit the Resurrection of Jesus into this scheme. So I for one would not rely on this further project of an eschatology coherent with the sciences.

An alternative is to appeal to the precedent of time reversibility in physics, and allow fusion as well as fission. Hence the side branches that split off containing the dead might fuse together into a heavenly realm. The Resurrection of the Dead would then consist of a final fusion of all existing branches of the universe. On this model the Heavenly realm could itself have undergone fission shortly after Jesus' death, with that branch coming to fuse with the Earthly branch. That is beginning, however, to look rather ad hoc, so I judge that while the Tree of Life hypothesis might be satisfactory for Jews and Muslims, Christians should seek something different. So I shall refer to this as the Christians' objection.

A further theological objection would hold to all the hypotheses proposed in this paper. I call it the Sophisticates' Objection. Surely we do not expect to survive death in a body like this one in a world like ours? Surely, the objection goes, there is a radical transformation into something

that we cannot envisage. I reply thus. However radical our eventual transformation turns out to be, we should doubt the metaphysical possibility of our surviving too sudden a change. Life in a side branch could be the first step with more radical changes to follow.

There are three other, non-theological, objections to the Tree of Life hypothesis, which I now note. The first is that this hypothesis does not cohere with the sciences as well as we might like. For although the natural order is not interfered with in the branches that continue, the pruning itself seems to be contrary to the natural order, involving the annihilation of what would be like a whole classical universe. In particular there is the problem with the conservation laws, notably that of mass energy. There are two ways of understanding these in the context of a branching universe. One is to take the mass energy within a branch; the other is to take the totality across branches. But neither works—unless, as Edward Tryon has suggested, the mass energy is zero.[7] If we take the totality across all branches then we would expect some extra energy in the side branches containing the dead. If we consider energy in each branch then pruning violates the conservation. So unless we speculate that the total mass energy is zero or that it is zero on the side branches in which the dead live on then an otherwise well-established conservation law is violated.

We may meet this objection if we allow, along with David Chalmers and Richard Swinburne, the possibility of "zombies", molecule for molecule replicas of human persons but with no consciousness. For simplicity let us temporarily adopt Swinburne's Substance Dualism. Then we may take the universe to branch repeatedly without pruning. At each branch the soul can only go with the one body. So we obtain something similar to the Tree of Life but with the conservation laws holding on each branch. (This is illustrated in Fig. 38.2, which is just like Fig. 38.1 except that branches are bezombied rather than pruned.) In Section 6, I shall offer a defence of zombies,

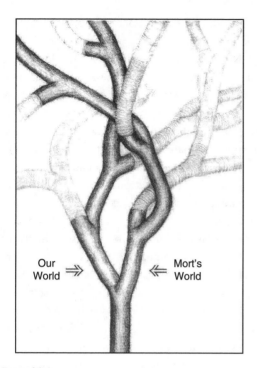

Our World ⟹   ⟸ Mort's World

Figure 38.2

but this would be premature here since there are other objections to the unmodified Tree of Life.

The next objection is that before mass and energy were equated the conservation of mass was taken to explicate the principle *ex nihilo nihil fit*. And that principle retains its intuitive appeal: stuff, we think, does not just come into existence. And even if the total mass energy is zero we might well consider that stuff would come to exist if the universe underwent fission. Therefore branching would be impossible. To this it might be replied that theists usually accept that God created *ex nihilo*. But if so that was a miraculous act and we should be reluctant to think that this miracle is repeated every fraction of a second as the Universe branches.

The final objection to the Tree of Life hypothesis is that many find the idea of spatially separated branches of the universe implausible. I suspect this is only a genuine problem for presentists for whom a branching universe consists of many unconnected universes. The rest of us may console ourselves with the real connections between the branches in the past.

In addition to these objections there are one or two further reasons for seeking a variant on the Tree of Life. One is that, as I explain in the Appendix, the unmodified Tree of Life is inferior in some respects to the Many Worlds interpretation of quantum theory. The other, for what it is worth, is that the Tree of Life coheres well only with a probabilistic physics and there might be a more fundamental deterministic physics might.

4. The Fibrous Universe

Because of the objections to the unmodified Tree of Life hypothesis, and even to its zombie variant, I now consider the Many Worlds interpretation of quantum theory, proposed by B. S. De Witt as an explication of Hugh Everett's interpretation, and currently championed by David Deutsch.[8] The idea is that a quantum state describes not just what is happening in one world but in many worlds. So, to take an example dear to Deutsch, a quantum computer will have enormous power because it is like a large collection of classical computers in different worlds. For a reason discussed in the Appendix, I hold that even "particles" such as electrons and quarks exist in many worlds simultaneously. And so do we. Therefore I prefer to think of these many "worlds" as themselves all embedded in the one hyperspace. As Dean Zimmerman has pointed out to me, hyperspace does little real work in explaining Mort's survival. It helps the exposition, however, first by overcoming any tendency to think of the separate "worlds" as possible worlds, and secondly as reminding us that we do not have many bodies in different "worlds" so much as one body with parts in different "worlds".

Geometers and topologists often talk of *fiber-bundles*. Why mention this esoteric mathematical terminology? It is because when philosophers talk of *many worlds* or even a *multiverse* this suggests many separate universes, perhaps branches in a

McCall branching universe but nonetheless not spatially connected now. As I have said, I want to resist this suggestion, and instead think of what classically we took to be a universe, with three spatial and one temporal dimension, as just one "fiber" in a bundle. So I am thinking of the universe as itself a bundle of universe-fibers, each of which has the usual number of spatial dimensions. Space is to be thought of as having enough dimensions to contain all the universe-fibers at a given time; so it is Hyperspace.

To illustrate the concept of a fiber-bundle consider a familiar three-dimensional space. Now pick a plane K. Then the three-dimensional space can be considered a fiber-bundle with the "fibers" being K and all the planes parallel to K. This does not mean that the planes are somehow separate like cards in a deck, or one dimensional like cotton fibers. All it means is that the three-dimensional space has some extra structure, namely an equivalence relation whose equivalence classes are the fibers.

As I have already mentioned, this way of thinking of the Many Worlds interpretation helps overcome resistance to individuals existing in many "worlds", that is, universe-fibers. When I suggest that the universe is a fiber-bundle, I am suggesting that the "multiverse" or ensemble of "universes" is in fact our universe, perhaps the only one there is, and that it has an equivalence relation on it so that the equivalence classes, which I call universe-fibers, have only three macroscopic spatial dimensions. The whole universe is thus vastly larger than we usually think, and, regrettably, vastly more complicated. It is, however, neither larger nor more complicated than a supposed multiverse made up of distinct universes in the standard version of the Many Worlds Interpretation.

In a classical mechanical theory we would say that each individual fiber evolved deterministically and perhaps hypothesize that nearby fibers had similar initial conditions. In a quantum theory the state of all the fibers taken together might evolve deterministically but not individual fibers.

Now consider an object, as it might be you or I or, again, as it might be an electron. Does it belong to a single fiber or extend across many fibers? If we thought of the fibers as separate universes, it would be natural to assume the former and talk of *counterparts* in neighboring fibers. But if we think of a bundle of fibers we may say that electrons and human beings extend across fibers. In fact I made the distinction between a universe made up of fibers and one that has separate sub-universes chiefly to motivate what might otherwise seem incoherent, the hypothesis that things as we know them extend across many of these universe-fibers. Strictly speaking, however, we do not require spatial relations between the different fibers, such as would exist if they were in a hyperspace. It suffices that there be some physically necessary correlations and that there be simultaneity relations across fibers.

My chief reason for suggesting that things, including we ourselves, extend across universe-fibers is that it is absurd to posit counterparts of ourselves, especially counterparts that are indistinguishable in all mental respects. So our minds extend across fibers. We could hypothesize that the one mind is correlated with a whole collection of brains, each one in a different fiber. Alternatively we could hypothesize that there is just the one brain itself spread out across the many fibers. Perhaps there is merely a verbal distinction between the two hypotheses, but, for reasons indicated in the Appendix, I prefer the hypothesis that objects, including our brains, are spread out across fibers.

Even if this is not merely a verbal dispute the choice of which hypothesis to adopt does not affect the discussion of an afterlife, provided we are convinced there is but a single mind corresponding to the bodies—or the body parts as the case might be—in the different fibers. Nonetheless the question is of intrinsic interest and it is worth noting that given the

Whiteheadian account of points as "constructs" (technically *filters*) of smaller and smaller regions this distinction between the two hypotheses would not be merely verbal. For in that case we might for the sake of uniformity take the universe-fibers themselves to be similar "constructs", made up of more and more narrow tubes each representable as, but not constituted by, many universe-fibers side by side.

As Zimmerman has pointed out, this Whiteheadian universe-tube hypothesis is open to the objection that there would then not be any completely determinate state of particles. For their locations and other properties would vary across the tubes, however small. In reply I note that on a Whiteheadian account it is natural to take the fundamental properties to correspond to the integrals of the quantities postulated in a point-based theory. For instance, instead of the mass or charge density at a point we consider the total mass or total charge of a region. This approach may easily be extended to tubes. For example, suppose there are two extra dimensions in the hyperspace, and to avoid confusion let us use the *schmeter* as the unit of length across the extra two dimensions. Then the fundamental unit of mass will not be the *gram* but the *schmam*, where a gram is a schmam per square schmeter. A certain region in a tube could have a total mass of, say, 12 schmams. If the tube was of cross-section 2 square schmeters, then on fiber-based theory we might say that its intersection with a given fiber had density of, say, 6 schmams per square schmeter, that is, 6 grams. And if the volume of the region were itself 3 cubic meters, then the density would be 2 schmams per square schmeter per cubic meter, that is, 2 grams per cubic meter. On a Whiteheadian tube-based account the fundamental mass properties are expressed in schmams, and the ones that appear in a point-based fiber-based account are derivatives. There is no indeterminacy, and there only seemed to be because it was assumed, incorrectly, that the fundamental mass property would be measured in grams not schmams.

Noting, then, that the fibrous universe may be adapted to a tube-based Whiteheadian account I shall, for the sake of exposition, consider fibers rather than tubes and suppose that familiar objects, including our bodies, extend across these fibers. If the neighboring universe-fibers differ just a little, then there is some indeterminacy in what happens to an object. Consider the famous Two Slit thought experiment, in which an electron is fired at a screen with two slits in it without the quantum state being able to specify which slit it went through. If we say that in one fiber one electron-part goes through one slit and in another fiber another electron-part through the other slit, then it is *as if* it is indeterminate which slit the while electron (extended across the fibers) goes through. This is a harmless quasi-indeterminacy due to the failure to distinguish fibers. Rather than say there is no fact of the matter we should say that there is a more complicated fact of the matter than we first supposed.

The fibrous universe hypothesis provides us with a modification of the Tree of Life. Call this the Pruned Dividing Bundle hypothesis. For a bundle of fibers can undergo fission into sub-bundles without any one fiber undergoing fission. (See Fig. 38.3.) If we observers extend across a bundle of universe-fibers and we observe whether or not something has occurred, then the bundle will divide into those fibers in which it has occurred and those in which it has not. Hence our minds would divide also, because in one bundle we observed one thing but in another the other. Given enough different results of observations, we would be forced to say that we do not just have a divided mind but have undergone fission. But that is contrary to the assumption being made in this paper that we survive without fission. Therefore we need something like pruning.

5. Three Fibrous Universe Theories

I am now going to a suppose that some version of the Many Worlds hypothesis holds, so that

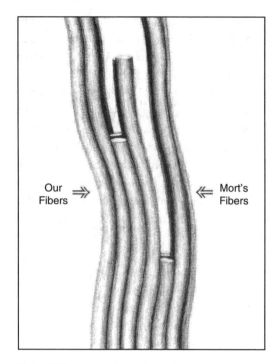

Figure 38.3

there is a fibrous Universe, and consider three versions of the Dividing Bundle hypothesis. In all three the Universe is made up of fibers that do not undergo fission. Nonetheless, being a bundle of fibers, it can undergo fission by means of the separation of the fibers into two or more sub-bundles. Without something like pruning we would have repeated fission of all of us each minute, and not merely the survival of death but over-survival. On the Pruned Dividing Bundle version whole sub-bundles are pruned, as in Fig. 38.3, where, however, the immense number of fibers cannot be depicted. That is tantamount to terminating many of the fibers.

When an agent X acts to bring about a situation of type T, then, on this Pruned Dividing Bundle hypothesis, X terminates universe-fibers so that of those that remain and contain X, all or most of them are ones in which a T occurs. I say "or most of them" because we would not notice a little bit of (quasi-) indeterminacy. Likewise when Y observes that a U occurs then either all or most of the fibers that remain and which contain Y are ones in which a U occurs.

Which of the objections to the simple Tree of Life hold for this Pruned Dividing Bundle hypothesis? The Christians' Objection will be dealt with in the Section 7. Here I consider the others. There is no insuperable problem due to spatially separate branches; for even if that was a genuine problem we could solve it by saying that the universe-fibers are packed into a higher dimensional Hyperspace rather than occupying separate spaces. Nor is there any violation of *ex nihilo nihil fit*.

The problem of mass-energy conservation still holds, however. Suppose we do not hold the total energy of the universe to be zero. Then terminating universe-fibers violate energy conservation. In any case there is an enormous intuitive difference between short-lived branches of a branching universe and the termination of universe-fibers which have existed from the beginning of the Universe and which are much like most people have thought of the whole Universe. No doubt God has the power to annihilate them, but I have glibly suggested that human beings annihilate them too. Thus if I scratch an itchy toe I have just annihilated half the Universe. Talk of delusions of grandeur! Surely this is crazy. The problem of what happens to the energy is, then, just one, rather minor, aspect of a more general problem, the counter-intuitive character of universe-fiber annihilation.

For fellow friends of zombies, I now present the Zombie Diving Bundle hypothesis in which the universe-fibers that are to be "pruned" are not annihilated so much as bezombied (Fig. 38.4). If there is no consciousness in these fibers, then they are as good as annihilated. This avoids any problems with conservation of energy, and agency is now just a matter of consciousness retreating away from the unwanted fibers, not massive annihilation.

Many will not only find the termination of fibers counter-intuitive but also dismiss zombification. For them I suggest a variant on which

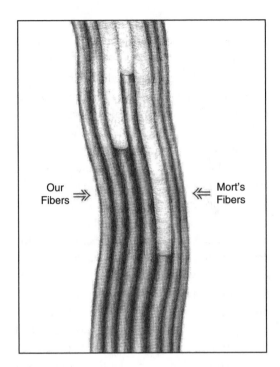

Figure 38.4

therefore, have to terminate in order to provide scope for action. All that is required for the agent to bring about a situation of type T is for the agent to "squeeze" the bundle of fibers in which a T does not occur and allow the corresponding expansion of the bundle in which a T does occur. That is, the action increases the volume of fibers in which a T occurs and decreases the volume in which T does not occur, keeping the total volume constant. Note that in this case the result will never be 100 percent determinate that T occurs, while if fibers are terminated or bezombied total determinacy can occur.

On the Squeeze hypothesis agency does not terminate fibers that have existed from the beginning. Agency, and observation, merely contract or expand the region of Hyperspace these fibers take up. If we picture Hyperspace as a Euclidean plane (so the volume is represented by area,) with time as a third dimension, then we could picture the universe-fibers as curves in the resulting three-dimensional space and it is easy to think of some curves coming closer together so as to occupy less volume while others grow further apart to occupy more.

This Squeeze hypothesis requires that the volume be a suitable measure of indeterminacy and hence be related systematically to the frequencies of types of observation, in such a way that relative frequencies tend to approximate the ratios of the volumes. Thus, if a beam of electrons passes through the twin slits, the relative frequency of detections in a given region R of the screen should approximate the ratio of: (a) the volume of the mereological sum of the universe tubes in which the electron hits R; to (b) the volume of the mereological sum of the universe tubes in which the electron hits the screen somewhere. Because of the need to posit this systematic connection between the expected frequencies and the volume, we might, on reflection, prefer the first two versions of the Dividing Bundle hypothesis to the Squeeze hypothesis.

fibers are neither annihilated nor bezombied, so it is not as if the bundle divides. This is the Squeeze hypothesis. On it we must take the supposition of hyperspace as of more than heuristic significance. The universe-fibers are, I am now supposing, packed into Hyperspace. Perhaps they are packed *densely*, in the sense that every (hyper) ball in Hyperspace, however small, intersects some universe-fiber. This is a consequence of a Whiteheadian account in which the fibers are "constructs" out of smaller and smaller tubes, and so is fairly plausible anyway if we adopt a Whiteheadian account of points and instants as "constructs" out of extended regions and intervals. In that case we may no longer equate the probability of an event of type T with the proportion of fibers in which a T occurs, for there will be infinitely many in which T occurs and infinitely many in which T does not occur. Rather, we should compare the volume occupied by the fibers in which T occurs with the volume occupied in which T does not occur. The fibers do not,

6. Zombies to the Rescue!

Any hypothesis that implies that for all we know most or all of those around us now are zombies should, I say, be rejected, as contrary to the pre-suppositions of morality. This is the *reductio ad zombidum*. Nonetheless we should not dismiss them too swiftly. For if the past but not the future is real then there is a strong case for saying the past is inhabited by zombies, so we need to posit them anyway. The case is that otherwise we cannot reply to the somewhat similar objections made by David Lewis (in conversation with John Bigelow) by Craig Bourne, by David Braddon-Mitchell, and by Trenton Merricks.[9] If the past is real, Lewis asks us to spare a thought for poor old Bonaparte suffering from the delusion that it was still early in the nineteenth century, and then asked how we are justified in our belief that we are not similarly deluded because the present might have already advanced to the year 2500 leaving us stranded in the past! His solution was to adopt the token-reflexive account of the present. Presentists solve the problem by denying Bonaparte any reality. But we Growing Block theorists take the present as an ontologically significant boundary between the actual past and the many merely possible futures. We should, therefore, take the past as zombie-land in order to avoid the Deluded Bonaparte objection.[10]

Likewise those who are realists about possible worlds but reject Lewis's token-reflexive account of actuality should take counterpart human beings in other possible worlds to be zombies. On the Zombie Dividing Bundle hypothesis we may take the bezombied fibers as mere might-have-beens, which have achieved a status like the past without ever having been actually present.

7. Mort's Fate

On the proposed Fibrous Universe variants on the Tree of Life there are three different ways of surviving death. First, as in Fig. 38.3 or Fig. 38.4, there could be a complete separation into a universe-bundle in which Mort lives on and a universe-bundle in which the rest of us live on. Or, secondly, the bundle in which Mort lives on might in fact be a very small part of a larger bundle. Or, thirdly, there could be overlap without Mort's sub-bundle being part of ours. Perhaps in these last two cases Mort would become a ghost, but in any case Mort could have little impact on our world as a whole, being reduced to near epiphenomenal status.

In the last two cases there could be an overlap between all the universe-bundles in which the dead live on their solitary lives and the mainstream Earthly bundle. Hence it might subsequently happen that the universe-fibers in the overlap were the only ones not to be terminated. In that case Mort and everyone else who died would, from the perspective of Earth, come back to life. This provides a model for the Resurrection of Jesus, as well as a general Resurrection of the Dead. After the Crucifixion, the fibers in which Jesus did not die but survived in the tomb were only a minute proportion of the actual ones, but at the Resurrection all the other fibers were terminated. As far as I can see this meets the Christians' objection to the unmodified Tree of Life hypothesis.

8. Is the Fibrous Universe too Complicated?

The fibrous universe seems rather complicated —neither the sort of thing God would create nor the sort of thing we should posit uncreated. It is, to be sure, no more complicated than other Many Worlds interpretations of quantum theory, but we might reject them as well on the grounds of undue complexity.

The fibrous universe might be too complicated to posit uncreated, but it coheres rather better with creation. To argue for this, I first submit that in addition to any non-sensory ways of knowing, God perceives the world, that is, God knows the world in a sensory fashion. For if God knows everything and if what it is like to see red is itself something to know, then God must know what it is like to see red.[11] It would be a strange imperfection if God knew what it was like to see red but lacked the capacity to see something red, and similarly for other perceptions. I infer that God can choose to perceive the world. Granted that we believe that God can choose to perceive the world, it is better not to multiply mysteries by positing Middle Knowledge as God's way of knowing creatures' choices. Instead we should suppose that God knows these choices by perceiving creatures.

I cannot understand how God could perceive the Universe unless Berkeleian idealism is correct and the Universe is made up of perceptions, some human perhaps but most divine. Conversely if, for some reason, the theist is already a Berkeleian idealist then this entails that God perceives.

Regardless of whether it is linked with Idealism in this way, the hypothesis of divine perception has considerable appeal. It is, however, threatened by the Perspectives Dilemma, namely: is divine perception perspectival or not? Perspectival perception such as vision contains as part of its content a spatial relation to the apparent object. For example, in out-of-body experiences things appear as if from a point of view which is in fact outside the body. Now for the dilemma: if the divine perception is not perspectival, then it conveys no knowledge of spatial relations and so is inadequate; but if the divine perception is perspectival, then it must be from a single perspective, otherwise it is non-veridical. For the awareness of A from point of view X and of B from point of view Y will in many cases misrepresent the spatial relation between A and B. Suppose, for instance, that X, A, B, and Y are in a straight line, with XA = 1 cm, AB = 3 cm, and BY = 1 cm. Then A and B seem to be 1 cm away from the perceiver, but both A and B being 1 cm away is incompatible with their being 3 cm apart. And presumably God would not create in such a way as to be subject to non-veridical perception.

The second horn of the Perspectives Dilemma is less sharp than the first. For divine perception could always be veridical provided God is confined to a single point of view. In that case we might even think of God as occupying a point. There are, however, two objections to the hypothesis of a single divine point of view. The first is that it is arbitrary where the divine point of view is. (And maybe in Special Relativity the frame of reference is also arbitrary.) The second is that, it could be said, one point of view is not enough for God to have the perfection of knowing every thing in every way. The only reply to these objections that I can think of is to suppose that God creates a fibrous universe, with every point being the divine point of view in some of the fibers. Given Special Relativity, we may also suppose that the divine point of view is in every frame of reference in some fiber. In passing I note that this reconciles Special Relativity with the idea of absolute time and an absolute present, by taking what is absolute to be that which God is aware of.

The resulting system is one in which God perceives everything in every universe-fiber and occupies every point of view in some fiber, without any arbitrary picking out of just one point of view. It therefore provides a satisfactory blunting of the second horn of the Perspectives Dilemma and hence a defense of the hypothesis that God knows things by perceiving them.

9. Conclusion

The aim of this paper has been to make progress towards the goal of a metaphysical hypothesis that provided scope for agency, survival of death, and the Resurrection, while cohering well with contemporary science. My best attempt at such a hypothesis is based upon the idea that the "worlds" of the Many Worlds interpretation of quantum theory should be thought of as universe-fibers.

Appendix: The Fibrous Universe and Quantum Theory

I have neither the space nor the expertise to expound the various interpretations of quantum theory, with their strengths and weaknesses. All I can do here is to note the sort of interpretation the simple Tree of Life model provides, the sort of interpretation the more complicated Fibrous Universe hypothesis provides, note the advantage of the latter, and leave it at that.

Interpretations of quantum theory answer the following questions:

- *The Structure Question*: What sort of structure do quantum systems and their states have?
- *The Dynamics Question*: What happens when a system evolves without interference?
- *The Measurement Question*: What if anything novel occurs if there is outside interference, in particular during observation?

The Tree of Life model has nothing to say about the Structure Question. Concerning the Dynamics Question it tell us that between branchings the Schrödinger equation or its relativistic analog holds, governing the deterministic evolution of the state of the system. Its answer to the Measurement Question is that observation is one of those occasions in which the system does not evolve deterministically, and, excepting cases of lasting universe-fission, it evolves probabilistically because just one branch survives more than a jiffy. If there are only finitely many branches then it is not surprising that the observed frequencies of an occurrence of type T would approximate the proportion of branches in which a T occurs. It could be queried whether this proportion of branches counts as a genuine probability of a T occurring, but that is no problem for we would not need to hypothesize any probability in addition to these proportions to explain the frequencies. In particular we need not posit irreducible propensities.

As far as it goes that sort of interpretation is entirely satisfactory. But it does not go far enough. The advantage of the Fibrous Universe is that it inherits the Many Worlds Interpretation's capacity to give more detailed answers to the Structure Question and the Dynamics Question. On the Many Worlds Interpretation we try to interpret the state as a probability distribution over various classical states, involving position and momentum of various particles. A well-known difficulty, pointed out by Eugene Wigner, is that the attempt to do so commits us to probabilities less than zero.[12] My preferred response to this is to reinterpret the state not as a probability distribution but in terms of the expected number of particles with given position and momentum.[13] I assume that the "quantum vacuum" is a flux of many short-lived particles so that the quantum state specifies the expected number above par where *par* is what occurs in the "vacuum". Then it is quite consistent to allow some expected values below par, holes in the "vacuum", as it were.

Given this interpretation, what we call a particle does not exist in just the one "world" but involves the distribution of position and momenta of particles in the various "worlds". Hence my preference for saying that we have one brain spread across many fibers rather than one mind corresponding to many brains.

On this interpretation an electron stands to the genuine, often short-lived particles much as an organism stands to its constituents, being a self-perpetuating pattern in the flux. Provided we grant that the "particles" that make us up are themselves constituted by what happens in many "worlds" and provided we grant that there is a probability measure over the "worlds" the further identification of the "worlds" as universe-fibers and the probability measure as a (hyper) volume is not strictly necessary, although it has heuristic value.

A little-known implication of this hypothesis about "particles" is that as Wigner also showed there is an informative answer to the dynamics question. The state evolves just as we would expect if the particles within the "worlds" bounce off each other conserving energy and momentum.[14]

Finally, as regards the Measurement Question, recent work on decoherence by Wojciech Zurek, Roland Omnès, and others suggests, although not conclusively proving,[15] that, when an observation is made of whether or not a T occurs, the state evolves into a good approximation to a mixture of states in one of which a T occurs in 100 percent of the "worlds" and in the other a T occurs in no "worlds". Hence the totality of all the "worlds" undergoes an almost complete fission into a T branch and a not-T branch. Moreover the probability of observing a T is equal to the probability measure of the set of "worlds" in which a T occurs. Without some device for pruning the tree, we would say that the observers underwent fission when an observation was made. The proposed Fibrous Universe hypotheses restore common sense while keeping the solution to the Measurement Question provided by the Many Worlds Interpretation.

The result is that the Fibrous Universe has the benefits of the Many Worlds Interpretation without the absurdity of the fission of observers. It is superior to the unmodified Tree of Life as an interpretation because it is more informative. It should be noted, however, that someone who considered some quite different interpretation of quantum theory to be correct would not be impressed. My response to the unimpressed would be that we should not make up our minds on the interpretation of quantum theory independently of the rest of metaphysics but seek a unified account of everything, including agency. If that inclines us one way rather than another when it comes to interpreting quantum theory, so be it.

Notes

Many thanks to the Pew Charitable Trusts, which funded a conference on *Persons: Human and Divine* held at the Nassau Inn, Princeton, on 8 & 9 February 2004, where I read a version of this paper. Many thanks also to all who participated in that conference, and to Dean Zimmerman for his helpful editorial comments. Finally I would like to thank Fiona Utley for drawing the diagrams.

1 Huw Price, *Time's Arrow & Archimedes Point: New Directions for the Physics of Time* (Oxford: Oxford University Press, 1996), ch. 9: David Lewis in his 2002 Jack Smart lecture, "How Many Lives has Schrödinger's Cat?" subsequently published in the *Australasian Journal of Philosophy*, 82 (2004), 3–22. David Lewis refers to Peter J. Lewis's paper, "What is it like to be Schrödinger's cat?", *Analysis*, 60 (2000), 22–9, as making the same sort of point. Peter Lewis, however, is relying on the Many Minds Interpretation of John Lockwood, in which many minds are posited. See John Lockwood, *Mind, Brain and Quantum* (Oxford: Blackwell, 1989).

2 There are two assumptions being made here. The first is that the vagueness of the time of death is not an issue, so we may ignore the point that the "corpse" might be not quite dead for a short while. The second is that "corpsism" is incorrect, where corpsism is the thesis that an animal is an enduring thing that survives death as a corpse, until the corpse disintegrates. Corpsism has been discussed but only as part of a *tu quoque* response to an argument for animalism. See Eric T. Olson, "Animalism and the Corpse Problem", *Australasian Journal of Philosophy*, 82 (2004), 265–74.

3 See Peter van Inwagen, "The Possibility of Resurrection", in Paul Edwards (ed.), *Immortality* (New York: Macmillan, 1992), 242–6, repr. from the *International Journal for the Philosophy of Religion*, 9 (1978).

4 Storrs McCall, *A Model of the Universe* (Oxford: Clarendon Press), 1994.

5 For convenience I am assuming that the only animals who are persons are human beings. Animals that are not persons might well have a will to survive but I doubt that they have a will not to undergo fission.

6 Peter Geach, *Providence and Evil* (Cambridge: Cambridge University Press, 1977), 141–3.

7 Edward P. Tryon, "Is the Universe a Vacuum Fluctuation?", *Nature*, 246/5433 (1990), 396–7, repr.

in John Leslie (ed.), *Physical Cosmology and Philosophy* (New York: Macmillan).

8 B. S. De Witt, "Quantum Mechanics and Reality", *Physics Today*, 23 (1970), 30–5; Hugh Everett, " 'Relative State' Formulation of Quantum Mechanics", *Review of Modern Physics*, 29 (1957), 452–64; David Deutsch, *The Fabric of Reality: The Science of Parallel Universes and its Implications* (New York: Penguin USA, 1997).

9 Craig Bourne, "When am I? A Tense Time for some Tense Theorists?" *Australasian Journal of Philosophy*, 80/3 (2002), 359–71; David Braddon-Mitchell, "How do We Know it is Now Now?" *Analysis*, 64/3 (2004), 199–202; Trenton Merricks, "Goodbye Growing Block", in D. W. Zimmerman (ed.), *Oxford Studies in Metaphysics*, ii (Oxford: Oxford University Press, 2006).

10 For some further details see my "The Real but Dead Past: A Reply to Braddon-Mitchell", *Analysis*, 64/4 (2004). Quentin Smith reaches a somewhat similar conclusion in *Language and Time* (New York: Oxford University Press, 1993), ch. 5.

11 Frank Jackson's Mary Argument depends on the premise that what it is like to see red is itself something that can be known. See Frank Jackson, "Epiphenomenal Qualia", *Philosophical Quarterly*, 32 (1982), 127–36.

12 Eugene Wigner, "On the Quantum Correction for Thermodynamic Equilibrium", *Physical Review*, 40 (1932), 749–59, repr. in Y. S. Kim and M. E. Noz, *Phase Space Picture of Quantum Mechanics: Group Theoretical Approach* (Singapore: World Scientific, 1991), 219–31.

13 See my "Common Sense and a 'Wigner-Dirac' Approach to Quantum Mechanics". *The Monist*, 89 (1997), 131–59; and my "In Defence of the Phase Space Picture", *Synthese*, 119 (1999), 299–311.

14 Kim and Noz, *Phase Space Picture of Quantum Mechanics*, 224.

15 Wojciech Zurek, "Decoherence and the Transition from Quantum to Classical", *Physics Today*, 44 (1991), 36–44; and Roland Omnès, *Understanding Quantum Mechanics* (Princeton: Princeton University Press, 1999).

Chapter 39

David Lewis

A PHILOSOPHER'S PARADISE

1 The Thesis of Plurality of Worlds

The world we live in is a very inclusive thing. Every stick and every stone you have ever seen is part of it. And so are you and I. And so are the planet Earth, the solar system, the entire Milky Way, the remote galaxies we see through telescopes, and (if there are such things) all the bits of empty space between the stars and galaxies. There is nothing so far away from us as not to be part of our world. Anything at any distance at all is to be included. Likewise the world is inclusive in time. No long-gone ancient Romans, no long-gone pterodactyls, no long-gone primordial clouds of plasma are too far in the past, nor are the dead dark stars too far in the future, to be part of this same world. Maybe, as I myself think, the world is a big physical object; or maybe some parts of it are entelechies or spirits or auras or deities or other things unknown to physics. But nothing is so alien in kind as not to be part of our world, provided only that it does exist at some distance and direction from here, or at some time before or after or simultaneous with now.

The way things are, at its most inclusive, means the way this entire world is. But things might have been different, in ever so many ways. This book of mine might have been finished on schedule. Or, had I not been such a commonsensical chap, I might be defending not only a plurality of possible worlds, but also a plurality of impossible worlds, whereof you speak truly by contradicting yourself. Or I might not have existed at all – neither I myself, nor any counterpart of me. Or there might never have been any people. Or the physical constants might have had somewhat different values, incompatible with the emergence of life. Or there might have been altogether different laws of nature; and instead of electrons and quarks, there might have been alien particles, without charge or mass or spin but with alien physical properties that nothing in this world shares. There are ever so many ways that a world might be; and one of these many ways is the way that this world is.

Are there other worlds that are other ways? I say there are. I advocate a thesis of plurality of worlds, or *modal realism*,[1] which holds that our world is but one world among many. There are countless other worlds, other very inclusive things. Our world consists of us and all our surroundings, however remote in time and space; just as it is one big thing having lesser things as parts, so likewise do other worlds have lesser other-worldly things as parts. The worlds are something like remote planets; except that most of them are much bigger than mere planets, and they are not remote. Neither are they nearby. They are not at any spatial distance whatever from here. They are not far in the past or future, nor for that matter near; they are not at any temporal distance whatever from now. They are isolated: there are no spatiotemporal relations at all between things that belong to different worlds. Nor does anything that happens at one world cause anything to happen at another. Nor do they overlap; they have no parts in common, with the exception, perhaps, of immanent universals exercising their characteristic privilege of repeated occurrence.

The worlds are many and varied. There are enough of them to afford worlds where (roughly speaking) I finish on schedule, or I write on behalf of *impossibilia*, or I do not exist, or there are no people at all, or the physical constants do not permit life, or totally different laws govern the doings of alien particles with alien properties. There are so many other worlds, in fact, that absolutely *every* way that a world could possibly be is a way that some world *is*. And as with worlds, so it is with parts of worlds. There are ever so many ways that a part of a world could be; and so many and so varied are the other worlds that absolutely every way that a part of a world could possibly be is a way that some part of some world is.

The other worlds are of a kind with this world of ours. To be sure, there are differences of kind between things that are parts of different worlds – one world has electrons and another has none, one has spirits and another has none – but these differences of kind are no more than sometimes arise between things that are parts of one single world, for instance in a world where electrons coexist with spirits. The difference between this and the other worlds is not a categorial difference.

Nor does this world differ from the others in its manner of existing. I do not have the slightest idea what a difference in manner of existing is supposed to be. Some things exist here on earth, other things exist extraterrestrially, perhaps some exist no place in particular; but that is no difference in manner of existing, merely a difference in location or lack of it between things that exist. Likewise some things exist here at our world, others exist at other worlds; again, I take this to be a difference between things that exist,

not a difference in their existing. You might say that strictly speaking, only this-worldly things *really* exist; and I am ready enough to agree; but on my view this 'strict' speaking is *restricted* speaking, on a par with saying that all the beer is in the fridge and ignoring most of all the beer there is. When we quantify over less than all there is, we leave out things that (unrestrictedly speaking) exist *simpliciter*. If I am right, other-worldly things exist *simpliciter*, though often it is very sensible to ignore them and quantify restrictedly over our worldmates. And if I am wrong, other-worldly things fail *simpliciter* to exist. They exist, as the Russell set does, only according to a false theory. That is not to exist in some inferior manner – what exists only according to some false theory just does not exist at all.

The worlds are not of our own making. It may happen that one part of a world makes other parts, as we do; and as other-worldly gods and demiurges do on a grander scale. But if worlds are causally isolated, nothing outside a world ever makes a world; and nothing inside makes the whole of a world, for that would be an impossible kind of self-causation. We make languages and concepts and descriptions and imaginary representations that apply to worlds. We make stipulations that select some worlds rather than others for our attention. Some of us even make assertions to the effect that other worlds exist. But none of these things we make are the worlds themselves.

Why believe in a plurality of worlds? – Because the hypothesis is serviceable, and that is a reason to think that it is true. The familiar analysis of necessity as truth at all possible worlds was only the beginning. In the last two decades, philosophers have offered a great many more analyses that make reference to possible worlds, or to possible individuals that inhabit possible worlds. I find that record most impressive. I think it is clear that talk of *possibilia* has clarified questions in many parts of the philosophy of logic, of mind, of language, and of science – not to mention metaphysics itself. Even those who officially scoff often cannot resist the temptation to help themselves abashedly to this useful way of speaking.

Hilbert called the set-theoretical universe a paradise for mathematicians. And he was right (though perhaps it was not he who should have said it). We have only to believe in the vast hierarchy of sets, and there we find entities suited to meet the needs of all the branches of mathematics;[2] and we find that the very meagre primitive vocabulary of set theory, definitionally extended, suffices to meet our needs for mathematical predicates; and we find that the meagre axioms of set theory are first principles enough to yield the theorems that are the content of the subject. Set theory offers the mathematician great economy of primitives and premises, in return for accepting rather a lot of entities unknown to *Homo javanensis*. It offers an improvement in what Quine calls ideology, paid for in the coin of ontology. It's an offer you can't refuse. The price is right; the benefits in theoretical unity and economy are well worth the entities. Philosophers might like to see the subject reconstructed or reconstrued; but working mathematicians insist on pursuing their subject in paradise, and will not be driven out. Their thesis of plurality of sets is fruitful; that gives them good reason to believe that it is true.

Good reason; I do not say it is conclusive. Maybe the price is higher than it seems because set theory has unacceptable hidden implications – maybe the next round of set-theoretical paradoxes will soon be upon us. Maybe the very idea of accepting controversial ontology for the sake of theoretical benefits is misguided – so a sceptical epistemologist might say, to which I reply that mathematics is better known than any premise of sceptical epistemology. Or perhaps some better paradise might be found. Some say that mathematics might be pursued in a paradise of *possibilia*, full of unactualised idealisations of things around us, or of things we do – if so, the parallel with mathematics serves my purpose

better than ever! Conceivably we might find some way to accept set theory, just as is and just as nice a home for mathematics, without any ontological commitment to sets. But even if such hopes come true, my point remains. It has been the judgement of mathematicians, which modest philosophers ought to respect, that if that is indeed the choice before us, then it is worth believing in vast realms of controversial entities for the sake of enough benefit in unity and economy of theory.

As the realm of sets is for mathematicians, so logical space is a paradise for philosophers. We have only to believe in the vast realm of *possibilia*, and there we find what we need to advance our endeavours. We find the wherewithal to reduce the diversity of notions we must accept as primitive, and thereby to improve the unity and economy of the theory that is our professional concern – total theory, the whole of what we take to be true. What price paradise? If we want the theoretical benefits that talk of *possibilia* brings, the most straightforward way to gain honest title to them is to accept such talk as the literal truth. It is my view that the price is right, if less spectacularly so than in the mathematical parallel. The benefits are worth their ontological cost. Modal realism is fruitful; that gives us good reason to believe that it is true.

Good reason; I do not say it is conclusive. Maybe the theoretical benefits to be gained are illusory, because the analyses that use *possibilia* do not succeed on their own terms. Maybe the price is higher than it seems, because modal realism has unacceptable hidden implications. Maybe the price is *not* right; even if I am right about what theoretical benefits can be had for what ontological cost, maybe those benefits just are not worth those costs. Maybe the very idea of accepting controversial ontology for the sake of theoretical benefits is misguided. Maybe – and this is the doubt that most interests me – the benefits are not worth the cost, because they can be had more cheaply elsewhere. Some of these doubts are too complicated to address here, or too simple to address at all; others will come in for discussion in the course of this book.

2   Modal Realism at Work: Modality

In the next four sections [of *On the Plurality of Words*], I consider what possible worlds and individuals are good for. Even a long discussion might be too short to convince all readers that the applications I have in mind are workable at all, still less that approaches employing *possibilia* are superior to all conceivable rivals. (Still less that *possibilia* are absolutely indispensable, something I don't believe myself.) Each application could have a book of its own. Here I shall settle for less.

The best known application is to modality. Presumably, whatever it may mean to call a world actual (see section 9), it had better turn out that the world we are part of is the actual world. What actually is the case, as we say, is what goes on here. That is one possible way for a world to be. Other worlds are other, that is unactualised, possibilities. If there are many worlds, and every way that a world could possibly be is a way that some world is, then whenever such-and-such might be the case, there is some world where such-and-such is the case. Conversely, since it is safe to say that no world is any way that a world could not possibly be, whenever there is some world at which such-and-such is the case, then it might be that such-and-such is the case. So modality turns into quantification: possibly there are blue swans iff, for some world W, at W there are blue swans.

But not just quantification: there is also the phrase 'at W' which appears within the scope of the quantifier, and which needs explaining. It works mainly by restricting the domains of quantifiers in its scope, in much the same way that the restricting modifier 'in Australia' does. In Australia, all swans are black – all swans are indeed black, if we ignore everything not in Australia; quantifying only over things in Australia, all swans are black. At some strange world W, all swans are blue – all swans are indeed blue,

if we ignore everything not part of the world W; quantifying only over things that are part of W, all swans are blue.

Such modifiers have various other effects. For one thing, they influence the interpretation of expressions that are not explicitly quantificational, but that reveal implicit quantification under analysis: definite descriptions and singular terms definable by them, class abstracts and plurals, superlatives, etc. An example: it is the case at world W that nine numbers the solar planets iff nine numbers those solar planets that are part of W. Another example: words like 'invent' and 'discover' are implicitly superlative, hence implicitly quantificational; they imply doing something *first*, before *anyone* else did. So the inventor of bifocals at W is the one who is part of W and thought of bifocals before anyone else who is part of W did. For another thing, besides restricting explicit or implicit quantifiers, our modifiers can restrict proper names. In Australia, and likewise at a possible world where the counterparts of British cities are strangely rearranged, Cardiff is a suburb of Newcastle – there are various places of those names, and we banish ambiguity by restricting our attention to the proper domain. Here I am supposing that the way we bestow names attaches them not only to this-worldly things, but also to other-worldly counterparts thereof. That is how the other-worldly Cardiffs and Newcastles bear those names in our this-worldly language. In the same way, the solar planets at W are those that orbit the star Sol of the world W, a counterpart of the Sol of this world. Natural language being complex, doubtless I have not listed all the effects of our modifiers. But I believe the principle will always stay the same: whatever they do, they do it by instructing us, within limits, to take account only of things that are part of a limited domain – the domain of things in Australia, or the domain of parts of a certain world.

Two qualifications concerning our restrictive modifiers. (1) I do not suppose that they must restrict all quantifiers in their scope, without exception. 'In Australia, there is a yacht faster than any other' would mean less than it does if the modifier restricted both quantifiers rather than just the first. 'Nowadays there are rulers more dangerous than any ancient Roman' would be trivialised if we ignored those ancient Romans who are not alive nowadays. 'At some small worlds, there is a natural number too big to measure any class of individuals' can be true even if the large number that makes it true is no part of the small world. (2) Of course there will usually be other restrictions as well; doubtless we are already ignoring various immigrant swans and their descendants, and also whatever freak or painted swans there may be in Australia or among the parts of world W, so our modifier 'in Australia' or 'at W' adds more restrictions to the ones already in force. In short, while our modifiers tend to impose restrictions on quantifiers, names, etc., a lot is left up to the pragmatic rule that what is said should be interpreted so as to be sensible. If that means adding extra tacit restrictions, or waiving some of the restrictions imposed by our modifiers, then – within limits – so be it.[3]

As possibility amounts to existential quantification over the worlds, with restricting modifiers inside the quantifiers, so necessity amounts to universal quantification. Necessarily all swans are birds iff, for any world W, quantifying only over parts of W, all swans are birds. More simply: iff all swans, no matter what world they are part of, are birds. The other modalities follow suit. What is impossible is the case at no worlds; what is contingent is the case at some but not at others.

More often than not, modality is *restricted* quantification; and restricted from the standpoint of a given world, perhaps ours, by means of so-called 'accessibility' relations. Thus it is nomologically necessary, though not unrestrictedly necessary, that friction produces heat: at every world that obeys the laws of our world, friction produces heat. It is contingent which world is ours; hence what are the laws of our world; hence which worlds are nomologically

'accessible' from ours; hence what is true throughout these worlds, i.e. what is nomologically necessary.

Likewise it is historically necessary, now as I write these words, that my book is at least partly written: at every world that perfectly matches ours up to now, and diverges only later if ever, the book is at least partly written.

Putting together nomological and historical accessibility restrictions, we get the proper treatment of predetermination – a definition free of red herrings about what can in principle be known and computed, or about the analysis of causation. It was predetermined at his creation that Adam would sin iff he does so at every world that both obeys the laws of our world and perfectly matches the history of our world up through the moment of Adam's creation.

As other worlds are alternative possibilities for an entire world, so the parts of other worlds are alternative possibilities for lesser individuals. Modality *de re*, the potentiality and essence of things, is quantification over possible individuals. As quantification over possible worlds is commonly restricted by accessibility relations, so quantification over possible individuals is commonly restricted by counterpart relations. In both cases, the restrictive relations usually involve similarity. A nomologically or historically accessible world is similar to our world in the laws it obeys, or in its history up to some time. Likewise a counterpart of Oxford is similar to Oxford in its origins, or in its location vis-à-vis (counterparts of) other places, or in the arrangement and nature of its parts, or in the role it plays in the life of a nation or a discipline. Thus Oxford might be noted more for the manufacture of locomotives than of motor cars, or might have been a famous centre for the study of paraconsistent hermeneutics, iff some other-worldly counterpart of our Oxford, under some suitable counterpart relation, enjoys these distinctions.

Sometimes one hears a short list of the restricted modalities: nomological, historical, epistemic, deontic, maybe one or two more. And sometimes one is expected to take a position, once and for all, about what is or isn't possible *de re* for an individual. I would suggest instead that the restricting of modalities by accessibility or counterpart relations, like the restricting of quantifiers generally, is a very fluid sort of affair: inconstant, somewhat indeterminate, and subject to instant change in response to contextual pressures. Not anything goes, but a great deal does. And to a substantial extent, saying so makes it so: if you say what would only be true under certain restrictions, and your conversational partners acquiesce, straightway those restrictions came into force.[4]

The standard language of modal logic provides just two modal expressions: the diamond, read as "possibly", and the box, read as "necessarily". Both are sentential operators: they attach to sentences to make sentences, or to open formulas to make open formulas. So a modal logician will write

◇ for some x, x is a swan and x is blue

to mean that possibly some swan is blue, i.e. that there might be a blue swan; or

□ for all x, if x is a swan then x is a bird

to mean that necessarily all swans are birds. Likewise

◇ x is blue

is a formula satisfied by anything that could possibly be blue, and

□ x is a bird

is a formula satisfied by anything that must necessarily be a bird. When they attach to sentences we can take the diamond and the box as quantifiers, often restricted, over possible worlds. How to take them when they attach to open

formulas – sentential expressions with unbound variables – is more questionable.

A simple account would be that in that case also they are just quantifiers over worlds. But that raises a question. Start with something that is part of this world: Hubert Humphrey, say. He might have won the presidency but didn't, so he satisfies the modal formula 'possibly x wins' but not the formula 'x wins'. Taking the diamond 'possibly' as a quantifier over worlds, (perhaps restricted, but let me ignore that), that means that there is some world W such that, at W, he satisfies 'x wins'. But how does he do that if he isn't even part of W?

You might reply that he *is* part of W as well as part of this world. If this means that the whole of him is part of W, I reject that for reasons to be given in section 4.2 [of *On The Plurality of Worlds*, not reproduced here]; if it means that part of him is part of W, I reject that for reasons to be given in section 4.3. Then to save the simple account, we have to say that Humphrey needn't be part of a world to satisfy formulas there; there is a world where somehow he satisfies 'x wins' *in absentia*.

We might prefer a more complex account of how modal operators work.[5] We might say that when 'possibly' is attached to open formulas, it is a quantifier not just over worlds but also over other-worldly counterparts of this-worldly individuals; so that Humphrey satisfies 'possibly x wins' iff, for some world W, for some counterpart of Humphrey in W, that counterpart satisfies 'x wins' at W. The satisfaction of 'x wins' by the counterpart is unproblematic. Now we need no satisfaction *in absentia*.

The simple and complex accounts are not in competition. Both do equally well, because there is a counterpart-theoretic account of satisfaction *in absentia* that makes them come out equivalent. Satisfaction *in absentia* is vicarious satisfaction: Humphrey satisfies 'x wins' vicariously at any world where he has a winning counterpart. Then according to both accounts alike, he satisfies 'possibly x wins' iff at some world he has a counterpart who wins.

The box and diamond are interdefinable: 'necessarily' means 'not possibly not'. So what I have said for one carries over to the other. According to the simple account, Humphrey satisfies the modal formula 'necessarily x is human' iff it is not the case that there is some world W such that, at W, he satisfies 'x is not human'; that is, iff at no world does he satisfy – in *absentia* or otherwise – 'x is not human'. According to the complex account, Humphrey satisfies 'necessarily x is human' iff it is not the case that for some world W, for some counterpart of Humphrey in W, that counterpart satisfies 'x is not human' at W; that is, iff there is no counterpart in any world of Humphrey who satisfies 'x is not human'. Taking satisfaction *in absentia* to be vicarious satisfaction through a counterpart, the simple and complex accounts again agree: Humphrey satisfies 'necessarily x is human' iff he has no non-human counterpart at any world.

(It is plausible enough that Humphrey has no non-human counterpart. Or, if I am right to say that counterpart relations are an inconstant and indeterminate affair, at any rate it is plausible enough that there is *some* reasonable counterpart relation under which Humphrey has no non-human counterpart – so let's fix on such a counterpart relation for the sake of the example.)

The alert or informed reader will know that if what I've said about how Humphrey satisfies modal formulas sounds right, that is only because I took care to pick the right examples. A famous problem arises if instead we consider whether Humphrey satisfies modal formulas having to do with the contingency of his existence. According to what I've said, be it in the simple or the complex formulation, Humphrey satisfies 'necessarily x exists' and fails to satisfy 'possibly x does not exist' iff he has no counterpart at any world W who does not exist at W. But what can it mean to say that the counterpart is 'at W' if not that, at W, the counterpart exists?[6] So it seems that Humphrey *does* satisfy 'necessar-

ily x exists' and *doesn't* satisfy 'possibly x does not exist'. That is wrong. For all his virtues, still it really will not do to elevate Humphrey to the ranks of the Necessary Beings.

What I want to say, of course, is that Humphrey exists necessarily iff at every world he has some counterpart, which he doesn't; he has the possibility of not existing iff at some world he lacks a counterpart, which he does. It's all very well to say this; but the problem is to square it with my general account of the satisfaction of modal formulas.

So shall we give a revised account of the satisfaction of modal formulas? Should we say that Humphrey satisfies 'necessarily ϕx' iff at every world he has some counterpart who satisfies 'ϕx'? Then, by the interdefinability of box and diamond, Humphrey satisfies 'possibly x is a cat' iff it is not the case that at every world he has some counterpart who satisfies 'not x is a cat'; and indeed that is not the case, since at some worlds he has no counterparts at all; so it seems that he *does* satisfy 'possibly x is a cat' even if he has not a single cat among his counterparts! This is no improvement. What next?

Shall we dump the method of counterparts? – That wouldn't help, because we can recreate the problem in a far more neutral framework. Let us suppose only this much. (1) We want to treat the modal operators simply as quantifiers over worlds. (2) We want to grant that Humphrey somehow satisfies various formulas at various other worlds, never mind how he does it. (3) We want it to come out that he satisfies the modal formula 'necessarily x is human', since that seems to be the way to say something true, namely that he is essentially human. (4) We want it to come out that he satisfies the modal formula 'possibly x does not exist', since that seems to be the way to say something else true, namely that he might not have existed. (5) We want it to come out that he does *not* satisfy the model formula 'possibly x is human and x does not exist' since that seems to be the way to say something false, namely that he might have been human without even existing. So he satisfies 'x is human' at all words and 'x does not exist' at some worlds; so he satisfies both of them at some worlds; yet though he satisfies both conjuncts he doesn't satisfy their conjunction! How can that be?

There might be a fallacy of equivocation. Maybe what it means for Humphrey to satisfy a formula in *absentia* is different in the case of different kinds of formulas, or in the case of different kinds of worlds. Maybe, for instance, he can satisfy 'x does not exist' at a world by not having a counterpart there; but to satisfy 'x is human' at a world he has to have a counterpart there who is human, and to satisfy 'x is human and x does not exist' he would have to have one who was human and yet did not exist. Or maybe the language is uniformly ambiguous, and different cases invite different disambiguations. Either way, that would disappoint anyone who hopes that the language of quantified modal logic will be a well-behaved formal language, free of ambiguity and free of devious semantic rules that work different ways in different cases.

Or maybe the satisfying of modal formulas does not always mean what we would intuitively take it to mean after we learn how to pronounce the box and diamond. Maybe, for instance, saying that Humphrey satisfies 'necessarily x is human' is *not* the right way to say that he is essentially human. That would disappoint anyone who hopes that the language of boxes and diamonds affords a good regimentation of our ordinary modal thought.

Whichever it is, the friend of boxes and diamonds is in for a disappointment. He can pick his disappointment to suit himself. He can lay down uniform and unambiguous semantic rules for a regimented formal language – and re-educate his intuitions about how to translate between that language and ordinary modal talk. He can discipline himself, for instance, never to say 'necessarily human' when he means 'essentially human'; but instead, always to say

'necessarily such that it is human if it exists'. Alternatively, he can build his language more on the pattern of what we ordinarily say – and equip it either with outright ambiguities, or else with devious rules that look at what a formula says before they know what it means to satisfy it.[7]

What is the correct counterpart-theoretic interpretation of the modal formulas of the standard language of quantified modal logic? – Who cares? We can make them mean whatever we like. We are their master. We needn't be faithful to the meanings we learned at mother's knee – because we didn't. If this language of boxes and diamonds proves to be a clumsy instrument for talking about matters of essence and potentiality, let it go hang. Use the resources of modal realism *directly* to say what it would mean for Humphrey to be essentially human, or to exist contingently.

In any case, modality is not all diamonds and boxes. Ordinary language has modal idioms that outrun the resources of standard modal logic, though of course you will be able to propose extensions. Allen Hazen mentions several examples of this in his 'Expressive Completeness in Modal Languages'. But let me mention some more.

There is what I take to be numerical quantification: it might happen in three different ways that a donkey talks iff three possible individuals, very different from one another, are donkeys that talk. It scarcely seems possible to cover the entire infinite family of numerical modalities unless we resort to the pre-existing apparatus of numerical quantification. Then we need some entities to be the 'ways' that we quantify over. My candidates are the possible worlds and individuals themselves, or else sets of these.

There are modalised comparatives: a red thing could resemble an orange thing more closely than a red thing could resemble a blue thing. I analyse that as a quantified statement of comparative resemblance involving coloured things which may be parts of different worlds.

For some x and y (x is red and y is orange and
for all u and v (if u is red and v is blue, then
x resembles y more than u resembles v))

Try saying that in standard modal logic. The
problem is that formulas get evaluated relative to
a world, which leaves no room for cross-world
comparisons.

Maybe you can solve the problem if you
replace the original comparative relation '. . .
resembles . . . more than . . . resembles . . .' by
some fancy analysis of it, say in terms of numerical measures of degrees of resemblance and
numerical inequalities of these degrees. After
that, you might be able to do the rest with
boxes and diamonds. The fancy analysis might
be correct. But still, I suggest that your solution
is no fair. For that's not how the English does
it. The English does not introduce degrees of
resemblance. It sticks with the original comparative relation, and modalises it with the auxiliary 'could'. But this 'could' does not behave
like the standard sentence-modifying diamond,
making a sentence which is true if the modified
sentence could be true. I think its effect is to
unrestrict quantifiers which would normally
range over this-worldly things. The moral for me
is that we'd better have other-worldly things to
quantify over. I suppose the moral for a friend of
primitive modality is that he has more on his
plate than he thinks he has: other primitive
modal idioms than just his boxes and diamonds.

Another modal notion which is badly served by
diamonds and boxes is supervenience. The idea
is simple and easy: we have supervenience when
there could be no difference of one sort without
differences of another sort. At least, this *seems*
simple and easy enough; and yet in recent discussions[8] we get an unlovely proliferation of
non-equivalent definitions. Some stick close to
the original idea but seem too weak; others seem
strong enough but out of touch with the original
idea. A useful notion threatens to fade away into
confusion. I offer this diagnosis of the trouble.

There really is just one simple, easy, useful idea.
However, it is unavailable to those who assume
that all modality must come packaged in boxes
and diamonds. Therefore we get a plethora of
unsatisfactory approximations and substitutes.

To see why there is a problem about formu-
lating supervenience theses, we need a few
examples. First, a fairly uncontroversial one. A
dot-matrix picture has global properties – it is
symmetrical, it is cluttered, and whatnot – and
yet all there is to the picture is dots and non-dots
at each point of the matrix. The global properties are nothing but patterns in the dots. They
supervene: no two pictures could differ in their
global properties without differing, somewhere,
in whether there is or isn't a dot.

A second example is more controversial and
interesting. The world has its laws of nature, its
chances and causal relationships; and yet – perhaps! – all there is to the world is its point-by-
point distribution of local qualitative character.
We have a spatiotemporal arrangement of points.
At each point various local intrinsic properties
may be present, instantiated perhaps by the
point itself or perhaps by point-sized bits of matter or of fields that are located there. There may
be properties of mass, charge, quark colour and
flavour, field strength, and the like; and maybe
others besides, if physics as we know it is
inadequate to its descriptive task. Is that all? Are
the laws, chances, and causal relationships nothing but patterns which supervene on this point-
by-point distribution of properties? Could two
worlds differ in their laws without differing,
somehow, somewhere, in local qualitative character? (I discuss this question of 'Humean supervenience', inconclusively, in the Introduction to
my *Philosophical Papers*, volume II.)

A third example. A person has a mental life of
attitudes and experiences and yet – perhaps! –
all there is to him is an arrangement of physical
particles, interacting in accordance with physical laws. Does the mental supervene on the physical? We can distinguish two questions. (1) *Narrow
psychophysical supervenience*: could two people

differ mentally without also themselves differing physically? (2) *Broad* psychophysical supervenience: could two people differ mentally without there being a physical difference somewhere, whether in the people themselves or somewhere in their surroundings? We can also distinguish questions in another way, cross-cutting the distinction of narrow and broad, depending on how restricted a range of possibilities we consider. If we restrict ourselves to worlds that obey the actual laws of nature, then even a dualist might accept some kind of psychophysical supervenience, if he believes in strict laws of psychophysical correlation. If we impose no restriction at all, then even a staunch materialist might reject all kinds of psychophysical supervenience, if he takes materialism to be a contingent truth. If we want to define materialism in terms of psychophysical supervenience, we will have to steer between these extremes.[9]

Supervenience means that there *could* be no difference of the one sort without difference of the other sort. Clearly, this 'could' indicates modality. Without the modality we have nothing of interest. No two dot-for-dot duplicate pictures differ in symmetry; they could not, and that is why symmetry is nothing but a pattern in the arrangement of dots. Maybe also it happens that no two dot-for-dot duplicate pictures differ in their origins. But if so, that just means that a certain sort of coincidence happens not to have occurred; it doesn't mean that the origin of a picture is nothing but a pattern in the arrangement of dots. Dot-for-dot duplicates perfectly well could come from different origins, whether or not they ever actually do.

So we might read the 'could' as a diamond – a modal operator "possibly" which modifies sentences. "There could be no difference of the one sort without difference of the other sort" – read this to mean that it is not the case that, possibly, there are two things which have a difference of the one sort without any difference of the other sort. That is: it is not the case that there is some world W such that, at W, two things have

a difference of the one sort but not the other. That is, taking 'at W' as usual as a restricting modifier: there is no world wherein two things have a difference of the one sort but not the other. Is this an adequate way to formulate supervenience?

Sometimes it is. It will do well enough to state our supervenience theses about dot-matrix pictures. Symmetry (or whatnot) supervenes on the arrangement of the dots iff there is no world wherein two pictures differ in symmetry without differing in their arrangement of dots. It will do also to state narrow psychophysical supervenience: that thesis says that there is no world (or, none within a certain restriction) wherein two people differ mentally without themselves differing physically. So far, so good.

But sometimes the formulation with a diamond is not adequate. We start to hit trouble with the thesis of broad psychophysical supervenience. The idea is that the mental supervenes on the physical; however, the physical pattern that is relevant to a given person's mental life might extend indefinitely far outside that person and into his surroundings. Then the thesis we want says that there could be no mental difference between two people without there being some physical difference, whether intrinsic or extrinsic, between them. Reading the 'could' as a diamond, the thesis becomes this: there is no world (or, none within a certain restriction) wherein two people differ mentally without there being some physical difference, intrinsic or extrinsic, between them. That is not quite right. We have gratuitously limited our attention to physical differences between two people in the same world, and that means ignoring those extrinsic physical differences that only ever arise between people in different worlds. For instance, we ignore the difference there is between two people if one inhabits a Riemannian and the other a Lobachevskian spacetime. So what we have said is not quite what we meant to say, but rather this: there could be no mental differences without some physical difference of *the sort that could arise between people in the same world*. The italicised part is a gratuitous addition. Perhaps it scarcely matters here. For it doesn't seem that the sort of very extrinsic physical difference that could never arise between people in the same world would make much difference to mental life. Nevertheless, insistence on reading the 'could' as a diamond has distorted the intended meaning.

For a case where the distortion is much more serious, take my second example: the supervenience of laws. We wanted to ask whether two worlds could differ in their laws without differing in their distribution of local qualitative character. But if we read the 'could' as a diamond, the thesis in question turns into this: it is not the case that, possibly, two worlds differ in their laws without differing in their distribution of local qualitative character. In other words: there is no world wherein two worlds differ in their laws without differing in their distribution of local qualitative character. That's trivial – there is no world wherein two worlds do anything. At any one world W, there is only the one single world W. The sentential modal operator disastrously restricts the quantification over worlds that lies within its scope. Better to leave it off. But we need *something* modal – the thesis is not just that the one actual world, with its one distribution of local qualitative character, has its one system of laws![10]

What we want is modality, but not the sentential modal operator. The original simple statement of supervenience is the right one, in all cases: there *could* be no difference of the one sort without difference of the other sort. What got us into trouble was to insist on reading 'could' as a diamond. Just as in the case of modalised comparatives, the real effect of the 'could' seems to be to unrestrict quantifiers which would normally range over this-worldly things. Among all the worlds, or among all the things in all the worlds (or less than all, in case there is some restriction), there is no difference of the one sort without difference of the other sort. Whether the things that differ are part of the same world is

neither here nor there. Again the moral is that we'd better have other-worldly things to quantify over – not just a primitive modal modifier of sentences.

When I say that possible worlds help with the analysis of modality, I do not mean that they help with the metalogical 'semantical analysis of modal logic'. Recent interest in possible worlds began there, to be sure. But wrongly. For that job, we need no possible worlds. We need sets of entities which, for heuristic guidance, 'may be regarded as' possible worlds, but which in truth may be anything you please. We are doing mathematics, not metaphysics. Where we need possible worlds, rather, is in applying the results of these metalogical investigations. Metalogical results, by themselves, answer no questions about the logic of modality. They give us conditional answers only: if modal operators can be correctly analysed in so-and-so way, then they obey so-and-so system of modal logic. We must consider whether they may indeed be so analysed; and then we are doing metaphysics, not mathematics.

Once upon a time, there were a number of formal systems of sentential modal logic. (Also of quantified modal logic, but I shall not discuss those further.) Their modal operators, box and diamond, were said to mean 'necessarily' and 'possibly', but were not interpreted as quantifiers over worlds. These systems differed from one another mostly by including or excluding various controversial axioms about iterated modality, most prominently these:

(B) If P, then necessarily possibly P.

(4) If necessarily P, then necessarily necessarily P.

(E) If possibly P, then necessarily possibly P.

It was possible to investigate the deductive interrelations and consequences of various modal principles. For instance, given the plausible further axiom

(T) If P, then possibly P.

and a fairly minimal (but not entirely uncontroversial) basic system K,[11] it turns out that (E) can be deduced from (B) and (4) together, and conversely. But what was not possible was to intuit clearly which of these principles were to be accepted, and why; or even to command a clear view of what was at issue.

At this point it was discovered, by several people at about the same time, that if you interpret the box and diamond as restricted quantifiers over a set of entities 'regarded as possible worlds', then (B), (4), (E), and (T) turn out to correspond to simple conditions on the relation whereby the box and diamond are restricted.[12] We spell this out as follows. A (*relational*) *frame* consists of a non-empty set – call it the set of *indices* – and a binary relation R on the indices. A *valuation* for the language of a system of modal logic over a frame specifies a truth value for every sentence of the language at every index, and does so in conformity to the standard rules for the truth-functional connectives together with the following rules for modal operators:

'Necessarily ϕ' is true at i iff ϕ is true at all j such that iRj.

'Possibly ϕ' is true at i iff ϕ is true at some j such that iRj.

(Here is where we treat the modal operators as restricted quantifiers.) A frame *validates* a sentence iff every valuation over that frame makes that sentence true at every index; and validates a system of modal logic iff it validates every theorem of that system. Given the following correspondence between our axioms and conditions on frames –

(B) corresponds to being symmetric: if iRj, then jRi

(4) corresponds to being transitive: if iRj and jRk, then iRk

(E) corresponds to being 'euclidean': if iRj and iRk, then jRk

(T) corresponds to being reflexive: iRi

it is easy to see that by adding any combination of zero or more axioms to the basic system K, we get a system that is validated by all frames that satisfy the corresponding combination of conditions. Further, every such system is *complete* in the sense that if any sentence is validated by all frames that validate the system, then that sentence already is a theorem of the system. The same is true for a very much longer list of corresponding axioms and conditions. The results can be extended to quantified modal logic, and related results are available for systems weaker than K.

These metalogical investigations seemed to cast light on the status of the controversial axioms. Maybe we didn't yet know whether the axioms were to be accepted, but at least we now knew what was at issue. Old questions could give way to new. Instead of asking the baffling question whether whatever is actual is necessarily possible, we could try asking: is the relation R symmetric?

But in truth the metalogical results, just by themselves, cast no light at all. If the modal operators can be correctly interpreted as quantifiers over the indices of some or other frame, restricted by the relation of that frame, *then* we have found out where to look for illumination about controversial axioms. If not, not. To apply the results, you have to incur a commitment to some substantive analysis of modality. To be sure, you might not have to be a genuine modal realist like me. You might prefer an analysis on which the modal operators are quantifiers over some sort of abstract ersatz worlds – linguistic descriptions, maybe. (If you meant that as a fully general analysis of modality, I would raise several objections; see section 3.2 [of *On the Plurality of Worlds*, not reproduced here]. If you meant it to apply only in certain limited cases, for instance to modal talk about how a chess game might have gone, I would not object at all.) But if the metalogical results are to be at all relevant to modality, *some* quantificational analysis has to be correct. If modal operators were quantifiers over towns restricted by the relation of being connected by rail, that would validate some system or other of modal logic. – So what, since modal operators are nothing of the sort? What good is it to know which misinterpretations would validate a system?

I myself, of course, do think that modal operators are quantifiers over possible worlds; that very often they are restricted; and that the applicable restriction may be different from the standpoint of different worlds, and so may be given by a relation of 'accessibility'. Therefore I do not just think that the indices of frames 'may be regarded as' possible worlds. I think that among all the frames, there are some whose indices *are* the possible worlds; and that among such frames there are some whose relations *do* give the correct restrictions on modal operators (correct for appropriate contexts). So for me, the metalogical results are applicable, because I believe that there exist frames which afford correct interpretations of the modal operators.

Return to an example I mentioned before: it is nomologically necessary that friction produces heat because at every world nomologically accessible from ours – every world that obeys the laws of ours – friction produces heat. Then, indeed, puzzling questions about the logic of iterated nomological necessity turn into more tractable questions about the relation of nomological accessibility. Is it symmetric? Transitive? Euclidean? Reflexive? In other words, is it so that whenever world W_1 obeys the laws of W_0, then also W_0 obeys the laws of W_1? Is it so that whenever W_2 obeys the laws of W_1 which in turn obeys the laws of W_0, then W_2 obeys the laws of W_0? Is it so that whenever W_1 and W_2 both obey the laws of W_0, then they obey each other's laws? Is it so that every world obeys its own laws? – A theory of lawhood can be expected to answer

these questions, and we can see how different theories would answer them differently. (For instance, my own views on lawhood answer all but the last in the negative.) This transformation of questions is helpful indeed. But the help comes from a substantive theory of what nomological necessity is – not from metalogical investigations that keep silent about which frames, if any, afford correct interpretations. It is the substantive theory, not the metalogic, for which we need possible worlds. [. . .]

6 Isolation

I hope that by saying what theoretical purposes it is meant to serve, I have helped to make clear what my thesis of plurality of worlds is. Now I shall address some further questions of formulation and state some further tenets of my position.

A possible world has parts, namely possible individuals. If two things are parts of the same world, I call them *worldmates*.[50] A world is the mereological sum[51] of all the possible individuals that are parts of it, and so are worldmates of one another. It is a maximal sum: anything that is a worldmate of any part of it is itself a part. (This is just a consequence of my denial that worlds overlap.) But not just any sum of parts of worlds is itself a world. It might, of course, be only part of a world. Or it might consist of parts of two or more different worlds; thus it might be spread over logical space, not wholly within any one world, and its parts might not all be worldmates of one another.

What, then, is the difference between a sum of possible individuals that is a possible world, and one that is not? What makes two things worldmates? How are the worlds demarcated one from another? Why don't all the *possibilia* comprise one big world? Or, at the other extreme, why isn't each possible neutrino a little world of its own? In Perry's terminology: what is the unity relation for possible worlds?[52]

I gave part of the answer in my opening section, when I said that nothing is so far away from us in space, or so far in the past or the future, as not to be part of the same world as ourselves. The point seems uncontroversial, and it seems open to generalisation: whenever two possible individuals are spatiotemporally related, they are worldmates. If there is any distance between them – be it great or small, spatial or temporal – they are parts of one single world.

(Better: for any two possible individuals, if every particular part of one is spatiotemporally related to every particular part of the other that is wholly distinct from it, then the two are worldmates. This formulation avoids difficults that might be raised concerning partial spatiotemporal relatedness of trans-world mereological sums; difficulties about multiply located universals; and difficulties about whether we ought to say that overlapping things are spatiotemporally related.)

This is perhaps more controversial than it seems. Didn't I speak, in connection with predetermination, of worlds that diverge? That is, of worlds that are exactly alike up to some time, and differ thereafter? Doesn't that presuppose trans-world comparison of times, simultaneity or succession between events of different worlds? Trans-world spatiotemporal relations between the participants in those events, or the spacetime regions in which they happen?

I think not. Trans-world comparisons, yes; trans-world spatiotemporal relations, no.

Suppose two worlds are exactly alike up to a certain time, and diverge thereafter. I explain it thus. There is an initial segment of one world, and there is an initial segment of the other, which are perfect duplicates. They are maximal such segments: they are not respectively included in two larger initial segments which are also duplicates. There is a correspondence between the parts of these two segments under which the corresponding parts also are duplicates; and under which corresponding parts are related alike spatiotemporally, and as whole to part. Therefore the corresponding parts are excellent counterparts. They are so whether you take a counterpart relation that stresses similarity of intrinsic character, or one that stresses extrinsic match of origins, or even one that stresses historical role. (Except insofar as something that is part of the duplicated region has a historical role lying partly outside that region.) Temporal cross-sections of the worlds, for instance, are excellent counterparts: there are counterpart centuries, or weeks, or seconds. Likewise there are counterpart places: galaxies, planets, towns. So things that are parts of the two worlds may be simultaneous or not, they may be in the same or different towns, they may be near or far from one another, in very natural counterpart-theoretic senses. But these are not genuine spatiotemporal relations across worlds. The only trans-world relations involved are internal relations of similarity; not indeed between the very individuals that are quasi-simultaneous (or whatever) but between larger duplicate parts of the two worlds wherein those individuals are situated.

Suppose you discovered – say, from a well-accredited oracle – that large parts of human history were re-enacted, with interesting variations, in remote galaxies at times in the distant past and future. In speaking of these re-enactments, you would surely introduce counterpart-theoretic comparisons of place and time. You might say that a remarkable event in one of them took place last year in Headington; when you would also say, without any conflict, that it will take place about 6.4×10^{12} years hence, 3.8×10^9 light years away in the general direction of the constellation Centaurus. You should have no greater difficulty in squaring talk about other-worldly goings-on last week in Didcot with my denial that there are any spatiotemporal relations between parts of different worlds.

So we have a sufficient condition: if two things are spatiotemporally related, then they are worldmates. The converse is much more problematic. Yet that is more or less the doctrine that I propose. Putting the two halves together: things are worldmates iff they are spatiotemporally related. A world is unified, then, by the spatiotemporal interrelation of its parts. There are no spatiotemporal relations across the boundary between one world and another; but no matter how we draw a boundary within a world, there will be spatiotemporal relations across it.

A first, and simplest, objection is that a world might possibly consist of two or more completely disconnected spacetimes. (Maybe our world does, if indeed such disconnection is possible.) But whatever way a world might be is a way that some world is; and one world with two disconnected spacetimes is a counterexample against my proposal. Against this objection, I must simply deny the premise. I would rather not; I admit some inclination to agree with it. But it seems to me that it is no central part of our modal thinking, and not a consequence of any interesting general principle about what is possible. So it is negotiable. Given a choice between rejecting the alleged possibility of disconnected spacetimes within a single world and (what I take to be the alternative) resorting to a primitive worldmate relation, I take the former to be more credible.

I cannot give you disconnected spacetimes within a single world; but I can give you some passable substitutes. One big world, spatiotemporally interrelated, might have many different world-like parts. Ex hypothesi these are not complete worlds, but they could seem to be. They might be four-dimensional; they might have no boundaries; there might be little or no causal interaction between them. Indeed, each of these world-like parts of one big world might be a duplicate of some genuinely complete world. There are at least four ways for one big world to contain many world-like parts. Each is a way that a world could be; and so, say I, each is a way that some world is.

(1) The spacetime of the big world might have an extra dimension. The world-like parts might then be spread out along this extra dimension, like a stack of flatlands in three-space.

(2) The world-like parts might share a common spacetime. There might be several populations, interpenetrating without interaction in the single spacetime where all of them live. If so, of course the inhabitants had better not interact with the shape of their spacetime as we do with the shape of ours; else this interaction enables the different populations to interact indirectly with one another.

(3) Time might have the metric structure not of the real line, but rather of many copies of the real line laid, end to end. We would have many different epochs, one after another. Yet each epoch would have infinite duration, no beginning, and no end. Inhabitants of different epochs would be spatiotemporally related, but their separation would be infinite. Or instead there might be infinitely many infinite regions laid out side by side in space; then there would have to be infinite spatial distances between points in different world-like regions.

(4) Or time might have the metric structure of the real line, as we normally suppose. And yet there might be infinitely many world-like epochs one after the other. Each might be of finite duration; but their finitude might be hidden from their inhabitants because, as the end of an epoch approaches, everything speeds up. Suppose that one generation lives and dies in twelve months, the next in six, the next in three, . . . so that infinitely many generations fit into the last two years of their epoch. Similarly, world-like regions of finite diameter might be packed spatially, with shrinkage as things approach the edge.

If you thought, as I did too, that a single world might consist of many more or less isolated world-like parts, how sure can you be that you really had in mind the supposed possibility that I reject? Are you sure that it was an essential part of your thought that the world-like parts were in no way spatiotemporally related? Or might you not have had in mind, rather, one of these substitutes I offer? Or might your thought have been sufficiently lacking in specificity that the substitutes would do it justice?

A second objection concerns spirits, and episodes in the mental lives of spirits, which are traditionally supposed to be outside of space. However sure we are that no such deficient things are worldmates of ours, is it not at least possible that the traditional story might be true? If so, then some world is populated by such spirits. But that is no objection. I do not say that all worlds are unified by spatiotemporal interrelatedness in just the same way. So the interrelation of a world of spirits might be looser than that of a decent world like ours. If the spirits and their doings are located in time alone, that is good enough. (To make sense of that, maybe time and space would have to be more separable at the world of the spirits than they are at our world; but that is surely possible.) I can even allow marvellous Spirits who are spatiotemporally related to other things by being omnipresent – for that is one way among others to stand in spatiotemporal relations. I am not sure why I need to defend the possibility of spirit tales – after all, people have been known to accept impossible theories, as witness naive set theory – but in fact I think I give them at least as much room in logical space as they deserve.

A third objection concerns the possibility that there might be nothing, and not rather something. If a world is a maximal mereological sum of spatiotemporally interrelated things, that makes no provision for an absolutely empty world. A world is not like a bottle that might hold no beer. The world is the totality of things it contains, so even if there's no beer, there's still the bottle. And if there isn't even the bottle, there's nothing there at all. And nothing isn't a very minimal something. Minimal worlds there

can indeed be. There can be nothing much: just some homogeneous unoccupied spacetime, or maybe only one single point of it. But nothing much is still something, and there isn't any world where there's nothing at all. That makes it necessary that there is something. For it's true at all worlds that there is something: it's true whenever we restrict our quantifiers to the domain of parts of a single world, even if the only part of some world is one indivisible nondescript point. Of course, if we don't restrict quantifiers from the standpoint of one world or another, then all the more is it true that there is something rather than nothing: there is logical space, the totality of the worlds in all their glory.

How bad is this? I think the worst of it is the fear that I might offer to *explain* why there is something rather than nothing, just by saying that this is a necessary truth. But don't fear; I do not think that would be an explanation. For an explanation, I think, is an account of etiology: it tells us something about how an event was caused. Or it tells us something general about how some, or many, or all events of a certain kind are caused. Or it explains an existential fact by telling us something about how several events jointly make that fact true, and then perhaps something about how those truthmaker events were caused. So I think there is nothing I might say that could count as explaining why there is something rather than nothing; and that includes saying, truly, that there is no world where there is nothing.[53]

So far I am stonewalling. I accept the unwelcome consequences of my thesis, and claim they are not as bad as you might think. But there is one more objection to consider, and this one really does seem to me to call for a retreat. The last resort would be a primitive worldmate relation, but I think it won't be necessary to fall back that far.

Imagine a theory of spacetime that is built for Newtonian mechanics, or for common sense. (Old-fashioned Newtonian mechanics, as opposed to recent reformulations that are still in a sense Newtonian, but do away with absolute rest.) This theory will say that any two spacetime points are related by a spatial distance and a temporal distance: two different distances. One but not both of these distances may be zero, thus absolute simultaneity and absolute rest both are well defined. I suppose this is a way the world might have been, therefore it is a way that some world is. But we have good reason to think that our world is different. In our relativistic world, any two spacetime points have only one distance between them; it may be a spatial distance, it may be a temporal distance, or it may be a zero distance which is neither spatial nor temporal ('space-like' interval coded by a positive real, 'time-like' interval coded by a positive imaginary, or "light-like" interval). Of course there are other differences between Newtonian and relativistic spacetime, but this difference of two distances versus one is the difference that matters to ontology.

We name the properties and relations that figure in our world; so what we call 'spatiotemporal relations' are relations that behave in the relativistic way, with spatial or temporal distance but not both. Now when we talk about the Newtonian world, are we talking about the possibility of different behaviour on the part of those same relations? Is it that those very relations might double up to give us two distances, one of each kind, between the same two points? Or are we talking instead about some different relations that might take the place of the spatiotemporal relations of our world?[54]

If it is the former, no worries. The Newtonian world is just as much spatiotemporally interrelated as ours is, even if the spatiotemporal relations behave differently there. But if it is the latter, then strictly speaking I cannot say that the Newtonian world is *spatiotemporally* interrelated. It has its system of external relations, whereby its parts are arranged, which are analogous to the spatiotemporal relations whereby the parts of our world are arranged. But these Newtonian impostors are not to be called the 'spatiotemporal relations', because that is the name we gave to the different relations that hold between the parts of our world. (It is beside the point that when we named the relations of our world, we may have thought they behaved in the Newtonian rather than the relativistic way. However much we intended to name relations that conformed to some theory, doubtless we intended much more to name relations that are pervasive in our world.) Similarly, *mutatis mutandis*, if the inhabitants of a Newtonian world talk about the possibility of a world like ours. Suppose they did pretty much what we did in naming what they call 'spatiotemporal relations'; and suppose it is not so that the very same relations behave in the Newtonian way at one world and in the relativistic way at the other. Then they should not say, strictly speaking, that our world is 'spatiotemporally interrelated'.

I do not know how to answer the question whether we have the same relations in the different worlds. It might even have different answers in different cases: some pairs of a Newtonian and a relativistic world use the same relations (doubled up for the Newtonian world), other pairs don't. Also, I suppose some worlds are interrelated by systems of external relations that differ more, at least in their behaviour, than Newtonian doubled-up distances differ from relativistic distances. It would be nice to suppose that all worlds are interrelated by the very same relations, namely the ones that we call 'spatiotemporal', despite whatever behavioural differences there may be. I do not reject this supposition. But I am unwilling to rely on it.

What I need to say is that each world is interrelated (and is maximal with respect to such interrelation) by a system of relations which, if they are not the spatiotemporal relations rightly so called, are at any rate analogous to them. Then my task is to spell out the analogy. At least some of the points of analogy should go as follows. (1) The relations are *natural*; they are not gruesome gerrymanders, not even mildly disjunctive.

(2) They are *pervasive*: mostly, or perhaps without exception, when there is a chain of relations in the system running from one thing to another, then also there is a direct relation. (3) They are *discriminating*: it is at least possible, whether or not it happens at every world where the relations are present, that there be a great many interrelated things, no two of which are exactly alike with respect to their place in the structure of relations. (4) They are *external*: they do not supervene on the intrinsic natures of the *relata* taken separately, but only on the intrinsic character of the composite of the *relata*. (See section 5. The definition of what it is for a relation to be external involved *possibilia* but not yet possible worlds, and so is available at this point without circularity.) When a system of relations is analogous to the spatiotemporal relations, strictly so called, let me call them *analogically* spatiotemporal.[55]

I have some hope that it might be possible to bypass the messy idea of analogically spatiotemporal relations. A much simpler alternative would be that worlds are unified by *external* interrelatedness, of whatever sort. On this suggestion, *any* natural external relations will do to unify a world. Every part of a world bears some such relation to every other part; but no part of one world ever bears any such relation to any part of another. Never mind whether the relations in question are spatiotemporal, either strictly or analogically.

If the simplification is to have a hope, the restriction to natural relations must bear a good deal of weight. It will have to exclude more than just the gruesome gerrymanders. For what about the relation of *non-identity*? (Here I am indebted to discussion with James Grieve.) It qualifies on my definition as an external relation, and it obtains invariably between the particular parts of different worlds. However, we may fairly deny it a place in our select inventory of the natural relations. It would be superfluous to include it if we have the resources to introduce it by definition; and we do, since X and Y are non-identical iff there is a class that one of X and Y belongs to and the other does not. (If you think there is need to cover non-identity of 'proper classes' you should add a clause: '. . . or there is something that belongs to one of X and Y but not the other'.)

I find it hard to say whether this simplification could succeed. My problem is a lack of test cases. What natural external relations could there be besides the (strictly or analogically) spatiotemporal relations? I would reject some candidates for further external relations that might be offered: for instance, primitive genidentity relations, non-qualitative counterpart relations [. . .], or a primitive worldmate relation.

Perhaps the following will do as a test case. If so, it looks unfavourable for the simplification. We tend to think that positive and negative charge are natural intrinsic properties of particles; but suppose not. Suppose instead there are natural external relations of like-chargedness and opposite-chargedness. (Then we can introduce extrinsic versions of the charge properties. To be neutral is to be like-charged to some particles and opposite-charged to none; to be negative is to be like-charged to most of the lightweight particles that orbit much heavier clumps of particles hereabouts; and to be positive is to be opposite-charged to a negative particle.) On this view, as opposed to the standard view, the relations of like- and opposite-chargedness do *not* supervene on the intrinsic natures of two particles taken separately; an electron and a positron may be perfect intrinsic duplicates. That is the point of calling the relations external. They are natural *ex hypothesi*. They are pervasive (at least, given the appropriate laws) in that whenever two particles are connected by a chain of such relations, they are connected directly. But they are very far from discriminating (again, given the appropriate laws): if there are as few as three particles, there must be two of them that are alike so far as these relations are concerned. If this story, or something like it, could be true, then here we have external relations that are not strictly or analogically spatiotemporal.

Could two particles in different worlds stand in these external relations of like- or opposite-chargedness? So it seems, offhand; and if so, then the simplification fails. I would welcome a reason why particles at different worlds cannot stand in these relations – other than a verificationist reason that I would find unpersuasive – but failing such a reason, I am inclined to reject the simplification. Then I must stick instead with my underdeveloped suggestion that the unifying external relations have to be, if not strictly spatiotemporal, at least analogically spatiotemporal.

There is a second way in which the worlds are isolated: there is no causation from one to another. If need be, I would put this causal isolation alongside spatiotemporal isolation as a principle of demarcation for worlds. But there is no need. Under a counterfactual analysis of causation, the causal isolation of worlds follows automatically. Therefore it contributes nothing to the demarcation of one world from another. No matter how we solve the demarcation problem, trans-world causation comes out as nonsense.

When we have causation within a world, what happens is roughly as follows. (For simplicity I ignore complications having to do with causal pre-emption and overdetermination, and with the idealisation of supposing that we always have closest antecedent-worlds. Taking these matters into account would do nothing in favour of trans-world causation.) We have a world W where event C causes event E. Both these events occur at W, and they are distinct events, and it is the case at W that if C had not occurred, E would not have occurred either. The counterfactual means that at the closest worlds to W at which C does not occur, E does not occur either.

Try to adapt this to a case of trans-world causation, in which the events of one world supposedly influence those of another. Event C occurs at world W_C, event E occurs at world E_E, they are distinct events, and if C had not occurred, E would not have occurred either. This

counterfactual is supposed to hold – where? It means that at the closest worlds to – where? – at which C does not occur, E does not occur – where? – either.

Normally the counterfactual is supposed to hold at the world where the one event causes the other; so maybe if the causation goes between two worlds, the counterfactual ought to hold at both. So we have:

(1) at the closest worlds to W_C at which C does not occur, E does not occur either, and

(2) at the closest worlds to W_E at which C does not occur, E does not occur either.

But (1) looks wrong: since we are looking at a supposed case of trans-world causation, it is irrelevant to ask whether we get E at worlds close to W_C; we ought to be looking at worlds close to W_E, the world where the supposed effect did take place. And (2) looks even worse: we ought to be hypothesising the removal of C from a world like W_C: removing it from a world like W_E is irrelevant. In fact, the closest world to W_E at which C does not occur might very well be W_E itself!

So should we make sure that we make our revisions to the right worlds by specifying explicitly which worlds the events are to be removed from? Like this:

(1′) at the closest worlds to W_C at which C does not occur at W_C, E does not occur at W_E, and

(2′) at the closest worlds to W_E at which C does not occur at W_C, E does not occur at W_E.

But this is worse than ever. What can these double modifications mean: at *this* world, an event does not occur at *that* world? C just *does* occur at W_C, E just *does* occur at W_E; there is no world at which these facts are otherwise. You might as well say that in Auckland it rains in Melbourne, but in Wellington it doesn't rain in Melbourne. There is no way to make literal sense of this, unless by taking the outer modifier as vacuous. (That is why you instantly thought of two ways to make non-literal sense of it: in Auckland they say it rains in Melbourne, but they don't say so in Wellington; it rains a lot in Melbourne compared to Auckland, but not compared to Wellington.)

Try this. As the one world is to ordinary causation, so the pair of worlds is to trans-world causation. So put pairs for single worlds throughout:

(3) at the closest world-pairs to the pair $\langle W_C, W_E \rangle$ such that C does not occur at the first world of the pair, E does not occur at the second world of the pair.

This makes sense, but not I think in a way that could make it true. For I suppose that the closeness of one world-pair to another consists of the closeness of the first worlds of the pairs together with the closeness of the second worlds of the pairs. We have to depart from W_C for the first world of a closest pair, since we have to get rid of C. But we are not likewise forced to depart from W_E for the second world of a closest pair, and what is so close to a world as that world itself? So the second world of any closest pair will just be W_E, at which E does occur, so (3) is false.

(If there were significant external relations between worlds, that might provide another respect of comparison for world-pairs. But to this I say, first, that even if trans-world external relations are not absolutely forbidden by our solution to the problem of demarcation, the permitted ones would be such things as our imagined relations of like- and opposite-chargedness, which don't seem to do anything to help (3) to come true; and second, that if our special world-pair counterfactuals are supposed to make for causal dependence, they had better be governed by the same sort of closeness that governs ordinary causal counterfactuals, but ordinary closeness of worlds does not involve any trans-world external relations that might make world-pairs close.)

When it seems to us as if we can understand trans-world causation, I think that what must be happening is as follows. We think of the totality of all the possible worlds as if it were one grand world, and that starts us thinking that there are other ways the grand world might have been. So perhaps what we really have in mind is:

(4) at the closest alternative grand worlds to ours where C does not occur in the part corresponding to W_C, E does not occur in the part corresponding to W_E.

But this is thoroughly misguided. If I am right, the many worlds already provide for contingency, and there is no sense in providing for it all over again. Or else I am wrong, and the many worlds do not provide for genuine contingency. [...] But then it makes no sense to repeat the very method you think has failed, only on a grander scale. The worlds are all of the maximal things that are suitably unified. If they fall into grand clusters, and yet grander clusters of clusters, and so on, that is neither here nor there. By 'worlds' I still mean *all* the worlds. (And how could they fall into clusters – what sort of relation could unify a cluster without also merging the worlds within it?) There is but one totality of worlds; it is not a world; it could not have been different. Therefore (4) is nonsense, intelligible only if taken as vacuous.

So there isn't any trans-world causation. And not because I so stipulate as a principle of demarcation, but as a consequence of my analyses of causation and of counterfactuals. This is the real reason why there couldn't be a very powerful telescope for viewing other worlds. The obstacle isn't that other worlds are too far away, as Kripke jokingly says; and it isn't that they're somehow 'abstract', as of course he really thinks. (See *Naming and Necessity*, pages 44 and 19.) Telescopic viewing, like other methods of gathering information, is a *causal* process: a 'telescope' which produced images that were causally independent of the condition of the thing 'viewed' would be a bogus telescope. No trans-world causation, no trans-world telescopes.

Likewise, if there is no trans-world causation, there is no trans-world travel. You can't get into a 'logical-space ship' and visit another possible world. You could get into what you confusedly think is a logical-space ship, turn the knob, and disappear. And a perfect duplicate of you at your disappearance, surrounded by a perfect duplicate of your ship, could appear *ex nihilo* at some other world. Indeed, there are plenty of worlds where aspiring logical-space travellers disappear, and plenty of worlds where they appear, and plenty of qualitative duplications between ones that disappear and ones that appear. But none of this is travel unless there is one surviving traveller who both departs and arrives. And causal continuity is required for survival; it is a principal part of what unifies a persisting person. It is so within a single world: if there is a demon who destroys people at random, and another who creates people at random, and by a very improbable coincidence the creating demon replaces a victim of the destroying demon, the qualitative continuity could be perfect, but the lack of causal dependence would still make it not be a genuine case of survival. Likewise across worlds. No trans-world causation, no trans-world causal continuity; no causal continuity, no survival; no survival, no travel. All those people in various worlds who meet their ends in 'logical-space ships', as well as the more fortunate ones who appear *ex nihilo* in such ships, are sadly deluded.

But if you'd like to see a world where Napoleon conquered all, don't give up hope. Maybe ours is one of those big worlds with many world-like parts, spatiotemporally related in some peculiar way. Then you might get your wish, near enough, by means of a special telescope or a special spaceship that operates entirely within our single world. You won't see the world-like part where Napoleon himself is, of course; you're there already, and he didn't conquer all. But I presume you'd be content with a world-like part where the conqueror was an

excellent counterpart of Napoleon. I would be the last to denounce decent science fiction as philosophically unsound. No; tales of viewing or visiting 'other worlds' are perfectly consistent. They come true at countless possible worlds. It's just that the 'other worlds' that are viewed or visited never can be what I call 'other worlds'.

7 Concreteness

Because I said that other worlds are of a kind with this world of ours, doubtless you will expect me to say that possible worlds and individuals are concrete, not abstract. But I am reluctant to say that outright. Not because I hold the opposite view; but because it is not at all clear to me what philosophers mean when they speak of 'concrete' and 'abstract' in this connection. Perhaps I would agree with it, whatever it means, but still I do not find it a useful way of explaining myself.

I can say this much, even without knowing what 'concrete' is supposed to mean. I take it, at least, that donkeys and protons and puddles and stars are supposed to be paradigmatically concrete. I take it also that the division between abstract and concrete is meant to divide entities into fundamentally different kinds. If so, then it is out of the question that an abstract entity and a concrete entity should be exactly alike, perfect duplicates. According to my modal realism, the donkeys and protons and puddles and stars that are parts of this world have perfect duplicates that are parts of other worlds. This suffices to settle, whatever exactly it may mean, that at least some possible individuals are 'concrete'. And if so, then at least some possible worlds are at least partly 'concrete'.

A spectator might well assume that the distinction between 'concrete' and 'abstract' entities is common ground among contemporary philosophers, too well understood and uncontroversial to need any explaining. But if someone does try to explain it, most likely he will resort to one (or more) of four ways.[56]

First, the Way of Example: concrete entities are things like donkeys and puddles and protons and stars, whereas abstract entities are things like numbers. That gives us very little guidance. First, because we have no uncontroversial account of what numbers are. Are the paradigms of abstractness meant to be the von Neumann ordinals – certain pure sets? Are they meant to be structural universals, instantiated here and there within our world, like the tripartiteness that is instantiated wherever there is a proton composed of quarks (if quarks themselves are mereological atoms)? Are they 'irreducible *sui generis* abstract entities'? And even given a useful account of the nature of numbers, there are just too many ways that numbers differ from donkeys *et al.* and we still are none the wiser about where to put a border between donkey-like and number-like.

At least the Way of Example has something to say about some parts of other worlds. As noted above, some parts of other worlds are *exactly* like donkeys, because they are donkeys, so those at any rate are paradigmatically concrete. Likewise for other-worldly puddles and protons and stars. So far, so good. But other parts of other worlds are, for instance, chunks of other-worldly spacetime – are those paradigmatically concrete? And if ordinary particulars contain universals or tropes as (non-spatiotemporal) parts, then worlds composed of ordinary particulars will in turn have universals or tropes as parts; in which case not all the parts of worlds are paradigmatically concrete. Indeed we might contemplate a theory of numbers – one which says, for instance, that the number three is the structural universal of tripartiteness – according to which some parts of worlds would turn out to be paradigmatically abstract.

And what of a whole world? Is it sufficiently donkey-like, despite its size? And perhaps despite the fact that it consists mostly of empty spacetime? I am inclined to say that, according to the Way of Example, a world is concrete rather than abstract – more donkey-like than number-like. I am also inclined to say that a world is more like a raven than a writing-desk; and that it is ping rather than pong. But I know not why.

Second, the Way of Conflation: the distinction between concrete and abstract entities is just the distinction between individuals and sets, or between particulars and universals, or perhaps between particular individuals and everything else. That accords well enough with our examples. It is safe to say that donkeys and the like are particular individuals, not universals or sets. It is a defensible, if not trouble-free, view that numbers are sets; alternatively, it is arguable that they are universals. So far, so good. I say that worlds are individuals, not sets. I say that worlds are particulars, not universals. So according to the Way of Conflation in either version, I say that worlds are concrete.

Third, the Negative Way: abstract entities have no spatiotemporal location; they do not enter into causal interaction; they are never indiscernible one from another.

The Negative Way and the Way of Conflation seem to disagree rather badly. As for the first part, the denial that abstract entities are located, I object that by this test some sets and universals come out concrete. Sets are supposed to be abstract. But a set of located things *does* seem to have a location, though perhaps a divided location: it is where its members *are*. Thus my unit set is right here, exactly where I am; the set of you and me is partly here where I am, partly yonder where you are; and so on. And universals are supposed to be abstract. But if a universal is wholly present in each of many located particulars, as by definition it is, that means that it is where its instances are. It is multiply located, not unlocated. You could just declare that an abstract entity is located only in the special way that a set or a universal is located – but then you might as well just say that to be abstract is to be a set or universal. Your talk of unlocatedness adds nothing. Maybe a *pure* set, or an *uninstantiated* universal, has no location. However these are the most dispensable and suspect of sets and universals. If it is said that sets or universals generally are unlocated, perhaps we have a hasty generalisation. Or perhaps we have an inference: they're unlocated because they're abstract. If so, we had better not also say that they're abstract because they're unlocated.

As for the second part, the denial that abstract entities enter into causal interaction, this too seems to disagree with the Way of Conflation. Is it true that sets or universals cannot enter into causal interaction? Why shouldn't we say that something causes a set of effects? Or that a set of causes, acting jointly, causes something? Or that positive charge causes effects of a characteristic kind whenever it is instantiated? Many authors have proposed to identify an event – the very thing that most surely can cause and be caused – with one or another sort of set. (For instance, in 'Events' I propose to identify an event with the set of spacetime regions where it occurs.) Must any such identification be rejected, regardless of the economies it may afford, just because sets are supposed to be 'abstract'?

As for the third part, the denial that abstract entities can be indiscernible, indeed I do not see what could be said in favour of indiscernible universals. But as for sets, I should think that if two individuals are indiscernible, then so are their unit sets; and likewise whenever sets differ only by a substitution of indiscernible individuals. So, *pace* the Way of Conflation, it seems that the Negative Way does not classify universals, or sets in general, as abstract.

What does it say about worlds? Other worlds and their parts certainly stand in no spatiotemporal or causal relations to *us*. Worlds are spatiotemporally and causally isolated from one another; else they would be not whole worlds, but parts of a greater world. But by the same token, we stand in no spatiotemporal or causal relation to *them*. That doesn't make us abstract. It's no good saying that, for us, we are concrete and an other-worldly being is abstract; whereas, for that other-worldly being, he is concrete and we are abstract. For one thing is certain: whatever the abstract-concrete distinction is, at least

it's supposed to be a very fundamental difference between two kinds of entities. It has no business being a symmetrical and relative affair.

So the right question is: do other worlds and their parts stand in spatiotemporal and causal relations to anything? Parts of worlds do: they stand in (strictly or analogically) spatiotemporal relations, and in causal relations, to other parts of their own worlds. (With exceptions. Maybe a tiny world might have only one part. A chaotic and lawless world might have no causation. But I presume we don't want to say that parts of worlds are abstract in these special cases, concrete otherwise.) Whole worlds, however, cannot stand in spatiotemporal and causal relations to anything outside themselves, and it seems that nothing can stand in such relations to its own parts. Should we conclude that worlds – including the one we are part of – are abstract wholes made of concrete parts? Perhaps, indeed, divisible exhaustively into concrete parts? That seems unduly literalistic – presumably the Negative Way should be construed charitably, so that wholes can inherit concreteness from their parts. As for indiscernibility, I have no idea whether there are indiscernible worlds; but certainly there are indiscernible parts of worlds, for instance indiscernible epochs of a world of two-way eternal recurrence. So according to the Negative Way, charitably read, I say that worlds and their parts – including the universals, if such there be! – are concrete.

Fourth, the Way of Abstraction: abstract entities are abstractions from concrete entities. They result from somehow subtracting specificity, so that an incomplete description of the original concrete entity would be a complete description of the abstraction. This, I take it, is the historically and etymologically correct thing to mean if we talk of 'abstract entities'. But it is by no means the dominant meaning in contemporary philosophy.

A theory of non-spatiotemporal parts of things, whether these be recurring universals or non-recurring tropes, makes good sense of some abstractions. We can say that unit negative charge is a universal common to many particles, and is an abstraction from these particles just by being part of each of them. Or we can say that the particular negative charge of this particular particle is part of it, but a proper part and in that sense an abstraction from the whole of it. But we cannot just identify abstractions with universals or tropes. For why can we not abstract some highly extrinsic aspect of something – say, the surname it bears? Or its spatiotemporal location? Or its role in some causal network? Or its role in some body of theory? All these are unsuitable candidates for genuine universals or tropes, being no part of the intrinsic nature of the thing whence they are abstracted.

We can also make good sense of abstractions, or an adequate imitation thereof, by the stratagem of taking equivalence classes. For instance, we abstract the direction of a line from the line itself by taking the direction to be the class of that line and all other lines parallel to it. There is no genuine subtraction of specific detail, rather there is multiplication of it; but by swamping if not by removal, the specifics of the original line get lost. For instance, the direction comprises many located lines; it is located where its members are, namely everywhere; so it is not located more one place than another, and that is the next best thing to not being anywhere. But sets in general cannot be regarded thus as abstractions: most sets are equivalence classes only under thoroughly artificial equivalences. (And the empty set is not an equivalence class at all.) Further, if we abstract by taking equivalence classes, we need not start with paradigmatically concrete things. Thus directions may be abstracted from lines, but the lines themselves may be taken as certain sets of quadruples of real numbers.

So even if universals and equivalence classes are abstractions, it remains that the Way of Abstraction accords badly with the Ways of Example and of Conflation. It accords no better with the Negative Way: if we can abstract the spatiotemporal location of something, that abstraction will not be unlocated; rather, there will be nothing to it except location. Likewise if we can abstract the causal role of something, then the one thing the abstraction will do is enter into causal interactions.

Unless understood as universals or tropes or equivalence classes, abstractions are obviously suspect. The inevitable hypothesis is that they are verbal fictions: we say 'in the material mode' that we are speaking about the abstraction when what's true is that we are speaking abstractly about the original thing. We are ignoring some of its features, not introducing some new thing from which those features are absent. We purport to speak of the abstraction 'economic man'; but really we are speaking of ordinary men in an abstract way, confining ourselves to their economic activities.

According to the Way of Abstraction, I say that worlds are concrete. They lack no specificity, and there is nothing for them to be abstractions from. As for the parts of worlds, certainly some of them are concrete, such as the other-worldly donkeys and protons and puddles and stars. But if universals or tropes are non-spatiotemporal parts of ordinary particulars that in turn are parts of worlds, then here we have abstractions that are parts of worlds.

So, by and large, and with some doubts in connection with the Way of Example and the Negative Way, it seems that indeed I should say that worlds as I take them to be are concrete; and so are many of their parts, but perhaps not all. But it also seems that to say that is to say something very ambiguous indeed. It's just by luck that all its disambiguations make it true.

8 Plenitude

At the outset, I mentioned several ways that a world might be; and then I made it part of my modal realism that

(1) absolutely every way that a world could possibly be is a way that some world is, and

(2) absolutely every way that a part of a world could possibly be is a way that some part of some world is.

But what does that mean? It *seems* to mean that the worlds are abundant, and logical space is somehow complete. There are no gaps in logical space; no vacancies where a world might have been, but isn't. It seems to be a principle of plenitude. But is it really?

Given modal realism, it becomes advantageous to identify 'ways a world could possibly be' with worlds themselves. Why distinguish two closely corresponding entities: a world, and also the maximally specific way that world is? Economy dictates identifying the 'ways' with the worlds.

But as Peter van Inwagen pointed out to me, that makes (1) contentless. It says only that every world is identical to some world. That would be true even if there were only seventeen worlds, or one, or none. It says nothing at all about abundance or completeness. Likewise for (2).

Suppose we thought a maximally specific 'way' should be the same kind of things as a less specific 'way': namely a property, taken as a set. Then a maximally specific 'way' would be a unit set. Now indeed the 'ways' are distinct from the worlds. Further, they are abstract in whatever sense sets are. But this does nothing to restore content to (1). A 'possible way' is a *non-empty* set, and (1) now says trivially that each of the unit sets has a member.[57]

Or perhaps a 'way' should be not a unit set, but an equivalence class under indiscernibility. I am agnostic about whether there are indiscernible worlds. If there are, I myself would wish to say that there are indiscernible ways a world could be, just as I would say that a world of two-way eternal recurrence affords countless indiscernible ways – one per epoch – for a person to be. But others might not like the idea of indiscernible 'ways'. They might therefore welcome a guarantee that, whether or not worlds ever are indiscernible, 'ways' never will be. Now

(1) says trivially that each of the equivalence classes has a member.

Or suppose we thought a 'way' should be the intrinsic nature of a world, a highly complex structural universal (as in Forrest, 'Ways Worlds Could Be'.) Given that thesis, a "possible way" is an *instantiated* universal. Now (1) says trivially that each of these has a world to instantiate it.

We might read (1) as saying that every way we think a world could possibly be is a way that some world is; that is, every seemingly possible description or conception of a world does fit some world. Now we have made (1) into a genuine principle of plenitude. But an unacceptable one. So understood, (1) indiscriminately endorses offhand opinion about what is possible.

I conclude that (1), and likewise (2), cannot be salvaged as principles of plenitude. Let them go trivial. Then we need a new way to say what (1) and (2) seemed to say: that there are possibilities enough, and no gaps in logical space.

To which end, I suggest that we look to the Humean denial of necessary connections between distinct existences. To express the plenitude of possible worlds, I require a *principle of recombination* according to which patching together parts of different possible worlds yields another possible world. Roughly speaking, the principle is that anything can coexist with anything else, at least provided they occupy distinct spatiotemporal positions. Likewise, anything can fail to coexist with anything else. Thus if there could be a dragon, and there could be a unicorn, but there couldn't be a dragon and a unicorn side by side, that would be an unacceptable gap in logical space, a failure of plenitude. And if there could be a talking head contiguous to the rest of a living human body, but there couldn't be a talking head separate from the rest of a human body, that too would be a failure of plenitude.

(I mean that plenitude requires that there could be a separate thing *exactly like* a talking head contiguous to a human body. Perhaps you would not wish to call that thing a 'head', or you would not wish to call what it does 'talking'. I am somewhat inclined to disagree, and somewhat inclined to doubt that usage establishes a settled answer to such a far-fetched question; but never mind. What the thing may be called is entirely beside the point. Likewise when I speak of possible dragons or unicorns, I mean animals that fit the stereotypes we associate with those names. I am not here concerned with Kripke's problem of whether such animals are rightly called by those names.)

I cannot altogether accept the formulation: anything can coexist with anything. For I think the worlds do not overlap, hence each thing is part of only one of them. A dragon from one world and a unicorn from a second world do not themselves coexist either in the dragon's world, or in the unicorn's world, or in a third world. An attached head does not reappear as a separated head in some other world, because it does not reappear at all in any other world.

Ordinarily I would replace trans-world identity by counterpart relations, but not here. I cannot accept the principle: a counterpart of anything can coexist with a counterpart of anything else. Counterparts are united by similarity, but often the relevant similarity is mostly extrinsic. In particular, match of origins often has decisive weight. Had my early years gone differently, I might be different now in ever so many important ways – here I envisage an other-worldly person who is my counterpart mainly by match of origins, and very little by intrinsic similarity in later life. It might happen (at least under some resolutions of the vagueness of counterpart relations) that nothing could be a counterpart of the dragon unless a large part of its surrounding world fairly well matched the dragon's world; and likewise that nothing could be a counterpart of the unicorn unless a large part of its surrounding world fairly well matched the unicorn's world; and that no one world matches both the dragon's world and the unicorn's world well enough; and therefore that there is no world

where a counterpart of the dragon coexists with a counterpart of the unicorn. Considered by themselves, the dragon and the unicorn are compossible. But if we use the method of counterparts, we do not consider them by themselves; to the extent that the counterpart relation heeds extrinsic similarities, we take them together with their surroundings.

It is right to formulate our principle of recombination in terms of similarity. It should say, for instance, that there is a world where something like the dragon coexists with something like the unicorn. But extrinsic similarity is irrelevant here, so I should not speak of coexisting *counterparts*. Instead, I should say that a *duplicate* of the dragon and a *duplicate* of the unicorn coexist at some world, and that the attached talking head has at some world a separated duplicate.

Duplication is a matter of shared properties, but differently situated duplicates do not share all their properties. In section 5, I defined duplication in terms of the sharing of perfectly natural properties, then defined intrinsic properties as those that never differ between duplicates. That left it open that duplicates might differ extrinsically in their relation to their surroundings. Duplicate molecules in this world may differ in that one is and another isn't part of a cat. Duplicate dragons in different worlds may differ in that one coexists with a unicorn and the other doesn't. Duplicate heads may differ in that one is attached to the rest of a human body and the other isn't.

Not only two possible individuals, but any number, should admit of combination by means of coexisting duplicates. Indeed, the number might be infinite. Further, any possible individual should admit of combination with itself: if there could be a dragon, then equally there could be two duplicate copies of that dragon side by side, or seventeen or infinitely many.

But now there is trouble. Only a limited number of distinct things can coexist in a spacetime continuum. It cannot exceed the infinite cardinal number of the points in a continuum. So if we have more than continuum many possible individuals to be copied, or if we want more than continuum many copies of any single individual, then a continuum will be too small to hold all the coexisting things that our principle seems to require.

Should we keep the principle of recombination simple and unqualified, follow where it leads, and conclude that the possible size of spacetime is greater than we might have expected? That is tempting, I agree. And I see no compelling reason why a possible spacetime can never exceed the size of a continuum. But it seems very fishy if we begin with a principle that is meant to express plenitude about how spacetime might be occupied, and we find our principle transforming itself unexpectedly so as to yield consequences about the possible size of spacetime itself.

Our principle therefore requires a proviso: 'size and shape permitting'. The only limit on the extent to which a world can be filled with duplicates of possible individuals is that the parts of a world must be able to fit together within some possible size and shape of spacetime. Apart from that, anything can coexist with anything, and anything can fail to coexist with anything.

This leaves a residual problem of plenitude: what are the possible sizes and shapes of spacetime? Spacetimes have mathematical representations, and an appropriate way to state plenitude would be to say that for every representation in some salient class, there is a world whose spacetime is thus represented. It is up to mathematics to offer us candidates for the 'salient class'. [. . .]

We sometimes persuade ourselves that things are possible by experiments in imagination. We imagine a horse, imagine a horn on it, and thereby we are persuaded that a unicorn is possible. But imaginability is a poor criterion of possibility. We can imagine the impossible, provided we do not imagine it in perfect detail and all at once. We cannot imagine the possible in perfect detail and all at once, not if it is at all complicated. It is impossible to construct a regular polygon of nineteen sides with ruler and compass; it is possible but very complicated to construct one of seventeen sides. In whatever sense I can imagine the possible construction, I can imagine the impossible construction just as well. In both cases, I imagine a texture of arcs and lines with the polygon in the middle. I do not imagine it arc by arc and line by line, just as I don't imagine the speckled hen speckle by speckle – which is how I fail to notice the impossibility.

We get enough of a link between imagination and possibility, but not too much, if we regard imaginative experiments as a way of reasoning informally from the principle of recombination. To imagine a unicorn and infer its possibility is to reason that a unicorn is possible because a horse and a horn, which are possible because actual, might be juxtaposed in the imagined way.

In 'Propositional Objects' Quine suggested that we might take a possible world as a mathematical representation: perhaps a set of quadruples of real numbers, regarded as giving the coordinates of the spacetime points that are occupied by matter. His method could be extended to allow for various sizes and shapes of spacetime, for occupancy by different kinds of matter and by point-sized bits of fields, and perhaps even for occupancy of times by non-spatial things. In section 3.2 [not reproduced here], I shall argue that we should not identify the worlds with any such mathematical representations. However we should accept a correspondence: for every Quinean ersatz world, there is a genuine world with the represented pattern of occupancy and vacancy. This is just an appeal to recombination. But we are no longer applying it to smallish numbers of middle-sized things, horses or horns of heads. Instead, we are applying it to point-sized things, spacetime points themselves or perhaps point-sized bits of matter or of fields. Starting with point-sized things that are uncontroversially possible, perhaps because actual, we patch together duplicates of them in great number (continuum many, or more) to make an entire world. The mathematical representations are a book-keeping device, to make sure that the 'size and shape permitting' proviso is satisfied.

Another use of my principle is to settle – or as opponents might say, to beg – the question whether laws of nature are strictly necessary. They are not; or at least laws that constrain what can coexist in different positions are not. Episodes of bread-eating are possible because actual; as are episodes of starvation. Juxtapose duplicates of the two, on the grounds that anything can follow anything; here is a possible world to violate the law that bread nourishes. So likewise against the necessity of more serious candidates for fundamental laws of nature – perhaps with the exception of laws constraining what can coexist at a single position, for instance the law (if such it be) that nothing is both positive and negative in charge. It is no surprise that my principle prohibits strictly necessary connections between distinct existences. What I have done is to take a Humean view about laws and causation, and use it instead as a thesis about possibility. Same thesis, different emphasis.

Among all the possible individuals there are, some are parts of this world; some are not, but are duplicates of parts of this world; some, taken whole, are not duplicates of any part of this world, but are divisible into parts each of which is a duplicate of some part of this world. Still other possible individuals are not thus divisible: they have parts, no part of which is a duplicate of any part of this world. These I call *alien* individuals. (That is, they are alien *to* this world; similarly, individuals could be alien to another world. For instance, many individuals in this world are alien to more impoverished worlds.) A world that contains alien individuals – equivalently, that is itself an alien individual – I call an alien world.

In 'New Work for a Theory of Universals', I defined an alien natural property as one that is not instantiated by any part of this world, and that is not definable as a conjunctive or structural property build up from constituents that are all instantiated by parts of this world.[58] Anything that instantiates an alien property is an alien individual; any world within which an alien property is instantiated is an alien world.

But not conversely: we could have an alien individual that did not instantiate any alien properties, but instead combined non-alien properties in an alien way. Suppose that positive and negative charge are not, strictly speaking, incompatible; but suppose it happens by accident or by contingent law that no this-worldly particle has both these properties. Then an other-worldly particle that does have both is an alien individual but needn't have any alien properties.

A world to which no individuals, worlds, or properties are alien would be an especially rich world. There is no reason to think we are privileged to inhabit such a world. Therefore any acceptable account of possibility must make provision for alien possibilities.

So it won't do to say that all worlds are generated by recombination from parts of this world, individuals which are possible because they are actual. We can't get the alien possibilities just by rearranging non-alien ones. Thus our principle of recombination falls short of capturing all the plenitude of possibilities.

A principle which allowed not only recombination of spatiotemporal parts of the world but also recombination of non-spatiotemporal parts – universals or tropes – would do a bit more. It would generate those alien individuals that do not instantiate alien properties. But I say (1) that such a principle, unlike mine, would sacrifice neutrality about whether there exist universals or tropes, and (2) that it still wouldn't go far enough, since we also need the possibility of alien properties.

Although recombination will not generate alien worlds out of the parts of this world, it nevertheless applies to alien worlds. It rules out that there should be only a few alien worlds. If there are some, there are many more. Anything alien can coexist, or fail to coexist, with anything else alien, or with anything else not alien, in any arrangement permitted by shape and size.

9 Actuality

I say that ours is one of many worlds. Ours is the actual world; the rest are not actual. Why so?—I take it to be a trivial matter of meaning. I use the word 'actual' to mean the same as 'this-worldly'. When I use it, it applies to my world and my worldmates; to this world we are part of, and to all parts of this world. And if someone else uses it, whether he be a worldmate of ours or whether he be unactualised, then (provided he means by it what we do) it applies likewise to his world and his worldmates. Elsewhere I have called this the 'indexical analysis' of actuality and stated it as follows.

> I suggest that 'actual' and its cognates should be analyzed as *indexical* terms: terms whose reference varies, depending on relevant features of the context of utterance. The relevant feature of context, for the term 'actual', is the world at which a given utterance occurs. According to the indexical analysis I propose, 'actual' (in its primary sense) refers at any world w to the world w. 'Actual' is analogous to 'present', an indexical term whose reference varies depending on a different feature of context: 'present' refers at any time t to the time t. 'Actual' is analogous also to 'here', 'I', 'you', and 'aforementioned'—indexical terms depending for their reference respectively on the place, the speaker, the intended audience, the speaker's acts of pointing, and the foregoing discourse.
>
> ('Anselm and Actuality', pages 184–5)

This makes actuality a relative matter: every world is *actual at* itself, and thereby all worlds are on a par. This is *not* to say that all worlds are actual – there's no world at which that is true, any more than there's ever a time when all times are present. The 'actual at' relation between worlds is simply identity.

Given my acceptance of the plurality of worlds, the relativity is unavoidable. I have no tenable alternative. For suppose instead that one world alone is *absolutely* actual. There is some special distinction which that one world alone possesses, not relative to its inhabitants or to anything else but *simpliciter*. I have no idea how this supposed absolute distinction might be understood, but let us go on as if we did understand it. I raise two objections.

The first objection concerns our knowledge that we are actual. Note that the supposed absolute distinction, even if it exists, doesn't make the relative distinction go away. It is still true that one world alone is ours, is this one, is the one we are part of. What a remarkable bit of luck for us if the very world we are part of is the one that is absolutely actual! Out of all the people there are in all the worlds, the great majority are doomed to live in worlds that lack absolute actuality, but we are the select few. What reason could we ever have to think it was so? How could we ever know? Unactualised dollars buy no less unactualised bread, and so forth. And yet we *do* know for certain that the world we are part of is the actual world – just as certainly as we know that the world we are part of is the very world we are part of. How could this be knowledge that we are the select few?

D. C. Williams asks the same question. Not about 'actuality' but about 'existence'; but it comes to the same thing, since he is discussing various doctrines on which so-called 'existence' turns out to be a special status that distinguishes some of the things there are from others. He complains that Leibniz 'never intimates, for example, how he can tell that *he* is a member of the existent world and not a mere possible monad on the shelf of essence' ('Dispensing with Existence', page 752).

Robert M. Adams, in 'Theories of Actuality', dismisses this objection. He says that a simple-property theory of absolute actuality can account for the certainty of our knowledge of our own actuality by maintaining that we are as immediately acquainted with our own absolute actuality as we are with our thoughts, feelings, and sensations. But I reply that if Adams and I and all the other actual people really have this immediate acquaintance with absolute actuality, wouldn't my elder sister have had it too, if only I'd had an elder sister? So there she is, unactualised, off in some other world getting fooled by the very same evidence that is supposed to be giving me my knowledge.

This second objection concerns contingency. (It is due to Adams, and this time he and I agree.) Surely it is a contingent matter which world is actual. A contingent matter is one that varies from world to world. At one world, the contingent matter goes one way; at another, another. So at one world, one world is actual; and at another, another. How can this be *absolute* actuality? – The relativity is manifest!

The indexical analysis raises a question. If 'actual' is an indexical, is it or is it not a rigidified indexical? In a context where other worlds are under consideration, does it still refer to the world of utterance, or does it shift its reference? Compare 'now', which is normally rigidified, with 'present', which may or may not be. So you say 'Yesterday it was colder than it is now', and even in the scope of the time-shifting adverb, 'now' still refers to the time of utterance. Likewise you say 'Yesterday it was colder than it is at present', and the reference of 'present' is unshifted. But if you say 'Every past event was once present', then the time-shifting tensed verb shifts the reference of 'present'. I suggest that 'actual' and its cognates are like 'present': sometimes rigidified, sometimes not. What if I'd had an elder sister? Then there would have been someone who doesn't actually exist. (Rigidified.)

Then she would have been actual, though in fact she is not. (Unrigidified.) Then someone would have been actual who actually isn't actual. (Both together.) In the passage just quoted I called the unrigidified sense 'primary'; but not for any good reason.[59]

I said that when I use it, 'actual' applies to my world and my worldmates; that is, to the world I am part of and to other parts of that world. Likewise, *mutatis mutandis*, when some other-worldly being uses the word with the same meaning. But that left out the sets. I would not wish to say that any sets are *parts* of this or other worlds,[60] but nevertheless I would like to say that sets of actual things are actual. Sometimes we hear it said that sets are one and all unlocated; but I don't know any reason to believe this, and a more plausible view is that a set is where its members are. It is scattered to the extent that its members are scattered; it is unlocated if, but only if, its members are unlocated. That applies as much to location among the worlds as it does to location within a single world. Just as a set of stay-at-home Australians is in Australia, so likewise a set of this-wordly things is this-worldly, in other words actual. In the same way, a set of sets that are all in Australia is itself in Australia, and likewise a set of actual sets is itself actual; and so on up the iterative hierarchy.

I might sometimes prefer to use the word 'actual' a bit more broadly still. There is no need to decide, once and for all and inflexibly, what is to be called actual. After all, that is not the grand question: what is there? It is only the question which of all the things there are stand in some special relation to us, but there are special relations and there are special relations. Suppose there are things that are not our world, and not parts of our world, and not sets built up entirely from things that are parts of our world – but that I might nevertheless wish to quantify over even when my quantification is otherwise restricted to this-worldly things. If so, no harm done if I sometimes call them 'actual' by courtesy. No harm done, in fact, if I decline to adopt any official position on the question whether they are actual or whether they are not! It is no genuine issue.

The numbers, for instance, might well be candidates to be called 'actual' by courtesy. But it depends on what the numbers are. If they are universals, and some or all of them are non-spatiotemporal parts of their this-worldly instances which in turn are parts of this world, then those numbers, at least, are actual not by courtesy but because they are parts of this world. Likewise for other mathematical entities.

Properties, taken as sets of all their this- and other-worldly instances, are another candidate. By what I said above about actuality of sets, only those properties are actual whose instances are confined to the actual world. But most of the properties we take an interest in have instances both in and out of this world. Those ones might be called 'partly actual'; or they might as well just be called 'actual', since very often we will want to include them in our otherwise this-worldly quantifications.

Events fall in with the properties; for I see no reason to distinguish between an event and the property of being a spatiotemporal region, of this or another world, wherein that event occurs. (See my 'Events'.) An event that actually occurs, then, is a set that includes exactly one this-worldly region. That makes it partly actual, and we may as well just call it 'actual'.

Propositions, being sets of worlds, also fall in with the properties taken as sets. A proposition is partly actual at just those worlds where it is true, for it has just those worlds as its members. So we might call at least the true propositions 'actual'; or we might just call all propositions 'actual', distinguishing however between those that are and are not actually true.

Not only sets but individuals may be partly actual – big individuals, composed of parts from more worlds than one, and so partly in each of several worlds. If there are any such trans-world individuals that are partly in this world, hence partly actual, should we call them 'actual'

simpliciter? – That depends. We needn't, if we think of them just as oddities that we can mostly ignore. I think they are exactly that. But if we were reluctant to ignore them in our quantifying, perhaps because we thought that we ourselves were among them, then we might appropriately call them 'actual'.[61]

Notes

1 Or 'extreme' modal realism, as Stalnaker calls it – but in what dimension does its extremity lie?

2 With the alleged exception of category theory – but here I wonder if the unmet needs have more to do with the motivational talk than with the real mathematics.

3 This discussion of restricting modifiers enables me to say why I have no use for impossible worlds, on a par with the possible worlds. For comparison, suppose travellers told of a place in this world – a marvellous mountain, far away in the bush – where contradictions are true. Allegedly we have truths of the form 'On the mountain both P and not P'. But if 'on the mountain' is a restricting modifier, which works by limiting domains of implicit and explicit quantification to a certain part of all that there is, then it has no effect on the truth-functional connectives. Then the order of modifier and connectives makes no difference. So 'On the mountain both P and Q' is equivalent to 'On the mountain P, and on the mountain Q'; likewise 'On the mountain not P' is equivalent to 'Not: on the mountain P'; putting these together, the alleged truth 'On the mountain both P and not P' is equivalent to the overt contradiction 'On the mountain P, and not: on the mountain P'. That is, there is no difference between a contradiction within the scope of the modifier and a plain contradiction that has the modifier within it. So to tell the alleged truth about the marvellously contradictory things that happen on the mountain is no different from contradicting yourself. But there is no subject matter, however marvellous, about which you can tell the truth by contradicting yourself. Therefore there is no mountain where contradictions are true. An impossible world where contradictions are true would be no better. The alleged truth about its contradictory goings-on

would itself be contradictory. At least, that is so if I am right that 'at so-and-so world' is a restricting modifier. Other modifiers are another story. 'According to the Bible' or 'Fred says that' are *not* restricting modifiers; they do not pass through the truth-functional connectives. 'Fred says that not P' and 'Not: Fred says that P' are independent: both, either, or neither might be true. If worlds were like stories or story-tellers, there would indeed be room for worlds according to which contradictions are true. The sad truth about the prevarications of these worlds would not itself be contradictory. But worlds, as I understand them, are *not* like stories or story-tellers. They are like this world; and this world is no story, not even a true story. Nor should worlds be replaced by their stories. [. . .]

4 See Kratzer, 'What "Must" and "Can" Must and Can Mean'; and my 'Scorekeeping in a Language Game'.

5 This is essentially the account I gave in 'Counterpart Theory and Quantified Modal Logic'.

6 We might just *say* it, and not mean anything by it. That is Forbes's solution to our present difficulty, in his so-called 'canonical counterpart theory' – my own version is hereby named 'official standard counterpart theory' – in which, if Humphrey has no ordinary counterpart among the things which exist at W, he does nevertheless have a counterpart at W. This extraordinary counterpart is none other than Humphrey himself—he then gets in as a sort of associate member of W's population, belonging to its 'outer domain' but not to the 'inner domain' of things that exist there fair and square. This isn't explained, but really it needn't be. It amounts to a stipulation that there are two different ways that Humphrey – he himself, safe at home in this world – can satisfy formulas *in absentia*. Where he has proper counterparts, he does it one way, namely the ordinary vicarious way. Where he doesn't, he does it another way – just by not being there he satisfies 'x does not exist'.

7 If he likes, he can give himself more than one of these disappointments. As I noted, Forbes's talk of non-existent counterparts in outer domains amounts to a stipulation that satisfaction *in absentia* works different ways in different cases; so I find it strange that he offers it in rejoinder to a proposal

of Hunter and Seager that modal formulas of parallel form needn't always be given parallel counterpart-theoretic translations. But this divided treatment does not pay off by making the modal formulas mean what we would offhand expect them to – it is exactly the non-existent counterparts in the outer domains that keep Humphrey from satisfying 'necessarily x is human' even if he is essentially human.

8 Surveyed in Teller, 'A Poor Man's Guide to Supervenience and Determination'.

9 See Kim, 'Psychophysical Supervenience', and my 'New Work for a Theory of Universals'.

10 One more example of the same sort of distortion. Let *naturalism* be the thesis that whether one's conduct is right supervenes on natural facts, so that one person could do right and another do wrong only if there were some difference in natural facts between the two – as it might be, a difference in their behaviour or their circumstances. Consider the theory that, necessarily, right conduct is conduct that conforms to divinely willed universal maxims. Suppose it is contingent what, if anything, is divinely willed. And suppose that facts about what is divinely willed are supernatural, not natural, facts. You might well expect that this divine-will theory of rightness would contradict naturalism; for if two people are alike so far as natural facts are concerned, but one of them lives in a world where prayer is divinely willed and the other lives in a world where blasphemy is divinely willed, then what is right for the first is not right for the second. But if we read the 'could' as a diamond, we get an unexpected answer. A difference in what universal maxims are divinely willed never could be a difference between two people in the same world. Within a single world, the only differences relevant to rightness are natural differences, such as the difference between one who prays and one who blasphemes. So indeed there is no world wherein one person does right and another does wrong without any difference in natural facts between the two. So either this divine-will theory of rightness is naturalistic after all; or else – more likely – something has gone amiss with our understanding of supervenience.

11 K is given by rules of truth-functional implication; the rule that any substitution instance of a

theorem is a theorem; the rule of interchange of equivalents, which says that if 'ϕ_1 iff ϕ_2' is a theorem, and -ϕ_2- comes from -ϕ_1- by substituting ϕ_2 for ϕ_1 at one or more places, then '-ϕ_1- iff -ϕ_2-' is a theorem; and three axioms:

Possibly P iff not necessarily not P.

Necessarily (P and Q) iff (necessarily P and necessarily Q).

Necessarily (P iff P).

When a new system is made by adding further axioms to K, it is understood that the word 'theorem' in the rules of substitution and interchange applies to all theorems of the new system.

12 The first discussions of this, some much more developed than others, are Hintikka, 'Quantifiers in Deontic Logic'; Kanger, *Provability in Logic*; Kripke, 'A Completeness Theorem in Modal Logic'; and Montague, 'Logical Necessity, Physical Necessity, Ethics, and Quantifiers'. There is also unpublished work of C. A. Meredith, reported in Prior, *Past, Present and Future*, page 42. A well known early discussion is Kripke, 'Semantical Considerations on Modal Logic'.

[. . .]

50 Worldmates are compossible in the strongest sense of the word. Two things are compossible in another sense if they are vicariously worldmates, in virtue of their counterparts; that is, iff some one world contains counterparts of both of them. Two things are compossible in yet another sense iff some one world contains intrinsic duplicates of both. In this third sense, any two possible individuals are compossible (except, perhaps, when one is too big to leave room for the other); see section 8.

51 The *mereological sum*, or *fusion*, of several things is the least inclusive thing that includes all of them as parts. It is composed of them and of nothing more; any part of it overlaps one or more of them; it is a proper part of anything else that has all of them as parts. Equivalently: the mereological sum of several things is that thing such that, for any X, X overlaps it iff X overlaps one of them. For background on the mereology that I shall be using extensively in this book, see Leonard and Goodman; or Goodman, *Structure of Appearance*, section 11.4.

52 The question is raised by Richards. I am grateful to

him, and to David Johnson, for helpful discussion of it.

53 I find it pleasing that another view, the one I like second best after my own, also seems to make it come out necessary that there is something rather than nothing. This is the 'combinatorial' view: in place of other worlds, we have constructions in which the elements of this world – elementary particulars and universals, perhaps – are put together in different combinations. [. . .] But as D. M. Armstrong has noted in discussion, there is no way to combine elements and make nothing at all. So there is no combinatorial possibility that there might be nothing.

54 What does this question mean? Maybe one thing, maybe another, depending on our underlying theory of natural properties and relations; and on that question I am staying neutral between three alternatives. (See section 5.) (1) Maybe naturalness is a primitive, applied to properties or relations understood as sets. Then we have families of relations that can serve as the common spatiotemporal relations of all the worlds, and we have other families of less inclusive relations that can serve as the different special spatiotemporal relations for different kinds of worlds, and the question is which relations are more natural. (2) Maybe a relation is natural when its instances share a relational universal; then the question is what universals there are. (3) Maybe a relation is natural when its instances contain duplicate tropes; then the question is what tropes there are.

55 There are three different conceptions of what the spatiotemporal relations might be. There is the dualist conception: there are the parts of spacetime itself, and there are the pieces of matter or fields or whatnot that occupy some of the parts of spacetime. Then the spatiotemporal relations (strict or analogical) consist of distance relations that hold between parts of spacetime; relations of occupancy that hold between occupants and the parts of spacetime they occupy; and, derivatively from these, further distance relations between the occupants, or between occupants and parts of spacetime.

There are two simpler monistic conceptions. One of them does away with the occupants as separate things: we have the parts of spacetime, and their distance relations are the only spatiotemporal relations. The properties that we usually ascribe to occupants of spacetime—for instance, properties of mass, charge, field strength—belong in fact to parts of spacetime themselves. When a part of spacetime has a suitable distribution of local properties, then it is a particle, or a piece of a field, or a donkey, or what have you.

The other monistic conception does the opposite: it does away with the parts of spacetime in favour of the occupants (now not properly so called), so that the only spatiotemporal relations are the distance relations between some of these. I tend to oppose the third conception, at least as applied to our world, for much the reasons given in Nerlich, *The Shape of Space*. I tend, more weakly, to oppose the dualist conception as uneconomical. I suppose it may be, however, that there are worlds of all three sorts; if so, that would give more reason than ever to doubt that the same system of spatiotemporal relations serves to unify all the worlds. Throughout this book, I shall presuppose that there are such things as spatiotemporal regions, whether or not there also are distinct things that occupy those regions. But I believe this presupposition plays no important role, and I could have been more neutral at the cost of clumsier writing. I certainly don't mean to suggest that the existence of spacetime and its parts is an essential tenet of modal realism.

56   I shall pass over a fifth way, offered by Dummett in chapter 14 of *Frege: Philosophy of Language*, in which the distinction between abstract and concrete entities is drawn in terms of how we could understand their names. Even if this fifth way succeeds in drawing a border, as for all I know it may, it tells us nothing directly about how the entities on opposite sides of that border differ in their nature. It is like saying that snakes are the animals we instinctively most fear – maybe so, but it tells us nothing about the nature of snakes.

57   Some critics have thought it very important that the 'ways' should be 'abstract' entities and distinct from the worlds. For instance, see Stalnaker, 'Possible Worlds'; and van Inwagen, who writes 'the cosmos, being concrete, is not a way things

could have been. . . . And surely the cosmos cannot itself be identical with any way the cosmos could have been: to say this would be like saying that Socrates is identical with the way Socrates is, which is plain bad grammar.' ('Indexicality and Actuality', page 406.) But to me, the choice whether to take a 'way' as a unit set or as its sole member seems to be of the utmost unimportance, on a par with the arbitrary choice between speaking of a set or of its characteristic function.

58   Perhaps, as Armstrong has suggested in discussion, I should have added a third clause: '. . . and that is not obtainable by interpolation or extrapolation from a spectrum of properties that are instantiated by parts of this world'.

59   For various examples that require or forbid rigidification if they are to make sense, see my *Philosophical Papers*, volume 1, page 22; for further discussion, see Hazen, 'One of the Truths about Actuality' and van Inwagen, 'Indexicality and Actuality'.

60   But not because I take it that the part – whole relation applies only to individuals and not sets, as I said in *Philosophical Papers*, volume I, page 40; rather, because I now take it that a set is never part of an individual.

61   In *Philosophical Papers*, volume I, pages 39–40, I distinguished three ways of 'being in a world': (1) being *wholly* in it, that is, being part of it; (2) being *partly* in it, that is, having a part that is wholly in it; and (3) existing *from the standpoint of* it, that is, 'belonging to the least restricted domain that is normally – modal metaphysics being deemed abnormal – appropriate in evaluating the truth at that world of quantifications'. If the world in question is actual, that is almost my present distinction between being actual, being partly actual, and being actual by courtesy; the only difference in the terminologies being that I would not now throw all sets into the lower grade. I distinguish all of the above from (4) existing *according to* a world: I claim that something exists according to a world – for instance, Humphrey both exists and wins the presidency according to certain worlds other than ours – by having a counterpart that is part of that world. On being part of versus existing according to, see section 4.1 [not reproduced here].

References

Adams, Robert M. 'Theories of Actuality', Noûs 8 (1974), pp. 211–31.

Hazen, Allen. 'One of the Truths about Actuality', Analysis 39 (1979), pp. 1–3.

Hintikka, Jaakko. 'Quantifiers in Deontic Logic', Societas Scientiarum Fennica, Commenationes Humanarum Litterarum 23 (1957), No. 4.

Kanger, Stig. Provability in Logic. Almqvist and Wiksell, 1957.

Kim, Jaegwon. 'Psychophysical Supervenience', Philosophical Studies 41 (1982), pp. 51–70.

Kratzer, Angelika. 'What "Must" and "Can" Must and Can Mean', Linguistics and Philosophy 1 (1977), pp. 337–55.

Kripke, Saul. 'A Completeness Theorem in Modal Logic', Journal of Symbolic Logic 24 (1959), pp. 1–14.

——. 'Semantical Considerations on Modal Logic', Acta Philosophical Fennica 16 (1963), pp. 83–94.

Lewis, David. 'Counterpart Theory and Quantified Modal Logic', Journal of Philosophy 65 (1968), pp. 113–26; reprinted with added postscripts in Lewis, Philosophical Papers, volume 1.

——. 'Anselm and Actuality', Noûs 4 (1970), pp. 175–88; reprinted with added postscripts in Lewis, Philosophical Papers, volume 1.

——. 'Scorekeeping in a Language Game', Journal of Philosophical Logic 8 (1979), pp. 339–59; reprinted in Lewis, Philosophical Papers, volume 1.

——. Philosophical Papers, volume 1. Oxford University Press 1983.

——. 'New Work for a Theory of Universals', Australasian Journal of Philosophy 61 (1983), pp. 343–77.

Montague, Richard. 'Logical Necessity, Physical Necessity, Ethics, and Quantifiers', Inquiry 3 (1960), pp. 259–69; reprinted in Montague, Formal Philosophy.

——. Formal Philosophy: Selected Papers of Richard Montague. Yale University Press, 1974.

Prior, Arthur N. Past, Present, and Future. Clarendon, 1967.

Quine, Willard van Orman. 'Propositional Objects' in Quine, Ontological Relativity and Other Essays, Columbia University Press, 1969.

Stalnaker, Robert. 'Possible Worlds', Noûs 10 (1976), pp. 65–75.

Teller, Paul. 'A Poor Man's Guide to Supervenience and Determination', Southern Journal of Philosophy, supplement to volume 22 (1984), pp. 137–62.

van Inwagen, Peter. 'Indexicality and Actuality', Philosophical Review 89 (1980), pp. 403–26.

Williams, Donald C. 'Dispensing with Existence', Journal of Philosophy 59 (1962), pp. 748–63.

Chapter 40

Alvin Plantinga

TWO CONCEPTS OF MODALITY
Modal Realism and Modal Reductionism

Necessary and contingent propositions, objects with accidental and essential properties, possible worlds, individual essences—these are the *phenomena of modality*. I shall contrast two opposed conceptions of modal phenomena[1]; one of them, as I see it, is properly thought of as *modal realism*; the other is *modal reductionism*. 'Modal realism', as I use the term, has nothing to do with whether certain sentences or propositions have truth values; it has equally little to do with the question whether it is possible that our most cherished theories should in fact be false. I speak rather of *existential* realism and antirealism.[2] The existential realist with respect to universals, for example, holds that there really are such things as universals; the antirealist holds that there are no such things, and may add that the role said by some to be played by them is in fact played by entities of some other sort. The existential realist with respect to so-called theoretical entities in science—quarks or chromosomes, say—claims that there really are things with at least roughly the properties scientists say such things have; the antirealist denies this. In the first part of this paper, I shall sketch a version of modal realism; in the second I shall outline and briefly explain modal reductionism. My chief example of reductionism will be the important modal theory of David Lewis: I shall argue that Lewis is a modal realist and/or a realist about possible worlds in approximately the sense in which

William of Ockham is a realist about universals: namely, not at all.

I. Modal Realism

A. *Grade I: Accidental and Essential Properties*

There are three grades of modal realism (to adapt a famous claim); so let us begin at the beginning and turn to the first. Here we may conveniently start with modality *de dicto* and the familiar distinction between necessary and contingent propositions. According to the modal realist, there are *propositions*: The things that are both true or false and capable of being believed or disbelieved. Every proposition is true or false (we may ignore the claim—misguided as I see it—that some propositions are neither); and every proposition is such that it is possibly believed or possibly disbelieved or both.[3] It is the *intentional* character of propositions that is most fundamental and important. Propositions are *claims*, or *assertions*; they *attribute* or *predicate* properties to or of objects; they *represent* reality or some part of it as having a certain character. A proposition is the sort of thing *according to which* things are or stand a certain way.

The modal realist therefore holds that there are propositions. What is specific to him as a *modal* realist, however, is the claim that true propositions come in two varieties: those that could have been false, and those that could not. Some but not all true propositions exclude falsehood by their very natures. In the first group would fall the theorems of first order logic, the truths of mathematics and perhaps set theory, and a miscellaneous host of less well regimented items, such as **no one is taller than himself, red is a color, no human beings are prime numbers**, and (at any rate according to some) **there is a being than which it is not possible that there be a greater**. Such propositions are necessarily true; they have the property of being true and have it esentially—i.e., they have it in such a way that they could not have lacked it. Other propositions, on the other hand, have the property of being true, all right, but have it accidentally: they could have lacked it. These are contingent propositions: for example, **Socrates was the teacher of Plato** and **Armidale, Australia, is about the same size as Saskatoon, Saskatchewan**. Necessary propositions are absolutely necessary; they are necessary in the strongest sense of the term. This sort of necessity—suppose we call it 'broadly logical necessity'[4]—is to be distinguished from causal or natural necessity (presumably our natural laws and physical constants could have been different in various subtle and not so subtle ways) as well as from self-evidence (in either the narrow or extended sense), from what is known or knowable *a priori*, and what (if there is any such thing) we cannot give up.[5]

A necessary proposition, therefore, has truth (the property of being true) essentially; a (true) contingent proposition has it accidentally. Here we have a special case of a more general distinction: that between an object's having a property essentially, on the one hand, or accidentally on the other. Modality *de dicto* is an important special case of modality *de re*: the special case where the object in question is a proposition and the property in question is truth. But it is only a special case; for according to the modal realist of the first grade, *all* objects have both essential and accidental properties: there are objects and there are properties and all of the first have some of the second accidentally and some of the second

essentially. The properties **being self-identical, being a person,** and **being possibly conscious** are essential to me; the properties **wearing shoes** and **liking mountains** are accidental to me. Nine, to take a famous example, has the property of being odd essentially but the property of numbering the planets accidentally. Of course there are variations on the theme of modal realism of the first grade; instead of saying that all objects have both essential and accidental properties, we could have said that *some* objects have both essential and accidental properties. More weakly still, we could have taken modal realism of the first grade as the claim that (*pace* Quine and others) there really is a distinction between necessity and possibility, counting as a modal realist anyone who affirms this, even if he also affirms (perhaps with Brand Blanshard and other idealists) that all objects have all their properties essentially.

B. Grade II: Possible Worlds

Not content with the claim that all objects have both essential and accidental properties, the modal realist of the second grade asserts that there are such things as *possible worlds* and that for any (temporally invariant) state of affairs or proposition **S**, **S** is possible if and only if there is a possible world that includes or entails it. She may think of possible worlds in more than one way. She may hold, for example, that there are states of affairs as well as propositions, where a state of affairs is such an item as **Socrates' being wise, 7 + 5's** equaling 12, and **there being no lions in Australia**. A state of affairs is *actual* and *obtains*, or else is not actual and fails to obtain; and a state of affairs **S** *includes* a state of affairs **S*** if and only if it is not possible that **S** be actual and **S*** fail to be actual. Like propositions, states of affairs have complements or negations: indeed, states of affairs and propositions are isomorphic, with **actuality** and **inclusion** for states of affairs replacing **truth** and **entailment** for propositions. She may also think, as I do, that some propositions (and states of affairs are) *temporally variant*; their truth values can vary over time. Thus the proposition **Paul is eating** is true at the present time, but not, fortunately enough, at every time. As I see it, a sentence like 'Paul is eating', assertively uttered at a time **t,** does not express the temporally invariant proposition **Paul eats at t** but a temporally variant proposition true at just the times Paul eats. Since states of affairs are isomorphic to propositions, there are also temporally variant states of affairs—**Paul's eating,** for example—which obtain at some times but not at others.[6] Possible worlds, then, are possible states of affairs: more specifically, they are temporally invariant states of affairs. Still more specifically, a possible world is a *maximal* possible state of affairs, where a state of affairs **S** is maximal if and only if for every state of affairs **S***, either **S** includes **S*** or **S** includes the complement ~**S*** of **S***. Alternatively, we could say that a possible world is a maximal possible *proposition*: a proposition that is possible, and for every proposition **p** either entails (in the broadly logical sense) **p** or entails ~**p**. (Of course if states of affairs just *are* propositions, then my "alternatively" was not appropriate.)

It is clear that the second grade is indeed a step beyond the first: even if there are both necessary and contingent states of affairs, both necessary and contingent propositions, it doesn't follow, at any rate just as a matter of logic, that there are *maximal* possible propositions or states of affairs.[7] Perhaps for every possible proposition **p**, there is a possible proposition **q** that properly entails it, but no proposition **q** that for every proposition **p** entails either **p** or its complement. (Or perhaps there are possible propositions or states of affairs that are not properly entailed or included by any propositions or states of affairs, but nonetheless are not maximal.) Further, suppose we agree that there is at least one possible world: it still requires a nontrivial argument to show that for any (temporally invariant) state of affairs or proposition **S**, **S** is possible if and only if there is a possible world that includes or entails it.[8]

According to the modal realist of the second grade, then, for every (possible) temporally invariant proposition or state of affairs there is a possible world in which it is true or obtains. Further, there is one possible world which includes every actual state of affairs[9]; this is the actual world, which I shall call 'alpha'. Alpha alone is actual, although of course all the worlds exist, and indeed *actually* exist. Still further, this vast assemblage of worlds is complete and world invariant: each of the worlds exists necessarily, and there could not have been a world distinct from each of the worlds that does in fact exist. (At any rate so I say; the existentialist[10] would disagree.) We can now make the traditional assertion connecting truth in worlds with modality *de dicto*: a proposition is necessarily true if and only if true in every possible world.

C. *Grade III: Things Have Properties in Worlds*

According to the modal realist of the third grade, concrete objects such as you and I have properties in worlds. This isn't as trifling as it sounds. An object **x** has a property **P** in a world **w** if and only if it is not possible that **w** be actual and **x** exist but fail to have **P**—alternatively, if and only if **w** includes **x**'s having **P**. An object's having a property in a world, obviously enough, is no more than a special case of an object's having a property in a proposition or state of affairs, where **x** has **P** in a proposition **A** if and only if it is not possible that **A** be true and **x** exist but fail to have **P**.

But isn't it just obvious and uncontroversial that Socrates, for example, has the property of being wise in the proposition **Socrates is wise?** It isn't obvious and non-controversial, because it isn't uncontroversial that there is such a proposition as **Socrates is wise** (or such a state of affairs as **Socrates' being wise**). More exactly, what isn't uncontroversial is that Socrates and the proposition expressed by 'Socrates is wise' are such that it isn't possible that the second be true and the first fail to be wise. For suppose a view of names like Frege's is true: such a proper name as 'Socrates', on this view, is semantically equivalent to such a definite description as 'the teacher of Plato' or 'the shortest Greek philosopher'. A proper name therefore expresses a property; it expresses such a property as **being the (sole) teacher of Plato** or **being the shortest Greek philosopher**. Such a property, of course, is accidental to Socrates—he could have existed but lacked it. If so, then the proposition expressed by the sentence 'Socrates is wise' could have been true even if Socrates (the person who actually *is* the teacher of Plato) were not wise, provided there existed someone who was wise and the sole teacher of Plato. If this view of names were correct, then the sentence 'Socrates is wise' would not express a proposition in which Socrates has wisdom. It could be held, more generally, that there are no sentences at all that express a proposition so related to Socrates, and that indeed there aren't any propositions so related to him. To hold this view is to hold that there is no proposition which is *singular* with respect to Socrates; for a proposition is singular with respect to an object **x** only if it is a proposition in which **x** has some property or other. So suppose there aren't any propositions singular with respect to concrete, contingent beings such as you and I: then there are no worlds singular with respect to us, and hence no worlds in which we have properties. On this view, worlds will be *Ramsified*: they will be general propositions or states of affairs specifying that certain properties and relation— certain *qualitative* (as opposed to *quidditative*[11]) properties and relations—are exemplified. Such worlds will specify, for each of us individually and all of us collectively, various roles we could have played; but no world will specify that you or I play a given role. An object **x** has a property **P** in a world, therefore, only if there are propositions singular with respect to **x** and **P**. But clearly if there is a proposition singular with respect to **x**, then there is a world in which **x** has **P**. Objects have properties in worlds,

therefore, if and only if there are singular propositions.

Further, objects have properties in worlds if and only if there are *individual essences*: properties essential to an object and essentially unique to that object.[12] First, it is obvious that if an object has an individual essence, then there are worlds in which it has properties. For suppose Socrates has an essence **E**: then there is a proposition and a state of affairs in which Socrates has wisdom: **E and wisdom are coexemplified** and **E's being coexemplified with wisdom**. And then, of course, there would be possible worlds in which Socrates has wisdom: those worlds including the states of affairs or propositions in question. So if there are individual essences, there are also singular propositions.

But it is also easy to see if there are singular propositions, then (given certain plausible assumptions) there are also individual essences. For suppose we know what it is for a proposition to *predicate a property* of an object. A proposition **A** predicates a property **P** of an object **x** only if necessarily, if **A** is true then **x** has **P**.[13] Given this notion, we can see that if there are singular propositions, there will also be essences. For consider the singular proposition **Socrates is wise**. This proposition predicates wisdom of Socrates and nothing else. So there is the property **being the person the proposition *Socrates is wise* predicates wisdom of** (or the property **standing to the proposition *Socrates is wise* in the relation in which an object stands to a proposition if and only if the later predicates wisdom of the former**); and this property is an essence of Socrates. Clearly it is *essential* to him: he could not have existed and been such that this proposition did not predicate wisdom of him. But it is also essentially unique to him; there could not have been someone distinct from Socrates who was such that this proposition predicated wisdom of him. It is therefore an essence of Socrates.

According to the modal realist of the third grade, then, objects have properties in worlds. In view of the above equivalences, he might as well have said that there are singular propositions; for objects have properties in worlds if and only if there are singular propositions. Or he might have said that there are individual essences; for objects have properties in worlds if and only if there are individual essences. And given that objects have properties in worlds, we can make the traditional assertions connecting essential property possession with having properties in worlds: an object **x** has a property **P** essentially if and only if **x** has **P** in every world in which **x** exists; **x** has **P** accidentally if and only if **x** has **P** and there is a world in which **x** exists but lacks **P**.

Now suppose we agree that things do in fact have properties in worlds, so that in fact there are individual essences. Then fascinating questions arise: questions I can only mention, not discuss. First: do objects have *qualitative* essences, i.e., essences constructible out of purely qualitative properties? Infinite disjunctions of infinite conjunctions of such properties, perhaps? Second: are there *haecceities*, where a haecceity of an object is the property of being that very object? If so, are haecceities non-qualitative? If they are, will there also be other non-qualitative essences? Third: an unusually interesting alleged special case of individual essences is presented by *unexemplified* individual essences: individual essences that could have been exemplified, but in fact are not. *Existentialists*—such philosophers as Robert Adams[14], Kit Fine[15] and Arthur Prior[16] deny that there are any such things—although at the high cost of denying one or more of three exceedingly plausible premisses.[17] Singular propositions and quidditative properties, they say, are dependent upon the individuals they involve; so if Socrates had not existed, then the same would have held for this individual essence.

D. *Actualism and Serious Actualism*

But what about possibilia—i.e., *mere* possibilia? A *possibile* would be a thing that does not exist although it could have; a thing that does not exist

in the actual world but does exist in some other world. Should we not add a fourth grade of modal realism, a grade occupied by those who hold that in addition to all the things that exist, there are some more that do not? I doubt it. There is nothing specifically modal about these alleged things that do not exist—or rather there is nothing any more modal about them than about anything else. Anything that does exist is a *possibile*; the claim to fame of these alleged nonexistents is not the modal claim that they possibly exist, but the ontological claim that while indeed there *are* such things, they do not *exist*. I therefore do not believe that we should spend a grade of modal realism on these disorderly elements. The compleat modal realist, however, must take a stand on the question whether there are any such things as mere possibilia. I suggest he reject them as a snare and a delusion and embrace what is sometimes called 'actualism'. Actualism is the view that there neither are nor could have been any entities that do not exist, (where our quantifiers are taken wholly unrestricted). 'Actualism' is not a good name for actualism; it slyly encourages a confusion that is apparently all too attractive on its own demerits: the confusion between actuality and existence. The actualist does not hold that everything is *actual* (he recognizes, of course, that some states of affairs are not actual and some propositions are false); what *he* holds is that everything *exists* (again, quantifier taken unrestrictedly); there are no things that do not exist. But the name seems to have become entrenched, so 'actualism' it shall be. The compleat modal realist, therefore, will be an actualist. There may be more things than are dreamt of in our philosophy, but there aren't more things than all the things that exist; and while there could have been things distinct from each of the things that exist, it does not follow that there are some things that do not exist but could have.[18] What does follow (as I see it) is that there are some unexemplified essences.

Let us therefore embrace actualism. We can take a further step; we can also embrace *serious* actualism. The serious actualist holds, naturally enough, that everything whatever exists, but he adds that nothing has properties in worlds in which it does not exist. That is, for any world **w**, if Socrates has a property in **w**, then Socrates exists in **w**; for any world **w**, if **w** is such that if it had been actual, then Socrates would have had **P**, then **w** is such that if it had been actual Socrates would have existed. Still another way to put it: Socrates could not have had a property without existing.

On the face of it, serious actualism certainly looks to be *de rigueur* for the actualist. If there could have been no objects that do not exist, how could it be that Socrates should have had some property but not existed? If he had some property or other, then there would have been such a thing as Socrates, in which case (by actualism) there would have *existed* such a thing as Socrates. Still, there are actualists who deny serious actualism. Kit Fine[19] and John Pollock[20], both sturdy actualists, maintain that Socrates does have properties in worlds in which he does not exist: they say he has *nonexistence*, the complement of existence, in such worlds. We all agree, say they, that there are worlds in which Socrates does not exist; what could be more sensible, then, than to say that in those worlds he has the property of non-existence? I concede a certain surface plausibility to this opinion; on a closer look, however, we can see, I think, both that serious actualism is a corollary of actualism *tout court*, and that the apparent plausibility of the contary opinion is merely apparent.

First, then, I propose to argue that if actualism is true, then Socrates has neither the property of existence nor the complement of that property in worlds in which he does not exist. My argument has the following two premises:

(1) Necessarily, for any property **P**, if **P** is exemplified, then there is something that exemplifies it,

and

(2) Necessarily, for any property **P**, whatever exemplifies **P** exists.

(1), I take it, is obvious; and (2) is an immediate consequence of actualism. (If, as actualism testifies, necessarily, everything exists, then necessarily, everything that meets any condition exists.) But (1) and (2) entail

(3) Necessarily, if nonexistence is exemplified, it is exemplified by something that exists.

Clearly enough, it is impossible that nonexistence (the complement of existence) be exemplified by something that exists; it is therefore impossible that nonexistence be exemplified. So suppose Socrates has a property **P** in a world **w** in which he does not exist: then if **w** had been actual, Socrates would have exemplified **P**. So if **w** had been actual, then either Socrates would have exemplified **P & existence** (the conjunction of **P** with existence) or **P & nonexistence**. He could not have exemplified the later; for if he had, then nonexistence would have been exemplified, and we have seen that this is impossible. Therefore he would have exemplified the former; hence he would have exemplified existence. But then Socrates exemplifies existence in any world in which he exemplifies any property at all, just as the serious actualist claims.

If this is so, however, whence the plausibility of the contrary opinion? Why does it seem no more than common sense to say that Socrates exemplifies nonexistence in worlds in which he does not exist? We can see why as follows. As realists of the third grade, we agree that there are singular propositions. Associated with every property **P**, therefore, is a propositional function: a function whose value, for a given object **x**, is the singular proposition that **x** has **P**. Call these functions *conditions*. Associated with the property **being wise**, then, is a condition that maps an object—Socrates, let's say—onto the proposition that it is wise. Of course there is also the condition that maps Socrates onto the proposition that he is unwise, has the complement of wisdom. But there is also a condition that maps Socrates onto the proposition **it is false that Socrates is wise**—which proposition, according to the serious actualist, is distinct from the proposition **Socrates is unwise**. (The latter proposition is true only in worlds in which Socrates exists and has the complement of wisdom; the former is true in those worlds, but also in the rest of the worlds in which Socrates does not have that property, namely, the worlds in which he does not exist.) So we have four conditions:

> **x is wise**
> **x is unwise**
> **~(x is wise)**

and

> **~(x is unwise).**

The first two of these, says the serious actualist, are *predicative*—i.e., their values, for any object **x** taken as argument, predicate a property of **x**; their values, for Socrates taken as argument, respectively predicate wisdom and unwisdom of him. The second two, on the other hand, are impredicative. Their values, for Socrates taken as argument, do indeed predicate a property (namely, falsehood) of the *propositions* **Socrates is wise** and **Socrates is unwise**; but they predicate no property of Socrates himself. More generally, the value of an impredicative condition for an object **x** predicates no property of **x**, although it may predicate a property of some proposition predicating a property of **x**.

Now perhaps it is plausible to think that properties just are conditions—or at any rate are so intimately connected with them that for each distinct condition there is a distinct property: the property the value of that condition, for a given object **x** taken as argument, predicates of **x**. That is, it is plausible to think that *predicative* conditions are or are intimately connected with properties;

as we have seen, says the serious actualist, the value of an impredicative condition, for an object **x** does not predicate a property of **x**. But clearly actualism implies (by the above argument) that no object can satisfy a predicative condition in a world in which it does not exist; thus serious actualism is vindicated.

Now here the actualist opponent of serious actualism (call him a 'frivolous actualist') is not without reply. "Is it so clear," he says, "that such a proposition as **it is false that Socrates is wise** predicates no property of Socrates? True, it predicates falsehood of the proposition **Socrates is wise**; but why should that prevent its also predicating a property of Socrates—the property, perhaps, of being such that the proposition that he is wise is false? But if this is correct, then the conditions you call impredicative are not really impredicative after all; and surely Socrates can satisfy *those* conditions in worlds in which he does not exist. Surely, for example, he can satisfy such conditions as **~(x exists)** and **~(x is wise)** in worlds in which he does not exist; after all, the values of those functions for Socrates taken as argument are true in those worlds."

But here we must pay careful attention to this idea of an object's satisfying a condition in a world—or rather, we must distinguish two related notions, both of which lurk in this area. On the one hand there is the idea that an object **x** satisfies a condition **C** in a world **w** if and only if necessarily, if **w** had been actual, then **x** would have satisfied **C**. On the other hand, there is the idea that an object **x** satisfies a condition **C** in a world **w** if and only if necessarily, **C(x)** is true in **w**—if and only if, that is, necessarily, if **w** had been actual, then the value of **C** for **x** taken as argument would have been true. We can put these two as follows:

> D1   **x** satisfies **C** in **w** iff necessarily, if **w** had been actual, then **x** would have satisfied **C**.

and

D2 **x** satisfies **C** in **w** iff necessarily, **C(x)** is true in **w**.

To mark the difference between these two, let's say that **x** satisfies **C** in **w** if **x, C** and **w** are related as in D1, and that **x** satisfies **C** *at* **w** if they are related as in D2. Then the thing to see is that if actualism is true, no object satisfies a condition (or has a property) in a world in which it does not exist, although an object such as Socrates satisfies a condition such as ∼**(x is wise)** *at* worlds in which it does not exist. We can see this via an argument that exactly parallels the argument I gave above (p. 523) for the conclusion that Socrates has no properties in worlds in which he does not exist. My premises are

(4) Necessarily, for any condition **C**, if **C** is satisfied, then there is something that satisfies it

and

(5) Necessarily, for any condition **C**, whatever satisfies **C** exists.

Again, (4) is obvious and (5) follows from actualism. But (4) and (5) together entail

(6) Necessarily, if the condition ∼**(x exists)** is satisfied, then it is satisfied by something that exists.

The consequent of (6), however, is impossible; it is therefore impossible that ∼**(x exists)** be satisfied. It may seem a bit bizarre that there are conditions that cannot be satisfied, even though there are worlds at which they are satisfied. This peculiarity is merely verbal, and is due to a quirk in our definition of 'satisfies at'. **C** is indeed satisfied in some possible world only if **C** is possibly satisfied; the same cannot be said for satisfaction *at*.

But now it follows that there is no possible world in which Socrates satisfies ∼**(x exists)**. For suppose he satisfies that condition in some possible world **w**: then if **w** had been actual, Socrates would have satisfied that condition, in which case it would have been satisfied—which, as we have just seen, is impossible. So if Socrates satisfies ∼**(x exists)** in **w**, then **w** is not possible after all, contrary to hypothesis. Neither Socrates nor anything else, therefore, satisfies ∼**(x exists)** in any world (although of course Socrates and many other things satisfy ∼**(x exists)** *at* many possible worlds). And as before we can easily go on to show that Socrates does not satisfy any condition at all in a world in which he does not exist. For suppose Socrates satisfies **C** (= **x is C**) in **w**. Then either Socrates satisfies **x is C & x exists** in **w**, or Socrates satisfies **x is C and** ∼**(x exists)** in **w**. As we have seen, the latter is impossible; hence if Socrates satisfies **C** in **w**, then he also satisfies **x exists** in **w**, in which case he exists in **w**. It is therefore a mistake to think that an object can satisfy any conditions at all, predicative or impredicative, in worlds in which it does not exist. An object satisfies a condition or exemplifies a property in a possible world, therefore, only if it exists in that world, just as the serious actualist claims. Serious actualism, therefore, follows from actualism *simpliciter*; the temptation to think otherwise, I believe, stems from a tendency to confuse *satisfaction at* with *satisfaction in*. It is easy to confuse these two, and this confusion leads immediately to the idea that Socrates satisfies nonexistence in worlds in which he does not exist. The modal realist of the first grade, therefore, holds that individuals in general and propositions in particular have both essential and accidental properties; the modal realist of the second grade adds that there exist possible worlds. According to modal realism of the third grade, objects have properties in worlds— alternatively, objects have essences. The modal realist will also hold, I hope, that there are no things that do not exist, although there could have been things that do not exist in the world that is in fact actual. Finally, since he is an actualist, he should also embrace serious actualism.

II. Modal Reductionism

Suppose you, like (say) W.v. Quine, are a lover of desert landscapes: you believe in nothing but concrete individuals and set-theoretic constructions on them. Suppose you are also inclined to accept our common modal opinions: you believe that things might have been different in many ways, that if things had been appropriately different, then you would have had some properties that in fact you lack, and that there could have been people distinct from each of the people there actually are. Then you have something of a problem: how to construe these modal facts without recourse to propositions that are true but possibly false, properties an object has accidentally, possible worlds that are merely possible, and essences that are not exemplified. For none of these things seems to fit with the idea that whatever there is, is either a concrete individual or a set.

So what to do? Well, you could *quine* the whole disorderly crew: there simply *are* no essences, possible worlds, properties, propositions, and the like, you say. Serious science, you proclaim, has no place for such unwholesome elements, and you go on to blame a bad upbringing for our powerful tendency to think in modal terms. But there is a more subtle alternative; you could embrace the whole motley menageries with an outward show of enthusiasm, but seek to introduce order and domesticity by analyzing them in terms of the objects you favor; you could *model* them and their properties in concreta and sets. That is the course taken by David Lewis, whose powerfully subtle modal thought will be my chief example of modal reductionism.

A. Lewis' Modal Theory

Lewis' theory of modality and possible worlds began life as "Counterpart Theory":

The counterpart relation is our substitute for identity between things in different worlds.

Where some would say that you are in several worlds, in which you have somewhat different properties and somewhat different things happen to you, I prefer to say that you are in the actual world and no other, but you have counterparts in several other worlds. Your counterparts resemble you closely in content and context in important respects. They resemble you more closely than do the other things in their worlds. But they are not really you. For each of them is in his own world, and only you are here in the actual world. Indeed we might say, speaking casually, that your counterparts are you in other worlds, that they and you are the same; but this sameness is no more a literal identity than the sameness between you today and you tomorrow. It would be better to say that your counterparts are men you would have been, had the world been otherwise.[21]

On this account, you and I exist in just one possible world: the actual world. Now why would Lewis say a thing like that? Why would he thus sharply diverge from the modal realist, who typically holds that each of us exists in many different possible worlds? His answer in "Counterpart Theory and Modal Logic": "P2, the postulate according to which nothing exists in more than one world, serves only to rule out avoidable problems of individuation" (Lewis 1968: 114). We can see a better answer, however, once we see clearly how Lewis thinks of possible worlds. Possible worlds, he says, are spatiotemporally isolated concrete individuals: concrete individuals that are spatiotemporally related only to themselves and their parts. This wasn't entirely clear from his early accounts. Consider this famous passage from *Counterfactuals*:

I believe that there are possible worlds other than the one we happen to inhabit. If an argument is wanted, it is this. It is uncontroversially true that things might have been otherwise than they are. I believe, and so do you, that things could have been different in countless ways. But what does this mean? Ordinary language permits the paraphrase: there are many ways things could have been besides the way they actually are. On the face of it, this is an existential quantification. It says that there exist many entities of a certain description, to wit 'ways things could have been'. I believe that things could have been different in countless ways; I believe permissible paraphrases of what I believe: taking the paraphrase at its face value, I therefore believe in the existence of entities that might be called 'ways things could have been'. I prefer to call them 'possible worlds'.[22]

This suggestion seems more than compatible with the idea that possible worlds are not concreta, such as you and I and God, but abstracta, like the null set and the number 7. "Ways things could have been", one might sensibly think, would be properties, perhaps, or possibly propositions, or states of affairs, or other abstracta.[23] But Lewis has recently clarified his view:

Are there other worlds? I say there are. I advocate a thesis of plurality of worlds, or *modal realism* . . . that holds that our world is but one world among many. There are countless other worlds, other very inclusive things. Our world consists of us and all our surroundings, however remote in time and space; just as it is one big thing having lesser things as parts, so likewise do other worlds have lesser otherworldly things as parts. The worlds are something like remote planets; except that most of them are much bigger than mere planets and they are not remote. Neither are they nearby. They are not at any spatial distance whatever from here. They are not far in the past or future, nor for that matter near; they are not at any temporal distance at all from now. They are isolated: there are no spatiotemporal relations at all between things that belong to different worlds. Nor does anything that happens at one world cause anything to happen at another.[24]

So worlds are concrete particulars—many of them enormous, but some no larger than a flea. (In fact, some of them *are* fleas; Lewis holds that every concrete particular has a duplicate that is coextensive with its world and hence *is* that world.) Each world, furthermore is *maximal* in the sense that each of its parts is spatiotemporally related to each of its parts and only to its parts. (So suppose we call them 'maximal objects'). Maximal objects, of course, are not individuals that do not exist but could have; each of them exists, all right, although (except for the one of which we are a part) they are not spatiotemporally related to you and me. What we ordinarily refer to as "the universe" is one of these maximal objects; Lewis calls it 'the actual world'. But if possible worlds are maximal objects and you and I are parts of such a maximal object, then it is easy to see a good reason for thinking you and I exist in just one maximal object: if we existed in more than one, then each would be spatiotemporally related to the other (by virtue of sharing us as parts) and hence would not be maximal after all.[25]

So I exist in just one world; how can it be, then, that I have accidental properties? If there is no other world in which I exist, then for any property I do not have, there is no world in which I have it; so how could I have such a property? Lewis' answer: I possibly have a property if I have a counterpart—someone in this world[26] or another who is sufficiently similar to me—who has it.[27] I am possibly going barefoot today; that is, in some world there is someone who appropriately resembles me and is going barefoot. An object has a property accidentally if and only if it has it and has a counterpart that lacks it; an object has a property essentially if and only if it and all its counterparts have it.

Possible worlds, therefore, are maximal objects. The actual world is the maximal object of which we are parts; other maximal objects and their parts are *possibilia*. On Lewis' view a *possibile* is a concrete individual that is part (or the whole) of a world and spatiotemporally unrelated to us. *Pace* Meinong, Castañeda and Parsons, possibilia are not things that do not exist but could have; instead they are things that exist as solidly as you and I, though (except for our worldmates) at no spatiotemporal distance from us. *Properties* are sets—any sets; and an object *has* a property if and only if it is a member of it. An *individual essence* is the set of some individual and its counterparts. *Propositions* (or states of affairs: Lewis does not distinguish them) are sets of possible worlds: a proposition is *true* if and only if the actual world is a member of it, *possibly true* if and only if it is not empty, *necessary* if and only if it is the set of all possible worlds, and *impossible* if and only if it is the null set. Some propositions, of course, are unit sets; and since some worlds are donkeys or fleas, some propositions are unit sets of donkeys or fleas.

B. Modal Realism?

At first glance Lewis looks like a paradigm modal realist; indeed, Robert Stalnaker and others call him an *extreme* modal realist. Take the first grade of modal realism, the view that there are objects that have both accidental and essential properties. Surely Lewis endorses this view? An object has a property **P** *essentially*, he says, if and only if it is a member of **P** and so are all its counterparts; it has **P** *accidentally* if and only if it is a member of **P** but has a counterpart that is not. He holds that each of us has counterparts that have properties we don't; he also holds that each of us and all our counterparts are members of the universal set of individuals; should we not conclude that on his view objects have properties essentially and accidentally? Take modality *de dicto*, that special case of the first grade. Lewis holds that among the sets of maximal objects containing the maximal object of which we are a part, some contain fewer than all those objects and some (one) contain them all; shouldn't we conclude that on his

view some true propositions are contingent and some necessary? Turn to the second grade of modal realism: don't we find Lewis claiming (indeed, stubbornly insisting) that there are possible worlds? Turn finally to the third grade of modal realism: don't we find Lewis affirming both that there are individual essences (the set of an individual and its counterparts) and that objects have properties in worlds (where an object has a property in a world if and only if it is a member of that property and is part of that world)? So doesn't it follow that Lewis' view is a case of modal realism and a case of realism about possible worlds?

It doesn't follow. Lewis' modal theory is *apparently* realistic; in fact, however, it is not realist at all—or so, at any rate, I shall argue. (Of course this is nothing against the view; nobody says you have to be a modal realist.) Turn first to modality *de dicto*, that special case of modal realism of the first grade according to which some true propositions are contingent and some necessary; and say that a theory is *realist*, if it asserts that indeed there are some things of this sort, *antirealist* if it asserts that there are no such things, and *nonrealist* if it is not realist. I believe Lewis' theory is an example of antirealism here. True enough, Lewis seems to *say* that there are necessary and contingent propositions, but he also says that they are *sets*. There are many contingent propositions; each is a set of maximal objects. There is just one necessary proposition: the set of all the maximal objects; there is just one necessarily false proposition: the null set.

My complaint is not just that on this view there is only one necessary (or necessarily false) proposition, when it is clear that in fact there are many. That is indeed a legitimate complaint: surely a person could know that $2 + 1 = 3$ even if he does not know that arithmetic is incomplete or that Goldbach's conjecture is true (if it is) or that there is such a person as God. This complaint is legitimate; but if it is multiplicity we want, Lewis is prepared to oblige. He has other set-theoretic constructions on offer to "play the role" of propositions, and among them are some with as much multiplicity as you please (57). But my complaint comes right at the beginning and is both much more obvious and much more radical: sets, as we all know, are not the sort of things that can be true or false at all. You are teaching a course in set theory. The first day an agressive but confused student demands to know your view of the null set: is it true, he asks, or is it false? He adds (a bit truculantly) that in his opinion it is clearly false. Your reply, appropriately enough, is that it is neither; sets aren't the sort of things that can be either true or false. When this student claims that the null set is false, what he says is obviously mistaken; and isn't that claim obviously mistaken, even if made, not by confused student, but by first-rate philosopher?

Perhaps Lewis' reply to this line of argument would go as follows: that there *are* such things as propositions—i.e., the things that are true or false and can be believed and disbelieved—that is a matter of common opinion and something we all know pretheoretically. But we don't know pretheoretically what these things are like, or what their nature is: *that* is a matter, not for common opinion, but for the theoretician.[28] (Perhaps Lewis would say here, as he does in another context, that "if naive intuition claims to decide such a recondite matter, we ought to tell it to hold its tongue" (246)). Here theory is under little pressure from common opinion or pretheoretical knowledge. But then no theory can be anti-realistic with respect to propositions just by saying that propositions are sets (or by attributing to them any other kind of nature).

Clearly this is partly right: there is much about the nature of propositions we don't pretheoretically know. Are they, as some have thought, sentences in some very large powerful language? Are they instead, as Augustine and the bulk of the medieval tradition insist, divine thoughts? Do they have an internal structure? Do they have properties as constituents? Do they have concrete objects as constituents? Are there singular propositions? Lewis is right; we don't

pretheoretically know the answer to these questions. But we do know *something* about the nature of propositions, prior to theory. (By virtue of this pretheoretical knowledge we know, for example, that propositions couldn't be sentences of English or German.) Conceivably they could turn out to be idealized sentences or divine thoughts; but they couldn't turn out to be just *anything*—donkeys, or fleas, or tables[29], for example. We know that no propositions are donkeys, and we know that none are fleas. We know that no one believes fleas or donkeys (and not because of a depressing tendency on their parts to prevaricate).

Now on Lewis' view, no propositions are donkeys or fleas (although some possible worlds are); but some of them—uncountably many of them—are unit sets of donkeys and fleas. I say this is something we pretheoretically know to be false. Even as we can see that a proposition can't be a donkey or a flea, so we can see that a proposition can't be the unit set of a flea, or any other set of fleas or donkeys, or other livestock—or a set of concrete objects of any sort. You can't believe a set, and a set can't be either true or false. The problem, fundamentally, is that sets, like donkeys, obviously lack the relevant intentional properties—the intentional properties propositions have. A set is neither a claim nor anything like a claim; it doesn't represent its members or anything else as being thus and so; it neither is nor makes a claim as to what things are like.[30] The unit set of a donkey, for example, doesn't represent its member as being a donkey, or a nondonkey, or anything else; it is mute on that topic, as on every other. It certainly doesn't represent things as being such that there are no horses and that all pigs can fly, as it would, on Lewis' theory, if its member were a maximal object. On Lewis' theory, the null set is the impossible proposition. (If it is necessary that there be a null set, then the null set, on his view, is the proposition that there is no null set!) But why say it is *that* proposition? If the null set is a proposition, why couldn't it be a necessary proposition, or any other proposition? I say it is obvious that the null set isn't any proposition at all. It isn't the claim that there are married bachelors or that $3 + 1 = 7$ or that there is no such thing as the null set; nor is it the denial of these claims. A set isn't a claim; it no more represents things as being a certain way than an elephant has subsets. On Lewis' view there are concrete *possibilia* and sets and nothing else[31]; but if so then on his view there are no propositions at all, and hence none that are necessary or contingent. I therefore believe that Lewis' theory is nonrealistic and indeed antirealistic with respect to this special case of modal realism of the first grade.

Now suppose we turn to the more general thesis of modal realism of the first grade: the claim that objects have properties both essentially and accidentally. Is this true, on Lewis' theory? Is it true, on Lewis' view, that Socrates could have had the property of being foolish? Of course he endorses the words 'Socrates could have had the property of being foolish'; on his theory this sentence is true, expresses a truth. But my assertively and sincerely uttering or writing the sentence 'There are X's' is insufficient for my holding that there are X's, as is my theory's assigning truth to this sentence. Perhaps, for example, I use the words involved in such a way that they do not in fact express the proposition in question. Compare the ultraliberal theologian who says that on his theory there is indeed such a person as God, all right—the sentence 'There is a God' expresses a truth—but there are no supernatural beings, and as he uses the word 'God' it denotes the 'evolutionary-historical' process that has brought us into being.[32] That theologian's theory, in all probability, is not realistic with respect to God.

On Lewis' theory, then: do individuals have accidental properties? According to the theory, you have counterparts who are members of sets you are not a member of; and this is offered as an analysis of your having some properties accidentally. But is the analysis correct? Suppose there exists a person who is very much like you

and is a member of some set you are not a member of: is that so much as *relevant* to your possibly having some property? It is hard to see how. On the face of it, there being a foolish person who is otherwise a great deal like Socrates has nothing whatever to do with the question whether Socrates could have been foolish. Surely it is not relevantly sufficient for Socrates' being possibly foolish; and the fact, if it is a fact, that this person is spatiotemporally unrelated to us and Socrates doesn't help. Nor, of course, is it necessary; even if everyone (even those, if any, who inhabit maximal objects distinct from ours) were wise, it would still be the case that Socrates could have been foolish. The existence of other maximal objects and counterparts who are members of sets I am not a member of is clearly irrelevant to the phenomena of modality. Surely I could have been barefoot even if everyone, even those in other maximal objects if there are any, were wearing shoes. Surely the proposed analysis is incorrect; it flouts the obvious pretheoretical truth that what is a possibility for me does not depend in this way upon the existence and character of other concrete objects.

Lewis sees his theory as "disagreeing with firm common sense opinion" (133) especially with respect to his ontology—that uncountable magnitude of donkeys spatiotemporally unrelated to us, and those more than uncountably many maximal objects. Firm common sense opinion is indeed incredulous here; there is no reason, pretheoretically, to believe that there is more than one maximal object; and considerable pretheoretical impulse to be at least agnostic about the matter. The idea that there are more than uncountably many of them, therefore, seems a great deal to swallow. Still, common opinion tends to be agnostic here, and could perhaps be convinced by enough of the right sort of evidence. (A traditional theist will be harder to convince; from his point of view there couldn't be all those donkeys spatiotemporally unrelated to us. Say that **x** has been *created** by God if either **x** has been created by God or has been created by something that has been created* by God. According to the traditional theist, it is a necessary truth that every nondivine concrete particular has been created* by God. All the donkeys there are, accordingly, are causally related to God. But (necessarily) things causally related to the same thing are causally related to each other; so there couldn't be any concrete paticulars that are causally unrelated to you and me). Where firm common opinion sticks in its heels is at the claim that it is *necessary* that there be all those donkeys and maximal objects. It seems clearly *possible* that there be at most one maximal object and only finitely many donkeys; and it is possible that all the donkeys there are be spatiotemporally related to us.

The idea that there are more than uncountably many donkeys and maximal objects is therefore problematic. But the real problem, from a modal point of view, is not with *that* idea but with the claim that a thing possibly has a property if and only if it has a counterpart that has the property. Perhaps I do indeed have a counterpart who can talk French; but clearly enough even if I don't, it is still possible that I talk French. Counterparts, concrete objects spatiotemporally unrelated to us, other maximal objects—these are all quite irrelevant to modality.

Still, even if this analysis is incorrect it does not follow that Lewis' theory is either nonrealistic or antirealistic with respect to objects that have properties essentially and accidentally; and that, after all, is the question at issue. (Even if my analysis of causation is incorrect, it does not follow that I do not believe in causation.) Nevertheless Lewis' theory, if taken at face value, is (as I see it) a radical rejection of essential and accidental property possession; on his theory, no objects have properties accidentally or essentially. The reason, fundamentally, is that on this theory there are no such things as properties at all. Lewis takes a property to be a set—in the first instance a set of all its this- and other-worldly members; but if we aren't satisfied with *those* sets in the role of properties, he has others on offer

(pp. 56–59). But clearly enough, properties are *not* sets. As Lewis sees things, we know pretheoretically that there are such things as properties—at any rate we firmly believe that there are entities that deserve the name—but (as in the case of propositions) we don't pretheoretically know much of anything about their nature. And indeed there *is* much we don't know about them. But we do know *something* about their nature, and enough to see that they could not be sets. Take, for example, the property of being a donkey, which Lewis proposes to identify with the set of donkeys (this- or other-worldly donkeys). *That* set, clearly enough, could not have been empty; it could not have been the null set. (Had there been no donkeys, that set would not have existed.) But the property of being a donkey could have been unexemplified; obviously there could have been no donkeys at all, here or on any other maximal object, if there are any others. Donkeyhood is contingently exemplified; the set of donkeys (since there are some donkeys) is esentially nonempty; hence the property of being a donkey is not the set of donkeys.[33] Of course Lewis can *get the effect* on contingency in his model; some but not all maximal objects **w** are such that the set of donkeys-in-**w** is empty. But how does this help? The set of donkeys—i.e., the set of all donkeys—still has a property donkeyhood lacks; hence the former is distinct from the latter. So I say it is obvious that properties are not sets. It is obvious that no property is the unit set of a donkey, or a larger set of donkeys, or any other set of animals or concreta (It is obvious that no properties are sets; but I must concede that it is not *as* obvious as that no propositions are sets.) But if it is obvious that no property is a set, then Lewis' theory is a rejection of modal realism of the first grade.

I turn now to the second grade of modal realism: the claim that there are possible worlds. How does Lewis' theory stand with respect to this claim? Are there any such things, on his theory? I think not. (Of course there are the things he *calls* possible worlds—at any rate there is *one* such thing.) First, it is clear, I think, that the phrase "possible world" is philosopher's talk for something like 'way things could have been', or better, 'total way things could have been'. (And so the use of 'world' in 'possible world' is quite different from its use in e.g., 'God created the world.'[34]) Now this pretheoretical idea of a way things could have been (like the ideas of proposition and property) pretheoretically displays a certain indefiniteness: a way things could have been could be a state of affairs, perhaps, or a property, or a proposition or perhaps even (cardinality problems aside) a set of propositions or states of affairs. But could possible worlds, ways things could have been, turn out to be maximal objects? It is hard to see how. There are at least two central and obvious characteristics of possible worlds (or total ways things could have been). First, they are such that if there is at least one object that has a property accidentally, then it follows that there are at least two possible worlds; if there are **n** properties such that I could have had any combination of those properties, then there are at least 2^n possible worlds. Second, possible worlds are such that if there is at least one contingent proposition, it follows that there are at least two possible worlds; more generally, if there are at least **n** appropriately independent propositions then there are at least 2^n possible worlds. Not so for maximal objects. If it is possible that there be more than one maximal object (and perhaps it isn't), it will be a contingent matter just how many there are in fact; there could be two, or six, or (less likely) countably infinitely many. (Could there be at least 2^c, as Lewis' theory requires?) But what is more important in the present context is this: the number of maximal objects, unlike the number of possible worlds, is independent of the number of logically independent propositions (and independent of the number of combinations of properties I could have had). There are objects that have properties contingently and propositions that are contingent; and that is true no matter how many maximal objects there are. I

have the property of wearing shoes accidentally; the proposition **Paul is over six feet tall** is contingent; and this is so even if, as most of us believe, there is only one maximal object. So possible worlds can't be maximal objects.[35] Lewis' Theory, then, is not a realism with respect to possible worlds.

Still further, this theory, I think, is an *antirealism* with respect to possible worlds. Like propositions, possible worlds have that intentional property: a possible world is such that things are thus and so *according to* it; a possible world *represents* things as being a certain way. But no concrete object or set theoretic construction does a thing like that. So if all there are are concrete individuals and set-theoretic constructions on them, then there are no possible worlds. On Lewis' ontology that is all there are; so on his theory there are no possible worlds; so Lewis' theory is an example of antirealism with respect to possible worlds. Suppose someone says: "On my theory there is another universe causally and spatiotemporally discontinuous with the universe we see around us. This universe contains duplicates of some of us, and things similar to others of us. But all the objects in either that universe or ours or anywhere else are concrete particular or set-theoretic constructions therefrom." Then on that person's theory there are no possible worlds, and adding more maximal objects won't help. So I believe Lewis' theory is antirealist about possible worlds. But if so, then on this theory it is not the case that objects have properties in worlds; so Lewis' theory is an antirealism of the third grade as well as of the second and the first. The just conclusion, I think, is that Lewis is about as much a modal realist as is W. v. Quine. (Let me hasten to add, once more, that this is no denigration of his views; nobody claims modal realism is *de rigueur* for modal theorists. I mean only to correct what I see as widespread misunderstanding.)

Of course there is *something* in the neighborhood with respect to which Lewis is a realist, and a pretty unusual and interesting thing at that: a plurality of maximal objects. Like Quine, he prefers desert landscapes: concrete objects and sets. Lewis' desert, however, with its 2^c or more spatiotemporally isolated maximal objects, is both more extensive and less continuous than Quine's. Lewis is certainly a realist of an interesting kind; but what he isn't is a *modal* realist. On his theory, as I see it, there are no propositions, states of affairs, possible worlds, essences or objects with essential and accidental properties; what there are instead are concrete objects and set theoretical constructions on them, some of which play roles formally similar to the roles in fact played by the phenomena of modality if the modal realist is right.

C. Lewis and Modal Reductionism

Lewis seems to say some puzzling things: that among the propositions there are some that are unit sets of donkeys, that the property of being a donkey is a set of this- and other-worldly donkeys, and that I could have been going barefoot now only if there is someone sufficiently like me who is going barefot now. These are things I said we know are false. Why, then, would Lewis say them? He seems to say puzzling things: what is most puzzling is that he should say them. But perhaps he isn't really saying them; perhaps there is something more subtle going on. (It's not entirely easy to see just what Lewis' project really is; but I shall do my best.) First, Lewis is a modal *reductionist*: He offers reductive analyses of the phenomena of modality: he reduces possible worlds to maximal objects, propositions and states of affairs to sets of maximal objects, essences to sets of concrete objects, and essential and accidental property possession to similarity and set membership.

There are at least two kinds of philosophical analysis: *reductive* and *explicative*. The explicative analyst gives analyses of the sort G.E. Moore said could not be given of goodness: he tries to penetrate a concept we already have, to discern the structure of such a concept, to resolve it into its

components (if any), and to show the relations in which those components stand.[36] The late lamented analysis of knowledge as justified true belief is of this sort. The *reductive* analyst, however, is stalking different game. One who reduces propositions to sets does not claim that when we reflect on our common concept of propositions, what we see is that propositions after all are really sets, or that the concept of propositions is really the same concept as that of a certain sort of set. Instead, he proposes what from the point of view of that common concept is a *substitute*; the whole point of his analysis is to provide a substitute for the suspect entities, thereby thinking perhaps, to reduce commitment to questionable ontology.

There are at least two kinds of reductive analyses: ontological and semantical. The first kind tells us that there really are such things as A's, but (contrary to what we might have thought) they are really B's: there are such things as houses and horses, but in fact they are really congeries of sense data; there are such things as mental states, but in fact each mental state is identical with some neurological state; there really are such things as propositions, but in fact they are sets of maximal objects. He then uses the relevant terms—'proposition', 'true', and the like—in their ordinary and established ways, and may seem to say quite outrageous things: that some sets are true, that some are necessarily true, that the null set represents Frege as a married bachelor, that the null set is necessarily false, and that Frege believed the null set until Russell showed him the error of his ways. But Lewis' analyses are not like this. He does not tell us that there really are such things as propositions and properties, and that *what* they really are are sets: "All this is a matter of fitting suitable entities to the various rather ill-defined roles that we rather indecisively associate with various familiar names. Don't think of it as a matter of discovering which entities *really are* the states of affairs, or the ways things might be, or the possibilities, or the propositions, or the structures!"

The *semantical* reductionist, by contrast, uses the relevant terms in a nonstandard way. By 'proposition' he might just *mean* 'set of maximal objects'; and by 'is true' he might mean 'has the maximal object of which we are parts as a member'.[37] Sometimes it looks as if this is the course Lewis takes: "Not everyone means the same thing by the word 'proposition'. I mean a set of possible worlds, a region of logical space. Others mean something more like a sentence, something with indexicality and syntactic structure, but taken in abstraction from any particular language." . . . "The word "property" is also used in many senses. I mean a set: the set of exactly those possible beings, actual or not, that have the property in question."[38] A semantical reductionist doesn't claim that propositions are sets; since by 'proposition' he means sets of maximal objects, when he says "propositions are sets of maximal objects" what he asserts is what the rest of us assert when we say "sets of maximal objects are sets of maximal objects". Then he doesn't really assert such peculiar items as that propositions are sets of maximal objects or that the property of being a donkey is the set of this and other worldly donkeys.

Is Lewis a semantical reductionist? I'm not quite sure. What is clearer, I think, is that he proposes *models*. He models our modal talk, or thought, or the modal phenomena in set-theoretic constructions on concrete individuals; he proposes models whose domains of interpretation contain only the sorts of entities of which he approves. He offers us semantics for our modal discourse, semantical systems that have recourse only to the sorts of things he believes in. Lewis thinks there are various *roles* associated with such words as 'proposition', 'property', 'state of affairs', 'possibility', and the like (and not just the roles of denoting the propositions, properties, states of affairs, possibilities, and the like); and the job of analysis or theory is to find the things that best fill these roles:

'Property', and the rest, are names associated

in the first instance with roles in our thought. It is a firm commitment of common sense that there are some entities or other that play the roles and deserve the names, but our practical mastery of uses of the names does not prove that we have much notion what manner of entities those are. That is a question for theorists. I believe in properties. That is, I have my candidates for entities to play the role and deserve the name. My principal candidates are sets of possible individuals. (But I can offer you alternatives—other set-theoretic constructions out of possible individuals—to suit different versions of the role.) (189)

And (speaking of states of affairs and ways things might be):

I suppose it is a firm commitment of common sense that there are some entities or other that fill the roles, and therefore deserve the names. But that is not to say that we have much notion of what sort of entities those are. We can toss the names around and never think what manner of entities we are talking about. Only when we want to improve on common sense and get something more systematic and unified and definite, does the question arise. The entities that deserve the names are the entities best suited to fill the roles. To figure out what those are, we must survey the candidates according to our best systematic theory of what there is. It's no good saying: which are they? Why they are the states of affairs! (185)

(To the question "Who shall play Polonius?", says Lewis, it's not good replying, "Why, Polonius, of course!").

Lewis *takes* properties to be certain sets; he *identifies* properties with those sets, in something like the way in which one might take the number 1 to be the unit set of the null set: "I identify propositions with certain properties: namely with those that are instantiated only by entire possible worlds" (50). To take properties or propositions to be sets is to endorse those sets as suited to play the relevant role:

> If we believe in possible worlds and individuals, and if we believe in set-theoretic constructions out of things we believe in, then we have entities suited to play the role of properties.
>
> The simplest plan is to take a property just as the set of all its instances—all of them, this- and other-worldly alike. Thus the property of being a donkey comes out as the set of all donkeys, the donkeys of other worlds along with the donkeys of ours.

Further, there may be several versions of the property role among which our use of the relevant terms does not make a choice. Thus we can't sensibly ask, for example, whether two properties are ever necessarily coextensive. We must recognize instead that the word has become associated with a variety of subtly different roles:

> Here there is a rift in our talk of properties, and we simply have two different conceptions. It's not as if we have fixed once and for all, in some perfectly definite and unequivocal way, on the things we call 'the properties', so that now we are ready to enter into debate about such questions as, for instance, whether two of them are ever necessarily coextensive. Rather, we have the word 'property' introduced by way of a varied repertory of ordinary and philosophical uses. To deserve the name of 'property' is to be suited to play the right theoretical role: or better, to be one of a class of entities which together are suited to play the right role collectively. But it is wrong to speak of the role associated with the word 'property' as if it were fully and uncontroversially settled. It comes in many versions, differing in a number of ways. The question worth asking is: which entities, if any, among

those we should believe in, can occupy which versions of the property role? (55)

Lewis models our modal thought and talk in concrete objects and set theoretical constructions therefrom. There are several different models on offer: the proposition **Sam is happy** could be a set of worlds, for example; but it could also be a pair set consisting of Sam and a property; and of course there are many other possibilities. There is something that represents *de re* of me that I am Fred: we can take Fred himself as the thing that does so (232). (Under a weaker counterpart relation there are things that represent me as being a poached egg: we can take the poached eggs to be those things.) What isn't wholly clear, however, is just what Lewis, qua theoretician, proposes to do with these models.[39] There they are: all those different models in which different things play the role of a given proposition or property. We are not to ask which really *is* that proposition or property; no model is endorsed to the exclusion of the others; all are acceptable, although some are more suitable for some purposes than for others. If you think there is only one necessary and one impossible proposition, there is an appropriate model; if what you want is multiplicity (many necessary propositions), that is easily arranged; if you think that concrete objects such as you and I are constituents of propositions, that too is no problem: there is a model to fit.

Now I find this puzzling. I'm not sure what claim, if any, is being made about propositions, properties, states of affairs, possibilities, and their like. But perhaps at any rate the following is clear. Lewis accepts what he calls the common opinion that indeed there are such things as propositions, properties, etc. He adds, however, that common opinion has no definite idea as to what these things are; this is up for theoretical grabs; so far as what we pretheoretically know, is concerned these things could be any of the objects presented by the proposed models.

But is this really true? Indeed there are those

roles of which Lewis speaks; but aren't they accompanied by much fuller stage directions—e.g., no proposition can be played by a set—than he supposes? Alternatively, don't we know a lot more about what fills them than he supposes? Do we have only those roles Lewis speaks of, so that it is up to theory to say what fills them? Or do we also know something about the sorts of things that occupy them—e.g., that no proposition is the unit set of a donkey, or any larger sets of donkeys, or indeed any set at all? The modal realist—my kind of modal realist—says there are such things as proposition, properties, worlds and their like. We know that these things play certain roles, sure enough; but we know more about them than that. We know, e.g., that they are not sets—although there might be interesting isomorphisms between propositions and certain set-theoretic structures, isomorphisms from which we can learn about propositions, even if we know that propositions aren't sets. We know that neither Paul nor any poached egg[40] can represent of me that I am Paul or a poached egg, although there are models of modality in which Paul or a poached egg could play the role of such a representer—models from which we may be able to learn something important about representation.

So I am not quite sure what Lewis' theory says about propositions and their like. But this much seems reasonably clear: according to this theory, any propositions (or property) you pick is at any rate some set or other. And if this is so, then I say his theory is antirealistic about these things.

It's Lewis concretism that is to blame—his view that all there are are concrete individuals and sets (and perhaps also immanent universals or tropes). For there are obvious truths which together with this claim entail that there are no propositions, properties, or possible worlds. It is not that concretism *as such* is incompatible with modal realism. According to another, more moderate if vaguer version of concretism, there are indeed such nonconcreta as propositions, properties, numbers, sets, states of affairs,

possible worlds and so on; but all of them must somehow be rooted in or dependent upon concrete objects. Sets, for example, are ontologically dependent upon their members; had Paul Zwier failed to exist, then so would his unit set. (Perhaps sets are also and essentially *collections*—as Cantor thought—and thus dependent upon some kind of collecting activity on the part of some individuals or other.) Propositions depend for their existence upon concrete thinkers: propositions, perhaps, just *are* thoughts (and even that allegedly arch-Platonist Frege called them *Gedanken*); and properties, perhaps, just are concepts. This view is open to obvious and crushing objection if the thinkers involved are *human* thinkers: for then there are far too many propositions and properties. Of course there is no problem here for the Augustinian view according to which propositions are *divine* thoughts (and properties divine concepts). Some might think explaining propositions as God's thought is at best a case of *obscurum per obscurius* (58).

But one man's cost is another man's benefit; if you already accept or are inclined to accept theism, then this suggestion may seem not just acceptable, but compelling.

D. Two Objections

(1) "You say Lewis is not a modal realist; but *he* says he is. And isn't he the authority on his own theory? Who are you to say that this theory is anti-realistic if he says it isn't?"

Reply: similar questions are regularly debated in theology. Someone might claim that according to his theory Christ indeed arose from the dead; what this means he says, is that the disciples "had an experience of forgiveness, which they expressed in categories of resurrection." It remains a question whether on his theory Christ arose from the dead. He assertively writes and utters such sentences as 'Christ arose from the dead'; on his theory, that sentence expresses a truth; but it doesn't follow that on his theory Christ arose from the dead. An even more liberal theologian might say: "Certainly on my theory there is such a person as God: when I say that, what I mean is that I face the Future with confidence."[41] It remains a question on his theory whether there is such a person as God. Consider a paradigm nominalist: he says that there are no universals, properties, or kinds; he adds that the role the realist thinks is played by such things is in fact played by utterances or inscriptions of words of natural languages. Such a nominalist is a reductionist with respect to universals; he is also an antirealist with respect to them. (Never mind whether his reduction is successful or not.) Compare this nominalist with someone who claims to be a realist with respect to universals but adds that universals are really inscriptions or utterances of words of natural language; that, he says, is what their nature is. This person's ontology, I suggest, is indistinguishable from the paradigm nominalist's views, despite his realist claims and aspirations. Claiming royalty at the font doesn't automatically confer sovereignty: claiming to be a realist with respect to universals is insufficient for being one. Suppose someone says he believes in elephants: only on his theory, he says, elephants are really numbers—numbers equal to the sum of their proper divisors. He adds that there are no material objects. Then according to his theory there are no elephants, despite his assertively writing or uttering "On my theory there are elephants, only as it happens they are perfect numbers." Lewis says he believes in the phenomena of modality—propositions, properties and the like:

> I believe in properties. That is, I have my candidates for entities to play the role and deserve the name. My principal candidates are sets of possible individuals. (But I can offer you alternatives. . .) (p. 189)

No doubt there are indeed set-theoretic constructions on individuals that can play the role of properties (or propositions) in one or another model of our modal talk; but saying so, I submit, is not sufficient for being a realist with respect to properties (or propositions).

(2) "In arguing that Lewis is a modal antirealist, you employ premises that he doesn't accept—such premises, for example, as the claim that no set can be believed, that no set is a claim or an assertion, that no set represents anything as being thus and so, and that no set could be true or false. But Lewis accepts none of these premises; so you can't properly employ them to determine the commitments of his theory."

Reply: the question is how to tell what a theory is committed to: what premises and arguments forms can be used along with what a theory explicitly asserts to reach propositions to which that theory is committed? This is a delicate question. Suppose my theory does not contain a given premise: does that show that it is not committed to any conclusion that can be derived from what it explicitly says only with the help of that premise? I don't think so. Consider someone with a theory according to which, oddly enough, there are two uniquely tallest men. You point out that according to his theory, there is more than one uniquely tallest human being; he demurs, replying that on his theory it is not true that two is greater than one. His theory is nonetheless committed, I think, to the proposition that there is more than one uniquely tallest human being. Suppose my theory contains **p** and also **if p then q**; then it is committed to **q**, even if I claim that *modus ponens* is no part of my theory. Return to the ultra-liberal theologian—a peculiarly rigid follower of Bultmann, for example—according to whose theory there is no person who is perfect in knowledge and power and who has created the worlds; in fact there are only material objects and no supernatural beings at all. We characterize his theory as atheism, i.e., anti-realism with respect to God. "Not at all," he says; "on my theory, to accept belief in God is to adopt a certain attitude or policy: it is to resolve to accept and embrace one's finitude, giving up the futile attempt to build hedges and walls against guilt, failure, and death." He adds that he rejects the premiss that any theory according to which there are only material objects and no supernatural beings is an atheist theory. The fact is, I think, that his theory is atheist, whether or not he accepts those premisses. (In the case of this theologian (and some of the others), there is a certain evasiveness, a certain deplorable deceptiveness, a certain lack of candor. No such thing characterizes Lewis' views; quite the contrary: Lewis is wholly forthright as to what it is he thinks.) In each of these cases, it is quite proper to use a premise not included in the theory in question in order to determine what that theory is committed to. I say the same goes with respect to the premisses that no sets predicate properties of objects, or represent things as being thus and so, or are true or false, or are assertions, or are believed. So I think it is quite proper to use these premisses to determine the commitments of Lewis' modal theory, even if he does not accept those premisses.

Of course the question what a theory is committed to is delicate. Let **T** be a theory: and suppose **T** entails (i.e., strictly implies) that there are no X's. It doesn't follow that according to **T** there are no X's. For perhaps **T** contains some false (and hence necessarily false) mathematics; it wouldn't follow that according to **T** there are no possible worlds, despite the fact that **T** entails that there are no possible worlds (as well as that there are some). Suppose **T** attributes to X's a property **P** such that every X has the complement of **P** essentially, or a property **Q** such that it is impossible that there be X's that have **Q**; or suppose there is some property **R** such that it is necessary that X's have **R** essentially and such that according to **T** nothing has **R**: it still doesn't follow that **T** is antirealist with respect to X's. Surely I could have a mistaken theory about quarks: a theory according to which there are such things as quarks and according to which quarks have a property **P** such that in fact it is a necessary truth that all quarks have ~ **P** essen-

tially. Then my theory attributes to quarks a property **P** such that every quark has the complement of **P** essentially; it also attributes to quarks a property such that it is impossible that there be any quarks that have that property; and there is a property **R**—namely, **being a quark not having P**—such that it is necessary that quarks have this property essentially, while according to my theory nothing has this property. But it doesn't follow that my theory is antirealist with respect to quarks. Suppose it is a necessary truth that every contingent object has essentially the property of having been created* by God;[42] and suppose someone's theory asserts that human beings have not been created* by God. It doesn't follow that on the theory in question there are no human beings.

On the other hand, as we have already seen, **T**'s (or **T**'s expression) containing a sentence like 'There are X's' is not sufficient for **T**'s being realistic with respect to X's (or even for its not being antirealistic with respect to X's). Still further, even if **T** asserts that according to **T** there are X's, it doesn't follow that according to **T** there are X's. A person might say that on his theory there are angels; it does not follow that on his theory there are angels. For if he goes on to say that on his theory angels are cats (and thinks of cats no differently from the rest of us), then it is not the case that his theory asserts that there are angels.

This question, therefore—the question just what a theory is committed to—is both vexed and delicate. What is it that determines which premises can be used in conjunction with what a theory explicitly asserts to reach propositions to which that theory is committed? I think it's a matter of *obviousness*; wholly obvious propositions can be used in that fashion. Of course there are problems here (problems I don't have the space to enter). We must remember Kreisel's dictum: "it ain't obvious what's obvious"; and to whom must the propositions be obvious? and since obviousness is a matter of degree, does it follow that commitment of a theory to a proposition is a matter of degree? I shall save these questions for another time and turn to a different objection. I say it is obvious that, e.g., no set represents anything as being thus and so; but is that really obvious, or better, is it relevantly obvious? According to some, there is theory, and then there is data, or evidence, or the appearances (the appearances a theory must save). A semantic theory such as Lewis' is accountable to the data—but not of course to other semantic theories.[43] The data are our linguistic intuitions as to which sentences express truths: "Our intuitive judgments, made 'upon reflection' after we have assured ourselves of the nonlinguistic fact, of what is true and what implies what, are the appearances that a semantic theory must save" (Hazen, 1979: 320). On this view, a satisfactory theory will assign the right truth values to the sentences; but if it turns out, on the theory, that these sentences express propositions quite different from the ones we thought they did, that is nothing against it[44] Further, the relevantly obvious truths, the ones we can properly use along with what a theory explicitly asserts to determine what the theory is committed to, are just those nontheoretical truths of linguistic intuition.

Now Lewis (sensibly enough) endorses no such facile bifurcation of theory and linguistic intuition:

> There is no sharp line between sacrosanct intuition and freewheeling theory. We start where we are—where else?—with a stock of initial opinions, and we try to rework them into something better Any revision of previous theory counts as some cost. But some of our opinions are firmer and less negotiable than others. And some are more naive and less theoretical than others. And there seems to be some tendency for the more theoretical ones to be more negotiable (241).

Among our firm opinions in this area are our "linguistic intuitions" to the effect that certain sentences—such sentences as 'Socrates could have been foolish'—do indeed express truths. Quite right. But aren't some of the "more theoretical" claims equally obvious? Clearly enough, 'Socrates could have been foolish' expresses a truth; but isn't it nearly as obvious that the truth it expresses does not require that Socrates have a foolish counterpart? Isn't it equally obvious that the truth in question is not a set of maximal objects, or of other concrete objects, or indeed a set of any kind at all? Isn't it equally obvious that no proposition is the unit set of a donkey, or the null set? Lewis once said he found it hard to believe that he and all his surroundings were a set of sentences.[45] That seems fair enough; but is it much easier to believe that the proposition **7 + 5 = 13**, say, or **there is no God** (if you are a classical theist) or **there is no null set** (if you are not) is really the null set? Or to believe that uncountably many propositions are unit sets of fleas or donkeys? I doubt it. And the same holds, I think, for the other premises I used to argue that Lewis' view is not a case of modal realism. (I must concede that some of these propositions are more obvious than others; it is clearer that Lewis' view is antirealistic with respect to propositions than with respect to properties, and clearer with respect to properties than with respect to possible worlds.) But even if I am wrong, even if the existence of these obvious truths is not sufficient for the theory's being antirealist, the most important point still remains: the theory in conjunction with obvious truths obviously entails modal antirealism of all grades.

E. Concluding Reflection

Although Lewis proposes semantical reductionist models for our modal discourse, it is less than clear that he is a semantical reductionist, because it isn't clear what it is he proposes that we do with these models. Still, his theory has some affinities with semantical reductionism, and in conclusion I wish to say briefly why I think semantical reductive analysis is unhopeful. For what is the point of the project? One begins with an ontological conviction—that all there are are concrete particulars and set theoretic constructions on them, perhaps. This conviction seems hard to square with common opinion, (including one's own opinion) about truths and falsehoods, properties, possibilities, and the like. One hopes to remedy the situation by giving the semantical reductive analysis in question. But how does the analysis help? Offering a semantical analysis does little to respect common opinion; for it preserves the sentences typically used to express common opinion, but not the opinion they express. It is common opinion that some propositions are true and other false, and that I could have been wearing my other shoes. The reductionist respects these *sentences*; they come out true on his analysis. But in his mouth what the first means is that some sets of maximal objects include the maximal object of which we are parts and some do not; and what the second means is that there exists (quantifier taken broadly) someone sufficiently like me who is wearing his other shoes. Clearly these are not the common opinions commonly expressed in the sentences he endorses; while he speaks with the vulgar, he thinks with the learned, and his agreement with common opinion is a merely verbal agreement. If divergence from common opinion is costly, semantical analysis does little to help.[46]

Insofar as he is concerned with divergence from common opinion, from what we all know or believe, the reductive analyst faces a dilemma. On the one hand, he can propose his theory as the sober metaphysical truth: there are possible worlds and they are maximal concrete objects; there are such things as propositions, and they are sets of maximal concrete objects. But these suggestions, of course, are wholly at variance with common opinion, according to which no possible worlds are donkeys (or other concreta) and no propositions are sets of concreta. On the other hand, he can propose a semantical analysis: he can assign a meaning to the relevant sentences—the sentences expressing common opinion about truth and modality—by way of a semantics whose domain of interpretation includes only objects of the sorts he approves of. The semantics then assigns propositions to these sentences, and when he affirms the sentences he affirms those propositions. Then, however, he winds up respecting not common opinion, but only the words in which common opinion is commonly expressed.

At the beginning of section II I said that one who believes only in sets and concreta has at least two options: on the one hand, she can quine what doesn't seem to fit, and on the other she can give a reductive analysis of these things. I implied that the second was subtler than the first. Perhaps it is; but so far as flouting what we pretheoretically know or believe is concerned, there is little real difference between them. The first, furthermore, is more straightforward, more conducive to clarity of thought than the second, at least if the reductive analysis in question is a semantical analysis. Return once more to the hyper-liberal theologian who insists that on his theory there is such a person as God all right, even though there are no supernatural beings: for the word 'God', as he uses it, he says, denotes the evolutionary-historical process (or perhaps "the forces not ourselves that make for goodness"). Suppose such a theologian goes on to model the rest of what theists ordinarily say in nonsupernatural beings: he doesn't share their belief that there is such a person as God, even though on his theory the words 'There is such a person as God' express a truth. His opinion differs from that of the plainspeaking atheist only by virtue of being less plainly spoken. Something similar goes for the semantical reductionist.[47] One who quines the modal phenomena rejects both common opinion and the sentence in which it is expressed; the semantical reductionist endorses the sentences but rejects the opinions. From the point of view of modal realism, it is hard to see a significant difference.

By way of conclusion then: the modal realist believes in necessary and contingent truths, object with essential and accidental properties, and individual essences. He will also, I hope, accept actualism; and if actualism, then serious actualism. By contrast the modal reductionist, whatever the virtues of his views, is not a modal realist at all.[48]

Notes

1 Modal phenomena are not, of course, to be contrasted with modal noumena; my use of the term is Platonic, not Kantian.

2 See my "How to be an Anti-Realist", *Proceedings of the American Philosophical Association*, Vol. 56, pp. 47–49.

3 According to the classical theist, every proposition is in *fact* (and, indeed, *necessarily*) believed or disbelieved—by God, who is a necessary being and essentially omniscient.

4 See my *The Nature of Necessity* (Oxford: At the Clarendon Press, 1974), p. 2.

5 *Op. Cit.* pp. 2–9

6 See "Self-Profile" in *Alvin Plantinga*, ed. James Tomberlin and Peter van Inwagen (Dordrecht: D. Reidel Publishing Co., 1985) (hereafter "*Profiles*") pp. 90–91 and John Pollock's "Plantinga on Possible Worlds" (*Op. Cit.*) p. 122.

7 See Pollock, *Op Cit.* pp. 121–126, and my reply in "Replies to my Colleagues" in *Profiles* (hereafter "Replies") pp. 327–329.

8 *Loc. Cit.*

9 Given a proposition (or state of affairs) **P**, there will typically be several distinct propositions (or states of affairs) equivalent to it; in the interests of brevity I ignore the question whether this also holds for possible worlds.

10 See my "On Existentialism", *Philosophical Studies* 1983 (Vol. 44) pp. 1–20; see also Pollock, *Op. Cit.*, pp. 134–140 and my reply (Replies, pp. 324–427).

11 See "On Existentialism" p. 2.

12 Examples of such properties would be **being Socrates, being identical with this very thing** (I am referring to the number 7), and such world-indexed properties unique to an object as **being**

the first dog to be born at sea in alpha. (For more about world-indexed properties, see *The Nature of Necessity* pp. 62–65.)

13 This condition is necessary but not sufficient. The proposition **7 is prime** predicates primeness of the number 7; it does not predicate primeness of the number 5, despite the equivalence, in the broadly logical sense, of **7 is prime** and **5 is prime**. The proposition **Socrates is wise** predicates wisdom of Socrates and does not predicate **being prime** of 7, despite its equivalence, in the broadly logical sense to **Socrates is wise and 7 is prime**.

14 See, for example, "Theories of Actuality" in *The Possible and the Actual* ed. by Michael Loux (Ithaca: Cornell University Press, 1976) and "Actualism and Thisness", *Synthese* (49) 1981.

15 See his Postscript in A.N. Prior and Kit Fine, *Worlds Times and Selves* (Amherst: University of Massachusetts Press, 1977, and "Plantinga on the Reduction of Possibilist Discourse" in *Profiles*.

16 See, for example, "Modal Logic and the Logic of Applicability" and "Supplement to 'Modal Logic and the Logic of Applicability'" in *Worlds Times and Selves* and "The Possibly True and the Possible" in *Papers in Logic and Ethics* (Amherst: University of Massachusetts Press, 1976).

17 See "On Existentialism", pp. 9–20 and "Replies" pp. 340–349.

18 See my "Actualism and Possible Worlds" (*Theoria* 42 (1976)) p. 160; reprinted in Loux, *The Possible and the Actual*, p. 272.

19 See "Plantinga on the Reduction of Possibilist Discourse" in *Profiles*, pp. 165–171.

20 *Ibid.* pp. 126–130.

21 "Counterpart Theory and Quantified Modal Logic", *Journal of Philosophy*, 1968, pp. 114–115. (Reprinted with postscript in Lewis: *Philosophical Papers* (Oxford: Oxford University Press, 1983).

22 *Counterfactuals* (Cambridge, Mass.: Harvard University Press, 1973), p. 84.

23 As I assumed in discussing Lewis' views in *The Nature of Necessity* pp. 102–114.

24 *On the Plurality of Worlds* (Oxford: Basil Blackwell Ltd., 1986), p. 2. (Hereafter "*Plurality*"; unless otherwise noted, page references in the text will be to this work.)

25 There is a more detailed account of Lewis' conception of possible worlds in Peter van Inwagen's

"Two Concepts of Possible Worlds" (*Midwest Studies in Philosophy*, XI, 1986 pp. 185–192) along with powerful criticism of this conception.

26 In *Plurality* as opposed to "Counterpart Theory and Modal Logic" Lewis allows that an object may have a counterpart in its own world.

27 A complication we may here ignore: Lewis holds that here are different counterpart relations appropriate to different contexts, so that an object may be my counterpart under one but not another of them.

28 " 'Property', and the rest/e.g., 'proposition'—AP/, are names associated in the first instance with roles in our thought. It is a firm commitment of common sense that there are some entities or other that play the roles and deserve the names, but our practical mastery of uses of the names does not prove that we have much notion what manner of entities those are. That is a question for theorists." (Plurality, 189)

29 According to Richard Cartwright, "Moore is reported to have once had a nightmare in which he was unable to distinguish propositions from tables" ("Propositions" in R.J. Butler, ed., *Analytical Philosophy* (New York: Barnes & Noble, Inc., 1962) p. 103).

30 Lewis, of course, would disagree; indeed, he suggests that a concrete object—another person, e.g.—can represent me as being thus and so; it can represent me as being it: "It is not some other world, differing haecceitistically from ours, which represent *de re* of me that I am Fred; it is Fred himself, situated as he is within our world" (232).

31 But things are not quite so simple; Lewis speaks of individuals and set-theoretic constructions on them as the things he is "most committed to"; and he is also sympathetic to the idea that there are immanent universals or tropes (but presumably not both) (64–69).

32 Gordon Kaufman, *Theology for a Nuclear Age* (Manchester: Manchester University Press, 1985) p. 43. (Of course I don't mean to suggest any real kinship between Lewis' thought and contemporary liberal theology.)

33 Strictly speaking, this argument requires the additional (and uncontroversial) premise that if the property of being a donkey is the set of donkeys, then the set of donkeys is essentially nonempty only if the property of being a donkey is essentially exemplified.

34 See footnote 4 of van Inwagen's "Two Concepts of Possible Worlds".

35 Purists may wish to state the above argument, not in terms of possible worlds and maximal objects, but in terms of the properties **being a possible world** and **being a maximal object**.

36 See Ernest Sosa's "Classical Analysis", *Journal of Philosophy*, v. LXXX, No 11 (November, 1983).

37 G. E. Moore in "A Defense of Common Sense" (*Philosophical Papers* (London: George Allen and Unwin Ltd., 1959) p. 36): "Some philosophers use the expression 'The earth has existed for many years past' to express, not what it would ordinarily be understood to express, but the proposition that some proposition, related to this in a certain way, is true; when all the time they believe that the proposition, which this expression would ordinarily be understood to express, is, at least partially, false."

38 "Attitudes *de dicto* and *de se*," *Philosophical Papers* 1 pp. 134–135. (On Lewis' view not everything that has properties is a *possible* (for example, sets, or the mereological sum of a couple of maximal objects, or of parts of a couple of such objects); in *Plurality* he therefore takes properties to be sets of any kind, not just sets of possibilia.

39 And hence it is not clear to me whether or not he is what above I called a *semantical* reductionist.

40 Nor any set theoretical construction on concrete individuals. Objection: "you say that no concrete objects or sets have that intentional property you attribute to propositions and states of affairs: the property of representing things as being thus and so, of being a thing **x** such that according to **x** things stand thus and so. But isn't this clearly mistaken? Surely *sentences of natural languages* are true or false, and thus such that according to them things stand a certain way; and sentences are sets: sets of sounds or shapes. Furthermore, sentences aren't the only things that represent: a scale model of the *Titanic*, for example, can represent it as having four smokestacks, and a topographical map of the North Cascades can represent Mt. Baker as being more than 10,700 feet high."

Reply: stipulate for purposes of argument that sentences are sets. The important point is that a sentence in itself does not have any such intentional property at all; rather sentences are used by speakers and writers to express the things that do have the relevant intentional property. The sequence of shapes "Socrates is wise" does not represent Socrates as being wise; instead, speakers of English use that sequence of shapes to express the proposition that Socrates is wise. Similarly for maps and models; the map doesn't (except in a derivative sense) represent Mt. Baker as being more than 10,700 feet high; instead, the cartographer uses the map to make that representation, i.e., to communicate that proposition. Similarly for models: an object that looks like a small Titanic isn't in itself any claim at all as to what the Titanic is like; but if I assert that it is a scale model of that ship, then I use it to make claims or assertions about what the Titanic is like—I use it, that is, to express propositions.

41 He might say something even more exciting: "God is the name of that center which is everywhere, but it is everywhere only by being nowhere where it is only itself, and therefore nowhere in the absence or silence of consciousness or speech." Thomas J.J. Altizer, "History as Apocalypse" in Deconstruction in Theology by Thomas J.J. Altizer, Max A. Myers, Carl A. Raschke, Robert P. Scharlemann, Mark C. Taylor, and Charles E. Winquist (New York: the Crossroad Publishing Co., 1982) p. 155.

42 See above, p. 531.

43 See. e.g., Allen Hazen, "Counterpart-theoretic Semantics for Modal Logic" in Journal of Philosophy, vol. 76 (1979) p. 323.

44 ". . . what Plantinga disparages as a merely verbal agreement about the truth value of the sentence 'Socrates could have been unwise' is the only agreement that can be demanded from the counterpart theorist: it is the only agreement that matters. Our logical intuition about such sentences of our ordinary modal language are the evidence that both Plantinga and the counterpart theorist must appeal to and explain. What proposition is expressed by such a sentence . . . is a matter of theory . . ." Loc Cit. p. 323.

45 Counterfactuals, p. 86.

46 As Lewis suggests in a different context (247), it may still do something. Perhaps it is more obvious that the words 'there could have been nothing that had the property of being a donkey' express a truth than that it is false that the proposition expressed by those words is really the proposition that there are maximal objects in which there are no members of the set of this- and otherworldly donkeys; then to claim the latter is less outrageous than to deny the former.)

47 Again, I do not mean for a moment to suggest that semantical reductionism shares the devious and deplorably deceptive character sometimes attaching to such theology.

48 I take this opportunity to record my gratitude to many—in particular David Lewis, Peter van Inwagen, Philip Quinn, Del Ratzsch, Nicholas Wolterstorff and the members of the Calvin Colloquium—for stimulating discussion and incisive criticism. I should also like again to call attention to van Inwagen's penetrating discussion of allied matters in "Two Concepts of Possible Worlds" (above, note 25).

References

Adams, Robert. "Theories of Actuality" in Loux, The Possible and the Actual.

Adams, Robert. "Actualism and Thisness", Synthese (49) 1981.

Altizer, Thomas J.J. "History as Apocalypse" in Deconstruction in Theology by Thomas J.J. Altizer, Max A. Myers, Carl A. Raschke, Robert P. Scharlemann, Mark C. Taylor, and Charles E. Winquist (New York: The Crossroad Publishing Co., 1982) p. 155.

Cartwright, Richard. "Propositions" in R.J. Butler, ed, Analytical Philosophy (New York: Barnes & Noble, Inc., 1962).

Fine, Kit, and Prior, Arthur. Worlds, Times and Selves (Amherst: University of Massachusetts Press, 1977.

Fine, Kit. "Plantinga on the Reduction of Possibilist Discourse" in van Inwagen, "Two Concepts of Possible Worlds".

Hazen, Allen. "Counterpart-theoretic Semantics for Modal Logic" in Journal of Philosophy, vol 76 (1979).

Kaufman, Gordon. Theology for a Nuclear Age (Manchester: Manchester University Press, 1985.

Lewis, David. "Counterpart Theory and Quantified Modal Logic", Journal of Philosophy, 1968, pp. 114–115. (Reprinted with postscript in Philosophical Papers I).

Lewis, David. *Philosophical Papers* I (Oxford: Oxford University Press, 1983).

Lewis, David. *Counterfactuals* (Cambridge, Mass.: Harvard University Press, 1973).

Lewis, David. *On the Plurality of Worlds* (Oxford: Basil Blackwell Ltd., 1986).

Lewis, David. "Attitudes *de dicto* and *de se*", *The Philosophical Review* 88 (1979). Reprinted in *Philosophical Papers* I.

Loux, Michael. *The Possible and the Actual* (Ithaca: Cornell University Press, 1976).

Moore, G. E. "A Defense of Common Sense" in *Philosophical Papers* (London: George Allen and Unwin Ltd., 1959).

Plantinga, Alvin. "How to be an Anti-Realist", *Proceedings of the American Philosophical Association*, vol 56.

Plantinga, Alvin. *The Nature of Necessity* (Oxford: Clarendon Press, 1974).

Plantinga, Alvin. "On Existentialism", *Philosophical Studies* 1983 (Vol. 44).

Plantinga, Alvin. "Actualism and Possible worlds" *Theoria* 42 (1976), reprinted in Loux, *The Possible and the Actual*.

Pollock, John. "Plantinga on Possible Worlds" in van Inwagen, "Two Concepts of Possible Worlds".

Prior, Arthur. *Worlds, Times and Selves* (Amherst: University of Massachusetts Press, 1976).

Prior, Arthur. "Modal Logic and the Logic of Applicability" in *Worlds, Times and Selves*.

Prior, Arthur. "Supplement to 'Modal Logic and the Logic of Applicability' " in *Worlds, Times and Selves*.

Prior, Arthur. *Papers in Logic and Ethics* (Amherst: University of Massachusetts Press, 1976).

Prior, Arthur. "The Possibly True and the Possible" in *Papers in Logic and Ethics*.

Sosa, Ernest. "Classical Analysis", *Journal of Philosophy*, v. LXXX, No 11 (November, 1983).

Tomberlin, James and van Inwagen, Peter. *Alvin Plantinga* (Dordrecht: D. Reidel Publishing Co., 1985).

van Inwagen, Peter. "Two Concepts of Possible Worlds" in *Midwest Studies in Philosophy*, XI, 1986.

Chapter 41

Nelson Goodman

WORDS, WORKS, WORLDS*

1. Questions

Countless worlds made from nothing by use of symbols – so might a satirist summarize some of Cassirer's major themes. These themes – the multiplicity of worlds, the speciousness of 'the given', the creative power of the understanding, the variety and formative function of symbols – are also integral to my own thinking. Sometimes, though, I forget that they have been so eloquently set forth by Cassirer,[1] partly perhaps because his emphasis on myth, his concern with the comparative study of cultures, and his talk of the human spirit have been mistakenly associated with current trends toward mystical obscurantism, anti-intellectual intuitionism, or anti-scientific humanism. Actually these attitudes are as alien to Cassirer as to my own skeptical, analytic, constructionalist orientation.

My aim in what follows is less to defend certain theses that Cassirer and I share than to take a hard look at some crucial questions they raise. In just what sense are there many worlds? What distinguishes genuine from spurious worlds? What are worlds made of? How are they made, and what role do symbols play in the making? And how is worldmaking related to knowing? These questions must be faced even if full and final answers are far off.

2. Versions and Visions

As intimated by William James's equivocal title *A Pluralistic Universe*, the issue between monism and pluralism tends to evaporate under analysis. If there is but one world, it embraces a multiplicity of contrasting aspects; if there are many worlds, the collection of them all is one. The one world may be taken as many, or the many worlds taken as one; whether one or many depends on the way of taking.

Why, then, does Cassirer stress the multiplicity of worlds? In what important and often neglected sense are there many worlds? Let it be clear that the question here is not of the possible worlds that many of my contemporaries, especially those near Disneyland, are busy making and manipulating. We are not speaking in terms of multiple possible alternatives to a single actual world but of multiple actual worlds. How to interpret such terms as "real", "unreal", "fictive", and "possible" is a subsequent question.

Consider, to begin with, the fact that the statements "the sun always moves" and "the sun never moves", though equally true, are at odds with each other. Shall we say, then, that they describe different worlds, and indeed that there are as many different worlds as there are such mutually exclusive truths? Rather, we are inclined to regard the two strings of words not as complete statements with truth-values of their own but as elliptical for some such statements as "Under frame of reference A, the sun always moves" and "Under frame of reference B, the sun never moves" – statements that may both be true of the same world.

Frames of reference, though, belong less to what is described than to systems of description; and each of the two statements relates what is described to such a system. If I ask about the world, you can offer to tell me how it is under one or more frames of reference; but if I insist that you tell me how it is apart from all frames, what can you say? We are confined to ways of describing whatever is described. Our universe, so to speak, consists of these ways rather than of a world or of worlds.

The alternative descriptions of motion, all of them in much the same terms and routinely transformable into one another, provide only a minor and rather pallid example of diversity in accounts of the world. Much more striking is the vast variety of versions and visions in the several sciences, in the works of different painters and writers, and in our perceptions as informed by these, by circumstances, and by our own insights, interests, and past experiences. Even with all illusory or wrong or dubious versions dropped, the rest exhibit new dimensions of disparity. Here we have no neat set of frames of reference, no ready rules for transforming physics, biology, and psychology into one another, and no way at all of transforming any of these into Van Gogh's vision, or Van Gogh's into Canaletto's. Such of these versions as are depictions rather than descriptions have no truth-value in the literal sense, and cannot be combined by conjunction. The difference between juxtaposing and conjoining two statements has no evident analogue for two pictures or for a picture and a statement. The dramatically contrasting versions of the world can of course be accommodated by relativization: each is right under a given system – for a given science, a given artist, or a given perceiver and situation.

Here again we turn from describing or depicting 'the world' to talking of descriptions and depictions, but now without even the consolation of intertranslatability among or any evident organization of the several systems in question.

Yet doesn't a right version differ from a wrong one just in applying to the world, so that rightness itself depends upon and implies a world? On the contrary, 'the world' depends upon rightness. We cannot test a version by comparing it with a world undescribed, undepicted, unperceived, but only by other means that I shall discuss later. While we may speak of determining what versions are right as 'learning about the world', 'the world' supposedly being that which all right versions describe, all we learn about the world is contained in right versions of it; and while the underlying world, bereft of these, need not be denied to those who love it, it is perhaps on the whole a world well lost. For some purposes, we may want to define a relation that will so sort versions into clusters that each cluster constitutes a world and the members of the cluster are versions of that world; but for many purposes, right world-descriptions and world-depictions and world-perceptions, the ways-the-world-is, or just versions can be treated as our worlds.[2]

Since the fact that there are many different world-versions is hardly debatable, and the question how many if any worlds-in-themselves there are is virtually empty, in what non-trivial sense are there, as Cassirer and like-minded pluralists insist, many worlds? Just this, I think: that many different world-versions are of independent interest and importance, without any requirement or presumption of reducibility to a single base. The pluralist, far from being anti-scientific, accepts the sciences at full value. His typical adversary is the monopolistic materialist or physicalist who maintains that one system, physics, is preeminent and all-inclusive, such that every other version must eventually be reduced to it or rejected as false or meaningless. If all right versions could somehow be reduced to one and only one, that one might with some semblance of plausibility[3] be regarded as the only truth about the only world. But the evidence for such reducibility is negligible, and even the claim is nebulous since physics itself is fragmentary and unstable and the kind and consequences of reduction envisaged are vague. (How do you go about reducing Constable's or James Joyce's world-view to physics?) I am the last person likely to underrate construction and reduction.[4] A reduction from one system to another can make a genuine contribution to understanding the interrelationships among world-versions; but reduction in any reasonably strict sense is rare, almost always partial, and seldom if ever unique. To demand full and sole reducibility to physics or any other one version is to forego nearly all other versions. The pluralists' acceptance of versions other than physics implies no relaxation of rigor but a recognition that standards different from yet no less exacting than those applied in science are appropriate for appraising what is conveyed in perceptual or pictorial or literary versions.

So long as contrasting right versions not all reducible to one are countenanced, unity is to be sought not in an ambivalent or neutral something beneath these versions but in an overall organization embracing them. Cassirer undertakes the search through a cross-cultural study of the development of myth, religion, language, art, and science. My approach is rather through an analytic study of types and functions of symbols and symbol systems. In neither case should a unique result be anticipated; universes of worlds as well as worlds themselves may be built in many ways.

3. How Firm a Foundation?

The non-Kantian theme of multiplicity of worlds is closely akin to the Kantian theme of the vacuity of the notion of pure content. The one denies us a unique world, the other the common stuff of which worlds are made. Together these theses defy our intuitive demand for something stolid underneath, and threaten to leave us uncontrolled, spinning out our own inconsequent fantasies.

The overwhelming case against perception without conception, the pure given, absolute immediacy, the innocent eye, substance as substratum, has been so fully and frequently set forth – by Berkeley, Kant, Cassirer, Gombrich,[5] Bruner,[6] and many others – as to need no restatement here. Talk of unstructured content or an unconceptualized given or a substratum without properties is self-defeating; for the talk imposes structure, conceptualizes, ascribes properties. Although conception without perception is merely *empty*, perception without conception is *blind* (totally inoperative). Predicates, pictures, other labels, schemata, survive want of application, but content vanishes without form. We can have words without a world but no world without words or other symbols.

The many stuffs – matter, energy, waves, phenomena – that worlds are made of are made along with the worlds. But made from what? Not from nothing, after all, but *from other worlds*. Worldmaking as we know it always starts from worlds already on hand; the making is a remaking. Anthropology and developmental psychology may study social and individual histories of such world-building, but the search for a universal or necessary beginning is best left to theology.[7] My interest here is rather with the processes involved in building a world out of others.

With false hope of a firm foundation gone, with the world displaced by worlds that are but versions, with substance dissolved into function, and with the given acknowledged as taken, we face the questions how worlds are made, tested, and known.

4. Ways of Worldmaking

Without presuming to instruct the gods or other world makers, or attempting any comprehensive or systematic survey, I want to illustrate and comment on some of the processes that go into worldmaking. Actually, I am concerned more with certain relationships among worlds than with how or whether particular worlds are made from others.

(a) Composition and Decomposition

Much but by no means all worldmaking consists of taking apart and putting together, often conjointly: on the one hand, of dividing wholes into parts and partitioning kinds into subspecies, analyzing complexes into component features, drawing distinctions; on the other hand, of composing wholes and kinds out of parts and members and subclasses, combining features into complexes, and making connections. Such composition and decomposition is normally effected or assisted or consolidated by the application of labels: names, predicates, gestures, pictures, etc. Thus, for example, temporally diverse events are brought together under a proper name or identified as making up 'an object' or 'a person'; or snow is sundered into several materials under terms of the Eskimo vocabulary. Metaphorical transfer – for example, where taste predicates are applied to sounds – may effect a double reorganization, both re-sorting the new realm of application and relating it to the old one.

Identification rests upon organization into entities and kinds. The response to the question "same or not the same?" must always be "same what?".[8] Different soandsos may be the same such-and-such: what we point to or indicate, verbally or otherwise, may be different events but the same object, different towns but the same state, different members but the same club or different clubs but the same members, different innings but the same ball game. 'The ball-in-play' of a single game may be comprised of temporal segments of a dozen or more baseballs. The psychologist asking the child to judge constancy when one vessel is emptied into another must be careful to specify *what* constancy is in question – constancy of volume or depth or shape or kind of material, etc.[9] Identity or constancy in a world is identity with respect to what to what is within that world as organized.

Motley entities cutting across each other in complicated patterns may belong to the same world. We do not make a new world every time we take things apart or put them together in another way; but worlds may differ in that not everything belonging to one belongs to the other. The world of the Eskimo who has not grasped the comprehensive concept of snow differs not only from the world of the Samoan but also from the world of the New Englander who has not grasped the Eskimo's distinctions. In other cases, worlds differ in response to theoretical rather than practical needs. A world with points as elements cannot be the Whiteheadian world having points as certain classes of nesting volumes, or having points as certain pairs of interesting lines or as certain triples of intersecting planes. That the points of our everyday world can be equally well defined in any of these ways does not mean that a point can be identified in any one world with a nest of volumes and a pair of lines and a triple of planes; for all these are different from each other. Again the world of a system taking minimal concrete phenomena as atomic cannot admit qualities as atomic parts of these concreta.[10]

Repetition as well as identification is relative to organization. A world may be unmanageably heterogeneous or unbearably monotonous according to how events are sorted into kinds. Whether or not today's experiment repeats yesterday's, however much the two events may differ, depends upon whether they test a common hypothesis; as Sir George Thomson puts it:

> There will always be something different . . . What it comes to when you say you repeat an experiment is that you repeat all the features of an experiment which a theory determines arerelevant. In other words you repeat the experiment as an example of the theory.[11]

Likewise, two musical performances that differ drastically are nevertheless performances of the same work if they conform to the same score. The notational system distinguishes constitutive from contingent features, thus picking out the performance-kinds that count as works.[12] And things 'go on in the same way' or not according to what is regarded as the same way; 'now I can go on',[13] in Wittgenstein's sense, when I have found a familiar pattern, or a tolerable variation of one, that fits and goes beyond the cases given. Induction requires taking some classes to the exclusion of others as relevant kinds. Only so e.g., do our observations of emeralds exhibit any regularity and confirm that all emeralds are green rather than that all are grue (i.e. examined before a given date and green, or not so examined and blue).[14] The uniformity of nature we marvel at or the unreliability we protest belongs to a world of our own making.

In these latter cases, worlds differ in the relevant kinds comprised in them. I say "relevant" rather than "natural" for two reasons: first, "natural" is an inapt term to cover not only biological species but such artificial kinds as musical works, psychological experiments, and types of machinery; and second, "natural" suggests some absolute categorical or psychological priority while the kinds in question are rather habitual or traditional or devised for a new purpose.

(b) *Weighting*

While we may say that in the cases discussed some relevant kinds of one world are missing from another, we might perhaps better say that the two worlds contain just the same classes sorted differently into relevant and irrelevant kinds. Some relevant kinds of the one world, rather than being absent from the other, are present as irrelevant kinds; some differences among worlds are not so much in entities comprised as in emphasis or accent, and these differences are no less consequential. Just as to stress all syllables is to stress none, so to take all classes as relevant

kinds is to take none as such. In one world there may be many kinds serving different purposes; but conflicting purposes may make for irreconcilable accents and contrasting worlds, as may conflicting conceptions of what kinds serve a given purpose. Grue cannot be a relevant kind for induction in the same world as green; for that would preclude some of the decisions, right or wrong, that constitute inductive inference.

Some of the most striking contrasts of emphasis appear in the arts. Many of the differences among portrayals by Daumier, Ingres, Michelangelo, and Rouault are differences in aspects accentuated. What counts as emphasis, of course, is departure from the relative prominence accorded the several features in the current world of our everyday seeing. With changing interests and new insights, the visual weighting of features of bulk or line or stance or light alters, and yesterday's level world seems strangely perverted − yesterday's realistic calendar landscape becomes a repulsive caricature.

These differences in emphasis, too, amount to a difference in relevant kinds recognized. Several portrayals of the same subject may thus place it according to different categorical schemata. Like a green emerald and a grue one, even if the same emerald, a Piero della Francesca *Christ* and a Rembrandt one belong to worlds organized into different kinds.

Works of art, though, characteristically illustrate rather than name or describe relevant kinds. Even where the ranges of application − the things described or depicted − coincide, the features or kinds exemplified or expressed may be very different. A line drawing of softly draped cloth may exemplify rhythmic linear patterns; and a poem with no words for sadness and no mention of a sad person may in the quality of its language be sad, and poignantly express sadness. The distinction between saying or representing on the one hand and showing or exemplifying on the other becomes even more evident in the case of abstract painting and music and dance that have no subject-matter but nevertheless manifest – exemplify or express – forms and feelings. Exemplification and expression, though running in the opposite direction from denotation – that is, from the symbol to a literal or metaphorical feature of it instead of to something the symbol applies to – are no less symbolic referential functions and instruments of worldmaking.[15]

Emphasis or weighting is not always binary as is a sorting into relevant and irrelevant kinds or into important and unimportant features. Ratings of relevance, importance, utility, value often yield hierarchies rather than dichotomies. Such weightings are also instances of a particular type of ordering.

(c) Ordering

Worlds not differing in entities or emphasis may differ in ordering; for example, the worlds of different constructional system differ in order of derivation. As nothing is at rest or is in motion apart from a frame of reference so nothing is primitive or is derivationally prior to anything apart from a constructional system. However, derivation unlike motion is of little immediate practical interest; and thus in our everyday world, although we almost always adopt a frame of reference at least temporarily, we seldom adopt a derivational basis. Earlier I said that the difference between a world having points as pairs of lines and a world having lines as composed of points is that the latter but not the former admits as entites nonlinear elements comprised within lines. But alternatively we may say that these worlds differ in their derivational ordering of lines and points of the not-derivationally-ordered world of daily discourse.

Orderings of a different sort pervade perception and practical cognition. The standard ordering of brightness in color follows the linear increase in physical intensity of light; but the standard ordering of hues curls the straight line of increasing wavelength into a circle. Order includes periodicity as well as proximity; and the standard ordering of tones is by pitch and octave. Orderings alter with circumstances and objectives. Much as the nature of shapes changes under different geometries, so do perceived patterns change under different orderings; the patterns perceived under a twelve-tone scale are quite different from those perceived under the traditional eight-tone scale, and rhythms depend upon the marking off into measures.

Radical reordering of another sort occurs in constructing a static image from the input from scanning a picture, or of a unified and comprehensive image of an object or a city from temporally and spatially and qualitatively heterogeneous observations and other items of information.[16] Some very fast readers recreate normal word-ordering from a series of fixations that proceed down the left-hand page and then up the right-hand page of a book.[17] And spatial order in a map or a score is translated into temporal sequence of a trip or a performance.

All measurement, furthermore, is based upon order. Indeed, only through suitable arrangements and groupings can we handle vast quantities of material perceptually or cognitively. Gombrich discusses the decimal periodization of historical time into decades, centuries, and millennia.[18] Daily time is marked off into twenty-four hours, and each of these into sixty minutes of sixty seconds each. Whatever else may be said of these modes of organization, they are not 'found in the world' but *built into a world*. Ordering, as well as composition and decomposition and weighting of wholes and kinds, participates in worldmaking.

(d) Deletion and Supplementation

Also, the making of one world out of another usually involves some extensive weeding out and filling in – actual excision of some old and supply of some new material. Our capacity for overlooking is virtually unlimited, and what we do take in usually consists of significant fragments and clues that need massive supplementation.

Artists often make skilful use of this; a lithograph by Giacometti fully presents a walking man by sketches of the head, hands, and feet only in just the right postures and positions against an expanse of blank paper, and a drawing by Katharine Sturgis conveys a hockey player in action by a single charged line.

That we find what we are prepared to find, what we look for or what forcefully affronts our expectations, that we are blind to what neither serves nor counters our interests, is a commonplace of everyday life and is amply attested by psychological experiments.[19] In the painful experience of proofreading and the more pleasurable one of watching a skilled magician, we incurably miss something that is there and see something that is not there. Memory edits more ruthlessly; a person with equal command of two languages may remember a learned list of items while forgetting in which language they were listed.[20] And even within what we do perceive and remember, we dismiss as illusory or negligible what cannot be fitted into the architecture of the world we are building.

The scientist is no less drastic, rejecting or purifying most of the entities and events of the world of ordinary things while generating quantities of filling for curves suggested by sparse data, and erecting elaborate structures on the basis of meagre observations. Thus does he build a world conforming to his chosen concepts and obeying his universal laws.

Replacement of a so-called analog by a so-called digital system involves deletion in the articulation of separate steps; for example, to use a digital thermometer with readings in tenths of a degree is to recognize no temperature as lying between 90 and 90.1 degrees. Similar deletion occurs under standard musical notation, which recognizes no pitch between c and c and no duration between a sixty-fourth and a one-hundred-and-twenty-eighth note. On the other hand, supplementation occurs when, say, an analog replaces a digital instrument for measuring mileage, or when a violinist performs from a score.

Perhaps the most spectacular cases of supplementation, though, are found in the perception of motion. Sometimes motion in the perceptual world results from intricate and abundant fleshing out of the physical stimuli. Psychologists have long known of what is called the 'phi phenomenon': under carefully controlled conditions, if two spots of light are flashed a short distance apart and in quick succession, the viewer normally sees a spot of light moving continuously along a path from the first position to the second. That is remarkable enough in itself since of course the direction of motion cannot have been determined prior to the second flash; but perception has even greater creative power. Paul Kolers has recently shown[21] that if the first stimulus spot is circular and the second square, the seen moving spot transforms smoothly from circle to square; and transformations between two-dimensional and three-dimensional shapes are often effected without trouble. Moreover, if a barrier of light is interposed between the two stimulus spots, the moving spot detours around the barrier. But what happens if the first flash is, say, red and the second pink (or blue)? Kolers and von Grünau[22] have found that, almost incredibly, while the seen spot moves and transforms its shape smoothly as before, it stays red to about the middle of the path and then abruptly changes to pink (or blue)! Just why these supplementations occur as they do is a fascinating subject for speculation.[23]

(e) Deformation

Finally, some changes are reshapings or deformations that may according to point of view be considered either corrections or distortions. The physicist smooths out the simplest rough curve that fits all his data. Vision stretches a line ending with arrowheads pointing in while shrinking a physically equal line ending with arrowheads pointing out, and tends to expand the size of a smaller more valuable coin in relation to that of a larger less valuable one.[24] Caricaturists often go beyond overemphasis to actual distortion. Picasso starting from Velasquez's *Las Meninas*, and Brahms starting from a theme of Haydn's, work magical variations that amount to revelations.

These then are ways that worlds are made. I do not say *the* ways. My classification is not offered as comprehensive or clearcut or mandatory. Not only do the processes illustrated often occur in combination but the examples chosen sometimes fit equally well under more than one heading; for example, some changes may be considered alternatively as reweightings or reorderings or reshapings or as all of these, and some deletions are also matters of differences in composition. All I have tried to do is to suggest something of the variety of processes in constant use. While a tighter systematization could surely be developed, none can be ultimate; for as remarked earlier, there is no more a unique world of worlds than there is a unique world.

5. Trouble with Truth

With all this freedom to divide and combine, emphasize, order, delete, fill in and fill out, and even distort, what are the objectives and the constraints? What are the criteria for success in making a world?

Insofar as a version is verbal and consists of statements, truth may be relevant. But truth cannot be defined or tested by agreement with 'the world'; for not only do truths differ for different worlds but the nature of agreement between a version and a world apart from it is notoriously nebulous. Rather – speaking loosely and without trying to answer either Pilate's question or Tarski's – a version is true when it offends no unyielding beliefs and none of its own precepts. Among beliefs unyielding at a given time may be long-lived reflections of laws of logic, short-lived reflections of recent observations, and other convictions and prejudices ingrained with varying degrees of firmness. Among precepts, for example, may be choices among alternative

frames of reference, weightings, and derivational bases. But the line between beliefs and precepts is neither sharp nor stable. Beliefs are framed in concepts informed by precepts; and if a Boyle ditches his data for a smooth curve just missing them all, we may say either that observational volume and pressure are different properties from theoretical volume and pressure or that the truths about volume and pressure differ in the two worlds of observation and theory. And the staunchest belief tends in time to admit alternatives; "the earth is at rest" passed from dogma to dependence upon precept.

Truth, far from being a solemn and severe master, is a docile and obedient servant. The scientist who supposes that he is single-mindedly dedicated to the search for truth deceives himself. He is unconcerned with the trivial truths he could grind out endlessly; and he looks to the multifaceted and irregular results of observations for little more than suggestions of overall structures and significant generalizations. He seeks system, simplicity, scope; and when satisfied on these scores he tailors truth to fit.[25] He as much decrees as discovers the laws he sets forth, as much designs as discerns the patterns he delineates.

Truth, moreover, pertains solely to what is said, and literal truth solely to what is said literally. We have seen, though, that worlds are made not only by what is said literally but also by what is said metaphorically, and not only by what is said either literally or metaphorically but also by what is exemplified and expressed – by what is shown as well as what is said. In a scientific treatise, only literal truth may count; but in a poem or novel, metaphorical or allegorical truth may matter more, for even a literally false statement may be metaphorically true[26] and may mark or make new associations and discriminations, change emphases effect exclusions and additions. And statements whether literally or metaphorically true or false may show what they do not say, may work as trenchant literal or metaphorical examples of unmentioned features and feelings. In Vachel Lindsay's *The Congo*, for example, the pulsating pattern of drumbeats is insistently exhibited rather than described.

Finally, for nonverbal versions and even for verbal versions without statements, truth is irrelevant. We risk confusion when we speak of pictures or predicates as "true of" what they depict or apply to; they have no truth-value, and may represent or denote some things and not others, while a statement does have truth-value and is true of everything if of anything.[27] And a nonrepresentational picture such as a Mondrian says nothing, denotes nothing, pictures nothing, and is neither true nor false, but shows much. Nevertheless, showing or exemplifying, like denoting, is a referential function; and much the same considerations count for pictures as for the concepts or predicates of a theory: their relevance and their revelations, their force and their fit – in sum their *rightness*. Rather than speaking of pictures as true or false we might better speak of theories as right or wrong; for the truth of the laws of a theory is but one special feature and is often, as we have seen, overridden in importance by the cogency and compactness and comprehensiveness, the informativeness and organizing power of the whole system.

"The truth, the whole truth, and nothing but the truth" would thus be a perverse and paralyzing policy for any worldmaker. The whole truth would be too much; it is too vast, variable, and clogged with trivia. The truth alone would be too little, for some right versions are not true – being either false or neither true nor false – and even for true versions rightness may matter more.

6. Relative Reality

Shouldn't we now return to sanity from all this mad proliferation of worlds? Shouldn't we stop speaking of right versions as if each were, or had, its own world, and recognize all as versions of one and the same neutral and underlying world? The world thus regained, as remarked earlier, is a world without kinds or order or motion or rest or pattern – a world not worth fighting for or against.

We might, though, take the real world to be that of some one of the alternative right versions (or groups of them bound together by some principle of reducibility or translatability) and regard all others as versions of that same world differing from the standard version in accountable ways. The physicist takes his world as the real one, attributing the deletions, additions, irregularities, emphases, of other versions to the imperfections of perception, the urgencies of practice, or poetic license. The phenomenalist regards the perceptual world as fundamental, and the excisions, abstractions, simplifications and distortions of other versions as resulting from scientific or practical or artistic concerns. For the man-in-the-street, most versions from science, art, and perception depart in some ways from the familiar serviceable world he has jerry-built from fragments of scientific and artistic tradition and from his own struggle for survival. This world, indeed, is the one most often taken as real; for reality in a world, like realism in a picture, is largely a matter of habit.

Ironically, then, our passion for *one* world is satisfied, at different times and for different purposes, in *many* different ways. Not only motion, derivation, weighting, order, but even reality is relative. And so also, of course, is fiction; for so long as one world is designated as real, one version or integrated group of versions as the standard of reality, differing versions are considered to be at least in part either false or figurative, and ontological disparities to be the result of omitting real or adding fictive entities. Incidentally, with one world designated as real, merely-possible worlds might naturally be identified with divergent true or right versions; but for some contemporary philosophers, merely-possible worlds seem rather to be identified with false versions or 'state-descriptions' constructed from the same vocabulary as the only true one.

That reality is relative, worlds and right versions many, does not imply that all alternatives are equally good for every or indeed for any purpose, or that every alternative is much good for some purpose or other, and by no means precludes preference among versions. Not even a fly is likely to take one of his wing-tips as a fixed point; we do not welcome molecules or concreta as elements of our everyday world, or combine tomatoes and triangles and typewriters and tyrants and tornadoes into a single kind; the physicist will count none of these among his fundamental particles; the painter who sees like the man-in-the-street will have more popular than artistic success. And the same philosopher who here metaphilosophically contemplates a vast variety of worlds finds that only versions meeting the demands of a dogged and deflationary nominalism suit his purposes in constructing philosophical systems.

Moreover, while readiness to recognize alternative worlds may be liberating, and suggestive of new avenues of exploration, a willingness to welcome all worlds builds none. Mere acknowledgement of the many available frames of reference provides us with no map of the motions of heavenly bodies; acceptance of the eligibility of alternative bases produces no scientific theory or philosophical system; awareness of varied ways of seeing paints no pictures. A broad mind is no substitute for hard work.

7. Notes on Knowing

What I have been saying bears on the nature of knowledge. On these terms, knowing cannot be exclusively or even primarily a matter of determining what is true. Discovery often amounts, as when I place a piece in a jigsaw puzzle, not to arrival at a proposition for declaration or defense, but to finding a fit. Much of knowing aims at something other than true, or any, belief. An increase in acuity of insight or in range of comprehension, rather than a change in belief, occurs when we find in a pictured forest a

face we already knew was there, or learn to distinguish stylistic differences among works already classified by artist or composer or writer, or study a picture or a concerto or a treatise until we see or hear or grasp features and structures we could not discern before. Such growth in knowledge is not by formation or fixation of belief[28] but by the advancement of understanding.[29]

Furthermore, if worlds are as much made as found, so also knowing is as much remaking as reporting. All the processes of worldmaking I have discussed enter into knowing. Perceiving motion, we have seen, often consists in producing it. Discovering laws involves drafting them. Recognizing patterns is very much a matter of inventing and imposing them. Comprehension and creation go on together.

I may not have given adequate answers to the questions I raised at the start; and you may feel that I have used far too freely all the processes I have described, from decomposition through deletion to distortion. But even if you feel that what I have said is not true, I hope you may find some of it right.

Notes

* Written for delivery at the meeting in honor of the 100th anniversary of the birth of Ernst Cassirer, held at the University of Hamburg on October 21, 1974.

1 E.g. in *Language and Myth*, translated by Suzanne Langer (Harper, 1946).

2 Cf. 'The Way the World Is' (1960), in my *Problem and Projects* [hereinafter PP] (Bobbs-Merrill, 1972), pp. 24–32.

3 But not much; for no one type of reducibility serves all purposes.

4 Cf. 'The Revision of Philosophy' (1956), in PP, pp. 5–23; and also my *The Structure of Appearance* [hereinafter SA] (Bobbs-Merrill, second ed., 1966).

5 In *Art and Illusion* (Pantheon Books, 1960), E. H. Gombrich argues in many passages against the notion of 'the innocent eye'.

6 See the essays in Jerome S. Bruner's *Beyond the Information Given* [hereinafter BI], ed. by Jeremy M. Anglin (W. W. Norton, 1973), Chapter I.

7 Cf. *SA*, pp. 127–145; and 'Sense and Certainty' (1952) and 'The Epistemological Argument' (1967), in PP, pp. 60–75. We might take construction of a history of successive development of worlds to involve application of something like a Kantian regulative principle, and the search for a first world thus to be as misguided as the search for a first moment of time.

8 This does not, as sometimes is supposed, require any modification of the Leibniz formula for identity, but merely reminds us that the answer to a question "Is this the same as that?" may depend upon whether the "this" and the "that" in the question refer to thing or event or color or species, etc.

9 See BI, pp. 331–340.

10 See further *SA*, pp. 3–22, 132–135, 142–145.

11 In 'Some Thoughts on Scientific Method' (1963), in *Boston Studies in the Philosophy of Science*, Vol. II (Humanities Press, 1965), p. 85.

12 See my *Languages of Art* [hereinafter LA], (Bobbs-Merrill, 1968), pp. 115–130.

13 Discussion of what this means occupies many sections, from about Section 142 on, of Ludwig Wittgenstein's *Philosophical Investigations*, translated by G. E. M. Anscombe, (Blackweli, 1953). I am not suggesting that the answer I give here is Wittgenstein's.

14 See my *Fact, Fiction, and Forecast* (Bobbs-Merrill, third ed., 1973), pp. 72–80.

15 On exemplification and expression as referential relations see *LA*, pp. 50–57, 87–95.

16 See *The Image of the City* by Kevin Lynch (Cambridge, Technology Press, 1960).

17 See E. Llewellyn Thomas 'Eye Movements in Speed Reading', in *Speed Reading: Practices and Procedures* (University of Delaware Press, 1962), pp. 104–114.

18 In *Zeit, Zahl, und Zeichen*, written for delivery at the meeting mentioned in the asterished note above.

19 See 'On Perceptual Readiness' (1957) in BI, pp. 7–42.

20 See Paul Kolers, 'Bilinguals and Information Processing', *Scientific American* **218** (1968), 78–86.

21 *Aspects of Motion Perception* (Pergamon Press, 1972), pp. 47ff.

22 This result is reported in 'Visual Construction of Color is Digital', forthcoming in *Science*. I am grateful to the authors, in the Department of Psychology at the University of Toronto, for permission to cite this paper prior to its publication.

23 I plan to write a paper 'Essay on a New Fact of Vision', on this matter.

24 See 'Value and Need as Organizing Factors in Perception' (1947), in BI, pp. 43–56.

25 See 'Science and Simplicity' (1963), in PP, pp. 337–346.

26 See *LA*, pp. 51, 68–70.

27 E.g. "2+2=4" is true of everything in that for every x, x is such that $2+2=4$. A statement S will normally not be *true about x* unless S is about x in one of the senses of "about" defined in "About" (PP, pp. 246–272); but definition of "about" depends essentially on features of statements that have no reasonable analogues for pictures.

28 I allude here to Charles S. Peirce's paper 'The Fixation of Belief' (1877), in *Collected Papers of Charles Sanders Peirce*, Harvard University Press, Vol. 5 (1934), pp. 223–247.

29 On the nature and importance of understanding in the broader sense, see M. Polanyi, *Personal Knowledge*, University of Chicago Press (1960).

Index

A-series 152–8, 169–70
abstract objects 10, 24, 26–8, 30–2, 34, 39–40, 43n5,
    44n8, 74n4; see also possible worlds: as abstract and
    concrete objects
accessibility relations 487–8, 495
actualism 134; serious 522–5
actuality 12, 511–13, 519
Adams, R. 130–1, 144n4, 145n15, 145n16, 512, 522
agent causation see causation; agent
alternate possibilities: principle of 440–6
animalism 320–30
anthropic principle 444, 463–4
Aristotle 1, 157–8, 160–2, 168, 320, 355, 357, 370n15,
    386n19, 447
Armstrong, D. 515n13
Ayer, A.J. 94

B-series 152–6, 170
bare particulars 41, 48
Bishop Butler 241
brain-transplant scenarios 306, 329

Carnap, R. 3, 5, 18
causation; agent 377–8, 386n19, 404, 406, 418n29;
    backwards see causation: reverse; reverse 202–3, 207,
    218–19, 222; singular 64
chaotic eternal inflation 443, 449
Chisholm, R. 129
closed timelike curves 142, 206, 214, 222n20
coercion: and moral responsibility 428–31
common sense 97; and presentism 127
compatibilism 390, 400–2, 416n2, 417n12; see also
    incompatibilism and determinism; soft
conceptualism 18; see also nominalism
concrete objects 26–7; vs. abstract objects 35
correspondence theory of truth 49; see also truthmakers

cosmic horizon 442
counterfactuals 83–4; and fiction 84; and trans-world
    causation 501–2
counterpart theory 486–90, 526–8; problems with
    530–1

deliberation: and the feeling of freedom 407–8, 424–5
determinism 423; hard 399, 407–9, 411–15, 418; soft 402,
    415–17

Edwards, J. 254–5, 262n46, 263n48, 380
endurantism 233
ens successivum 245–6, 248; definition of 260
essential properties see properties: accidental vs. essential
eternalism 109
external time 194–6

facts 45, 50–2; general 50; see also states of affairs; particulars:
    thick and particulars: thin
fatalism 160–2, 335, 351–71
fibrous universes 473–7
fictional characters 78–80, 85, 146n26; see also fictions
fictions 81; impossible 88–90
fine-tuning 452–5, 458–67
Fischer, J. 400–1, 404, 410
four-dimensionalism 109, 111n1; see also eternalism;
    presentism and temporal parts
Frankfurt, H. 381–3, 400–1, 403–4
free will 335, 347–8, 369n1; and causal loops 220; see also
    freedom
freedom: Lockean see Locke, J.: on freedom; metaphysical
    421–7; Reidian see Reid, T.: on freedom
Frege, G. 18, 521

general facts see facts: general
grandfather paradox 198–201, 219, 221

haecceity 41, 48, 522; and presentism 130–2, 144n4; *see also* individual essence
Honderich, T. 399–400, 409, 413, 416–19
Hume, David 94, 320, 323, 421

identity: criterion of personal *see* identity: personal; "is" of 241–4; "loose and popular" vs. "strict" sense 244–8; personal 229, 238, 254, *see also* psychological continuity: and personal identity; through time 254, 259n11; trans-world 82, 508
incompatibilism 390, 399, 402–4, 407, 417; *see also* compatibilism *and* libertarianism
individual essence 41, 518, 521–2, 528; *see also* haecceity
inevitably 351–4
intrinsic properties *see* properties: intrinsic
island universes 442

Kant, I. 249, 261n 33, 405, 407
Kripke, S. 81, 89, 92, 438,

law of excluded middle 367–9
Leibniz, G. 152, 375–6, 379–80, 385n9
Lewis, D.: on modality 526–44, *see also* possible worlds; as concrete *and* counterpart theory; on properties 34–5; on the role of properties 35–8
libertarianism 406; *see also* incompatibilism
Locke, J. 48, 249–50, 259n9, 322, 328; on freedom 372–6, 381
loops: causal 110, 197, 203–24; information 212–17; intentional 219–21; object 208–11; person 217–18

many-worlds interpretations of quantum mechanics 445–7, 473–9
material constitution: problem of 228
materialism *see* animalism
McTaggart's proof 152–9
Meinong, A. 59–63, 74n4, 74n7
metaphysics 1–6
modal operators 438, 488–9, 493–5
modality 486–7, 518–20, *see also* Lewis, D.; on modality *and* possible worlds; *de dicto* 64–5, 518–19, 528; *de re* 487–8, 519; and time *see* time; and modality
moral responsibility *see* alternate possibilities: principle of; autonomy view of 389–90, 393–5, 397–8; nonautonomy views of 389–92
multiverses 441–52

necessity *see* modality
negative states of affairs *see* states of affairs: negative
nominalism 10, 18, 22–3, 34, 50
non-existent objects *see* noneism *and* Meinong, A.
non-present objects *see* presentism
noneism 61

ontology 3, 10, 11–12, 15, 17–20, 34

particulars: thick 49; thin 49–50
perdurantism 233–4
personal time 194–5
personhood 197
platonism 24
plenitude 506–9; principle of 37; *see also* recombination: principle of
possibility *see* modality
possible objects 13, 35–7; *see also* possible worlds
possible worlds 438, 483–4; as abstract 519–20; as concrete 503–6
presentism 109–10, 127–50; and absolute simultaneity 128, 140–1
Prior, A.N. 134
properties: as abundant 41–2; accidental vs. essential 519, 525, 533, 541; alien 510; and conditions 523–5; intrinsic 234–5, 508; problem of temporary intrinsic 234–5; role of 34–5; as sets 35–8, 513, 533–6; as sparse 41; as unsaturated assertibles 38–43
propositions 38, 44n17, 69, 356–8, 370n8, 370n10, 513, 528–40
psychological continuity: and personal identity 249–51, 309–16

Quine, W.V. 5, 9–10, 30–1, 42, 43n5, 59–74, 74n9, 75n19, 76n24, 76n26, 122–3, 144n7, 257–8

rational intuitions 4
Real Self View 392–5
realism *see* platonism
recombination: principle of 507–11
Reid, T. 4–5, 239, 243–4; on freedom 372, 374–86; *see also* Locke, J: on freedom
restoration problem 210–11, 217, 221
reverse causation *see* causation: reverse
Russell, Bertrand 13–15, 62

Ship of Theseus *see* material constitution: problem of
sorites of decomposition 92–9
special relativity *see* presentism; and absolute simultaneity
states of affairs 45–53, 437, 519–23; negative 51
Strawson, P.F. 122, 262n37, 412–14
structural universals *see* universals; structural
substance 237, 249–51
substance-language 122–3
supervenience 491–3

Taylor, R.: on fatalism 363–7, 371n19, 371n20
temporal parts 233–5, 254–8, 264–71, 322; and time travel 194
Thomson, J. 264–5, 269–71
time *see* presentism *and* eternalism; abstract and concrete 142; and modality 133–6, 141; and space 133–6
Tooley, M. 156n7
trans-world identity *see* identity: trans-world

Tree of Life hypothesis 470–3, 475
tree model of reality 151–5, 157–60, 162–3
truthmakers 46–51

universals 14–18, 45–7; structural 47
unsaturated assertibles *see* properties: as unsaturated
    assertibles

van Inwagen, P. 264–5, 403, 407, 470, 507

Wolf, S. 409–10
world ensemble 455
worldmates 495–8